dividual justices, but also the deep and unremitting problems which face the Court in building a structure of law on the foundation of the Constitution.

From "Abstraction" through "History" to "Zoning," it is clearly evident that the nation's highest court has, in shaping the course of justice in American democracy, produced writings of a judicial and literary aptness which should prove highly interesting not only to lawyers, but to writers, teachers, students, and laymen everywhere.

THE EDITOR

PERCIVAL E. JACKSON, who has been a practicing lawyer in New York City for nearly half a century, is the author of several books on law and the legal profession, including *Look at the Law* (New York, 1940) and *What Every Corporation Director Should Know* (New York, 1949).

THE WISDOM OF THE

SUPREME COURT

THE WISDOM OF THE
SUPREME COURT

SELECTED AND ARRANGED BY

PERCIVAL E. JACKSON

UNIVERSITY OF OKLAHOMA PRESS

NORMAN

BY PERCIVAL E. JACKSON

Law of Cadavers (New York, 1936, 1950)
Look at the Law (New York, 1940)
What Every Corporation Director Should Know (New York, 1949)
Corporate Management (Charlottesville, Virginia, 1955)
Justice and the Law (Charlottesville, Virginia, 1960)
The Wisdom of the Supreme Court (Norman, 1962)

LIBRARY OF CONGRESS CATALOG CARD NUMBER: 62–10764

COPYRIGHT 1962 BY THE UNIVERSITY OF OKLAHOMA PRESS,
PUBLISHING DIVISION OF THE UNIVERSITY.
COMPOSED AND PRINTED AT NORMAN, OKLAHOMA, U.S.A.,
BY THE UNIVERSITY OF OKLAHOMA PRESS. FIRST EDITION.

DEDICATED TO THE MEMORY OF LEARNED HAND
JURIST AND LEGAL SCHOLAR
(WHOSE OPPORTUNITY TO WRITE A FOREWORD FOR THIS BOOK
WAS FORECLOSED BY HIS DEATH)
AND TO THE MANY OTHERS
WHO SERVED BUT WERE NOT CALLED

PREFACE

FOR MORE THAN A CENTURY AND A HALF, the pens of the learned, and often venerable, justices of our high court have been engaged in fashioning, on a foundation of our Constitution, a structure of law designed, and frequently redesigned, to protect the liberties and to advance the private and public well-being of our people. Over these years, there has gone into the building of that structure words of profound courage and wisdom which with rare exception have lain buried in its walls.

Until now, this wealth of expression has remained unexplored except by lawyers and judges seeking solace for contemporary controversy and by biographers of a few of the more prominent members of the Court. Thus unexposed to popular gaze, the reputations of all but a few of the toilers, as one of them, Mr. Justice Story, remarked, have been "confined to the narrow limits which embrace the votaries of jurisprudence," and, it may be added, in these days of haste and superficiality, to a comparatively small percentage of the latter.

The products of the talents and labors of these builders are entitled to a greater public knowledge and recognition. Their dissemination should serve to make our citizens more conscious of their democratic heritage, more worthy of its privileges, and more assiduous in protecting and furthering its growth. Indeed, in this time of periodic controversy over the Court, a more widespread appreciation of the wisdom of its members can serve none but a useful purpose.

One need not argue the value of apposite quotation. As Mr. Justice Cardozo said, "I may seem to quote overmuch. My excuse is the desire to make manifest the truth that back of what I write is the sanction of something stronger than my own unaided thought."

On the score of accuracy, one may look to the words of Mr. Justice McKenna: "When we depart from the words, ambiguity comes."

Attesting effectiveness, Mr. Justice Story is found saying, "The utility of abridgments, in all departments of learning, will scarcely be doubted by any person who is accustomed to due reflection on the subject."

In selecting these quotations, effort has been made to avoid statement of legal rule. Instead, choice has been dictated by what was said and the manner in which it was said, so that for the lawyer's brief, the newspaperman's article, the student's theme, it may supply the substance and color of information and knowledge garnered from a storehouse of historic and philosophic understanding that has moulded the American way of life in all its complexities.

PERCIVAL E. JACKSON

NEW YORK, NEW YORK
January 5, 1962

ACKNOWLEDGMENTS

I WISH TO THANK the publishers of the following copyrighted works for permission to quote from them: *Life of John Marshall,* by Albert J. Beveridge, Houghton Mifflin Company (1919); *Other People's Money,* by Louis D. Brandeis, J. B. Lippincott Company, successor to Frederick A. Stokes Co. (1932); *The Nature of the Judicial Process,* by Benjamin N. Cardozo, Yale University Press (1921); *The Growth of the Law,* by Benjamin N. Cardozo, Yale University Press (1924); *Law and Literature,* by Benjamin N. Cardozo, Harcourt, Brace & World, Inc., successor to Harcourt, Brace & Co., Inc. (1931); *Paradoxes of Legal Science,* by Benjamin N. Cardozo, Columbia University Press (1928); *We the Judges,* by William O. Douglas, Doubleday & Company, Inc. (1956); *The Common Law,* by Oliver Wendell Holmes, Little, Brown & Company (1881, 1909, 1923); *Speeches,* by Oliver Wendell Holmes, Little, Brown & Company (1891, 1895, 1896, 1900, 1913); *Holmes-Pollock Letters* (1874-1932), edited by Mark De Wolfe Howe, Harvard University Press (1941); *Holmes-Laski Letters* (1916-1935), edited by Mark De Wolfe Howe, Harvard University Press (1953, 1957); *The Struggle for Judicial Supremacy,* by Robert H. Jackson, Alfred A. Knopf, Inc. (1941); *Brandeis: A Free Man's Life,* by Alpheus Thomas Mason, The Viking Press, Inc. (1946); *Harlan Fiske Stone: Pillar of the Law,* by Alpheus Thomas Mason, The Viking Press, Inc. (1956); *Charles Evans Hughes,* by Merlo J. Pusey, The MacMillan Company, (1952); *Justice Oliver Wendell Holmes: His Book Notices and Uncollected Letters and Papers,* edited and annotated by Harry C. Schriver, Central Book Company (1936); *Stephen J. Field: Craftsman of the Law,* by Carl Brent Swisher, The Brookings Institution (1930); and for permission to quote from the following articles by the respective publishers: *Harvard Law Review,* "The Ministry of Justice," by Benjamin N. Cardozo (1921), "Mr. Justice Holmes and the Constitution," by Felix Frankfurter (1929), "The Path of the Law," by Oliver Wendell Holmes (1896), "The Theory of Legal Interpretation," by Oliver Wendell Holmes (1899), "Natural Law," by Oliver Wendell Holmes (1918), "Law in Science and Science in Law," by Oliver Wendell Holmes (1899), "The Common Law in the United States," by Harlan Fiske Stone (1934), "The Public Influence of the Bar," by Harlan Fiske Stone (1934); *Stanford Law Review,* "Training the Trial Lawyer: A Neglected Area of Legal Education," by Robert H. Jackson (1950); *Columbia University Quarterly,* "The Conscientious Objector," by Harlan Fiske Stone (1919); *Cornell Law Quarterly,* "The Lawyer and His Neighbors," by Harlan Fiske Stone (1919); *Illinois Law Review* (Northwestern University School of Law), "Ideals and Doubts," by Oliver Wendell Holmes, excerpts reprinted by special permission of the *Illinois Law Review* (Northwestern University School of Law), Vol. X, No. 1 (1915).

Percival E. Jackson

CONTENTS

KEY TO CITATION REFERENCES

1. *United States Supreme Court Reports.* The citations do not include the dates; these may be found, together with a list of the early reporters, in Appendix I.

2. Other court reports. In addition to the quotations taken from the official Supreme Court reports, quotations have been taken from opinions by Judge Holmes reported in the official *Massachusetts Supreme Court Reports* and identified in the text as "Mass." Quotations have also been taken from opinions by Judge Cardozo in the official *New York Court of Appeals Reports,* identified in the text as "N.Y." In a few instances, quotations have been found elsewhere: in the *Lawyers' Edition, United States Supreme Court Reports,* identified as "L. Ed.," and in early reports containing opinions of the Supreme Court judges rendered at circuit, e.g., "Sumner," "Fed. Cas."

3. Text references to books other than official reports.

BRANDEIS

Business—A Profession refers to *Business—A Profession,* by Louis D. Brandeis. Boston, Small, Maynard & Co., 1914. Republished, Boston, Hale, Cushman & Flint, 1933 (edition used).

Other People's Money refers to *Other People's Money and How the Bankers Use It,* by Louis D. Brandeis. New York, Frederick A. Stokes & Co., 1914;

republished Washington, National Home Library Foundation, 1933 (edition used).

Mason, *Brandeis* refers to *Brandeis: A Free Man's Life,* by Alpheus Thomas Mason: New York, The Viking Press, 1946.

CARDOZO

Growth of the Law refers to *The Growth of the Law,* by Benjamin N. Cardozo: New Haven, Yale University Press, 1924.

Law and Literature refers to *Law and Literature,* by Benjamin N. Cardozo: New York, Harcourt, Brace & Co., 1931.

Nature of Judicial Process refers to *The Nature of the Judicial Process,* by Benjamin N. Cardozo: New Haven, Yale University Press, 1921.

Paradoxes refers to *Paradoxes of Legal Science,* by Benjamin N. Cardozo: New York, Columbia University Press, 1928.

DOUGLAS

We the Judges refers to *We the Judges,* by William O. Douglas: New York, Doubleday & Co., 1956.

FIELD

Swisher, *Field* refers to *Stephen J. Field: Craftsman of the Law,* by Carl Brent Swisher: Washington, The Brookings Institution, 1930.

HOLMES

Collected Legal Papers refers to *Collected Legal Papers,* by Oliver Wendell Holmes: New York, Harcourt, Brace & Howe, 1920.

The Common Law refers to *The Common Law,* by Oliver Wendell Holmes, Jr.: Boston, Little, Brown & Co., 1938.

Holmes-Laski Letters refers to *Holmes-Laski Letters: The Correspondence of Mr. Justice Holmes and Harold J. Laski, 1916–1935,* ed. by Mark De Wolfe Howe: Cambridge, Harvard University Press, 1953.

Holmes-Pollock Letters refers to *Holmes-Pollock Letters: The Correspondence of Mr. Justice Holmes and Sir Frederick Pollock, 1874–1932,* ed. by Mark De Wolfe Howe: Cambridge, Harvard University Press, 1941.

Speeches refers to *Speeches,* by Oliver Wendell Holmes: Boston, Little, Brown & Co., 1934.

Uncollected Letters refers to *Justice Oliver Wendell Holmes: His Book Notices and Uncollected Letters and Papers,* ed. and annotated by Harry C. Schriver: New York, Central Book Co., 1936.

HUGHES

Pusey, *Hughes* refers to *Charles Evans Hughes,* by Merlo J. Pusey: New York, The Macmillan Company, 1952.

JACKSON

Struggle for Judicial Supremacy refers to *The Struggle for Judicial Supremacy,* by Robert H. Jackson: New York, Alfred A. Knopf, 1941.

MARSHALL

Beveridge, *Life of Marshall* refers to *The Life of John Marshall,* by Albert J. Beveridge, 4 vols.: Boston and New York, Houghton Mifflin Co., 1916–19.

STONE

Mason, *Stone* refers to *Harlan Fiske Stone: Pillar of the Law,* by Alpheus Thomas Mason: New York, The Viking Press, 1956.

STORY

Life and Letters refers to *Life and Letters of Joseph Story,* ed. by W. W. Story, 2 vols.: Boston, C. C. Little & J. Brown, 1851.

Misc. Writings refers to *Story's Miscellaneous Writings,* by Joseph Story: Boston, James Munroe Company, 1835.

4. Text references to articles.

FRANKFURTER

"Holmes and the Constitution" refers to "Mr. Justice Holmes and the Constitution," by Felix Frankfurter, 41 *Harvard Law Review,* 121–64.

HOLMES

"Ideals and Doubts" refers to "Ideals and Doubts," by Oliver Wendell Holmes, 10 *Illinois Law Review,* 1–4.

"Law in Science and Science in Law" refers to "Law in Science and Science in Law," by Oliver Wendell Holmes, 12 *Harvard Law Review* 443–63.

"Natural Law" refers to "Natural Law," by Oliver Wendell Holmes, 32 *Harvard Law Review,* 40–44.

"The Path of the Law" refers to "The Path of the Law," by Oliver Wendell Holmes, 10 *Harvard Law Review* 457–78.

5. Some confusion may be thought to arise from the use of uninitialled surnames of the justices in the text, since coincidence of surname occurs with the following: Harlan, John Marshall (the grandfather), and Harlan, John Marshall (the grandson); Jackson, Howell E., and Jackson, Robert H.; and

Lamar, Joseph R., and Lamar, Lucius Q. C. However, since in no case did any of these justices bearing the same surname serve simultaneously, reference to the date of the report from which the quotation was taken will identify the justice responsible for it.

THE WISDOM OF THE

SUPREME COURT

Supreme Court of the *United States;*

February Term, 1790.

This being the period prescribed by law, for holding the first term of the SUPREME COURT of the UNITED STATES, the Judges met at *New-York,* the seat of the Federal Government, their respective commissions were read, and they were qualified according to law.

2 Dallas 399

THE WISDOM OF THE SUPREME COURT

ABRIDGMENT

The utility of abridgments, in all departments of learning, will scarcely be doubted by any person, who is accustomed to due reflection on the subject.—Story: *Misc. Writings,* 321.

ABSENCE

Absence may be a policy.—Jackson: Boone v. Lightner, 319 U.S. 561, 575.

ABSOLUTE

Nothing is more certain in modern society than the principle that there are no absolutes, that a name, a phrase, a standard has meaning only when associated with the considerations which gave birth to the nomenclature. —Vinson: Dennis v. United States, 341 U.S. 494, 508.

See also Rights, absolute; Truth 8.

ABSOLUTISM

Related subjects: Despotism; Oligarchy. *See also* Communism 1; Democracy, industrial 1, 5; Equality 28; Legislature 3; Power 8–10.

ABSTRACTION

We would, with becoming modesty, inquire whether every axiom or precept, either in politics or ethics, or in any other science, is not an abstraction. Whether truth itself, whether justice or common honesty, is not an abstraction? — Daniel: Marshall v. Baltimore & O. R.R., 16 How. (57 U.S.) 314, 346.

Related subject: Generality. *See also* Caution; Experience 6; Tariff.

ABSURDITY

See Extravagance 1.

ABUSE

1. Error or unwisdom is not equivalent to abuse.—Cardozo: American Tel. & Tel. v. United States, 299 U.S. 232, 236.

2. We do not discard a useful tool

because it may be misused.—Frankfurter: Dennis v. United States, 341 U.S. 494, 546.

See also Freedom 28; Labor union, abuse; Legislation 5; Majority-minority, abuse; Political party 9, 10; Power 33 ff.; Public official, power abuse; Publicity 3; Tax, abuse.

ACCEPTANCE

Acceptance undoubtedly includes approbation.—Marshall: Bank of U. S. v. Dandridge, 12 Wheat. (25 U.S.) 64, 112.

Related subject: Acquiescence.

ACCIDENT

1. Accidents do not conform to types; . . . they are one thing that happen "simply because"—they *are* accidents.—Pitney: Ward v. Krinsky, 259 U.S. 503, 524.

2. Laws cannot prevent accidents nor can a law equally protect all against them.—Reed: Louisiana v. Resweber, 329 U.S. 459, 465.

Related subjects: Liability; Negligence; Tort. See also Insurance 16; Liability 14; Mistake 1; Motor vehicle; Negligence, industrial accidents; Occupation 5; Unemployment 3.

ACCOUNTING

It may be said that in commercial or investment banking or any business extending credit success depends on knowing what not to believe in accounting.—Jackson: Federal Power Comm'n v. Hope Nat. Gas Co., 320 U.S. 591, 643.

Related subject: Bookkeeping. See also Arithmetic 2; Estimate 3; Symbol 12; Tax 128.

ACCURACY

See Detail 2.

ACCUSATION, ACCUSER

1. The law does not expect a man to be prepared to defend every act of his life which may be suddenly and without notice alleged against him.—Marshall: Beveridge, *Life of Marshall,* III, 619.

2. It is not uncommon for ignorant and corrupt men to falsely charge others with doing what they imagine that they themselves, in their narrow minds and experience, would have done under the circumstances.—Clarke: Valdez v. United States, 244 U.S. 432, 450.

3. Justice, though due to the accused, is due to the accuser also.—Cardozo: Snyder v. Massachusetts, 291 U.S. 97, 122.

See also Defense (legal) 7, 11; Innocence 1; Judge 44, 45, 48.

ACHIEVEMENT

If you want to hit a bird on the wing, you must have all your will in a focus, you must not be thinking about yourself, and equally, you must not be thinking about your neighbor; you must be living in your eye on that bird. Every achievement is a bird on the wing.—Holmes: *Speeches,* 85.

See also Effort 12; Will 1.

ACQUIESCENCE

We glide into acquiescence when negation seems to question our kinship with the crowd.—Cardozo: *Law and Literature,* 19.

See also Silence 4, 5, 8.

ACQUITTAL

See Reputation 10.

ACT, ACTION

1. An act which, in itself, is merely

a voluntary muscular contraction, derives all its character from the consequences which will follow it under the circumstances in which it is done. —Holmes: Aikens v. Wisconsin, 195 U.S. 194, 205.

2. An act is to be viewed, not singly and *in vacuo*, but in the setting of the whole occasion, if we would judge its moral quality.—Cardozo: In the Matter of Shaddock v. Schwartz, 246 N.Y. 288, 294.

3. We call that action reasonable which an informed, intelligent, just-minded, civilized man could rationally favor.—Brandeis: Quaker City Cab Co. v. Pennsylvania, 277 U.S. 389, 406.

4. There is no surer way to find out what parties meant, than to see what they have done.—Swayne: Brooklyn Ins. Co. v. Dutcher, 5 Otto (95 U.S.) 269, 273.

5. Environment illuminates the meaning of acts, as context does that of words.—Jackson: Cramer v. United States, 325 U.S. 1, 33.

6. Action can tell a story, display all the most vivid relations between men, and depict every kind of human emotion, without the aid of a word.— Holmes: Kalem Co. v. Harper Bros., 222 U.S. 55, 61.

7. The place for a man who is complete in all his powers is in the fight. The professor, the man of letters, gives up one-half of life that his protected talent may grow and flower in peace. But to make up your mind at your peril upon a living question, for purposes of action, calls upon your whole nature.—Holmes: "Law in Science

and Science in Law," 12 Harv. L. Rev. 452.

8. One cannot frustrate the doing of an act already done.—Cardozo: People v. Ruskay, 243 N.Y. 58, 62.

9. The moving waters are full of life and health; only in the still waters is stagnation and death.—Brewer: "Government by Injunction," 15 Nat. Corp. Rep. 849.

See also Advocacy 3; Choice 4; Crime; Criminal law; Duty 12; Effort; End-means 5; Equity court 30; Fact; Freedom 92, 138; Guilt 1; Intent 3, 8, 12; Judgment 4; Knowledge 4; Legislation 17; Liability 6, 13, 15, 16; Life 2, 3, 7; Mind 15; Motive; Punishment; State, acts; Wrong 5, 6.

ACTIVITY
Related subjects: Behavior; Conduct.

ACTUALITY
The only cosmic possibilities that I know anything about are the actualities. I do not know whether our ultimates such as good and bad, ideals, for the matter of that, consciousness, are cosmic ultimates or not. They seem to me to bear marks of the human and the finite. All that I know is that they are ultimates for us.— Holmes: *Uncollected Letters,* 165–66.

Related subject: Reality. *See also* Law 71; Truth 1.

ADAGE
1. To adopt a homely form of words, the complainants have been crying before they are really hurt.— Cardozo: Carter v. Carter Coal Co., 298 U.S. 238, 341.

2. He who must search a haystack for a needle is likely to end up with the attitude that the needle is not

worth the search.—Jackson: Brown v. Allen, 344 U.S. 443, 537.

> Related subjects: Axiom; Maxim. *See also* Extreme.

ADJUDICATION
See Remedy 2; Supreme Court, functions.

ADJUSTMENT
See Formula 12; Freedom, speech 106, 107; Punishment 26.

ADMINISTRATION
Administration is more than a means of regulation; administration is regulation.—Frankfurter: San Diego Council v. Garmon, 359 U.S. 236, 243.

> *See also* Court 54; Government (U.S.), federal 49.

ADMIRALTY
1. Our law of the sea has an ancient history. While it has not been static, the needs and interests of the interrelated worldwide seaborne trade which it reflects are very very deeply rooted in the past.—Frankfurter: Mitchell v. Trawler Racer, 362 U.S. 539, 551.

2. No area of federal law is judge-made at its source to such an extent as is the law of admiralty.—Frankfurter: *ibid.*, 550.

> Related subjects: Maritime law; Maritime lien; Ocean; Seaman; Ship.

ADMISSION
> Related subjects: Confession and related subjects. *See also* Evidence, admissions.

ADVERTISEMENT, ADVERTISING
1. Advertisements as a whole may be completely misleading although every sentence separately considered is literally true.—Black: Donaldson v. Read Magazine, 333 U.S. 178, 188.

2. A picture is none the less a picture, and none the less a subject of copyright, that it is used as an advertisement.—Holmes: Bleistein v. Donaldson Co., 188 U.S. 239, 251.

> *See also* Flag 11; Label 4; Patent 13; Premium system; Proprietary medicine; Trade-mark 6.

ADVICE
1. The advice of the elders to young men is very apt to be as unreal as a list of the hundred best books.—Holmes: "The Path of the Law," 10 Harv. L. Rev. 475.

2. When the task that is set before one is that of cleaning house, it is prudent as well as usual to take counsel of the dwellers.—Cardozo: Schechter v. United States, 295 U.S. 495, 552.

> *See also* Command 2.

ADVOCACY
1. What a man thinks is of no concern to government.... Advocacy and belief go hand in hand. For there can be no true freedom of mind if thoughts are secure only when they are pent up.—Douglas: Speiser v. Randall, 357 U.S. 513, 536.

2. Advocacy which is in no way brigaded with action should always be protected by the First Amendment. That protection should extend even to the ideas we despise.—Douglas: *ibid.*, 536-37.

3. There is still a clear constitutional line between advocacy of abstract doctrine and advocacy of action.—Douglas: *ibid.*, 537.

> *See also* Association; Freedom 72; Freedom, speech, limitations; Idea 4.

AFTERTHOUGHT

1. The confident conclusion which can be formed after experience.—McKenna: Brown v. Schleier, 194 U.S. 18, 23.

2. After a misfortune has happened, it is easy to see how it might have been avoided.—McLean: Goslee v. Shute's Ex'rs, 18 How. (59 U.S.) 463, 466.

3. No argument can be drawn from the wisdom that comes after the fact. —Davis: United States v. Union Pac. R.R., 1 Otto (91 U.S.) 72, 81.

Related subjects: Hindsight.

AGE (era)

Every age is modern to those who are living in it.—Cardozo: *Paradoxes,* 21.

See also Practical 4.

AGE, AGED (years)

1. A man must accept limits, at least after eighty. He must accept Hegel's notion that one becomes a person only by determination, that is, by accepting limits. To be *this* is to be *not that.*—Holmes: *Uncollected Letters,* 153.

2. A man is or may be young after sixty, and not old before eighty.—Holmes: *ibid.,* 163.

3. In one sense a man is no longer young at twenty-four. He has reached an age when his opinions are entitled to respect, when in a general way he is anybody's equal, when at least no one is entitled to bully him.—Holmes: *ibid.,* 163.

4. My reason tells me not to expect much now, although my feelings still have some of the illusions of youth.—Holmes: *ibid.,* 182.

5. I have gone on feeling young, but I have noticed that I met fewer of the old to whom to show my deference.—Holmes: *Speeches,* 83.

6. As I grow older, I grow calm.—Holmes: *ibid.,* 102.

7. An old man ought to be sad.—Holmes: *Holmes-Pollock Letters,* I, 37.

See also Infant; Public expenditure 4; Unemployment 6–8.

AGREEMENT

Related subject: Contract. *See also* Freedom 3; Monopoly 15; Restraint of trade 3, 9, 10.

AIR (atmosphere)

Atmospheric air is itself an agent of decay.—Swayne: Brown v. Piper, 1 Otto (91 U.S.) 37, 40.

AIR (aviation)

Aviation has added a new dimension to travel and to our ideas. The ancient idea that landlordism and sovereignty extend from the center of the world to the periphery of the universe has been modified. Today the landowner no more possesses a vertical control of all the air above him than a shore owner possesses horizontal control of all the sea before him. The air is too precious as an open highway to permit it to be "owned" to the exclusion or embarrassment of air navigation by surface landlords who could put it to little real use.—Black: Northwest Airlines v. Minnesota, 322 U.S. 292, 302–303.

ALARM
> Related subject: Warning. *See also* Argument 1.

ALIEN

1. All residents of this nation are kin in some way by blood or culture to a foreign land.—Murphy: Korematsu v. United States, 323 U.S. 214, 242.

2. The alien retains immunities from burdens which the citizen must shoulder. — Jackson: Harisiades v. Shaughnessy, 342 U. S. 580, 585.

3. We do not confiscate the lands or goods of the stranger within our gates. —Cardozo: Techt v. Hughes, 229 N. Y. 222, 244.

4. The story of the American melting pot is the story of how peoples of many tongues and many races became one.—Douglas: *We the Judges,* 18.

> Related subjects: Citizen; Denationalization; Denaturalization; Deportation; Naturalization. *See also* Citizen 3; Constitution 69; Democracy 22.

ALLEGIANCE

1. Such is the contradictoriness of the human mind that the expression of the views which may collide with cherished American ideals does not necessarily prove want of devotion to the Nation. It would be foolish to deny that even blatant intolerance toward some of the presuppositions of the democratic faith may not imply rooted disbelief in our system of government. — Frankfurter: Baumgartner v. United States, 322 U.S. 665, 674.

2. Surely it cannot show lack of attachment to the principles of the Constitution that she thinks that it can be improved. I suppose that most intelligent people think that it might be.—

Holmes: United States v. Schwimmer, 279 U.S. 644, 654.

3. Loyalty is a matter of mind and of heart not of race. That indeed is the history of America.—Douglas: Hirabayashi v. United States, 320 U.S. 81, 107.

4. Where there is a sense of belonging, there are ties of loyalty and devotion that no strains of politics can ever sever or destroy.—Douglas: *We the Judges,* 426–27.

5. Loyalty and the desire to work for the welfare of the state . . . are individual rather than group characteristics.—Murphy: Oyama v. California, 332 U.S. 633, 666.

6. In peace, too, men may differ widely as to what loyalty to our country demands; and an intolerant majority, swayed by passion or by fear, may be prone in the future, as it has often been in the past, to stamp as disloyal opinions with which it disagrees.—Brandeis: Schaefer v. United States, 251 U.S. 466, 495.

7. This country demands that its sons and daughters whatever their race—however intense or diverse their religious connections—be politically merely American citizens.—Brandeis: Mason, *Brandeis,* 442.

8. There is room here for men of any race, of any creed, or any condition in life, but not to Protestant-Americans, or Catholic-Americans, or Jewish-Americans, nor for German-Americans, Irish-Americans, or Russian-Americans.—Brandeis: *ibid.*

9. Old social or cultural loyalties may still exist, though basic alle-

giance is transferred here.—Douglas: Knauer v. United States, 328 U.S. 654, 659.

> Related subjects: Citizen; Disloyalty; Naturalization; Patriotism; Treason. *See also* Nationalism 6.

ALTERNATIVE
Alternatives are deceptive. Their very statement conveys the impression that one possibility is as effective as the next.—Murphy: Wolf v. Colorado, 338 U.S. 25, 41.

AMBIGUITY
> *See* Commerce 6; Conclusion 10; Construction 28; Generality 14; Reform 13.

AMBITION
> *See* War 4.

AMENDMENT
> *See* Construction 8; Legislation, amendment.

AMORTIZATION
> *See* Depreciation 5.

AMOUNT
> *See* Right 17.

ANALOGY
While it is not always profitable to analogize "fact" to "fiction," La Fontaine's fable of the crow, the cheese, and the fox demonstrates that there is a substantial difference between holding a piece of cheese in the beak and putting it in the stomach.—Frankfurter: Alleghany Corp. v. Breswick & Co., 353 U.S. 151, 170.

> Related subject: Illustration. *See also* Precedent 30.

ANALYSIS
> *See* Maxim 1.

ANARCHIST, ANARCHY
> *See* Constitution 37; Crime 8; Entrap-

ment 2; Freedom 19–21, 27; Lawlessness 2; Rights 33.

ANNUITY
> *See* Insurance.

ANONYMITY
> *See* Freedom, speech 109; Freedom, press 176.

ANSWER
1. Answers are not obtained by putting the wrong question and thereby begging the real one.—Frankfurter: Priebe & Sons v. United States, 332 U.S. 407, 420.

2. Silence and a steady devotion to duty are the best answers to irresponsible criticism.—Murphy: Craig v. Harney, 331 U.S. 367, 383.

> *See also* Argument 5, 7; Inquiry 1; Question.

ANTIDOTE
Give the antidote with the bane.—Holmes: Herring Co. v. Halls Safe Co., 208 U.S. 554, 559.

ANTIQUITY
1. Antiquity has its charms but it may be doubted whether wisdom is not more frequently found in experience and the gradual progress of human affairs.—McLean: Jacobson v. James, 20 How. (61 U.S.) 296, 307.

2. It is not necessarily error to follow the footsteps of ancient philosophy, to reverence the precepts of ancient criticism, to meditate over the pages of ancient exploits, or to listen to the admonitions of ancient oratory. —Story: *Misc. Writings,* 18.

APPEAL (legal)
1. The right to a judgment from more than one court is a matter of

grace and not a necessary ingredient of justice.—Frankfurter: Cobbledick v. United States, 309 U.S. 323, 325.

2. Judicial review gives time for the sober second thought.—Douglas: *We the Judges,* 445.

3. According to an early English judge, "The devil himself knoweth not the mind of man," and a modern reviewing court is not much better equipped to lay bare unexposed mental process.—Frankfurter: NLRB v. Donnelly Co., 330 U.S. 219, 229.

4. A few minutes' observation of the parties in the courtroom is more informing than reams of cold record. —Jackson: Ashcraft v. Tennessee, 322 U.S. 143, 169.

5. In this living record, there are many guideposts to the truth which are not in the printed record. Without seeing them ourselves, we will do well to give heed to those who have seen them.—Burton: Haley v. Ohio, 232 U.S. 596, 625.

6. Enough can be squeezed from these poor and puny anonymities to turn the color of legal litmus paper.— Holmes: Abrams v. United States, 250 U.S. 616, 629.

7. Disappointed litigants and losing lawyers like to have another go at it. —Frankfurter: Ferguson v. Moore-McCormack Lines, 352 U.S. 521, 542.

8. The grounds for uneasiness can be considered only by another power. —Holmes: Casey v. United States, 276 U.S. 413, 419.

See also Supreme Court, functions.

APPEARANCE
See Military 10; Truth 16.

APPETITE
The stealthy invasions of inordinate appetites. — McKenna: Grogan v. Walker & Co., 259 U.S. 80, 96.

APPROBATION
See Acceptance.

ARBITRATION
Arbitration is a matter of contract and a party cannot be required to submit to arbitration any dispute which he has not agreed so to submit.— Douglas: United Steelworkers v. Warrior & Gulf Nav. Co., 363 U.S. 574, 582.

ARGUMENT
1. Alarms ... are not arguments.— McKenna: United States v. Ohio Oil Co., 234 U.S. 548, 575.

2. The power of subtle argument to give an appearance of difficulty to what is relatively simple.—Frankfurter: People of Puerto Rico v. Hermanos, 309 U.S. 543, 547.

3. Cost and importance, while they add to the solemnity of our duty, do not increase the difficulty of decision except as they induce argument upon matters that, with less mighty interests, no one would venture to dispute. —Holmes: Sanitary District v. United States, 266 U.S. 405, 425.

4. To waste time and argument ... would be not much less idle than to hold a lighted taper to the sun.—Marshall: McCulloch v. Maryland, 4 Wheat. (17 U.S.) 316, 419.

5. The elaborate argument ... does not need an elaborate answer. — Holmes: United States v. Wurzbach, 280 U.S. 396, 399.

6. This argument has a superficial plausibility on the word level, but if our attention is directed to substance rather than symbols the speciousness of the argument is exposed.—Black: United States v. Wallace & Tiernan Co., 336 U.S. 793, 799.

7. Argument is all right. Everyone has a right to use it and no one is free from the need of being ready to answer it.—Holmes: *Holmes-Pollock Letters*, I, 133.

Related subjects: Contention; Controversy. *See also* Afterthought 3; Construction 35, 147; Distinction 7; Expediency 1; Extreme 3; Foundation 1; History 9; Lawyer 75; Preference.

ARGUMENT (in court)

1. *You wish the Court to hear, and listen too?*
   Then speak with point, be brief, be close, be true.
   Cite well your cases; let them be in point;
   Not learned rubbish, dark, and out of joint;
   And be your reasoning clear, and closely made,
   Free from false taste, and verbiage, and parade.
   Stuff not your speech with every sort of law,
   Give us the grain, and throw away the straw.
   Books should be read; but if you can't digest,
   The same's the surfeit, take the worst or best.
   Clear heads, sound hearts, full minds, with point may speak,
   All else how poor in fact, in law how weak.

Who's a great lawyer? He, who aims to say
The least his cause requires, not all he may.

. . . .

Whoe'er in law desires to win his cause,
Must speak with point, not measure our "wise saws,"
Must make his learning apt, his reasoning clear,
Pregnant in matter, but in style severe;
But never drawl, nor spin the thread so fine,
That all becomes an evanescent line.

—Story: *Life and Letters*, II, 89–90.

2. Argument is likely to leave each judge just where it found him.—Jackson: *Struggle for Judicial Supremacy*, 301.

3. I used to say that, as Solicitor-General, I made three arguments of every case. First came the one that I planned—as I thought, logical, coherent, complete. Second was the one actually presented—interrupted, incoherent, disjointed, disappointing. The third was the utterly devastating argument that I thought of after going to bed that night.—Jackson: 99 L. Ed. 1318.

4. The argument in the case has been like a theological debate over the number of angels who can stand on the head of a pin.—Douglas: Johnston v. United States, 351 U.S. 215, 223.

ARISTOCRACY
See Democracy 18.

ARITHMETIC

1. Bare figures have a way of acquiring an existence of their own, independent of the evidence which gave rise to them.—Clark: Holland v. United States, 348 U.S. 121, 128.

2. Two and two will always make four, despite the reports of presidents and financial advisers who insist on stretching it into five.—Brandeis: Mason, *Brandeis,* 213.

3. Obsessed with the delusion that two and two make five, he fell at last a victim of the relentless rules of humble arithmetic. Remember, O Stranger! Arithmetic is the first of the sciences and the mother of safety.—Brandeis: *ibid.,* 200.

See also Question 4.

ARMY

1. An army is not a deliberative body. It is the executive arm. Its law is that of obedience.—Brewer: *In re* Grimley, 137 U.S. 147, 153.

2. The armed services must protect a society, not merely its Constitution.—Jackson: Korematsu v. United States, 323 U.S. 214, 244.

3. Discrimination is unavoidable in the Army. Some must be assigned to dangerous missions; others find soft spots.—Jackson: Orloff v. Willoughby, 345 U.S. 83, 94.

4. The Government has the right to bury its own soldiers and to see to it that their graves shall not remain unknown or unhonored. — Peckham: United States v. Gettysburg Elec. Ry., 160 U.S. 668, 683.

Related subjects: Conscription; Military; Selective service (military). *See also* President 2.

ARREST

1. An arrest shows nothing more than that someone probably suspected the person apprehended of an offense. —Black: Schware v. Board of Bar Exam'rs, 353 U.S. 232, 241.

2. The period of detention before the magistrate is the awful lull.—Douglas: *We the Judges,* 364.

3. It is better, so the Fourth Amendment teaches, that the guilty sometimes go free than that citizens be subject to easy arrest.—Douglas: Henry v. United States, 361 U.S. 98, 104.

4. Under our system suspicion is not enough for an officer to lay hands on a citizen.—Douglas: *ibid.*

5. An arrest is not justified by what the subsequent search discloses. — Douglas: *ibid.,* 103.

6. An arrest, though by no means probative of any guilt or wrongdoing, is sufficiently significant as an episode in a man's life that it may often be material at least to further enquiry.—Douglas: Chaunt v. United States, 364 U.S. 350, 354.

See also Reputation 11; Witness 12.

ART, ARTIST

1. All art is caricature, that is, it emphasizes what the artist wants to call attention to at the expense of other elements that may have a cosmic equality but that are not relevant to what he wants to make you see, feel, or think.—Holmes: *Uncollected Letters,* 157.

2. The object of art is to pull the trigger of an emotion. — Holmes: *Holmes-Pollock Letters,* II, 49.

3. Certainly works are not the less

connected with the fine arts because their pictorial quality attracts the crowd, and therefore gives them a real use—if use means to increase trade and to help to make money.—Holmes: Bleistein v. Donaldson Co., 188 U.S. 239, 251.

4. Individual perception of the beautiful is too varied a power to permit a narrow or rigid concept of art.—Reed: Mazer v. Stein, 347 U.S. 201, 214.

Related subjects: Illustration; Picture. *See also* Censor; Lawyer 40.

ARTIFICIALITY
See Imitation 4.

ASPIRATION
The society for which many philanthropists, labor reformers and men of fashion unite in longing is one in which they may be comfortable and may shine without much trouble or any danger.—Holmes: *Speeches,* 56.
Related subject: Desire.

ASSAULT
An assault is ordinarily held to be committed merely by putting another in apprehension of harm whether or not the actor actually intends to inflict or is capable of inflicting that harm.—Brennan: Ladner v. United States, 358 U.S. 169, 177.
Related subject: Attack.

ASSEMBLY
See Freedom, assembly; Street 3.

ASSOCIATION
1. Associations, the organs of its common will.—Cardozo: People *ex rel.* Karlin v. Culkin, 248 N.Y. 465, 468.

2. Effective advocacy of both public and private points of view, particularly controversial ones, is undeniably enhanced by group association .... It is beyond debate that freedom to engage in association for the advancement of beliefs and ideas is an inseparable aspect of the "liberty" assured by . . . the 14th Amendment.—Harlan: National A. A. C. P. v. Alabama, 357 U.S. 449, 460.

3. Inviolability of privacy in group association may in many circumstances be indispensable to preservation of freedom of association, particularly where a group espouses dissident beliefs.—Harlan: *ibid.,* 462.
Related subject: Organization. *See also* Corporation 5, 7, 8, 14; Freedom, assembly; Guilt 5–7; Political party; Race 23; Reputation 3, 4.

ATHEISM
See Freedom, religion 121.

ATMOSPHERE (environment)
See Trial 15, 35, 36; Trial, unfair.

ATROCITY
See War 19.

ATTACK
The attack was not the less inexcusable because the consequences were not as injurious as . . . intended.—Story: The Marianna Flora, 11 Wheat. (24 U.S.) 1, 51.
Related subject: Assault. *See also* Self-defense 1.

ATTEMPT
See Effort 8, 13; Gesture 1; Intent 4.

AUTHOR
1. While authors may have habits making for intermittent want, they

may have no less a spirit of independence which would resent treatment of them as wards under guardianship of the law.—Frankfurter: Fisher Music Co. v. Witmark, 318 U.S. 643, 657.

2. Ghost-writing has debased the intellectual currency in circulation here and is a type of counterfeiting which invites no defense. Perhaps this Court renders a public service in treating phantom authors and ghost-writers as legal frauds and disguised authorship as a deception.—Jackson: Kingsland v. Dorsey, 338 U.S. 318, 324.

See also Copyright.

AUTHORITY

1. Divided authority breeds friction.—Black: Burford v. Sun Oil Co., 319 U.S. 315, 335.

2. When authority can say, "The State—it is I!" it meets with no impediments to its exercise.—McKenna: United States v. Ohio Oil Co., 234 U.S. 548, 564.

See also Autocracy; Constitution (U.S.), authority; Discipline 1; Government (U.S.), authority; Government, federal, authority; Government, federal-state, authority; Jurisdiction 1; Legislation, authority; Legislature, authority; Precedent; Public official, authority; Sovereignty 6; Speculation (conjecture); Supreme Court, authority.

AUTOCRACY
See Authority 2.

AUTOMATION

It had to keep up with the mechanical march; to fall back would have been its destruction. — McKenna: United States v. United Shoe Mach.

Co., 247 U.S. 32, 55.
Related subject: Machine.

AUTOMOBILE
See Motor Vehicle.

AVARICE
See War 4.

AVERAGE
See Remedy 22.

AVERSION
See Fear 2.

AVIATION
See Air (aviation).

AVOIDANCE
See Tax, avoidance.

AXIOM
Related subjects: Adage; Maxim. *See also* Construction 17; White-slave traffic.

BAD FAITH
See Faith 14, 15.

BAIL

1. Unless this right to bail before trial is preserved, the presumption of innocence, secured only after centuries of struggle, would lose its meaning—Vinson: Stack v. Boyle, 342 U.S. 1, 4.

2. Why fix bail at any reasonable sum if a poor man can't make it?—Burton, Minton: Griffin v. Illinois, 351 U.S. 12, 29.

3. The purpose of bail is to insure the defendant's appearance and submission to the judgment of the court. It is never denied for the purpose of punishment.—Douglas: Reynolds v. United States, 4 L.Ed. 2d, 46, 48.

4. We have held that an indigent defendant is denied equal protection

of the law if he is denied an appeal on equal terms with other defendants, solely because of his indigence. Can an indigent be denied freedom, where a wealthy man would not, because he does not happen to have enough property to pledge for his freedom?—Douglas: Bandy v. United States, 5 L.Ed. 2d, 218, 219.

5. The fundamental tradition in this country is that one charged with a crime is not, in ordinary circumstances, imprisoned until after a judgment of guilt. . . . This traditional right to freedom during trial and pending judicial review has to be squared with the possibility that the defendant may flee or hide himself. Bail is the device which we have borrowed to reconcile these conflicting interests.—Douglas: *ibid*.

BAIT
See Novelty.

BANK, BANKER, BANKING
See Accounting; Money 3; Purpose 2; Stockbroker.

BANKRUPTCY
See Insolvency; Creditor 2.

BAR ASSOCIATION
1. Bar organizations have generally taken only a perfunctory interest in the real problems of the profession. They have been chiefly organizations which, when not given over to petty politics, have been devoted to honoring the leaders of the profession and to describing in sonorous phrases the noble traditions of the bar and the perfection of the common law.—

Stone: Mason, *Stone*, 377.

2. Movements toward reform in bar organizations have been of a perfunctory character and usually fall into the hands of those who are more interested in the self-advertising to be gained from them than in real accomplishment.—Stone: *ibid*.

BARGAIN
Related subjects: Buyer; Contract; Vendor-vendee. *See also* Equity court 27, 29; Freedom, contract 178.

BARGAINING (collective)
See Labor union, collective bargaining.

BARTER
See Exchange.

BEGINNING
1. The classic admonition to begin at the beginning.—Frankfurter: Vanston Bondholders Prot. Comm. v. Green, 329 U.S. 156, 169.

2. Against the first step . . . this court has warned, expressing a maxim of experience,—"Withstand beginnings." . . . Who can know to what end they will conduct.—McKenna: Block v. Hirsh, 256 U.S. 135, 160.

3. One cannot jump at once to great ends. Therefore I hope you will not shirk the details and drudgery that life offers, but will master them as the first step to bigger things. One must be a soldier before one can be a general.—Holmes: *Uncollected Letters*, 151.

4. Every journey to a forbidden end begins with the first step.—Sutherland: Carter v. Carter Coal Co., 298 U.S. 238, 295–96.

BEHAVIOR
Related subjects: Act; Conduct; Misbehavior; Misconduct. *See also* Formula 9; Freedom, belief 136; Law 70; Wrong 4.

BELIEF
1. It is enough that I cannot characterize their belief as a vagary of the mind, an idle dream or phantasy, an irrational pretense.—Cardozo: People v. Westchester Co. Nat'l Bank, 231 N.Y. 465, 491.

2. The concept may be right or wrong. At least it corresponds to an intelligible belief, and one widely prevalent today among honest men and women.—Cardozo: Liggett Co. v. Lee, 288 U.S. 517, 586.

See also Debtor 5; Experience 2; Freedom, religion, belief, conscience, thought, learning; Patriotism 7; Proof 2; Religion, belief.

BENEFIT
The benefit but a shadow.—Cardozo: Snyder v. Massachusetts, 291 U.S. 97, 106–107.

See also River; Tax 7, 53, 65.

BEQUEST
Every bequest is but a bounty, and a bounty must be taken as it is given. —Johnson: Hunter v. Bryant, 2 Wheat. (15 U.S.) 32, 37.

BIAS
Bias or prejudice is such an elusive condition of the mind that it is most difficult, if not impossible, to always recognize its existence.—Peckham: Crawford v. United States, 212 U.S. 183, 196.

Related subjects: Bigotry; Prejudice. *See also* Constitutional adjudication, bias; Judge 45, 46; Jury, challenge.

BIBLE
Where can the purest principles of morality be learned so clearly or so perfectly as from the New Testament? Where are benevolence, the love of truth, sobriety, and industry, so powerfully and irresistibly inculcated as in the sacred volume?—Story: Vidal v. Girard's Ex'rs, 2 How. (43 U.S.) 127, 200.

BIGAMY
See Freedom 77.

BIGOTRY
Bigotry has traced out the march of its persecutions in footsteps of blood.—Story: *Misc. Writings,* 4.

Related subjects: Bias; Oppression; Persecution; Prejudice.

BILL OF RIGHTS
Bills of rights give assurance to the individual of the preservation of his liberty. They do not define the liberty they promise.—Cardozo: *Paradoxes,* 97.

Related subject: Constitution (U.S.), amendments 1–10. *See also* Constitution (U.S.) 2; Constitution (U.S.), Bill of Rights; Constitutional law 1; Freedom, petition 162; Government (U.S.) 9; Military 15; Supreme Court 57.

BIRTH
Birth must precede, but it is no part of either funeral or apotheosis.—McReynolds: Newberry v. United States, 256 U.S. 232, 257.

BIRTHRIGHT
See Citizen 25, 34.

BLACKSTONE'S COMMENTARIES

Of a work, which has been so long before the public as Blackstone's Commentaries, it cannot be necessary for us to utter one word of approbation. For luminous method, for profound research, for purity of diction, for comprehensive brevity, and pregnancy of matter, for richness in classical allusions, and for extent and variety of knowledge of foreign jurisprudence, whether introduced for illustration, or ornament, or instruction, it is not too much to say, that it stands unrivalled in ours, and, perhaps, in every other language.—Story: *Misc. Writings,* 230.

BLAME
Related subject: Fault. *See also* Liability 7; Punishment 4.

BLASPHEMY

Although Christianity be a part of the common law of the State, yet it is so in this qualified sense, that its divine origin and truth are admitted, and therefore it is not to be maliciously and openly reviled and blasphemed against, to the annoyance of believers or the injury of the public.—Story: Vidal v. Girard's Ex'rs, 2 How. (43 U.S.) 127, 198.

BLIND
See Conduct 4.

BODY

The lack of a bone mars the symmetry of the body.—Reed: Edwards v. United States, 312 U.S. 473, 482.
See also Identity; Punishment 37.

BOND
Related subject: Securities. *See also* Investment 6; Tax 43, 110.

BONE
See Body.

BOOK

1. A book is valuable on account of the matter it contains, the ideas it communicates, the instruction or entertainment it affords. — McLean: Wheaton v. Peters, 8 Pet. (33 U.S.) 591, 653.

2. In this age, books, to be read, must be succinct, and direct to their purpose.—Story: *Misc. Writings,* 319.

3. Books must serve as powerful agencies of social, economic, or political reform. They may enable us to gain a keener insight into our society and its problems.—Douglas: *We the Judges,* 335.

4. No man of literary culture . . . would call a book, paper or a manufacture of paper, any more than he would designate a masterpiece of Raphael, as canvas or a manufacture of canvas.—Bradley: Pott v. Arthur, 14 Otto (104 U.S.) 735, 736.
See also Blackstone's Commentaries; Censor; Classics; Federalist 1; Identity; Intolerance 6; Law reports; Learning 4; Literature; Patent 15.

BOOKKEEPING

Bookkeeping is hardly an exact science. As a representation of the condition and trend of a business, it uses symbols of certainty to express values that actually are in constant flux.— Jackson: Federal Power Comm'n v.

Hope Nat. Gas Co., 320 U.S. 591, 643.
Related subject: Accounting. *See also* Depreciation 1.

BORROWING
Borrowing is borrowing, no matter
from whom.—McKenna: Auten v.
United States Nat'l Bank, 174 U.S.
125, 143.
Related subjects: Lender; Loan.

BOUNDARY
A boundary line is none the worse
for being narrow.—Frankfurter: Mc-
Leod v. Dilworth Co., 322 U.S. 327,
329.
See also Sovereignty 5.

BOUNTY
See Bequest.

BRAVERY
Related subject: Heroism. *See also* Classification 1.

BREVITY
Brevity becomes of itself a source of
obscurity.—Story: *Misc. Writings*,
153.

BRIBERY
Men are more often bribed by their
loyalties and ambitions than by money.—Jackson: United States v. Wunderlich, 342 U.S. 98, 103.
Related subject: Corruption.

BUCCANEER
Such men are the proper instruments of belligerent or neutral fraud;
they are the avowed panders of the
mercantile world; their consciences
are in the market.—Johnson: The St.
Nicholas, 1 Wheat. (14 U.S.) 417,
419.

BURDEN
1. Special burdens are often necessary for general benefits.—Field: Bar-
bier v. Connolly, 113 U.S. 27, 31.
2. There is a distinction between
imposing a burden and withholding
a favor.—Stone: National Life Ins.
Co. v. United States, 277 U.S. 508,
536.

BURIAL
1. A benevolent discretion, giving
heed to all those promptings and emotions that men and women hold sacred in the disposition of their dead,
must render judgment as it appraises
the worth of the competing forces.—
Cardozo: Yome v. Gorman, 242 N.Y.
395, 402.
2. Separation after death from the
resting place of wife or child may
have seemed an evil more poignant
than separation after death from the
faithful of the church.—Cardozo:
ibid., 404.
See also Army 4.

BUSINESS
1. All the protean arrangements
which the wit of man can devise that
are not business transactions within
the meaning of ordinary speech.—
Frankfurter: Comm'r of Int. Rev. v.
Wemyss, 324 U.S. 303, 306.
2. Business men as a rule are not
wholly in the dark as to the ways of
their competitors.—Cardozo: Norwegian Nitrogen Prod. Co. v. United
States, 288 U.S. 294, 323.
3. In the transactions of business
life, sanity of end and aim is at least
a presumption, albeit subject to be re-

butted.—Cardozo: Outlet Embroidery Co. v. Derwent Mills, 254 N.Y. 179, 183.

4. The most enlightened judicial policy is to let people manage their own business in their own way.—Holmes: Dr. Miles Medical Co. v. John D. Park & Sons Co., 220 U.S. 373, 411.

5. There may be necessaries that sooner or later must be dealt with like short rations in a shipwreck.—Holmes: *ibid.,* 412.

6. It [the statute] burdens honest business, it is true, but burdens it only that, under its forms, dishonest business may not be done.—McKenna: Merrick v. Halsey 242 U.S. 568, 587.

7. Certainly there is no profession, possibly no business, which does not offer peculiar opportunities for reprehensible practices. — McReynolds: Adams v. Tanner, 244 U.S. 590, 594.

8. A business never stands still. It either grows or decays.—Cardozo: West Ohio Gas Co. v. Public Util. Comm'n, 294 U.S. 63, 72.

9. Men have not made inventions in business, men have not made economies to any great extent because they wanted to. They have made them because they had to, and the proposition that "necessity is the mother of inventions" is just as true today, in the era of the trusts, as it was hundreds of years before.—Brandeis: Mason, *Brandeis,* 355–56.

10. If a business is unsuccessful, it means that the public does not care enough for it to make it pay. —

Holmes: Arizona Copper Co. v. Hammer, 250 U.S. 400, 433.

11. Business has little patience with the suitor for ease and favor.—Cardozo: In the Matter of Jordan v. Decorative Co., 230 N.Y. 522, 525.

12. In any great and extended change in the manner or method of doing business it seems to be an inevitable necessity that distress, and perhaps, ruin, shall be its accomplishment in regard to some of those who were engaged in the old methods.—Peckham: United States v. Trans-Missouri Fr. Assoc., 166 U.S. 290, 323.

13. There is no duty resting upon a citizen to suspect the honesty of those with whom he transacts business.—Black: Federal Trade Comm'n v. Standard Educ. Soc., 302 U.S. 112, 116.

Related subjects: Business (big) and related subjects; Commerce; Corporation; Industry; Labor. *See also* Accounting; Bookkeeping; Charity; Commerce 4; Competition 5; Corporation, importance; Democracy (industrial); Exploitation 1; Fiduciary 5, 6; Foreman; Good will; Judicial notice 4; Lawyer 27; Occupation 10; Pension 1; Press 7; Privacy 2; Production; Profit; Public interest, business; Radio 3; Sherman Antitrust Law 4; Sovereignty 13; Tax 18, 71, 77, 112; Trademark; Unemployment; Value 8, 10; Wages 3.

BUSINESS (big)

1. Size alone gives to giant corporations a social significance not attached ordinarily to smaller units of private enterprise.—Brandeis: Ligget Co. v. Lee, 288 U.S. 517, 565.

2. In final analysis, size in steel is

the measure of the power of a handful of men over our economy. That power can be utilized with lightning speed. It can be benign or it can be dangerous.—Douglas: United States v. Columbia Steel Co., 334 U.S. 495, 536.

3. All power tends into a government in itself. Power that controls the economy should be in the hands of elected representatives of the people, not in the hands of an industrial oligarchy. Industrial power should be decentralized. It should be scattered into many hands so that the fortunes of the people will not be dependent on the whim or caprice, the political prejudices, the emotional stability of a few self-appointed men. The fact that they are not vicious men but respectable and social-minded is irrelevant.—Douglas: *ibid*.

4. The evils of bigness are something different from and additional to the evils of monopoly. A business may be too big to be efficient without being a monopoly; and it may be a monopoly and yet (so far as size is concerned) may be well within the limits of efficiency.—Brandeis: Mason, *Brandeis*, 202.

5. When ... you increase your business to a very great extent, and the multitudes of problems increase with its growth, you will find, in the first place, that the man at the head has a diminishing knowledge of the facts, and in the second place, a diminishing opportunity of exercising a careful judgment upon them. Furthermore— and this is one of the most important grounds of the inefficiency of large in-

stitutions—there develops a centrifugal force greater than the centripetal force. Demoralization sets in; a condition of lessened efficiency presents itself. . . . These are the disadvantages that attend bigness.—Brandeis: *ibid.*, 354–55.

6. If business is to go on, men must unite to do it and must sell their wares. — Holmes: International Harvester Co. v. Kentucky, 234 U.S. 216, 223.

7. The history of combinations has shown that what one may do with impunity may have intolerable results when done by several in co-operation. —Brandeis: Federal Trade Comm'n v. Gratz, 253 U.S. 421, 438.

8. Overshadowing combinations having financial resources without limit and an audacity in the accomplishment of their objects that recognizes none of the restraints of moral obligations controlling the action of individuals; combinations governed entirely by the law of greed and selfishness—so powerful that no single state is able to overthrow them and give the required protection to the whole country, and so all-pervading that they threaten the integrity of our institutions.—Harlan: United States v. E. C. Knight Co., 156 U.S. 1, 44.

9. It is plain from the slightest consideration of practical affairs, or the most superficial reading of industrial history, that free competition means combination, and that the organization of the world, now going on so fast, means an ever-increasing might and scope of combination. It seems to me futile to set our faces against this

tendency. Whether beneficial on the whole, as I think it, or detrimental, it is inevitable, unless the fundamental axioms of society, and even the fundamental conditions of life are to be changed. — Holmes: Vegelahn v. Guntner, 167 Mass. 92, 108.

Related subjects: Business; Competition; Corporation; Monopoly and related subjects; Trust. *See also* Corporation, importance.

BUYER

Related subjects: Vendor-vendee. *See also* Equity court; Falsity 5, 6; Fiduciary 3; Litigation 21.

CALAMITY

See Government (general) 4.

CALMNESS

See Judgment 6.

CAMERA

Disclosure conveyed by the limitations and power of the camera does not convey the same things to the mind as disclosure made by the limitations and power of pen or voice.— Frankfurter: Radio Corp. v. United States, 341 U.S. 412, 425–26.

CANON

Related subjects: Rule and related subjects. *See also* Construction, rules; Equity court 7.

CAPITAL

1. A man's capital may be rated by the use of a cipher as truly as by the use of any other symbol.—Cardozo: Paskusz v. Phila. Cas. Co., 213 N.Y. 22, 25.

2. The fundamental relation of "capital" to "income" has been much discussed by economists, the former

being likened to the tree or the land, the latter to the fruit or the crop; the former depicted as a reservoir supplied from springs, the latter as the outlet stream, to be measured by its flow during a period of time.—Pitney: Eisner v. Macomber, 252 U.S. 189, 206.

Related subject: Investment. *See also* Corporation 68; Income; Monopoly 4.

CAPITALIST

1. It always will be true that the wealth of a nation is in the hands of the few, while the many subsist upon the proceeds of their daily toil.—Brewer: N.Y. State Bar Assoc. Bul., XVI, 37–47.

2. Great undertakings like this, whose future is at the time uncertain, requiring as they do large amounts of money to carry them on seem to make it necessary that extraordinary inducements should be held out to capitalists to enter upon them, since a failure is almost sure to involve those who make the venture in financial ruin.—Waite: Sinking Fund Cases, 9 Otto (99 U.S.) 700, 723.

3. Another kind of slavery sought to be fastened on the American people; namely, the slavery that would result from aggregations of capital in the hands of a few individuals and corporations controlling, for their own profit and advantage exclusively, the entire business of the country, including the production and sale of the necessities of life.—Harlan: Standard Oil Co. v. United States, 221 U.S., 1, 83.

CAPITAL PUNISHMENT
Related subject: Death penalty. *See also* Murder 2.

CARE
See Negligence 4, 7; Precaution; Vigilance.

CARICATURE
See Art 1.

CASES (legal)
1. Great cases, like hard cases, make bad law. For great cases are called great, not by reason of their real importance in shaping the law of the future, but because of some accident of immediate overwhelming interest which appeals to the feelings and distorts the judgment. These immediate interests exercise a kind of hydraulic pressure which makes what previously was clear seem doubtful, and before which even well-settled principles of law will bend.—Holmes: Northern Sec. Co. v. United States, 193 U.S. 197, 400–401.

2. Mr. Justice Fuller has, somewhere, emphatically said, that he had a dread of hard cases; they were the shipwrecks of the law.—Story: *Misc. Writings*, 283.
Related subject: Litigation. *See also* Justice.

CATCH PHRASE
1. Ready-made catch-phrases may conceal but do not solve serious constitutional problems. — Frankfurter: Shapiro v. United States, 335 U.S. 1, 50.

2. It is not the first use but the tiresome repetition of inadequate catch words upon which I am observing—

phrases which originally were contributions, but which, by their very felicity, delay further analysis for fifty years. That comes from the same source as dislike of novelty,—intellectual indolence or weakness—a slackening in the eternal pursuit of the more exact.—Holmes: "Law in Science and Science in Law," 12 Harv. L. Rev. 455.
Related subjects: Label; Language; Word.

CAUSE, CAUSATION
1. A failure to stop a man from doing what he knows that he ought not to do, hardly can be called a cause of his act.—Holmes: Unadilla V. Ry. v. Caldine, 278 U.S. 139, 142.

2. One could carry the search for causes backward, almost without end.—Cardozo: Gully v. First Nat'l Bank, 299 U.S. 109, 117.
See also Probable cause; War, cause.

CAUSE-EFFECT
1. When the root is cut the branches fall.—Holmes: Smallwood v. Gallardo, 275 U.S. 56, 62.

2. It was the fruit for which the seed was planted.—Cardozo: Buffum v. Peter Barceloux Co., 289 U.S. 227, 233.

3. Every effect is natural when there is complete knowledge of the cause.—Cardozo: Kerr S. S. Co. v. Radio Corp., 245 N.Y. 284, 290.

4. I believe with Montesquieu that if the chance of a battle—I may add, the passage of a law—had ruined a state, there was a general cause at work that made the state ready to

perish by a single battle or law.— Holmes: *Speeches,* 102.

5. Everything in nature is cause and effect by turns.—Cardozo: Bird v. St. Paul Fire & Marine Ins. Co., 224 N.Y. 47, 55.

CAUTION

Caution often seeks shelter in meaningless abstractions, devoid of guiding concreteness.—Frankfurter: Andres v. United States, 333 U.S. 740, 766.

See also Lawyer 69; Progress 8.

CAVEAT EMPTOR

Caveat emptor is a maxim that will often have to be followed when the morality which it expresses is not that of sensitive souls.—Cardozo: *Nature of Judicial Process,* 109.

CENSOR, CENSORSHIP

1. Censorship has had a long history in the western world. Book banning is as old as books.—Douglas: *We the Judges,* 323.

2. A requirement that literature or art conform to some norm prescribed by an official smacks of an ideology foreign to our system.—Douglas: Hannegan v. Esquire, 327 U.S. 146, 158.

3. We could justify any censorship only when the censors are better shielded against error than the censored. — Jackson: American Com. Assoc. v. Douds, 339 U.S. 382, 443.

4. In this Nation every writer, actor, or producer, no matter what medium of expression he may use, should be freed from the censor.—Douglas: Superior Films v. Dept. of Educ., 346 U.S. 587, 589.

5. To paraphrase Doctor Johnson, if nothing may be shown but what licensors may have previously approved, power, the yea or nay saying by officials, becomes the standard of the permissible.—Frankfurter: Burstyn v. Wilson, 343 U.S. 495, 532.

6. In seeking to apply the broad and all - inclusive definition of "sacrilegious" given by the New York courts, the censor is set adrift upon a boundless sea amid a myriad of conflicting currents of religious views, with no charts but those provided by the most vocal and powerful orthodoxies. — Clark: Burstyn v. Wilson, *ibid.,* 504–505.

7. The censor is beholden to those who sponsored the creation of his office, to those who are most radically preoccupied with the suppression of communication. The censor's function is to restrict and to restrain; his decisions are insulated from the pressures that might be brought to bear by public sentiment if the public were given an opportunity to see that which the censor has curbed. — Warren: Times Film Corp. v. Chicago, 365 U.S. 43, 67–68.

8. The censor's sword pierces deeply into the heart of free expression.—Warren: *ibid.,* 75.

9. The problems of the wayward mind concern the clerics, the psychiatrists, and the philosophers. Few groups have hesitated to create the political pressures that translate into secular law their notions of morality. —Douglas: *ibid.,* 80.

10. No more powerful weapon for

sectarian control can be imagined than governmental censorship.—Douglas: *ibid.*

11. The forces that build up demands for censorship are heterogeneous.—Douglas: *ibid.*, 81.

12. The regime of the censor is deadening. . . . The result is a pattern of conformity.—Douglas: *ibid.*, 82.

13. Under a censor's regime the weights are cast against freedom.—Douglas: *ibid.*, 86.

See also Constitution (U.S.), First Amendment 102, 103; Freedom, speech 103; Majority-minority 10; Teacher 7.

CENSURE

The most exemplary conduct and conscientious discharge of duty may not protect an individual from censure.—McLean: Goesele v. Bimeler, 14 How. (55 U.S.) 589, 609.

CERTAINTY

1. Out of the domain of the exact sciences and actual observation there is no absolute certainty.—Field: Hopt v. Utah, 120 U.S. 430, 439.

2. But certainty generally is illusion, and repose is not the destiny of man. —Holmes: "The Path of the Law," 10 Harv. L. Rev. 465.

3. Certitude is not the test of certainty. We have been cock-sure of many things that were not so.—Holmes: "Natural Law," 32 Harv. L. Rev. 40.

4. We are left to float on a sea of uncertainty.—Johnson: Green v. Biddle, 8 Wheat. (21 U.S.) 1, 103.

Related subjects: Definiteness; Definitiveness; Uncertainty. See also Fact 10; Law, certainty; Mind 11, 12; Political economy; Rule 5; Supreme Court 63; Tax 128.

CERTITUDE
See Certainty 3; Construction 85; Symbol 12.

CHALLENGE
See Jury, challenge.

CHAMPAGNE
Champagne is a beverage singularly grateful to the taste, and is indulged in by those who are supposed to be able and willing to pay the tax upon it. It is an article of high luxury.—Hunt: DeVary v. Arthur, 3 Otto (93 U.S.) 420, 423.

CHANCE
1. What a man does not know and cannot find out is chance as to him, and is recognized as chance by the law.—Holmes: Dillingham v. McLaughlin, 264 U.S. 370, 373.

2. They took the chances of the future. They must abide by its vicissitudes. — Cardozo: In the Matter of Berkovitz v. Arbib & Houlberg, 230 N.Y. 261, 274.

Related subjects: Gamble and related subjects.

CHANGE
1. Time works changes, brings into existence new conditions and purposes.—McKenna: Weems v. United States, 217 U.S. 349, 373.

2. The mystery of change and motion still vexes the minds of men as it baffled the Eleatics of old in the beginnings of recorded thought.—Cardozo: *The Growth of the Law*, 143.

3. I hope it is something more than timidity, dread of the new, that makes me fear that it is a step from the deck to the sea—the metaphor suggests a peril in consequences. — McKenna: Arizona Copper Co. v. Hammer, 250 U.S. 400, 434.

4. The elements of change and of certainty cannot exist in the same thing at the same time.—Hunt: Lapeyre v. United States, 17 Wall. (84 U.S.) 191, 205.

5. The metamorphosis is too great to be viewed without a shock.—Cardozo: Woolford Realty Co. v. Rose, 286 U.S. 319, 327.

See also Business 12; Despotism 1; Human nature and related subjects; Government (general) 6; Government (U.S.), change; Law 27, 45, 49; Legislation 8; Legislation, amendment; Legislation, repeal; Liability 17; Manufacture 2; Mind 1; Politics 3; Precedent 37; Proposition 2; Public welfare 21, 22; Reform 3; Remedy, change; Rule 9; Standard 2; Taste 2; Tax 39; Zoning 2.

CHAOS

Chaos serves no social end.—Jackson: Tax Comm'n v. Aldrich, 316 U.S. 174, 196.

CHARACTER, CHARACTERISTIC

1. The sportsman's spirit, which is only another word for character. This is the chief thing, more important far than skill, for skill without this will be palsied and perverted.—Cardozo: Law and Literature, 169.

2. Our vices as well as our virtues have been imputed to bodily derangements till character has become identified with a chemical reaction.—Cardozo: ibid., 83.

3. The tests of character come to us silently, unawares, by slow and inaudible approaches. We hardly know that they are here, till lo! the hour has struck, and the choice has been made, well or ill, but whether well or ill, a choice.—Cardozo: ibid., 170.

4. Many men are all wool, but none is more than a yard wide.—Brandeis: Mason, Brandeis, 620.

5. Men are not bad, men are not degraded, because they desire to be so; they are degraded largely through circumstances.—Brandeis: ibid., 91.

6. It is not, as a rule, the good people who commit crime.—Brewer: Hawker v. New York, 160 U.S. 189, 196.

7. He was a strong man, physically and mentally. Such a nature forms strong likes and strong dislikes; and at no time are such likes and dislikes so potent as when the thought of approaching death suggests the last action in respect thereto.—Brewer: Mackall v. Mackall, 135 U.S. 167, 171.

8. It is most idle to take a man apart from the circumstances which, in fact, were his. To be sure, it is easier in fancy to separate a person from his riches than from his character. But it is just as futile.—Holmes: Speeches, 88.

Related subjects: Evidence, character; Reputation. See also Corporation, characteristics; Dominance 1; Evidence, character; Government (general); Government (U.S.), characteristics; Grand jury 2; Human nature 1, 3; Idea 6; Insanity; Judge, qualifications; Judge, disabilities; Lawyer, characteristics; Lawyer 45; Legislation 43; Liability 7, 8; Merchant; Nation; Parent-child 5; Prosecutor 6; Public official 16; Seaman; Self incrimination 10; Supreme Court, characteristics; Witness, characteristics.

CHARITY

1. Charity, in a legal sense, is rather a matter of description than of definition.—Wayne: Perin v. Carey, 24 How. (65 U.S.) 465, 494.

2. Charity ministers to the mind as well as to the body.—Cardozo: Butterworth v. Keeler, 219 N.Y. 446, 450.

3. Charity kindly throws a mantle of oblivion over these matters of long ago.—Brewer: Mackall v. Mackall, 135 U.S. 167, 170.

4. It is only when income may be applied to the profit of the founders that business has a beginning and charity an end.—Cardozo: Butterworth v. Keeler, 219 N.Y. 446, 449.

See also Justice 3; Tax 108.

CHARTER

See Corporation, charter.

CHILD, CHILDREN

A democratic society rests, for its continuance, upon the healthy, well-rounded growth of young people into full maturity as citizens, with all that implies.—Rutledge: Prince v. Commonwealth of Mass., 321 U.S. 158, 168.

Related subjects: Infant; Parent-child; Youth. *See also* Education, public; Illegitimacy; Polygamy; Public school 4.

CHILD LABOR

If there is any matter upon which civilized countries have agreed . . . it is the evil of premature and excessive child labor.—Holmes: Hammer v. Dagenhart, 247 U.S. 251, 280.

CHINESE

1. They [Chinese] seem in the United States to have remained pilgrims and sojourners as all their fathers were.—Fuller: United States v. Wong Kim Ark, 169 U.S. 649, 726.

2. The time has been when many young men from China came to our educational institutions to pursue their studies; when her commerce sought our shores, and her people came to build our railroads, and when China looked upon this country as her best friend. If all this be reversed and the most populous nation on earth becomes the great antagonist of this republic, the careful student of history . . . for cause of such antagonism need look no further than the treatment accorded during the last twenty years by this country to the people of that nation.—Brewer: United States v. Sing Tuck, 194 U.S. 161, 182.

CHOICE

1. Inaction without more is not tantamount to choice. — Cardozo: Richard v. Credit Suisse, 242 N.Y. 346, 351.

2. Choice has not been made until choice has been allowed.—Cardozo: Fitzgerald v. Harbor Lighterage Co., 244 N.Y. 132, 137.

3. Conduct under duress involves a choice.—Holmes: Union Pac. R.R. v. Public Serv. Comm'n, 248 U.S. 67, 70.

4. An act implies a choice, and . . . it is felt to be impolitic and unjust to make a man answerable for harm, un-

less he might have chosen otherwise. —Holmes: *The Common Law,* 54.

5. We must consider the two objects of desire both of which we cannot have and make up our minds which to choose.—Holmes: Olmstead v. United States, 277 U.S. 438, 470.

6. The right to choose is not destroyed by the unwisdom of the choice.—Cardozo: Pallocco v. Lehigh Valley R.R., 236 N.Y., 110, 114.

7. A choice between the rock and the whirlpool. — Sutherland: Frost Truck Co. v. Railroad Comm'n, 271 U.S. 583, 593.

8. There was no choice but Hobson's.—Rutledge: Canizio v. New York, 327 U.S. 82, 92.

9. Choice, as it happens, is not free. —Cardozo: Michigan v. Michigan Tr. Co., 286 U.S. 334, 342.

Related subject: Election (choice). *See also* Duress 2; Freedom 158; Judicial process 11, 12.

CHRISTIANITY

To the benign influence of the Christian religion it remained to shed a few faint rays upon the gloom of war; a feeble light but barely sufficient to disclose its horrors.—Johnson: The Rapid, 8 Cranch (12 U.S.) 155, 161.

See also Blasphemy.

CHURCH

The congregation had the same right to the comfortable enjoyment of its house for church purposes that a private gentleman has to the comfortable enjoyment of his own house. —Field: Baltimore & P. R.R. v. Fifth Bapt. Church, 108 U.S. 317, 335.

See also Papacy; Pipe: Religion: Roman Catholic Church.

CHURCH-STATE SEPARATION

See Freedom, religion 119, 122, 123, 124.

CIGARETTE

Cigarettes are but one of the numerous manufactures of tobacco, and we cannot take judicial notice of the fact that it is more noxious in this form than in any other. . . . Cigarettes do not seem until recently to have attracted the attention of the public as more injurious than other forms of tobacco. . . . Nor are we now prepared to take judicial notice of any special injury resulting from their use or to indorse the opinion of the Supreme Court of Tennessee that "they are inherently bad and bad only."— Brown: Austin v. Tennessee, 179 U.S. 343, 348.

CIRCUMSPECTION

If the duty of circumspection has need of other emphasis, we may find it in the consequences.—Cardozo: Browne v. City of New York, 241 N.Y. 96, 112.

CITIZEN, CITIZENSHIP

1. Citizens are the members of the political community to which they belong. They are the people who compose the community, and who, in their associated capacity, have established or submitted themselves to the dominion of a government for the promotion of their individual as well as their collective rights.—Waite: United States v. Cruikshank, 2 Otto (92 U.S.) 542, 549.

2. Under that constitution there are citizens, but no subjects.—Wilson: Chisholm v. Georgia, 2 Dall. (2 U.S.) 419, 456.

3. No citizen of the United States is an alien in any state of the Union. —Sutherland: Colgate v. Harvey, 296 U.S. 404, 426.

4. A clergyman, no less than a judge, is a citizen.—Reed: Murdock v. Pennsylvania, 319 U.S. 105, 135.

5. A citizen is still a citizen, though guilty of crime and visited with punishment. His political rights may be put in abeyance or forfeited. . . . If he loses his rights he escapes none of his disabilities and liabilities which before subsisted.—Swayne: White v. Hart, 13 Wall. (80 U.S.) 646, 651.

6. Citizenship is a privilege not due of common right.—Cardozo: Morrison v. California, 291 U.S. 82, 89.

7. Citizenship obtained through naturalization is not a second-class citizenship. — Douglas: Knauer v. United States, 328 U.S. 654, 658.

8. State citizenship is ephemeral. It results only from residence and is gained or lost therewith.—Jackson: Edwards v. California, 314 U.S. 160, 183.

9. The life and liberty of the citizen are precious things—precious to the state as to the citizen.—McKenna: Trono v. United States, 199 U.S. 521, 539.

10. Not only is United States citizenship a "high privilege," it is a priceless treasure.—Black: Johnson v. Eisentrager, 339 U.S. 763, 791.

11. It certainly can be no humiliation to the citizen of a Republic to yield a ready obedience to the laws as administered by the constituted authorities. On the contrary, it is among his first and highest duties as a citizen, because free government cannot exist without it.—Taney: Ableman v. Booth, 21 How. (62 U.S.) 506, 521.

12. It is not to rulers and statesmen alone, that the science of government is important and useful. It is equally indispensable for every American citizen, to enable him to exercise his own rights, to protect his own interests, and to secure the public liberties and the just operations of public authority. —Story: *Misc. Writings,* 155.

13. The citizen should be able to comprehend among other things the great and difficult problems of industry, commerce, and finance, which with us necessarily become political questions. He must learn about men as well as things. Our great beneficent experiment in democracy will fail unless the people, our rulers, are developed in character and intelligence.— Brandeis: Mason, *Brandeis,* 151–52.

14. To take an interest in public affairs, and to further and promote those principles which are believed to be vital or important to the general welfare, is every citizen's duty. It is a just complaint that so many good men abstain from taking such an interest.—Bradley: *Ex parte* Curtis, 106 U.S. 371, 376.

15. In a republic, every citizen is himself in some measure entrusted with the public safety, and acts an im-

portant part for its weal or woe.—
Story: *Misc. Writings,* 448.

16. Our highest civil duty is to serve
our country when in danger.—Davis:
Ex parte Milligan, 4 Wall. (71 U.S.)
2, 130.

17. Still as in the days of Edward I,
the citizenry may be called upon to
enforce the justice of the State, not
faintly and with lagging steps, but
honestly and bravely and with whatever implements and facilities are convenient and at hand.—Cardozo: In
the Matter of Barington v. Yellow
Taxi Corp., 250 N.Y. 14, 17.

18. The duty to disclose knowledge
of crime rests upon all citizens.—Jackson: Stein v. New York, 346 U.S. 156,
184.

19. Jury service is a duty as well as
a privilege of citizenship; it is a duty
that cannot be shirked on a plea of
inconvenience or decreased earning
power.—Murphy: Thiel v. Southern
Pac. Co., 328 U.S. 217, 224.

20. Under our system, the *people*
. . . are the sovereign. Their rights,
whether collective or individual, are
not bound to give way to a sentiment
of loyalty to the person of a monarch.
The citizen here knows no person,
however near to those in power or
however powerful himself, to whom
he need yield the rights which the
law secures to him when it is well administered.—Miller: United States v.
Lee, 106 U.S. 196, 208–209.

21. A citizen of the United States
. . . is not bound to cringe to any
superior, or to pray for any act of
grace, as a means of enjoying all the
rights and privileges enjoyed by other
citizens. And when the spirit of lawlessness, mob violence, and sectional
hate can be so completely repressed
as to give full practical effect to this
right, we shall be a happier nation,
and a more prosperous one than we
now are.—Bradley: Slaughter House
Cases, 16 Wall. (83 U.S.) 36, 113.

22. What is there in the exalted station of the officer, which shall bar a
citizen from asserting, in a court of
justice, his legal rights, or shall forbid
a court to listen to the claim.—Marshall: Marbury v. Madison, 1 Cranch
(5 U.S.) 137, 170.

23. The privilege of bringing every
law to the test of the constitution belongs to the humblest citizen, who
owes no obedience, to any legislative
act, which transcends the constitutional limits.—Story: *Misc. Writings,* 428.

24. One of the great ends of the
constitution, one which it never loses
sight of in any of its provisions—that
of making an American citizen as
free in one state as he was in another.
—Johnson: Ogden v. Saunders, 12
Wheat. (25 U.S.) 213, 274.

25. It is the birthright of every
American citizen when charged with
crime, to be tried and punished according to law.—Davis: *Ex parte* Milligan, 4 Wall. (71 U.S.) 2, 119.

26. American citizenship should be
a sure guaranty of safety . . . in which
every citizen of the United States
might stand erect in every portion of
its soil, in the full enjoyment of every
right and privilege belonging to a freeman, without fear of violence or mo-

lestation.—Bradley: Slaughter House Cases, 16 Wall. (83 U.S.) 36, 123.

27. The interests of every citizen are bound up with the fate of the government. None can claim exemption. —Bradley: Legal Tender Cases, 12 Wall. (79 U.S.) 457, 561.

28. The power of citizenship as a shield against oppression was widely known from the example of Paul's Roman citizenship, which sent the centurion scurrying to his higher-ups with the message: "Take heed what thou doest; for this man is a Roman." —Jackson: Edwards v. California, 314 U.S. 160, 182.

29. Possession by an American citizen of the rights and privileges that constitute citizenship imposes correlative obligations, of which the most indispensable may well be "to take his place in the ranks of the army of his country and risk the chance of being shot down in its defense."—Frankfurter: Trop v. Dulles, 356 U.S. 86, 121.

30. The civilized nations of the world are in virtual unanimity that statelessness is not to be imposed as punishment for crime. — Warren: *ibid.,* 102.

31. Use of denationalization as a punishment is barred by the Eighth Amendment. There may be involved no physical mistreatment, no primitive torture. There is instead the total destruction of the individual's status in organized society. It is a form of punishment more primitive than torture, for it destroys for the individual the political existence that was cen-

turies in the development.—Warren: *ibid.,* 101.

32. Citizenship is not a license that expires upon misbehavior.—Warren: *ibid.,* 92.

33. Citizenship, like freedom of speech, press, and religion, occupies a preferred position in our written Constitution, because it is a grant absolute in terms.—Warren: Perez v. Brownell, 356 U.S. 44, 84.

34. United States citizenship is . . . the constitutional birthright of every person born in this country.—Warren: *ibid.,* 66.

35. Citizenship is man's basic right for it is nothing less than the right to have rights.—Warren: *ibid.,* 64.

36. Acquisition of American citizenship is a solemn affair.—Douglas: Chaunt v. United States, 364 U.S. 350, 352.

Related subjects: Denationalization; Denaturalization; Naturalization; Nationality. *See also* Democracy 21; Deportation 4; Education; Election; Eminent domain 13; Equality 9; Freedom, thought 149; Government (general) 12, 13; Government (U.S.), 18; Language 1; Litigant 7; Military 17; Nationality; Negro; Politician 2; Poverty 2; Public official 3, 4, 5; Rights 24; Rights, limitations; State 5; Sunday 1; Vote 1; War 3; War, consequences.

CITY
Related subjects: Municipal planning; Municipality. *See also* Railroad 1.

CIVILIZATION
1. To be civilized is to be potentially master of all possible ideas, and that means that one has got beyond being shocked, although one preserves one's

own moral and aesthetic preferences. —Holmes: *Holmes-Pollock Letters,* I, 105.

2. The degree of civilization which a people has reached, no doubt, is marked by their anxiety to do as they would be done by.—Holmes: *The Common Law,* 44.

3. For most of the things that properly can be called evils in the present state of the law I think the main remedy, as for the evils of public opinion, is for us to grow more civilized.— Holmes: *Speeches,* 102.

4. The mark of a truly civilized man is confidence in the strength and security derived from the inquiring mind. — Frankfurter: D e n n i s v. United States, 341 U.S. 494, 556.

5. The progress of civilization is to a considerable extent the displacement of error which once held sway as official truth by beliefs which in turn have yielded to other beliefs.—Frankfurter: Kovacs v. Cooper, 336 U.S. 77, 95.

> See also Court 22; Doubt 2; Freedom 53; Law 61; Lawyer 21; Litigation 29; Majority-minority 9; Marriage 3; Polygamy 3; Real property 8; Tax 15.

CIVIL SERVICE

The civil service system has been called "the one great political invention" of nineteenth century democracy.—Douglas: United Pub. Workers v. Mitchell, 330 U.S. 75, 121.

CLAIM

1. A mistaken claim is nonetheless a claim.—Vinson: Healy v. Comm'r of Int. Rev., 345 U.S., 278, 282.

2. The claim had been swollen in disfigurement of truth.—Cardozo: Thomann v. City of Rochester, 256 N.Y. 165, 172.

> See also Limitation; Litigation 1; Value 28.

CLARITY

That may be very clear to one intellect, which is far from being so to another.—Marshall: Ogden v. Saunders, 12 Wheat. (25 U.S.) 213, 339.

> See also Opinion 19.

CLASS HATRED

The unfortunately growing hatred of the poor for the rich seems to me to rest on the belief that money is the main thing (a belief in which the poor have been encouraged by the rich), more than on any grievance.— Holmes: *Speeches,* 56–57.

> See also Property 36.

CLASSICS

1. Age increases my conviction that one cannot afford to give much time to the classics. Some time, yes. But one needs to enlarge and enrich one's view of life and the universe. The ideas of the classics, so far as living, are our commonplaces. It is the modern books that give us the latest and the most profound conceptions. It seems to me rather a lazy makeshift to mumble over the familiar. — Holmes: *Uncollected Letters,* 178.

2. Subject to such private exceptions as one would make, the literature of the past is a bore—(It has not our emphasis. It does not ask, still less answer, our questions. It comes from

a different intellectual and emotional *milieu*).—Holmes: *ibid.*, 182.

CLASSIFICATION

1. Some qualities, such as those of bravery or heroism, are unique and incommensurable. They refuse, like originality or genius, to stay within a class.—Cardozo: Barlow v. Berry, 245 N.Y. 500, 504.

2. Plodding virtues are not so rare that their possessors, however estimable cannot be classified in groups. —Cardozo: *ibid*.

3. The fact that women may now have achieved the virtues that men have long claimed as their prerogatives and now indulge in vices that men have long practiced, does not preclude the States from drawing a sharp line between the sexes.—Frankfurter: Coesaert v. Cleary, 335 U.S. 464, 466.

4. There may even be a need to make a regulation based on race, the source of the most vicious discriminations man has made . . . by reason of the special traits of those races, such, for example, as their susceptibility to particular diseases.—Douglas: *We the Judges,* 399.

5. The very idea of classification is that of inequality.—Brewer: Atchison, T. & S. F. R.R. v. Matthews, 174 U.S. 96, 106.

CLASS LEGISLATION
See Legislation, discriminatory.

CLEMENCY

1. At such a time [appeal for clemency] anything is pertinent that may move the mind to doubt or the heart to charity. It is not necessary that reason be convinced; it is enough that compassion be stirred.—Cardozo: Andrews v. Gardiner, 224 N.Y. 440, 447.

2. The right to plead for clemency is not a monopoly of the bar.—Cardozo: *ibid*.
Related subjects: Pardon; Parole; Probation. *See also* Wrongdoer 7.

CLERGYMAN
Related subject: Preacher. *See also* Citizen 4.

CLICHÉ
One finds it hard to believe that a cliché so inveterate is devoid of meaning altogether.—Cardozo: Campbell v. City of New York, 244 N.Y. 317, 329.

CLIENT
See Lawyer, obligations; Lawyer 61.

CLOSED SHOP
See Labor union.

COAL INDUSTRY
This history of the bituminous coal industry is written in blood as well as in ink.—Douglas: Sunshine Anth. Coal Co. v. Adkins, 310 U.S. 381, 395.

CODE (legal)

1. Another mistake, as we cannot but think, is that a code is to be short. This probably springs from the thoroughly exploded notion that it is to make every man his own lawyer. . . . A code will not get rid of lawyers, and should be written for them much more than the laity.—Holmes: *Uncollected Letters,* 64–65.

2. Justinian's prohibition of any commentary on the product of his

codifiers is remembered only for its futility.—Cardozo: *Nature of Judicial Process,* 18.

See also Constitution 52.

COERCION

1. Coercion might be the product of subtlety as well as of violence.—Douglas: Breithaupt v. Abram, 352 U.S. 432, 443.

2. The rightfulness of coercion must depend on the pre-existing obligation to do that for which compulsion is used. It is no objection to the principle, that the injured party may be of the weakest.—Marshall: Ogden v. Saunders, 12 Wheat. (25 U.S.) 213, 345.

3. Words uttered under coerion are proof of loyalty to nothing but self-interest.—Black and Douglas: West Va. State Bd. of Educ. v. Barnette, 319 U.S. 624, 644.

Related subjects: Compulsion; Duress; Pressure. See also Court 23; Motive 10; Witness 16.

COHABITATION
See Marriage 5.

COINCIDENCE

1. If we may not say of such a coincidence that it literally is impossible, at least we may say that one would be surprising, and several would be marvellous.—Cardozo: In the Matter of Mayor of New York, 246 N.Y. 72, 78.

2. If one factor is uniform in a continuing series of events that are brought to pass through human intervention, the law would have to have the blindness of impartiality not to attribute the uniform factor to man's purpose.—Frankfurter: Cassell v. Texas, 339 U.S. 282, 293.

3. The mind of justice, not merely its eyes, would have to be blind to attribute such an occurrence to mere fortuity. — Frankfurter: Avery v. Georgia, 345 U.S. 559, 564.

COLLECTIVE BARGAINING
See Labor union.

COLLUSION
See Fraud 1.

COLONIES
See Commerce 2.

COMBAT
See Self-defense 2.

COMBINATION
Related subjects: Monopoly and related subjects. See also Business (big) 6, 9; Labor union; Restraint of trade.

COMMA
See Punctuation.

COMMAND

1. An absolute command does not exist—penalty or no penalty—unless a breach of it is deprived of the protection of the law.—Holmes: *Uncollected Letters,* 27.

2. The personal ascendancy of one man may be such that it would give to his advice the effect of a command.—Holmes: Northern Sec. Co. v. United States, 193 U.S. 197, 403.

See also Compulsion 2; Construction 42.

COMMERCE

1. Thus we read in a great poet of "looks commercing with the skies"; but this sublimated application of the

term would badly accord with the views of commerce in a mercantile sense, or with the utilitarian spirit of this calculating and prosaic age. — Daniel: Passenger Cases, 7 How. (48 U.S.) 283, 501.

2. The colonies of modern nations owe their origin almost exclusively to the spirit of commerce.—Story: *Misc. Writings,* 50.

3. Past experience teaches us, that however the facilities of commerce may be multiplied, her tracks will be filled with productions which enrich the country and add to the comforts and enjoyments of its rapidly increasing population.—McLean: Pennsylvania v. Wheeling & Belmont Bridge Co., 13 How. (54 U.S.) 518, 576.

4. Free access to the markets through unobstructed channels of commerce is the very breath of the life of . . . manufacturing establishments. —Pitney: Paine Lumber Co. v. Neal, 244 U.S. 459, 474.

5. The laws of the Union protect our commerce wherever the flag of the country may float.—McLean: United States v. Guthrie, 17 How. (58 U.S.) 284, 309.

6. Uncertainty and ambiguity are the bane of commerce.—Bradley: Merritt v. Welsh, 14 Otto (104 U.S.) 694, 702.

> See also Constitution, commerce clauses; Manufacture 1; Mining; Restraint of trade 8; Tax 81.

COMMON DENOMINATOR

The common denominator silences and satisfies.—Cardozo: *Law and Literature,* 19.

COMMON LAW

1. The common law is not a brooding omnipresence in the sky, but the articulate voice of some sovereign or quasi-sovereign that can be identified. —Holmes: Southern Pac. Co. v. Jensen, 244 U.S. 205, 222.

2. The common law is the *lex non scripta,* that is, the unwritten law, which cannot now be traced back to any positive text; but is composed of customs, and usages, and maxims, deriving their authority from immemorial practice, and the recognitions of courts of justice. . . . It is the law of liberty, and the watchful and inflexible guardian of private property and public rights.—Story: *Misc. Writings,* 442.

3. The history of the common law may be divided into three great epochs; the first extending from the reign of William the Conqueror to the Reformation; the second from the reign of Elizabeth to the Revolution, which placed the house of Brunswick on the throne; and the third including the period which has since elapsed, down to our time.—Story: *ibid.,* 407.

4. The common law had its origin in ignorant and barbarous ages; it abounded with artificial distinctions and crafty subtilities, partly from the scholastic habits of its early clerical professors, and partly from its subserviency to the narrow purposes of feudal polity.—Story: *ibid.,* 412-13.

5. The common law is gradually changing its old channels, and wearing new. It has continual accessions on some sides; and, on others, leaves

behind vast accumulations, which now serve little other purpose than to show, what were its former boundaries.—Story: *ibid.,* 307.

6. The responses from the other [common law] are the voice of the law, speaking through all ages in one unvarying tone; delivering the results of human wisdom, developed in principles, matured, digested, explained, enforced and supported during five centuries, amidst all the conflicts of party vengeance, civil war, and regal o p p r e s s i o n. — Baldwin: *Ex parte* Crane, 5 Pet. (30 U.S.) 189, 221.

7. Malleability, to suit the necessities and usages of the mercantile and commercial world, is one of the most valuable characteristics of the common law.—Grier: Mercer County v. Hackett, 1 Wall. (68 U.S.) 83, 95.

8. The common law rules . . . are not the particular rules which were in force in 1791, but are those rules adapted to present day conditions, "in accordance with present day standards of wisdom and justice rather than in accordance with some outworn and antiquated rules of the past."—Stone: Dimick v. Schiedt, 293 U.S. 474, 496 (quot. 290 U.S. 371, 382).

9. Common law, . . . in its early history freely blended religious conceptions of sin with legal conceptions of crime.—Jackson: Jordan v. De George, 341 U.S. 223, 237.

10. The common law, unless bound and riveted by statute, has instruments at hand of many varieties and shapes for the molding of that justice which is the end of her endeavor.—Cardozo: *Law and Literature,* 187.

11. The common law begins and ends with the solution of a particular case.—Holmes: *Uncollected Letters,* 19.

12. The State of Georgia is the only State—indeed, apparently the only jurisdiction in the common-law world —to retain the common-law rule that a person charged with a criminal offense is incompetent to testify under oath in his own behalf at his trial.—Brennan: Ferguson v. Georgia, 365 U.S. 570.

Related subject: Law, development. *See also* Construction 141; Government (U.S.), state 80; Interest 1; Labor 102; Labor, history; Reputation 7; Restraint of trade 1; Sunday 5; Witness 5.

COMMONPLACE

These are commonplaces, but at times—it may be always—commonplaces are our best guides when rights are concerned.—McKenna: United States v. Ohio Oil Co., 234 U.S. 548, 571.

See also Dissent 1.

COMMON SENSE

1. Common sense often makes good law.—Douglas: Peak v. United States, 353 U.S. 43, 46.

2. That which makes no sense to the common understanding surely is not required by any fictive notions of law or even by the most sentimental attitude toward criminals.—Frankfurter: Milanovich v. United States, 365 U.S. 551, 559–60.

Related subject: Practical. *See also* Construction, practical; Faith 3.

COMMUNISM,
COMMUNIST PARTY

1. It is the doctrine of absolutism, pure, simple and naked; and of communism, which is its twin; the double progeny of the same evil birth.—Matthews: Poindexter v. Greenhow, 114 U.S. 270, 291.

2. Their whole philosophy is to minimize man as an individual and to increase the power of man acting in the mass. If any single characteristic distinguishes our democracy from Communism it is our recognition of the individual as a personality rather than as a soulless part in the jigsaw puzzle that is the collectivist state.—Jackson: American Com. Assoc. v. Douds, 339 U.S. 382, 443.

3. An exaction of some profession of belief or nonbelief is precisely what the Communists would enact—each individual must adopt the ideas that are common to the ruling group.—Jackson: *ibid.,* 443.

4. There are, however, contradictions between what meets the eye and what is covertly done, which, in my view of the issues, provide a rational basis upon which Congress reasonably could have concluded that the Communist Party is something different in fact from any other substantial party we have known, and hence may constitutionally be treated as something different in law.—Jackson: *ibid.,* 423.

5. Communism in the world scene is no bogey-man; but Communism as a political faction or party in this country plainly is. Communism has been so thoroughly exposed in this country that it has been crippled as a political force. Free speech has destroyed it as an effective political party.—Douglas: Dennis v. United States, 341 U.S. 494, 588.

6. They are miserable merchants of unwanted ideas; their wares remain unsold. The fact that their ideas are abhorrent does not make them powerful.—Douglas: *ibid.,* 589.

7. Communism will not go to jail with these Communists.—Jackson: *ibid.,* 578.

8. History overwhelmingly establishes that many youths like the petitioner were drawn by the mirage of communism during the depression era, only to have their eyes later opened to reality. Such experiences no doubt may disclose wooly mind or naive notions regarding the problems of society.—Frankfurter: Schware v. Board of Bar Exam'rs, 353 U.S. 232, 251.

9. In the atmosphere existing in this country today, the charge that someone is a Communist is so common that hardly anyone active in public life escapes it.—Black: Wilkinson v. United States, 365 U.S. 399, 419.

See also Investigation 5; Legislation 57.

COMMUNITY
See Society.

COMMUNITY OF PROPERTY

The notion of a community of property and profits was utterly incompatible with the growth of a state. It cut off, at a blow, every excitement to individual enterprise; and, by its unequal distribution of burthens and benefits, sowed far and wide the elements of discord.—Story: *Misc. Writings,* 37.

COMMUNITY PROPERTY

We shall not attempt to epitomize a legal system at least as ancient as the custom of the Visigoths, but we must note that the community property principle rests upon something more than the moral obligation of supporting spouse and children: the business relationship of man and wife for their mutual monetary profit.— Clark: Wissner v. Wissner, 338 U.S. 655, 659–60.

COMPANY TOWN

A company-owned town is a town. In its community aspects it does not differ from other towns.—Frankfurter: Marsh v. Alabama, 326 U.S. 501, 510.

COMPANY UNION

See Labor union, abuse.

COMPENSATION

Related subjects: Interest; Wage. *See also* Eminent domain; Injury 1; Interest; Lawyer, compensation; Penalty 2, 3; Public official, compensation.

COMPENSATION (wages)

We know . . . that professional services are offered in the industrial and business field; and that while there is no hard and fast standard of compensation, and men bargain for their rewards, salaries do bear some relation to experience and ability.—Roberts: Brush v. Comm'r of Int. Rev., 300 U.S. 352, 376.

COMPETENCE, COMPETENCY

Related subjects: Incompetence; Insanity; Mental disease. *See also* Witness, competency.

COMPETITION

1. If the policy on which our law is founded is too narrowly expressed in the term free competition, we may substitute free struggle for life. Certainly, the policy is not limited to struggles between persons of the same class, competing for the same end. It applies to all conflicts of temporal interests. — Holmes: Vegelahn v. Guntner, 167 Mass. 92, 107.

2. Free competition means a free and open market among both buyers and sellers for the sale and distribution of commodities.—Stone: Maple Floor Mfrs. Assoc. v. United States, 268 U.S. 563, 583.

3. Effective competition requires that traders have large freedom of action when conducting their own affairs.—McReynolds: Federal Trade Comm'n v. Curtis Pub. Co., 260 U.S. 568, 582.

4. The free competition so often figured as a social good imports order and moderation and a decent regard for the welfare of the group.—Cardozo: Carter v. Carter Coal Co., 298 U.S. 238, 331.

5. The doctrine generally has been accepted that free competition is worth more to society than it costs. —Holmes: Vegelahn v. Guntner, 167 Mass., 92, 106.

6. I think we greatly exaggerate the value and importance to the public

of competition ... as fixing a fair price. What really fixes that is the competition of conflicting desires.—Holmes: Dr. Miles Medical Co. v. John D. Park & Sons Co., 220 U.S. 373, 412.

7. No system of regulation can safely be substituted for the operation of individual liberty as expressed in competition.—B r a n d e i s : Mason, *Brandeis,* 181.

8. The wastes of democracy are among the greatest obvious wastes, but we have compensations in democracy which far outweigh that waste, and make it more efficient than absolutism. So it is with competition. Incentive and development which are incident to the freer system of business result in so much greater achievement that the waste is relatively insignificant. The margin between that which men naturally do, and that which they can do, is so great that a system which urges men on to action and develops individual enterprise and initiative is preferable, in spite of the wastes that necessarily attend that process.—Brandeis: *ibid.,* 382.

9. If experience did not teach that economic advantage goes along with larger sales, there would be an end to the hot pursuit for wide and wider markets. — Cardozo: Stewart Dry Goods Co. v. Lewis, 294 U.S. 550, 570.

10. At least since Adam Smith wrote, unhampered competition has not generally been considered immoral.—Black: Mercoid Corp. v. Mid-Cont. Inv. Co., 320 U.S. 661, 673.

11. Success alone does not show reprehensible methods, although it may increase or render insuperable the difficulties which rivals must face.—McReynolds: Federal Trade Comm'n v. Curtis Pub. Co., 260 U.S. 568, 582.

12. The careless and the unscrupulous must rise to the standards of the scrupulous and diligent.—Cardozo: Federal Trade Comm'n v. Alcoma Lumber Co., 291 U.S. 67, 79.

13. A trader may not, by pursuing a dishonest practice, force his competitors to choose between its adoption or the loss of their trade.—Stone: Federal Trade Comm'n v. Keppel, 291 U.S. 304, 313.

14. Competition, not combination, should be the law of trade.—McKenna: National Cotton Oil Co. v. Texas, 197 U.S. 115, 129.

15. True, of course, it is that the weaker members of the group . . . may find themselves unable to keep pace with the stronger, but it is their comparative inefficiency, not tyrannical compulsion, that make them laggards in the race.—Cardozo: Hegeman Farms Corp. v. Baldwin, 293 U.S. 163, 171.

16. I cannot believe that in the long run the public will profit by this court permitting knaves to cut reasonable prices for some ulterior purpose of their own, and thus to impair, if not to destroy, the production and sale of articles which it is assumed to be desirable that the public should be able to get.—Holmes: Dr. Miles Medical Co. v. John D. Park & Sons Co., 220 U.S. 373, 412.

17. Unfair competition involves not only an offender but also a victim.—

Douglas: Federal Trade Comm'n v. Bunte Bros., 312 U.S. 349, 356.

18. Men will pay for any privilege that gives a reasonable expectancy of preference in the race of competition.—Cardozo: In the Matter of Brown, 242 N.Y. 1, 6.

19. The conflict for advantage called competition—the play of the contending forces ordinarily engendered by an honest desire for gain.—McReynolds: United States v. Am. Linseed Oil Co., 262 U.S. 371, 388.

Related subjects: Monopoly and related subjects. *See also* Business 2; Business (big) 9; Corporation 63, 64; Lawyer 79; Production 4; Tax 80.

COMPLAINT

Complaints . . . may be interested lament but, on the other hand, they may be the expression of real grievance and demand redress. — McKenna: United States v. United Shoe Mach. Co., 247 U.S. 32, 56.

COMPROMISE

1. The question has been discussed, until discussion has become useless. It has been argued, until argument is exhausted. We have now met on the ground of compromise. — Marshall: Beveridge, *Life of Marshall,* IV, 505.

2. To obtain a just compromise, concession must not only be mutual —it must be equal also. . . . There can be no hope that either will yield more than it gets in return.—Marshall: *ibid.,* 506.

3. If we cannot meet on the line that divides us equally, then take the hand of friendship, and make an equal compromise.—Marshall: *ibid.*

4. Some middle point must be found between the horns of this dilemma. — Holmes: *The Common Law,* 107.

5. Everyone cannot have his own way and each must yield something to the reasonable satisfaction of the needs of all.—Reed: Breard v. Alexandria, 341 U.S. 622, 626.

6. Of what use would it be to attempt to bring bodies of men to agreement and compromise of controversies if you put out of view the influences which move them or the fellowship which binds them—maybe controls and impels them, whether rightfully or wrongfully, to make the cause of one the cause of all?—McKenna: Adair v. United States, 208 U.S. 161, 185.

7. Nowadays at least, men are seldom sure enough of their convictions to be willing to put inflexibility in the forefront of the virtues and compromise behind it.—Cardozo: *Law and Literature,* 158.

8. The seductions of a dinner were thought to have a tendency to mollify convictions and stimulate with the gastric juices a tendency to compromise.—Cardozo, *ibid.*

See also Contention 1; Judicial process 13; Jury 43.

COMPULSION

1. The location of the point at which pressure turns into compulsion, and ceases to be inducement, would be a question of degree—at times, perhaps, of fact. — Cardozo: Steward Mach. Co. v. Davis, 301 U.S. 548, 590.

2. Compulsion which comes from

circumstances can be as real as compulsion which comes from a command.—Douglas: Pub. Util. Comm'n v. Pollak, 343 U.S. 451, 468.

Related subjects: Coercion; Pressure. *See also* Law 70.

CONCEALMENT

1. Concealment is as frequently the refuge of error as it is of crime.—Wayne: Patterson v. Gaines, 6 How. (47 U.S.) 550, 593.

2. In a court of conscience deliberate concealment is equivalent to deliberate falsehood.—Waite: Crosby v. Buchanan, 23 Wall. (90 U.S.) 420, 454.

3. Honesty of purpose prompts frankness of statement. Concealment is indicative of fraud.—Waite: *ibid.,* 457.

4. The fundamental truth, evolved from the experience of mankind, that the innocent do often conceal through fear or other emotion.—White: Hickory v. United States, 160 U.S. 408, 421.

See also Construction 79; Silence 2.

CONCEPT

1. All concepts are relative.—Vinson: Dennis v. United States, 341 U.S. 494, 508.

2. A conception so general cannot be without cause.—McKenna: German Alliance Ins. Co. v. Lewis, 233 U.S. 389, 412.

3. The conceptions of the infancy of the race.—Holmes: Wheeler v. Sohmer, 233 U.S. 434, 438.

CONCESSION

See Compromise 2.

CONCLUSION

1. This was but the usual error of arriving at a false conclusion by the use of equivocal or ambiguous terms. —Grier: Hogg v. Ruffner, 1 Black (66 U.S.) 115, 120.

2. The facts are such that different minds may honestly draw different conclusions from them. — Clarke: United Zinc & Chem. Co. v. Britt, 258 U.S. 268, 277.

3. The statement may be called a conclusion, but it is a conclusion of fact, just as the statement that a certain liquid was beer is a conclusion of fact from certain impressions of taste, smell, and sight. — Holmes: Southern Ry. v. King, 217 U.S. 524, 538.

4. That a conclusion satisfied one's private conscience does not attest its reliability. The validity and moral authority of a conclusion largely depend on the mode by which it was reached.—Frankfurter: Joint Anti-Fascist Ref. Comm. v. McGrath, 341 U.S. 123, 171.

Related subjects: Belief and related subjects. *See also* Dictum 2, 3; Liberalism; Mind 3; Reason 6.

CONCUBINE

The prostitute may, in the popular sense, be more degraded in character than the concubine, but the latter none the less must be held to lead an immoral life, if any regard whatever be had to the views that are almost universally held in this country as to the relations which may rightfully, from the standpoint of morality, exist between man and woman in the matter

of sexual intercourse. — H a r l a n:
United States v. Bitty, 208 U.S. 393,
402.

CONDEMNATION (legal)
See Eminent domain.

CONDITION
See Privilege 2, 5; Promise 3; Public expenditure 6.

CONDUCT

1. The moral connotation of behavior is conduct.—Murphy: Schneiderman v. United States, 320 U.S. 118, 133.

2. The standards for a very large part of human conduct do not vary from century to century.—Holmes: *The Common Law,* 126

3. A blind man is not required to see at his peril.—Holmes: *ibid.,* 109.

4. When men live in society, a certain average of conduct, a sacrifice of individual peculiarities going beyond a certain point, is necessary to the general welfare.—Holmes: *ibid.,* 108.

5. Not all the precepts of conduct precious to the hearts of many of us are immutable principles of justice, acknowledged *semper ubique et ab omnibus,* wherever the good life is a subject of concern.—Cardozo: Snyder v. Massachusetts, 291 U.S. 97, 122.

6. The practical business of government and administration of the law is obliged to proceed on more or less rough and ready judgments based on the assumption that mature and rational persons are in control of their own conduct.—Jackson: Gregg Cartage & Storage Co. v. United States, 316 U.S. 74, 80.

7. The question is not whether the defendant thought his conduct was that of a prudent man, but whether you think it was.—Holmes: *The Common Law,* 107.

8. He who is intelligent and prudent does not act at his peril, in theory of law.—Holmes: *ibid.,* 108.

9. The question what a prudent man would do under given circumstances is equivalent to the question what are the teachings of experience as to the dangerous character of this or that conduct under these or those circumstances.—Holmes: *ibid.,* 150.

10. If a man's conduct is such as would be reckless in a man of ordinary prudence, it is reckless in him. —Holmes: Commonwealth v. Pierce, 138 Mass. 165, 176.

11. Conduct may be regulated which cannot be initially commanded. —McKenna: United States v. Ohio Oil Co., 234 U.S. 548, 565.

12. It is common experience that men conform their conduct to regulations by governmental authority so as to avoid the unpleasant legal consequences which failure to conform entails.—Stone: Columbia Broadcasting Sys. v. United States, 316 U.S. 407, 418.

13. Where a rule of conduct applies to more than a few people, it is impracticable that everyone should have a direct voice in its adoption.— Holmes: Bi-Metallic Inv. Co. v. State Bd. Equal., 239 U.S. 441, 445.

14. A man does not make conduct otherwise lawful unlawful simply by yearning that it should be so.—

Holmes: Continental Co. v. Louis Co., 212 U.S. 227, 271.

15. Misbehavior, though without taint of corruption or fraud, may be born of indiscretion.—Cardozo: Berizzi Co. v. Krause, 239 N.Y. 315, 318.

16. Prohibited conduct may result from misconception of what duty requires.—Frankfurter: Cassell v. Texas, 339 U.S. 282, 293.

17. No man should profit from his own inequity or take advantage of his own wrong.—Cardozo: *Nature of Judicial Process,* 41.

18. The springs of conduct are subtle and varied.—Cardozo: DeCicco v. Schweizer, 221 N.Y. 431, 438.

19. The pattern of past conduct is not easily f o r s a k e n. — Douglas: United States v. Crescent Amusement Co., 323 U.S. 173, 186.

20. The history of the past conduct is the foundation for the judgment as to what the future conduct is likely to be. — Vinson: American Com. Assoc. v. Douds, 339 U.S. 382, 413-14.

21. Our conduct would always manifest the firmness of men who were determined, and never the violence of passionate men.—Marshall: Beveridge, *Life of Marshall,* II, 320.

22. The familiar presumption of rightfulness which attaches to human conduct in general.—Sutherland: International Shoe Co. v. Federal Trade Comm'n, 280 U.S. 291, 302.

23. Conduct "wrongful" because unsocial, but not "a wrong" to any one.—Cardozo: Palsgraf v. Long Island R.R., 248 N.Y. 339, 344.

24. A man may have as bad a heart as he chooses, if his conduct is within the rules.—Holmes: *The Common Law,* 110.

25. Varying conceptions regarding the "mainsprings of human conduct" are derived from a variety of experiences or assumptions about the nature of man, and "experience with human affairs," is not only diverse but often drastically conflicting.—Black: Comm'r of Int. Rev. v. Duberstein, 363 U.S. 278, 297.

Related subjects: Act; Behavior; Misbehavior; Misconduct; Negligence; Order; Practice; Standard. *See also* Censure; Corporation, conduct; Crime; Criminal law; Evidence, inferences; Fidelity 3; Fraud 13; Freedom 8, 125, 126; Government, employee 2; Idea 5; Illegality 2; Immoral; Intent 4, 13, 15; Jury, function; Law 23; Lawyer, functions; Lawyer, characteristics; Motive; Opinion 6; Principle 6; Prohibition 3; Punishment; Standards; Symbol 4; Test 1.

CONFEDERACY

1. The Government of the Confederate States . . . had no existence, except as a conspiracy to overthrow lawful authority. Its foundation was treason against the existing Federal Government. Its single purpose, so long as it lasted, was to make that treason successful. . . . When it was overthrown it perished totally. . . . What of good or evil has flowed from it remains for the consideration and discussion of the philosophical statesman and historian.—Miller: Sprott v. United States, 20 Wall. (87 U.S.) 459, 463.

2. The State remained a State of the Union. She never escaped the obliga-

tions of the Constitution, though for a while she may have evaded their enforcement.—Miller: Keith v. Clark, 7 Otto (97 U.S.) 454, 461.

3. It is not too much to say that the life of the Confederacy depended as much upon its cotton as it did upon its men.—Waite: Lamar v. Browne, 2 Otto (92 U.S.) 187, 194.

CONFEDERATION

The Constitution of the United States was not only not then in existence, but it was not then even dreamed of. The union of the States was crumbling into ruins, under the old confederation. Agriculture, manufacturers and commerce were at their lowest ebb. There was infinite danger to all the States from local interests and jealousies, and from the apparent impossibility of a much longer adherence to that shadow of a government, the Continental Congress.—Story: Charles River Bridge v. Warren Bridge, 11 Pet. (36 U.S.) 420, 610.

CONFESSION

1. A confession is wholly and incontestably voluntary only if a guilty person gives himself up to the law and becomes his own accuser.—Jackson: Ashcraft v. Tennessee, 322 U.S. 143, 161.

2. The term "voluntary" confession does not mean voluntary in the sense of a confession to a priest merely to rid one's soul of a sense of guilt. "Voluntary confessions" in criminal law are the product of calculations of a different order, and usually proceed from belief that further denial is use-

less and perhaps prejudicial.—Jackson: *ibid*.

3. Actual or threatened violence have no place in eliciting truth and it is fair to assume that no officer of the law will resort to cruelty if truth is what he is seeking.—Jackson: *ibid.*, 160.

4. Men are so constituted that many will risk the postponed consequences of yielding to a demand for a confession in order to be rid of present or imminent physical suffering.—Jackson: *ibid*.

5. The tendency of the innocent, as well as the guilty, to risk remote results of a false confession rather than suffer immediate pain is so strong that judges long ago found it necessary to guard against miscarriages of justice by treating any confession made concurrently with torture or threat of brutality as too untrustworthy to be received as evidence of guilt. —Jackson: Stein v. New York, 346 U.S. 156, 182.

6. No confession that has been obtained by any form of physical violence to the person is reliable. . . . Such treatment not only breaks the will to conceal or lie, but may even break the will to stand by the truth.—Jackson: Watts v. Indiana, 338 U.S. 49, 59–60.

7. Every man can be "broken." There is a point where the nervous system can take no more pain, shock, or fatigue, where it will pay any price for relief. A few minutes, a few days, or a few weeks, may be required, depending upon the individual and the

torture device that is employed. Once that point has been reached the accused becomes, for the moment, putty in the hands of the police and will admit what they charge and sign what they want.—Douglas: *We the Judges,* 366.

8. Conduct devoid of physical pressure but not leaving a free exercise of choice is the product of duress as much so as choice reflecting physical constraint.—Frankfurter: Haley v. Ohio, 332 U.S. 596, 606.

9. It would disregard standards that we cherish as part of our faith in the strength and well-being of a rational, civilized society to hold that a "confession" is voluntary simply because the confession is the product of a sentient choice.—Frankfurter: *ibid.*

10. Once a confession is obtained it supplies ways of verifying its trustworthiness.—Jackson: Watts v. Indiana, 338 U.S. 49, 60.

11. It is common courtroom knowledge that extortion of confessions by "third-degree" methods is charged falsely as well as denied falsely.—Jackson: Stein v. New York, 346 U.S. 156, 181.

12. The abhorrence of society to the use of involuntary confessions does not turn alone on their inherent untrustworthiness. It also turns on the deep-rooted feeling that the police must obey the law while enforcing the law; that in the end life and liberty can be as much endangered from illegal methods used to convict those thought to be criminals as from actual criminals themselves.—Warren: Spano v. New York, 360 U.S. 315, 320–21.

Related subjects: Admission; Evidence, admissions; Third degree; Self incrimination. *See also* Criminal law 25; Tax 149.

CONFISCATION
See Fiction 5; Forfeiture; Property 20, 29; Public utility 5–7, 9; Tax 25.

CONFLICT
The most constructive way of resolving conflicts is to avoid them.—Frankfurter: Western Pac. R. Corp. v. Western Pac. R. Co., 345 U.S. 247, 270.

CONFORMITY
See Censor 12.

CONFUSION
1. They confuse, "make not light but darkness visible."—McKenna: Rhode Island v. Palmer, 253 U.S. 350, 404.

2. Old confusions die hard.—Rutledge: Owens v. Union Pac. R.R., 319 U.S. 703, 721.
See also Witness 1.

CONGRESS
1. In the legislature of the Union alone, are all represented.—Marshall: McCulloch v. Maryland, 4 Wheat. (17 U.S.) 316, 431.

2. It is difficult to say that any power can be exercised by Congress which is not derived from the Constitution. Without that instrument, it is as powerless as any other association of men.—McLean: United States v. Guthrie, 17 How. (58 U.S.) 284, 309.

3. Congress have the power to do much which is not probable they will

44

do.—McLean: Parsons v. Bedford, 3 Pet. (28 U.S.) 433, 456.

4. The Founders of this Nation entrusted the lawmaking power to the Congress alone in both good and bad times.—Black: Youngstown Sheet & Tube Co. v. Sawyer, 343 U.S. 579, 589.

5. Congress does in truth regulate by its silence as much as by its action. —Woodbury: Passenger Cases, 7 How. (48 U.S.) 283, 562.

6. What Congress has created Congress can refashion.—Douglas: United Steelworkers v. United States, 361 U.S. 39, 68.

7. Even if Congress has chosen the wrong way to accomplish its aim, that choice is binding.—Black: NLRB v. Radio & Tel. B. E. Union, 364 U.S. 573, 583.

8. The Congress is predominantly a lawyers' body. — Frankfurter: 364 U.S. 587, 594

9. When Congress has the will it has no difficulty in expressing it.— Frankfurter: Bell v. United States, 349 U.S. 81, 3.

Related subjects: Constitutional adjudication; Contempt (of Congress); Legislature; Lobbying; Supreme Court. *See also* Delay 3; Freedom, belief 137; Government (U.S.), federal-state, authority; Income 3; Public building; Public welfare 2; Symbol 5.

CONJECTURES

1. We may indulge conjectures; but the law does not decide upon conjectures.—Story: Wright v. Denn, 10 Wheat. (23 U.S.) 204, 239.

2. This is no more than a confident conjecture.—Catron: Allen's Ex'rs v.

Wilkins, 18 How. (59 U.S.) 385, 392.

Related subjects: Speculation (conjecture); Suspicion. *See also* Inference 2; Law 85.

CONSCIENCE

1. Conscience . . . is known to be inadequate in individuals. In large numbers, little is to be expected from it.—Douglas: *We the Judges,* 259.

2. Law only works within the sphere of the senses. If the external phenomena, the manifest acts and omissions, are such as it requires, it is wholly indifferent to the internal phenomena of conscience.—Holmes: *The Common Law,* 110.

See also Court 25, 28; Equity 5; Equity court 17; Freedom, conscience; Judge 8; Judicial process 10; Legislature 9; Majority-minority 17.

CONSCIENTIOUS OBJECTION, OBJECTOR

1. Conscientious resistance is a matter of conscience not of law; for that very reason, the servants of the law can take notice of it only *de gratia* or as an element in guiding judicial discretion. —Holmes: *Holmes-Pollock Letters,* II, 27.

2. We are a nation with the duty to survive; a nation whose Constitution contemplates war as well as peace; whose government must go forward upon the assumption, and safely can proceed upon no other, that unqualified allegiance to the nation and submission and obedience to the laws of the land, as well those made for war as those made for peace, are not inconsistent with the will of God.

Sutherland: United States v. Macintosh, 283 U.S. 605, 625.

3. Refusal to bear arms is not necessarily a sign of disloyalty or a lack of attachment to our institutions. One may serve his country faithfully and devotedly, though his religious scruples make it impossible for him to shoulder a rifle. Devotion to one's country can be as real and as enduring among non-combatants as among combatants.—Douglas: Girouard v. United States, 328 U.S. 61, 64.

> Related subjects: Conscription; Military service; Selective service (military).

CONSCRIPTION

1. The government has the right to the military service of all its able-bodied citizens.—Brewer: *In re* Grimley, 137 U.S. 147, 153.

2. Conscription is an awesome business.—Jackson: Dickinson v. United States, 346 U.S. 389, 401.

3. The Due Process Clause does not shield the citizen from conscription ... to stem the tide of Communism. If Communist aggression creates such hardships for loyal citizens, it is hard to find justification for holding that the Constitution requires that its hardships must be spared the Communist alien.—Jackson: Harisiades v. Shaughnessy, 342 U.S. 580, 591.

> Related subjects: Military service: Selective service (military).

CONSENT

1. Consent does not depend on some ritualistic formula. — Frankfurter: Great Northern Life Ins. Co. v. Read, 322 U.S. 47, 59.

2. Consent will not protect if reason and moderation are not made to mark the boundaries of what is done under its shelter.—Stone: Rogers v. Guaranty Tr. Co., 288 U.S. 123, 150.

See also Permission.

CONSEQUENCE

1. There is no fear that the nation will drift from its ancient moorings as the result.—Cardozo: Panama Ref. Co. v. Ryan, 293 U.S. 388, 443.

2. A guillotine for cutting off all the consequences.—Holmes: Francis v. McNeal, 228 U.S. 695, 700.

> Related subject: Result. *See also* Attack; Circumspection; Constitutional adjudication, consequences; Construction 41; Construction, consequences; Denaturalization; Intent 15; Legislation, effectiveness; Legislation, inadequacies; Litigation 20; Logic 3; Punishment 6; Rights 12; Silence 7; War, consequences.

CONSERVATIVE, CONSERVATISM

1. True conservatism involves progress, and ... unless our financial leaders are capable of progress, the institutions which they are trying to conserve will lose their foundation.—Brandeis: Mason, *Brandeis,* 162–63.

2. The conservative classes in the community are not those who wish to leave unrestricted the power of wealth, but those who in economic relations are working for justice to capitalists and to public alike.—Brandeis, *ibid.,* 130.

3. Loads the dice in favor of the *status quo.*—Jackson: *Struggle for Judicial Supremacy,* 320.

See also Intolerance 2; Judge 6; Lawyer,

criticism; Legislator 23; Mind 9; Orthodoxy; Supreme Court 12, 20.

CONSISTENCY
See Law, consistency; Legislation 35;
Litigation 28; Truth 17; Uniformity.

CONSPIRACY
1. A conspiracy is a partnership in
criminal purposes.—Holmes: United
States v. Kissel, 218 U.S. 601, 608.

2. Just as the mechanism of a watch
affords evidence of a design, and
hence of a designer, so a systematic
course of action, pursued at one and
the same time by many persons, and
affecting their mutual interests, raises
a fair inference of an agreement between them to pursue that course of
action.—Pitney: Frey & Son v. Cuda-
hy Packing Co., 256 U.S. 208, 217-18.

3. It is perfectly possible and even
may be rational to enact that a conspiracy to accomplish what an individual is free to do shall be a crime.
—Holmes: Drew v. Thaw, 235 U.S.
432, 438.

4. The liability for conspiracy is not
taken away by its success.—Holmes:
Heike v. United States, 227 U.S. 131,
144.

5. It is impossible in the nature of
things for a man to conspire with himself.—Cardozo: Morrison v. California, 291 U.S. 82, 92.

6. The modern law of conspiracy
was largely evolved by the judges.—
Jackson: Krulewitch v. United States,
336 U.S. 440, 456.

See also Crime 21; Restraint of trade.

CONSTITUTION (general)
1. A constitution is framed for ages

to come, and is designed to approach
immortality as nearly as human institutions can approach it. Its course cannot always be tranquil. It is exposed to
storms and tempests.—Marshall: Cohens v. Virginia, 6 Wheat. (19 U.S.)
264, 387.

2. A constitution states or ought to
state not rules for the passing hour,
but principles for an expanding future.—Cardozo: *Nature of Judicial
Process*, 83.

3. A principle, to be vital, must be
capable of wider application than the
mischief which gave it birth. This is
peculiarly true of constitutions. They
are not ephemeral enactments, designed to meet passing occasions. . . .
The future is their care, and provision
for events of good and bad tendencies
of which no prophecy can be made.—
McKenna: Weems v. United States,
217 U.S. 349, 373.

4. Frame constitutions of government with what wisdom and foresight
we may, they must be imperfect, and
leave something to discretion, and
much to public virtue.—Story: *Misc.
Writings*, 430.

5. Constitutions are intended to preserve practical and substantial rights,
not to maintain theories.—Holmes:
Davis v. Mills, 194 U.S. 451, 457.

6. A Constitution has an organic
life in such a sense, and to such a degree, that changes here and there do
not sever its identity.—Cardozo:
Browne v. City of New York, 241
N.Y. 96, 111.

7. A Constitution is not intended
to embody a particular economic the-

ory, whether of paternalism and the organic relation of the citizen to the state or of *laissez faire*. It is made for people of fundamentally different views.—Holmes: Lochner v. New York, 198 U.S. 45, 75–76.

> Related subjects: Constitution (U.S.); Sovereignty. *See also* Court 4; Legislature 8; Rights 47.

CONSTITUTION (U.S.)

> Defined 1–5; framers 6–13; adoption 14–18; authority 19–30; purposes 31–43; construction, general 44–47, flexibility 48–55, liberal 56–60, limitations 61–62, powers 63–67; protections 68–73; requirements 74–77; restraints 78–79; perversion 80–86; miscellaneous 87–89; Preamble 90; commerce clauses 91–93; Bill of Rights 94–97; First Amendment 98–104; Fourth Amendment 105–107; Fifth Amendment 108–110; Thirteenth Amendment 111; Fourteenth Amendment 112–122; Fourteenth and Fifteenth Amendments 123; Fifteenth Amendment 124.

> Related subjects: Citizen; Constitution (general); Constitutional adjudication; Freedom; Government (U.S.); Rights, constitutional; Sovereignty; Supreme Court, functions.

——, defined

1. The Constitution is a compact between sovereigns.—Douglas: New York v. United States, 362 U.S. 572, 595.

2. The Constitution of the United States contains what may be deemed a bill of rights for the people of each state.—Marshall: Fletcher v. Peck, 6 Cranch (10 U.S.) 87, 138.

3. It is an experiment, as all life is an experiment.—Holmes: Abrams v. United States, 250 U.S. 616, 630.

4. The Constitution, we cannot re-call too often, is an organism, not merely a literary composition. — Frankfurter: Burstyn v. Wilson, 343 U.S. 495, 518.

5. The Constitution is not a formulary.—Frankfurter: Wisconsin v. J. C. Penney Co., 311 U.S. 435, 444.

——, framers

6. Those who won our independence by revolution were not cowards. They did not fear political change. They did not exalt order at the cost of liberty. — Brandeis: Whitney v. California, 274 U.S. 357, 377.

7. The makers of our Constitution undertook to secure conditions favorable to the pursuit of happiness. They recognized the significance of man's spiritual nature, of his feelings and of his intellect. They knew that only a part of the pain, pleasure and satisfactions of life are to be found in material things. They sought to protect Americans in their beliefs, their thoughts, their emotions and their sensations. They conferred, as against the government, the right to be let alone—the most comprehensive of rights and the right most valued by civilized men.—Brandeis: Olmstead v. United States, 277 U.S. 438, 478.

8. From their own experience and their deep reading in history, the Founders knew that Law alone saves a society from being rent by internecine strife or rule by mere brute power however disguised. "Civilization involves subjection of force to reason and the agency of this subjec-

tion is law."—Frankfurter: United States v. UMW, 330 U.S. 258, 308.

9. The Constitution is a practical instrument, made by practical men, and suited to the territory and circumstances on which it was intended to operate.—Catron: Passenger Cases, 7 How. (48 U.S.) 283, 449.

10. The Constitution was written to be understood by the voters.—Roberts: United States v. Sprague, 282 U.S. 716, 731.

11. The Framers of the Constitution knew human nature as well as we do. They too had lived in dangerous days; they too knew the suffocating influence of orthodoxy and standardized thought. They weighed the compulsions for restrained speech and thought against the abuses of liberty. They chose liberty.—Douglas: Beauharnais v. Illinois, 343 U.S. 250, 287.

12. Those who won our independence believed that the final end of the state was to make men free to develop their faculties; and that in its government the deliberative forces should prevail over the arbitrary. . . . They believed liberty to be the secret of happiness and courage to be the secret of liberty.—Brandeis: Whitney v. California, 274 U.S. 357, 375.

13. Those who formed the Constitution struck out anew free of previous shackles in an effort to obtain a better order of government more congenial to human liberty and welfare.—Black: Green v. United States, 356 U.S. 165, 212.

See also Constitution (U.S.) 14–18, 68,

90; Conviction 5; Government, federal 44; Liquor 5; Search and seizure 7.

———, adoption

14. The constitution of the United States, was ordained and established, not by the states in their sovereign capacities, but emphatically, as the preamble of the constitution declares, by "the people of the United States."—Story: Martin v. Hunter's Lessee, 1 Wheat. (14 U.S.) 305, 324.

15. The framers of the Constitution wished its adoption, and well knew that it would be endangered by its strength, not by its weakness.—Marshall: McCulloch v. Maryland, 4 Wheat. (17 U.S.) 316, 420.

16. The constitution was formed in and for an advanced state of society.—Johnson: Anderson v. Dunn, 6 Wheat. (19 U.S.) 204, 232

17. The Constitution was formed for our whole country.—McLean: Dred Scott v. Sandford, 19 How. (60 U.S.) 204, 232.

18. It was against a background poignant with memories of evil procedures that our Constitution was drawn.—Douglas: *We the Judges,* 379.

———, authority

19. The people made the constitution, and the people can unmake it. It is the creature of their own will, and lives only by their will.—Marshall: Cohens v. Virginia, 6 Wheat. (19 U.S.) 264, 389

20. If there be any who deny its necessity; none can deny its authority. —Marshall: *ibid.,* 381.

21. If such be the constitution, it is the duty of the court to bow with respectful submission to its provisions.—Marshall: *ibid.,* 377.

22. This is the authoritative language of the American people; and, if gentlemen please, of the American States.—Marshall: *ibid.,* 381.

23. Whenever the Constitution commands, discretion terminates.—Daniel: Marshall v. Baltimore & O. R.R., 16 How. (57 U.S.) 314, 344.

24. The Constitution is supreme because the people who ratified it have made it so.—Wayne: Dodge v. Woolsey, 18 How. (59 U.S.) 331, 347.

25. The Constitution of the United States is a law for rulers and people, equally in war and in peace, and covers with the shield of its protection all classes of men, at all times, and under all circumstances.—Davis: *Ex parte* Milligan, 4 Wall. (71 U.S.) 2, 120–21.

26. To the Constitution of the United States the term sovereign, is totally unknown.—Wilson: Chisholm v. Georgia, 2 Dall. (2 U.S.) 419, 454.

27. Under our Constitution it is We The People who are sovereign. The people have the final say. The legislators are their spokesmen. The people determine through their votes the destiny of the nation.—Douglas: United States v. UAW, 352 U.S. 567, 593.

28. Constitutional mandates are imperative.—Brewer: Fairbank v. United States, 181 U.S. 283, 291.

29. What the Constitution grants the Constitution can take away.—

Warren: Perez v. Brownell, 356 U.S. 44, 79.

30. No state legislator or executive or judicial officer can war against the Constitution without violating his undertaking to support it.—Per curiam: Cooper v. Aaron, 358 U.S. 1, 18.

See also Legislation 13; Public official 1.

———, purposes

31. The Constitution establishes a representative government, not a pure democracy.—Holmes: Opinions of the Justices, 160 Mass., 586, 594.

32. The Constitution, in all its provisions, looks to an indestructible Union, composed of indestructible States.—Chase: Texas v. White, 7 Wall. (74 U.S.) 700, 725.

33. The Constitution of the United States was designed for the common and equal benefit of all the people of the United States.—Story: Martin v. Hunter's Lessee, 1 Wheat. (14 U.S.) 305, 348.

34. Among the great cardinal principles of that instrument, no one is more conspicuous or more venerable than the establishment of justice.—Chase: Hepburn v. Griswold, 8 Wall. (75 U.S.) 603, 622.

35. The Constitution deals with substance, not shadows. Its inhibition was leveled at the thing, not the name.—Field: Cummings v. Missouri, 4 Wall. (71 U.S.) 277, 325.

36. The Constitution does not limit the useful to that which satisfies immediate bodily needs. — Holmes: Bleistein v. Donaldson Co., 188 U.S. 239, 249.

37. While the Declaration was directed against an excess of authority, the Constitution was directed against anarchy.—Jackson: *Struggle for Judicial Supremacy,* 8.

38. The Constitution circumscribes the field of privilege and favor.—Cardozo: In the Matter of Barthelmess v. Cukor, 231 N.Y. 435, 441.

39. The Constitution has not ordained that the forms of business shall be cast in imperishable moulds.—Cardozo: Hartford A. & I. Co. v. Nelson Co., 291 U.S. 352, 361.

40. The great purposes of the Constitution do not depend on the approval or convenience of those they restrain.—Jackson: Everson v. Bd. of Educ., 330 U.S. 1, 28.

41. The Constitution created a government dedicated to equal justice under law.—Per curiam: Cooper v. Aaron, 358 U.S. 1, 19.

42. The provisions of the Constitution are not time-worn adages or hollow shibboleths. They are vital, living principles that authorize and limit governmental powers in our Nation. They are the rules of government.—Warren: Trop v. Dulles, 356 U.S. 86, 103.

43. The Constitution favors no racial group, no political or social group.—Douglas: Uphaus v. Wyman, 364 U.S. 388, 406.

See also Constitution, framers, adoption; Equality; Fraud 14.

———, construction, general

44. We must never forget that it is a constitution we are expounding.—Marshall: McCulloch v. Maryland, 4 Wheat. (17 U.S.) 316, 407.

45. We are under a Constitution, but the Constitution is what the judges say it is, and the judiciary is the safeguard of our liberty and of our property under the Constitution. — Hughes: Pusey, *Hughes,* 204.

46. The great ordinances of the Constitution do not establish and divide fields of black and white. Even the more specific of them are found to terminate in a penumbra shading gradually from one extreme to the other.—Holmes: Springer v. Philippine Islands, 277 U.S. 189, 209.

47. All the notions of society, particularly in their jurisprudence, are more or less artificial; our Constitution nowhere speaks the language of men in a state of nature.—Johnson: Ogden v. Saunders, 12 Wheat. (25 U.S.) 213, 290.

Related subjects: Construction; Constitutional adjudication.

———, construction, flexibility

48. A constitution intended to endure for ages to come, and, consequently, to be adapted to the various crises of human affairs.—Marshall: McCulloch v. Maryland, 4 Wheat. (17 U.S.) 316, 415

49. The instrument was not intended to provide merely for the exigencies of a few years, but was to endure through a long lapse of ages, the events of which were locked up in the inscrutable purposes of Providence.—Story: Martin v. Hunter's Lessee, 1 Wheat. (14 U.S.) 305, 326.

50. The great generalities of the Constitution have a content and a significance that vary from age to age.—Cardozo: *Nature of Judicial Process,* 17.

51. The greatest expounders of the Constitution, from John Marshall to Oliver Wendell Holmes, have always insisted that the strength and vitality of the Constitution stem from the fact that its principles are adaptable to changing events.—Jackson: *Struggle for Judicial Supremacy,* 174.

52. The Constitution was designed for the vicissitudes of time. It should never become a code, which carries overtones of one period that may be hostile to another.—Douglas: *We the Judges,* 433.

53. That instrument must be understood as an Eighteenth-Century sketch of a government hoped for, not as a blueprint of the Government that is.—Jackson: Youngstown Sheet & Tube Co. v. Sawyer, 343 U.S. 579, 653.

54. The constitutional fathers, fresh from a revolution, did not forge a political strait-jacket for the generations to come.—Murphy: Schneiderman v. United States, 320 U.S. 118, 137.

55. The meaning of the Constitution does not change with the ebb and flow of economic events.—Sutherland: West Coast Hotel Co. v. Parrish, 300 U.S. 379, 402.

————, construction, liberal

56. Constitutional interpretation should involve more than dialectics.

—Black: Feldman v. United States Oil & Ref. Co., 322 U.S. 487, 499.

57. It is an inadmissibly narrow conception of American constitutional law to confine it to the words of the Constitution and to disregard the gloss which life has written upon them. — Frankfurter: Youngstown Sheet & Tube Co. v. Sawyer, 343 U.S. 579, 610.

58. To approximate the constitutional policy would be better than to nullify it.—Murphy: Williams v. North Carolina, 325 U.S. 226, 261.

59. The provisions of the Constitution are not mathematical formulas having their essence in their form; they are organic, living institutions transplanted from English soil. Their significance is vital, not formal; it is to be gathered not simply by taking the words and a dictionary, but by considering their origin and the line of their growth.—Holmes: Gompers v. United States, 233 U.S. 604, 610.

60. It well may be that guarantees which must be written are less secure than those so embedded in the hearts of men that they need not be written. —Douglas: *We the Judges,* 259.

————, construction, limitations

61. In construing the Constitution we should remember that it is a frame of government for men of opposite opinions and for the future, and therefore not hastily import into it our own views, or unexpressed limitations derived merely from the practice of the past.—Holmes: Opinion of the Justices, 160 Mass. 586, 594.

62. Humility . . . means an alert self scrutiny so as to avoid infusing into the vagueness of a constitutional command one's merely private notions.—Frankfurter: Haley v. Ohio, 332 U.S. 596, 602.

———, construction, powers

63. Let the end be legitimate, let it be within the scope of the constitution, and all means which are appropriate, which are plainly adapted to that end, which are not prohibited, but consistent with the letter and spirit of the constitution, are constitutional. —Marshall: McCulloch v. Maryland, 4 Wheat. (17 U.S.) 316, 421.

64. The Constitution everywhere assumes, as a postulate, that wherever power is given it will be used, or at least, used as far as the interests of the American people require it.—Johnson: Martin v. Hunter's Lessee, 1 Wheat. (14 U.S.) 305, 375.

65. Extraordinary conditions do not create or enlarge constitutional power. —Hughes: Schechter v. United States, 295 U.S. 495, 528.

66. Beneficent aims, however great or well directed, can never serve in lieu of constitutional power.—Sutherland: Carter v. Carter Coal Co., 298 U.S. 238, 291.

67. The Constitution was built for rough as well as smooth roads. In time of war the nation simply changes gears and takes the harder going under the same power.—Burton: Duncan v. Kahanamoku, 327 U.S. 304, 342.

———, protections

68. The illustrious men who framed that instrument were guarding the foundations of civil liberty against the abuses of unlimited power.—Davis: *Ex parte* Milligan, 4 Wall. (71 U.S.) 2, 126.

69. The protection of the Constitution extends to all,—to those who speak other languages as well as to those born with English on the tongue.—McReynolds: Meyer v. Nebraska, 262 U.S. 390, 401.

70. The idea that a Constitution should protect individual nonconformity is essentially American.— Jackson: American Com. Assoc. v. Douds, 339 U.S. 382, 443.

71. Our protection against all kinds of fanatics and extremists, none of whom can be trusted with unlimited power over others, lies not in their forbearance but in the limitations of our Constitution.—Jackson: *ibid.,* 439.

72. The Constitution was adopted to preserve our government, not to serve as a protecting screen for those who, while claiming its privileges, seek to destroy it.—Clarke: United States *ex rel.* Milwaukee Soc. Dem. Pub. Co. v. Burleson, 255 U.S. 407, 414.

73. The Constitution of the United States is not intended as a facility for crime. It is intended to prevent oppression.—McKenna: Brown v. Elliott, 225 U.S. 392, 402.

See also Criminal 43; Equality; Equal protection; Public welfare 14, 24; Self incrimination 12.

————, requirements

74. The Constitution is not to be satisfied with a fiction.—Holmes: Hyde v. United States, 225 U.S. 347, 390.

75. The Constitution as a continuously operating charter of government does not demand the impossible or the impractical.—Stone: Hirabayashi v. United States, 320 U.S. 81, 104.

76. The Constitution commands neither logical symmetry nor exhaustion of a principle. — Frankfurter: Hughes v. Superior Court, 339 U.S. 460, 468.

77. Constitutionality does not exact a sense of proportion or the sanity of humor or an absence of fear.—Frankfurter: Dennis v. United States, 341 U.S. 494, 556.

————, restraints

78. Its language is the language of restraint, not of coercion.—Marshall: Ogden v. Saunders, 12 Wheat. (25 U.S.) 213, 351.

79. Its words are a restraint upon power, intended as such in deliberate persuasion of its wisdom as against unrestrained freedom. — McKenna: Block v. Hirsh, 256 U.S. 135, 163.

————, perversion

80. Powerful and ingenious minds ... may, by a course of well digested, but refined and metaphysical reasoning ... explain away the Constitution of our country, and leave it a magnificent structure indeed, to look at, but totally unfit for use.—Marshall: Gibbons v. Ogden, 9 Wheat. (22 U.S.) 1, 222.

81. It depends upon the present age, whether the national constitution shall descend to our children in its masculine majesty, to protect and unite the country; or whether, shorn of its strength, it shall become an idle mockery, and perish before the grave has closed upon the last of its illustrious founders.—Story: *Misc. Writings,* 432.

82. Of what avail are written constitutions whose bills of right for the security of individual liberty have been written, too often, with the blood of martyrs shed upon the battle field and the scaffold, if their limitations and restraints upon power may be overpassed with impunity by the very agencies created and appointed to guard, defend and enforce them; and that, too, with the sacred authority of law, not only compelling obedience, but entitled to respect?—Matthews: Virginia Coupon Cases, 114 U.S. 270, 291.

83. Life, liberty, property, and the equal protection of the law, grouped together in the Constitution, are so related that the deprivation of any one of those separate and independent rights may lessen or extinguish the value of the other three.—Lamar: Smith v. Texas, 233 U.S. 630, 636.

84. Once let the barriers of the Constitution be removed, and the march of abuse will be onward and without bounds.—Daniel: Passenger Cases, 7 How. (48 U.S.) 283, 518.

85. The introduction of new subjects of doubt, contest and contradiction, is the fruit of abandoning the

constitutional land marks.—Campbell: Marshall v. Baltimore & O. R.R., 16 How. (57 U.S.) 314, 353.

86. If the provisions of the Constitution be not upheld when they pinch as well as when they comfort, they may as well be abandoned.—Sutherland: Home Bldg. & Loan Assoc. v. Blaisdell, 290 U.S. 398, 483.

————, miscellaneous

87. Constitutional provisions are based on the possibility of extremes. —McKenna: General Oil Co. v. Crain, 209 U.S. 211, 226-27.

88. Our Constitution is not a covenant of nonresistance toward organized efforts at disruption and betrayal, either of labor or of the country.— Jackson: America Com. Assoc. v. Douds, 339 U.S. 382, 434.

89. The integrity of the basic law is to be preserved against hasty or ill-considered changes, the fruit of ignorance or passion.—Cardozo: Browne v. City of New York, 241 N.Y. 96, 109.

See also Treaty 1.

————, Preamble

90. The preamble declares domestic tranquility as well as liberty to be an object in founding a Federal Government and I do not think the Forefathers were naive in believing both can be fostered by the law.—Jackson: Terminiello v. Chicago, 337 U.S. 1, 34.

————, commerce clauses (Article I, Secs. 8, 10)

91. The power of Congress to regulate commerce among the States is perhaps the most benign gift of the Constitution.—Brown: Cook v. County of Marshall, 196 U.S. 261, 272.

92. The Commerce Clause . . . creates an area of free trade.—Douglas: *We the Judges,* 222.

93. The Commerce Clause . . . does, indeed, contain an arsenal of power. It has done great service in creating one nation out of many States.— Douglas: *ibid.,* 221.

See also Commerce.

————, Bill of Rights

94. Man being what he is cannot safely be trusted with complete immunity from outward responsibility in depriving others of their rights. At least such is the conviction underlying our Bill of Rights.—Frankfurter: Joint Anti-Fascist Ref. Comm. v. McGrath, 341 U.S. 123, 171.

95. We have enjoyed so much freedom for so long that we are perhaps in danger of forgetting how much blood it cost to establish the Bill of Rights. — Frankfurter: Dennis v. United States, 341 U.S. 494, 549.

96. When we are dealing with the Constitution of the United States, and more particularly with the great safeguards of the Bill of Rights, we are dealing with principles of liberty and justice "so rooted in the traditions and conscience of our people as to be ranked as fundamental"—something without which "a fair and enlightened system of justice would be impossible." —Frankfurter: West Va. State Bd. of Educ. v. Barnette, 319 U.S. 624, 652.

97. The protections explicitly afforded the individual by the Bill of

Rights represent a large part of the characteristics which distinguish free from totalitarian government. — Black: Feldman v. United States Oil & Ref. Co., 322 U.S. 487, 502.

> See also Bill of Rights; Constitution (U.S.) 2; Freedom, various subdivisions.

————, First Amendment

98. Not the least of the virtues of the First Amendment is its protection of each member of the smallest and most unorthodox minority.— Black: American Com. Assoc. v. Douds, 339 U.S. 382, 448.

99. The First Amendment makes confidence in the common sense of our people and in their maturity of judgment the great postulate of our democracy. — Douglas: Dennis v. United States, 341 U.S. 494, 590.

100. The First Amendment gives freedom of mind the same security as freedom of conscience. — Rutledge: Thomas v. Collins, 323 U.S. 516, 531.

101. Do the people of this land— in the providence of God, favored, as they sometimes boast, above all others in the plenitude of their liberties.— desire to preserve those so carefully protected by the First Amendment; liberty of religious worship, freedom of speech and of the press, and the right as freemen peaceably to assemble and petition their government for a redress of grievances? If so, let them withstand all *beginnings* of encroachment. For the saddest epitaph which can be carved in memory of a vanished liberty is that it was lost because its possessors failed to stretch forth a

saving hand while yet there was time. —Sutherland: Assoc. Press v. NLRB, 301 U.S. 103, 141.

102. As long as the First Amendment survives, the censor, no matter how respectable his cause, cannot have the support of government. It is not for government to pick and choose according to the standards of any religious, political, or philosophical group.—Douglas: Times Film Corp. v. Chicago, 365 U.S. 43, 81.

103. The First Amendment was designed to enlarge, not to limit, freedom in literature and in the arts as well as in politics, economics, law, and other fields. . . . Its aim was to unlock all ideas for argument, debate, and dissemination. No more potent force in defeat of that freedom could be designed than censorship. It it a weapon that no minority or majority group, acting through government, should be allowed to wield over any of us.—Douglas: *ibid.*, 84.

104. Only by a dedicated preservation of the freedoms of the First Amendment can we hope to preserve our Nation and its traditional way of life.—Black: Braden v. United States, 365 U.S. 431, 444.

> See also Advocacy; Criticism 6; Freedom; Majority-minority 17; Motion picture 2.

————, Fourth Amendment

105. The clue to the meaning and scope of the Fourth Amendment is John Adams' characterization of Otis' argument against search by the police that "American independence was then and there born."—Frankfurter:

United States v. Rabinowitz, 339 U.S. 56, 69–70.

106. It [the Fourth Amendment] marks the right of privacy as one of the unique values of our civilization. —Douglas: McDonald v. United States, 335 U.S. 451, 453.

107. It is precisely because the appeal to the Fourth Amendment is so often made by dubious characters that its infringements call for alert and strenuous resistance. — Frankfurter: Harris v. United States, 331 U.S. 145, 156.

See also Arrest 3; Police 3; Privacy; Search and seizure.

————, Fifth Amendment

108. This command of the Fifth Amendment ("nor shall any person . . . be compelled in any criminal case to be a witness against himself . . .") registers an important advance in the development of our liberty—"one of the great landmarks in man's struggle to make himself civilized." Time has not shown that protection from the evils against which this safeguard was directed is needless or unwarranted. — Frankfurter: Ullman v. United States, 350 U.S. 422, 426.

109. Magna Charta declared that no man should be taken or imprisoned, or be disseized of his freehold or liberties or free customs, or be outlawed or exiled or in any way destroyed, or be passed upon or condemned, but by the lawful judgment of his peers, or by the law of the land; which is the origin of the provision, embodied in the Fifth Amendment, . . . that no man shall be deprived of life, liberty or property, without due process of law.—Gray: United States v. Lee, 106 U.S. 196, 227–28.

110. The privilege [5th Amendment] serves to protect the innocent who otherwise might be ensnared by ambiguous circumstances. — Clark: Slochower v. Bd. of Higher Educ., 350 U.S. 551, 557, 558.

See also Self incrimination; Tax 135.

————, Seventh Amendment
See Expert 4.

————, Eighth Amendment
See Citizen 31; Punishment 9.

————, Thirteenth Amendment

111. It [the Thirteenth Amendment] is the denunciation of a condition, and not a declaration in favor of a particular people. It reaches every race and every individual, and if in any respect it commits one race to the nation, it commits every race and every individual thereof. Slavery or involuntary servitude of the Chinese, of the Italian, of the Anglo-Saxon, are as much within its compass as slavery or involuntary servitude of the African.—Brewer: Hodges v. United States, 203 U.S. 1, 16–17.

————, Fourteenth Amendment

112. The traditions and habits of centuries were not intended to be overthrown when that Amendment [the F o u r t e e n t h] was passed.—Holmes: Interstate Consol. St. Ry. v. Massachusetts, 207 U.S. 79, 87.

113. The 14th Amendment does not enact Mr. Herbert Spencer's Social Statics.—Holmes: Lochner v. New York, 198 U.S. 45, 75.

114. The "liberty" secured by the Fourteenth Amendment summarizes the experience of history.—Frankfurter: Bridges v. California, 314 U.S. 252, 284.

115. By the term "liberty," as used in the provision [Fourteenth Amendment], something more is meant than mere freedom from physical restraint or the bounds of a prison. It means freedom to go where one may choose, and to act in such a manner, not inconsistent with the equal rights of others, as his judgment may dictate for the promotion of his happiness; that is, to pursue such callings and avocations as may be most suitable to develop his capacities, and give to them their highest enjoyment.—Field: Munn v. People of Illinois, 4 Otto (94 U.S.) 113, 142.

116. I cannot believe that the liberty guaranteed by the 14th Amendment includes only liberty to acquire and to enjoy property.—Brandeis: Gilbert v. Minnesota, 254 U.S. 325, 343.

117. The Due Process Clause embodies a system of rights based on moral principles so deeply embedded in the traditions and feelings of our people as to be deemed fundamental to a civilized society as conceived by our whole history. Due process is that which comports with the deepest notions of what is fair and right and just.—Frankfurter: Solesbee v. Balkcom, 339 U.S. 9, 16.

118. The judicial enforcement of the Due Process Clause is the very antithesis of a Procrustean rule.—Frankfurter: Irvine v. California, 347 U.S. 128, 143.

119. It [Fourteenth Amendment] introduced all of that race, whose ancestors had been imported and sold as slaves, at once, into the political community known as the "People of the United States."—Harlan: Civil Rights Cases, 109 U.S. 3, 46.

120. The 14th Amendment, . . . was adopted with a view to the protection of the colored race, but has been found to be equally important in its application to the rights of all. —Holmes: United States v. Mosley, 238 U.S. 383, 388.

121. The rudiments of fair play required by the 14th Amendment.—Holmes: Chicago, M. & St.P. Ry. v. Polt, 232 U.S. 165, 168.

122. By the term "life" as here used, something more is meant than mere animal existence. . . . The deprivation not only of life, but of whatever God has given to everyone with life, for its growth and enjoyment, is prohibited by the provision . . . if its efficacy be not frittered away by judicial decision.—Field: Munn v. Illinois, 4 Otto (94 U.S.) 113, 142.

See also Association; Constitutional adjudication 28, 29; Corporation 27; Criminal law 29; Freedom; Hearing 7; Labor 102; Race, equality.

———, Fourteenth and Fifteenth Amendments

123. They are a bulwark of defense, and can never be made an engine of oppression. — Swayne: S l a u g h t e r House Cases, 16 Wall. (83 U.S.) 36, 128.

58

————, Fifteenth Amendment

124. The Amendment nullifies sophisticated as well as simple-minded modes of discrimination.—Frankfurter: Lane v. Wilson, 307 U.S. 268, 275.
See also Negro 7; Race, equality.

————, Sixteenth Amendment
See Income 2.

————, Eighteenth Amendment
See Liquor 5.

————, Nineteenth Amendment
See Woman 5, 6.

CONSTITUTIONAL ADJUDICATION

Defined 1–5; power 6–8; power, exercise 9–12, presumptions 13–16, policy 17, 18, judgment 19–21, consequences 22–26, novelty 27, bias of standards 28–33, stare decisis 34–39; invalidity 40, 41; miscellaneous 42–45.

————, defined

1. The most delicate, and, at the same time, the proudest attribute of American jurisprudence is the right of its judicial tribunals to decide questions of constitutional law. In other governments, these questions cannot be entertained or decided by courts of justice; and, therefore, whatever may be the theory of the constitution, the legislative authority is practically omnipotent, and there is no means of contesting the legality or justice of a law, but by an appeal to arms.—Story: *Misc. Writings,* 428.

2. This is government by lawsuit. These constitutional lawsuits are the stuff of power politics in America.—Jackson: *Struggle for Judicial Supremacy,* 287.

3. With the great men of the Supreme Court, constitutional adjudication has always been statecraft.—Frankfurter: "Holmes and the Constitution," 41 Harv. L. Rev. 121, 126.

4. The reason why from the beginning even the narrow judicial authority to nullify legislation has been viewed with a jealous eye is that it serves to prevent the full play of the democratic process. — Frankfurter: West Va. State Bd. of Educ. v. Barnette, 319 U.S. 624, 650.

5. In nations like America that have written constitutions, the judiciary must do more than dispense justice in cases and controversies. It must also keep the charter of government current with the times and not allow it to become archaic or out of tune with the needs of the day.—Douglas: *We the Judges,* 428.

Related subjects: Constitution, general; Constitution (U.S.), construction; Courts, construction; Dissent; Freedom; Judicial process; Supreme Court.

————, power

6. The perpetuity of our institutions and the liberty which is enjoyed under them depend, in no small degree, upon the power given the judiciary to declare null and void all legislation that is clearly repugnant to the supreme law of the land.—Harlan: Smyth v. Ames, 169 U.S. 466, 528.

7. Research has shown and practice has established the futility of the charge that it was a usurpation when this court undertook to declare an act of Congress unconstitutional.—Holmes: Blodgett v. Holden, 275 U.S.

142, 147.

8. I do not think the United States would come to an end if we lost our power to declare an Act of Congress void. I do think the Union would be imperiled if we could not make that declaration as to the laws of the several States.—Holmes: *Speeches,* 102.

—————, power, exercise

9. Judges do not sit on cushions of down while administering the supreme law of the land in this court. —Baldwin: *Ex parte* Crane, 5 Pet. (30 U.S.) 189, 222.

10. The court struggles to preserve, and surrenders to nothing short of obvious compulsion.—Cardozo: In the Matter of Gallien, 247 N.Y. 195, 200.

11. Our right to destroy is bounded by the limits of necessity.—Cardozo: People *ex rel*. Alpha Portland Cement Co. v. Knapp, 230 N.Y. 48, 62–63.

12. History may satisfy constitutionality, but constitutionality need not produce the title-deeds of history. —Frankfurter: Hannah v. Larche, 363 U.S. 420, 493.

—————, power, exercise, presumptions

13. It is but a decent respect due to the wisdom, the integrity, and the patriotism of the legislative body, by which any law is passed, to presume in favour of its validity.—Washington: Ogden v. Saunders, 12 Wheat. (25 U.S.) 213, 270.

14. The presumption of validity should be more than a pious formula, to be sanctimoniously repeated at the opening of an opinion and forgotten at the end.—Cardozo: *Paradoxes,* 125.

15. The legislature, acting within its sphere, is presumed to know the needs of the people of the State.— Hughes: Townsend v. Yeomans, 301 U.S. 441, 451.

16. Laws are not to be sacrificed by courts on the assumption that legislation is the play of whim and fancy.—Cardozo: People *ex rel*. Alpha Portland Cement Co. v. Knapp, 230 N.Y. 48, 62.

—————, power, exercise, policy

17. To be able to dispute the policy of a law is not to establish its invalidity.—McKenna: National Cotton Oil Co. v. Texas, 197 U.S. 115, 129.

18. Matters of policy . . . are by definition matters which demand the resolution of conflicts of value, and the elements of conflicting values are largely imponderable. Assessment of their competing worth involves differences of feeling; it is also an exercise in prophecy. Obviously the proper forum for mediating a clash of feelings and rendering a prophetic judgment is the body chosen for those purposes by the people.—Frankfurter: A. F. of L. v. Am. Sash & Door Co., 335 U.S. 538, 557.

—————, power, exercise, judgment

19. Within the field where men of reason may reasonably differ, the legislature must have its way.—Cardozo: Williams v. Baltimore, 289 U.S. 36, 42.

20. For the removal of unwise laws from the statute books appeal lies not to the courts but to the ballot and to the processes of democratic govern-

ment.—Stone: United States v. Butler, 297 U.S. 1, 79.

21. To be able to find fault with a law is not to demonstrate its invalidity.—McKenna: Metropolis Theatre Co. v. Chicago, 228 U.S. 61, 69.

———, power, exercise, consequences

22. I should have my doubts, as I have them about this statute; but they would be whether the bill that has to be paid for every gain, although hidden as interstitial detriments, was not greater than the gain was worth,—a matter that is not for me to decide.— Holmes: Adkins v. Children's Hosp., 261 U.S. 525, 571.

23. The judicial function is exhausted with the discovery that the relation between means and end is not wholly vain and fanciful, an illusory pretense.—Cardozo: Williams v. Baltimore, 289 U.S. 36, 42.

24. The correcting statute may be as narrow as the mischief.—Cardozo: *ibid.,* 46.

25. Legislation is not void because it hits the evil that is uppermost. Equally it is not void because it hits the evil that is nearest.—Cardozo: People v. Teuscher, 248 N.Y. 454, 460.

26. Legislation may begin where an evil begins.—Holmes: Truax v. Corrigan, 257 U.S. 312, 343.

———, power, exercise, novelty

27. The accident of our finding certain opinions natural and familiar, or novel, and even shocking, ought not to conclude our judgment upon the question whether statutes embodying

them conflict with the Constitution of the United States.—Holmes: Lochner v. New York, 198 U.S. 45, 76.

———, power, exercise, bias of standards

28. There is nothing that I more deprecate than the use of the 14th Amendment beyond the absolute compulsion of its words to prevent the making of social experiments that an important part of the community desires, in the insulated chambers afforded by the several states, even though the experiments may seem futile or even noxious to me and to those whose judgment I most respect. —Holmes: Truax v. Corrigan, 257 U.S. 312, 344.

29. I cannot believe that the [Fourteenth] Amendment was intended to give us carte blanche to embody our economic or moral beliefs in its prohibitions.—Holmes: Baldwin v. Missouri, 281 U.S. 586, 595.

30. State constitutions and state laws may regulate life in many ways which we as legislators might think as injudicious, or if you like as tyrannical.—Holmes: Lochner v. New York, 198 U.S. 45, 75.

31. From age to age, the problem of constitutional adjudication is the same. . . . It is to keep one age unfettered by the fears or limited vision of another.—Douglas: *We the Judges,* 429, 430.

32. No court would declare a usury law unconstitutional, even if every member of it believed that Jeremy Bentham had said the last word on

that subject, and had shown for all time that such laws did more harm than good.—Holmes: Otis v. Parker, 187 U.S. 606, 609.

33. The Sunday laws, no doubt, would be sustained by a bench of judges, even if every one of them thought it superstitious to make any day holy.—Holmes: *ibid*.

————, power, exercise, stare decisis

34. A reversal of a long current of decisions can be justified only if rooted in the Constitution itself as an historic document designed for a developing nation. — F r a n k f u r t e r : Graves v. New York, 306 U.S. 466, 488.

35. The conservation and orderly development of our institutions rests on our acceptance of the results of the past, and their use as lights to guide our steps in the future. . . . In the discharge of its function of interpreting the Constitution, this court exercises an august power. . . . If the permanency of its conclusions is to depend upon the personal opinions of those who, from time to time, may make up its membership, it will inevitably become a theatre of political strife.—White: Pollock v. Farmers Loan & Tr. Co., 157 U.S. 429, 650–51.

36. In a very large number of cases where questions of strict law are before the Court we have to accept the decision of the Court as the highest authority. But on a question of public policy it is no disrespect to the Supreme Court to say that the majority of the Court were mistaken. There is no reason why five gentlemen of the Supreme Court should know better what public policy demands than five gentlemen of Congress.—Brandeis: Mason: *Brandeis*, 427.

37. When the Court announces a rule that strikes down a law, it not only binds the executive and judicial departments; it does far more than this. It binds *itself* and its *successors* and all inferior courts and future judges to decide similar cases by like logic. It not only limits the judgment of other judges, but, so long as the rule stands, it destroys the discretion even of the men who made it.—Jackson: *Struggle for Judicial Supremacy*, 295–96.

38. The overruling of a decision on constitutional law is, at times, not the true measure of the change. Commonly the change extends over a long period; the erosion of a precedent is gradual. The overruling does not effect an abrupt change in the law; it rather recognizes a *fait accompli*.—Douglas: *We the Judges*, 432.

39. A constitutional interpretation that is wrong should not stand.—Black: Connecticut Gen. Life Ins. Co. v. Johnson, 303 U.S. 77, 85.

————, invalidity

40. An unconstitutional Act is not a law; it confers no rights; it imposes no duties; it affords no protection; it creates no office; it is, in legal contemplation, as inoperative as though it had never been passed.—Field: Norton v. Shelby County, 118 U.S. 425, 442.

41. A law which cannot endure the test of the Constitution without judicial amendment must perish. — Moody: Howard v. Illinois Cent. R.R. 207 U.S. 463, 515.

———, miscellaneous

42. Congressional incoherence of thought or of speech is not unconstitutional.—Jackson: United States v. Spelar, 338 U.S. 217, 225.

43. Constitutional questions, it is true, are not settled by even a consensus of present public opinion. . . .—Brewer: Muller v. Oregon, 208 U.S. 412, 420–21.

44. Lessening the power to enact bad laws likewise lessens the power to enact good ones.—Stone: Mason, *Stone,* 412.

45. It can hardly be denied that Mr. Justice Holmes and Mr. Justice Brandeis were the originators and formulators of the body of our present constitutional law pertaining to civil liberties; pronouncements since have merely been echoes and applications, when not distortions, of principles laid down by them.—Frankfurter: Rio v. United States, 364 U.S. at p. 233.

CONSTITUTIONAL LAW

1. The fundamental rights to life, liberty, and the pursuit of happiness, considered as individual possessions, are secured by those maxims of constitutional law which are the monuments showing the victorious progress of the race in securing to me the blessings of civilization under the reign of just and equal laws, so that, in the

famous language of the Massachusetts Bill of Rights, the government of the Commonwealth "may be a government of laws and not of men."—Matthews: Yick Wo v. Hopkins, 118 U.S. 356, 368.

2. This Court is forever adding new stories to the temples of constitutional law, and the temples have a way of collapsing when one story too many is added.—Jackson: Douglas v. Jeannette, 319 U.S. 157, 181.

Related subject: Constitutional adjudication.

CONSTRUCTION (legal)

Functions 1–5, particular 6–22; rules, literal 23–46, technical terms 47–51, penal statutes 52–58; rules, liberal 59–63, sensible and practical 64–72, ambiguity 73–79, uncertainty 80–94; meaningless 95–101, consequences 102–105; context 106–109, usage 110–115, purpose 116–121, punctuation 122, 123, miscellaneous 124–133; perversion 134–152.

Related subjects: Constitution (U.S.), construction; Constitutional adjudication.

———, functions

1. The legislature does not speak with finality as to the meaning of its own powers. The final word is for the courts.—Cardozo: *Paradoxes,* 99.

2. Ours is the simple service of interpretation.—McKenna: Sandberg v. McDonald, 248 U.S. 185, 201.

3. The very office of construction is to work out, from what is expressly said and done, what would have been said with regard to events not definitely before the minds of the parties, if those events had been considered.—Holmes: *The Common Law,* 303.

4. The difficulties of so-called interpretation arise when the Legislature has had no meaning at all; when the question which is raised on the statute never occurred to it; when what the judges have to do is, not to determine what the legislature did mean on a point which was present to its mind, but to guess what it would have intended on a point not present to its mind, if the point had been present.—Cardozo: *Nature of Judicial Process*, 15.

5. There can be no construction when there is nothing to construe.—Swayne: United States v. Hartwell, 73 U.S. 385, 396.

————, functions, particular

6. It is not our province to make contracts, but to construe them.—McLean: Perrine v. Chesapeake & Del. Canal Co., 9 How. (50 U.S.) 172, 195.

7. Courts cannot make for the parties better agreements than they themselves have been satisfied to make.—Moody: Green Co., Ky. v. Quinlan, 211 U.S. 582, 596.

8. The judicial function is that of interpretation; it does not include the power of amendment under the guise of interpretation.—Sutherland: West Coast Hotel Co. v. Parrish, 300 U.S. 379, 404.

9. We are not at liberty to revise while professing to construe.—Cardozo: Sun Print. & Pub. Assoc. v. Remington Paper & Power Co., 235 N.Y. 338, 346.

10. There is a difference between reading what is and rewriting it.—Frankfurter: Shapiro v. United States, 335 U.S. 1, 43.

11. Judicial construction, constitutional or statutory, always is subject to hazards of judicial reconstruction.—Jackson: United States v. Harriss, 347 U.S. 612, 635.

12. The loss to business would in the long run be greater than the gain if judges were clothed with power to revise as well as to interpret.—Cardozo: *Growth of the Law*, 111.

13. To supply omissions transcends the judicial function.—Brandeis: Iselin v. United States, 270 U.S. 245, 251.

14. I think this court ought not to interject what it can only suppose the lawmakers would have inserted if they had thought long enough.—McReynolds: Federal Trade Comm'n v. Klesner, 274 U.S. 145, 159.

15. Where the legislature has failed to make its intention manifest courts should proceed cautiously, remaining sensitive to the interests of defendant and society alike.—Warren: Gore v. United States, 357 U.S. 386, 394.

16. The Court's task is to construe not English but congressional English. Our problem is not what do ordinary English words mean, but what did Congress mean them to mean. — Frankfurter: Commissioner of Int. Rev. v. Acker, 361 U.S. 87, 95.

17. The so-called canons of construction are not technical rules of law, they are "axioms of experience."—Frankfurter: Mastro Plastics Corp. v.

NLRB, 350 U.S. 270, 293 (quot. 278 U.S. 41, 48).

18. To read legislation. Literalism and evisceration are equally to be avoided.—Frankfurter: United States v. Dotterweich, 320 U.S. 277, 284.

19. Like all truths, Marshall's canons of construction had to be revivified for new demands made upon them by a new generation.—Frankfurter: "Holmes and the Constitution," 41 Harv. L. Rev. 132.

20. We do not inquire what the legislature meant; we ask only what the statute means.—Holmes: "The Theory of Legal Interpretation," 12 Harv. L. Rev. 419

21. The intention of the law maker constitutes the law.—Swayne: Stewart v. Kahn, 11 Wall. (78 U.S.) 493, 504.

22. We mean, of course, his intention as expressed. Not, what did he intend to say? must be the test.—Pitney: Chater v. Carter, 238 U.S. 572, 584.

————, rules, literal

23. A law is the best expositor of itself.—Marshall: Pennington v. Coxe, 2 Cranch (6 U.S.) 34, 52.

24. The only sound principle is to declare *ita lex scripta est,* to follow and to obey.—Clifford: Legal Tender Cases, 12 Wall. (79 U.S.) 457, 633.

25. If this be the literal construction, it is still more apparently its real meaning.—Marshall: Schooner Paulina's Cargo v. United States, 7 Cranch (11 U.S.) 52, 61.

26. Whatever the consequences, we must accept the plain meaning of plain words.—Holmes: United States v. Brown, 206 U.S. 240, 244.

27. There is no warrant for seeking refined arguments to show that the statute does not mean what it says.—Holmes: United States v. Wurzbach, 280 U.S. 396, 398.

28. When we depart from the words, ambiguity comes.—McKenna: Rhode Island v. Palmer, 253 U.S. 350, 398.

29. Good c o n s c i e n c e would be flouted ... with injustice ... if charity were to lead to a refusal to enforce the bond as written.—Cardozo: Burston v. Garrett Bldg. Corp., 252 N.Y. 230, 235.

30. There is no latitude in a taxing statute,—you must adhere to the very words.—Sutherland: Irwin v. Gavit, 268 U.S. 161, 169.

31. To tamper with the words is to eliminate them.—Fuller: Territory of Hawaii v. Mankichi, 190 U.S. 197, 223.

32. Analysis . . . shows that there is no gap between what they wrote and what in reason they must have meant.—Cardozo: Woolford Realty Co. v. Rose, 286 U.S. 319, 330.

33. The poignant significance attributed to every word of legislation. —Holmes: United States v. Sischo, 262 U.S. 165, 168.

34. We have not traveled, in our search for the meaning of the lawmakers, beyond the borders of the statute.—Cardozo: United States v.

Great Northern Ry., 287 U.S. 144, 154.

35. Argument hardly can make the intent of the statute clearer.—Holmes: Robertson v. Gordon, 226 U.S. 311, 316.

36. Whatever the reason, words mean what they say.—Douglas: Singer v. United States, 323 U.S. 338, 346.

37. The grant is its own dictionary. —Holmes: Damon v. Hawaii, 194 U.S. 154, 161.

38. As unambiguous as language can be.—Jackson: Adams v. Maryland, 347 U.S. 379, 384.

39. These words cannot be meaningless, else they would not have been used.—Roberts: United States v. Butler, 297 U.S. 1, 65.

40. These words . . . carry the Constitution with them. — B r o w n : Downes v. Bidwell, 182 U.S. 244, 286.

41. These are words of weighty import. They involve consequences of the most momentous character.—Harlan: *ibid.,* 379.

42. This is language of command. —Taft: United States *ex rel.* McAlester-Edwards Co., 262 U.S. 200, 208.

43. Phrasing mirrors thought. — Frankfurter: Brown v. Allen, 344 U.S. 443, 501.

44. We do nothing to the words of the Act; we merely accept them.— Jackson: SEC v. C. M. Joiner Leasing Corp., 320 U.S. 344, 355.

45. Apter words could hardly have been chosen.—Cardozo: Altz v. Leiberson, 233 N.Y. 16, 18.

46. The literal catholicity of its terminology.—Jackson: Lauritzen v. Larsen, 345 U.S. 571, 576.

———, rules, literal,
technical terms

47. This is tax language and should be read in its tax sense.—Frankfurter: United States v. Ogilvie Hardware Co., 330 U.S. 709, 721.

48. When an astronomer reports that a comet is to be seen with the telescope in the constellation of Auriga, in so many degrees of declination, and so many hours and minutes of right ascension, it is all Greek to the unskilled in science; but other astronomers will instantly direct their telescopes to the very point in the heavens where the stranger has made his entrance into our system. They understand the language of their brother scientist.—Bradley: Webster Loom Co. v. Higgins, 15 Otto (105 U.S.) 580, 585.

49. We must talk as one lawyer to another, or we shall be talking at cross purposes.—Cardozo: *Growth of the Law,* 98.

50. This precision of content . . . differentiates scientific from most political, legislative and legal language. —Frankfurter: United States v. Spelar, 338 U.S. 217, 223.

51. The peculiar idiom of the industry.—Frankfurter: Federal Com. Comm'n v. Columbia Broadcasting Sys., 311 U.S. 132, 135.

———, rules, literal, penal statutes

52. Nothing short of obvious compulsion will lead us to a reading of the statute whereby the pains and penalties of crimes are shorn of all terrors more poignant than a form of

words.—Cardozo: People v. Ingber, 248 N.Y. 302, 306.

53. Although it is not likely that a criminal will carefully consider the text of the law before he murders or steals, it is reasonable that a fair warning should be given to the world in language that the common world will understand, of what the law intends to do if a certain line is passed. To make the warning fair, so far as possible the line should be clear. — Holmes: McBoyle v. United States, 283 U.S. 25, 27.

54. Blurred signposts to criminality will not suffice to create it.—Rutledge: United States v. CIO, 335 U.S. 106, 142.

55. A definiteness which requires so much subtlety to expound is hardly definite.—Roberts, Frankfurter, and Jackson: Screws v. United States, 325 U.S. 91, 153.

56. It would be highly inconvenient, not to say unjust, to make every doubtful phrase a dragnet for penalties.—Story: United States v. Shackford, 5 Mason 445.

57. It is not permissible to enact a law which, in effect, spreads an all-inclusive net for the feet of everybody upon the chance that, while the innocent will surely be entangled in its meshes, some wrongdoers also may be caught.—Sutherland: Ryson v. Banton, 273 U.S. 418, 443.

58. Words which are vague and fluid . . . may be as much of a trap for the innocent as the ancient laws of Caligula.—Douglas: United States v. Cardiff, 344 U.S. 174, 176.

———, rules, liberal

59. A rigid adherence to the letter often leads to erroneous results.—Bradley: Reed v. Merchants Mut. Ins. Co., 5 Otto (95 U.S.) 23, 30.

60. Literalness may strangle meaning.—Frankfurter: Utah Junk Co. v. Porter, 328 U.S. 39, 44.

61. The notion that because the words of a statute are plain, its meaning is also plain, is merely pernicious oversimplification. — Frankfurter: United States v. Monia, 317 U.S. 424, 431.

62. The spirit which vivifies, and not the letter which killeth, is the proper guide by which to correctly interpret a statute. — White: United States v. Trans-Missouri Fr. Assoc., 166 U.S. 290, 354.

63. A fine sense of honor had brought the statute into being. We are to read it in a kindred spirit.—Cardozo: Moore Ice Cream Co. v. Rose, 289 U.S. 373, 379.

———, rules, sensible and practical

64. Common sense accepts the ruling, cited by Plowden, that the Statute of 1 Edward II., which enacts that a prisoner who breaks prison shall be guilty of a felony, does not extend to a prisoner who breaks out when the prison is on fire—"for he is not to be hanged because he would not stay to be burnt."—Field: United States v. Kirby, 7 Wall. (74 U.S.) 482, 487.

65. The common sense of man approves the judgment mentioned by Puffendorf, that the Bolognian law which enacted, "That whoever drew

blood in the streets should be punished with the utmost severity," did not extend to the surgeon who opened the vein of a person that fell down in the street in a fit.—Field, *ibid.*

66. There is no canon against using common sense in construing laws as saying what they obviously mean.—Holmes: Boschen v. Ward, 279 U.S. 337, 339.

67. Some reference to matters extrinsic is inevitable. Words are symbols, and we must compare them with things and persons and events.—Cardozo: In the Matter of Fowles, 222 N.Y. 222, 232.

68. The law, in construing the common speech of men, is not so nice in its judgments as the defendant's argument assumes. It does not look for precise balance of phrase, promise matched against promise in perfect equilibrium. — Cardozo: Moran v. Standard Oil Co., 211 N.Y. 187, 197.

69. Business contracts must be construed with business sense, as they naturally would be understood by intelligent men of affairs.—Holmes: North German Lloyd v. Guaranty Tr. Co., 244 U.S. 12, 24.

70. A law must be framed and judged of in consideration of the practical affairs of man.—White: American Co. v. Zeiss, 219 U.S. 47, 68–69.

71. The conflict is over semantics rather than over practical realities.—Jackson: Regal Knitwear Co. v. NLRB, 324 U.S. 9, 11.

72. This Court naturally does not review congressional enactments as a panel of grammarians; but neither do we regard ordinary principles of English prose as irrelevant to a construction of those enactments.—Warren: Flora v. United States, 362 U.S. 145, 150.

———, rules, ambiguity

73. If it takes nine pages to determine the scope of a statute, its meaning can hardly be so clear that he who runs may read. . . . Generalities regarding the effect to be given to the "clear meaning" of a statute do not make the meaning of a particular statute "clear." — Frankfurter: United States v. Sullivan, 322 U.S. 689, 705.

74. How often words introduced for the purpose of explanation are themselves the means of creating doubt or ambiguity!—Daniel: License Cases, 5 How. (46 U.S.) 504, 612.

75. Words cannot change the fact, though they may mislead and bewilder.—Field: United States v. Erie Ry., 106 U.S. 327, 332.

76. Nobody would express such an intent in such words unless in a contest of opposing interests, where the two sides both hoped to profit by an ambiguous phrase.—Holmes: United States v. Pulaski Co., 234 U.S. 97, 106.

77. Ambiguous clauses should not be permitted to serve as traps.—Hughes: Williams v. Union Cent. Life Ins. Co., 291 U.S. 170, 180.

78. We think the light is so strong as to flood whatever places in the statute might otherwise be dark.—Cardozo: Hopkins Fed. Sav. & Loan Assoc. v. Cleary, 296 U.S. 315, 334.

79. Its i n v o l v e d and intricate

phraseology . . . bears many evidences of being framed to conceal rather than to make clear its real meaning and purpose.—Clarke: Straus v. Victor Talking Mach. Co., 243 U.S. 490, 501.

————, rules, uncertainty

80. There is scarcely any law which does not admit of some ingenious doubt. — Story: Barlow v. United States, 7 Pet. (32 U.S.) 404, 411.

81. Has skill in the use of language ever been so universal, or will it ever be so universal, as to make indubitably clear the meaning of legislation? —McKenna: Citizens' Bank v. Parker, 192 U.S. 73, 86.

82. Such is the character of human language, that no word conveys to the mind, in all situations, one single definite idea.—Marshall: McCulloch v. Maryland, 4 Wheat (17 U.S.) 316, 414.

83. Words after all are symbols, and the significance of the symbols varies with the knowledge and experience of the mind receiving them. —Cardozo: Cooper v. Dasher, 290 U.S. 106, 109.

84. Different and metaphorical significations of the term can doubtless be suggested by ingenious imaginations.—Daniel: Passenger Cases, 7 How. (48 U.S.) 283, 501.

85. The words have the sound of certainty which simple, everyday language gives forth. The certainty is only illusion.—Rutledge: Robinson v. United States, 324 U.S. 282, 287.

86. Words are flexible.—Holmes:

International Stevedoring Co. v. Haverty, 272 U.S. 50, 52.

87. Words express whatever meaning convention has attached to them. —Holmes: Trimble v. Seattle, 231 U.S. 683, 688.

88. It [the word] comes down to its interpreters freighted with subtle implications, with the "tacit assumptions," the "unwritten practices," the "thousand influences" and "values" that "logic and grammar never could have got from the books."—Cardozo: Hawks v. Hamill, 288 U.S. 52, 57.

89. I often doubt whether it would not be a gain if every word of moral significance could be banished from the law altogether, and other words adopted which should convey legal ideas uncolored by anything outside the law.—Holmes: "The Path of the Law," 10 Harv. L. Rev. 464.

90. Then, as often happens, language reacted upon thought, so that conclusions were drawn . . . from the terms in which they happened to be expressed.—Holmes: *The Common Law,* 382.

91. It is one of the misfortunes of the law that ideas become encysted in phrases and thereafter for a long time cease to provoke further analysis.— Holmes: Hyde v. United States, 225 U.S. 347, 391.

92. We seek to find peace of mind in the word, the formula, the ritual. The hope is an illusion.—Cardozo: *Growth of the Law,* 66–67.

93. The search is for the just word, the happy phrase, that will give ex-

pression to the thought, but somehow the thought itself is transfigured by the phrase when found.—Cardozo: *ibid.,* 89.

94. Shifting shades of meaning are a fruitful source of error.—Cardozo: Glass & Co. v. Mizroch, 239 N.Y. 475, 481.

———, rules, meaningless

95. Little had been accomplished beyond the addition of a phrase to the rigmarole of parchments.—Cardozo: In the Matter of Mayor of New York, 246 N.Y. 72, 76.

96. The word is one of the most featureless known even to the language of those who are incapable of discriminating speech. — Holmes: Coca-Cola Co. v. Koke Co., 254 U.S. 143, 147.

97. Minutiae of expression may be found.—Holmes: United States v. N. Y. Cent. R.R., 279 U.S. 73, 79.

98. If the language of fiction be preferred. . . .—Holmes: Nash v. Minn. Title Ins. & Tr. Co., 163 Mass. 574, 586.

99. A bit of verbal logic from which the meaning of things has evaporated.—Frankfurter: Phelps Dodge Corp. v. NLRB, 313 U.S. 177, 191.

100. An addition of nothing but words.—McKenna: Rhode Island v. Palmer, 253 U.S. 350, 402.

101. The one is but another phrasing of the other.—Rutledge: Prince v. Mass., 321 U.S. 158, 170.

———, rules, consequences

102. Consequences c a n n o t alter statutes, but may help to fix their meaning.—Cardozo: In the Matter of Rouss, 221 N.Y. 81, 91.

103. Courts have striven mightily at times to canalize construction along the path of safety.—Cardozo: Hopkins Fed. Sav. & Loan Assoc. v. Cleary, 296 U.S. 315, 334.

104. Whatever the scope of power, we are reminded of our duty to strain constructions to the uttermost if by so doing we can give relief from injustice or oppression. — Cardozo: Thomann v. City of Rochester, 256 N.Y. 165, 173–74.

105. The one construction invigorates the act; the other saps its life. A choice between them is not hard.—Cardozo: Panama Ref. Co. v. Ryan, 293 U.S. 388, 439.

———, rules, context

106. The word to be defined, in common with words generally, will have a color and a content that will vary with the setting. — Cardozo: Hawks v. Hamill, 288 U.S. 52, 57.

107. That a word may be known by the company it keeps is, however, not an invariable rule, for the word may have a character of its own not to be submerged by its association.—Sutherland: Russell Motor Car Co. v. United States, 261 U.S. 514, 519.

108. This is to ignore the transforming power of association for phrases as for men.—Cardozo: In the Matter of Merchant v. Mead-Morrison Mfg. Co., 252 N.Y. 284, 299–300.

109. To strip from words the limits

inherent in their context.—Frankfurter: Amalgamated Assoc. v. Wisconsin Emp. Rel. Bd., 340 U.S. 383, 405.

————, rules, usage

110. An interpretation of language by its traditional use.—Holmes: New York Tr. Co. v. Eisner, 256 U.S. 345, 349.

111. If a man uses a word to which he knows the other party attaches, and understands him to attach, a certain meaning, he may be held to that meaning, and not be allowed to give it any other.—Holmes: *The Common Law*, 310.

112. However colloquial and uncertain the words had been in the beginning, they had won for themselves finally an acceptance and a definiteness that made them fit.—Cardozo: Duparquet H. & M. Co. v. Evans, 297 U.S. 216, 220.

113. The words . . . had come down through the centuries, freighted with a significance which they had gained under the old order.—Cardozo: Techt v. Hughes, 229 N.Y. 222, 232.

114. Words must be read with the gloss of the experience of those who framed them.—Frankfurter: United States v. Rabinowitz, 339 U.S. 56, 70.

115. We do not . . . parse the statute as grammarians or treat it as an abstract exercise in lexicography. We read it in the animating context of well-defined usage. — Frankfurter: Beauharnais v. Illinois, 343 U.S. 250, 253.

See also Mistake 3.

————, rules, purpose

116. As the meaning of the lawmaker is the law, so the meaning of the contracting parties is the agreement. Words are merely the symbols they employ to manifest their purpose that it may be carried into execution.—Swayne: Whitney v. Wyman, 11 Otto (101 U.S.) 392, 396.

117. An ancient evil was to be uprooted, and uprooted altogether. It was not to be left with fibres still clinging to the soil.—Cardozo: Warner v. Goltra, 293 U.S. 155, 159.

118. There is a unity of verbal structure that is a symptom of an inner unity, a unity of plan and function.—Cardozo: Moore Ice Cream Co. v. Rose, 289 U.S. 373, 378.

119. To let general words draw nourishment from their purpose is one thing. To draw on some unexpressed spirit outside the bounds of the normal meaning of words is quite another. — Frankfurter: Addison v. Holly Hill Fruit Prod., 322 U.S. 607, 617.

120. They came there freighted with the meaning imparted to them by the mischief to be remedied.—Cardozo: Duparquet H. & M. Co. v. Evans, 297 U.S. 216, 221.

121. When Congress has the will it has no difficulty in expressing it.—Frankfurter: Bell v. United States, 349 U.S. 81, 83.

————, rules, punctuation

122. Singular as it may appear, it really is the fact in this case, that these

men's lives may depend upon a comma more or less.—Johnson: United States v. Palmer, 3 Wheat. (16 U.S.) 610, 636.

123. The use of the comma is exceedingly arbitrary and indefinite.—Johnson, *ibid.,* 638.

———, rules, miscellaneous

124. The meaning of a sentence is to be felt rather than to be proved.—Holmes: United States v. Johnson, 221 U.S. 488, 496.

125. The sentence is as significant for what it omits as for what it says.—Cardozo: Moskowitz v. Marrow, 251 N.Y. 380, 397.

126. Words acquire scope and function from the history of events which they summarize. — Frankfurter: Phelps Dodge Corp. v. NLRB, 313 U.S. 177, 186.

127. Legislatively speaking as in ordinary life, silence in some instances may give consent.—Rutledge: Cleveland v. United States 329 U.S. 14, 22.

128. The search for significance in the silence of Congress is too often the pursuit of a mirage.—Frankfurter: Scripps-Howard Radio v. Federal Com. Comm'n, 316 U.S. 4, 11.

129. What it said must be interpreted in the light of what it thought.—Cardozo: City Bank Farmers' Tr. Co. v. N. Y. Cent. R.R., 253 N.Y. 49, 60.

130. Through all the verbal variances, however, there runs this common core of thought and truth.—Cardozo: Radio Corp. v. Radio Eng'r Labs. Inc., 293 U.S. 1, 8.

131. The dictionaries, the last resort of the baffled judge.—Jackson: Jordon v. De George, 341 U.S. 223, 234.

132. It is an aid merely; not an inexorable command.—Brandeis: Dorchy v. Kansas, 264 U.S. 286, 290.

See also Precedent 33; Public official 18.

———, perversion

133. The solemn pledge of the United States to its wards is not to be construed like a money-lender's mortgage. — Black: Federal Power Comm'n v. Tuscarora Ind. Nat., 362 U.S. 99, 137.

134. An order may be as effectively annulled by misconstruction as by avowedly setting it aside.—Brandeis: American Exp. Co. v. So. Dakota *ex rel.* Caldwell, 244 U.S. 617, 628.

135. It is easy, by very ingenious and astute construction, to evade the force of almost any statute, where a court is so disposed.—Grier: Pillow v. Roberts, 13 How. (54 U.S.) 472, 476.

136. Respect for law does not thrive on captious interpretations.— Douglas: Delgadillo v. Carmichael, 332 U.S. 388, 391.

137. It is not an adequate discharge of duty for courts to say: "We see what you are driving at, but you have not said it, and therefore we shall go on as before."—Black: United States v. Atlantic Mut. Ins. Co., 343 U.S. 236, 245–46 (quot. Holmes).

138. It is useless to attempt to deceive ourselves by an adroit use of words, or by a train of metaphysical reasoning. We cannot, in that way,

change the nature of things.—Bradley: Marye v. Parsons, 114 U.S. 323, 337.

139. The fact that it required so ingenious and labored an argument to vindicate such a construction seems to me, of itself, conclusive evidence that the construction should not be given to it. — Grier: The Binghamton Bridge, 3 Wall. (70 U.S.) 51, 83.

140. The parties are bound by the contract as it is interpreted by the court, yet neither of them meant what the court declares that they have said. —Holmes: "The Path of the Law," 10 Harv. L. Rev. 463–64.

141. Legislation was read in this hostile spirit in the mid-Victorian days when it was regarded, in the main, as wilful and arbitrary interference with the harmony of the common law and with its rational unfolding by judges.—Frankfurter: Pope v. Atlantic Coast Line R.R., 345 U.S. 379, 390.

142. Would substitute for the natural meaning of the expression used . . . the artificial meaning which might be given to it by the law and by lawyers.—Clarke: Seufert Bros. Co. v. United States, 249 U.S. 194, 199.

143. The perturbation of mind and opinions produced by departure from the words.—McKenna: Rhode Island v. Palmer, 253 U.S. 350, 404.

144. So to read the statute is to misread it.—Cardozo: People *ex rel.* Clark v. Gilchrist, 243 N.Y. 173, 183.

145. Devitalizing the essence to preserve the husk alone.—Cardozo: Interstate Com. Comm'n v. Oregon-Wash. R.R. & Nav. Co., 288 U.S. 14, 49.

146. The latitudinarian attitude of Alice in Wonderland toward language.—Frankfurter: National Mut. Ins. Co. v. Tidewater Transfer Co., 337 U.S. 582, 654.

147. To stick in the bark of a hard and narrow verbalism. — Cardozo: Schuylkill Tr. Co. v. Pennsylvania, 296 U.S. 113, 129.

148. A pedantically literal reading. —Murphy: Morris v. McComb, 332 U.S. 422, 438.

149. To read with a hostile eye.— Mackson: United States v. Carolina Ft. Carriers Corp., 315 U.S. 475, 491.

150. Read with an adverse mind.— Holmes: Leary v. United States, 224 U.S. 567, 576.

151. A construction that is not interpretation, but p e r v e r s i o n.— Holmes: United States v. Pulaski Co., 243 U.S. 97, 106.

152. To smuggle in . . . muffled words.—Holmes: Davis v. Pringle, 268 U.S. 315, 318.

CONTEMPT (of Congress)

1. That a d e l i b e r a t e assembly, clothed with the majesty of the people . . . whose deliberations are required by public opinion to be conducted under the eye of the public . . . should not possess the power to suppress rudeness, or repel insult, is a supposition too wild to be suggested. —Johnson: Anderson v. Dunn, 6 Wheat (19 U.S.) 204, 228–29.

——— (of court)

2. Any man, counsel or witness,

who comes into a court of justice armed ought to be punished, and if he is a member of the bar, he ought to be suspended or removed permanently.—Field: *In re* Sharon v. Hill, 11 Sawyer 122.

3. Misbehavior means something more than adverse comment or disrespect.—Holmes: Toledo Newspaper Co. v. United States, 247 U.S. 402, 423.

4. When a case is finished courts are subject to the same criticism as other people.—Holmes: Patterson v. Colorado, 205 U.S. 454, 463.

5. A publication intended to teach the judge a lesson, or to vent spleen, or to discredit him, or to influence him in his future conduct, would not justify exercise of the contempt power.—Frankfurter: Bridges v. California, 314 U.S. 252, 291.

6. The danger of confusing correction of interference with judicial action with concern over a court's dignity. — Frankfurter: Pennekamp v. Florida, 328 U.S. 331, 368.

7. The power to punish for contempt of court is a safeguard not for judges as persons but for the function which they exercise. — Frankfurter: *ibid.,* 366.

8. The power of courts to punish for contempt is a means of assuring the enforcement of justice according to law. — Frankfurter: Sacher v. United States, 343 U.S. 1, 24.

9. The grounds upon which contempts are punished are impersonal. —Holmes: Patterson v. Colorado, 205 U.S. 454, 463.

10. If imprisoned, "he carries the keys of his prison in his own pocket." —Lamar: Gompers v. Bucks Stove & Range Co., 221 U.S. 418, 442 (quot. 54 C. C. A. 622).

11. The court protects itself.—Brandeis: Olmstead v. United States, 277 U.S. 438, 485.

Related subject: Court, criticism. *See also* Judge 70, 71; Trial 36.

CONTENTION

1. That which is settled beyond dispute may not be disregarded and be brought into the realm of that which is controvertible and questionable by the mere garb in which propositions are clothed. — White: Billings v. United States, 232 U.S. 261, 284.

2. But a spider's web, which the first breath of the law blows away.— Bradley: *In re* Glen Iron Works, 20 Fed. 674, 681.

3. This is a desperate contention.— Holmes: Lenman v. Jones, 222 U.S. 51, 54.

4. The contention puts out of view all of the facts of the case.—McKenna: United States v. Gay, 264 U.S. 353, 357.

5. The contention gets a semblance of strength from the ability of counsel. — McKenna: Oregon & C. R.R. v. United States, 243 U.S. 549, 561.

Related subjects: Argument; Controversy. *See also* Epithet 4.

CONTEXT

Related subject: Construction, context. *See also* Act 2, 5; Evidence 24; Necessary 2; Rights 50; Word 1.

CONTINGENT FEE

See Lawyer, compensation.

CONTRACT

1. A compact lies at the foundation of all national life. Contracts mark the progress of communities in civilization and prosperity. They guard, as far as is possible, against the fluctuations of human affairs. They seek to give stability to the present and certainty to the future. They gauge the confidence of man in the truthfulness and integrity of his fellow-man. They are the springs of business, trade and commerce. Without them, society could not go on.—Swayne: Farrington v. Tennessee, 5 Otto (95 U.S.) 679, 682.

2. A large proportion of the property of the world exists in contracts.—Field: Legal Tender Case, 110 U.S. 421, 451.

3. The making of a contract depends not on the agreement of two minds in one intention, but on the agreement of two sets of external signs—not on the parties' having *meant* the same thing but on their having *said* the same thing.—Holmes: "The Path of the Law," 10 Harv. L. Rev. 464.

4. There can be no bargain without two parties.—Miller: Grafton v. Cummings, 9 Otto (99 U.S.) 100, 107.

5. If the contract did not express the true agreement, it was the claimant's folly to have signed it.—Bradley: Brawley v. United States, 6 Otto (96 U.S.) 168, 173.

6. Whether the agreement was made reluctantly, or appellant got the worst of the bargain, are matters unnecessary to be considered. It is enough that, without fraud or coercion, it did agree.—Sutherland: Savage Arms Corp. v. United States, 266 U.S. 217, 221.

7. Every contract is the acceptance of some inequality.—Holmes: Power Mfg. Co. v. Saunders, 274 U.S. 490, 498.

8. Nothing could be more remote from an actual contract than the wrongful extortion of money by threats.—Holmes: Wallace v. Hines, 253 U.S. 66, 68.

9. A contract existing, its obligation is impregnable.—McKenna: Block v. Hirsh, 256 U.S. 135, 163.

10. There is a well recognized distinction between the expectation of parties to a contract and the duty imposed by it.—Strong: Legal Tender Cases, 12 Wall. (79 U.S.) 457, 548.

11. It will not do for a man to enter into a contract and, when called upon to respond to its obligations, to say that he did not read it when he signed it, or did not know what it contained. If this were permitted, contracts would not be worth the paper on which they are written.—Hunt: Upton v. Tribilcock, 1 Otto (91 U.S.) 45, 50.

12. If the government will not keep its faith, little better can be expected from the citizen. If contracts are not observed, no property will in the end be respected, and all history shows that rights of persons are unsafe when property is insecure. Protection to one goes with protection to the other, and there can be neither prosperity nor progress when this foundation of all

just government is unsettled.—Field: Sinking Fund Cases, 9 Otto (99 U.S.) 700, 767.

13. It is true that . . . people when contracting contemplate performance, not breach.—Holmes: Globe Ref. Co. v. Landa Cotton Oil Co., 190 U.S. 540, 543.

14. In most contracts men take the risk of events over which they have imperfect or no control.—Holmes: Ferry v. Ramsey, 277 U.S. 88, 95.

15. Self-interest is quick to discern the extent of rights or obligations, and never yield more than the written or spoken words require.—McKenna: Lowrey v. Hawaii, 206 U.S. 206, 222.

16. The bargain is equally affected whichever half you regulate. — Holmes: Adkins v. Children's Hosp., 261 U.S. 525, 569.

17. Through the instrumentality of contracts, the machinery of the government is carried on. — McLean: Piqua Branch of State Bank of Ohio v. Knoop, 16 How. (57 U.S.) 369, 389.

18. Wherever the right of private property and the right of free contract coexist, each party when contracting is inevitably more or less influenced by the question whether he has much property, or little, or none; for the contract is made to the very end that each may gain something that he needs or desires more urgently than that which he proposes to give in exchange. — Pitney: Coppage v. Kansas, 236 U.S. 1, 17.

19. Any legal liability for breach of a contract is a disagreeable consequence which tends to make the con-

tractor do as he said he would.— Holmes: Bailey v. Alabama, 219 U.S. 219, 246.

20. Agreements are made to be performed—no less by the Government than by any other.—Whittaker: Federal Power Comm'n v. Tuscarora Ind. Nat., 362 U.S. 99, 124.

Related subject: Agreement. *See also* Arbitration 1; Constitution, Fourteenth Amendment; Construction 6, 7, 69, 116, 140; Freedom, contract; Freedom 96; Intent 6, 7; Judgment 12; Legislature 15; Marriage; Rights 25; Seaman 3; Sovereignty 15; State 10; Sunday 4.

CONTRACTOR
See Lawyer 6.

CONTRIBUTION
Contributions of a few for the satisfaction of the many. — Cardozo: *Law and Literature,* 143.

CONTROVERSY
1. To attempt now to throw considerations of principle into either scale, is to add fuel to a flame which it is our purpose of extinguish.—Marshall: Beveridge, *Life of Marshall,* IV, 505.

2. Of this troubled stream of controversy we may indeed say, "It flows, and flows, and flows, and ever will flow on."—Story: *Misc. Writings,* 427.

3. Let us not leave to them the bitter inheritance of our contentions.—Story: *ibid.,* 525.

4. Each party to the controversy was standing on his legal rights, and was willing to abate no fragment of them. — Cardozo: Tismer v. N.Y. Edison Co., 228 N.Y. 156, 163.

5. The controversy will not down.

—Jackson: *Struggle for Judicial Supremacy,* 270.

6. As sterile as abstract controversies usually are. — Jackson: Regal Knitwear Co. v. NLRB, 324 U.S. 9, 15.

7. The subject matter perhaps too often has been generative of heat rather than light.—Rutledge: Oklahoma Press Pub. Co. v. Walling, 327 U.S. 186, 202.

8. The cooling period is good for most hotly-contested issues.—Douglas: *We the Judges,* 445.

Related subjects: Argument; Contention.

CONVERSION

Probably every stealing is a conversion, but certainly not every knowing conversion is a stealing.—Jackson: Morissette v. United States, 342 U.S. 246, 271.

Related subjects: Larceny; Theft.

CONVICTION (belief)

Related subjects: Belief and related subjects. *See also* Compromise 7; Intolerance 1; Law 9.

CONVICTION (crime)

1. The rule that a man shall not be charged with one crime and convicted of another, may sometimes cover real guilt, but its observance is essential to the preservation of innocence.—Marshall: Schooner Hoppet v. United States, 7 Cranch (11 U.S.) 389, 394.

2. The difficulty of proving a fact will not justify conviction without proof.—Marshall: Beveridge, *Life of Marshall,* III, 512.

3. The defendant stands convicted; he faces punishment and cannot insist on terms or strike a bargain.—

Hughes: Burns v. United States, 287 U.S. 216, 220.

4. The dignity of the United States Government will not permit the conviction of any person on tainted testimony.—Warren: Mesarosh v. United States, 352 U.S. 1, 9.

5. Cheap, easy convictions were not the primary concern of those who adopted the Constitution and the Bill of Rights.—Black: Green v. United States, 356 U.S. 165, 216.

Related subjects: Crime; Criminal law. *See also* Citizen 5; Lawyer 99; Probation 3; Reputation 7, 8, 9.

COPY

The copy is the personal reaction of an individual upon nature.—Holmes: Bleistein v. Donaldson Co., 188 U.S. 239, 250.

COPYRIGHT

1. A copyright, like a patent, is "at once the equivalent given by the public for benefits bestowed by the genius and meditations and skill of individuals and the incentive to further efforts for the same important objects. —Hughes: Fox Film Corp. v. Doyal, 286 U.S. 123, 127–28 (quot. 21 How. [62 U.S.] 167, 168.

2. Where the truths of a science or the methods of an art are the common property of the whole world, any author has the right to express the one, or explain and use the other, in his own way.—Bradley: Baker v. Selden, 11 Otto (101 U.S.) 99, 100–101.

3. No reporter has or can have any copyright on the written opinions delivered by this court; and . . . the

judges . . . cannot confer on any reporter any such right. — McLean: Wheaton v. Peters, 8 Pet. (33 U.S.) 591, 668.

4. A person is not excluded from using any combination of words merely because someone has used it before, even if it took labor and genius to make it.—Holmes: International News Serv. v. Assoc. Press, 248 U.S. 235, 246.

See also Advertising 2; Design 1.

CORNELL UNIVERSITY, founder

A reference to Mr. Cornell, and his connection with this transaction, is appropriate. A man acquiring wealth by his own exertions, the dream of his later years was a university, bearing his name, and so munificently endowed as to become, like Yale and Harvard, a centre of learning. . . . It was the glory of a great university which he hoped to realize —one which would link his name with its glory. The glory and strength of Cornell University was the purpose. — Brewer: Cornell Univ. v. Fiske, 136 U.S. 152, 205.

CORPORATION

Defined 1–6; charter, objects 7–10; identity 11, 12; characteristics 13–18; conduct 19–22; importance 23–25; rights 26, 27; duties, obligations 28, 29; stockholders 30–42; dividends 43–45, stock 46–48; directors, duties, obligations 49–64; miscellaneous 65–69; holding companies 70–76; reorganization 77–85.

Related subject: Business (big).

———, defined

1. A corporation is an artificial being, invisible, intangible, and existing only in contemplation of law. Being the mere creature of law, it possesses only those properties which the charter of its creation confers upon it, either expressly or as incidental to its very existence. — Marshall: Trustees of Dartmouth College v. Woodward, 4 Wheat. (17 U.S.) 518, 636.

2. They [corporations] are not novelties. They are institutions of very ancient date. — Marshall: Bank of U. S. v. Dandridge, 12 Wheat. (25 U.S.) 64, 92.

3. The corporation is a creature of the state.—Brown: Hale v. Henkel, 201 U.S. 43, 74.

4. It leads nowhere to call a corporation a fiction. If it is a fiction, it is a fiction created by law with intent that it should be acted on as if true.— Holmes: Klein v. Board, 282 U.S. 19, 24.

5. The corporate device is one form of associated enterprise. — Frankfurter: Nierbo Co. v. Bethlehem Ship. Corp., 308 U.S. 165, 169.

6. The corporation, a creature of the legal imagination.—Jackson: Tax Comm'n v. Aldrich, 316 U.S. 174, 186–87.

See also Fiction 10.

———, charter, objects

7. The great object of an incorporation is to bestow the character and properties of individuality on a collective and changing body of men.— Marshall: Providence Bank v. Billings & Pittman, 4 Pet. (29 U.S.) 514, 562.

8. The great object of an act of incorporation is, to enable a body of men to exercise the faculties of an individual. — McLean: West River Bridge v. Dix, 6 How. (47 U.S.) 507, 537.

9. The privilege is a mere private corporate privilege for the benefit of the stockholders, to be used or not at their own pleasure—to operate when they please, and to stop when they please.—Story: Charles River Bridge v. Warren Bridge, 11 Pet. (36 U.S.) 420, 639.

10. Every corporation necessarily carries its charter wherever it goes, for that is the law of its existence.—Waite: Reffe v. Rundle, 13 Otto (103 U.S.) 222, 226.

———, identity

11. The name of a corporation is the symbol of its personal existence.—Johnson: Osborn v. Bank of U. S., 9 Wheat. (22 U.S.) 738, 877.

12. Legally speaking, a corporation does not change its identity by adding a cubit to its stature.—Holmes: Old Dominion Copper Min. & Smelt. Co. v. Lewisohn, 210 U.S. 206, 213.

———, characteristics

13. For the general purposes and objects of a law, this invisible, incorporeal creature of a law may be considered as having corporeal qualities. —Marshall: Bank of U. S. v. Deveaux, 5 Cranch (9 U.S.) 61, 89.

14. The will to be announced is the aggregate will. The voice which utters it must be the aggregate voice. Human organs belong only to individuals. The words they utter are the words of individuals. These individuals must speak collectively to speak corporately, and must use a collective voice. — Marshall: Bank of U.S. v. Dandridge, 12 Wheat. (25 U.S.) 64, 92.

15. Corporations have neither race nor color.—Black: Connecticut Gen. Life Ins. Co. v. Johnson, 303 U.S. 77, 87.

16. A corporation is never "found" anywhere except metaphorically. . . . But in the case of a natural person, he can be "found" not metaphorically but physically. And when a person is not actually physically present in a place, he is not, "so to speak," "found" there except in the world of Alice in Wonderland. — Frankfurter: Freeman v. Bee Mach. Co., 319 U.S. 448, 461.

17. It is but another instance of the absence of human affections which is said to characterize all corporations. —Miller: United States v. Union Pac. R.R., 8 Otto (98 U.S.) 569, 620.

18. A corporation is an artificial, legally created entity that can have no "knowledge" itself and is said to have "knowledge" only through its employees.—Douglas: United States v. A. & P. Trucking Co., 358 U.S. 121, 127.

———, conduct

19. A corporation necessarily acts through human beings. — Douglas: Coryell v. Phipps, 317 U.S. 406, 410.

20. The prevalence of the corporation in America has led men of this

generation to act, at times, as if the privilege of doing business in corporate form were inherent in the citizen; and has led them to accept the evils attendant upon the free and unrestricted use of the corporate mechanism as if these evils were the inescapable price of civilized life and, hence, to be borne with resignation. Throughout the greater part of our history a different view prevailed.— Brandeis: Liggett Co. v. Lee, 288 U.S. 517, 548.

21. The separation of ownership from management, the development of the corporate structure as to vest in small groups control over the resources of great numbers of small and uninformed investors, make imperative a fresh and active devotion to that [fiduciary] principle if the modern world of business is to perform its proper function. — Stone: Mason, *Stone,* 379.

22. A command to the corporation is in effect a command to those who are officially responsible for the conduct of its affairs.—Hughes: Wilson v. United States, 221 U.S. 361, 376.

———, importance

23. There is scarcely a business pursued requiring the expenditure of large capital, or the union of large numbers, that is not carried on by corporations. It is not too much to say that the wealth and business of the country are to a great extent controlled by them.—Field: Paul v. Virginia, 8 Wall. (75 U.S.) 168, 181–82.

24. Of relatively recent growth, the corporation has become almost the unit of organization of our economic life. Whether for good or ill, the stubborn fact is that in our present system the corporation carries on the bulk of production and transportation, is the chief employer of both labor and capital, pays a large part of our taxes, and is an economic institution of such magnitude and importance that there is no present substitute for it except the state itself. — Jackson: Tax Comm'n v. Aldrich, 316 U.S. 174, 192.

25. Through size, corporations, once merely an efficient tool employed by individuals in the conduct of private business, have become an institution — an institution which has brought such concentration of economic power that so-called private corporations are sometimes able to dominate the State.—Brandeis: Liggett Co. v. Lee, 288 U.S. 517, 565.

———, rights

26. A corporation . . . is not endowed with the inalienable rights of a natural person. — Brewer: Northern Sec. Co. v. United States, 193 U.S. 197, 362.

27. Corporations cannot claim for themselves the "liberty" which the Due Process Clause guarantees. That clause protects only their property.— Frankfurter: Bridges v. California, 314 U.S. 252, 280–81.

———, duties, obligations

28. The obligation to do justice rests upon all persons, natural and artificial.—Field: Marsh v. Fulton Co., 10 Wall. (77 U.S.) 676, 684.

29. A corporation, quite as much as an individual, is held to a careful adherence to truth in their dealings with mankind.—Campbell: Zabriskie v. Cleveland, C. & C. R.R., 23 How. (64 U.S.) 381, 400–401.

———, stockholders

30. The act of becoming a member [of a corporation] is something more than a contract, it is entering into a complex and abiding relation. — Holmes: Modern Woodman v. Mixer, 267 U.S. 544, 551.

31. Whenever the public interest requires the employment of a great aggregation of capital, exposed to immense risk, some limitation of responsibility is necessary in order that men may be induced to contribute to the enterprise. — Bradley: The Scotland, 15 Otto (105 U.S.) 24, 31.

32. The existence of a corporation is a fiction, but the very meaning of that fiction is that the liability of its members shall be determined as if the fiction were the truth. — Holmes: Remington v. Samana Bay Co., 140 Mass. 494, 501.

33. It is the right and duty of the shareholders to vote. They in this way give continuity to the life of the corporation, and may thus control and direct its management and operations. —Swayne: Farrington v. Tennessee, 5 Otto (95 U.S.) 679, 687.

34. The owner of preferred stock is not without substantial interest in the affairs of the issuing corporation, although denied voting rights.—Mc-

Reynolds: Nelson Co. v. Helvering, 296 U.S. 374, 377.

35. The majority are participants in a corporate enterprise. In entrusting their capital to the corporation, they accept the disadvantages of the corporate system along with its advantages. — Black: Voeller v. Neilston Ware Co., 311 U.S. 531, 536.

36. The shareholders must suffer for the wrongs committed by their officers.—Cardozo: Marr v. Tumulty, 256 N.Y. 15, 24.

37. A court of equity will not hear a stockholder assert that he is not interested in preventing the law of the corporation from being broken. — Campbell: Zabriskie v. Cleveland, C. & C. R.R., 23 How. (64 U.S.) 381, 395.

38. The majority has the right to control; but when it does so, it occupies a fiduciary relation toward the minority; as much so as the corporation itself or its officers and directors. —Brandeis: Southern Pac. Co. v. Bogert, 250 U.S. 483, 487–88.

39. A standing criticism of the use of corporations in business is that it causes such business to be owned by people who do not know anything about it. Argument has not been supposed to be necessary in order to show that the divorce between the power of control and knowledge is an evil.— Holmes: Liggett Co. v. Baldrige, 278 U.S. 105, 114.

40. Ownership has been separated from control; and this separation has removed many of the checks which

formerly operated to curb the misuse of wealth and power. And as ownership of the shares is becoming continually more dispersed, the power which formerly accompanied ownership is becoming increasingly concentrated in the hands of a few.—Brandeis: Liggett Co. v. Lee, 288 U.S. 517, 565.

41. In numbers there is strength. In organization there is effectiveness. Often a small minority of stockholders control a corporation. Indeed, it is almost an axiom of corporate management that a small, cohesive group may control, especially in the larger corporations where the holdings are widely diffused. — Minton: Terry v. Adams, 345 U.S. 461, 493.

42. The financial burden and the risks incident to any attempt of individual stockholders to interfere with an existing management is ordinarily prohibitive. — Brandeis: *Other People's Money,* 41.

———, dividends

43. Large dividends are the bribes which managers tender the small investor for the power conferred to use other people's money.—Brandeis, Mason, *Brandeis,* 356.

44. Every dividend distribution diminishes by just so much the assets of the corporation, and in a theoretical sense reduces the intrinsic value of the stock. But, at the same time, it demonstrates the capacity of the corporation to pay dividends, holds out a promise of further dividends in the future, and quite probably increases the market value of the shares.—Pit-

ney: Lynch v. Hornby, 247 U.S. 339, 346.

45. To withhold dividends from preferred stockholders, in order to make good a deficiency caused by payments to common shareholders which ought not to have been made, was practically to destroy the right of preference.—Harlan: New York, L. E. & W. R.R. v. Nickals, 119 U.S. 296, 310.

———, stock dividends

46. A stock dividend may be likened to a mere exchange of coins.— Cardozo: Equitable Tr. Co. v. Prentice, 250 U.S. 1, 9.

47. The corporation is no poorer and the stockholder no richer than they were before.—Holmes: Towne v. Eisner, 245 U.S. 418, 426.

48. A "stock dividend" shows that the company's accumulated profits have been capitalized, instead of distributed to the stockholders or retained as surplus available for distribution in money or in kind should opportunity offer. Far from being a realization of profits of the stockholder, it tends rather to postpone such realization.—Pitney: Eisner v. Macomber, 252 U.S. 189, 211.

———, directors, duties, obligations

49. The diligent director is the one who exhibits in the performance of his trust "the same degree of care and prudence that men prompted by self-interest generally exercise in their own affairs." — Cardozo: People v. Mancuso, 255 N.Y. 463, 469.

50. Obviously, the only justification

for the director's existence is that he should direct. — Brandeis: Mason, *Brandeis*, 417.

51. For the proper exercise of the functions of director, it is essential that he be disinterested; that is, be free from any conflicting interest.— Brandeis: *ibid.*, 417-18.

52. It is also essential that he [the director] have knowledge. Facts, facts, facts, are the only basis on which he can properly exercise his judgment. It is as necessary that he know intimately the facts concerning the business, as that he have only one interest to subserve. Now, no man can have such detailed knowledge of the facts of many enterprises.—Brandeis: *ibid.*, 418.

53. Directors cannot, in justice to those who deal with the Bank, shut their eyes to what is going on around them. It is their duty to use ordinary diligence in ascertaining the condition of its business, and to exercise reasonable control and supervision of its officers. They have something more to do than, from time to time, to elect the officers of the Bank and to make declarations of dividends. — Harlan: Martin v. Webb, 110 U.S. 7, 15.

54. Directors must exercise ordinary care and prudence in the administration of the affairs of a bank, and . . . this includes something more than officiating as figure-heads. — Fuller: Briggs v. Spaulding, 141 U.S. 132, 165.

55. Their business competence did not confer on them the privileges of making concealed or unauthorized profits.—Stone: Rogers v. Guaranty Tr. Co., 288 U.S. 123, 143.

56. Everyone should know that the denial of minority representation on boards of directors has resulted in the domination of most corporations by one or two men; and in practically banishing all criticism of the dominant power. And even where the board is not so dominated, there is too often that "harmonious cooperation" among directors which secures for each, in his own line, a due share of the corporation's favors. — Brandeis: *Other People's Money*, 40.

57. They came to the board as the eyes of the bank.—Holmes: Curtis v. Connly, 257 U.S. 260, 264.

58. He was a man of such importance and reputation that the use of his name must have contributed to securing the confidence of the community and of depositors for the bank.— Clarke: Bowerman v. Hamner, 250 U.S. 504, 513.

59. Prudent and fair directors would prefer to have the sanction of the stockholders to their acts.—Bradley: Chicago City Ry. Co. v. Allerton, 18 Wall. (85 U.S.) 233, 236.

60. For erring directors, however, there may at times be absolution if all the shareholders are satisfied.— Cardozo: McCandless v. Furlaud, 296 U.S. 140, 157.

61. The practice of interlocking directorates is the root of many evils.— Brandeis: *Other People's Money*, 35.

62. The mazes of . . . interlocking directorates are not easily unraveled.

—Cardozo: Marr v. Tumulty, 256 N.Y. 15, 23.

63. The whole history of finance urges caution when one investment banker stakes out his claim to two competing companies. Experience shows that when one gains a seat at his competitor's table, it is the beginning of the end of competition. A new zone of influence has been created. Its efficacy turns not on the amount of stock ownership but on a host of subtle and imponderable considerations. Such an intertwined relationship has been "the root of many evils" and so demonstrably inimical to the "public interest" in the past as not to be disregarded today.—Douglas: McLean Truck Co. v. United States, 321 U.S. 67, 95.

64. Interlocking directorates between companies which compete stifle the competition. Or to use the words of Mr. Justice Brandeis, the practice substitutes "the pull of privilege for the push of manhood." Moreover, those entwined relations are the stuff out of which concentration of financial power over American industry was built and is maintained.—Douglas: United States v. Grant Co., 345 U.S. 629, 636.

———, miscellaneous

65. The stock of the company is a vendible security, and the community expects statements of its condition and management.—Campbell: Philadelphia, W. & B. R.R. v. Quigley, 21 How. (62 U.S.) 202, 211.

66. It is the accumulation of corporate earnings over a period of time which marks any real accrual of wealth to the stockholders.—Douglas: Helvering v. Griffiths, 318 U.S. 371, 411.

67. What is income for a corporation may not be income for a shareholder.—Cardozo: Equitable Tr. Co. v. Prentice, 250 N.Y. 1, 8.

68. The idea that the capital of a corporation is a football to be thrown into the market for the purposes of speculation, that its value may be elevated or depressed to advance the interests of its managers, is a modern and wicked invention. — Hunt: Upton v. Tribilcock, 1 Otto (91 U.S.) 45, 48.

69. The property and expectations of the corporation are the backbone of the value of its shares.—Holmes: Klein v. Board, 282 N.Y. 19, 23.

———, holding companies

70. The whole problem of the relation between parent and subsidiary corporations is one that is still enveloped in the mists of metaphor.—Cardozo: Berkey v. Third Ave. Co., 244 N.Y. 84, 94.

71. Some of us feel that as utilized in this country it [the holding company] is, with a few exceptions, a menace to responsible management and to sound finance, shifting control of local institutions to absentee managements and centralizing in few hands control of assets and enterprises bigger than they are able well to man-

age—views which are matters of record.—Jackson: Anderson v. Abbott, 321 U.S. 349, 380.

72. Domination may spring as readily from subtle or unexercised power as from arbitrary imposition of command. To conclude otherwise is to ignore the realities of intercorporate relationships. — Murphy: North Am. Co. v. SEC, 327 U.S. 686, 693.

73. Historical ties and associations, combined with strategic holdings of stock, can on occasion serve as a potent substitute for the more obvious modes of control. — Murphy: *ibid.*, 693.

74. It was its brain or at least the efferent nerve without which that company could not move.—Holmes: Edward v. Chile Copper Co., 270 U.S. 452, 456.

75. Intercorporate relations, linked in a web of baffling intricacy.—Cardozo: Landis v. North Am. Co., 299 U.S. 248, 256.

76. A finding of dominion so absolute and abdication so complete.—Cardozo: People *ex rel.* Studebaker Corp. v. Gilchrist, 224 N.Y. 114, 123.

————, reorganization

77. A court in ascertaining whether a plan is fair and equitable is not engaged in ascertaining indisputable facts. It is forming a judgment, and largely a prophetic judgment, regarding a maze of factors, and as to each factor there is usually room for considerable difference of opinion. — Frankfurter: Reconstruction Fin.

Corp. v. Denver & R. G. W. R.R., 328 U.S. 495, 547.

78. Abstractly, no one will reject what the President has called the principle that "reorganizations must give primary consideration to the public interest." But that public interest is in the keeping of the courts. It must be safeguarded by them without regard to the manner in which those who have also private interests represent the public interest.—Reed: Insurance Gr. Comm. v. Denver & R. G. W. R.R., 329 U.S. 607, 630.

79. A basic requirement of any reorganization is the determination of a capitalization which makes it possible not only to respect the priorities of the various classes of claimants but also to give the new company a reasonable prospect for survival.—Douglas: Institutional Investors v. Chicago, M. & St. P. R.R., 318 U.S. 523, 540–41.

80. The scourge of overcapitalization.—Douglas: *ibid.*, 541.

81. There is no constitutional reason why earning power may not be utilized as the criterion for determining value for reorganization purposes.—Douglas: *ibid.*

82. A determination of earning power of an enterprise "requires a prediction as to what will occur in the future, an estimate, as distinguished from mathematical certitude." — Douglas: *ibid.*, 565.

83. The bulge of war earnings per se is unreliable for use as a norm unless history is to be ignored.—Douglas: *ibid.*, 543.

84. The history of fees in corporate reorganizations contains many sordid chapters.—Douglas: Dickinson Indust. Site v. Cowan, 309 U.S. 382, 388.

85. The whole undertaking . . . was in fact an elaborate and devious form of conveyance masquerading as a corporate reorganization, and nothing else.—Sutherland: Gregory v. Helvering, 293 U.S. 465, 470.

CORRUPTION

1. Corruption is always the forerunner of despotism. — Swayne: Meguire v. Corwine, 11 Otto (101 U.S.) 108, 111–12.

2. Personal influence to be exercised over an officer of government, in the procurement of contracts . . . is not a vendible article in our system of laws and morals.—Field: Oscanyan v. Winchester Rep. Arms Co., 13 Otto (103 U.S.) 261, 273.

Related subject: Bribery. *See also* Court 3; Democracy 6; Discretion 8; Election; Freedom 42; Judge 34; Judicial process 15; Legislature 21, 22; Public interest 5; Public official 8; Standard 3.

COST

Related subject: Price. *See also* Original cost; Value 14.

COUNSEL

See Lawyer.

COURAGE

1. If we but face our difficulties, they will fly before us.—Story: *Misc. Writings,* 27.

2. The courage of adventurous youth. There are some unquenchable spirits who never lose it, though the calendar may say that they have left youth behind and reached manhood or old age.—Cardozo: *Law and Literature,* 171.

3. Have courted danger and defied it.—Cardozo: *ibid.,* 125.

See also Freedom, thought 154; Judge 7; Legislator 19.

COURT

General 1–6; importance 7–11; functions 12–36; power 37–48; operation 49–56; influences 57–64; criticism 65–70.

Related subjects: Appeal; Constitution (U.S.); Constitutional adjudication; Contempt (of court); Equity court; Judge; Judgment (legal); Judicial notice; Judicial process; Litigation; Military, tribunal; Opinion, judicial; Supreme Court; Tax court; Trial.

———, general

1. A judicial tribunal, where all action which precedes judgment is upon oath and has its assurance and sanctions.—McKenna: United States v. Woo Jan, 245 U.S. 552, 556.

2. The right to resort to the courts, when exercised in good faith, shall be kept free from the menace of unknown and unknowable penalties which intimidate the suitor, and clog his liberty of action.—Cardozo: City of Yonkers v. Fed. Sug. Ref. Co., 221 N.Y. 206, 212–13.

3. It is not enough that the doors of the temple of justice are open; it is essential that the ways of approach are kept clean.—Brewer: Hatfield v. King, 184 U.S. 162, 168.

4. Constitutions and laws precede the judiciary.—Woodbury: Luther v. Borden, 7 How. (48 U.S.) 1, 52.

5. Under the Constitution courts

86

are merely one of the coordinate agencies which hold and exercise governmental power. — Black: Green v. United States, 356 U.S. 165, 219.

6. Courts are not omniscient. Like every other human agency, they too can profit from trial and error, from experience and reflection. — Black: *ibid.,* 195.

————, importance

7. There must be a final tribunal somewhere for deciding every question in the world.—Bradley: Chicago, M. & St. P. Ry. v. Minnesota, 134 U.S. 418, 465.

8. The Judicial Department comes home in its effects to every man's fireside; it passes on his property, his reputation, his life, his all.—Marshall: quot. O'Donoghue v. United States, 289 U.S. 516, 532.

9. If the judicial power fall short of giving effect to the laws of the Union, the existence of the federal government is at an end.—Marshall: Worcester v. Georgia, 6 Pet. (31 U.S.) 515, 570.

10. Legislatures and courts are not merely cherished American institutions; they are indispensable to our government.—Black: Duncan v. Kahanamoku, 327 U.S. 304, 322.

11. Under our constitutional system, courts stand against any winds that blow as havens of refuge for those who might otherwise suffer because they are helpless, weak, outnumbered, or because they are non-conforming victims of prejudice and public ex-citement.—Black: Chambers v. Florida, 309 U.S. 227, 241.

————, functions

12. The courts are creatures of the state and of its power, and while their life as courts continues, they must obey the law of their creator.—Cardozo: *Growth of the Law,* 49.

13. The function of the judges "is to determine controversies between litigants."Cardozo: In the Matter of Richardson, 247 N.Y. 401, 411.

14. A court does all that its duty compels when it confines itself to the controversy before it.—Holmes: Barker Paint Co. v. Painter's Union 734, 281 U.S. 462, 463.

15. We have no concern with the future. It has not come yet.—Holmes: Union Tr. Co. v. Grosman, 245 U.S. 412, 417.

16. For protection against abuses by Legislatures the people must resort to the polls, not to the courts.—Waite: Munn v. Illinois, 4 Otto (94 U.S.) 113, 134.

17. If the majority of the legislature be corrupted, it may well be doubted, whether it be within the province of the judiciary to control their conduct.—Marshall: Fletcher v. Peck, 6 Cranch (10 U.S.) 87, 130.

18. It is the province of a court to expound the law, not to make it.—Taney: Luther v. Borden, 7 How. (48 U.S.) 1, 41.

19. Our province is to decide what the law is, not to declare what it should be. . . . If the law is wrong, it

ought to be changed; but the power for that is not with us.—Waite: Minor v. Happersett, 21 Wall. (88 U.S.) 162, 178.

20. The power to declare the law carries with it the power, and within limits the duty, to make law when none exists.—Cardozo: *Nature of Judicial Process*, 124.

21. I recognize without hesitation that judges do and must legislate, but they can do so only interstitially; they are confined from molar to molecular motions. — Holmes: Southern Pac. Co. v. Jensen, 244 U.S. 205, 220.

22. Our function as judges is not to transform civilization, but to regulate and order it.—Cardozo: *Paradoxes*, 59.

23. He [the judge] may advise; he may persuade; but he may not command or coerce. He does coerce when, without convincing the judgment, he overcomes the will by the weight of his authority.—Brandeis: Horning v. Dist. of Columbia, 254 U.S. 135, 139.

24. One of the highest functions of the judge is to establish the true relation between conduct and profession. —Cardozo: *Nature of Judicial Process*, 109.

25. The judge interprets the social conscience, and gives effect to it in law, but in so doing he helps to form and modify the conscience he interprets. Discovery and creation react upon each other.—Cardozo: *Growth of the Law*, 96–97.

26. It is the function and duty of courts to resolve doubts. — Stone: White v. United States, 305 U.S. 281, 292.

27. The judiciary plays an important role in educating the people as well as in deciding cases.—Douglas: *We the Judges*, 443.

28. The judiciary is in a high sense the guardian of the conscience of the people as well as of the law of the land.—Douglas: *ibid.*, 445.

29. It may be said to be generally true that the weaker a party and the smaller his interest the greater the need of the strong hand of the court to ascertain and protect his rights.— Brewer: Montana Co. v. St. Louis M. & M. Co., 152 U.S. 160, 170.

30. The protection of the public interest in the special keeping of the Court is more imperative than the despatch of judicial business.—Reed: Insurance Gr. Comm. v. Denver & R. G. W. R.R., 329 U.S. 607, 631.

31. When the legislative will is clouded, what is called judicial construction has an inevitable element of judicial creation.—Frankfurter: Andres v. United States, 333 U. S. 740, 752–53.

32. The courts of no country execute the penal laws of another.—Marshall: The Antelope, 10 Wheat (23 U.S.) 66, 123.

33. The courts were established and are maintained to provide impartial tribunals of strictly disinterested arbiters to resolve charges of wrongdoing between citizen and citizen or citizen and state. — Black: Green v. United States, 356 U.S. 165, 200.

34. If the federal court is to be merely an automaton stamping the papers an Attorney General presents, the judicial function rises to no higher level than an IBM machine.—Douglas: United Steelworkers v. United States, 361 U.S. 39, 71.

35. The underlying aim of judicial inquiry is ascertainable truth. — Frankfurter: Rios v. United States, 364 U.S. at p. 234.

36. We live in the jurisdiction of two sovereignties. Each has its own system of courts to interpret and enforce its laws, although in common territory. — Whittaker: W i l s o n v. Schnettler, 365 U.S. 381, 385.

See also Constitution (U.S.) 21; Constitutional adjudication; Legislature 4.

————, power

37. The possession of judicial power imposes an obligation to exercise it.—Johnson: Bank of Columbia v. Okely, 4 Wheat. (17 U.S.) 235, 243.

38. One often-declared difference between judicial and legislative power is that . . . the one construes what has been; the other determines what shall be.—Brewer: ICC v. Brimson, 154 U.S. 447; 155 U.S. 3, 9.

39. Judicial power, as contradistinguished from the power of the laws, has no existence.—Marshall: Osborn v. Bank of U. S., 9 Wheat (22 U.S.) 738, 866.

40. Courts cannot give or withhold at pleasure.—Holmes: Southern Pac. Co. v. Jensen, 244 U.S. 205, 220.

41. The court's power cannot be enlarged by its emotions.—McKenna: Herrera v. United States, 22 U.S. 558, 572.

42. The courts are without authority to repress evil save as the law has proscribed it and then only according to law.—Stone: Viereck v. United States, 318 U.S. 236, 245.

43. While by the Constitution the judicial department is recognized as one of the three great branches . . . it is inherently the weakest of them all. Dependent as its courts are for the enforcement of their judgments, upon officers appointed by the Executive . . . with no patronage and no control of purse or sword, their power and influence rest solely upon the public sense of the necessity for the existence of a tribunal to which all may appeal . . . and on the confidence reposed in the soundness of their decisions and the purity of their motives.—Miller: United States v. Lee, 106 U.S. 196, 223.

44. The strength of the judiciary is in the command it has over the hearts and minds of men.—Douglas: *We the Judges,* 445.

45. The laws of our country take care, or should take care, that not the weight of a judge's finger shall fall upon any one except as specifically authorized.—Field: *In re* Bonner, 151 U.S. 242, 259.

46. No court can make time stand still. — Frankfurter: Scripps-Howard Radio v. Federal Com. Comm'n, 316 U.S. 4, 9.

47. The judge, if you fall into his clutches, is still the Themis of the Greeks, announcing mystic dooms.

You may not understand his words, but their effects you can be made to feel.—Cardozo: *Law and Literature,* 71.

48. No court of justice can in its nature be made the handmaid of iniquity.—Johnson: Bank of U. S. v. Owens, 2 Pet. (27 U.S.) 527, 538.

————, operation

49. While the facts are uncertain, as they are still only motives for decision upon the law,—grounds for legislation, so to speak,—the judges may ascertain them in any way which satisfies their conscience.—Holmes: *The Common Law,* 151.

50. The process of determining facts will inevitably be misleading unless each step bears a close relation to the realities of life.—Brandeis: McCardle v. Indianapolis Water Co., 272 U.S. 400, 424.

51. It is a constituent part of the judicial system that the judge sees only with judicial eyes, and knows nothing respecting any particular case, of which he is not informed judicially.—Marshall: United States v. Wilson, 7 Pet. (32 U.S.) 150, 161.

52. Our concern is with realities, not nomenclature.—McReynolds: Senior v. Braden, 295 U.S. 422, 429.

53. Courts proceed step by step.—Holmes: Johnson v. United States, 228 U.S. 457, 458.

54. To be effective, judicial administration must not be leaden-footed.—Frankfurter: Cobbledick v. United States, 309 U.S. 323, 325.

55. Our process does not issue unless the path is clear. — Cardozo: Hawks v. Hamill, 288 U.S. 52, 61.

56. In lawsuits generally the courts must rest their determination on the evidence exhibited by counsel. They are helpless, except in rare instances, to speak the word of truth if the facts are not uncovered for them.—Cardozo: In the Matter of Edge Ho Holding Corp., 256 N.Y. 374, 379.

See also Dictum 4, 5; Dissent 3; Human nature 5; Intolerance 4; Mind 16.

————, influences

57. How can it be reasonably expected, that the law should flourish as a science, when the judges are doomed to resist the humors of the prince, or the clamors of the populace, at the peril of those stations, which may constitute their only refuge from pecuniary distress?—Story: *Misc. Writings,* 415.

58. It is in vain, that we insert bills of rights in our constitutions, as checks upon legislative power, unless there be firmness in courts, in the hour of trial, to resist the fashionable opinions of the day.—Story: *ibid.,* 430.

59. Politicians may protest and orators may declaim, but this does not affect the case.—Story: Wilkinson v. Leland, 2 Pet. (27 U.S.) 627, 653.

60. It is not for judges to listen to the voice of persuasive eloquence or popular appeal.—Story: Trustees of Dartmouth College v. Woodward, 4 Wheat. (17 U.S.) 518, 713.

61. The sole end of courts of justice is to enforce the laws uniformly and impartially, without respect of persons or times or the opinions of men.

—Curtis: United States v. Morris, 1 Curt. 62, 63.

62. Those who have brought public opinion to bear on this subject, act under a mere moral responsibility; under no oath which binds their movements to the straight and narrow line drawn by the Constitution. —Baldwin: Cherokee Nation v. Georgia, 5 Pet. (30 U.S.) 1, 50.

63. Judges, however they may conscientiously seek to discipline themselves against it, unconsciously are too apt to be moved by the deep undercurrents of public feeling.—Frankfurter: Dennis v. United States, 341 U.S. 494, 556.

64. A court which yields to the popular will thereby licenses itself to practice despotism, for there can be no assurance that it will not on another occasion indulge its own will.— Frankfurter: AFL v. Am. Sash & Door Co., 335 U.S. 538, 557.

——, criticism

65. Whenever the liberties of this country are to be destroyed, the first step in the conspiracy will be to bring courts of justice into odium; and, by overawing the timid, and removing the incorruptible, to break down the last barrier between the people and universal anarchy or despotism.— Story: *Misc. Writings,* 430.

66. The attack upon the judiciary is in fact an attack upon the union. The judicial department is well understood to be that through which the government may be attacked most successfully, because it is without

patronage, and of course without power. And it is equally well understood that every subtraction from its jurisdiction is a vital wound to the government itself. — Marshall: Beveridge, *Life of Marshall,* IV, 365–66.

67. I feel very profoundly that much of the criticism of courts and many of the blunders of courts have their origin in false conceptions, or at any rate in varying conceptions, of the limits of judicial power, the essence of the judicial function, the nature of the judicial process.—Cardozo: *Growth of the Law,* 144–45.

68. The need is great that courts be criticized but just as great that they be allowed to do their duty.—Frankfurter: Bridges v. California, 314 U.S. 252, 284.

69. A judge . . . cannot engage in political debate or make public defense of his acts. When his action is judicial he may always rely upon the support of the defined record upon which his action is based. . . . But when he participates in the action of the executive or legislative departments of governments he is without these supports. He exposes himself to attack and indeed invites it, which because of his peculiar situation inevitably impairs his value as a judge and the appropriate influence of his office.—Stone: Mason, *Stone,* 711.

70. The assumption that respect for the judiciary can be won by shielding judges from published criticism wrongly appraises the character of American public opinion. For it is a prized American privilege to speak

one's mind, although not always with perfect good taste, on all public institutions. And an enforced silence, however, limited, solely in the name of preserving the dignity of the bench, would probably engender resentment, suspicion, and contempt much more than it would enhance respect.—Black: Bridges v. California, 314 U.S. 252, 270–71.

COURT-MARTIAL
See Military tribunal.

COVENANT
1. Words of prophecy, encouragement, or bounty, holding out a hope but not amounting to a covenant.—Holmes: Wisconsin & Mich. Ry. v. Powers, 191 U.S. 379, 386.
2. We do not refuse to enforce a covenant while it lasts because it may not last forever.—Cardozo: Booth v. Knipe, 225 N.Y. 390, 396.
3. One does not commonly pledge one's self to generosity in the language of a covenant.—Cardozo: De Cicco v. Schweitzer, 221 N.Y. 431, 439.
See also Regulation 1; Religion 19.

CREDIBILITY
See Witness, credibility.

CREDIT
A man who has property usually has friends and credit.—Pitney: Ownbey v. Morgan, 256 U.S. 94, 111.
See also Tax 150.

CREDITOR
1. Real creditors are rarely unwilling to receive their debts from any hand which will pay them. — Marshall: Brooks v. Marbury, 11 Wheat. (24 U.S.) 79, 97.

2. Is it worse for the creditor to lose a little by depreciation than everything by the bankruptcy of his debtor?—Bradley: Legal Tender Cases, 12 Wall. (79 U.S.) 457, 564.
See also Debtor 6; Equality 17; Municipality 8.

CREDULITY
1. It would be a stout credulity that could accept this explanation. — McKenna: United States v. United Shoe Mach. Co., 247 U.S. 32, 43.
2. Save credulity and ignorance from imposition.—McKenna: Hall v. Geiger-Jones Co., 242 U.S. 539, 551.

CREED
Related subject: Religion. *See also* Punishment 7.

CRIME, CRIMINAL,
CRIMINALITY
1. A crime is made up of acts and intent. — Waite: United States v. Cruikshank, 2 Otto (92 U.S.) 542, 558.
2. Crime, as a compound concept, generally constituted only from concurrence of an evil-meaning mind with an evil-doing hand, was congenial to an intense individualism and took deep and early root in American soil. — Jackson: Morissette v. United States, 342 U.S. 246, 251–52.
3. Criminality is one thing—a matter of law—and . . . morality, ethics and religious teachings are another. Their relations have puzzled the best of men. — Jackson: Jordan v. De George, 341 U.S. 223, 241.
4. In morals and the eye of the law,

there is a vast difference between the criminality of a person acting mistakenly from a worthy motive, and one committing the same act from a wanton and malignant spirit, and with a corrupt and wicked design.—Harlan: Beckwith v. Bean, 8 Otto (98 U.S.) 266, 277.

5. Willful fault is generally, though not invariably, the determining mark of crime.—Cardozo: Fougera & Co. v. City of New York, 224 N.Y. 269, 279.

6. The contention that an injury can amount to a crime only when inflicted by intention is no provincial or transient notion. — Jackson: Morissette v. United States, 342 U.S. 246, 250.

7. Criminality does not rid of its evil quality by the precautions it takes against consequences, personal or pecuniary.—McKenna: United States v. Russell, 255 U.S. 138, 143.

8. The anarchist is not at liberty to break the law because he reasons that all government is wrong.—Cardozo: People v. Schmidt, 216 N.Y. 324, 342.

9. Old crimes . . . may be committed under new conditions. — Reed: Browder v. United States, 312 U.S. 335, 339.

10. There are no crimes against the United States except by statute.—Holmes: *Holmes-Pollock Letters,* II, 32.

11. Few instruments of injustice can equal that of implied or presumed or constructive crimes. — Jackson: Krulewitch v. United States, 336 U.S. 440, 457.

12. One may press a charge or withhold it as one will. One may not make action or inaction dependent on a price. — Cardozo: Union Exchange Nat. Bank v. Joseph, 231 N.Y. 250, 253.

13. There is to be no traffic in the privilege of invoking the public justice of the state.—Cardozo: *ibid.*

14. Crime is contagious. — Brandeis: Olmstead v. United States, 277 U.S. 438, 485.

15. Crimes of violence flourish under cover of the night and darkness.—Cardozo: In the Matter of Heidemann v. Am. Dist. Tel. Co., 230 N.Y. 305, 308.

16. An English historian, contrasting the London of his day with the London of the time when its streets, supplied only with oil lamps, were scenes of nightly robberies, says that "the adventurers in gas lights did more for the prevention of crime than the government had done since the days of Alfred."—Harlan: New Orleans Gas Co. v. Louisiana Light Co., 115 U.S. 650, 658.

17. He must be a bold man indeed who is confident that he knows what causes crime. Those whose lives are devoted to an understanding of the problem are certain only that they are uncertain regarding the role of the various alleged "causes" of crime.—Frankfurter: Winters v. New York, 333 U.S. 507, 526, 527.

18. Crimes so atrocious as those which have for their object the subversion by violence of those laws and those institutions which have been ordained in order to secure the peace

and happiness of society, are not to escape punishment because they have not ripened into treason.—Marshall: *Ex parte* Bollman, 4 Cranch (8 U.S.) 75, 126–27.

19. We do not go with Blackstone in saying that "a vicious will" is necessary to constitute a crime . . . for conduct alone without regard to the intent of the doer is often sufficient.—Douglas: Lambert v. California, 355 U.S. 225, 228.

20. Past crimes do not forever outlaw the criminal and open him to police practices, aimed at securing his repeated conviction, from which the ordinary citizen is protected.—Frankfurter: Sherman v. United States, 356 U.S. 369, 383.

21. Group association for criminal purposes often, if not normally, makes possible the attainment of ends more complex than those which one criminal could accomplish.—Frankfurter: Callanan v. United States, 364 U.S. 587, 593.

Related subjects: Criminal law; Penal; Wrong; Wrongdoer. *See also* Assault; Conspiracy; Constitution (U.S.) 73; Construction, penal statutes; Court 32, 33; Defense, legal 2, 5; Embezzlement; Entrapment; Forgery 1; Freedom 97, 127; Guilt; Illegitimacy; Immunity: Imprisonment; Inducement 1; Larceny; Lawyer, importance; Libel, criminal; Liquor 2; Lynching; Moral turpitude 2; Motor vehicle 1, 2; Murder; Numbers racket; Pardon; Police 1; Polygamy; Punishment; Search and seizure 15, 16; Security; Self incrimination 10; Supreme Court 49, 60; Tax 68, 135; Theft; Treason; Trial, requirements; White-slave traffic; wire tapping; Wrongdoer 4.

CRIMINAL LAW

General 1–3; enforcement 4–17; principles 18–25; technicalities 26–29; interrogation 30–36; prosecution 37–41; miscellaneous 42–47.

Related subjects: Crime and related subjects.

——, general

1. Civil society has deprived us of the natural right of avenging ourselves, but it has preserved to us, all the more jealously, the right of bringing the offender to justice.—Bradley: Blyew v. United States, 13 Wall. (80 U.S.) 581, 598.

2. For the most part, the purpose of the criminal law is only to induce external conformity to rule.—Holmes: *The Common Law*, 49.

3. Most of us do not commit crimes, yet we nevertheless are subject to the criminal law, and it affords one of the motives for our conduct.—Holmes: Blackstone v. Miller, 188 U.S. 189, 206.

——, enforcement

4. In a criminal case not merely the liberty of individuals is at stake. Law itself is on trial as the "stern daughter of the voice of God."—Frankfurter: Sacher v. United States, 343 U.S. 1, 38.

5. The safety of society and the security of the innocent alike depend upon wise and impartial criminal justice. Misuse of its machinery may undermine the safety of the State; its misuse may deprive the individual of all that makes a free man's life dear.—

94

Frankfurter: Pennekamp v. Florida, 328 U.S. 331, 356–57.

6. There is much in our whole system of penology that seems archaic and vindictive and badly managed.—Jackson: Ashcraft v. Tennessee, 322 U.S. 143, 169.

7. Unhappily the enforcement of our criminal laws is scandalously ineffective. Crimes of violence multiply; punishment walks lamely. — McReynolds: Aldridge v. United States, 283 U.S. 308, 318.

8. No informed person can be other than unhappy about the serious defects of present-day American criminal justice.—Frankfurter: Leland v. Oregon, 343 U.S. 790, 802.

9. American criminal procedure has its defects, though its essentials have behind them the vindication of long history. But all systems of law, however wise, are administered through men and therefore may occasionally disclose the frailties of men. Perfection may not be demanded of law, but the capacity to counteract inevitable, though rare, frailties is the mark of a civilized legal mechanism. —Frankfurter: Rosenberg v. United States, 346 U.S. 271, 310.

10. Encouragement of delay is fatal to the vindication of the criminal law. — Frankfurter: Cobbledick v. United States, 309 U.S. 323, 325.

11. At the present time in this country there is more danger that criminals will escape than that they will be subjected to tyranny. — Holmes: Kepner v. United States, 195 U.S. 100, 134.

12. We have to choose, and for my part I think it a less evil that some criminals should escape than that the Government should play an ignoble part.—Holmes: Olmstead v. United States, 277 U.S. 438, 470.

13. We must not, in too great a solicitude for the criminal, give him a kind of immunity from punishment because of the difficulty in convicting him—indeed, of even detecting him. —McKenna: Hyde v. United States, 225 U.S. 347, 363.

14. On the one side is the social need that crime shall be repressed. On the other, the social need that law shall not be flouted by the insolence of office.—Cardozo: People v. Defore, 242 N.Y. 13, 24–25.

15. Whenever a court has a case where behavior that obviously is sordid can be proved to be criminal only with great difficulty, the effort to bridge the gap is apt to produce bad law. — Jackson: Lutwak v. United States, 344 U.S. 604, 620.

16. The moral health of the community is strengthened by according even the most miserable and pathetic criminal those rights which the Constitution has designed for all.—Frankfurter: Stroble v. California, 343 U.S. 181, 202.

17. Our system of justice rests on the conception of impersonality in the criminal law.—Black: Berra v. United States, 351 U.S. 131, 140.

———, principles

18. The laws which protect the liberties of the whole people must not be

violated or set aside in order to inflict, even upon the guilty, unauthorized though merited justice.—Chase: *Ex parte* Milligan, 4 Wall. (71 U.S.) 2, 132.

19. The efforts of the courts and their officials to bring the guilty to punishment, praiseworthy as they are, are not to be aided by the sacrifice of those great principles established by years of endeavor and suffering which have resulted in their embodiment in the fundamental law of the land.— Day: Weeks v. United States, 232 U.S. 383, 393.

20. If great principles sometimes appear as finicky obstructions in bringing a criminal to heel, this admonition of a wise judge gives the final answer: "Such constitutional limitations arise from grievances, real or fancied, and should go *pari passu* with the supposed evil. They withstand the winds of logic by the depth and toughness of their roots in the past. Nor should we forget that what seems fair enough against a squalid huckster of bad liquor may take on a very different face, if used by a government determined to suppress political opposition under the guise of sedition." — Frankfurter: Davis v. United States, 328 U.S. 582, 616 (quot. 16 F. 2d 202, 203).

21. Ancient evils historically associated with the possession of unqualified power to impose criminal punishment on individuals have a dangerous habit of reappearing when tried safeguards are removed. — Black: Feld-

man v. United States Oil & Ref. Co., 322 U.S. 487, 502.

22. There is, of course, strong temptation to relax rigid standards when it seems the only way to sustain convictions of evildoers.—Jackson: Krulewich v. United States, 336 U.S. 440, 457.

23. A shocking crime puts law to its severest test. Law triumphs over natural impulses aroused by such a crime only if guilt be ascertained by due regard for those indispensable safeguards which our civilization has evolved for the ascertainment of guilt. — Frankfurter: Fisher v. United States, 328 U.S. 463, 477.

24. Respect and obedience in this country are not engendered—and rightly not—by arbitrary and autocratic procedures.—Black: Green v. United States, 356 U.S. 165, 218.

25. Ours is an accusatorial and not an inquisitorial system—a system in which the State must establish guilt by evidence independently and freely secured and may not by coercion prove its charge against an accused out of his own mouth.—Frankfurter: Rogers v. Richmond, 365 U.S. 534, 541.

———, technicalities

26. All those technical niceties which the astuteness of ancient judges and lawyers has introduced into criminal proceedings at common law, and which time and long usage have sanctioned. — Marshall: The Samuel, 1 Wheat. (14 U.S.) 9, 15.

27. No one can think it desirable

that criminals should escape through technicalities which are useless as safeguards to liberty, and only serve to make conviction more a matter of chance. — Holmes: *Uncollected Letters*, 111.

28. At a certain period of English history, when an accused person had no right to be represented by counsel, and when the punishments for crimes were so severe . . . it was natural that technical objections . . . should be accorded great weight. . . . These times have passed and the reasons for the strict and slavish adherence to mere form have passed with them.—Peckham: Crain v. United States, 162 U.S. 625, 646.

29. There is danger that the criminal law will be brought into contempt—that discredit will even touch the great immunities assured by the Fourteenth Amendment — if gossamer possibilities of prejudice to a defendant are to nullify a sentence . . . and set the guilty free.—Cardozo: Snyder v. Massachusetts, 291 U.S. 97, 122.

———, interrogation

30. Ours is the accusatorial as opposed to the inquisitorial system. Such has been the characteristic of Anglo-American criminal justice since it freed itself from practices borrowed by the Star Chamber from the Continent whereby an accused was interrogated in secret for hours on end.—Frankfurter: Watts v. Indiana, 338 U.S. 49, 54.

31. Interrogation per se is not, while violence per se is, an outlaw. Questioning is an indispensable instrumentality of justice.—Jackson: Ashcraft v. Tennessee, 322 U.S. 143, 160.

32. Interrogation is not inherently coercive, as is physical violence. Interrogation does have social value in solving crime, as physical force does not. . . . Indeed, interrogation of those who know something about the facts is the chief means to solution of crime. —Jackson: Stein v. New York, 346 U.S. 156, 184.

33. Respect for law by law officers promotes respect generally, just as lawlessness by law officers sets a contagious and competitive example to others. — Frankfurter: Harris v. United States, 331 U.S. 145, 172.

34. In this country police testimony is often rejected by juries precisely because of a widely entertained belief that illegal methods are used to secure testimony. Thus, dubious police methods defeat the very ends of justice by which such methods are justified.—Frankfurter: *ibid*.

35. What happens behind doors that are opened and closed at the sole discretion of the police is a black chapter in every country—the free as well as the despotic, the modern as well as the ancient.—Douglas: United States v. Carignan, 342 U.S. 36, 46.

36. Easy but self-defeating ways in which brutality is substituted for brains as an instrument of crime detection. — Frankfurter: McNabb v. United States, 318 U.S. 332, 344.

———, prosecution

37. Criminal prosecutions do not recover concealed treasure.—Jackson: Maggio v. Zeitz, 333 U.S. 56, 62.

38. The state has, indeed, no interest to be promoted by the prosecution of the innocent.—Cardozo: Union Exch. Nat'l Bank v. Joseph, 231 N.Y. 250, 253.

39. In criminal prosecutions the Government is acting simply as the instrument of the public in enforcing penal laws for the protection of society. In that enforcement all citizens are interested. — Hughes: United States v. Wood, 299 U.S. 123, 149.

40. The interest of the United States in a criminal prosecution ". . . is not that it shall win a case, but that justice shall be done. . . ."—Brennan: Campbell v. United States, 365 U.S. 85, 96.

41. Bad men, like good men, are entitled to be tried and sentenced in accordance with law.—Black: Green v. United States, 365 U.S. 301, 309.

———, miscellaneous

42. Defendants charged with crime are as slow as are men generally to borrow trouble of the future.—Cardozo: Herndon v. Georgia, 295 U.S. 441, 448.

43. Criminals do not normally choose to engage in felonious enterprises before an audience of police officials. — Vinson: Trupiano v. United States, 334 U.S. 699, 715.

44. The assets of men engaged in criminal activities are rarely equal to the discharge of their obligations.—

Jackson: United States *ex rel*. Marcus v. Hess, 317 U.S. 537, 561.

45. Society is at war with the criminal classes. — Roberts: Sorrells v. United States, 287 U.S. 435, 453.

46. Even they [criminals] live under the Constitution.—McReynolds: Casey v. United States, 276 U.S. 413, 421.

47. Frontiers of criminal law, frontiers that are slowly but undeniably expanding under the impact of our increasing knowledge of psychology and psychiatry. — Murphy: Fisher v. United States, 328 U.S. 463, 491.

See also Accusation; Defense, legal; Double jeopardy; Due process; Dying declaration; Entrapment; Equal protection 6; Evidence; Ex post facto; Government (U.S.), federal 42; Grand Jury; Guilt; Habeas corpus; Hearing; Imprisonment; Impulse 2; Lawyer; Insanity; Intent 4; Jurisdiction 8; Presumption; Prosecutor 2; Punishment; Search and seizure; Self incrimination; Third degree; Trial; Wire tapping.

CRITICISM

1. Criticism is the spur of reform; and Burke's admonition that a healthy society must reform in order to conserve has not lost its force.—Frankfurter: Dennis v. United States, 341 U.S. 494, 549.

2. One may criticize even what one reveres.—Holmes: "The Path of the Law," 10 Harv. L. Rev. 473.

3. It is easier to point out defects than to devise remedies; to touch blemishes than to extract them; to demolish an edifice than to erect a convenient substitute. — Story: *Misc. Writings*, 447.

4. True, many criticisms may be, like their authors, devoid of good taste, but better all sorts of criticism than no criticism at all.—Brewer: "Government by Injunction," 15 Nat. Corp. Rep. 849.

5. Any summary suppression of unjust criticism carries with it an ominous threat of summary suppression of all criticism.—Murphy: Craig v. Harney, 331 U.S. 367, 383.

6. Criticism of government finds sanctuary in several portions of the First Amendment. It is part of the right of free speech. It embraces freedom of the press.—Black: Wilkinson v. United States, 365 U.S. 399, 425–26.
See also Contempt (of court); Court, criticism; Freedom 69, 70; Law 108; Lawyer, criticism; Public official, criticism; Reform 10; Supreme Court, public opinion; Thought 5.

CROSS-EXAMINATION
Related subjects: Testimony; Trial; Witness. See also Informer 4; Trial, requirements.

CRUEL AND UNUSUAL PUNISHMENT
See Punishment.

CRUELTY
1. Cruelty was once identified with physical abuse. Insult and derision, mental torture as well as physical, have come within its range.—Cardozo: Paradoxes, 18.

2. Cruelty might become an instrument of tyranny; of zeal for a purpose, either honest or sinister.—McKenna: Weems v. United States, 217 U.S. 349, 373.
See also Death penalty 6; Tax 89.

CURRENCY
See Money 3.

CUSTOM
1. Manners and customs (if we may not label them as law itself) are at least a source of law.—Cardozo: Paradoxes, 15.

2. Manners and customs are equally a source of morals.—Cardozo: ibid.

3. A thing which you have enjoyed and used as your own for a long time, whether property or an opinion, takes root in your being and cannot be torn away without your resenting the act and trying to defend yourself, however you came by it.—Holmes: "The Path of the Law," 10 Harv. L. Rev. 477.

4. It is clear that in many cases custom and mercantile usage have had as much compulsory power as law could have, in spite of prohibitory statutes. —Holmes: Uncollected Letters, 24.

5. When men's minds are preoccupied by systems and pursuits, which have received the sanction of many generations, every effort to overcome errors is like the effort to carry an enemy's fortress. It can rarely be accomplished by storm. It must be subdued by patient mining, by a gradual destruction of outposts, and by advances under cover of powerful batteries.—Story: Misc. Writings, 115.

6. Local institutions, customs and policies will not be overridden without fighting for consideration.—Jackson: Davies Warehouse Co. v. Bowles, 321 U.S. 144, 154.

7. We do not readily uproot the

growths of centuries. — Cardozo: Techt v. Hughes, 229 N.Y. 222, 240.

8. There is force in the argument that wider freedom of choice through the spontaneous flowerings of custom would work a social gain.—Cardozo: Manhattan Co. v. Morgan, 242 N.Y. 38, 52.

9. The time might be found to be too short for custom to develop.—Cardozo: *ibid.,* 53.

10. A valid custom cannot be based on so turbulent and discordant a history.—Murphy: Tennessee Coal, Iron & R.R. Co. v. Muscoda Local 123, 321 U.S. 590, 602.

11. It is an excellent custom, but it binds no man's conscience.—Grier: Richardson v. Goddard, 23 How. (64 U.S.) 28, 43.

12. We reproduce the ways of our predecessors as children and grandchildren recall the gait and manners of their ancestors.—Cardozo: *Law and Literature,* 149.

13. Local customs, however hardened by time, are not decreed in heaven. Habits and feelings they engender may be counteracted and moderated. Experience attests that such local habits and feelings will yield, gradually though this be, to law and education.—Frankfurter: Cooper v. Aaron, 358 U.S. 1, 25.

Related subjects: Habit; Mores; Practice; Tradition; Usage.

DAMAGES (legal)

1. As with a blow on the face, there may be no arithmetical rule for the estimate of damages.—Field: Balti-more & P. R.R. v. Fifth Bapt. Church, 108 U.S. 317, 335.

2. Probably in the end the public pays the damages in most cases of compensated torts.—Holmes: Southern Pac. Co. v. Darnell-Taenzer Lumber Co., 245 U.S. 531, 534.

3. In general it is not plain that a man's misfortunes or necessities will justify his shifting the damages to his neighbor's s h o u l d e r s. — Holmes: Pennsylvania Coal Co. v. Mahon, 260 U.S. 393, 416.

4. The rule of damages must give true expression to the realities of life. —Cardozo: Broadway Photoplay Co. v. World Film Corp., 225 N.Y. 104, 108.

5. We shall not feel the pricks of conscience if the offender pays the survivors in proportion to the measure of his offense. — Cardozo: Loucks v. Standard Oil Co., 224 N.Y. 99, 113.

See also Estimate 4; Freedom, contract 179; Injury 1; Interest 3; Litigation 7; Tort.

DANGER

1. When we say that a man appreciates a danger, we mean that he forms a judgment as to the future, and that his judgment is right.—Holmes: McKee v. Tourtellotte, 167 Mass. 69, 70–71.

2. The tourist on his first voyage may go down with the ship if evil winds arise.—Cardozo: In the Matter of Heidemann v. Am. Dist. Tel. Co., 230 N.Y. 305, 308.

3. The sudden brawl, the "chance medley" are dangers of the streets,

confronting with steady menace the men who watch while others sleep.—Cardozo: *ibid*.

Related subjects: Freedom, speech, limitations; Hazard. *See also* Courage 3; Duty 12; Freedom, speech 103; Generality 2; Motor vehicle 5, 7, 8; Negligence, standards; Occupation 4, 5; Rescue 1; Vendor 2.

DEATH

Every society is founded on the death of men. In one way or another some are always and inevitably pushed down the dead line. — Holmes: *Uncollected Letters,* 181.

Related subject: Dying declaration. *See also* Character 7; Improvement; Injury 3; Life 9; Motive 12; Railroad 2; Tax, inheritance.

DEATH PENALTY

1. When a prisoner sentenced by a court to death is confined in the penitentiary awaiting the execution of the sentence, one of the most horrible feelings to which he can be subjected during that time is the uncertainty during the whole of it . . . as to the precise time when his execution shall take place.—Miller: Medley v. Petitioner, 134 U.S. 160, 172.

2. The suggestion that the punishment of death, in order not to be unusual, must be accomplished by molar rather than by molecular motion seems to us a fancy unwarranted by the Constitution.—Holmes: Storti v. Commonwealth, 178 Mass. 549, 554.

3. The suffering is due not to its being more horrible to be struck by lightning than to be hanged with the chance of slowly strangling, but to the general fear of death. The suffering due to that fear the law does not seek to spare. It means that it shall be felt. —Holmes: *ibid*.

4. There is something pretty final about a death sentence. — Burton, Minton: Griffin v. Illinois, 351 U.S. 12, 28.

5. With the patient care exacted by the life that is at stake.—Cardozo: People v. Lytton, 257 N.Y. 310, 313.

6. The death penalty has been employed throughout our history, and, in a day when it is still widely accepted, it cannot be said to violate the constitutional concept of cruelty.—Warren: Trop v. Dulles, 356 U.S. 86, 99.

See also Imprisonment 4.

DEATH STATUTE

Death statutes have their roots in dissatisfaction with the archaisms of the law.—Cardozo: Van Beeck v. Sabine Tow. Co., 300 U.S. 342, 350.

See also Life 11.

DEBT

1. Debt, in its ultimate conception, is a dismemberment of ownership, and the power which it confers over an owner is, by the common knowledge of mankind, often the equivalent of the control which would result from ownership itself.—White: Lewis Pub. Co. v. Morgan, 229 U.S. 288, 315.

2. A debt is a legal relation between two parties.—Holmes: Safe Dep. & Tr. Co. v. Virginia, 280 U.S. 83, 97.

3. It is not in accordance with common experience for one man to pay

the debt of another, without receiving any benefit from the act. — Strong: Ketchum v. Duncan, 6 Otto (96 U.S.) 659, 662–63.

4. It is common for both solvent and insolvent men to pay some of their debts and to leave some unpaid. —Woods: First Nat'l Bank of Xenia v. Stewart, 114 U.S. 224, 231.

5. The Latin proverb: *Qui cito dat bis dat,* he who gives quickly gives twice, has its counterpart in a maxim equally sound: *Qui serius solvit, minus solvit;* he who pays too late, pays less.—Field: Louisiana v. New Orleans, 12 Otto (102 U.S.) 203, 207.

6. No man promises to pay money with any view to being released from that obligation by lapse of time.— Miller: Campbell v. Holt, 115 U.S. 620, 628.

7. Parties do not usually contract heavy pecuniary obligations without some object in view.—Clifford: Barreda v. Sulsbee, 21 How. (62 U.S.) 146, 164.

8. Imprisonment for debt is a relic of ancient barbarism. . . . It has descended with the stream of time. It is a punishment rather than a remedy. It is right for fraud, but wrong for misfortune. It breaks the spirit of the honest debtor, destroys his credit, which is a form of capital, and dooms him, while it lasts, to helpless idleness. —Swayne: Edwards v. Kearzey, 6 Otto (96 U.S.) 595, 602.

9. To say that a debt has a situs with the creditor is merely to clothe a foregone conclusion with a fiction.—

Holmes: Safe Dep. & Tr. Co. v. Virginia, 280 U.S. 83, 98.

Related subjects: Debtor; Obligation, Obligor; Public debt; Securities. *See also* State 14, Tax 3.

DEBTOR

1. The obligation of the debtor to pay his debt clings to and accompanies him wherever he goes.—Peckham: Harris v. Balk, 198 U.S. 215, 222.

2. The debtor interest of the country represents its bone and sinew, and must be encouraged to pursue its avocations. — Bradley: Legal Tender Cases, 12 Wall. (79 U.S.) 457, 564.

3. A dishonest person is an unsafe debtor.—Hunt: Memphis v. Brown, 20 Wall. (87 U.S.) 289, 318.

4. The debtor is often buoyed up by the hope of being able to get through with his difficulties long after his case is desperate and his creditors if they know anything of his embarrassments, either participate in the same feeling, or at least are willing to think that there is a possibility of his succeeding.—Bradley: Grant v. First Nat'l Bank, 7 Otto (97 U.S.) 80, 81–82.

5. Many an embarrassed debtor holds the genuine belief that if suits can be staved off for a season, he will weather a financial storm.—Cardozo: Shapiro v. Wilgus, 287 U.S. 348, 354.

6. Debtors are often benefited by delay, but creditors are usually sufferers.—Clifford: Brooklyn City & N. R.R. v. Nat'l Bank, 12 Otto (102 U.S.) 14, 51.

7. The doctrine that "necessitous

men are not free men," a doctrine evolved by the English courts of chancery in the eighteenth century for the protection of harassed debtors.—Murphy: United States v. Bethlehem Steel Corp., 315 U.S. 289, 310–11.

8. The unfortunate mortgagor who sees his farm sold by his rigid creditor for half of its value, for the want of money to redeem it, receives our sympathy, but the rules of law cannot be altered or suspended to aid him.—Hunt: Memphis v. Brown, 20 Wall. (87 U.S.) 289, 305.

> Related subjects: Debt and related subjects. *See also* Creditor 1; Equality 17; Sovereignty 14.

DECAY
> Related subject: Destruction. *See also* Air (atmosphere); Business 8.

DECEIT
1. Deceit is a notion drawn from the moral world, and in its popular sense distinctly imports wickedness. —Holmes: *The Common Law,* 132.

2. Recklessness and deceit do not automatically excuse themselves by notice of repentance.—Cardozo: Jones v. SEC, 298 U.S. 1, 30.

> Related subjects: Falsity and related subjects. *See also* Fraud 11.

DECISION (judicial)
1. The decision will depend on a judgment or intuition more subtle than any articulate major premise.—Holmes: Lochner v. New York, 198 U.S. 45, 76.

2. The grounds of decision are purely practical, and can never be elicited from grammar or from logic. —Holmes: *The Common Law,* 338.

3. In cases of first impression Lord Mansfield's often-quoted advice to the business man who was suddenly appointed judge, that he should state his conclusions and not give his reasons, as his judgment would probably be right and the reasons certainly wrong, is not without its application to more educated courts.—Holmes: *Uncollected Letters,* 63.

4. Its basis is "not in legal learning but in the realities of the record."—Jackson: Indianapolis v. Chase Nat'l Bank, 314 U.S. 63, 83.

5. Judicial decisions have had retrospective operation for near a thousand years.—Holmes: Kuhn v. Fairmont Coal Co., 215 U.S. 349, 372.

6. The fact that the decision was written at once being regarded as evidence of inadequate consideration. Such humbugs prevail! If a man keeps a case six months it is supposed to be decided on "great consideration." It seems to me that intensity is the only thing. A day's impact is better than a month of dead pull. — Holmes: *Holmes-Pollock Letters,* I, 154.

7. It does not change the significance of the Court's decision to coat it with the sugar of equity maxims.—Frankfurter: Alabama Pub. Serv. Comm'n v. Southern Ry. 341 U.S. 341, 359.

8. It is difficult for a court to decide issues of fact upon which experts equal in number and standing differ flatly.—Taft: North Dakota v. Minnesota, 263 U.S. 365, 385.

9. One of those cases in which the ground of the decision is more im-

portant than the decision itself, except to the parties. — Frankfurter: Bingham's Trust v. Comm'r of Int. Rev., 325 U.S. 365, 377.

10. Lower court decisions have no finality as to the law. The lawyers who fight them and the judges who write them know that they are inconclusive. — Jackson: *Struggle for Judicial Supremacy,* 303.

Related subjects: Dissent; Judicial process; Jury, verdict; Opinion, judicial; Precedent. *See also* Dictum; Hearing; Judgment, legal 14, 15; Military 11; Opinion 24, 25; Power 33; Question 1; Res Judicata 2, 5, 6; Solution 2; Supreme Courts, 5, 10; Tax 130.

DECLARATION OF INDEPENDENCE
See Constitution (U.S.) 37; Equality 11.

DEDUCTION
Related subject: Logic. *See also* Inference 2.

DEFAMATION
Many things that are defamatory may be said with impunity through the medium of speech. Not so, however, when speech is caught upon the wing.—Cardozo: Ostrowe v. Lee, 256 N.Y. 36, 39.

Related subjects: Epithet; Insult; Libel; Slander. *See also* Press 3.

DEFENSE
It is, indeed, the law of nature, and is possessed by man in his individual capacity. He may resist that which does him harm, whether he be assailed by an assassin, or approached by poison.—McLean: License Cases, 5 How. (46 U.S.) 504, 589.

Related subject: Self-defense. *See also*

Hearing 2; Insanity; Lawyer, importance; Lawyer 108; Notice 1; Witness 1.

DEFENSE (legal)
1. No man is to be condemned without the opportunity of making a defense. — Clifford: Ray v. Norseworthy, 23 Wall. (90 U.S.) 128, 136.

2. This right of defense belongs to all—good or bad, one who has violated laws the same as one who has not.—Black: National Union of M. C. & S. v. Arnold, 348 U.S. 37, 47.

3. Groundless defenses are the more oppressive where the amount involved is small.—Pitney: Missouri, K. & T. Ry. v. Cade, 233 U.S. 640, 651.

4. We may assume that the defendant will have no easy task in making proof of its defense. We are not at liberty for that reason to bar it from its day in court. — Cardozo: Susquehanna S.S. Co. v. Andersen & Co., 239 N.Y. 285, 297.

5. A criminal may not experiment with one defense, and then when it fails him, invoke the aid of the law which he has flouted, to experiment with another defense, held in reserve for that emergency.—Cardozo: People v. Schmidt, 216 N.Y. 324, 329.

6. I trust no man will ever be able to defend himself in an American court of justice upon the ground of his own turpitude.—Iredell: Fenemore v. United States, 3 Dall. (3 U.S.) 357, 364.

7. Still less is there anything new in the ineradicable tendency of the guilty, or even of the innocent, to divert the issue from themselves and

direct it to the conduct and motives and reputation of the complainant, the source of all the trouble.—Cardozo: *Law and Literature,* 150.

8. Every person prosecuted for crime, as a part of the strategy of defeating conviction, wants civil actions brought against him, and oftentimes wants to confess them or settle them in order to plead that he has squared his accounts with the law.—Jackson: United States *ex rel.* Marcus v. Hess, 317 U.S. 537, 561.

9. Mistaken notions about one's legal rights are not sufficient to bar prosecution for crime. — Frankfurter: Williams v. North Carolina, 325 U.S. 226, 238.

10. The Government, as a defendant, can exert an unctuous persuasiveness because it can clothe official carelessness with a public interest.—Jackson: Dalehite v. United States, 346 U.S. 15, 50.

11. The charge of taking indecent liberties with a child is, like rape, "an accusation easily to be made and hard to be proved, and harder to be defended by the party accused, tho never so innocent."—Douglas: Bute v. Illinois, 333 U.S. 640, 681.

Related subjects: Hearing and related subjects. *See also* Accusation 1; Innocence 1; Litigation 10; Trial 34; Witness 8, 9.

DEFINITENESS

Related subjects: Certainty; Definitiveness. *See also* Construction 55.

DEFINITION

1. To define is to limit.—Hughes: Cincinnati v. Vester, 281 U.S. 439, 448.

2. While for the purposes of judicial decision dictionary definitions often are not controlling, they are at least persuasive that meanings which they do not embrace are not common. —Stone: Aschenbrenner v. United States Fid. & Guar. Co., 292 U.S. 80, 85.

3. The rule may be and often is rendered obscure by attempts at definition, which serve to create doubts instead of removing them.—Field: Hopt v. Utah, 120 U.S. 430, 440–41.

4. Description may serve where definition would be hazardous.— Cardozo: *Growth of the Law,* 24.

5. We do not "make a fortress out of the dictionary."—Vinson: Farmers Res. & Irr. Co. v. McComb, 337 U.S. 755, 764 (quot. L. Hand, 148 F. 2d 737, 739).

6. Doctrinaire definitions, heedless of practical results.—Cardozo: Schuylkill Tr. Co. v. Pennsylvania, 296 U.S. 113, 127.

7. Definition . . . by the ordinary dictionary with its studied enumeration of subtle shades of meaning.— Cardozo: Fox v. Standard Oil Co., 294 U.S. 87, 96.

Related subject: Meaning. *See also* Insanity; Negligence 5; Reputation 2.

DEFINITIVENESS

The versatility of circumstances often mocks a natural desire for definitiveness.—Frankfurter: Weiner v. United States, 357 U.S. 349, 352.

Related subject: Definiteness. *See also* Prohibition 3.

DEGREE

See Hinterland; Negligence 2; Offensiveness 1; Right 20; Truth, degree; Value 19, 23.

DELAY

1. It was inaction and postponement. Responsibility was shifted from the shoulders of the present to the shoulders of the days to come.—Cardozo: United States v. Chicago, M., St. P. & P. R.R., 294 U.S. 499, 510.

2. Adjournment, it may be suggested, is sometimes a constructive interim solution to avoid a temporizing and premature measure giving rise to new difficulties.—Frankfurter: United States v. Pink, 315 U.S. 203, 237.

3. The achievement of the ends of Congress, already long deferred, will be put off till the Greek Kalends.—Cardozo: ICC v. New York, N. H. & H. R.R., 287 U.S. 178, 205.

See also Criminal law 10; Debtor 6; Decision 6; Law 35; Litigation 16–18, 25; Mistake 5; Remedy 10; Trial 41; War 9.

DELEGATION

See Duty 6, 8; Power 43.

DELINQUENCY

Science has found and the law has recognized that there are certain types of mental deficiency associated with delinquency which are inheritable.—Stone: Skinner v. Oklahoma, 316 U.S. 535, 545.

DEMAND

A demand, accompanied with rudeness and insult, is not a legal demand. —Grier: Boyden v. Burke, 14 How. (55 U.S.) 575, 583.

See also Price 2.

DEMOCRACY

1. What are the . . . maxims of democracy? . . . A strict observance of justice and public faith, and a steady adherence to virtue.—Marshall: Beveridge, *Life of Marshall,* I, 410.

2. The government is mild. The press is free. Religion is free. Knowledge reaches, or many reach, every home. What fairer prospect of success could be presented? — Story: *Misc. Writings,* 86.

3. We stand, the latest, and, if we fail, probably the last experiment of self-government by the people. — Story: *ibid.*

4. Unless the people do at all times possess virtue, and firmness, and intelligence enough, to reject mischievous influence; unless they are well instructed in public affairs, and resolutely maintain the principles of the constitution, it is obvious, that the government itself must soon degenerate into an oligarchy; and the dominant faction will rule with an unbounded and desolating energy. — Story: *ibid.,* 158.

5. The principles of the constitution, under which we live; the principles, upon which republics generally are founded, by which they are sustained, and through which they must be saved; the principles of public policy, by which national prosperity is secured, and national ruin averted; these, certainly, are not party creeds, or party dogmas.—Story: *ibid.,* 163.

6. Governments are not always overthrown by direct and open assaults. . . . The continual drippings

of corruption may wear away the solid rock, when the tempest has failed to overturn it.—Story: *ibid.*, 448.

7. Democracy is the least static form of society. Its basis is reason not authority.—Frankfurter; Pennekamp v. Florida, 328 U.S. 331, 350–51.

8. Power in a democracy implies responsibility in its exercise. No institution in a democracy, either governmental or private, can have absolute power. Nor can the limits of power which enforce responsibility be finally determined by the limited power itself. — Frankfurter: *ibid.*, 355–56.

9. The power of the people of the states to make and alter their laws at pleasure is the greatest security for liberty and justice. — Frankfurter: Bridges v. California, 314 U.S. 252, 281.

10. The heart of the matter is that democracy implies respect for the elementary rights of men, however suspect or unworthy; a democratic government must therefore practice fairness; and fairness can rarely be obtained by secret, one-sided determination of facts decisive of rights.—Frankfurter: Joint Anti-Fascist Ref. Comm. v. McGrath, 341 U.S. 123, 170.

11. A constitutional democracy like ours is perhaps the most difficult of man's social arrangements to manage successfully. Our scheme of society is more dependent than any other form of government on knowledge and wisdom and self-discipline for the achievement of its aims. For our democracy implies the reign of reason on the most extensive scale.—Frankfurter: Youngstown Sheet & Tube Co. v. Sawyer, 343 U.S. 579, 593.

12. The great postulate of our democracy is confidence in the common sense of the people and in their maturity of judgment, even on great issues—once they know the facts.—Douglas: *We the Judges*, 320.

13. The hope and safeguard of democracy is education . . . the education which enlightens the masses as to the right relationship of the individual to the organization of society and inculcates a sense of individual responsibility for the preservation of that relationship on a sound basis of which law is only the outgrowth.—Stone: Mason, *Stone*, 100.

14. It is true that democracy cannot live without respect for law, but it must be remembered that law in democracy will have only the respect it deserves.—Hughes: Pusey, *Hughes*, I, 394.

15. If the world is to be made safe for democracy, it must be a world in which the nations recognize and maintain the supremacy of law.—Hughes: *ibid.*, 369.

16. Democracy in any sphere is a serious undertaking. It substitutes self-restraint for external restraint. It is more difficult to maintain than to achieve. It demands continuous sacrifice by the individual and more exigent obedience to the moral law than any other form of government. — Brandeis: Mason, *Brandeis*, 585.

17. We Americans are committed . . . primarily to democracy. The so-

cial justice for which we are striving is an incident of our democracy, not the main end. It is rather the result of democracy—perhaps its finest expression—but it rests upon democracy, which implies the rule by the people.—Brandeis: *ibid.*, 430.

18. Democracy rests upon two pillars; one, the principle that all men are equally entitled to life, liberty, and the pursuit of happiness; and the other, the conviction that such equal opportunity will most advance civilization. Aristocracy, on the other hand, denies both these postulates. It rests upon the principle of the superman. It willingly subordinates the many to the few, and seeks to justify sacrificing the individual by insisting that civilization will be advanced by such sacrifices.—Brandeis: *ibid.*, 439.

19. In a democracy it is the part of statesmanship to prevent the development of power which overawes the ordinary forces of man. Where such power exists, it must be broken. The privilege which begets it must be destroyed.—Brandeis: *ibid.*, 419.

20. Discipline is not common in democracies, and it is particularly difficult to introduce it where the ranks of the privates are largely composed of thinkers.—Brandeis: *ibid.*, 312.

21. The gains, social and economic, which the miners and other citizens have realized in the past, are ultimately due to the fact that they enjoy the rights of free men under our system of government. Upon the maintenance of that system depends all future progress to which they may justly aspire. In our complex society, there is a great variety of limited loyalties, but the overriding loyalty of all is to our country and to the institutions under which a particular interest may be pursued.—Vinson: United States v. UMW, 330 U.S. 258, 306.

22. To say that any group cannot be assimilated is to admit that the great American experiment has failed, that our way of life has failed when confronted with the normal attachment of certain groups to the lands of their forefathers. — Murphy: Hirabayashi v. United States, 320 U.S. 81, 111.

23. The very ability of democracies to settle issues peaceably may depend on responding to them before they have developed the bitterness which comes of long-endured injustices.—Jackson: *Struggle for Judicial Supremacy*, 318.

24. The strength of democracy is its recognition of the rights of each and every minority in society.—Douglas: *We the Judges*, 353.

25. Democracy c a n n o t, indeed, flourish with political power concentrated at distant points. Democracy must have healthy roots at the town and village level.—Douglas: *ibid.*, 38.

26. Democracy cannot survive without the guidance of a creative minority.—Stone: Mason, *Stone*, 95.

27. Ultimately all the questions in this case really boil down to one—whether we as a people will try fearfully and futilely to preserve Democracy by adopting totalitarian methods, or whether in accordance with our

traditions and our Constitution we will have the confidence and courage to be free.—Black: Barenblatt v. United States, 360 U.S. 109, 162.

28. No longer are there vassals trembling at the rapacity of kings and lords.—Cardozo: In the Matter of the People (Melrose Ave.), 324 N.Y. 48, 53.

29. In days of great tension when feelings run high, it is a temptation to take short-cuts by borrowing from the totalitarian techniques of our opponents. But when we do, we set in motion a subversive influence of our own design that destroys us from within.—Douglas: Joint Anti-Fascist Ref. Comm. v. McGrath, 341 U.S. 123, 174.

30. A democracy is effective only if the people have faith in those who govern, and that faith is bound to be shattered when high officials and their appointees engage in activities which arouse suspicions of malfeasance and corruption.—Warren: 364 U.S. 520, 562.

31. The very foundation of a true democracy and the foundation upon which this Nation was built is the fact that government is responsive to the views of its citizens. — Black: Braden v. United States, 365 U.S. 431, 444.

Related subjects: Citizen; Constitution (U.S.); Freedom; Government (U.S.); Republic; Sovereignty. *See also* Competition 7, 8; Constitutional adjudication 4; Election; Equality; Good will 1; Power 17, 18; Property 25; Public opinion 10; Public school 1; Tyranny 6.

DEMOCRACY (industrial)

1. The next generation must witness a continuing and ever-increasing contest between those who have and those who have not. The industrial world is in a state of ferment. The ferment is in the main peaceful, and, to a considerable extent, silent; but there is felt today very widely the inconsistency in this condition of political democracy and industrial absolutism. The people are beginning to doubt whether in the long run democracy and absolutism can co-exist in the same community; beginning to doubt whether there is justification for the great inequalities in the distribution of wealth, for the rapid creation of fortunes, more mysterious than the deeds of Aladdin's lamp.—Brandeis: *Business—A Profession,* 342.

2. The end for which we must strive is the attainment of rule by the people, and that involves industrial democracy as well as political democracy. — Brandeis: Mason, *Brandeis,* 430.

3. We must avoid industrial despotism, even though it is a benevolent despotism.—Brandeis: *ibid.,* 141.

4. The American people have as little need of oligarchy in business as in politics. — Brandeis: *Other People's Money,* 141.

5. If the industrial democracy—true cooperation—should be substituted for industrial absolutism, there would be no lack of industrial leaders. —Brandeis: *ibid.,* 142.

6. In things economic, as well as in

things political, wisdom and safety lie in direct appeals to the people.—Brandeis: *ibid.,* 89.

7. Democracy is compatible with the division of labor based on fitness for the function to be performed, provided only that each function shall remain open to those who are fitted to perform it regardless of their social or economic status.—Stone: Mason, *Stone,* 95.

8. The problem of the hour is the reconciliation of the principles of liberty with the type of economic society we have constructed. — Stone: *ibid.,* 374.

Related subject: Labor.

DENATIONALIZATION

Related subjects: Denaturalization; Naturalization. *See also* Citizen 5, 30–32; Naturalization 6.

DENATURALIZATION

Denaturalization consequences may be more grave than consequences that flow from conviction for crime.—Black: Klapprott v. United States, 335 U.S. 601, 611.

Related subjects: Denationalization; Naturalization.

DEPENDENCE

The two are so tied together that either in its overthrow will drag the other down with it.—Cardozo: City Bank Farmers' Tr. Co. v. N. Y. C. R.R., 253 N.Y. 49, 60.

See also Judge 34; Woman 2, 5.

DEPORTATION

1. The expulsion of a race may be within the inherent powers of a despotism.—Brewer: Fong Yue Ting v. United States, 149 U.S. 698, 737.

2. Nor is the deportation a punishment; it is simply a refusal by the government to harbor persons whom it does not want.—Holmes: Bugajewitz v. Adams, 228 U.S. 585, 591.

3. Deportation can be the equivalent of banishment or exile. The stakes are indeed high for the alien who has acquired his residence here.—Douglas: Delgadillo v. Carmichael, 332 U.S. 388, 391.

4. To deport one who . . . claims to be a citizen obviously deprives him of liberty. It may result also in loss of both property and life; or of all that makes life worth living.—Reed: Ng Fung Ho v. White, 259 U.S. 276, 284.

5. That aliens remain vulnerable to expulsion after long residence is a practice that bristles with severities.—Jackson: Harisiades v. Shaughnessy, 342 U.S. 580, 587.

Related subject: Alien.

DEPRECIATION

1. The depreciation charge . . . is a bookkeeping device introduced in the exercise of practical judgment. . . . It preserves the integrity of the investment.—Brandeis: United Ry. & Elec. Co. v. West, 280 U.S. 234, 264.

2. A depreciation charge resembles a life insurance premium. The depreciation reserve, to which it is credited, supplies insurance for the plant against its inevitable decadence, as the life insurance reserve supplies the fund to meet the agreed value of the lost human life.—Holmes: Pacific Gas & Elec. Co. v. San Francisco, 265 U.S. 403, 423.

3. As a layman might put it, the machine in its lifetime must pay for itself before it can be said to pay anything to its owner.—Jackson: Detroit Edison Co. v. Comm'r of Int. Rev., 319 U.S. 98, 101.

4. There is a broad twilight zone between depreciation and maintenance.—Brandeis: United Ry. & Elec. Co. v. West, 280 U.S. 234, 259.

5. The l a b e l is unimportant, whether depreciation or amortization, if the substance of allowance is adequately preserved.—Cardozo: American Tel. & Tel. Co. v. United States, 299 U.S. 232, 244.

6. Wear and tear do not wait on net income.—Douglas: Virginian Hotel Corp. v. Helvering, 319 U.S. 523, 525.

DEPRESSION

Related subject: Public emergency. *See also* Tax 118.

DERISION

If we cannot understand, let us show that the superiority is ours by combining to deride. — Cardozo: *Growth of the Law,* 22.

DESCRIPTION

1. A description which distinguishes it from any other, although a better or still more certain description might be given, is all that is required.—Marshall: Matson v. Hord, 1 Wheat. (14 U.S.) 130, 138.

2. Some description there must be. Its adequacy depends upon the degree of certainty attained when the words are applied to things.—Car-

dozo: Marks v. Cowdin, 226 N.Y. 138, 144.

3. There are times when a description is deceptive from the very fact of its simplicity.—Cardozo: Federal Trade Comm'n v. Alcoma Lumber Co., 291 U.S. 67, 75.

See also Definition 4.

DESIGN

1. Ornamental designs, or pictorial illustrations addressed to the taste . . . may be said . . . their form is their essence, and their object the production of pleasure in their contemplation. This is the final end. They are as much the product of genius and the result of composition as are the lines of the poet or the historian's periods. —Bradley: Baker v. Selden, 11 Otto (101 U.S.) 99, 103–104.

2. A design or pattern in ornamentation or shape appeals only to the taste through the eye, and is often a matter of evanescent caprice.—Blatchford: Dobson v. Hartford Carpet Co., 114 U.S. 439, 445.

DESIRE

1. There is every reason . . . for trying to make our desires intelligent.— Holmes: "Ideals and Doubts," 10 Ill. L. Rev. 2.

2. There is in all men a demand for the superlative, so much so that the poor devil who has no other way of reaching it attains it by getting drunk. —Holmes: "Natural Law," 32 Harv. L. Rev. 40.

3. Consciously or unconsciously we all strive to make the kind of a

world we like.—Holmes: "Ideals and Doubts," 10 Ill. L. Rev. 2.

Related subject: Aspiration. *See also* Freedom 185; Reform 5; Value 2; Wealth 3.

DESPAIR

See Hindrance.

DESPOTISM

1. There is in such governments, what may be called a desolating calm, a universal indisposition to changes, and a fearfulness of reform on all sides; on the part of the people, lest it should generate some new oppression; and on the part of the ruler, lest it should introduce some jealousy or check of his arbitrary power.—Story: *Misc. Writings,* 405.

2. In governments purely despotic, the laws rarely undergo any considerable changes through a long series of ages. The fundamental institutions (for such there must be in all civilized societies), whether modelled at first by accident or by design, by caprice or by wisdom, assume a settled course, which is broken in upon only by the positive edicts of the sovereign, suited to some temporary exigency.—Story: *ibid.*

3. The laws of the Medes and Persians were proverbially immutable.—Story: *ibid.,* 406.

4. Despotism, be it financial or political, is vulnerable, unless it is believed to rest upon a moral sanction.—Brandeis: *Other People's Money,* 31.

5. From time immemorial despots have used real or imagined threats to the public welfare as an excuse for needlessly abrogating human rights.—Murphy: Duncan v. Kahanamoku, 327 U.S., 304, 330.

6. Despotic governments cannot exist without stifling the voice of opposition to their oppressive practices.—Black: Barenblatt v. United States, 360 U.S. 109, 145.

7. The laws of an absolute monarchy are not its legislative acts; they are the will and pleasure of the monarch expressed in various ways—if expressed in any, it is a law.—Baldwin: United States v. Arredondo. 6 Pet. (31 U.S.) 691, 714.

Related subjects: Absolutism; Oligarchy; Tyranny. *See also* Constitution (U.S.) 97; Corruption 1; Democracy (industrial) 3; Deportation 1; Freedom, thought 148; Government, general 8; Idea 9; Majority-minority 6; Public official 25; Rights 2; Search and seizure 5.

DESTRUCTION

Related subject: Decay. *See also* Property 23; Protection; Rule 17, 18; Tax, abuse; War 35.

DETAIL

1. Details are apt to seem sordid and uninteresting, but a horse must eat hay as well as oats and it is in transfiguring details that a man shows his power.—Holmes: *Uncollected Letters,* 166.

2. There is an accuracy that defeats itself by the over-emphasis of details.—Cardozo: *Law and Literature,* 7.

DEVICE

A device need not be necessarily

fraudulent; the term includes anything which is a plan or contrivance. —Day: Armour Packing Co. v. United States, 209 U.S. 56, 71.

DICTIONARY

See Construction 37; Definition.

DICTUM (legal)

1. We emphasize the distinction between dictum and decision.—Cardozo: Dayton Power & Light Co. v. Pub. Util. Comm'n, 292 U.S. 290, 302.

2. We must distinguish "between what was said and what was done," between "dictum and decision," between reasoning and conclusion.— Hughes: United Gas Pub. Serv. Co. v. Texas, 303 U.S. 123, 144.

3. The disclosure of the reasoning by which a conclusion is reached cannot remotely be deemed dictum.— Frankfurter: Darr v. Burford, 339 U.S. 200, 225–26.

4. I own that it is a good deal of a mystery to me how judges, of all persons in the world, should put their faith in dicta. A brief experience on the bench was enough to reveal to me all sorts of cracks and crevices and loopholes in my own opinions when picked up a few months after delivery, and reread with due contrition.—Cardozo: *Nature of Judicial Process,* 29–30.

5. Courts do not weary of cautioning counsel to distinguish dictum from decision. They must heed their own warnings.—Cardozo: Smith v. Hedges, 223 N.Y. 176, 184.

6. Reiteration may have given them an authority not otherwise belonging to them.—Cardozo: Cullings v. Goetz, 256 N.Y. 287, 292.

See also Judge 64; Precedent 23.

DIFFERENCE

Related subject: Distinction. *See also* Faith 10; Morality 6; Name 5, 9; Number; Optional, 2; Value 21; Whole, part 1; Woman.

DIFFICULTY

See Argument 2, 3; Courage 1; Tax, difficulties; Wisdom 7.

DIGRESSION

If a boy gets his fingers pinched between two inward revolving wheels, it probably will only distract attention and bore the reader to describe the machinery. — Holmes: *Uncollected Letters,* 156.

DILEMMA

1. Necessarily subject to being impaled on one or the other of two horns of a dilemma, either inflicting a fatal wound.—Fuller: *In re* Chapman, 166 U.S. 661, 671.

2. The petitioner's problem is to avoid Scylla without being drawn into Charybdis.—Jackson: Montana–Dakota Util. Co. v. Northwestern Pub. Serv. Co., 341 U.S. 246, 250.

DILIGENCE

Ordinary diligence, like most other human qualifications or characteristics, is a relative term, to be judged of by the nature of the subject to which it is directed.—Bradley: Holladay v. Kennard, 12 Wall. (79 U.S.) 254, 258.

Related subjects: Effort; Industry. *See also* Self-restraint 2.

DIPLOMACY

See Foreign affairs.

113

DIRECTOR

See Corporation, directors.

DISAPPOINTMENT

Disappointment crowds fast upon human footsteps, in whatever paths they tread.—Story: *Misc. Writings,* 9.

DISBARMENT

See Lawyer, disbarment, misconduct.

DISCHARGE

"Discharge" . . . usually . . . is a slightly discrediting verb.—Holmes: United States v. Sweet, 189 U.S. 471, 473-74.

See also Labor 22; Public official 41.

DISCIPLINE

The strategy of discipline is not simple. The maintenance of authority hinges upon a delicate complex of human factors. — Byrnes: Southern S.S. Co. v. NLRB, 316 U.S. 31, 46.

See also Democracy 20.

DISCLOSURE

1. Disclosure is the antidote to partiality and favor.—Cardozo: People *ex rel.* Fordham M. R. Church v. Walsh, 244 N.Y. 280, 291.

2. If dual interests are to be served, the disclosure to be effective, must lay bare the truth, without ambiguity or reservation, in all its stark significance. —Cardozo: Wendt v. Fisher, 243 N.Y. 439, 443.

See also Fiduciary 13, 14, 18; Will 5; Wire tapping 3.

DISCOURAGEMENT

At times, indeed, we shall seem to have learned nothing, and shall wonder whether there was profit in the labor and the sacrifice.—Cardozo: *Growth of the Law,* 108.

DISCOVERY

To discover and to suspect are wholly different things.—McKenna: Carroll v. United States, 267 U.S. 132, 166.

2. Their dance was over and the time had come to pay the fiddler.— Jackson: Stein v. New York, 346 U.S. 156, 186.

Related subjects: Invention; Patent. *See also* Mistake 4.

DISCRETION

1. The term "discretion" denotes the absence of a hard and fast rule. —Sutherland: Langnes v. Green, 282 U.S. 531, 541.

2. Discretion "must be regulated upon grounds that will make it judicial."—Cardozo: Rudiger v. Coleman, 228 N.Y. 225, 236.

3. The discretion . . . is not unregulated by principle.—Cardozo: Beecher v. Vogt Mfg. Co., 227 N.Y. 468, 473.

4. The discretion of the court, guided, it is true, by precedent, but controlled, in its final exercise, by a sense of equity and justice.—Cardozo: Central Tr. Co. v. Pittsburgh S. & N. R.R., 229 N.Y. 68, 71.

5. Discretion is not unconfined and vagrant. It is canalized within banks that keep it from overflowing.—Cardozo: Panama Ref. Co. v. Ryan, 293 U.S. 388, 440.

6. There is a middle ground or certainly a penumbra in which discretion is at large.—Cardozo: Helvering v. Davis, 301 U.S. 619, 640.

7. We must not invite the exercise of judicial impressionism. Discretion

there may be, but "methodized by analogy, disciplined by system." . . . Discretion without a criterion for its exercise is authorization of arbitrariness.—Frankfurter: Brown v. Allen, 344 U.S. 443, 496 (quot. Cardozo: *Nature of Judicial Process,* 139, 141).

8. Absolute discretion, like corruption, marks the beginning of the end of liberty.—Douglas: New York v. United States, 342 U.S. 882, 884.

9. Absolute discretion is a ruthless master. It is more destructive of freedom than any of man's other inventions.—Douglas: United States v. Wunderlich, 342 U.S. 98, 101.

10. Discretion is never without limits. — Harlan: System Fed. v. Wright, 364 U.S. 642, 648.

Related subject: Judicial process. *See also* Jury 42; State 13.

DISCRIMINATION

1. Discrimination is the act of treating differently two persons or things, under like circumstances.—Brandeis: National Life Ins. Co. v. United States, 277 U.S. 508, 530.

2. Discrimination . . . is a practical conception.—Hughes: Gregg Dye Co. v. Query, 286 U.S. 472, 481.

3. Ungenerous and unwise such discrimination may be. It is not for that reason unlawful.—Cardozo: People v. Crane, 214 N.Y. 140, 161.

4. Nor can discrimination be corrected by retaliation.—Pitney: Travis v. Yale & Towne Mfg. Co., 252 U.S. 60, 82.

See also Army 3; Classification 4; Constitution 43; Constitution, Fourteenth Amendment, Fifteenth Amendment; Equality; Equal protection; Intolerance; Labor, abuse; Legislation, discriminatory; Negro; Preference; Race; Religion, discrimination; Speech 8; Treaty 3; Trial 29, 30, 31.

DISCUSSION

If you simply say all rights shall be so, that is only a pontifical or imperial way of forbidding discussion. — Holmes: "Law in Science and Science in Law," 12 Harv. L. Rev. 462.

See also Freedom, speech.

DISEASE

1. It has in modern times become apparent that the physical health of the community is more efficiently promoted by hygienic and preventive means, than by the skill which is applied to the cure of disease after it has become fully developed.—Miller: *In re* Neagle, 135 U.S. 1, 59.

2. Many bodily sensations and ailments are of such a character that they can only be known to the person who experiences them.—Clifford: Travelers Ins. Co. v. Mosley, 8 Wall. (75 U.S.) 397, 417.

3. That he was treated for them is not conclusive that he had them. The most skillful treatment sometimes is given when the existence of a particular disease is only suspected, not known, and when afterwards it appears the physician was mistaken.— Strong: Moulor v. Am. Life Ins. Co., 11 Otto (101 U.S.) 708, 710.

Related subjects: Medicine; Physician. *See also* Invalid; Mental healing 1.

DISHONESTY

1. The measure of its [dishonesty's]

115

meaning is not a standard of perfection, but an infirmity of purpose so opprobrious or furtive as to be fairly characterized as dishonest in the common speech of men. — Cardozo: World Exch. Bank v. Commercial Cas. Ins. Co., 255 N.Y. 1, 5.

2. Dishonesty, unlike embezzlement or larceny, is not a term of art. —Cardozo: *ibid.*

Related subjects: Falsity and related subjects; Honesty. *See also* Competition 13; Debtor 3; State 10.

DISINTERMENT
The dead are to rest where they have been laid unless reason of substance is brought forward for disturbing their repose.—Cardozo: Yome v. Gorman, 242 N.Y. 395, 403.

DISLOYALTY
Disloyalty may have its origin in ignorance as well as fraud.—Cardozo: Roman v. Lobe, 243 N.Y. 51, 55.

Related subjects: Loyalty and related subjects. *See also* Conscientious objection; Labor 22; Public office 3; Trial 48.

DISOBEDIENCE
Disobedience is impossible unless there is something to be obeyed.— Cardozo: Standard Chem. & Met. Corp. v. Waugh Chem. Corp., 231 N.Y. 51, 55.

Related subjects: Law, obedience; Obedience. *See also* Law 109.

DISPUTE
There can be no dispute without disputants.—Butler: Lauf v. E. G. Shinner & Co., 303 U.S. 323, 337.

See also Freedom, religion; Labor, dispute; Risk 2.

DISSENT (judicial)
General 1–7; duty, right 8–11; value 12–18; miscellaneous 19–22.

Related subjects: Decision and related subjects.

———, general
1. I have written more dissents than I liked to this term, but they are dissents from decisions that I regretted and as to which I felt deeply.— Holmes: *Uncollected Letters,* 196.

2. The closeness of the division attests the measure of the doubt.—Cardozo: People *ex rel.* Hayes v. Mc-Laughlin, 247 N.Y. 238, 242.

3. The fact that there is a five-to-four decision usually means that there is at hand a five-to-four problem. Judges are not perverse; they look for unanimity, not disagreement.—Douglas: *We the Judges,* 255.

4. Dissenters are not empowered to define the scope of a decision, but the way they read it may induce dissent. —Frankfurter: Reed v. Pennsylvania R.R., 351 U.S. 502, 508.

5. In the nature of Supreme Court litigation must be sought the explanation for the large incidence of dissent.—Frankfurter: "Holmes and the Constitution," 41 Harv. L. Rev. 122.

6. An exaggerated view of the power of *camaraderie* neglects the deeper influences behind constitutional adjudications. Divisions of the Court in decisive issues are not due to want of "tact and good humor" in the "moderator," nor is accord secured through genial and irenic personalities.—Frankfurter: *ibid.,* 121.

7. Conflicts which have divided the Justices always mirror a conflict which pervades society. . . . The student of our times will nowhere find the deeper conflicts of American political philosophy and economic policy more authentically and intelligently portrayed than in the opinions and dissents of members of the Supreme Court.—Jackson: *Struggle for Judicial Supremacy,* 312.

———, duty, right

8. Upon constitutional questions I ever thought it my duty to give a public expression of my opinions, when they differed from that of the court.—Story: Briscoe v. Bank of Ky., 11 Pet. (36 U.S.) 257, 329.

9. Upon constitutional questions, the public have a right to know the opinion of every judge who dissents from the opinion of the court, and the reasons of his dissent.—Story: *ibid.,* 350.

10. The oath which he takes as a judge is not a composite oath, but an individual one. And in passing upon the validity of a statute, he discharges a duty imposed upon him, which cannot be consummated justly by an automatic acceptance of the views of others which have neither convinced, nor created a reasonable doubt in, his mind. He cannot subordinate his convictions to that extent and keep faith with his oath or retain his judicial and moral independence. — Sutherland: West Coast Hotel Co. v. Parrish, 300 U.S. 379, 401–402.

11. There are obvious limits of pro-

priety to the persistent expression of opinions that do not command the agreement of the court.—Holmes: Federal Trade Comm'n v. Beech-Nut P. Co., 257 U.S. 441, 456.

———, value

12. Dissent is essential to an effective judiciary in a democratic society, and especially for a tribunal exercising the powers of this Court.—Frankfurter: Ferguson v. Moore McCormack Lines, 352 U.S. 521, 528.

13. They are dissents that record prophecy and shape history.—Frankfurter: "Holmes and the Constitution," 41 Harv. L. Rev. 165.

14. The strongest guarantee for the permanent survival of a system of government based on a written constitution, interpreted by a court, is that its pronouncements be supported by written opinions, freely examined and criticized by the members of the Court who do not agree with them.—Stone: Mason, *Stone,* 575.

15. A considered and well-stated dissent sounds a warning note that legal doctrine must not be pressed too far.—Stone: *ibid.,* 591.

16. Dissent is of little worth unless it is read.—Stone: *ibid.,* 608.

17. The only purpose which an elaborate dissent can accomplish, if any, is to weaken the effect of the opinion of the majority, and thus engender want of confidence in the conclusions of courts of last resort.—White: Pollock v. Farmers Loan & Tr. Co., 157 U.S. 429, 608.

18. If the Court is to dispatch its

business as an institution, some accommodation of views is necessary and, where no principle of importance is at stake, there are times when an insistence upon a division is not in the interests of the best administration of justice. — Jackson: United States v. Swift & Co., 318 U.S. 442, 446.

————, miscellaneous

19. I once heard a very eminent judge say that he never let a decision go until he was absolutely sure that it was right. So judicial dissent often is blamed, as if it meant simply that one side or the other were not doing their sums right, and, if they would take more trouble, agreement inevitably would come.—Holmes: "The Path of the Law," 10 Harv. L. Rev. 465.

20. The judge who stands alone in decided dissent on matters of the infinite magnitude which the case presents, must sink under the continued and unequal struggle unless he can fix himself by a firm hold on the Constitution and the laws of the country. He must be presumed to be in the wrong, until he proves himself to be in the right.—Baldwin: Cherokee Nation v. Georgia, 5 Pet. (30 U.S.) 1, 32.

21. More truly characteristic of dissent is a dignity, an elevation, of mood and thought and phrase. Deep conviction and warm feeling are saying their last say with knowledge that the cause is lost. The voice of the majority may be that of force triumphant, content with the plaudits of the hour, and

recking little of the morrow. The dissenter speaks to the future, and his voice is pitched to a key that will carry through the years.—Cardozo: *Law and Literature,* 36.

22. One fears to say anything when the peril of misunderstanding puts a warning finger to the lips. Not so, however, the dissenter.—Cardozo: *ibid.,* 34.

See also Judgment 14.

DISSENT (disagreement), DISSENTER, DISSENSION

1. To those who agree with me I am uttering commonplaces and to those who disagree I am ignoring the necessary foundations of thought.—Holmes: "Natural Law," 32 Harv. L. Rev. 42.

2. Political or religious dissenters are . . . the plague of every totalitarian regime.—Douglas: *We the Judges,* 322.

3. The way of the religious dissenter has long been hard.—Douglas: Murdock v. Pennsylvania, 319 U.S. 105, 115.

4. When dissensions cut too deeply, men will fight, even hopelessly, before they will submit.—Jackson: American Com. Assoc. v. Douds, 339 U.S. 382, 426.

5. Those who begin coercive elimination of dissent soon find themselves exterminating dissenters. Compulsory unification of opinion achieves only the unanimity of the graveyard.—Jackson: West Va. State Bd. of Educ. v. Barnette, 319 U.S. 624, 641.

See also Freedom.

DISTINCTION

1. It is easy to distinguish between the full light of day and the darkness of midnight, but often very difficult to determine whether a given moment in the twilight hour is before or after that in which the light predominates over the darkness.—Brewer: Atchison, T. & S. F. R.R. v. Matthews, 174 U.S. 96, 103.

2. The very meaning of a line in the law is that right and wrong touch each other, and that anyone may get as close to the line as he can if he keeps on the right side.—Holmes: Louisville & Nashville R.R. v. United States, 242 U.S. 60, 74.

3. It may be said that the difference is only one of degree; most differences are, when nicely analyzed.—Holmes: Rideout v. Knox, 148 Mass. 368, 372.

4. In some fields, the bad fades into the good by such insensible degrees that the two are not capable of being readily distinguished and separated.—Sutherland: Euclid v. Ambler Realty Co., 272 U.S. 365, 389.

5. The passing years . . . have at least opened my eyes to the perception that distinctions which in . . . early years seemed sharp and obvious are in truth shadowy and blurred; the walls of the compartments in no wise watertight or rigid.—Cardozo: *Growth of the Law,* 36.

6. Lines are not the worse for being narrow if they are drawn on rational considerations. — Frankfurter: 10 E. 40th St. v. Callus, 325 U.S. 578, 584.

7. Of course an argument can be made on the other side. That is what is meant by a question of degree.—Frankfurter, *ibid.*

8. Nice distinctions are to be expected.—Holmes: Galveston, H. & S. A. Ry. v. Texas, 210 U.S. 217, 225.

Related subject: Difference. *See also* Formula 5; Precedent 38, 45; Tax 35, 40, 41, 43, 70.

DISTORTION

1. Lights and shadows were so adjusted that the picture was unreal.—Cardozo: In the Matter of Santrucek, 239 N.Y. 59, 62.

2. It is common knowledge that a camera can be so placed, and lights and shadows so adjusted, as to give a distorted picture of reality.—Cardozo: Snyder v. Massachusetts, 291 U.S. 97, 115.

DISTRUST

1. Universal distrust creates universal incompetence.—Holmes: Graham v. United States, 231 U.S. 474, 480.

2. Melancholy . . . would be that state of distrust which rests not a hope upon a moral influence.—Johnson: Anderson v. Dunn, 6 Wheat. (19 U.S.) 204, 232.

DIVIDEND
See Corporation, dividends.

DIVORCE

1. Divorce, like marriage, is of concern not merely to the immediate parties. It affects personal rights of the deepest significance. It also touches basic interests of society.—Frankfurter: Williams v. North Carolina, 325 U.S. 226, 230.

2. Statistics indicate that approximately five million divorced persons are scattered throughout the forty-eight states. More than 85% of these divorces were granted in uncontested proceedings.—Black: *ibid.,* 262–63.

3. Certain States make an industry of their easy divorce laws, and encourage inhabitants of other States to obtain "quickie" divorces which their home States deny them. To permit such States to bind all others to their decrees would endow with constitutional sanctity a Gresham's Law of domestic relations. — Frankfurter: Sherrer v. Sherrer, 334 U.S. 343, 366–67.

4. Conduct by parties and counsel, which, in any other type of litigation, would be regarded as perjury, but which is not so regarded where divorce is involved because ladies and gentlemen indulge in it.—Frankfurter: *ibid.,* 367.

5. Five States have divorce laws that certainly attract out-of-staters. Clark: Granville-Smith v. Granville-Smith, 349 U.S. 1, 21.

6. The Nevada divorce machinery has become so smooth that the husband-to-be often flies out to be present at the divorce, gets married in the church next door, and then accompanies his new wife to their "new" domicile. Secondly, Nevada does a thriving business not only in divorcing out-of-staters but in marrying them as well; by requiring no waiting period before marriage, Nevada steals a march on nearby California and other States which attempt to force their often impatient residents to wait three days.—Clark: *ibid.,* 23.

7. To me *ex parte* divorce is a concept as perverse and unrealistic as an *ex parte* marriage.—Jackson: Rice v. Rice, 336 U.S. 674, 678.

Related subjects: Domestic relations and related subjects.

DOCTRINE

1. A doctrine capable of being stated only in obscure and involved terms is open to reasonable suspicion of being either crude or erroneous.—Holmes: *Holmes-Pollock Letters,* II, 38.

2. It is a commonplace that there may be a grain of truth in the most uncouth doctrine, however false and repellent the balance may be.—Frankfurter: Dennis v. United States, 341 U.S. 494, 549.

3. A well settled legal doctrine embodies the work of many minds, and has been tested in form as well as substance by trained critics whose practical interest it is to resist it at every step.—Holmes: *Uncollected Letters,* 63–64.

4. Winds of doctrine should freely blow for the promotion of good and the correction of evil.—Frankfurter: Bridges v. California, 314 U.S. 252, 291.

See also Dissent 15; History 5.

DOGMA

1. The dogmatism of a little education is hopeless.—Holmes: *Holmes-Pollock Letters,* II, 11.

2. A tendency . . . whereby phrases are made to do service for critical

analysis by being turned into dogma. —Frankfurter: Pennekamp v. Florida, 328 U.S. 331, 352.

3. To dogmatize beyond the bounds of learning or experience.—Frankfurter: Adams v. United States, 317 U.S. 269, 279.

See also Repetition 4.

DOLLAR

Dollars are fungibles.—Cardozo: Hennings v. United States Fid. & Guar. Co., 294 U.S. 216, 224.

See also Inflation.

DOMESTIC RELATIONS

1. All know that the sweetness of social intercourse, the harmony of society, the happiness of families, depend on that mutual partiality which they feel, or that delicate forbearance which they manifest towards each other.—Marshall: Sexton v. Wheaton, 8 Wheat. (21 U.S.) 229, 239.

2. That society has a vital interest in the domestic relations of its members will be almost impatiently conceded. But it is not enough to pay lip-service to the commonplace as an abstraction. Its implications must be respected.—Frankfurter: Sherrer v. Sherrer, 334 U.S. 343, 359.

Related subjects: Divorce; Husband and wife; Marriage. *See also* Flag 10; Freedom, religion 129; Government (U.S.), state 81.

DOMICILE

1. Domicile means a relationship between a person and a locality. It is the place, and the one place, where he has his roots and his real, perma-

nent home.—Jackson: Williams v. North Carolina, 317 U.S. 287, 322.

2. The essential fact that raises a change of abode to a change of domicile is the absence of any intention to live elsewhere.—Holmes: Williamson v. Osenton, 232 U.S. 619, 624.

3. Renunciation of one home is not sufficient without the acquisition of another.—Cardozo: In the Matter of Blankford, 241 N.Y. 180, 183.

4. This term does not have the magic qualities of a divining rod in locating domicile. In fact, the search for the domicile of any person capable of acquiring a domicile of choice is but a search for his "home."—Jackson: District of Columbia v. Murphy, 314 U.S. 441, 455.

Related subject: Home.

DOMINANCE

His natural fitness to control became habitual, as his wealth and standing increased, and it was exercised and involuntarily yielded to by all who associated or who were in business with him.—Wayne: Patterson v. Gaines, 6 How. (47 U.S.) 550, 596.

See also Command 2; Freedom, thought 152.

DOUBLE JEOPARDY

1. Fear and abhorrence of governmental power to try people twice for the same conduct is one of the oldest ideas found in western civilization.—Black: Bartkus v. Illinois, 359 U.S. 121, 151.

2. The right not to be placed in jeopardy more than once for the same offense is a vital safeguard in our

society, one that was dearly won and one that should continue to be highly valued.—Black: *ibid*.

Related subject: Trial.

DOUBT

1. One-half the doubts in life arise from the defects of language.—Johnson: Gibbons v. Ogden, 9 Wheat. (22 U.S.) 1, 232.

2. To have doubted one's own first principles is the mark of a civilized man.—Holmes: "Ideals and Doubts," 10 Ill. L. Rev. 3.

3. To pile one doubt upon another till all that is certain in the conclusion is the assurance of uncertainty.—Cardozo: Standard Chem. & Met. Corp. v. Waugh Chem. Corp., 231 N.Y. 51, 56–57.

4. The phantoms of attenuated and unfounded doubts.—White: Newberry v. United States, 256 U.S. 232, 268.

Related subject: Uncertainty. *See also* Construction 80; Court 26; Dissent 2; Ignorance 6; Law, certainty; Legislation 48.

DRUMMER

The drummer is a figure representative of a by-gone day. But his modern prototype persists under more euphonious appellations. — Rutledge: Nippert v. Richmond, 327 U.S. 416, 435.

DRUNKARD,
DRUNKENNESS

Habitual drunkards are not competent to properly transact business. . . . Men so reduced will sacrifice their property, as they have sacrificed themselves, to the craving for strong drink. —Clarke: Kendall v. Ewert, 259 U.S. 139, 146–47.

Related subject: Liquor. *See also* Desire 2.

DUE PROCESS (legal)

1. What is due process of law depends on circumstances. It varies with the subject matter and the necessities of the situation.—Holmes: Moyer v. Peabody, 212 U.S. 78, 84.

2. There is no table of weights and measures for ascertaining what constitutes due process. — Frankfurter: Burns v. Wilson, 346 U.S. 137, 149.

3. The words "due process of law," were undoubtedly intended to convey the same meaning as the words "by the law of the land" in Magna Charta. —Curtis: Murray's Lessee v. Hoboken Loan & Impr. Co., 18 How. (59 U.S.) 272, 276.

4. Due process is not measured by the yardstick of personal reaction or the sphygmogram of the most sensitive person, but by that whole community sense of "decency and fairness" that has been woven by common experience into the fabric of acceptable conduct.—Clark: Breithaupt v. Abram, 352 U.S. 432, 436.

5. Fairness of procedure is "due process in the primary sense."—Frankfurter: Joint Anti-Fascist Ref. Comm. v. McGrath, 341 U.S. 123, 161 (quot. 281 U.S. 673, 681).

6. Due process is perhaps the most majestic concept in our whole constitutional system. While it contains the garnered wisdom of the past in assuring fundamental justice, it is also a

living principle not confined to past instances.—Frankfurter: *ibid.,* 174.

7. Due process of law is not for the sole benefit of an accused. It is the best insurance for the Government itself against those blunders which leave lasting stains on a system of justice. — Jackson: S h a u g h n e s s y v. United States, 345 U.S. 206, 224–25.

8. The requirement of "due process" is not a fair-weather or timid assurance. It must be respected in periods of calm and in times of trouble.—Frankfurter: Joint Anti-Fascist Ref. Comm. v. McGrath, 341 U.S. 123, 162.

9. The safeguards of "due process of law" and "the equal protection of the laws" summarize the history of freedom of English-speaking peoples running back to Magna Carta and reflected in the constitutional development of our people.—Frankfurter: Malinski v. New York, 324 U.S. 401, 413–14.

10. It is in the nature of the concept of Due Process, and . . . its high serviceability in our constitutional system, that the judicial enforcement of the Due Process Clause is the very antithesis of a Procrustean rule.—Frankfurter: Kingsley Co. v. Regents, 360 U.S. 684, 697.

11. Mere age may establish due process, but due process does not preclude new ends of government or new means of achieving them.—Frankfurter: Hannah v. Larche, 363 U.S. 420, 493.

Related subject: Constitution (U.S.), Fourteenth Amendment; Constitutional adjudication; Law of the Land. *See also* Equal protection 6; Hearing 2, 7; Law of the Land; Tax 30; Trial 22.

DURESS

1. The word duress implies feebleness on one side, overpowering strength on the other.—Black: United States v. Bethlehem Steel Corp., 315 U.S. 289, 300.

2. It always is for the interest of a party under duress to choose the lesser of two evils. But the fact that a choice was made according to interest does not exclude duress. It is the characteristic of duress properly so called.—Holmes: Union Pac. R.R. v. Public Serv. Comm'n, 248 U.S. 67, 70.

3. To draw the line intelligently between duress and inducement.—Cardozo: Steward Mfg. Co. v. Davis, 301 U.S. 495, 586.

See also Choice 3; Confession; Tax 123.

DUTY

1. A bare sense of duty is too feeble to induce men to comply with obligations.—Marshall: Beveridge, *Life of Marshall,* I, 416.

2. Some relations in life impose a duty to act in accordance with the customary morality and nothing more.—Cardozo: *Nature of Judicial Process,* 109.

3. Obedience to the law is itself a moral duty. — Cardozo: People v. Schmidt, 216 N.Y. 324, 340.

4. The conviction of an inability to accomplish result, is with me no dispensation from the duty of resistance. Daniel: Ward v. Peck, 18 How. (59 U.S.) 267, 271.

5. A neglected duty often works as

much against the interests . . . as a duty wrongfully performed.—Brewer: Keim v. United States, 177 U.S. 290, 295.

6. He who assumes duties may be required to perform them.—McKenna: Miller v. Strahl, 239 U.S. 426, 432.

7. A default in exercising a duty may not be resorted to as a reason for denying its existence.—White: Arver v. United States, 245 U.S. 366, 381.

8. The command is addressed to him. Since the duty is his, he may not escape it by delegating it to others.—Cardozo: People *ex rel*. Price v. Sheffield Farms Co., 225 N.Y. 25, 29.

9. The duty to inquire existing, there is no safety in ignorance if proper inquiry would avail.—Cardozo: *ibid.*, 30.

10. As often as the need arises, the call is to be met.—Cardozo: In the Matter of Richardson, 247 N.Y. 401, 419.

11. They were none the less on duty when inactive. Their duty was to stand and wait.—Holmes: Missouri, K. & T. R.R. v. United States, 231 U.S. 112, 119.

12. The dismays and perils of an extreme situation, and what then might be expected of courage or excused to timidity . . . what better test could be devised than the doing of "all in one's power" as determined by the circumstances?—McKenna: Miller v. Strahl, 239 U.S. 426, 433, 434.

Related subject: Obligation.

———, legal

13. A legal duty so called is nothing but a prediction that if a man does or omits certain things he will be made to suffer in this or that way by judgment of the court; and so of a legal right.—Holmes: "The Path of the Law," 10 Harv. L. Rev. 458.

14. Duties precede rights logically and chronologically. Even those laws which in form create a right directly, in fact either tacitly impose a duty on the rest of the world or confer an immunity from a duty previously or generally imposed.—Holmes: *Uncollected Letters*, 66.

15. A legal duty cannot be said to exist if the law intends to allow the person supposed to be subject to it an option at a certain price. The test of a legal duty is the absolute nature of the command.—Holmes: *ibid.*, 26.

16. The notion of duty involves something more than a tax on a certain course of conduct. A protective tariff on iron does not create a duty not to bring it into the country. The word imports the existence of an absolute wish on the part of the power imposing it to bring about a certain course of conduct, and to prevent the contrary.—Holmes, *ibid*.

17. A duty declared by Congress does not evaporate for want of a formulated s a n c t i o n. — Frankfurter: Montana-Dakota Util. Co., v. Northwestern Pub. Serv. Co., 341 U.S. 246, 261.

See also Citizen; Corporation, duties; Corporation, directors; Court, functions;

Dissent, duty; Faith 9; Judge 69; Knowledge 5; Lawyer, obligations; Lawyer 93; Legislature, duties; Liability 1; President 9; Rights 14, 15, 36; Risk 4; State 9; Supreme Court, duty; Tax 146.

DYING DECLARATION

1. In that last moment of life when that which presses most upon the parting spirit, is revealed in its naked truth.—Wayne: Gaines v. Relf, 12 How. (53 U.S.) 472, 558.

2. There is no unyielding ritual of words to be spoken by the dying. Despair may even be gathered though the period of survival outruns the bounds of expectation. — Cardozo: Shepard v. United States, 290 U.S. 96, 100.

3. There must be "a settled hopeless expectation" that death is near at hand, and what is said must have been spoken in the hush of its impending presence.—Cardozo: *ibid.*

4. A dying declaration by no means imports absolute verity. The history of criminal trials is replete with instances where witnesses even in the agonies of death, have, through malice, misapprehension, or weakness of mind, made declarations that were inconsistent with the actual facts.—Brown: Carver v. United States, 164 U.S. 694, 697.

5. The certain expectation of almost immediate death will remove all temptation to falsehood and enforce as strict adherence as the obligation of an oath could impose.—Fuller: Mattox v. United States, 146 U.S. 140, 152.

EARNINGS
See Value 8, 11.

ECCENTRICITY
See Individual 4.

ECONOMICS

1. It is only by divesting our minds of questions of ownership and other machinery of distribution, and by looking solely at the question of consumption—asking ourselves what is the annual product, who consumes it, and what changes would or could we make—that we can keep in the world of realities.—Holmes: Plant v. Woods, 176 Mass. 492, 505.

2. The price of a commodity is a great regulator of its market.—Douglas: *We the Judges,* 211.

3. In a changing economy, mere material gain to the individual may not in itself be the social good it was once conceived to be.—Stone: Mason, *Stone,* 380.

See also Efficiency 1; Lawyer 13; Science 9.

ECONOMY (thrift)

1. Economy and industry are essential to our happiness.—Marshall: Beveridge, *Life of Marshall,* I, 416–17.

2. To those who practice economy, a given sum will afford comfort, while to those of contrary habit the same sum will be wholly inadequate.—Sutherland: Adkins v. Children's Hosp., 261 U.S. 525, 555.

3. A policy of economy may be unenlightened, but it is certainly not capricious.—Harlan: Griffin v. Illinois, 351 U.S. 12, 37–38.

EDUCATION, general

1. We too need education in the obvious—to learn to transcend our own convictions and to leave room for much that we hold dear to be done away with short of revolution by the orderly change of law.—Holmes: *Speeches,* 102.

2. The way to gain a liberal view of your subject is not to read something else, but to get to the bottom of the subject itself.—Holmes: "The Path of the Law," 10 Harv. L. Rev. 475.

3. The growth of education is an increase in the knowledge of measure. To use words familiar to logic and to science, it is a substitution of quantitative judgments.—Holmes: "Law in Science and Science in Law," 12 Harv. L. Rev. 456.

4. There is education in books but education in life also; education in solitude, but education also in the crowd; education in study, but education even greater in the contagion of example.—Cardozo: *Law and Literature,* 145.

5. What is the business of education, but to fit men to accomplish their duties and their destiny?—Story: *Misc. Writings,* 163.

6. Youth is the time when familiarity with a language is established.—Holmes: Meyer v. Nebraska, 262 U.S. 390, 412.

7. By making the science of government an indispensable branch of popular education, we may gradually prepare the way for such a mastery of its principles, by the people at large, as shall confound the sophist, repress the corrupt, disarm the cunning, animate the patriotic, and sustain the moral and religious.—Story: *Misc. Writings,* 159.

————, public

8. The truest glory of our forefathers is in that system of public instruction, which they instituted by law, and to which New England owes more of its character, its distinction, and its prosperity, than to all other causes.—Story: *ibid.,* 72.

9. Every successive generation becomes a living memorial of our public schools, and a living example of their excellence. Never, never may this glorious institution be abandoned or betrayed by the weakness of its friends, or the power of its adversaries.—Story: *ibid.,* 73.

10. Today, education is perhaps the most important function of state and local governments. Compulsory school attendance laws and the great expenditures for education both demonstrate our recognition of the importance of education to our democratic society. It is required in the performance of our most basic public responsibilities, even service in the armed forces. It is the very foundation of good citizenship. Today it is a principal instrument in awakening the child to cultural values, in preparing him for later professional training, and in helping him to adjust normally to his environment. — Warren: Brown v. Bd. of Educ., 347 U.S. 483, 493.

11. Free public education, if faithful to the ideal of secular instruction and political neutrality will not be partisan or enemy of any class, creed, party, or faction.—Jackson: West Va. State Bd. of Educ. v. Barnette, 319 U.S. 624, 637.

12. Transportation, where it is needed, is as essential to education as any other element.—Rutledge: Everson v. Bd. of Educ., 330 U.S. 1, 47.

13. In these days, it is doubtful that any child may reasonably be expected to succeed in life if he is denied the opportunity of an education. Such an opportunity, where the state has undertaken to provide it, is a right which must be made available to all on equal terms.—Warren: Brown v. Bd. of Educ., 347 U.S. 483, 493.

14. In the field of public education the doctrine of "separate but equal" has no place. Separate educational facilities are inherently unequal.—Warren: *ibid.*, 495.

15. Education has been fostered better to fit people for self-expression and good citizenship.—Black: United Pub. Workers v. Mitchell, 330 U.S. 75, 114.

16. The fundamental theory of liberty upon which all governments in this Union repose excludes any general power of the state to standardize its children by forcing them to accept instruction from public teachers only. McReynolds: Pierce v. Society of Sisters, 268 U.S. 510, 535.

Related subjects: Knowledge; Learning; School; Wisdom. *See also* Citizen 12; Court 27; Democracy 13; Dogma 1; Lawyer, education; Parent-child 4; Public opinion 10; Television.

EFFECT

See Cause-effect.

EFFICIENCY

Efficiency and economy imply employment of the right instrument and material as well as their use in the right manner.—Brandeis: St. Louis & O. Ry. v. United States, 279 U.S. 461, 517.

See also Business (big) 4, 5; Monopoly 11, 13; Power 15.

EFFORT

1. That the joy of life is living, is to put out all one's powers as far as they will go; that the measure of power is obstacles overcome, to ride boldly at what is in front of you, be it fence or enemy; to pray, not for comfort, but for combat; to keep the soldier's faith against the doubts of civil life, more besetting and harder to overcome than all the misgivings of the battle-field, and to remember that duty is not to be proved in the evil day, but then to be obeyed unquestioning; to love glory more than the temptations of wallowing ease, but to know that one's final judge and only rival is oneself.—Holmes: *Speeches*, 64.

2. More complex and intense intellectual efforts mean a fuller and richer life. They mean more life. Life is an end in itself, and the only question as to whether it is worth living is whether you have enough of it.— Holmes: *ibid.*, 86.

3. All that is required of you is that you should go some-whither as hard as ever you can. The rest belongs to fate.—Holmes: *ibid.*, 3.

4. It is not well for soldiers to think much about wounds. Sooner or later we shall fall; but meantime it is for us to fix our eyes upon the point to be stormed, and to get there if we can. —Holmes: *ibid.,* 58.

5. So long as I am capable of my best, I want to put it to my work. A man's spiritual history is best told in what he does in his chosen line.— Holmes: *Uncollected Letters,* 167.

6. There is the problem you have to tackle, and it can't be done except by putting your neck into the collar and pulling long and hard.—Holmes: *ibid.,* 194.

7. The mode in which the inevitable comes to pass is through effort.— Holmes: *ibid.,* 201.

8. Successful or not, it is enough for the present argument that the attempt has been made.—Holmes: *The Common Law,* 120.

9. The great truth will have been learned that the quest is greater than what is sought, the effort finer than the prize, or, rather, that the effort is the prize—the victory cheap and hollow were it not for the rigor of the game.—Cardozo: *Law and Literature,* 163–64.

10. A gospel of effort takes the place of a gospel that has vacillated between inaction and despair.—Cardozo: *ibid.,* 121.

11. The ceaseless drive is there; the lure that prods and teases; the shining, if shifting, goal, which, like the lighthouses of today, may summon with a revolving light, but ever swings full

circle, a beacon to the wandering traveler. — Cardozo: *ibid.,* 175.

12. We will not sit by and refuse to do anything because the voice of pessimism may remind us with labored demonstration that try as hard as we may, we shall be unable to do everything.—Cardozo: *ibid.,* 121.

13. Little is the positive contribution that any one of us can give, to the movement forward through the ages. That little will call for the straining of every faculty, the bending of every energy, the appeal to every available resource, within us or without. —Cardozo: *Growth of the Law,* 141.

14. It is the effort—the attempt— that tells.—Brandeis: Mason, *Brandeis,* 94.

15. The only way to tell whether conditions can be improved is to try. —Brandeis: *ibid.,* 165.

Related subjects: Diligence; Industry; Spirit, human. *See also* Business 10; Faith 6; Genius 4; Law 9; Life 3, 5; Mystery; Occupation 9; Retirement; Skill.

EGOTISM
See Judge 37.

ELECTION (choice)
Election is simply what its name imports; a choice, shown by an overt act, between two inconsistent rights, either of which may be asserted at the will of the chooser alone. . . . In all such cases the characteristic fact is that one party has a choice independent of the assent of anyone else.—

Holmes: Bierce v. Hutchins, 205 U.S. 340, 346.

Related subject: Choice.

ELECTION

1. Where all power is derived from the people, and public functionaries, at short intervals, deposit it at the feet of the people, to be resumed again only at their will, individual fears may be alarmed by the monsters of imagination, but individual liberty can be in little danger.—Johnson: Anderson v. Dunn, 6 Wheat (19 U.S.) 204, 226.

2. Frequent elections by the people furnish the only protection, under the constitution, against the abuse of acknowledged l e g i s l a t i v e power. —Field: *Ex parte* Newman, 9 Cal. 502.

3. Free and honest elections are the very foundation of our republican form of government. — D o u g l a s: United States v. Classic, 313 U.S. 299, 329.

4. Our Constitution sought to leave no excuse for violent attack on the status quo by providing a legal alternative—attack by ballot.—Jackson: Harisiades v. Shaughnessy, 342 U.S. 580, 592.

5. It must be remembered that our democratic system can succeed in composing oppositions only if the effort is made while the separation is not extreme. When the separation becomes wide or deep, as that over slavery finally became, the contest gets beyond the capacity of elective processes to compose.—Jackson: *Struggle for Judicial Supremacy,* 316.

6. Our representative federation was not devised to arrest change, but to provide peaceful and orderly methods for the continuous changes which were recognized to be inevitable. The device of periodic election was chosen to register and remedy discontents and grievances in time to prevent them from growing into underground or violent revolutionary movements. —Jackson: *ibid.*

7. The measure of success of a democratic system is found in the degree to which its elections really reflect rising discontent before it becomes unmanageable, by which government responds to it with timely redress, and by which losing groups are self-disciplined to accept election results.—Jackson: *ibid.*

8. It is the duty of that [the national] government to see that he may exercise this right [of franchise] freely and to protect him from violence while so doing or on account of so doing. This duty does not arise solely from the interest of the party concerned, but from the necessity of the government itself, that its service shall be free from the adverse influence of force and fraud practiced on its agents, and that the votes by which its members of Congress and its President are elected shall be the free votes of the electors. — Miller: *Ex parte* Yarbrough, 110 U.S. 651, 662.

9. In a republican government, like ours, where political power is reposed

in representatives of the entire body of the people, chosen at short intervals by popular elections, the temptations to control these elections by violence and by corruption is a constant source of danger. Such has been the history of all republics and . . . no lover of his country can shut his eyes to the fear of future danger from both sources.—Miller: *ibid., 666–67.*

10. If the very sources of power [elections] may be poisoned by corruption or controlled by violence and outrage, without legal restraint, then, indeed, is the country in danger and its best powers, its highest purposes, the hopes which it inspires and the love which enshrines it, are at the mercy of the combinations of those who respect no right but brute force, on the one hand, and unprincipled corruptionists on the other.—Miller: *ibid., 667.*

11. We need not be told, how many secret springs are at work, to obstruct that perfect freedom and independence of choice, which are so essential to make the ballot-box the just index of public opinion.—Story: *Misc. Writings,* 158.

12. When corruption enters, the election is no longer free, the choice of the people is affected.—Douglas: United States v. Classic, 313 U.S. 299, 330.

13. Many things are prerequisites to elections or may affect their outcome —voters, education, means of transportation, health, public discussion, immigration, p r i v a t e animosities, even the face and figure of the candi-

date. — McReynolds: Newberry v. United States, 256 U.S. 232, 257.

14. The United States is a constitutional democracy. Its organic law grants to all citizens a right to participate in the choice of elected officials without restriction by any state because of race.—Reed: Smith v. Allwright, 321 U.S. 649, 664.

15. There is more to the right to vote than the right to mark a piece of paper and drop it in a box or the right to pull a lever in a voting booth. . . . It also includes the right to have the vote counted at full value without dilution or discount.—Douglas: South v. Peters, 339 U.S. 276, 279.

16. As a practical matter, the ultimate choice of the mass of voters is predetermined when the nominations have been made.—Pitney: Newberry v. United States, 256 U.S. 232, 286.

17. Candidates are carefully selected by both parties to give proper weight to Jew, Protestant and Catholic, and certain posts are considered the sole possession of certain ethnic groups. The propriety of these practices is something the courts sensibly have left to the good or bad judgment of the electorate.—Minton: Terry v. Adams, 345 U.S. 461, 493–94.

18. It must be recognized that elections and other public business are influenced by all sorts of pressures from carefully organized groups.—Minton: *ibid., 494.*

19. The relation between money and politics generally—and more particularly the cost of campaigns and contributions by prospective office-

holders, especially judges—involves issues of far-reaching importance to a democracy.—Frankfurter: McDonald v. Comm'r of Int. Rev., 323 U.S. 57, 63.

20. Petitioner's money was not spent to buy the election but to buy the opportunity to persuade the electors. His campaign contribution was not an insurance of victory frustrated by "an act of God" but the price paid for an active share in the hazards of popular elections.—Frankfurter: *ibid.,* 61.

21. Unless our democratic philosophy is wrong, there can be no evil in a candidate spending a legally permissible and necessary sum to approach the electorate and enable them to pass an informed judgment upon his qualifications.—Black: *ibid.,* 69.

22. I suppose a State itself has considerable latitude to offer inducements to voters who do not value their franchise enough to vote on their own time, even if they seem to me corrupting or discriminating ones. Perhaps my difficulty with today's decision is that I cannot rise above an old-fashioned valuation of American citizenship which makes a state-imposed pay-for-voting system appear to be a confession of failure of popular representative government.—Jackson: Day-Brite Light v. Missouri, 342 U.S. 421, 428.

23. It is common experience that when the candidate must seek support from all levels of his community, his political creed will be tolerance, not hatred; equal protection for every minority, not discrimination.—Douglas: *We the Judges,* 413.

24. Our American elections have been fought between parties which, roughly, have represented the forces advocating change and those preferring stability.—Jackson: *Struggle for Judicial Supremacy,* 318.

Related subjects: Elector; Vote. *See also* Corporation, stockholder; Court 16.

ELECTOR, ELECTORAL SYSTEM

1. Doubtless it was supposed that the electors would exercise a reasonable independence and fair judgment in the selection of the Chief Executive, but experience soon demonstrated that, whether chosen by the legislatures or by popular suffrage on general ticket or in districts, they were so chosen simply to register the will of the appointing power in respect of a particular candidate. In relation, then, to the independence of the electors the original expectation may be said to have been frustrated.—Fuller: McPherson v. Blacker, 146 U.S. 1, 36.

2. Electors, although often personally eminent, independent, and respectable, officially became voluntary party lackeys and intellectual nonentities to whose memory we might justly paraphrase a tuneful satire:

They always voted at their Party's call
And never thought of thinking for themselves at all.

As an institution the Electoral College suffered atrophy almost indistinguishable from *rigor mortis.*—Jackson: Ray v. Blair, 343 U.S. 214, 232.

3. The demise of the whole electoral system would not impress me as a disaster. At its best it is a mystifying and distorting factor in presidential elections which may resolve a popular defeat into an electoral victory. At its worst it is open to local corruption and manipulation, once so flagrant as to threaten the stability of the country. To abolish it and substitute direct election of the President, so that every vote wherever cast would have equal weight in calculating the result, would seem to me a gain for simplicity and integrity of our governmental processes.—Jackson: *ibid.*, 234.

Related subjects: Election; Vote.

ELECTRICITY

Electrical energy is not a substance—at least in common meaning. It cannot be bought and sold as so many ounces or pounds, or so many quarts or gallons. It has neither length, breadth nor thickness. But that it has actual content of some kind is clear, since it is susceptible of mechanical measurement with the necessary certainty to permit quantitative units to be fixed for purposes of barter, sale and exchange.—Sutherland: Utah Power & Light Co. v. Pfost, 286 U.S. 165, 180.

ELECTRIC LIGHT
See Publicity 2.

ELOQUENCE

Eloquence may set fire to reason.—Holmes: Gitlow v. New York, 268 U.S. 652, 673.

See also Court 60.

EMBEZZLEMENT
See Dishonesty 2.

EMERGENCY

1. The emergency begets the man.—Cardozo: Wagner v. Int'l Ry., 232 N.Y. 176, 180.

2. Emergency does not create power.—Hughes: Home Build. & Loan Assoc. v. Blaisdell, 290 U.S. 398, 425.

3. Although an emergency may not call into life a power which has never lived, nevertheless emergency may afford a reason for the exercise of a living power already enjoyed.—White: Wilson v. New, 243 U.S. 332, 348.

See also Rights 21; Speed.

EMINENT DOMAIN
(legal condemnation)

1. All private property is held subject to the demands of a public use. The constitutional guaranty of just compensation is not a limitation of the power to take, but only a condition of its exercise.—Brewer: Long Island Water Supp. Co. v. Brooklyn, 166 U.S. 685, 689.

2. The exercise of the power of eminent domain is against common right. It subverts the usual attributes of the ownership of property.—McKenna: Western Union Tel. Co. v. Pennsylvania R.R., 195 U.S. 540, 569.

3. The power of eminent domain is essential to a sovereign government.—Burton: United States v. Carmack, 329 U.S. 230, 236.

4. The power of eminent domain is merely the means to the end.—Douglas: Berman v. Parker, 348 U.S. 26, 33.

5. The law of eminent domain is

fashioned out of the conflict between the people's interest in public projects and the principle of indemnity to the landowner.—Douglas: United States *ex rel.* TVA v. Powelson, 319 U.S. 266, 280.

6. But to gather the streams from waste and to draw from them energy, labor without brains, and so to save mankind from toil that it can be spared, is to supply what, next to intellect, is the very foundation of all our achievements and all our welfare. If that purpose is not public, we should be at a loss to say what is.—Holmes: Mr. Vernon–Woodberry Cotton Duck Co. v. Alabama I. P. Co., 240 U.S. 30, 32.

7. A road need not be for a purpose of business to create a public exigency; air, exercise, and recreation are important to the general health and welfare; pleasure travel may be accommodated as well as business travel; and highways may be condemned to places of pleasing natural scenery.—Sanford: Rindge Co. v. Los Angeles County, 262 U.S. 700, 708.

8. The political ethics reflected in the Fifth Amendment reject confiscation as a measure of justice.—Douglas: United States v. Cors, 337 U.S. 325, 332.

9. Property must not be taken without compensation, but with the help of a phrase (the police power) some property may be taken or destroyed for public use without paying for it, if you do not take too much.—Holmes: Springer v. Philippine Islands, 277 U.S. 189, 209–10.

10. The question is, What has the owner lost? not, What has the taker gained?—Holmes: Boston C. of C. v. Boston, 217 U.S. 189, 195.

11. It is the property and not the cost of it that is protected by the Fifth Amendment.—Butler: Brooks-Scanlon Corp. v. United States, 265 U.S. 106, 123.

12. Condemnation is a means by which the sovereign may find out what any piece of property will cost.—Reed: Danforth v. United States, 308 U.S. 271, 284.

13. In view . . . of the liability of all property to condemnation for the common good, loss to the owner of nontransferable values deriving from his unique need for property or idiosyncratic attachment to it . . . is properly treated as part of the burden of common citizenship. — Frankfurter: Kimball Laundry Co. v. United States, 338 U.S. 1, 5.

14. Frustration and appropriation are essentially different things. — Sutherland: Omnia Com. Co. v. United States, 261 U.S. 502, 513.

Related subject: Public use.

EMOTION

1. Neither philosophy nor policy can shut out the feelings of nature.—Story: *Misc. Writings,* 80.

2. A man's state of mind or feeling can only be manifested to others by countenance, attitude or gesture, or by sounds or words, spoken or written.—Gray: Mutual Life Ins. Co. v. Hillman, 145 U.S. 285, 295.

Related subject: Passion(s). *See also* Act

6; Art 2; Court 41; Memorial 2; Treason 4, 5, 9.

EMPHASIS

1. The statement is aided by dramatic reinforcement. — Holmes: *The Common Law,* 215.

2. In law also the emphasis makes the song. — Frankfurter: Bethlehem Steel Co. v. N.Y. Lab. Rel. Bd., 330 U.S. 767, 780.

EMPLOYEE

See Juror 3, 31; Labor, employee.

EMPLOYER

See Labor, employer.

EMPLOYMENT

Related subjects: Labor, employment; Occupation. *See also* Seaman.

ENCOMIA

See Judge, encomia; Opinion 26–28.

ENCROACHMENT

If we can go so far, I see not where we are to stop.—Johnson: Rose v. Himley, 4 Cranch (8 U.S.) 241, 292

END

Related subject: End-means. *See also* Science 6; Word 3.

END-MEANS

1. No one may do evil that good may come.—Hunt: Jeffries v. Econ. Mut. Life Ins. Co., 22 Wall (89 U.S.) 47, 52.

2. An end although apparently desirable cannot justify inhibited means. —McReynolds: Nebbia v. New York, 291 U.S. 502, 558.

3. The end does not always sanctify the means.—Bradley: *Ex parte* Curtis, 106 U.S. 371, 378.

4. A given result at the end of a straight path is not made a different result because reached by following a devious path. — Sutherland: Minnesota Tea Co. v. Helvering, 302 U.S. 609, 613.

5. The relation between the action and the end, is not always so direct and palpable as to strike the eye of every observer.—Johnson: Anderson v. Dunn, 6 Wheat. (19 U.S.) 204, 226.

6. We should not so exalt the means as to lose sight of the end.—Pitney: Pennsylvania R.R. v. Int'l Co., 230 U.S. 184, 245.

7. A first principle of Anglo-American jurisprudence is that the ends do not justify the means.—Douglas: *We the Judges,* 354.

8. A civilized system of law is as much concerned with the *means* employed to bring people to justice as it is with the *ends* themselves.—Douglas: *ibid.*

9. To a constitutional end many ways are open; but to an end not within the terms of the Constitution, all ways are closed.—Sutherland: Carter v. Carter Coal Co., 298 U.S. 238, 291.

10. It is a means to an end, and not the end itself.—White: Marshall v. Gordon, 243 U.S. 521, 541.

Related subject: Means. *See also* Constitution 63; Freedom, press 169; Politics 2; Power 29; Property 22; Public official 22; Punishment 12; Remedy 14, 15; Wire tapping 5; Wrong 7.

ENGLISHMEN

It cannot, however, be disguised, that there are a national pride and loftiness of pretension occasionally

134

mixed up in the character of Englishmen, which lead them, especially as public men, to look down, sometimes with contempt, but more generally with indifference, upon the usages, laws, and institutions of other countries. . . . The English Bar is not exempt from this infirmity.—Story: *Misc. Writings,* 306.

See also Opinion 27.

ENLIGHTENMENT
See Self-interest 2.

ENTRAPMENT

1. The government may set decoys to entrap criminals. But it may not provoke or create a crime, and then punish the criminal, its creature.— Brandeis: Casey v. United States, 276 U.S. 413, 423.

2. If the government becomes a lawbreaker, it breeds contempt for law; it invites every man to become a law unto himself; it invites anarchy. — Brandeis: Olmstead v. United States, 277 U.S. 438, 485.

3. In earlier times, some Rulers placed their criminal laws where the common man could not see them, in order that he might be entrapped into their violation. Others imposed standards of conduct impossible of achievement to the end that those obnoxious to the ruling powers might be convicted under the forms of law.—Black: Williams v. North Carolina, 325 U.S. 226, 278.

4. Human nature is weak enough and sufficiently beset by temptations without government adding to them and generating crime.—Frankfurter:

Sherman v. United States, 356 U.S. 369, 384.

5. The function of law enforcement is the prevention of crime and the appehension of ciminals. Manifestly, that function does not include the manufacturing of crime.—Warren: Sherman v. United States, 356 U.S. 369, 372.

ENTREATY
See Remedy 3.

EPITHET

1. These terse epithets come down to our generation weighted with hatreds accumulated through centuries of bloodshed. They are recognized words of art in the profession of defamation. They are not the kind of insult that men bandy and laugh off when the spirits are high and the flagons are low. They are not in that class of epithets whose literal sting will be drawn if the speaker smiles when he uses them. They are always, and in every context, insults which do not spring from reason and can be answered by none. Their historical associations with violence are well understood, both by those who hurl and those who are struck by these missiles. —Jackson: Kunz v. New York, 340 U.S. 290, 299.

2. Nothing is added to the case by calling the arrangements set forth a scheme.—Holmes: Continental Wall Paper Co. v. Louis Voight Co., 212 U.S. 227, 272.

3. If the act was legal, it is not made illegal by a mere epithet.—Brewer: McLane v. King, 144 U.S. 260, 263.

4. The characterization does not aid the contention.—Hughes: Burnet v. Leininger, 285 U.S. 136, 141.

5. The derogatory epithet assumes the point to be decided. — Cardozo: Stewart Dry Goods Co. v. Lewis, 294 U.S. 550, 577.

6. All this is well enough if the picturesqueness of the epithets does not lead us to forget.—Cardozo: Berkey v. Third Ave. Ry., 244 N.Y. 84, 95.

7. The passages on their face are so obviously intemperate and so patently unwarranted that if . . . they should come under future observation, they would but serve to indicate to what intemperance of statement an absence of self restraint or forgetfulness of decorum will lead. — White: Cox v. Wood, 247 U.S. 3, 7.

Related subjects: Defamation and related subjects. *See also* Inquisition 2; Liar.

EQUALITY

1. Equality is equity.—Swayne: Pacific Ins. Co. v. Soule, 7 Wall. (74 U.S.) 433, 442.

2. The same fluid and dynamic conception which underlies the modern notion of liberty, as secured to the individual by the constitutional immunity, must also underlie the cognate notion of equality. — Cardozo: *Nature of Judicial Process,* 81–82.

3. Restrictions, viewed narrowly, may seem to foster inequality. The same restrictions, when viewed broadly, may be seen "to be necessary in the long run in order to establish the equality of position between the parties in which liberty of con-

tract begins."—Cardozo: *ibid*. (quot. Holmes: 236 U.S. 1, 27).

4. Equality of privilege and equality of obligation should be inseparable associates. — Black: Oklahoma Tax Comm'n v. United States, 319 U.S. 598, 610.

5. The dogma of equality makes an equation between individuals only, not between an individual and the community. No society has ever admitted that it could not sacrifice individual welfare to its own existence. —Holmes: *The Common Law,* 43.

6. It might be suggested that the dogma of equality applied even to individuals only within the limits of ordinary dealings in the common run of affairs.—Holmes: *ibid*.

7. It was a wise man who said that there is no greater inequality than the equal treatment of unequals.—Frankfurter: Dennis v. United States, 339 U.S. 162, 184.

8. The rule of equality permits many practical inequalities.—McKenna: Magoun v. Illinois Tr. & Sav. Bank, 170 U.S. 283, 296.

9. The equality of the rights of citizens is a principle of republicanism.—Waite: United States v. Cruikshank, 2 Otto (92 U.S.) 542, 555.

10. The theme of the Constitution is equality among citizens in the exercise of their political rights.—Douglas: MacDougall v. Green, 335 U.S. 281, 289–90.

11. Equality in right, in protection, and in burden is the thought which has run through the life of this Nation and its constitutional enactments

from the Declaration of Independence to the present hour. — Brewer: Magoun v. Illinois Tr. & Sav. Bank, 170 U.S. 283, 301.

12. America . . . has always declared herself for equality of nationalities as well as for equality of individuals. It recognizes racial equality as an essential of true brotherhood, and that racial equality is the complement of democracy. — Brandeis: Mason, *Brandeis,* 439.

13. Equality among men of all creeds, nationalities, and colors is the great curative of social ills. No one segment of society can long be set apart in a ghetto of second- or third-class citizenship. Once that happens, a divisive influence is at work, one that will sooner or later tear the community apart. — Douglas: *We the Judges,* 425.

14. But what is it to justice, how many, or how few; how high or how low; how rich, or how poor; the contending parties may chance to be? Justice is indiscriminately due to all, without regard to numbers, wealth, or rank.—Jay: Georgia v. Brailsford, 3 Dall. (3 U.S.) 483, 484.

15. If there is one place under our system of government where all should be in a position to have equal and exact justice done to them, it is a court of justice—a principle which I had supposed was as old as Magna Charta.—Harlan: Atchison, T. & S.F. R.R. v. Matthews, 174 U.S. 96, 124.

16. The law that protects the wealth of the most powerful, protects also the earnings of the most humble;

and the law which would confiscate the property of the one would in the end take the earnings of the other.— Field: Sinking Fund Cases, 9 Otto (99 U.S.) 727, 767.

17. There cannot be one law for debtors and another law for creditors. —Field: Legal Tender Cases, 12 Wall. (79 U.S.) 457, 670.

18. From the moment of birth onward, humankind, as the law views it, is a society of equals.—Cardozo: *Law and Literature,* 110.

19. Nothing is written more firmly into our law than the compact of the Plymouth voyagers to have just and equal laws. — Murphy: Hirabayashi v. United States, 320 U.S. 81, 110-11.

20. The law must reach all in like circumstances or conditions.—Douglas: *We the Judges,* 409.

21. A State need not equalize economic conditions. A man of means may be able to afford the retention of an expensive, able counsel not within reach of a poor man's purse. Those are contingencies of life which are hardly within the power, let alone the duty, of a State to correct or cushion.— Frankfurter: Griffin v. Illinois, 351 U.S. 12, 23.

22. The rights of all parties should be measured by the same yard-stick. —Shiras: Byers v. McAuley, 149 U.S. 608, 628.

23. Just as a life may not be shortened, so its value must be held as equal to that of any other, the mightiest or the lowliest. — Cardozo: *Law and Literature,* 109.

24. In our country, the highest man

is not above the people. If the rich may be said to have additional protection, they have not additional power.—Story: *Misc. Writings,* 514.

25. The passion for equality sometimes leads to hollow formulas.—Holmes: Postal Tel. Co. v. Tonopah & T. W. R.R., 248 U.S. 471, 475.

26. Wherever equality is the theme, men live together in peace. Wherever inequality is the practice, grievances and complaints fester.—Douglas: *We the Judges,* 425.

27. The sum is the same when the reckoning is closed.—Cardozo: Henneford v. Silas Mason Co., 300 U.S. 577, 584.

28. No absolutist is so intransigent as to assert that there can be literal adherence to a standard of equality or liberty.—Cardozo: *Growth of the Law,* 75.

Related subjects: Equal protection; Equity; Inequality. *See also* Freedom 25; Government (U.S.), state 72, 78; Nation 1; Negro 6; Ocean 1; Race; Sherman Antitrust Law 2; Supreme Court 69; Tax, equality; Woman 7.

EQUAL PROTECTION

1. The "equal protection of the laws" places all upon a footing of legal equality and gives the same protection to all for the preservation of life, liberty and property, and the pursuit of happiness.—Swayne: Slaughter House Cases, 16 Wall. (83 U.S.) 36, 127.

2. Equal protection is the most important single principle that any nation can take as its ideal.—Douglas: *We the Judges,* 426.

3. What the equal protection of the law requires is equality of burdens upon those in like situation or condition.—Day: South Carolina *ex rel.* Phoenix Mut. Life Ins. Co. v. McMaster, 237 U.S. 63, 72–73.

4. Constitutional protection is more essential in times of unrest and agitation than it can be in the security of less turbulent periods.—Day: Wilson v. New, 243 U.S. 332, 371.

5. The equal protection clause does not forbid discrimination with respect to things that are different.—Stone: Puget Sound Power & Light Co. v. Seattle, 291 U.S. 619, 624.

6. Both equal protection and due process emphasize the central aim of our entire judicial system—all people charged with crime must, so far as the law is concerned, "stand on an equality before the bar of justice in every American court." — Douglas: Griffin v. Illinois, 351 U.S. 12, 17 (quot. 309 U.S. 277, 241).

7. It is no requirement of equal protection that all evils of the same genus be eradicated or none at all.—Douglas: Railway Exp. Agency v. New York, 336 U.S. 106, 110.

8. Rights intended to protect all must be extended to all, lest they so fall into desuetude in the course of denying them to the worst of men as to afford no aid to the best of men in time of need.—Murphy: Goldman v. United States, 316 U.S. 129, 142.

Related subjects: Constitution (U.S.), Fourteenth Amendment; Equality, protection. *See also* Bail 4; Labor 32; Race; Tax 60.

EQUITY

1. Equity implies equality — equal fairness and honesty on both sides.— Pitney: United States v. St. Paul, M. & M. Ry., 247 U.S. 310, 320.

2. The only real equity is not to disturb the equilibrium established by the parties. — Holmes: Mitchell v. Hampel, 276 U.S. 299, 302.

3. Equity and honor are the same as in olden days. The Constitution does not define them, nor seek to circumscribe their content. — Cardozo: People v. Westchester Co. Nat'l Bank, 231 N.Y. 465, 486.

4. I do not know the equity that is incapable of being reduced to an absurdity when extended by some process of analogy to varying conditions.—Cardozo: *ibid.,* 490.

5. Equity is rooted in conscience.— Frankfurter: Hurd v. Hodge, 334 U.S. 24, 36.

6. If equities are equal, the first in time is best in right.—Butler: Salem Tr. Co. v. Mfrs. Fin. Co., 264 U.S. 182, 199.

7. His conception of equity and fairness, the thing demanded by good conscience, is one of justice unrelieved by tenderness or charity.—Cardozo: In the Matter of Shaddock v. Schwartz, 246 N.Y. 288, 294.

8. The call of these and kindred equities has been heard and answered in the past.—Cardozo: People v. Westchester Co. Nat'l Bank, 231 N.Y. 465, 486.

Related subjects: Equality; Equity court; Equity of redemption; Trust. *See also*

Fiduciary 11; Form 10; Tax, equity; Tax 133.

EQUITY COURT

Functions 1–5; principles, standards 6–12; powers 13–15; operations 16–31.

———, functions

1. A court of equity is not just an umpire between two litigants. In a very special sense, the public interest is in its keeping as the conscience of the law. — Frankfurter: Chrysler Corp. v. United States, 316 U.S. 556, 570.

2. The qualities of mercy and practicality have made equity the instrument for nice adjustment and reconciliation between the public interest and private needs as well as between competing private claims.—Douglas: Hecht Co. v. Bowles, 321 U.S. 321, 329–30.

3. That court [of equity] is not a divider of the inheritance of iniquity between the respective heirs of two confederates in fraud.—Lamar: Dent v. Ferguson, 132 U.S. 50, 66.

4. A court of equity is not called upon to do a vain thing. — Brown: Foster v. Mansfield, C. & L. M. R.R., 146 U.S. 88, 101.

5. The development of the jurisdiction of the chancery is lined with historic monuments.—Cardozo: Graf v. Hope Bldg. Corp., 254 N.Y. 1, 8.

———, principles, standards

6. The principles of equity jurisprudence are of a very enlarged and elevated nature. They are essentially rational, and moulded into a degree of moral perfection, which the law has

rarely aspired to.—Story: *Misc. Writings,* 433.

7. There are canons of the court of equity which have their foundation, not in the actual commission of fraud, but in that hallowed orison, "lead us not into temptation." — Johnson: Wormley v. Wormley, 8 Wheat. (21 U.S.) 421, 463.

8. Equity has its distinctive standards of fidelity and honor, higher at times than the standards of the market place.—Cardozo: Buffum v. Peter Barceloux Co., 289 U.S. 227, 237.

9. Equity does not demand that its suitors shall have led blameless lives.—Brandeis: Loughran v. Loughran, 292 U.S. 216, 229.

10. The maxim that he who comes into equity must come with clean hands is not applied by way of punishment for an unclean litigant but "upon considerations that make for the advancement of right and justice."—Black: Johnson v. Yellow Cab Transp. Co., 321 U.S. 383, 387.

11. Equity in the historical sense—equity jurisprudence — has no guidance to give beyond maxims.—Jackson: Federal Power Comm'n. v. Interstate Nat. Gas Co., 336 U.S. 577, 592.

12. In equity as at law there are signposts for the traveler.—Cardozo: Evangelical Luth. Church v. Sahlem, 254 N.Y. 161, 167.

———, powers

13. The flexibility of decrees of a court of equity will enable it to meet every emergency.—Field: Sharon v. Tucher, 144 U.S. 533, 548.

14. The plastic remedies of the chancery are moulded to the needs of justice. — Cardozo: Foreman v. Foreman, 251 N.Y. 237, 242.

15. Equity is not crippled ... by an inexorable formula.—Cardozo: Marr v. Tumulty, 256 N.Y. 15, 21.

———, operations

16. Equity follows the law, but not slavishly nor always.—Cardozo: Graf v. Hope Bldg. Corp., 254 N.Y. 1, 9.

17. A court of equity acts only when and as conscience commands.—Brewer: Deweese v. Reinhard, 165 U.S. 386, 390.

18. "A court of equity ought to do justice completely and not by halves."—Sutherland: Rice & Adams Corp. v. Lathrop, 278 U.S. 509, 515.

19. Equity looks in all directions.—Murphy: Comstock v. Institutional Investors, 355 U.S. 211, 238.

20. Equity will not reach out its hand to disturb that which all parties have considered settled for so many years.—Brewer: Randolph's Ex'r v. Quidnick Co., 135 U.S. 457, 465.

21. Equity looks through forms to substance.—Chase: Texas v. Hardenberg, 10 Wall. (77 U.S.) 68, 89.

22. Courts of equity are not to be misled by mere devices, nor baffled by mere forms.—Harlan: White v. Cotzhausen, 129 U.S. 329, 344.

23. In such circumstances, equity would be sacrificing the substance to the shadow if the tyranny of a for-

mula, the mirage of an unattainable condition, should lead it to stay its hand.—Cardozo: Kittredge v. Langley, 252 N.Y. 405, 412.

24. Equity does not act for every shadowy or unsubstantial wrong.—Cardozo: Nann v. Raimist, 255 N.Y. 307, 319.

25. Equity will not suffer a wrong without a remedy.—Taft: Independent Wireless Tel. Co. v. Radio Corp., 269 U.S. 459, 472.

26. Equity, it is said, will not be overnice in balancing the efficacy of one remedy against the efficacy of another when action will baffle, and inaction may confirm, the purpose of the wrongdoer. — Cardozo: Rogers v. Guaranty Tr. Co., 288 U.S. 123, 151.

27. Equity does not relieve from hard bargains simply because they are such.—Day: Columbus Ry., P. & L. Co. v. Columbus, 249 U.S. 399, 414.

28. Let the hardship be strong enough, and equity will find a way, though many a formula of inaction may seem to bar the path.—Cardozo: Graf v. Hope Bldg. Corp., 254 N.Y. 1, 13.

29. Equity . . . compels the buyer to exhibit an involuntary charity if he is found to have taken advantage of the necessities of the seller.—Cardozo: *ibid.,* 9.

30. In equity as in mechanics action and reaction are equal and opposite. The equity that one asks one must be ready to concede.—Cardozo: *ibid.,* 13.

31. Equity decrees are not like the packaged goods this machine age produces. They are uniform only in that they seek to do equity in a given case. —Douglas: United Steelworkers v. United States, 361 U.S. 44, 71.

See also Laches 2; Mandate 1; Trustee 3.

EQUITY OF REDEMPTION
(legal)
The "equity of redemption" is the creature of equity. . . . This principle of equity was victorious against the strong opposition of the common law judges, who thought that by "the Growth of Equity on Equity the Heart of the Common Law is eaten out."—Hughes: Home Build. & Loan Assoc. v. Blaisdell, 290 U.S. 398, 446–47.

ERROR

1. If there was any omission, under the circumstances it was an error and not a fault. In the eye of the law the former does not rise to the grade of the latter, and is always venial.—Swayne: Lockwood v. The Grace Girdler, 7 Wall. (74 U.S.) 196, 201.

2. The line which separates error in judgment from the usurpation of power is very definite. — Baldwin: Voorhees v. Jackson, 10 Pet. (35 U.S.) 474, 475.

3. The separating line between nullity and error is not an easy one to draw.—Cardozo: In the Matter of Marchant v. Mead-Morrison Mfg. Co., 252 N.Y. 284, 296.

4. One thinks that an error exposed is dead, but exposure amounts to nothing when people want to believe.—Holmes: *Holmes-Pollock Letters,* I, 219.

5. Error of judgment alone does not carry liability with it, for error of judgment alone is consistent with reasonable care.—Cardozo: Stern v. Int'l Ry., 220 N.Y. 284, 293.

6. I have an abiding faith that this, like other errors, will, in the end "die among its worshippers."—Field: Baltimore & O. R.R. v. Baugh, 149 U.S. 368, 403.

7. The error must be attributed to one of those failings which lean to virtue's side.—Miller: Washington Univ. v. Rouse, 8 Wall. (75 U.S.) 439, 443.

8. It is this right, the right to err politically, which keeps us strong as a nation. — Black: Barenblatt v. United States, 360 U.S. 109, 144.

Related subjects: Mistake; Omission. *See also* Abuse; Concealment 1; Construction 94; Custom 5; Judge 63; Jury 37; Litigation 26; Opinion 3, 4, 20, 22; Precedent 44; Promise 4; Supreme Court 3, 33, 55; Trial 19.

ESTIMATE

1. The law is full of instances where a man's fate depends on his estimating rightly, that is, as the jury subsequently estimates it, some matter of degree.—Holmes: Nash v. United States, 229 U.S. 373, 377.

2. Very often the bearing of information is not susceptible of intelligent estimate until it is placed in its setting, a tile in the mosaic.—Cardozo: In the Matter of Edge Ho Holding Corp., 256 N.Y. 374, 382.

3. Estimates are at times inevitable in any system of accounts.—Cardozo: American Tel. & Tel. Co. v. United States, 299 U.S. 232, 245.

4. Legal fiction never reached the height of holding a defendant bound to know the estimate that a jury would put upon the damage he had caused. — Holmes: Boston Sand & Gravel Co. v. United States, 278 U.S. 41, 48–49.

See also Evidence 23; Exchange 1; Value 22.

ESTOPPEL (by judgment)

See Res judicata.

ESTOPPEL (legal)

1. An estoppel has sometimes been quaintly defined, the stopping a man's mouth from speaking the truth; and would seem, in some measure, to partake of severity, if not of injustice. But it is in reality founded upon the soundest principles. — Thompson: Sprigg v. Bank of Mt. Pleasant, 10 Pet. (35 U.S.) 257, 265.

2. The principle of estoppel . . . has its foundation in a wise and salutary policy. It is a means of repose. It promotes fair dealing. It cannot be made an instrument of wrong or oppression, and it often gives triumph to right and justice where nothing else known to our jurisprudence can, by its operation, secure those ends. Like the Statute of Limitations, it is a conservator, and without it society could not well go on.—Swayne: Daniels v. Tearney, 12 Otto (102 U.S.) 415, 420.

3. A party is . . . always estopped by his own grant.—Marshall: Fletcher v. Peck, 6 Cranch (10 U.S.) 87, 137.

4. There can be no irrevocable estoppel when the truth has been with-

held. — Cardozo: Buffum v. Peter Barceloux Co., 289 U.S. 227, 235.

ETHICS
See Propaganda 1; Standard 7.

EVANGELISM, EVANGELIST
See Freedom, thought 153; Religion 18.

EVASION
See Innocence 2; Law 102; Tax, avoidance.

EVIDENCE (legal)
Rules 1–5; admissions 6–9; availability 10–13; inferences 14–18; weight 19–24; circumstantial 25–28; hearsay 29; character 30–38; miscellaneous 39–41.

Related subjects: Expert; Perjury; Proof; Testimony; Witness.

———, rules

1. Rules of evidence are adopted for practical purposes in the administration of justice, and must be so applied as to promote the ends for which they are designed. — Thompson: United States v. Reyburn, 6 Pet. (31 U.S.) 352, 367.

2. The rules of evidence are of great importance, and cannot be departed from without endangering private as well as public rights.—Story: Nicholls v. Webb, 8 Wheat. (21 U.S.) 326, 332.

3. Rules of evidence for criminal trials in the federal courts are made a part of living law and not treated as a mere collection of wooden rules in a game.—Frankfurter: United States v. Mitchell, 322 U.S. 65, 66.

4. The rules of evidence in the main are based on experience, logic and common sense, less hampered by history than some parts of the substan-

tive law. — Holmes: Donnelly v. United States, 228 U.S. 243, 277–78.

5. It is for ordinary minds, and not for psychoanalysts, that our rules of evidence are framed. — Cardozo: Shepard v. United States, 290 U.S. 96, 104.

———, admissions

6. In the affairs of human life, it is a salutary practical rule that a man shall not be permitted to deny what he has once solemnly acknowledged. —Thompson: Sprigg v. Bank of Mt. Pleasant, 10 Pet. (35 U.S.) 257, 265.

7. Verbal confessions or admissions, made in the presence of the witness alone, constitute, it is true, very unsatisfactory evidence, partly because of the facility with which they may be fabricated. — Harlan: Beckwith v. Bean, 8 Otto (98 U.S.) 266, 280.

8. They are admissions made in circumstances precluding the likelihood of haste and inadvertence. As such they are high evidence.—Cardozo: Prager v. N.J. Fid. & Plate Glass Inc. Co., 245 N.Y. 1, 4.

9. Legislation apart, no social policy calls for the adoption by the courts of an inexorable rule that guilt must be determined only by trial and not by admission.—Frankfurter: Adams v. United States, 317 U.S. 269, 276.

———, availability

10. In this as in all other cases, no testimony will be required which is shown to be unattainable.—Marshall: Church v. Hubbart, 2 Cranch (6 U.S.) 187, 237.

143

11. Evidence cannot always be produced to establish something declared to be true in entire good faith.—McReynolds: Soler v. United Fire Ins. Co., 299 U.S. 45, 50.

12. All evidence is to be weighed according to the proof which it was in the power of one side to have produced and in the power of the other side to have contradicted.—Cardozo: Cooper v. Dasher, 290 U.S. 106, 109 (quot. 98 Eng. Rep. 969).

13. The stranger from afar, unacquainted with the local ways, permits himself to be guided by the best evidence available, the directions or the counsel of those who dwell upon the spot. — Cardozo: Hawks v. Hamill, 288 U.S. 52, 60.

———, inferences

14. The production of weak evidence when strong is available can lead only to the conclusion that the strong would have been adverse. . . . Silence then becomes evidence of the most convincing character.—Stone: Interstate Circuit v. United States, 306 U.S. 208, 226.

15. Conduct which forms a basis for inference is evidence. Silence is often evidence of the most persuasive character.—Brandeis: United States *ex rel.* Bilokumsky v. Tod, 263 U.S. 149, 153–54.

16. Flight, even after accusation, is some evidence of guilt; but flight before accusation is persuasive evidence. —Cardozo: People v. Shilitano, 218 N.Y. 161, 182.

17. It is a matter of common knowledge that men who are entirely innocent do sometimes fly from the scene of a crime through fear of being apprehended as the guilty parties, or from an unwillingness to appear as witnesses.—Brown: Alberty v. United States, 162 U.S. 499, 511.

18. Inferences from circumstantial facts may frequently amount to full proof of a given theory.—Clifford: Fraser v. The Wenona, 19 Wall. (86 U.S.) 41, 58.

———, weight

19. Substantial evidence is more than a mere scintilla. It means such relevant evidence as a reasonable mind might accept as adequate to support a conclusion.—Hughes: Consolidated Edison Co. v. NLRB, 305 U.S. 197, 229.

20. It is still the rule . . . even in this Court that "insufficient evidence is, in the eye of the law, no evidence." —Cardozo: In the Matter of Case, 214 N.Y. 199, 203.

21. Small things may turn the scale. But something there must be.—Cardozo: People v. Galbo, 218 N.Y. 283, 294.

22. Elaborate calculations which are at war with realities are of no avail. — Hughes: Lindheimer v. Ill. Bell Tel. Co., 292 U.S. 151, 164.

23. The Company has submitted elaborate estimates and computations, but these have overshot the mark. Proving too much, they fail of the intended effect.—Hughes: *ibid.,* 175.

24. Evidence which would be colorless if it stood alone may get a new

complexion from other facts. — Holmes: Commonwealth v. Mulrey, 170 Mass. 103, 110.

———, circumstantial

25. Circumstantial evidence is often as convincing to the mind as direct testimony, and often more so. A number of concurrent facts, like rays of light, all converging to the same center, may throw not only a clear light but a burning conviction. . . . A cord of sufficient strength to suspend a man may be formed of threads, each of which would not support the weight of a pound or even of an ounce.— Grier: Thompson v. Bowie, 4 Wall. (71 U.S.) 463, 473.

26. It may be circumstantial, but it must be persuasive. — Peckham: Lalone v. United States, 164 U.S. 255, 257.

27. Experience shows that positive proof of fraudulent acts is not generally to be expected, and for that reason, among others, the law allows a resort to circumstances, as a means of ascertaining the truth.—Clifford: Castle v. Ballard, 21 How. (62 U.S.) 172, 187.

28. Circumstantial evidence may in some cases point to a wholly incorrect result. Yet this is equally true of testimonial evidence. — Clark: Holland v. United States, 348 U.S. 121, 140.

———, hearsay

29. The "hearsay" rule is often grossly artificial. Again in a different context it may be the very essence of justice, keeping out gossip, rumor, unfounded report, second-, third-, or further-hand stories.—Rutledge: Kotteakos v. United States, 328 U.S. 750, 761.

———, character

30. Very often the difference between liberty and imprisonment in cases where the direct evidence offered by the government and the defendant is evenly balanced depends upon the presence of character witnesses.—Murphy: United States v. Johnson, 323 U.S. 273, 279.

31. To thus digress from evidence as to the offense to hear a contest as to the standing of the accused, at its best opens a tricky line of inquiry as to a shapeless and elusive subject matter. At its worst it opens a veritable Pandora's box of irresponsible gossip, innuendo and smear. — Jackson: Michelson v. United States, 335 U.S. 469, 480.

32. In the frontier phase of our law's development, calling friends to vouch for defendant's good character, and its counterpart—calling the rivals and enemies of a witness to impeach him by testifying that his reputation for veracity was so bad that he was unworthy of belief on his oath—were favorite and frequent ways of converting an individual litigation into a community contest and a trial into a spectacle.—Jackson: *ibid*.

33. The evidence which the law permits is not as to the personality of defendant but only as to the shadow his daily life has cast in the neighborhood.—Jackson: *ibid., 477.

34. The law apparently ignores the existence of such human ciphers as Kipling's Tomlinson, of whom no ill is reported but no good can be recalled. They win seats with the righteous for character evidence purposes, however hard their lot in literature.—Jackson: *ibid.,* 478 n.

35. It [the law] subjects his proof to tests of credibility designed to prevent him from profiting by a mere parade of partisans.—Jackson: *ibid.,* 479.

36. It is not the man that he is, but the name that he has which is put in issue.—Jackson: *ibid.*

37. It illustrates Judge Hand's suggestion that the system may work best when explained least.—Jackson: *ibid.,* 481.

38. The evidence of general regard by one's fellows may be the weight which turns the scales of justice.—Jackson: *ibid.,* 490.

―――, miscellaneous

39. Society can ill afford to throw away the evidence produced by the falling out, jealousies, and quarrels of those who live by outwitting the law. —Jackson: On Lee v. United States, 343 U.S. 747, 756.

40. The statement of a non-professional witness as to the sanity or insanity, at a particular time, of an individual, whose appearance, manner, habits and conduct came under his personal observation, is not the expression of mere opinion. In form, it is opinion. . . . But, in a substantial sense and for every purpose essential to a safe conclusion, the mental condition of an individual, as sane or insane, is a fact, . . . and the expressed opinion . . . is but the statement of a fact.—Harlan: Connecticut Mut. Life Ins. Co. v. Lathrop, 111 U.S. 612, 620.

41. Society is entitled to every man's evidence.—Frankfurter: Rios v. United States, 364 U.S. at p. 234.

See also Court 56; Dying declaration; Hearing 5, 6; Informer; Patent 14; Result 2; Search and seizure 14; Silence; Theory 2; Wire tapping.

EVIL

1. Acknowledged evils, however grave and urgent they may appear to be, had better be borne, than the risk be run, in the effort to suppress them, of more serious consequences by resort to expedients of even doubtful constitutionality. — Fuller: United States v. E. C. Knight Co., 156 U.S. 1, 13.

2. What is evil may not always be clear. — McKenna: National Cotton Oil Co. v. Texas, 197 U.S. 115, 129.

See also Business (big) 4; Civilization 3; Constitutional adjudication 24–26; Corporation 20; Corruption; Court 42; Doctrine 4; End-means 1; Equal protection 7; Freedom, thought 151; Iniquity; Law 62; Malevolence; Remedy 13, 17; Vice; Wickedness.

EXAGGERATION
See Vanity 1.

EXCELLENCE
We ought not to rest satisfied with mediocrity, when excellence is within our reach. — Story: *Misc. Writings,* 433.

EXCEPTION
See Rule, exception.

EXCHANGE

"Exchange" is barter, and carries with it no implication of reduction to money as a common denominator. It contemplates simply an estimate, determined by self-interest, of the relative value and importance of the services rendered and those received.—Holmes: Postal Tel. Co. v. Tonopah & T. W. R.R., 248 U.S. 471, 474.
See also Money.

EXCUSE

Excuse would seldom fail if temptation could supply it.—Cardozo: Union Exch. Nat'l Bank v. Joseph, 231 N.Y. 250, 254.

EXECUTION (legal)

An execution is the fruit and end of the suit, and is very aptly called the life of the law.—Thompson: Bank of U.S. v. Halstead, 10 Wheat. (23 U.S.) 51, 64.

EXEMPTION

See Tax, exemption; Tax 134.

EXONERATION

Exoneration . . . is not to be confused with regulation. — Cardozo: Murray v. Cunard S.S. Co., 235 N.Y. 162, 165.

EXPATRIATION

Traditionally the United States has supported the right of expatriation as a natural and inherent right of all people. — Burton: Savorgnan v. United States, 338 U.S. 491, 497.

EXPECTANCY, EXPECTATION

1. In the heyday of gladsome expectation when the venture was still young.—Cardozo: In the Matter of Raymond v. Davis, 248 N.Y. 67, 71.

2. Expectancy may be said to have reached the vanishing point at which it merges in illusion.—Cardozo: In the Matter of Brown, 242 N.Y. 1, 12.
See also Fulfillment; Possible; Representation; Right 16; Value 9.

EXPEDIENCY

Expediency may tip the scales when arguments are nicely balanced.—Cardozo: Woolford Realty Co. v. Rose, 286 U.S. 319, 330.
See also Safety 1.

EXPERIENCE

1. Experience is of all teachers the most dependable, and . . . experience also is a continuous process.—Sutherland: Funk v. United States, 290 U.S. 371, 381.

2. Opportunity must be allowed for vindicating reasonable belief by experience.—Frankfurter: "Holmes and the Constitution," 41 Harv. L. Rev. 145.

3. Experience is the test by which it is decided whether the degree of danger attending given conduct under certain known circumstances is sufficient to throw the risk upon the party pursuing it. — Holmes: *The Common Law,* 149.

4. While the workings of a novel method are untested by a rich experience . . . there must be advance by trial and error. — Cardozo: Liggett Co. v. Lee, 288 U.S. 517, 586.

5. Experience is . . . available to correct uncertain prophecy. Here is a book of wisdom that courts may

not neglect. We find no rule of law that sets a clasp upon its pages, and forbids us to look within.—Cardozo: Sinclair Ref. Co. v. Jenkins Pet. Proc. Co., 289 U.S. 689, 698.

6. Often a liberal antidote of experience supplies a sovereign cure for a paralyzing abstraction built upon a theory.—Cardozo: *Paradoxes*, 125.

7. In the revealing light of experience the hazards to be avoided are disclosed to us as the hazards that ensued.—Cardozo: De Haen v. Rockwood Spr. Co., 258 N.Y. 350, 355.

8. Our surest recourse is in what has been done.—McKenna: Merrick v. Halsey, 242 U.S. 568, 587.

9. Life in all its fulness must supply the answer to the riddle.—Cardozo: Welch v. Helvering, 290 U.S. 111, 115.

10. Only time and costly experience can give the answers.—Stone: United States v. South-East Underwriters Assoc., 322 U.S. 533, 582.

See also Afterthought 1; Antiquity 1; Dogma 3; Judicial process 2; Jury 15, 16; Law 25; Prophecy 1; Supreme Court 14; Virtue 4.

EXPERIMENT

1. There is no "of course" as to what nature can do, except as proved by observation and experiment.—Holmes: Minerals Sep. No. Am. Corp. v. Magma Copper Co., 280 U.S. 400, 403.

2. To stay experimentation in things social and economic is a grave responsibility.—Brandeis: New State Ice Co. v. Liebmann, 285 U.S. 262, 311.

3. The discoveries in physical science, the triumphs in invention, attest the value of the process of trial and error. In large measure, these advances have been due to experimentation.—Brandeis: *ibid.*, 310.

4. For social development of trial and error, the fullest possible opportunity for the free play of the human mind is an indispensable prerequisite.— Frankfurter: Dennis v. United States, 341 U.S. 494, 550.

5. The rational process of trial and error implies a wary use of novelty and critical adoption of change.—Frankfurter: Radio Corp. v. United States, 341 U.S. 412, 425.

6. In the science of medicine, as in other sciences, experimentation is the spur of progress.—Black: Reilly v. Pinkus, 338 U.S. 269, 274.

Related Subject: Trial and error. See also Democracy 3; Government, general; Judicial process 3; Legislation, experimental; Policy; Truth 15.

EXPERT

1. Here, as elsewhere, we are driven to ask the opinions of those having superior knowledge.—Brewer: Montana Ry. v. Warren, 137 U.S. 348, 353.

2. In questions of science their [experts'] opinions are received, for in such questions scientific men have superior knowledge, and generally think alike. Not so in matters of common knowledge.—Strong: Milwaukee & St. P. Ry. v. Kellogg, 4 Otto (94 U.S.) 469, 473.

3. Where experts are introduced to testify as to opinions on matters peculiar to their art or trade, there is usually some conflict in their testi-

mony.—Grier: Ogden v. Parsons, 23 How. (64 U.S.) 167, 169–70.

4. It [the Seventh Amendment] permits expert opinion to have the force of fact when based on facts which sustain it.—Rutledge: Galloway v. United States, 319 U.S. 372, 396.

5. An expert in real estate is no more competent than anyone else to determine just what effect, measured in money, the dislike of litigation may have on a given person's mind.—Holmes: Sawyer v. City of Boston, 144 Mass. 470, 471.

6. An opinion, especially an opinion by an expert, may be found to be fraudulent if the grounds supporting it are so flimsy as to lead to the conclusion that there was no genuine belief back of it. — Cardozo: Ultramares Corp. v. Touche, 255 N.Y. 170, 186.

7. The record is redolent with familiar dogmatic assertions by experts equally confident of contradictory contentions. — Frankfurter: Railroad Comm'n v. Rowan & Nichols Oil Co., 310 U.S. 573, 583.

> Related subject: Opinion. *See also* Decision 8; Insanity.

EXPLOITATION

1. Also, if there is a form of speech for which I have less sympathy than another it is talk about "exploitation," as a hostile characterization of modern commercial life, and an implication that dominant brains are to blame. I think it is drivelling cant.—Holmes: *Uncollected Letters,* 197.

2. There are always those who are ready to gather where they have not sown.—Swayne: Providence Rubber Co. v. Goodyear, 9 Wall. (76 U.S.) 788, 793.

EXPOSITION

Exposition seems to be that of demonstrating the certainty and self-evidence of an axiom. — McKenna: United States v. New River Co., 265 U.S. 533, 543.

EX POST FACTO

1. It is not in our tradition for anyone to be charged with crime which is defined after his conduct, alleged to be criminal, has taken place.—Rutledge: In the Matter of Yamashita, 327 U.S. 1, 43.

2. To open the door to retroactive criminal statutes would rightly be regarded as a most serious blow to one of the civil liberties protected by our Constitution.—Jackson: Rosenberg v. United States, 346 U.S. 271, 290.

See also Legislation 75.

EXPOSURE

See Error 4; Investigation 3; Person 2.

EXPRESSION

1. The inadvertence of expressing one thing when another was meant.—McKenna: Fullinwider v. Southern Pac. R.R., 248 U.S. 409, 412.

2. The expression is made to carry too heavy a burden.—Hughes: Helvering v. Canfield, 291 U.S. 163, 169.

EXTORTION

See Contract 8.

EXTRAORDINARY

See Remedy 23; Test 2.

EXTRAVAGANCE

The extravagance is more violent, it approaches an absurdity.—Cardozo: In the Matter of Findlay, 253 N.Y. 1, 10.

See also Speculation (conjecture); Unrest.

EXTREME

1. The comparison of extremes is forensic, and it may be, fallacious.—McKenna: International Harvester Co. v. Missouri, 234 U.S. 199, 213.

2. To push propositions to the extreme to which they naturally lead is often an unsafe guide.—White: Northern Sec. Co. v. United States, 193 U.S. 197, 397.

3. By arguing from extremes almost every exercise of government can be shown to be a deprivation of individual liberty. — McKenna: National Cotton Oil Co. v. Texas, 197 U.S. 115, 129.

4. The baby is not to be thrown out with the bath.—Frankfurter: International Salt Co. v. United States, 332 U.S. 392, 405.

5. The law ... respects the wisdom of not burning even part of a house in order to roast a pig.—Frankfurter: *ibid.*, 403.

6. There is no need to be "more Roman than the Romans."—Frankfurter: Hughes v. Fetter, 341 U.S. 609, 621.

See also Proposition 4.

FACT

1. They are matters capable of precise ascertainment, and in no sense depending upon estimate, opinion or mere probability. — Harlan: First Nat'l Bank v. Hartford Fire Ins. Co., 5 Otto (95 U.S.) 673, 677.

2. A fact which has existed cannot be made never to have existed.—Marshall: Marbury v. Madison, 1 Cranch (5 U.S.) 137, 167.

3. Without considering how far motives commonly classed as ignoble have covered themselves with a high sounding name, or how far discontent means inadequacy of temperament or will, the first step toward improvement is to look the facts in the face.—Holmes: *Uncollected Letters,* 141.

4. It was said by *Chief Justice* Marshall, many years ago, that Congress could do many things, but that it could not alter a fact. — McLean: Pennsylvania v. Wheeling Bridge Co., 18 How. (59 U.S.) 421, 439.

5. If justice requires the fact to be ascertained, the difficulty of doing so is no ground for refusing to try.—Holmes: *The Common Law,* 48.

6. Facts do not often exactly repeat themselves in practice; but cases with comparatively small variations from each other do.—Holmes: *ibid.,* 124.

7. Many things must be learned as facts in law as in other sciences. They are the coin which we must have in our pocket if we are to pay our way with legal tender. Until we are provided with a plentiful supply of it, we shall do better to stay at home, and not go forth upon our journey.—Cardozo: *Growth of the Law,* 98.

8. State of mind is itself a fact, and may be a material fact, and false and fraudulent representations may be

made about it.—Hughes: Seven Cases v. United States, 239 U.S. 510, 517.

9. Nothing is so fallacious as facts, except figures. For figures which do not reveal the peculiar facts of each case cannot reflect a policy of any kind. — Murphy: Griffin v. United States, 336 U.S. 704, 723.

10. Fact finding does not require mathematical certainty. — B l a c k : Schulz v. Pennsylvania R.R., 350 U.S. 523, 526.

11. No finder of fact can see through the eyes of any other finder of fact.—Frankfurter: Commissioner of Int. Rev. v. Culbertson, 337 U.S. 733, 753.

12. Right and wrong are not objectively ascertainable, that in fact there is no right and wrong when two equally competent and equally independent judges, equally devoid of any bias or possessed of the same bias, could by the same reasoning process reach opposite conclusions on the facts.—Frankfurter: Stone v. N.Y., C. & St. L. R.R., 344 U.S. 407, 411–12.

13. Only lawyers know, unless now it is taxpayers and persons divorced, how rambling is the scope of facts from which proof is ever drawn to show and negate the ultimate conclusion of subjective "fact." They know, as do the courts and other tribunals which wrestle with the problem, how easily facts procreative of conflicting inferences may be marshalled and how conjectural is the outcome. There is no greater legal gamble. Rare is the situation, where much is at stake, in which conflicting circumstances cannot be shown and where accordingly conflicting ultimate inferences cannot be drawn.—Murphy: Williams v. Carolina, 325 U.S. 226, 258–59.

14. "Facts," except the most rudimentary, are not like members of a lodge who identify themselves by badges.—Frankfurter: Stroble v. California, 343 U.S. 181, 203.

Related subjects: Actuality; Reality. *See also* Court 49, 50; Fiction 4; Formula 8; Jury, function; Jury 33; Theory 3.

FACULTY

By practice and tradition, the members of the faculty are masters, and not servants, in the conduct of the class room. They have the independence appropriate to a company of scholars. —Cardozo: Hamburger v. Cornell Univ., 240 N.Y. 328, 336–37.

FAIRNESS

1. Fairness is a relative, not an absolute concept. It is fairness with reference to particular conditions or particular results.—Cardozo: Snyder v. Massachusetts, 291 U.S. 97, 116.

2. What is fair in one set of circumstances may be an act of tyranny in others.—Cardozo: *ibid.,* 117.

3. The concept of fairness must not be strained till it is narrowed to a filament. We are to keep the balance true.—Cardozo: *ibid.,* 122.

Related subject: Equity. *See also* Freedom, speech 98; Prosecutor; Public official 24; Tax, fairness; Trial, requirements; Trial, unfair.

FAITH

1. "Faith means belief in something concerning which doubt is still theor-

etically possible." Belief in what one may demonstrate to the senses is not faith.—Jackson: United States v. Ballard, 322 U.S. 78, 94.

2. I do not know what is true. I do not know the meaning of the universe. But in the midst of doubt, in the collapse of creeds, there is one thing I do not doubt, that no man who lives in the same world with most of us can doubt, and that is that the faith is true and adorable which leads a soldier to throw away his life in obedience to a blindly accepted duty, in a cause which he little understands, in a plan of compaign of which he has no notion, under tactics of which he does not see the use. — Holmes: *Speeches,* 59.

3. Most men who know battle know the cynic force with which the thoughts of common-sense will assail them in times of stress; but they know that in their greatest moments faith has trampled those thoughts under foot.—Holmes: *ibid*.

4. You know your own weakness and are modest; but you know that man has in him that unspeakable somewhat which makes him capable of miracle, able to lift himself by the might of his own soul, unaided, able to face annihilation for a blind belief. —Holmes: *ibid.,* 60.

5. For high and dangerous action teaches us to believe as right beyond dispute things for which our doubting minds are slow to find words of proof. Out of heroism grows faith in the worth of heroism. The proof comes later, and even may never come.— Holmes: *Speeches,* 63.

6. Part of life is to feel a direction for effort before it is definitely and articulately known and to persevere with faith. . . . If I were dying my last words would be: Have faith and pursue the unknown end.—Holmes: *Uncollected Letters,* 175.

7. For me at least there came moments when faith waivered. But there is the great lesson and the great triumph if you keep the fire burning until, by and by, out of the mass of sordid details there comes some result, be it some new generalization or be it a transcending spiritual repose.— Holmes: *ibid.,* 176-77.

8. The troubles will emerge as triumphs; the travail and the doubt will yield an unexpected peace.—Cardozo: *Law and Literature,* 163.

9. The measure of our faith is in some sense the measure of our duty to see to it that faith is justified.—Cardozo: People v. Dixon, 231 N.Y. 111, 128.

10. In the realm of religious faith, and in that of political belief, sharp differences arise. In both fields the tenets of one man may seem the rankest error to his neighbor.—Roberts: Cantwell v. Connecticut, 310 U.S. 296, 310.

11. Faith in his loyalty disarmed suspicion.—Cardozo: Globe Woolen Co. v. Utica Gas & Elec. Co., 224 N.Y. 483, 490.

12. An eighteenth century faith in human nature. — Holmes: Cole v.

Norborne Land Drain. Dist., 270 U.S. 45, 47.

13. His good faith did not purge him of the guilt of crime, though it called for mercy in the sentence.— Cardozo: *Law and Literature,* 113.

14. There are degrees of bad faith. —Bradley: New Orleans v. Christmas (Gaines Adm'r), 131 U.S. 191, 218.

15. Possessors in legal bad faith but in moral good faith. — Sutherland: Gulf Ref. Co. v. United States, 269 U.S. 125, 137.

> Related subjects: Belief and related subjects; Creed; Religion. *See also* Freedom 37; Heart; Hope.

FALLACY

1. It is a fallacy to break the fagot stick by stick. — Holmes: Schlitz Brew. Co. v. Houston Ice & Brew. Co., 250 U.S. 28, 29.

2. A century ago Malthus ran his sword through fallacies that one would have thought must die then and there, but men didn't like to believe him, and the humbugs that he killed are as alive as ever today.— Holmes: *Uncollected Letters,* 153.

> Related subjects: Falsity and related subjects. *See also* Generalization 3; Right 18.

FALLIBILITY

> *See* Judgment 8; Supreme Court 9, 15.

FALSITY

1. A suppression of the truth may amount to a suggestion of falsehood. —Gray: Stewart v. Wyoming Cattle Ranche Co., 128 U.S. 383, 388.

2. The fact that a false statement may be obviously false to those who are trained and experienced does not change its character, nor take away its power to deceive others less experienced. — Black: F e d e r a l T r a d e Comm'n v. Standard Educ. Soc., 302 U.S. 112, 116.

3. Such a statement of a half truth is as much a misrepresentation as if the facts stated were untrue.—Stone: Equitable Life Ins. Co. v. Halsey Stuart & Co., 312 U.S. 410, 426.

4. The reminder, as a host of impoverished investors will be ready to attest, that there are dangers in untruths and half truths when certificates masquerading as securities pass current in the market. — Cardozo: Jones v. SEC, 298 U.S. 1, 32.

5. There are dangers in spreading a belief that untruths and half truths, designed to be passed on for the guidance of confiding buyers, are to be ranked as peccadillos or even perhaps as part of the amenities of business.— Cardozo: *ibid.*

6. The mere exaggeration of the qualities which the article has; but when a proposed seller goes beyond that, assigns to the article qualities which it does not possess, does not simply magnify in opinion the advantages which it has, but invents advantages and falsely asserts their existence, he transcends the limits of "puffing" and engages in false representations and pretenses.—McKenna: United States v. New South Farm & Home Co., 241 U.S. 64, 71.

7. No man is justified in the utterance of a falsehood. It is an equal offense in morals, whether committed

for his own benefit or that of another. —Hunt: Jeffries v. Econ. Mut. Life Ins. Co., 22 Wall. (89 U.S.) 47, 52.

8. No man can be permitted to say, in respect to his own statements upon a material matter, that he did not expect to be believed.—Matthews: Glaflin v. Commonwealth Ins. Co., 110 U.S. 81, 95.

9. The defendants touched every string of desire by false statements, and sounded every note that could excite and delude.—McKenna: United States v. New South Farm & Home Co., 241 U.S. 64, 71.

10. The delusive apparatus of a promise known to be false when made. — Holmes: United States v. Moist, 231 U.S. 701, 702.

11. The various itinerant venders of patented articles, whose fluency of speech and carelessness regarding the truth of their representations might almost be said to have become proverbial. — Peckham: Ozan Lumber Co. v. Union Co. Nat'l Bank, 207 U.S. 251, 255–56.

> Related subjects: Dishonesty; Fallacy; Fraud; Misrepresentation; Perjury; Representation; Truth. *See also* Advertising 1; Concealment 2; Fact 8; Freedom 76, 95; Misbranding: Opinion 8–11; Speech 5.

FAME

Who does not prefer good to ill report of his work? And if fame—a good public name—is, as Milton said, the "last infirmity of noble mind," it is frequently the first infirmity of a mediocre one.—Frankfurter: Craig v. Harney, 331 U.S. 367, 396.

FAMILY

See Domestic relations and related subjects; Tradition 9.

FANATIC

1. No one but a fanatic can be *sure* that his opinions—political, economic, or social—are correct.—Brandeis: Mason, *Brandeis,* 506.

2. Fanatics should be sacrificed when the end is accomplished—like animals which had borne the gods to sacrificial feasts.—Brandeis: *ibid.,* 133.
See also Constitution 71.

FARM, FARM CO-OPERATIVE, FARMER

1. Congress intended cooperatives to be what they actually have been—the backbone of the farm market system and the dynamo which makes the system function.—Black: Brannan v. Stark, 342 U.S. 451, 470.

2. Agricultural producers, spread often over wide areas, and thus deficient in cohesion, but yielding up new energies when functioning together.—Cardozo: People v. Teuscher, 248 N.Y. 454, 463.

3. A farmer remains a farmer, just as a lawyer remains a lawyer, though the returns on his investments, while not enough to keep him going, are larger, none the less, than the profits of his labor.—Cardozo: First Nat'l Bank & Tr. Co. v. Beach, 301 U.S. 435, 440.

4. One does not cease to be a farmer because drought or wind or pest may have rendered the farm barren.—Cardozo: *ibid.,* 439.

5. The roots of the respondent's in-

come go down into the soil.—Cardozo: *ibid.*, 441.

See also Notice 5.

FASHION

1. The law of fashion is a law of life. The crest of the wave of human interest is always moving.—Holmes: "Law in Science & Science in Law," 12 Harv. L. Rev. 493.

2. Fashion is potent in science as well as elsewhere. — Holmes: *ibid.*, 447.

See also Opinion 23.

FATE

Our fates are in our own hands. We make and remake our own selves.... Nature pants with the desire to make us what we wish to be. The wish is the reality. What we think, that we are.—Cardozo: *Law and Literature,* 173.

FAULT

1. The criterion which is thought to be free from constitutional objection, the criterion of fault, is the application of an external standard, the conduct of a prudent man in the known circumstances, that is, in doubtful cases, the opinion of the jury, which the defendant has to satisfy at his peril, and which he may miss after giving the matter his best thought. — Holmes: Arizona Copper Co. v. Hammer, 250 U.S. 400, 432.

2. The gravity of the fault must be compared with the gravity of the hardship. — Cardozo: Graf v. Hope Bldg. Corp., 254 N.Y. 1, 13.

3. The fault was less theirs than that of the age in which they lived.—Story: *Misc. Writings,* 12.

Related subjects: Blame; Negligence and related subjects. *See also* Crime 5; Error 1; Liability 10–12.

FAVOR, FAVORITISM

The reproach of favoritism for the powerful to the prejudice of the lowly.—Cardozo: Hegeman Farms Corp. v. Baldwin, 293 U.S. 163, 172.

Related subject: Partiality. *See also* Burden 2; Disclosure 1; Jurisdiction 6; Majority-minority 7, 8; Regulation 4.

FEAR, FEARLESSNESS

1. Fear is a phase or symptom of distress.—Cardozo: Bishop v. New York Times Co., 233 N.Y. 446, 462.

2. Fear is a token of aversion.—Cardozo: *ibid.*

See also Assault; Concealment 4; Freedom 82; Judgment 6; Nation 7; Power 6; Violence 2.

FEDERALIST

The opinion of the Federalist has always been considered as of great authority. It is a complete commentary on our constitution; and is appealed to by all parties in the questions to which that instrument has given birth. Its intrinsic merit entitles it to high rank.—Marshall: Cohens v. Virginia, 6 Wheat. (19 U.S.) 264, 418.

FENCER

A fencer accepts the risk of a thrust by his antagonist or a spectator at a ball game the chance of contact with the ball.—Cardozo Murphy v. Steeplechase Amus. Co., 250 N.Y. 479, 482.

155

FETTER

The fetters which bind the people are forged from the people's own gold.
—Brandeis: Mason, *Brandeis*, 410.

FEW-MANY

See Greater-less; Power 22.

FICTION (legal)

1. Fictions are sometimes invented in order to realize the judicial conception of justice.—Stone: Curry v. McCanless, 307 U.S. 357, 374.

2. John Doe and Richard Roe, those fictional gentlemen of the law, are men of straw where once they were flesh and blood, but they enable lawyers to use old forms and procedures to gain new ends.—Jackson: *Struggle for Judicial Supremacy*, 293.

3. Fictions are often the hostages that the forces of movement give to the forces of position. But frequently lawyers' fictions serve no such useful purpose; too often they are employed as a screen to cover up a retreat.—Jackson: *ibid.*, 293-94.

4. Being a fiction, it is not allowed to obscure the facts, when the facts become important.—Holmes: Blackstone v. Miller, 188 U.S. 189, 204.

5. A fiction is not a satisfactory ground for taking one man's property to satisfy another man's wrongs.—Holmes: The Eugene F. Moran, 212 U.S. 466, 474.

6. Fiction always is a poor ground for changing substantial rights.—Holmes: Haddock v. Haddock, 201 U.S. 562, 630.

7. To speak of constructive presence is to use the language of fiction, and so to hinder precise analysis.—Holmes: Hyde v. United States, 225 U.S. 347, 386.

8. It overworks legal fiction to say that one is free in law when by the commonest of common sense he is bound. — Jackson: Shaughnessey v. United States, 345 U.S. 206, 220.

9. There is a fiction of law that a term consists of but one day; but such a fiction is only tolerated by the courts for the purpose of justice.—Davis: Newhall v. Sanger, 2 Otto (92 U.S.) 761, 766.

10. The law finds no difficulty in disregarding the corporate fiction whenever that is deemed necessary to attain a just result.—Brandeis: Eisner v. Macomber, 252 U.S. 189, 231.

11. The situs of intangibles is in truth a legal fiction.—Cardozo: Severnoe Sec. Corp. v. L. & L. Ins. Co., 255 N.Y. 120, 123.

12. It is a fiction created by law with intent that it should be acted on as if true.—Holmes: Klein v. Tax Supers, 282 U.S. 19, 24.

13. Fictions are commonplace to lawyers. — Douglas: Parker v. Ellis, 362 U.S. 574, 595.

See also Constitution 74; Corporation 4, 32; Debt 9; Juror 28; Principal, agent 1.

FIDELITY

1. There is great strength in serving with singleness of purpose one master only.—Brandeis: *Other People's Money*, 142.

2. An impairment of impartial judgment can occur in even the most well-meaning men when their per-

sonal economic interests are affected by the business they transact on behalf of the Government.—Warren: United States v. Mississippi Val. Gen. Co., 364 U.S. 520, 549.

3. The Biblical admonition that no man may serve two masters . . . is especially pertinent if one of the masters happens to be economic self-interest. —Warren: *ibid*.

Related subject: Fiduciary.

FIDUCIARY
Defined 1–4; standards 5–16; abuses 17–19; miscellaneous 20–22.

Related subjects: Fidelity; Trustee.

———, defined

1. A person acting in two distinct characters must in many respects be considered as two distinct persons.—Marshall: Pennington v. Coxe, 2 Cranch (6 U.S.) 34, 63.

2. He is one being, but acts in more than one capacity, and in all of his capacities he has duties and obligations.—McKenna: Clarke v. Rogers, 228 U.S. 534, 545.

3. The general rule stands upon our great moral obligation to refrain from placing ourselves in relations which ordinarily excite a conflict between self-interest and integrity.—Wayne: Michoud v. Girod, 4 How. (45 U.S.) 503, 555.

4. The character of vendor and that of purchaser cannot be held by the same person. They impose different obligations. Their union in the same person would at once raise a conflict between interest and duty, and constituted as humanity is, in the major-

ity of cases duty would be overborne in the struggle.—Field: Marsh v. Whitmore, 21 Wall. (88 U.S.) 178, 183–84.

———, standards

5. It was no more vital to that day (in the 1790's) that free speech should be preserved than it is to our own that those who act as fiduciaries in the strategic positions of our business civilization should be held to those standards of scrupulous fidelity which society has a right to demand.—Stone: Mason, *Stone,* 380.

6. Many forms of conduct permissible in a workaday world for those acting at arm's length, are forbidden to those bound by fiduciary ties.—Cardozo: Meinhard v. Salmon, 249 N.Y. 458, 464.

7. Uncompromising rigidity has been the attitude of courts of equity when petitioned to undermine the rule of undivided loyalty by the "disintegrating erosion" of particular exceptions. Only thus has the level of conduct for fiduciaries been kept at a level higher than that trodden by the crowd.—Cardozo: *ibid*.

8. The standard of loyalty for those in trust relations is without the fixed divisions of a graduated scale.—Cardozo: *ibid., 466.*

9. The rule of undivided loyalty is relentless and supreme. — Cardozo: *ibid., 468.*

10. Thought of self was to be renounced, however hard the abnegation.—Cardozo: *ibid*.

11. Equity refuses to confine within

the bounds of classified transactions its precept of a loyalty that is undivided and unselfish.—Cardozo: *ibid.,* 467.

12. The "great rule of law" which holds a trustee to the duty of constant and unqualified fidelity, is not a thing of forms and phrases. — Cardozo: Globe Woolen Co. v. Utica Gas & Elec. Co., 224 N.Y. 483, 489.

13. There must be candor and equity in the transaction, and some reasonable proportion between benefits and burdens.—Cardozo: *ibid,* 490.

14. The trustee is free to stand aloof, while others act, if all is equitable and fair. He cannot rid himself of the duty to warn and to denounce, if there is improvidence or oppression, either apparent on the surface, or lurking beneath the surface, but visible to his practiced eye.—Cardozo: *ibid.,* 489.

15. Only by . . . uncompromising rigidity has the rule of undivided loyalty been maintained against disintegrating erosion.—Cardozo: Wendt v. Fischer, 243 N.Y. 439, 444.

16. Preference of self is made subordinate to loyalty to others.—Cardozo: Meinhard v. Salmon, 249 N.Y. 458, 467.

————, abuses

17. When the history of the financial era which has just drawn to a close (1929) comes to be written, most of its mistakes and its major faults will be ascribed to the failure to observe the fiduciary principle, the precept as old as holy writ, that "a man cannot serve two masters." — Stone: Mason, *Stone,* 379.

18. A beneficiary, about to plunge into a ruinous course of dealing, may be betrayed by silence as well as by the spoken word. — Cardozo: Globe Woolen Co. v. Utica Gas & Elec. Co., 224 N.Y. 483, 489.

19. Abuse of corporate position, influence, and access to information may raise questions so subtle that the law can deal with them effectively only by prohibitions not concerned with the fairness of a particular transaction.—Frankfurter: SEC v. Chenery Corp., 318 U.S. 80, 92.

————, miscellaneous

20. One does not divest oneself so readily of one's duties as trustee.—Cardozo: Globe Woolen Co. v. Utica Gas & Elec. Co., 224 N.Y. 483, 489.

21. He might steal a march on his comrade under cover of the darkness, and then hold the captured ground. Loyalty and comradeship are not so easily abjured.—Cardozo: Meinhard v. Salmon, 249 N.Y. 458, 466.

22. Everything of profit arising out of the abused relation must now be yielded up.—Cardozo: McCandless v. Furlaud, 296 U.S. 140, 164.

See also Corporation 2, 38, 51, 55; Disclosure 2; Lawyer 51; Lawyer, misconduct; Principal, agent 3; Public official 10, 26.

FIGURE (numeral)
See Arithmetic; Fact 9.

FILE, FILING
The word "file" is derived from the

Latin word "filum," and relates to the ancient practice of placing papers on a thread or wire for safe-keeping and ready reference.—McKenna: United States v. Lombardo, 241 U.S. 73, 76.

FLAG

1. The only American flag known throughout the world is the flag of the United States. — Gray: Fong Yue Ting v. United States, 149 U.S. 698, 711.

2. It is all a symbol, if you like, but so is the flag. The flag is but a bit of bunting to one who insists on prose. Yet . . . its red is our life-blood, its stars our world, its blue our heaven. It owns our land. At will it throws away our lives. — Holmes: *Speeches*, 91.

3. The American people, acting through the legislative branch of the government, early in their history, prescribed a flag as symbolical of the existence and sovereignty of the nation. . . . For that flag every true American has not simply an appreciation, but a deep affection. No American, nor any foreign-born person who enjoys the privileges of American citizenship, ever looks upon it without taking pride in the fact that he lives under this free government.—Harlan: Halter v. Nebraska, 205 U.S. 33, 41.

4. The flag is the symbol of the nation's power—the emblem of freedom in its truest, best sense. It is not extravagant to say that to all lovers of the country it signifies government resting on the consent of the governed; liberty regulated by law; the protection of the weak against the strong; security against the exercise of arbitrary power; and absolute safety for free institutions against foreign aggression.—Harlan: *ibid.*, 43.

5. From the earliest periods in the history of the human race, banners, standards, and ensigns have been adopted as symbols of the power and history of the peoples who bore them. —Harlan: *ibid.*, 41.

6. It has often occurred that insults to a flag have been the cause of war, and indignities put upon it, in the presence of those who revere it, have often been resented and sometimes punished on the spot.—Harlan: *ibid*.

7. The use of an emblem or flag to symbolize some system, idea, institution, or personality, is a short cut from mind to mind.—Jackson: West Va. State Bd. of Educ. v. Barnette, 319 U.S. 624, 632.

8. There is no doubt that, in connection with the pledges, the flag salute is a form of utterance.—Jackson: *ibid*.

9. "We live by symbols." The flag is the symbol of our national unity, transcending all internal differences, however large, within the framework of the Constitution. — Frankfurter: Minersville School Dist. v. Gobitis, 310 U.S. 586, 596.

10. The preciousness of the family relation, the authority and independence which give dignity to parenthood, indeed the enjoyment of all freedom, presuppose the kind of ordered society which is summarized by our flag.—Frankfurter: *ibid.*, 600.

11. No one can be said to have the right, secured by the Constitution, to use the country's flag merely for purposes of advertising articles of merchandise. — Harlan: Halter v. Nebraska, 295 U.S. 33, 45.

See also Ship 3.

FLATTERY

See Imitation 3.

FLIGHT

1. The very meaning of flight is desistance or abandonment, unless, indeed, in special circumstances as in cases where a thief is fleeing with his loot.—Cardozo: People v. Moran, 246 N.Y. 100, 103.

2. Flight is for sanctuary and shelter, and shelter, if not sanctuary, is in the home. — Cardozo: People v. Tomlins, 213 N.Y. 240, 243.

See also Evidence 16, 17; Self-defense 3–5.

FLOOD

Floods pay no respect to state lines. —Douglas: Oklahoma *ex rel.* Phillips v. Atkinson Co., 313 U.S. 508, 521.

FOLLY

Men of the world shun more than anything else the exposure of their follies, more especially such as the world may think to be so.—Wayne: Paterson v. Gaines, 6 How. (47 U.S.) 550, 593.

FOOD

By means of food preserved in a compact and nutritious form, protected from its natural tendency to decay, deserts are traversed, seas navigated, distant regions explored. It is less brilliant, but more useful, than all the inventions for the destruction of the human race that have ever been known. — Hunt: Sewall v. Jones, 1 Otto (91 U.S.) 171, 187.

FORCE

1. Not an appeal to laws, but to force. A case in which a sovereign undertakes to assert his right upon his sovereign responsibility; to right himself, and not to appeal to any arbiter, but the sword, for the justice of his cause.—Johnson: Cherokee Nation v. Georgia, 5 Pet. (30 U.S.) 1, 29.

2. Force, under our system of government is eliminated. — Brewer: Kansas v. Colorado, 206 U.S. 46, 97.

3. I believe that force, mitigated so far as may be by good manners, is the *ultima ratio,* and between two groups that want to make inconsistent worlds I see no remedy except force. — Holmes: *Holmes-Pollock Letters,* II, 36.

4. Speech may be fought with speech. . . . But force may and must be met with force.—Vinson: American Com. Assoc. v. Douds, 339 U.S. 382, 396.

5. To put a premium on resort to force instead of legal remedies and to subvert the principles of law and order which lie at the foundation of society.—Hughes: NLRB v. Fansteel Met. Corp., 306 U.S. 240, 253.

6. What is gained by skill in the manipulation, is lost in the vigor of the blow.—Story: *Misc. Writings,* 314.

Related subjects: Mob; Violence. *See also* Freedom 93; Law 106; Litigation 3; Marriage 7; Moral 5; Revolution.

FORECAST
> Related subjects: Estimate; Prophecy. *See also* Value 11–13, 24.

FOREIGN AFFAIRS, FOREIGN RELATIONS

1. The whole of my politics respecting foreign nations, are reducible to this single position: . . . Commercial intercourse with all, but political ties with none . . . never connect ourselves politically with any nation whatever. —Marshall: Beveridge, *Life of Marshall,* II, 388.

2. In this cast external realm [foreign affairs] with its important, complicated, delicate and manifold problems, the President alone has the power to speak or listen as a representative of the nation.—Sutherland: United States v. Curtiss-Wright Exp. Corp., 299 U.S. 304, 319.

3. In our dealings with the outside world the United States speaks with one voice and acts as one, unembarrassed by the complications as to domestic issues which are inherent in the distribution of political power between the national government and the individual states. — Frankfurter: United States v. Pink, 315 U.S. 203, 242.

4. International relations are preeminently a matter of public policy.— Reed: National Bank v. Republic of China, 348 U.S. 356, 370.

5. To the legislative power alone it must belong to determine when the violence of other nations is to be met by violence; to the judiciary to administer law and justice as it is, not as it is made to be by the folly or caprice of other nations. — Johnson: The Nereide, 9 Cranch (13 U.S.) 388, 432.

6. Recognition of a foreign country is not a theoretical problem or an exercise in abstract symbolism. It is the assertion of national power directed towards safeguarding and promoting our interests and those of civilization. —Frankfurter: United States v. Pink, 315 U.S. 203, 241.

7. In all cases where the United States have been called upon to recognize the existence of the government or the independence of any other country, they have looked only to the fact, and not to right. Such has been the uniform course of our government.—Swayne: Phillips v. Payne, 2 Otto (92 U.S.) 130, 134.

8. The practice, now a growing one, of withholding recognition whenever it is thought that a government, functioning unhampered, is unworthy of a place in the society of nations.— Cardozo: Sokoloff v. Nat'l City Bank, 239 N.Y. 158, 165–66.

9. Characteristically delicate and elusive expressions of diplomacy. The draftsmen of such notes must have sensibilities and avoid the explicitness on which diplomatic negotiations so easily founder.—Frankfurter: United States v. Pink, 315 U.S. 203, 241.

10. Experience amply attests that, in this day of extensive international travel, rapid communication and widespread use of propaganda, the activities of the citizens of one nation when in another country can easily cause serious embarrassments to the

government of their own country as well as to their fellow citizens.—Frankfurter: Perez v. Brownell, 356 U.S. 44, 59.

Related subjects: Peace; Treaty. *See also* President.

FOREMAN

1. There is no magic in the word foreman. Whether it stands for a workman or something else cannot be known in advance as a matter of dictionary definition, without knowledge or heed of the conditions of the job. —Cardozo: Austin v. City of New York, 258 N.Y. 113, 116.

2. Trade union history shows that foremen were the arms and legs of management in executing labor policies.—Douglas: Packard Mot. Co. v. NLRB, 330 U.S. 485, 496.

FORESIGHT

1. The future would have to be scanned with microscopical powers of vision to foresee and forestall every possible diversity.—Cardozo: Binney v. Long, 299 U.S. 280, 299.

2. Some one must be the loser; it is part of the game of life; we have to pay in countless ways for the absence of prophetic vision.—Cardozo: *Nature of Judicial Process*, 143.

3. Life will have to be made over, and human nature transformed, before prevision so extravagant can be accepted as the norm of conduct, the customary standard to which behavior must confirm.—Cardozo: Palsgraf v. Long Island R.R., 248 N.Y. 339, 343.

Related subject: Prophecy. *See also* Liability 15, 16.

FOREST

See Public Domain.

FORFEITURE

1. Forfeitures are not favored in the law. They are often the means of great oppression and injustice. — Bradley: Knickerbocker Ins. Co. v. Norton, 6 Otto (96 U.S.) 234, 242.

2. We are not . . . to be astute in searching for reasons to confiscate a man's property because he has too much.—Grier: United States v. Vallejo, 1 Black (66 U.S.) 541, 558.

See also Life 12.

FORGERY

Forgery can confer no power nor transfer any rights.—Field: Western Union Tel. Co. v. Davenport, 7 Otto (97 U.S.) 369, 371.

See also Will 4.

FORGETFULNESS

It is possible to forget a thing that did happen. It is not possible to remember a thing that never existed.—Miller: Stitt v. Huidekopers, 17 Wall. (84 U.S.) 384, 394.

Related subject: Memory.

FORM (substance)

1. We can as little dispence with forms as with substance.—Story: The Amiable Isabella, 6 Wheat. (19 U.S.) 1, 73.

2. Form is not to be insisted upon beyond the requirements of safety and justice.—Holmes: Fernandez v. Phillips, 268 U.S. 311, 312.

3. It is the substance of what they do, and not the form in which they clothe their transactions, which must

afford the test.—Hughes: Electric Bond & Sec. Co. v. SEC, 303 U.S. 419, 440.

4. It would be strange, indeed, if parties could be allowed, under the protection of its forms, to defeat the whole objects and purposes of the law itself.—Story: Welch v. Mandeville, 1 Wheat. (14 U.S.) 233, 236.

5. Form is not something added to substance as a mere protuberant adornment. The two are fused into a unity.—Cardozo: *Law and Literature*, 5.

6. One cannot always segregate the technique from the substance or the form from the reality.—Rutledge: Kotteakos v. United States, 328 U.S. 750, 761.

7. The strength that is born of form and the feebleness that is born of the lack of form are in truth qualities of the substance. They are the tokens of the thing's identity. They make it what it is.—Cardozo: *Law and Literature*, 6.

8. Sometimes secreted in ancient forms and ceremonies one finds the inner life and meaning of an institution revealed in all its essence.—Cardozo: *ibid.*, 118.

9. We shall hesitate to lay emphasis upon differences of form where there is no difference in effect.—Cardozo: In the Matter of Horner, 237 N.Y. 489, 496.

10. Neither law nor equity requires a meaningless form, *"Bona sed impossibilia non cogit lex."*—Strong: Case v. New Orleans & C. R.R., 11 Otto (101 U.S.) 688, 690.

11. To wrest it from its purpose and turn it into a shallow form by taking refuge in a disingenuous silence or in subtle and adroit evasions.—Cardozo: Newburger v. Lubbell, 257 N.Y. 383, 387.

12. The form might remain, but the vital essence would have departed. —Swayne: Farmers and Mechanics Nat'l Bank v. Dearing, 1 Otto (91 U.S.) 29, 34.

13. To disregard the niceties of form, which often stand in the way of justice.—Taney: Parks v. Turner, 12 How. (53 U.S.) 39, 46.

14. An empty form—a mere concession to technicality. — Holmes: Saunders v. Shaw, 244 U.S. 317, 319.

15. "Grasp at a shadow while the substance escapes." — Stone: Chase Nat'l Bank v. United States, 278 U.S. 327, 338.

16. We cheat ourselves with words and forms.—Cardozo: McGovern v. City of New York, 234 N.Y. 377, 392.

17. The underlying reality rather than the form or label.—Cardozo: Worthen Co. v. Kavanaugh, 295 U.S. 56, 62.

18. We exalt form above substance. Cardozo: People v. Defore, 242 N.Y. 13, 23.

19. Make a fetish of form.—Douglas: Pearson v. McGraw, 308 U.S. 313, 318.

Related subjects: Formalism; Substance; Technicality. *See also* Equity Court 21, 22; Fiction 2.

FORMALISM

1. The mind rebels against the

formalism.—Cardozo: In the Matter of Rausch, 258 N.Y. 327, 331.

2. A sterile formalism would quickly lead to an impasse.—Cardozo: Schuylkill Tel. Co. v. Pennsylvania, 296 U.S. 113, 127.

3. An excessive regard for formalism. — Frankfurter: Great Northern Life Ins. Co. v. Read, 322 U.S. 47, 57–58.

Related subjects: Form (substance); Technicality.

FORMS

Whatever the value of the notion of forms, the only use of the forms is to present their contents.—Holmes: *Uncollected Letters,* 167.

FORMULA

1. To rest upon a formula is a slumber that, prolonged, means death.—Holmes: "Ideals and Doubts," 10 Ill. L. Rev. 3.

2. Few formulas are meant to serve as universals.—Cardozo: Schubert v. Schubert Wagon Co., 249 N.Y. 253, 256.

3. No formula will be adequate unless its breadth of view and flexibility of adaptation are fitted and proportioned to the scheme and purpose.—Cardozo: New York, W. & W. Ry. v. Livingston, 238 N.Y. 300, 306.

4. Few formulas are so absolute as not to bend before the blast of extraordinary circumstances. — Cardozo: Evangelical Luth. Church v. Sahlem, 254 N.Y. 161, 167.

5. Where the line is to be drawn between the important and the trivial cannot be settled by a formula.—Cardozo: Jacob & Youngs v. Kent, 230 N.Y. 239, 243.

6. To rely on a tidy formula for the easy determination of what is a fundamental right for purposes of legal enforcement may satisfy a longing for certainty but ignores the movements of a free society.—Frankfurter: Wolf v. Colorado: 338 U.S. 25, 27.

7. The misapplication of a formula into which a complicated idea is compressed and thereby mutilated is a poor excuse for rejecting the idea.—Frankfurter: Mercoid Corp. v. Mid-Cont. Inv. Co., 320 U.S. 661, 678.

8. Formulas of respect for constitutional safeguards cannot prevail over the facts of life which contradict them. They may not become a cloak for inquisitorial practices and make an empty form of the due process of law for which free men fought and died to obtain.—Douglas: Haley v. Ohio, 332 U.S. 596, 601.

9. We have refused to compress within a formula the extenuating possibilities of behavior in all its myriad diversities.—Cardozo: Mirizio v. Mirizio, 248 N.Y. 175, 179.

10. To sacrifice the substance of the right to the magic of a formula.—Cardozo: Cooper v. Dasher, 290 U.S. 106, 110.

11. The possibilities of injustice inherent in a changeless formula.—Cardozo: Moskowitz v. Marrow, 251 N.Y. 380, 398.

12. Practical adjustments, rather than a rigid formula, are necessary.—Douglas: Consolidated Rock Prod. Co. v. Du Bois, 312 U.S. 510, 529.

Related subjects: Principle; Rule; Standard. *See also* Equality 25; Equity 15, 23; Generality 15; Human nature 4; Self incrimination.

FOUNDATION

If the foundation fails the entire superstructure reared upon it must fall.—Swayne: Township of Pine Grove v. Talcott, 86 U.S. 666, 673.

FOUNDLING

Hospitals for foundlings existed in the Roman Empire. They increased when Christianity triumphed. They exist in all countries of Europe, and they exist in this country. There are no beneficiaries more needing protection care and kindness, none more blameless, and there are none who have stronger claims than these waifs, helpless and abandoned upon the sea of life.—Swayne: Ould v. Washington Hosp., 5 Otto (95 U.S.) 303, 311–12.

FRAGMENT

A congeries of fragments.—Cardozo: ICC v. N. Y., N. H. & H. R.R., 287 U.S. 178, 202.

FRANKNESS

See Honesty 11.

FRAUD

1. The existence of collusion implies the existence of fraud.—McKenna: Wheeler v. Denver, 229 U.S. 342, 350.

2. Fraud includes the pretense of knowledge when knowledge there is none.—Cardozo: Ultramares Corp. v. Touche, 255 N.Y. 170, 179.

3. There is a kind of fraud . . . in clinging to a benefit which is the product of misrepresentation, however innocently made. — Cardozo: Federal Trade Comm'n v. Alcoma Lumber Co., 291 U.S. 67, 81.

4. Upon the very same state of facts, an intelligent man, acting deliberately, might well be regarded as guilty of fraud, and an ignorant and inexperienced person might be entitled to a more charitable view.—Shiras: Wasatch Min. Co. v. Crescent Min. Co., 148 U.S. 293, 298.

5. It is a question of how strong an infusion of fraud is necessary to turn a flavor into a poison.—Holmes: International News Serv. v. Assoc. Press, 248 U.S. 235, 247.

6. The phases of fraud are manifold.—Cardozo: Sleicher v. Sleicher, 251 N.Y. 366, 371.

7. A representation may be morally innocent, and yet fraudulent in theory of law.—Holmes: *The Common Law*, 325.

8. The state of one's mind is a fact as capable of fraudulent misrepresentation as is one's physical condition or the state of his bodily health.—Stone: United States v. Ballard, 322 U.S. 78, 90.

9. I do not know what degree of skepticism or disbelief in a religious representation amounts to actionable fraud.—Stone: *ibid.*, 93.

10. The traditional badges of fraud are spread over the transaction in prodigal profusion.—Cardozo: Brody v. Pecoraro, 250 N.Y. 56, 61.

11. Deceit is not put beyond the power of the state because the cheat

is a laborer nor because the device for swindling is an agreement to labor.—Jackson: Pollock v. Williams, 322 U.S. 4, 24.

12. No fraud is more odious than an attempt to subvert the administration of justice.—Roberts: Hazel-Atlas Glass Co. v. Hartford-Empire Co., 322 U.S. 238, 251.

13. Fraud vitiates nearly every form of conduct affected by its taint.—Cardozo: Smyth v. United States, 302 U.S. 329, 358.

14. The Constitution of the United States does not secure to any one the privilege of defrauding the public.—Harlan: Plumley v. Massachusetts, 155 U.S. 461, 479.

15. I doubt if the vigilance of the law is equal to making money stick by over-credulous people.—Jackson: United States v. Ballard, 322 U.S. 78, 94.

16. The belief that their affected ignorance, or the impudence of the fraud, would screen them from the penalties of the laws.—Johnson: The Arrogante Barcelones, 7 Wheat. (20 U.S.) 496, 518.

17. Men do not perpetrate frauds upon the revenue from the mere love of mischief, or the wanton disregard of duty.—Story: The Apollon, 9 Wheat. (22 U.S.) 362, 443.

18. The elusiveness of a fraud well concocted and unsuspected while going on. . . .—Lurton: United States v. Carter, 217 U.S. 286, 302.

19. Mute and helpless victims of deception and fraud.—Black: Hazel-Atlas Glass Co. v. Hartford-Empire Co., 322 U.S. 238, 246.

Related subjects; Falsity and related subjects. *See also* Concealment 3; Device 1; Disloyalty 1; Evidence 27; Expert 6; Marriage 7; Moral turpitude 2; Speculation (financial) 1; Will 4.

FREEDOM (liberty)

Defined, scope 1–10; limitations 11–30; history 31–35; requirements 36–46; assembly 47–48; speech, importance 49–60, permissible 61–87, limitations 88–110; religion 111–131; belief 132–140; conscience 141–144; thought 145–157; learning 158–159; petition 160-162; privacy 163–165; press 166–176; contract 177–180; miscellaneous 181–190.

Related subjects: Advocacy; Association; Bill of Rights; Citizen; Constitution (U.S.), First Amendment, Fourteenth Amendment; Constitutional adjudication; Democracy; Democracy (industrial).

———, defined, scope

1. It is merely an example of doing what you want to do, embodied in the word "liberty."—Holmes: Adkins v. Children's Hosp., 261 U.S. 525, 568.

2. The very essence of civil liberty, is the right of every individual to claim the protection of the laws, whenever he receives an injury.—Marshall: Marbury v. Madison, 1 Cranch (5 U.S.) 137, 163.

3. The very idea that one man may be compelled to hold his life, or the means of living, or any material right essential to the enjoyment of life, at the mere will of another, seems to be intolerable in any country where freedom prevails, as being the essence of slavery itself.—Matthews: Yick Wo v. Hopkins, 118 U.S. 350, 370.

4. Life, liberty, and property stand upon equal grounds in the just estimate of freemen; and one becomes almost worthless without the security of the others.—Story: *Misc. Writings,* 152.

5. Freedom of speech, freedom of the press, and freedom of religion all have a double aspect—freedom of thought and freedom of action.—Murphy: Jones v. Opelika, 316 U.S. 584, 618.

6. Personal freedom has at least as much constitutional dignity as property.—Douglas: Ullman v. United States, 350 U.S. 422, 443.

7. But freedom to differ is not limited to things that do not matter much. That would be a mere shadow of freedom. The test of its substance is the right to differ as to things that touch the heart of the existing order. —Jackson: West Va. State Bd. of Educ. v. Barnette, 319 U.S. 624, 642.

8. Liberty under law extends to the full range of conduct which the individual is free to pursue.—Warren: Bolling v. Sharpe, 347 U.S. 497, 499.

9. All declare for liberty and proceed to disagree among themselves as to its true meaning.—Reed: Breard v. Alexandria, 341 U.S. 622, 625.

10. Among the liberties of the citizens that are guaranteed by the Fourteenth Amendment are those contained in the First Amendment. . . . These include the right to believe what one chooses, the right to differ from his neighbor, the right to pick and choose the political philosophy that he likes best, the right to associate with whomever he chooses, the right to join the groups he prefers, the privilege of selecting his own path to salvation.—Douglas: Lerner v. Casey, 357 U.S. 468, 409, 412-13.

————, limitations

11. Complete freedom—unfettered and undirected—there never is.—Cardozo: *Growth of the Law,* 61.

12. Narrow at best is any freedom that is allotted to us.—Cardozo: *ibid.*

13. The Constitution does not recognize an absolute and uncontrollable liberty.—Hughes: West Coast Hotel Co. v. Parrish, 300 U.S. 379, 391.

14. The Constitutional guaranties of personal liberty are not always absolutes. Government has a right to survive and powers conferred upon it are not necessarily set at naught by the express prohibitions of the Bill of Rights.—Stone: Minersville School Dist. v. Gobitis, 310 U.S. 586, 602.

15. Liberty can be pushed to a point at which liberty is destroyed.—Cardozo: *Paradoxes,* 120.

16. Liberty regulated by law is the underlying principle of our institutions. — Harlan: Sparf v. United States, 156 U.S. 51, 103.

17. Freedom is the general rule, and restraint the exception.—Van Devanter: Wolff Packing Co. v. Court of Ind. Rel. 267 U.S. 552, 566.

18. Liberty implies only freedom from arbitrary restraint. — Stone: Hardware Dealer's Mut. Fire Ins. Co. v. Glidden Co., 284 U.S. 151, 157.

19. Liberty as a legal concept contains an underlying paradox. Liberty

in the most literal sense is the negation of law, for law is restraint, and the absence of restraint is anarchy. On the other hand, anarchy by destroying restraint would leave liberty the exclusive possession of the strong or the unscrupulous.—Cardozo: *Paradoxes,* 94.

20. Unsocial freedom is the right of a man to use his powers without regard to the wishes and interests of any one except himself. Such freedom is theoretically possible for an individual. It is antithetic to all public control. It is theoretically impossible for a plurality of individuals living in mutual contact.—Cardozo: *ibid.,* 118.

21. Liberty in the literal sense is desired only by the anarchists.—Cardozo: *ibid.,* 6.

22. Liberty is an attractive theme, but the liberty which is exercised in sheer antipathy does not plead strongly for recognition.—McKenna: Adair v. United States, 208 U.S. 161, 186.

23. To use the words of one of the supporters of the Constitution, "the natural order of things is for liberty to yield and for government to gain ground."—McKenna: Block v. Hirsh, 256 U.S. 135, 163.

24. Some compromise is inevitable between liberty and license. — Cardozo: *Growth of the Law,* 75.

25. We are to reconcile liberty with equality, and both of them with order.—Cardozo: *Paradoxes,* 5.

26. There is no basis for saying that freedom and order are not compatible. That would be a decision of des-

peration. — Reed: Poulos v. New Hampshire, 345 U.S. 395, 408.

27. The choice is not between order and liberty. It is between liberty with order and anarchy without either.—Jackson: Terminiello v. Chicago, 337 U.S. 1, 37.

28. No liberty is made more secure by holding that its abuses are inseparable from its enjoyment.—Jackson: *ibid.*

29. Suppression has never been a successful permanent policy; any surface serenity that it creates is a false security.—Jackson: *ibid.,* 36.

30. Every agreement curtails the liberty of those who enter into it.—Brandeis: Hitchman Coal & Coke Co. v. Mitchell, 245 U.S. 229, 270.

———, history

31. Man's struggle for freedom in the western world has largely been an effort to be free from the inquisition.—Douglas: *We the Judges,* 441.

32. Those who won our independence had confidence in the power of free and fearless reasoning and communication of ideas to discover and spread political and economic truth. Noxious doctrines in those fields may be refuted and their evil averted by the courageous exercise of the right of free discussion.—Murphy: Thornhill v. Alabama, 310 U.S. 88, 95.

33. History teaches us that there have been but few infringements of personal liberty by the state which have not been justified, . . . in the name of righteousness and the public

good, and few which have not been directed, as they are now, at politically helpless minorities.—Stone: Minersville School Dist. v. Gobitis, 310 U.S. 586, 604.

34. It is fair summary of history to say that the safeguards of liberty have frequently been forged in controversies involving not very nice people. —Frankfurter: United States v. Rabinowitz, 339 U.S. 56, 69.

35. History indicates that individual liberty is intermittently subjected to extraordinary perils. Even countries dedicated to government by the people are not free from such cyclical dangers.—Black: Wieman v. Updegraff, 344 U.S. 183, 192.

———, requirements

36. The cardinal precept upon which the constitutional safeguards of personal liberty ultimately rest— that this shall be a government of laws. —Sutherland: Jones v. SEC, 298 U.S. 1, 23.

37. Civil liberties had their origin and must find their ultimate guaranty in the faith of the people.—Jackson: Douglas v. Jeannette, 319 U.S. 157, 182.

38. Our liberty is maintained only so long as justice is secure.—Clark: Rosenberg v. United States, 346 U.S. 271, 296.

39. My belief is that we must have freedom of speech, press and religion for all or we may eventually have it for none.—Black: Carlson v. Landon, 342 U.S. 524, 555.

40. Experience should teach us to be most on our guard to protect liberty when the government's purposes are beneficent. Men born to freedom are naturally alert to repel invasion of their liberty by evil-minded rulers. The greatest dangers to liberty lurk in insidious encroachment by men of zeal, well-meaning, but without understanding.—Brandeis: Olmstead v. United States, 277 U.S. 438, 479.

41. The virtue and talents of the members of the general government will tend to the security instead of the destruction of our liberty.—Marshall: Beveridge, *Life of Marshall*, I, 419.

42. It is utterly impossible, that real liberty can long remain among a people sunk in vice and indifferent to crimes. The forms and shadows of its institutions may remain, to deceive the idle spectator; but that spirit, which can alone quicken into life the principles of freedom, is gone for ever. —Story: *Misc. Writings,* 351.

43. The strength of this nation is weakened more by those who suppress the freedom of others than by those who are allowed freely to think and act as their consciences dictate.—Murphy: Bridges v. Wixon, 326 U.S. 135, 165.

44. Only by zealously guarding the rights of the most humble, the most unorthodox and the most despised among us can freedom flourish and endure in our land.—Murphy: *ibid.,* 166.

45. Personal liberty is a poor and shrunken thing, incapable of satisfying our aspirations or our wants, if it does not exact as its minimal require-

ment that there shall be the maintenance of opportunity for the growth of personality.—Cardozo: *Paradoxes,* 103–104.

46. In breaking one set of shackles, we are not to substitute another.—Cardozo: *Growth of the Law,* 10.

———, assembly

47. The very idea of a government, republican in form, implies a right on the part of its citizens to meet peaceably for consultation in respect to public affairs and to petition for a redress of grievances.—Waite: United States v. Cruikshank, 2 Otto (92 U.S.) 542, 552.

48. Freedom of assembly and freedom of speech, indeed, go hand in hand. Abuse of freedom of assembly, as for example, inciting a riot, can be curtailed. But the right itself cannot be.—Douglas: *We the Judges,* 319.

———, speech, importance

49. Full and free discussion had indeed been the first article of our faith. We have founded our political system on it. It has been the safeguard of every religious, political, philosophical, economic, and racial group amongst us. We have counted on it to keep us from embracing what is cheap and false; we have trusted the common sense of our people to choose the doctrine true to our genius and to reject the rest.—Douglas: Dennis v. United States, 341 U.S. 494, 584–85.

50. Our Constitution assumes that the common sense of the people and their attachment to our country will enable them, after free discussion, to withstand ideas that are wrong.—Black: Barenblatt v. United States, 360 U.S. 109, 146.

51. Like the course of the heavenly bodies, harmony in national life is a resultant of the struggle between contending forces. In frank expression of conflicting opinion lies the greatest promise of wisdom in governmental action; and in suppression lies ordinarily the greatest peril.—Brandeis: Gilbert v. Minnesota, 254 U.S. 325, 338.

52. Because freedom of public expression alone assures the unfolding of truth, it is indispensable to the democratic process. — Frankfurter: Bridges v. California, 314 U.S. 252, 293.

53. Freedom of expression is the well-spring of our civilization.—Frankfurter: Dennis v. United States, 341 U.S. 494, 550.

54. The principle of "the consent of the governed" would have no meaning if public discussion were banned.—Douglas: *We the Judges,* 353.

55. Our whole history teaches that adjustment of social relations through reason is possible while free speech is maintained.—Reed: Milk Wagon Drivers Union v. Meadowmoor Dairies, 312 U.S. 287, 320.

56. Of that freedom [of thought, speech] one may say that it is the matrix, the indispensable condition, of nearly every other form of freedom. With rare aberrations a pervasive recognition of that truth can be traced in our history, political and

legal.—Cardozo: Palko v. Connecticut, 302 U.S. 319, 327.

57. Without freedom of expression, thought becomes checked and atrophied.—Frankfurter: Kovacs v. Cooper, 336 U.S. 77, 95.

58. Free speech and fair trials are two of the most cherished policies of our civilization, and it would be a trying task to choose between them.—Black: Bridges v. California, 314 U.S. 252, 260.

59. We must have freedom of speech for all or we will in the long run have it for none but the cringing and the craven.—Black: Wieman v. Updegraff, 344 U.S. 183, 193.

60. The First Amendment and the Fourteenth Amendment, insofar as it protects freedom of speech are no exception to the law of life enunciated by Ecclesiastes: "For everything there is a season, and a time for every purpose under Heaven."—Frankfurter: *In re* Sawyer, 360 U.S. 622, 666.

———, speech, permissible

61. Time, place and circumstances determine the constitutional protection of utterance.—Frankfurter: *ibid*.

62. The First Amendment . . . protects the impassioned plea of the orator as much as the quiet publication of the tabulations of the statistician or economist. — Douglas: United States v. UAW, 352 U.S. 567, 595.

63. One has a right to freedom of speech whether he talks to one person or to one thousand. One has a right to freedom of speech not only when he talks to his friends but also when he talks to the public.—Douglas: *ibid*.

64. These days free speech includes more than talk to a crowd from a platform. It includes the movies, radio and television.—Douglas: *We the Judges,* 319.

65. Freedom of speech in America is not reserved for a select few. It extends to labor as well as capital, to farmers as well as to merchants, to socialists and communists as well as to republicans and democrats, to Catholics as well as to Protestants.—Douglas: *ibid*.

66. The authors of the First Amendment knew that novel and unconventional ideas might disturb the complacent, but they chose to encourage a freedom which they believed essential if vigorous enlightenment was ever to triumph over slothful ignorance.—Black: Martin v. Struthers, 319 U.S. 141, 143.

67. I do not suppose that anyone would say that the freedom of written speech is less protected by the First Amendment than the freedom of spoken words.—Holmes: Leach v. Carlile, 258 U.S. 138, 140.

68. Wholly neutral futilities, of course, come under the protection of free speech as fully as do Keats' poems or Donne's sermons.—Frankfurter: Winters v. New York, 333 U.S. 507, 528.

69. One of the prerogatives of American citizenship is the right to criticize public men and measures—and that means not only informed and responsible criticism but the freedom to speak foolishly and without moder-

171

ation.—Frankfurter: Baumgartner v. United States, 322 U.S. 665, 673–74.

70. The First Amendment means to me ... that the only constitutional way our Government can preserve itself is to leave its people the fullest possible freedom to praise, criticize or discuss, as they see fit, all governmental policies and to suggest, if they desire, that even its most fundamental postulates are bad and should be c h a n g e d. — Black: Barenblatt v. United States, 360 U.S. 109, 145–46.

71. Freedom to speak and write about public questions is as important to the life of our government as is the heart to the human body. In fact, this privilege is the heart of our government. If that heart be weakened, the result is debilitation; if it be stilled, the result is death.—Black: Milk Wagon Drivers Union v. Meadowmoor Dairies, 312 U.S. 287, 302.

72. It is the legal right of any American citizen to advocate a peaceful adoption of fascism or communism, socialism or capitalism. He may go far in expressing sentiments whether pro-semitic or anti-semitic, pro-negro, or anti-negro, pro-Catholic or anti-Catholic. He is legally free to argue for some anti-American system of government to supersede by constitutional methods the one we have. It is our philosophy that the course of government should be controlled by a consensus of the governed.—Jackson: Terminiello v. Chicago, 337 U.S. 1, 32.

73. The First Amendment is a charter for government, not for an institution of learning. "Free trade in ideas" means free trade in the opportunity to persuade to action, not merely to describe facts. — Rutledge: Thomas v. Collins, 323 U.S. 516, 537.

74. A function of free speech under our system of government is to invite dispute. It may indeed best serve its high purpose when it induces a condition of unrest, creates dissatisfaction with conditions as they are, or even stirs people to anger. Speech is often provocative and challenging. It may strike at prejudices and preconceptions and have profound unsettling effects as it presses for acceptance of an idea. — Douglas: Terminiello v. Chicago, 337 U.S. 1, 4.

75. Freedom of speech undoubtedly means freedom to express views that challenge deep-seated, sacred beliefs and to utter sentiments that may provoke resentment.—Frankfurter: *ibid.,* 11.

76. Nor should restrictions be permitted that cramp the feeling of freedom in the use of tongue or pen regardless of the temper or the truth of what may be uttered.—Frankfurter: Bridges v. California, 314 U.S. 252, 291.

77. Bigamy may be outlawed; but the discussion of it, even its defense as a religious custom, may not be made illegal. — Douglas: *We the Judges,* 309.

78. Too many settled beliefs have in time been rejected to justify this generation in refusing a hearing to its own dissentients.—Reed: Jones v. Opelika, 316 U.S. 584, 594.

79. The channels of inquiry and

thought must be kept open to new conquests of reason, however odious their expression may be to the prevailing climate of opinion.—Frankfurter: Bridges v. California, 314 U.S. 252, 282.

80. We do not lose our right to condemn either measures or men because the country is at war.—Holmes: Frohwerk v. United States, 249 U.S. 204, 208.

81. As against dangers peculiar to war, as against others, the principle of the right to free speech is always the same. — Holmes: Abrams v. United States, 250 U.S. 616-28.

82. Fear of serious injury cannot alone justify suppression of free speech and assembly. Men feared witches and burned women. It is the function of speech to free men from bondage of irrational fears.—Brandeis v. California, 274 U.S. 357, 376.

83. The naturalized citizen has as much right as the natural born citizen to exercise the cherished freedoms of speech, press and religion.—Murphy: Baumgartner v. United States, 322 U.S. 665, 679-80.

84. The right to speak one's mind would often be an empty privilege in a place and at a time beyond the protecting hand of the guardians of public order.—Reed: Kovacs v. Cooper, 336 U.S. 77, 86.

85. Where conduct is within the allowable limits of free speech, the police are peace officers for the speaker as well as for his hearers. — Frankfurter: Niemotko v. Maryland, 340 U.S. 268, 289.

86. Silencing a speaker by authorities as a measure of mob control, is like dynamiting a house to stop the spread of conflagration. . . . But this kind of disorder does not abridge the right to speak except for the emergency.—Jackson: Kunz v. New York, 340 U.S. 290, 301-302.

87. No one may be required to obtain a license in order to speak. . . . As long as he does no more than speak he has the same unfettered right, no matter what side of an issue he espouses.—Douglas: Thomas v. Collins, 323 U.S. 516, 543-44.
See also Censor, 8, 13; Constitution 103; Criticism 6.

———, speech, limitations
88. Freedom of speech exists only under law and not independently of it.—Jackson: Terminiello v. Chicago, 337 U.S. 1, 31.

89. Free speech is the rule, not the e x c e p t i o n. — Douglas: Dennis v. United States, 341 U.S. 494, 585.

90. Even juristic or philosophic authority recognized in this field admits that there are some speeches one is not free to make.—Jackson: Kunz v. New York, 340 U.S. 290, 300.

91. The First Amendment, while prohibiting legislation against free speech as such, cannot have been, and obviously was not, intended to give immunity for every possible use of language. — Holmes: Frohwerk v. United States, 249 U.S. 204, 206.

92. The liberty that is assured to us is not liberty to act. It is liberty to think and speak. Thought and speech in certain contexts may be equivalent

to acts. When this boundary is reached, we reach the limit of immunity.—Cardozo: *Paradoxes,* 112.

93. Utterance in a context of violence can lose its significance as an appeal to reason and become part of an instrument of force.—Frankfurter: Milk Wagon Drivers Union v. Meadowmoor Dairies, 312 U.S. 287, 293.

94. We should be eternally vigilant against attempts to check the expression of opinions that we loathe and believe to be fraught with death, unless they so imminently threaten immediate interference with the lawful and pressing purposes of the law that an immediate check is required to save the country.—Holmes: Abrams v. United States, 250 U.S. 616, 630.

95. The most stringent protection of free speech would not protect a man in falsely shouting fire in a theater, and causing a panic.—Holmes: Schenck v. United States, 249 U.S. 47, 52.

96. The petitioner may have a constitutional right to talk politics, but he has no constitutional right to be a policeman. There are few employments for hire in which the servant does not agree to suspend his constitutional rights of free speech as well as of idleness by the implied terms of his contract.—Holmes: McAuliffe v. New Bedford, 155 Mass. 216, 220.

97. We venture to believe that neither Hamilton nor Madison, nor any other competent person then or later, ever supposed that to make criminal the counseling of a murder within the jurisdiction of Congress would be an unconstitutional interference with free speech.—Holmes: Frohwerk v. United States, 249 U.S. 204, 206.

98. Free speech is essential to a republic, but free speech without the insistent demand by the community for fair speech is the opportunity of rogues and demagogues. — Hughes: Pusey, *Hughes,* 393.

99. In securing freedom of speech, the Constitution hardly meant to create the right to influence judges or juries. That is no more freedom of speech than stuffing a ballot box is an exercise of the right to vote.—Frankfurter: Pennekamp v. Florida, 328 U.S. 331, 366.

100. We should weigh the value of insulting speech against its potentiality for harm.—Jackson: Kunz v. New York, 340 U.S. 290, 302.

101. A hostile reception of his subject certainly does not alone destroy one's right to speak.—Jackson: *ibid.,* 301.

102. When a nation is at war many things that might be said in time of peace are such a hindrance to its effort that their utterance will not be endured so long as men fight, and . . . no court could regard them as protected by any constitutional right.—Holmes: Schenck v. United States, 249 U.S. 47, 52.

103. Censorship or suppression of expression of opinion is tolerated by our Constitution only when the expression presents a clear and present danger of action of a kind the State is empowered to prevent and punish.

—Jackson: West Va. State Bd. of Educ. v. Barnette, 319 U.S. 624, 633.

104. Just as there are those who regard as invulnerable every measure for which the claim of national survival is invoked, there are those who find in the Constitution a wholly unfettered right of expression.—Frankfurter: Dennis v. United States, 341 U.S. 494, 521.

105. When legislation touches freedom of thought and freedom of speech, such a tendency is a formidable enemy of the free spirit. —Frankfurter: *ibid.*, 556.

106. By adjustment of rights, we can have both full liberty of expression and an orderly life.—Reed: Breard v. Alexandria, 341 U.S. 622, 642.

107. Adjustment of the inevitable conflict between free speech and other interests is a problem as persistent as it is perplexing.—Frankfurter: Niemotko v. Maryland, 340 U.S. 268, 275.

108. Speech can be effectively limited by the exercise of the taxing power.—Brennan: Speiser v. Randall, 357 U.S. 513, 518.

109. The Constitution says nothing about the freedom of anonymous speech.—Clark: Talley v. California, 362 U.S. 60, 70.

110. The public has some rights against which the enforcement of freedom of speech would be "harsh and arbitrary in itself."—Clark: *ibid.*, 71.

See also Labor, disputes, communication; Label 2, 3; Mail 2; Radio 6; Street 3.

———, religion

111. The great truth . . . that religious freedom is the birthright of man . . . and that to worship God according to our own belief is not only our privilege, but it is our duty. . . . —Story: *Misc. Writings,* 61.

112. Official compulsion to affirm what is contrary to one's religious beliefs is the antithesis of freedom of worship.—Murphy: West Va. State Bd. of Educ. v. Barnette, 319 U.S. 624, 646.

113. Like St. Paul's freedom, religious liberty with a great price must be bought.—Rutledge: Everson v. Bd. of Educ., 330 U.S. 1, 59.

114. State power is no more to be used so as to handicap religions than it is to favor them.—Black: *ibid.*, 18.

115. The right given by the First and Fourteenth Amendments freely to practice and proclaim one's religious convictions . . . extends to the aggressive and disputatious as well as to the meek and acquiescent.—Murphy: Martin v. Struthers, 319 U.S. 141, 149.

116. The protection of the First Amendment is not restricted to orthodox religious practices any more than it is to the expression of orthodox economic views.—Douglas: Follett v. McCormick, 321 U.S. 573, 577.

117. Freedom of thought, which includes freedom of religious belief, is basic in a society of free men. . . . It embraces the right to maintain theories of life and of death and of the hereafter which are rank heresy to followers of the orthodox faith.—

Douglas: United States v. Ballard, 322 U.S. 78, 86.

118. The realm of religious training and belief remains, as the Amendment made it, the kingdom of the individual man and his God.—Rutledge: Everson v. Bd. of Educ., 330 U.S. 1, 57–58.

119. The First Amendment . . . does not say that in every and all respects there shall be a separation of Church and State. Rather, it studiously defines the manner, the specific ways, in which there shall be no concert or union or dependency one on the other. That is the common sense of the matter.—Douglas: Zorach v. Clauson, 343 U.S. 306, 312.

120. One cannot speak of religious liberty, with proper appreciation of its essential and historic significance, without assuming the existence of a belief in supreme allegiance to the will of God.—Hughes: United States v. Macintosh, 283 U.S. 605, 634.

121. The day that this country ceases to be free for irreligion it will cease to be free for religion—except for the sect that can win political power.—Jackson: Zorach v. Clauson, 343 U.S. 306, 325.

122. We have staked the very existence of our country on the faith that complete separation between the state and religion is best for the state and best for religion.—Rutledge: Everson v. Bd. of Educ., 330 U.S. 1, 59.

123. Religion is outside the sphere of political government.—Frankfurter: West Va. State Bd. of Educ. v. Barnette, 319 U.S. 624, 654.

124. If nowhere else, in the relation between Church and State, "good fences make good neighbors." — Frankfurter: Illinois v. Bd. of Educ., 333 U.S. 203, 232.

125. We do not intimate or suggest . . . that any conduct can be made a religious rite and by the zeal of the practitioners swept into the First Amendment.—Douglas: Murdock v. Pennsylvania, 319 U.S. 105, 109.

126. No doubt the Thugs of India imagined that their belief in the right of assassination was a religious belief; but their thinking so did not make it so. The practice of suttee by the Hindu widows may have sprung from a supposed religious conviction. . . . But no one, on that account, would hesitate to brand these practices, now, as crimes against society, and obnoxious to condemnation and punishment by the civil authority.—Bradley: Late Corp. of Latter Day Saints v. United States, 136 U.S. 1, 49–50.

127. Crime is not the less odious because sanctioned by what any particular sect may designate as religion.—Field: Davis v. Beason, 133 U.S. 333, 342–43.

128. One would not be justified in ignoring the familiar red traffic light because he thought it his religious duty to disobey the municipal command or sought by that means to direct public attention to an announcement of his opinions.—Hughes: Cox v. New Hampshire, 312 U.S. 569, 574.

129. The family itself is not beyond regulation in the public interest, as against a claim of religious liberty.

—Rutledge: Prince v. Massachusetts, 321 U.S. 158, 166.

130. The price of freedom of religion or of speech or of the press is that we must put up with and even pay for, a good deal of rubbish.—Jackson: United States v. Ballard, 322 U.S. 78, 95.

131. No chapter in human history has been so largely written in terms of persecution and intolerance as the one dealing with religious freedom. From ancient times to the present day, the ingenuity of man has known no limits in its ability to forge weapons of oppression for use against those who dare to express or practice unorthodox religious beliefs.—Murphy: Prince v. Massachusetts, 321 U.S. 158, 175-76.

See also Heresy 1; Nation (U.S.) 13; Rights 40; Tax 93.

———, belief

132. The great truth . . . that governments have no authority to inflict punishment for conscientious differences of opinion.—Story: Misc. Writings, 61.

133. Any person may . . . believe or disbelieve what he pleases. He may practice what he will in his own house of worship or publicly within the limits of public order. — Frankfurter: West. Va. State Bd. of Educ. v. Barnette, 319 U.S. 624, 654.

134. The liberty of man to search for truth ought not to be fettered, no matter what orthodoxies he may challenge. — Frankfurter: D e n n i s v. United States, 341 U.S. 494, 550.

135. Political beliefs, like religious convictions, are one's own business. One should not be subject to an accounting for anything but his conduct.—Douglas: We the Judges, 441.

136. Delicate must be the scales for the weighing of the interactions between behavior and belief. If the reading of the balance is doubtful, the presumption in favor of liberty should serve to tilt the beam. — Cardozo: Paradoxes, 115.

137. Congress certainly cannot forbid all effort to change the mind of the country.—Holmes: Abrams v. United States, 250 U.S. 616, 628.

138. If power to forbid acts includes power to forbid contemplating them, then the power of government over beliefs is as unlimited as its power over conduct and the way is open to force disclosure of attitudes on all manner of social, economic, moral and political issues.—Jackson: American Com. Assoc. v. Douds, 339 U.S. 382, 438.

139. The Constitution expresses more than the conviction of the people that democratic processes must be preserved at all costs. It is also an expression of faith and a command that freedom of mind and spirit must be preserved, which government must obey, if it is to adhere to that justice and moderation without which no free government can exist.—Stone: Minersville School Dist. v. Gobitis, 310 U.S. 586, 606-607.

140. There are areas where government may not probe. Private citizens, private clubs, private groups may

make such deductions and reach such conclusions as they choose from the failure of a citizen to disclose his beliefs, his philosophy, his associates. But government has no business penalizing a citizen merely for his beliefs or associations.—Douglas: Lerner v. Casey, 357 U.S. 468, 409, 414.

———, conscience

141. Government may enforce obedience to laws regardless of scruples. When one's belief collides with the power of the state, the latter is supreme within its sphere and submission or punishment follows. But, in the forum of conscience, duty to a moral power higher than the state has always been maintained. — Hughes: United States v. Macintosh, 283 U.S. 605, 633.

142. There can be no real freedom unless the conscience is free to express itself and unless man is free to obey its small voice.—Douglas: *We the Judges,* 353.

143. Courts, no more than Constitutions, can intrude into the consciences of men or compel them to believe contrary to their faith or think contrary to their convictions.—Reed: Jones v. Opelika, 316 U.S. 584, 593–94.

144. It may well be questioned whether the State which preserves its life by a settled policy of violation of the conscience of the individual will not in fact ultimately lose it by the process.—Stone: Mason, *Stone,* 108.

———, thought

145. If there is any principle of the Constitution that more imperatively calls for attachment than any other it is the principle of free thought— not free thought for those who agree with us but freedom for the thought that we hate.—Holmes: United States v. Schwimmer, 279 U.S. 644, 654–55.

146. Individual freedom and governmental thought-probing cannot live together. — Black: American Com. Assoc. v. Douds, 339 U.S. 382, 446.

147. Probing into men's thoughts trenches on those aspects of individual freedom which we rightly regard as the most cherished aspects of Western civilization. —Frankfurter: *ibid.,* 421.

148. The priceless heritage of our society is the unrestricted constitutional right of each member to think as he will. Thought control is a copyright of totalitarianism, and we have no claim to it.—Jackson: *ibid.,* 442.

149. The danger that citizens will think wrongly is serious, but less dangerous than atrophy from not thinking at all.—Jackson: *ibid.*

150. Intellectual freedom means the right to re-examine much that has been long taken for granted. A free man must be a reasoning man. And he must dare to doubt what a legislative or electoral majority may most passionately assert.—Jackson: *ibid.*

151. Our forefathers found the evils of free thinking more to be endured than the evils of inquest or suppression.—Jackson: *ibid.*

152. All ideological struggles, religious or political, are primarily battles for dominance over the minds of people.—Jackson: *ibid.,* 438.

153. We must not forget that in our country are evangelists and zealots of many different political, economic and religious persuasions whose fanatical conviction is that all thought is divinely classified into two kinds—that which is their own and that which is false and dangerous.—Jackson: *ibid.*

154. We need be bold and adventuresome in our thinking to survive.—Douglas: Adler v. Bd. of Educ., 342 U.S. 485, 511.

155. Under our Constitution men are punished for what they do or fail to do and not for what they think and believe.—Black: *In re* Summers, 325 U.S. 561, 578.

156. Liberty of thought soon shrivels without freedom of expression.—Frankfurter: Dennis v. United States, 341 U.S. 494, 550.

157. Our Constitution, in unequivocal terms, gives the right to each of us to say what we think without fear of the power of the Government.—Black: Wilkinson v. United States, 365 U.S. 399, 422.

See also Censor 9.

———, learning

158. There is no freedom without choice, and there is no choice without knowledge—or none that is not illusory. Implicit, therefore, in the very notion of liberty is the liberty of the mind to absorb and to beget. . . . At the root of all liberty is the liberty to know.—Cardozo: *Paradoxes,* 104.

159. The Constitution guarantees freedom of thought and expression to everyone in our society. All are entitled to it; and none needs it more than the teacher.—Douglas: Adler v. Bd. of Educ., 342 U.S. 485, 508.

———, petition

160. In a representative democracy such as this . . . the whole concept of representation depends upon the ability of the people to make their wishes known to their representatives.—Black: Eastern R.R. Conf. v. Noerr Motor Fr., 365 U.S. 127, 137.

161. The right of the people to inform their representatives in government of their desires with respect to the passage or enforcement of laws cannot properly be made to depend upon their intent in doing so. It is neither unusual nor illegal for people to seek action on laws in the hope that they may bring about an advantage to themselves and a disadvantage to their competitors. . . . Indeed, it is quite probably people with just such a hope of personal advantage who provide much of the information upon which governments must act.—Black: *ibid.,* 137.

162. The right of petition is one of the freedoms protected by the Bill of Rights.—Black: *ibid.,* 138.

———, privacy

163. Men cannot enjoy their right to personal f r e e d o m if fanatical masses, whatever their mission, can strangle individual thoughts and invade personal privacy. — Jackson: American Com. Assoc. v. Douds, 339 U.S. 382, 444.

164. The right to be let alone is

indeed the beginning of all freedom. —Douglas: Public Util. Comm'n v. Pollak, 343 U.S. 451, 467.

165. Inviolability of privacy in group association may in many circumstances be indispensable to preservation of freedom of association particularly where a group espouses dissident beliefs.—Douglas: Uphaus v. Wyman, 364 U.S. 388, 406.

———, press

166. Among those p r i n c i p l e s deemed sacred in America ... there is no one ... more deeply impressed on the public mind, than the liberty of the press. That this liberty is often carried to excess, that it has sometimes degenerated into licentiousness, is seen and lamented; but the remedy has not been discovered. Perhaps it is an evil inseparable from the good with which it is allied.—Marshall: Beveridge, *Life of Marshall,* II, 329–30.

167. No man can now doubt the fact, that wherever the press is free, it will emancipate the people; wherever knowledge circulates unrestrained it is no longer safe to oppress; wherever public opinion is enlightened, it nourishes an independent, masculine, and healthful spirit.—Story: *Misc. Writings, 7.*

168. A free press stands as one of the great interpreters between the government and the people. To allow it to be fettered is to fetter ourselves.—Sutherland: Grosjean v. Am. Press Co., 297 U.S. 233, 250.

169. Freedom of the press ... is not an end in itself but a means to the end of a free society.—Frankfurter: Pennekamp v. Florida, 328 U.S. 331, 354–55.

170. The purpose of the Constitution was not to erect the press into a privileged institution but to protect all persons in their right to print what they will as well as to utter it.—Frankfurter: *ibid.,* 364.

171. In plain English, freedom carries with it responsibility even for the press; freedom of the press is not a freedom from responsibility for its exercise.—Frankfurter: *ibid.,* 356.

172. One of the potent means for assuring judges their independence is a free press.—Frankfurter: *ibid.,* 355.

173. Liberty of circulation is the very life blood of a free press.—Murphy: Jones v. Opelika, 316 U.S. 584, 616.

174. The liberty of the press ... necessarily embraces pamphlets and leaflets. These indeed have been historic weapons in the defense of liberty, as the pamphlets of Thomas Paine and others in our own history abundantly attest.—Hughes: Lovell v. Griffin, 303 U.S. 444, 452.

175. Liberty of circulating is as essential to that freedom as liberty of publishing; indeed, without the circulation, the publication would be of little value.—Field: *Ex parte* Jackson, 6 Otto (96 U.S.) 727, 728–29.

176. Anonymous pamphlets, leaflets, brochures and even books have played an important role in the progress of mankind. Persecuted groups

180

and sects from time to time throughout history have been able to criticize oppressive practices and laws either anonymously or not at all.—Black: Talley v. California, 362 U.S. 60, 64.

See also Rights 40.

———, contract

177. Freedom of contract, from the very nature of the thing, can be enjoyed only by being exercised; and each particular exercise of it involves making an engagement which, if fulfilled, prevents for the time any inconsistent course of conduct.—Pitney: Coppage v. Kansas, 236 U.S. 1, 21.

178. The right of an individual or a corporation to make an unwise bargain is as complete as that to make a wise bargain.—Hunt: Jeffries v. Econ. Mut. Life Ins. Co., 22 Wall. (89 U.S.) 47, 53.

179. Illegality apart, a man may make himself answerable in damages for the happening or not happening of what event he likes. — Holmes: Beasley v. Texas & Pac. Ry., 191 U.S. 492, 497.

180. There is grim irony in speaking of the freedom of contract of those who, because of their economic necessities, give their service for less than is needful to keep body and soul together.—Stone: Morehead v. New York, 298 U.S. 587, 632.

———, miscellaneous

181. We shall remain free if we do not deserve to be slaves.—Marshall: Beveridge, *Life of Marshall,* II, 353.

182. There can be no independent action without a freedom of the will.

—McLean: Fox v. State of Ohio, 5 How. (46 U.S.) 410, 436.

183. I . . . probably take the extremest view in favor of free speech, in which, in the abstract, I have no very enthusiastic belief, though I hope I would die for it.—Holmes: *Holmes-Pollock Letters,* II, 29.

184. The value of their freedom is not susceptible of a pecuniary valuation.—Thompson: Lee v. Lee, 8 Pet. (33 U.S.) 44, 48.

185. The longing for freedom is ineradicable. It will express itself in protest against servitude and inaction unless the striving for freedom be made to seem immoral.—Brandeis: *Other People's Money,* 31.

186. There are some who think that the way to save freedom in this country is to adopt the technique of tyranny.—Warren: Jay v. Boyd, 351 U.S. 345, 367.

187. There are many appeals these days to liberty, often by those who are working for an opportunity to taunt democracy with its stupidity in furnishing them the weapons to destroy it.—Jackson: Terminiello v. Chicago, 337 U.S. 1, 35.

188. Freedom of speech, freedom of the press, freedom of religion are available to all, not merely to those who can pay their own way.—Douglas: Murdock v. Pennsylvania, 319 U.S. 105, 111.

189. Experience should teach us to be most on our guard to protect liberty when the Government's purposes are beneficent.—Brandeis: Olmstead v. United States, 277 U.S. 438, 479.

190. There are grim reminders all around this world that the distance between individual liberty and firing squads is not always as far as it seems. —Black: Braden v. United States, 365 U.S. 431, 445–46.

> See also Censor 13; Constitution 103, 104; Constitutional law; Debtor 7; Deportation 4; Discretion 8, 9; Due process; Election; Government 15; History 4; Idea 3; Independence 2; Military 5; Mob 1, 3; Ocean 4; Occupation; Police 2; Property 28; Public official 21; Rights 19; School 2; Security 2; Travel; War 26, 40.

FRICTION
See Authority 1.

FRIEND, FRIENDSHIP
See Credit; Notice 2.

FULFILLMENT
Fulfillment may fall short of expectation.—Cardozo: Walton Water Co. v. Village of Walton, 238 N.Y. 46, 51.

FUNGIBLE
See Dollar.

FUTILITY
Why should we employ the energy that is furnished to us by the cosmos to defy it and shake our fist at the sky? It seems to me silly.—Holmes: "Natural Law," 32 Harv. L. Rev. 40, 43.

> *See also* Scrutiny 2.

FUTURE
The important thing now is the future, not the past. — Brandeis: Mason, *Brandeis,* 213.

> *See also* Judgment 9; Value 11, 24–26.

FUTURES (trading)
See Speculation 4.

GADGET
See Patent 9.

GAMBLE
1. The event is none the less uncertain, that the chances of the event are certain. The chances only represent the average of a long series of events.—Holmes: Commonwealth v. Wright, 137 Mass. 250, 251.

2. He b l a m e d the situation on "chance." But the fickle goddess is hardly to be blamed for the result when it can be seen that the cards were stacked from the beginning.— Jackson: Frazier v. United States, 335 U.S. 457, 517.

> Related subjects: Chance; Danger; Hazard; Lottery; Risk; Speculation (financial); Venture; Wager. *See also* Fact 13; Insurance 5, 10; Punishment 39.

GASLIGHT
See Crime 16.

GENERALITY, GENERALIZATION
1. To generalize is to omit.— Holmes: Donnell v. Herring Co., 208 U.S. 267, 273.

2. It has become an aphorism that there is danger in generalities.—McKenna: United States v. U. S. Steel Corp., 251 U.S. 417, 448.

3. Too broadly generalized conceptions are a constant source of fallacy. —Holmes: Lorenzo v. Wirth, 170 Mass. 596, 600.

4. The generalizing principle will prevail, as generalization so often prevails, even in advance of evidence, because of the ease of mind and comfort which it brings.—Holmes: "Law in

Science and Science in Law," 12 Harv. L. Rev. 451.

5. The danger of reasoning from generalizations unless you have the particulars which they embrace in mind.—Holmes: *ibid.*, 461.

6. A generalization is empty so far as it is general. Its value depends on the number of particulars which it calls up to the speaker and the hearer. —Holmes: *ibid.*

7. For the incompetent, it sometimes is true, as has been said, that an interest in general ideas means an absence of particular knowledge. — Holmes: "The Path of the Law, 10 Harv. L. Rev. 477.

8. The men who teach us to disbelieve general propositions are only less valuable than those who encourage us to make them.—Holmes: *Uncollected Letters*, 173.

9. All these generalities are as easy as they are obvious, but, alas! the implication is an ordeal to try the souls of men.—Cardozo: *Law and Literature*, 8.

10. Modern scholarship warns us to swallow with a grain of salt these sweeping generalities, yet they have at least a core of truth.—Cardozo: *ibid.*, 70.

11. General terms get precision from the sense and experience of men, and become certain and useful guides in reasoning and conduct.—McKenna: Mutual Film Corp. v. Industrial Comm'n, 236 U.S. 230, 246.

12. Ignorance or indolence may take shelter behind generalities.— —Cardozo: *Growth of the Law*, 59.

13. There may be more of honest truth in the inspiring generality than in many an arid phrase of a colder, if exacter, science.—Cardozo: *ibid.*, 142.

14. Ambiguity lurks in generality and may thus become an instrument of severity. — Frankfurter: McComb v. Jacksonville Power Co., 336 U.S. 187, 197.

15. Formulas embodying vague and uncritical generalizations offer tempting opportunities to evade the need for continuous thought.—Frankfurter: Pennekamp v. Florida, 328 U.S. 331, 351.

Related subject: Abstraction. *See also* Constitution 50; Jury 40; Moral 3; Rule 12; Truth 6, 7.

GENERAL WELFARE
See Public welfare.

GENEROSITY
See Covenant; Liberality.

GENIUS
1. Genius is a word that ought to be reserved for the rarest of gifts.—Frankfurter: Marconi Wireless Tel. Co. v. United States, 320 U.S. 1, 62.

2. At such an altitude, to work at all with success is to qualify for genius. Rutledge: *ibid.*, 65.

3. Genius and talent are limited to no rank or condition of life.—Story: *Misc. Writings*, 123.

4. He knew well, that genius without labor could accomplish little.— Story: *ibid.*, 216.

See also Indifference; Science 2.

GESTURE
The attempt is but a gesture.—Car-

dozo: City Bank Farmers Tr. Co. v. N. Y. Cent. R.R., 253 N.Y. 49, 63.

GHOST-WRITING
See Author 2.

GIFT
1. A gift is none the less a gift because inspired by gratitude for the past faithful service of the recipient. —Sutherland: Bogardus v. Comm'r of Int. Rev., 302 U.S. 34, 44.

2. A gift in the statutory sense . . . proceeds from a "detached and disinterested generosity; out of affection, respect, admiration, charity or like impulses."—Brennan: Commissioner of Int. Rev. v. Duberstein, 363 U.S. 278, 285.

GOAL
Not the origin, but the goal, is the main thing. There can be no wisdom in the choice of a path unless we know where it will lead.—Cardozo: *Nature of Judicial Process,* 102.
See also Effort 11.

GOD
See Justice 1; Life 1; Power 5.

GOING CONCERN
See Value 17–19.

GOOD FAITH
Related subjects Faith; Honesty. *See also* Labor union, collective bargaining.

GOOD FORTUNE
Eminent good fortune is a prize rarely given even to the foremost in the race.—Story: *Misc. Writings,* 9.

GOOD WILL
1. The American political creed rests on the sovereignty of good-will. —Douglas: *We the Judges,* 151.

2. We . . . know that the sovereignty of good-will is vastly more powerful than the sovereignty of force and coercion.—Douglas: *ibid.,* 23–24.

GOOD WILL (business)
1. Good will is property in a very real sense.—Sutherland: Old Dearborn Distrib. Co. v. Seagram Distil. Corp., 299 U.S. 183, 194.

2. Earning a living is dependent upon securing work; and securing work is dependent upon public favor. —Brandeis: Senn v. Tile Layers Union, 301 U.S. 468, 482.
See also Reputation 1; Trade-mark 1; Value 17–19.

GOVERNMENT (general)
1. The science of government is the most abstruse of all sciences; if, indeed, that can be called a science which has but few fixed principles, and practically consists in little more than the exercise of sound discretion, applied to the exigencies of the state as they arise. It is the science of experiment. —Johnson: Anderson v. Dunn, 6 Wheat. (19 U.S.) 204, 226.

2. Government in a just sense, is, if one may so say, the *science of adaptations*—variable in its elements, dependent upon circumstances, and incapable of a rigid mathematical demonstration.—Story: *Misc. Writings,* 149.

3. What are the great objects of all free governments? They are, the protection and preservation of the personal rights, the private property, and

the public liberties of the whole people.—Story: *ibid.*, 151.

4. The great mass of human calamities, in all ages, has been the result of bad government, or ill adjusted government; of a capricious exercise of power, a fluctuating public policy, a degrading tyranny, or a desolating ambition.—Story: *ibid.*, 150.

5. A free people rarely bestow on good rulers the powers necessary for their own permanent protection, and as rarely withhold from bad ones those, which may be used for their own destruction.—Story: *ibid.*, 157.

6. Unhappily for m a n k i n d, a change of government has rarely taken place without involving evils of the most serious nature. It has been but the triumph of tyranny in the overthrow of the liberties of the people; or the sudden reaction of popular resentment, indignant at wrongs, and stimulated to criminal excesses.—Story: *ibid.*, 348.

7. In the formation of a government, the people may confer upon it such powers as they choose.—Waite: United States v. Cruikshank, 2 Otto (92 U.S.) 542, 549.

8. The power existing in every body politic is an absolute despotism; in constituting a government, the body politic distributes that power as it pleases and in the quantity it pleases, and imposes what checks it pleases upon its public functionaries. The natural distribution and the necessary distribution to individual security, is into legislative, executive and judicial; but it is obvious that every commu-

nity may make a perfect or imperfect separation and distribution of these powers at its will.—Johnson: Lessee of Livingston v. Moore, 7 Pet. (32 U.S.) 469, 546.

9. All governments which are not extremely defective in their organization, must possess, within themselves, the means of expounding, as well as enforcing, their own laws.—Marshall: Osborn v. Bank of U. S., 9 Wheat. (22 U.S.) 738, 818–19.

10. There are limitations upon the powers of all governments, without any express designation of them in their organic law; limitations which inhere in their very nature and structure.—Field: United States v. Erie Ry., 106 U.S. 327, 334.

11. It has always seemed to us a singular anomaly that believers in the theory of evolution and in the natural development of institutions by successive adaptations to the environment, should be found laying down a theory of government intended to establish its limits once for all by a logical deduction from axioms. — Holmes: *Uncollected Letters,* 106–107.

12. Government cannot exist if the citizen may at will use his property to the detriment of his fellows, or exercise his freedom of contract to work them harm.—Roberts: Nebbia v. New York, 291 U.S. 502, 523.

13. Every government is deemed to be just to its citizens.—Catron: Decatur v. Paulding, 14 Pet. (39 U.S.) 497, 522.

14. The consent upon which free

government rests is the consent that comes from sharing in the process of making and unmaking laws.—Frankfurter: West Va. State Bd. of Educ. v. Barnette, 319 U.S. 624, 655.

15. Even though the governmental purpose be legitimate and substantial, that purpose cannot be pursued by means that broadly stifle fundamental personal liberties when the end can be more narrowly achieved.—Stewart: Shelton v. Tucker, 364 U.S. 479, 488.

Related subjects: Legislation; Legislature; Sovereignty. *See also* Contract 12, 17; Dissent 14; Freedom 23; Justice 11; Law 12; Marriage 2; Police power 2; Political party 5, 6; Property 24; Public expenditure; Public welfare; Sovereignty; State; Tax, power; Tax, need for.

GOVERNMENT (U.S.)

General, defined, characteristics 1–6; general, authority 7–9, change 10, 11, powers 12–18, privileges 19–21, miscellaneous 22, 23; federal, basis 24–30, authority, supremacy 31–33; federal powers 34–37, separation 38–42, limitations 43–47; federal, miscellaneous 48, 49; federal-state, defined, authority 50–56, powers, accommodation 57–61, conflict 62–68; state, status 69–74; state powers, functions, rights 75–81, limitations 82–86; state, local, importance 87–91, miscellaneous 92, 93.

Related subjects: Congress; Constitution (U.S.); Democracy; Foreign affairs; Legislation; Legislature; President; Senate; Sovereignty.

———, general, defined, characteristics

1. Our government is emphatically a government of the people, in all its departments. It purports to be a government of laws, and not of men; and yet, beyond all others, it is subject to the control and influence of public opinion. Its whole security and efficiency depend upon the intelligence, virtue, independence, and moderation of the people. It can be preserved no longer than a reverence for settled, uniform laws constitutes the habit, I had almost said the passion, of the community.—Story: *Misc. Writings,* 446–47.

2. Our political system, different from many others, rests on the foundation of a belief in rule by the people—not some, but all the people.—Black: United Pub. Workers v. Mitchell, 330 U.S. 75, 114.

3. "A government of laws and not of men" was the rejection in positive terms of rule by fiat, whether by the fiat of governmental or private power. —Frankfurter: United States v. UMW, 330 U.S. 258, 307–308.

4. The essence of our free Government is "leave to live by no man's leave, underneath the law"—to be governed by those impersonal forces which we call law. Our Government is fashioned to fulfill this concept so far as humanly possible.—Jackson: Youngstown Sheet & Tube Co. v. Sawyer, 343 U.S. 579, 654–55.

5. We submit ourselves to rulers only if under rules.—Jackson: *ibid.,* 646.

6. This Government does not engage in sharp practices with its wards. —Black: Federal Power Comm'n v. Tuscarora Ind. Nat., 362 U.S. 99, 138.

———, general authority

7. The people are the recognized source of all authority, state or municipal, and to this authority it must come at last, whether immediately or by a circuitous route.—Hunt: Barnes v. Dist. of Columbia, 1 Otto (91 U.S.) 540, 545.

8. It is the theory, and I may add the glory, of our institutions that they are founded upon law, that no one can exercise any authority over the rights and interests of others except pursuant to and in the manner authorized by law.—Field: United States v. San Jacinto Tin Co., 125 U.S. 273, 307.

9. There is no mysticism in the American concept of the State or of the nature or origin of its authority. We set up government by consent of the governed, and the Bill of Rights denies those in power any legal opportunity to coerce that consent.—Jackson: West Va. State Bd. of Educ. v. Barnette, 319 U.S. 624, 641.

———, general, change

10. The . . . right of Americans to preserve, and to establish from time to time, such institutions, social and economic, as seem to them desirable; and, likewise, to end those which they deem undesirable.—Brandeis: Liggett Co. v. Lee, 288 U.S. 517, 578–79.

11. It is a principle of our Constitution that change in the organization of our government is to be effected by the orderly procedures ordained by the Constitution and not by force or fraud.—Stone: Schneiderman v. United States, 320 U.S. 118, 181.

———, general, powers

12. The government, within the Constitution, has all the powers granted to it which are necessary to preserve its existence.—Davis: *Ex parte* Milligan, 4 Wall. (71 U.S.) 2, 121.

13. Governmental power must be flexible and adaptive.—McKenna: Eubank v. Richmond, 226 U.S. 137, 143.

14. The power to commit violence, perpetrate injustice, take private property by force without compensation to the owner, and compel the receipt of promises to pay in place of money, may be exercised, as it often has been, by irresponsible authority, but it cannot be considered as belonging to a government founded upon law.—Field: Legal Tender Cases, 110 U.S. 421, 467.

15. A scheme of government like ours no doubt at times feels the lack of power to act with complete, all-embracing, swiftly moving authority. No doubt a government with distributed authority, subject to be challenged in the courts of law, at least long enough to consider and adjudicate the challenge, labors under restrictions from which other governments are free. It has not been our tradition to envy such governments. —Frankfurter: Youngstown Sheet & Tube Co. v. Sawyer, 343 U.S. 579, 613.

16. The state has as much right to guard, by anticipation, against the commission of an offense against its

laws, as to inflict punishment upon the offender after it shall have been committed.—Barbour: Mayor of New York v. Miln, 11 Pet. (36 U.S.) 102, 140.

17. Every exercise of governmental power must find its source in the Constitution. — Warren: Perez v. Brownell, 356 U.S. 44, 78.

18. When the Government becomes the moving party and levels its great powers against the citizen, it should be held to the same standards of fair dealing as we prescribe for other legal contests. To let the Government adopt such lesser ones as suits the convenience of its officers is to start down the totalitarian path.—Douglas: Anti-Fascist Ref. Comm. v. McGrath, 341 U.S. 123, 177.

———, general, privileges

19. There are certain immutable principles of justice which inhere in the very idea of free government which no member of the Union may disregard.—Brown: Holden v. Hardy, 169 U.S. 366, 389.

20. In any society the fullness and sufficiency of the securities which surround the individual in the use and enjoyment of his property constitute one of the most certain tests of the character and value of government.—Brewer: Monongahela Nav. Co. v. United States, 148 U.S. 312, 324.

21. The people have reason to prize and rejoice in such valuable privileges: and they ought not to forget that nothing but the free course of constitutional law and government can insure the continuance and enjoyment of them.—Jay: Chisholm v. Georgia, 2 Dall. (2 U.S.) 419, 479.

———, general, miscellaneous

22. Men must turn square corners when they deal with the Government. —Holmes: Rock Island R.R. v. United States, 254 U.S. 141, 143.

23. The might and power of the Federal Government have no equal. —Douglas: Hannah v. Larche, 363 U.S. 420, 500.

See also Construction 133; Contract 20, 85; Criminal law 39; Court 7, 8; Defense (legal) 10; Force 2; Freedom 189; Labor 33; Military 3, 4; Progress 2; Supreme Court; Tax, exemption; Veteran 1, 6.

———, federal, basis

24. The government of the United States was born of the Constitution. —White: Downes v. Bidwell, 182 U.S. 244, 288.

25. The American States, as well as the American people, have believed a close and firm Union to be essential to their liberty and to their happiness. —Marshall: Cohens v. Virginia, 6 Wheat. (19 U.S.) 264, 380.

26. Our very existence as a nation may depend on our union.—Marshall: Beveridge, *Life of Marshall*, II, 389.

27. The Union existed before the Constitution, which was ordained and established among other things to form "a more perfect union."— Sutherland: United States v. Curtiss-Wright Exp. Corp., 299 U.S. 304, 317.

28. In war, we are one people. In making peace, we are one people. In all commercial regulations, we are one and the same people.—Marshall: Co-

hens v. Virginia, 6 Wheat. (19 U.S.) 264, 413.

29. This country is one composed of many, and must on occasion be animated as one.—McKenna: Gilbert v. Minnesota, 254 U.S. 325, 329.

30. We are today one people, with one flag, one political creed, one loyalty.—Douglas: *We the Judges*, 17.

———, federal, authority, supremacy

31. The American people . . . did not design to make their government dependent on the states.—Marshall: McCulloch v. Maryland, 4 Wheat. (17 U.S.) 316, 432.

32. All constitutional laws are binding on the people, in the new States and the old ones, whether they consent to be bound by them or not.—McKinley: Pollard v. Hagan, 3 How. (44 U.S.) 212, 224.

33. The law of the State must bend to the supreme law of the land and the power of the nation.—Cardozo: Fitzgerald v. Harbor Lighterage Co., 244 N.Y. 132, 138.

———, federal, powers

34. They [powers] are given by all, for the benefit of all—and upon theory, should be subjected to that government only which belongs to all.—Marshall: McCulloch v. Maryland, 4 Wheat. (17 U.S.) 316, 429.

35. The United States has the powers inseparable from a sovereign nation.—Frankfurter: Dennis v. United States, 341 U.S. 494, 519.

36. A central authority must reconcile the clashing action of localities. . . .

In the phrase of Hobbes, there is need of "a common power to keep them in awe."—Cardozo: Penn. Gas Co. v. Public Serv. Comm'n, 225 N.Y. 397, 408.

37. No union can stand without some central veto over local encroachments.—Jackson: *Struggle for Judicial Supremacy*, 15.

———, federal, powers, separation

38. The legislature makes, the executive executes, and the judiciary construes the law.—Marshall: Wayman v. Southard, 10 Wheat. (23 U.S.) 1, 46

39. Where is there a more enduring monument of political wisdom than the separation of the judicial from the legislative power?—Story: *Misc. Writings*, 19.

40. One branch of the Government cannot encroach on the domain of another without danger. The safety of our institutions depends in no small degree on a strict observance of this salutary rule.—Waite: Sinking Fund Cases, 9 Otto (99 U.S.) 700, 718.

41. The sound application of a principle that makes one master in his own house precludes him from imposing his control in the house of another who is master there.—Sutherland: Rathbun v. United States, 295 U.S. 602, 630.

42. The act of hanging a criminal is executive; but to say when and where and how he shall be hanged is clearly legislative. — McReynolds:

Myers v. United States, 272 U.S. 108, 186.

———, federal powers, limitations

43. In this government, balances and checks have been carefully adjusted, with a view to secure public and private rights, and any departure from this organization endangers all. —McLean: Cary v. Curtis, 3 How. (44 U.S.) 236, 266.

44. The wise men who framed the Constitution, and the patriotic people who adopted it, . . . proceeded upon the theory—the wisdom of which experience has vindicated—that the only safe guaranty against governmental oppression was to withhold or restrict the power to oppress. — H a r l a n: Downes v. Bidwell, 182 U.S. 244, 381.

45. The country will not be saved by even the best motives in Washington. . . . Thank God for the limitations inherent in our federal system. —Brandeis: Mason: *Brandeis*, 621.

46. The system of checks and balances still functions as a vital force in American life.—Douglas: *We the Judges*, 31.

47. We pay a price for our system of checks and balances, for the distribution of power among the three branches of government. — Douglas: Youngstown Sheet & Tube Co. v. Sawyer, 343 U.S. 579, 633.
See also Constitution (U.S.), 104.

———, federal, miscellaneous

48. On this government, thus depending on ourselves for its existence, I will rest my safety.—Marshall: Beveridge, *Life of Marshall,* I, 437.

49. Simplicity of administration is a merit that does not inhere in a federal system of government.—Jackson: Davies Warehouse Co. v. Bowles, 321 U.S. 144, 153.

———, federal-state, defined, authority

50. No political dreamer was ever wild enough to think of breaking down the lines which separate the states, and of compounding the American people into one common mass. —Marshall: McCulloch v. Maryland, 4 Wheat. (17 U.S.) 316, 403.

51. The federal government is neither foreign to the State governments, nor is it hostile to them. It proceeds from the same people, and is as much under their control as the State governments. — Marshall: Worcester v. Georgia, 6 Pet. (31 U.S.) 515, 571.

52. The preservation of the just authority of the states is an object of deep concern to every lover of his country. . . . But it is equally true that the preservation of the just authority of the general government is essential as well to the safety of the states as to the attainment of the important ends for which that government was ordained by the people of the United States.—Harlan: United States v. E. C. Knight Co., 156 U.S. 1, 19.

53. Those who act on state authority alone necessarily assume all the risks of legitimate congressional interference. — Waite: Newport & C.

Bridge Co. v. United States, 15 Otto (105 U.S.) 470, 479.

54. When Congress has taken the particular subject-matter in hand, co-incidence is as ineffective as opposition.—Holmes: Charleston & W. C. Ry. v. Varnville Furn. Co., 237 U.S. 597, 604.

55. The national welfare as understood by Congress may require a different attitude within its sphere from that of some self-seeking state.—Holmes: Hammer v. Dagenhart, 247 U.S. 251, 281.

56. Peculiarities of local law may not gnaw at rights rooted in federal legislation.—Clark: South Buffalo Ry. v. Ahern, 344 U.S. 367, 372.

——, federal-state, powers, accommodation

57. If we are to survive as the United States, the balance between the powers of the nation and those of the states must be maintained.—McReynolds: Steward Mach. Co. v. Davis, 301 U.S. 548, 616.

58. The extension of federal control in these traditional local domains is a "delicate exercise of legislative policy in achieving a wise accommodation between the needs of central control and the lively maintenance of local institutions."—Douglas: Yonkers v. United States, 320 U.S. 685, 690 (quot. 308 U.S. 79, 84).

59. The sovereign rights in this dual relationship are not antagonistic. Accommodation and cooperation are their aim. It is friction, not fiction, to which we must give heed.—Minton:

Howard v. Comm'rs of Louisville, 344 U.S. 624, 627.

60. Harmony has an opportunity to maintain essential discipline, without that objectionable domination which is so inconsistent with our constitutional democracy.—Reed: Brown v. Allen, 344 U.S. 443, 487.

61. The mistaken supposition, which is sometimes indulged in, that the calling into being of the government under the Constitution, had the effect of destroying obvious powers of government instead of preserving and distributing such powers.—Hughes: Burnet v. Brooks, 288 U.S. 378, 404.

——, federal-state, powers, conflict

62. Two governments acting independently of each other cannot exercise the same power for the same object.—McLean: Fox v. Ohio, 5 How. (46 U.S.) 410, 436.

63. In the argument we have been reminded by one side of the dignity of a sovereign state; of the humiliation of her submitting herself to this tribunal; of the dangers which may result from inflicting a wound on that dignity; by the other, of the still superior dignity of the people of the United States, who have spoken their will in terms which we cannot misunderstand.—Marshall: Craig v. Missouri, 4 Pet. (29 U.S.) 410, 437.

64. Why may not these powers be exercised by the respective States? The answer is because they have parted with them, expressly for the

191

general good.—Marshall: Worcester v. Georgia, 6 Pet. (31 U.S.) 515, 592.

65. The state law yields only to the extent of the collision.—Fuller: McPherson v. Blacker, 146 U.S. 1, 41.

66. Our dual form of government has its perplexities.—McKenna: Hoke v. United States, 227 U.S. 308, 322.

67. Whatever inconvenience and embarrassments may be involved, they are the price we pay for our federalism, for having our people amenable to—as well as served and protected by—two governments.—Frankfurter: Knapp v. Schweitzer, 375 U.S. 371, 380.

68. The very essence of a healthy federalism depends upon the avoidance of needless conflict between state and federal courts.—Stewart: Elkins v. United States, 364 U.S. 206, 221.

See also Tax, exemption.

————, state, status

69. These states are constituent parts of the United States. They are members of one great empire—for some purposes sovereign, for some purposes subordinate.—Marshall: Cohens v. Virginia, 6 Wheat. (19 U.S.) 264, 414.

70. The States are not Nations, either as between themselves or towards foreign Nations. They are sovereign within their spheres, but their sovereignty stops short of nationality. Their political *status* at home and abroad is that of States in the United States.—Waite: New Hampshire v. Louisiana, 108 U.S. 76, 90.

71. The continued existence of the States, under a republican form of government, is made essential to the existence of the national government. —Curtis: Florida v. Georgia, 17 How. (58 U.S.) 478, 506.

72. Our Union is one of equal sovereigns, none entitled to preferment denied the others.—Douglas: Alabama v. Texas, 347 U.S. 272, 283.

73. The interpretations of modern society have not wiped out state lines. —Frankfurter: Polish Nat'l Alliance v. NLRB, 322 U.S. 643, 649.

74. Every State is more or less dependent on those which surround it. —Marshall: Worcester v. Georgia, 6 Pet. (31 U.S.) 515, 582.

————, state powers, functions, rights

75. The right of local self-government . . . belongs, under the Constitution, to the States and to the people thereof.—Matthews: Murphy v. Ramsey, 114 U.S. 15, 44-45.

76. The preservation of the just powers of the states is quite as vital as the preservation of the powers of the general government. — Harlan: Lochner v. New York, 198 U.S. 45, 74.

77. That the States might be so foolish as to kill a goose that lays golden eggs for them has no bearing on their constitutional rights.—Holmes: Erie R.R. v. Board of Pub. Util. Comm'r, 254 U.S. 394, 410.

78. Equality of constitutional right and power is the condition of all the states of the Union, old and new.— Lurton: Coyle v. Smith, 221 U.S. 559, 575.

79. Every State has a sphere of action where the authority of the National Government may not intrude. Within that domain the State is as if the Union were not.—Swayne: Farrington v. Tennessee, 5 Otto (95 U.S.) 679, 685.

80. There are many things that a man might do at common law that the states may forbid. — Holmes: Noble State Bank v. Haskell, 219 U.S. 104, 113.

81. Each state as a sovereign has a rightful and legitimate concern in the marital status of persons domiciled within its borders.—Douglas: Williams v. North Carolina, 317 U.S. 287, 298.

———, state powers, limitations

82. The powers of the Union, on the great subjects of war, peace, and commerce, and on many others, are in themselves limitations of the sovereignty of the States.—Marshall: Cohens v. Virginia, 6 Wheat. (19 U.S.) 264, 382.

83. That the members of the American family possess ample means of defence under the constitution, we hope ages to come will verify. But happily for our domestic harmony, the power of aggressive operation against each other is taken away.—Johnson: Burton's Lessee v. Williams, 3 Wheat. (16 U.S.) 529, 538.

84. The State cannot speak through an enactment which contravenes the Federal Constitution.—Field: Louisiana v. Jumel, 107 U.S. 711, 742.

85. We ought to remember the great caution shown by the Constitution in limiting the power of the states.—Holmes: Baldwin v. Missouri, 281 U.S. 586, 595.

86. What the state may not do directly it may not do indirectly.—Hughes: Bailey v. Alabama, 219 U.S. 219, 244.

———, state, local, importance

87. In the maintenance of local self-government, on the one hand, and the national power, on the other, our country has been able to endure and prosper for near a century and a half.—Taft: Child Labor Tax Case, 259 U.S. 20, 37.

88. Local self-government is undoubtedly desirable where there are not forcible reasons against its exercise. But it is not required by any inexorable principle.—Bradley: Metropolitan R.R. v. Dist. of Columbia, 132 U.S. 1, 8.

89. For a century our growth has come through natural expansion and the increase of the functions of the federal government. The growth of the future—at least of the immediate future—must be in quality and spiritual value. And that can come only through the concentrated, intensified strivings of smaller groups. — Brandeis: Mason, *Brandeis,* 603.

90. The differing needs and customs of the respective states and even of the respective communities within each state emphasize the principle that familiarity with, and complete understanding of, local characteristics, customs and standards are foundation

stones of successful self-government.
—Burton: Bute v. Illinois, 333 U.S.
640, 652.

91. Local processes of law are an essential part of any government conducted by the people. No national authority, however benevolent, that governs over 130,000,000 people in 48 states, can be as closely in touch with those who are governed as can the local authorities in the several states and their subdivisions.—Burton: *ibid*.

———, state, miscellaneous

92. Great states have a temper superior to that of private litigants.—Holmes: Virginia v. West Virginia, 220 U.S. 1, 36.

93. So firmly am I persuaded that the American people can no longer enjoy the blessings of a free government, whenever the state sovereignties shall be prostrated at the feet of the general government, nor the proud consciousness of equality and security, any longer than the independence of judicial power shall be maintained consecrated and intangible, that I could borrow the language of a celebrated orator, and exclaim, "I rejoice that Virginia has resisted."—Johnson: Martin v. Hunter's Lessee, 1 Wheat. (14 U.S.) 305, 363.
See also Tax, exemption.

GOVERNMENT EMPLOYEE

1. I do not doubt that the government employees as a class possess a normal independence and fortitude. But we have grounds to assume also that the normal proportion of them are subject to that very human weakness, especially displayed in Washington, which leads men to "crook the pregnant hinges of the knee where thrift may follow fawning."—Jackson: Frazier v. United States, 335 U.S. 457, 515.

2. The [conflict of interest] statute is . . . directed not only at dishonor, but also at conduct that tempts dishonor.—Warren: United States v. Mississippi Val. Gen. Co., 364 U.S. 520, 549.
See also Fidelity 2.

GRAND JURY

1. In the secrecy of the investigations by grand juries, the weak and helpless (proscribed, perhaps, because of their race, or pursued by an unreasoning public clamor), have found and will continue to find security against official oppression, the cruelty of mobs, the machinations of falsehood and the malevolence of private persons who would use the machinery of the law to bring ruin upon their personal enemies.—Harlan: Hurtado v. California, 110 U.S. 516, 554–55.

2. The traditional English and American grand jury . . . bring into the grand jury room the experience, knowledge, and viewpoint of all sections of the community. They have no axes to grind and are not charged personally with the administration of the law.—Black: *In re* Groban, 352 U.S. 330, 346–47.

3. The difference between the function of the trial jury and the function of the grand jury is all the difference between deciding a case and merely

194

deciding that a case should be tried. —Clark: Cassell v. Texas, 339 U.S. 282, 302.

4. To make of the grand jury a pawn in a technical game instead of respecting it as a great historic instrument of lay inquiry into criminal wrongdoing. — Frankfurter: United States v. Johnson, 319 U.S. 503, 512.

5. Grand juries ... "are not appointed for the prosecutor or for the court; they are appointed for the government and for the people."—Black: Levine v. United States, 362 U.S. 610, 624 (quot. 201 U.S. 43, 61).

6. In this country as in England of old, the grand jury is convened as a body of laymen, free from technical rules, acting in secret, pledged to indict no one because of prejudice and to free no one because of special favor.— Douglas: Hannah v. Larche, 363 U.S. 420, 499.

GREATER-LESS

1. It is true that the greater does not always include the less. A man may give his property away, yet he may not contract with a carrier to take the risk of the latter's negligently injuring it, or part with it on the valuable consideration of a wager. But, in general, the rule holds good.—Holmes: Rippey v. Texas, 193 U.S. 504, 509–10.

2. The greater includes the less, but that does not make them identical. In their totality they are as different as if the partial sameness did not exist.— Swayne: Scott v. United States, 12 Wall. (79 U.S.) 443, 444.

Related subject: Whole-part. *See also* Power 30.

GREATNESS

1. There are few great men, to whom one is brought near, however dazzling may be their talents or actions, who are not painfully diminished in the estimate of those, who approach them. The mist of distance sometimes gives a looming size to their character; but more often conceals its defects.—Story: *Misc. Writings,* 199.

2. A great man represents a great ganglion in the nerves of society, or, to vary the figure, a strategic point in the campaign of history, and part of his greatness consists in his being there.—Holmes: *Speeches,* 88.

3. We need have no fear in thus subordinating the individual to the community that great minds and great souls will be without an opportunity to reveal themselves.—Cardozo: *Growth of the Law,* 95.

See also Taste 1.

GROWTH

See Business 8; Identity; Law 32, 40; Skill.

GUESS

Related subject: Prophecy. *See also* Judgment 1.

GUIDE

See Commonplace; Self-interest 3.

GUILT

1. Although human laws punish actions, the human mind spontaneously attaches guilt to intentions.— Marshall: Beveridge, *Life of Marshall,* III, 486.

2. Guilt under our system of government is personal. When we make

guilt vicarious we borrow from systems alien to ours and ape our enemies. Those short-cuts may at times seem to serve noble aims; but we depreciate ourselves by indulging in them.—Douglas: Joint Anti-Fascist Ref. Comm. v. McGrath, 341 U.S. 123, 179.

3. If any fundamental assumption underlies our system, it is that guilt is personal and not inheritable.—Jackson: Korematsu v. United States, 323 U.S. 214, 243.

4. The doctrine of personal guilt is one of the most fundamental principles of our jurisprudence. — Murphy: Bridges v. Wixon, 326 U.S. 135, 163.

5. Guilt should not be imputed solely from association or affiliation with political parties or any other organization, however much we abhor the ideas which they advocate.—Black: American Com. Assoc. v. Douds, 339 U.S. 382, 452.

6. "Guilt by association" is an epithet frequently used and little explained, except that it is generally accompanied by another slogan, "guilt is personal." Of course it is: but personal guilt may be incurred by joining a conspiracy.—Jackson: *ibid.*, 433.

7. Many join associations, societies, fraternities with less than full endorsement of all their aims.—Douglas: Beilan v. Bd. of Educ., 357 U.S. 399, 414.

8. Variant degrees of mitigation may permit variant conclusions.—Cardozo: Union Exch. Nat'l Bank v. Joseph, 231 N.Y. 250, 254.

9. The inference of guilt to be drawn from possession is never one of law. It is an inference of fact. Other facts may neutralize it, or repel it, or render it so remote or tenuous or uncertain that in a given case we should reject it.—Cardozo: People v. Galbo, 218 N.Y. 283, 291.

10. Deliberate guilt — we say deliberate guilt, for it is not a question of ignorance or imbecility—is usually not so bold. It masks its purpose to hide it from prevention and penalty. —McKenna: United States v. United Shoe Mach. Co., 247 U.S. 32, 43.

11. I cannot think of any explanation consistent with innocence.—Cardozo: People v. Shilitano, 218 N.Y. 161, 182.

See also Evidence 9; Faith 13; Jury 48; Law 107; Murder 7; Presumption 6; Punishment 21; Self incrimination 13.

HABEAS CORPUS

1. The great writ of *habeas corpus* has been for centuries esteemed the best and only sufficient defense of personal freedom. . . . It was brought to America by the colonists, and claimed as among the immemorial rights descended to them from their ancestors.—Chase: *Ex parte* Yerger, 8 Wall. (75 U.S.) 85, 95.

2. By immemorial tradition the aim of *habeas corpus* is a justice that is swift and summary. — Cardozo: People *ex rel.* McCanliss v. McCanliss, 255 N.Y. 456, 459.

3. The law does not wait upon these niceties of practice, it does not dally and dawdle. . . . It leaps to the rescue

196

with the aid of its historic writ.—Cardozo: *ibid.,* 462.

4. Certain it is at least that the writ may not be thwarted at the pleasure of the jailer.—Cardozo: People *ex rel.* Sabatino v. Jennings, 246 N.Y. 258, 260–61.

5. The writ has no enemies so deadly as those who sanction the abuse of it, whatever their intent.—Jackson: Brown v. Allen, 344 U.S. 443, 544.

6. *Habeas Corpus,* like the currency, can be debased by overissue quite as certainly as by niggardly use.—Jackson: United States v. Shaughnessy, 347 U.S. 260, 271.

7. *Habeas corpus,* with an ancestry reaching back to Roman Law, has been over the centuries a means of obtaining justice and maintaining the rule of law when other procedures have been unavailable or ineffective.—Warren: Parker v. Ellis, 362 U.S. 574, 583.

HABIT
Related subjects: Custom and related subjects. *See also* Imitation 1; Legislation 6; Religion 15; Skill.

HAPPINESS
1. Happiness is not the constant attendant of the highest public favor; and it rather belongs to those, who, if they seldom soar, seldom fall.—Story: *Misc. Writings,* 9.

2. Happiness, I am sure from having known many successful men, cannot be won simply by being counsel for great corporations and having an income of fifty thousand dollars.

An intellect great enough to win the prize needs other food beside success.—Holmes: "The Path of the Law," 10 Harv. L. Rev. 478.
See also Knowledge 2; Virtue 4, 5.

HARDSHIP
See Equity Court 28; Law 100.

HARM
Related subject: Injury. *See also* Assault.

HASTE
See Premeditation.

HAZARD
1. The night too has its own hazards, for watchman and for wayfarer.—Cardozo: In the Matter of Heidemann v. Am. Dist. Tel. Co., 230 N.Y. 305, 308.

2. The moral hazard is increased with the increase of temptation.—Cardozo: Suetterlein v. Northern Ins. Co., 251 N.Y. 72, 77.
Related subjects: Gamble and related subjects. *See also* Experience 7.

HEALTH
Economic welfare is always related to health, for there can be no health if men are starving.—Cardozo: Baldwin v. Seelig, 294 U.S. 511, 523.
See also Women.

HEARING (legal)
1. It is a rule as old as the law, and never more to be respected than now, that no one shall be personally bound until he has had his day in court.—Field: Galpin v. Page, 18 Wall. (85 U.S.) 350, 368.

2. Can it be doubted that due process of law signifies a right to be heard

in one's own defense? — White: Hovey v. Elliott, 167 U.S. 409, 417.

3. He who demands decision without permitting inquiry, affirms that the decision he asks does not depend on inquiry. — Marshall: Cohens v. Virginia, 6 Wheat. (19 U.S.) 264, 377.

4. The judge is without the light whereby his discretion must be guided until a hearing, however summary, has been given the supposed offender. —Cardozo: Escoe v. Zerbst, 295 U.S. 490, 494.

5. A hearing is not judicial, at least in any adequate sense, unless the evidence can be known.—Cardozo: West Ohio Gas Co. v. Public Util. Comm'n, 294 U.S. 63, 69.

6. A hearing is not a hearing in the American sense if faceless informers or confidential information may be used to deprive a man of his liberty.— Douglas: Jay v. Boyd, 351 U.S. 345, 376.

7. *Audi alteram partem*—hear the other side!—a demand made insistently through the centuries, is now a command, spoken with the voice of the Due Process Clause of the Fourteenth Amendment, against state governments, and every branch of them ... whenever any individual, however lowly and unfortunate, asserts a legal claim. — Frankfurter: Caritativo v. California, 357 U.S. 549, 558.

8. He shall have a chance to say his say before the word of his pursuers is received to his undoing. — Cardozo: Escoe v. Zerbst, 295 U.S. 490, 493.

Related subjects: Accusation; Defense

(legal); Inquiry; Inquisition; Interrogation; Investigation; Trial. *See also* Lawyer 30.

HEARSAY
See Evidence, hearsay; Trial 19.

HEART
Heart and mind are not identical. Intuitive faith and reasoned judgment are not the same. Spirit is not always thought.—Rutledge: Prince v. Massachusetts, 321 U.S. 158, 165.

HERESY
1. The law knows no heresy, and is committed to the support of no dogma, the establishment of no sect. —Miller: Watson v. Jones, 13 Wall. (80 U.S.) 679, 728–29.

2. Heresy induces strong expressions of opposition. — Reed: Joint Anti-Fascist Ref. Com. v. McGrath, 341 U.S. 123, 200.
See also Religion 9.

HEROISM
See Classification 1; Faith 5.

HIGHWAY
The State maintains the highways upon which its people are dependent for their economic and social life.— Cardozo: Williams v. Baltimore, 289 U.S. 36, 44.
See also Ocean 1, 2.

HINDRANCE
The hindrances that are conjured up are counsels of despair.—Frankfurter: Harris v. United States, 331 U.S. 145, 172.

HINDSIGHT
Related subject: Afterthought. *See also* Invention; Military 9; Success 1; Wisdom 3–5.

HINTERLAND

The hinterland may be plain when the frontier is uncertain.—Cardozo: In the Matter of Richardson, 247 N.Y. 401, 413.

HISTORY

1. Upon this point a page of history is worth a volume of logic.—Holmes: New York Tr. Co. v. Eisner, 256 U.S. 345, 349.

2. It is refreshing to turn to the early incidents of our history, and learn wisdom from the acts of the great men who have gone to their account. — McLean: Dred Scott v. Sandford, 19 How. (60 U.S.) 393, 545.

3. What of the end when the lessons of history are ignored, when the barriers erected by wisdom gathered from experience are weakened or destroyed. And weakened or destroyed they may be when interest and desire feel their restraint. What, then of the end? Will history repeat itself?—McKenna: Wilson v. United States, 221 U.S. 361, 394.

4. Old and established freedoms vanish when history is forgotten.—Rutledge: Screws v. United States, 325 U.S. 91, 120.

5. In law also, doctrine is illuminated by history.—Frankfurter: Kovacs v. Cooper, 336 U.S. 77, 95.

6. The history of the world had taught . . . that what was done in the past might be attempted in the future.—Davis: *Ex parte* Milligan, 4 Wall. (71 U.S.) 2, 120.

7. We take a false and one-sided view of history when we ignore its dynamic aspects.—Cardozo: *Growth of the Law,* 104.

8. History but repeats itself. — Swayne: Farrington v. Tennessee, 5 Otto (95 U.S.) 679, 682.

9. Significant, also, is the argument from history. — Cardozo: Roman v. Lobe, 243 N.Y. 51, 56.

See also Antiquity 2; Coal industry; Common law; Communist 8; Confederacy; Confederation; Constitution; Constitutional adjudication 12; Dissent 13; Freedom, history; Freedom 55, 56; Independence (U.S.); Interest 1; Labor union, history; Law, development; Law of the Land 2; Lawyer 8, 11, 23, 106; Legislation 5, 52; Liquor 1, 7; Litigant 10; Magna Charta; Mail 1; Minority-majority 12, 14; Minority-majority, abuse; Money 1; Municipality 7; Municipal Planning 1; Opinion 15; Park; Pawnshop; Pioneer; Political party 1; Polygamy 1; Polygyny; Punishment 18; Republic; Roman Catholic Church; Search and seizure 2, 3, 11; Sherman Antitrust Law; Slavery 3; Smithsonian Institution; Sovereignty 16; Tax, history; Tax 138; Telephone 1, 2; Theater 3; Tobacco; Tyranny 2; Unemployment 4; Writing 1; Zoning 1, 2.

HOLDING COMPANY
See Corporation, holding company.

HOLIDAY

1. The duties of fasting and prayer are voluntary, and not of compulsion, and holiday is a privilege, not a duty. —Grier: Richardson v. Goddard, 23 How. (64 U.S.) 28, 43.

2. Saint's days and church fasts or festivals are treated as voluntary holidays, not as Sabbaths of compulsory rest.—Grier: *ibid.,* 42.

3. The class of persons most anxious to multiply holidays were the public

199

officers, apprentices, clerks, and others receiving yearly salaries.—Grier: *ibid.,* 43.

HOME

"Home" in the modern world is often a trailer or a tourist camp.—Murphy: Williams v. North Carolina, 325 U.S. 226, 257.

> Related subject: Domicile. *See also* Flight 2.

HONESTY

1. Honesty of purpose prompts frankness of statement.—Waite: Cosby v. Buchanan, 23 Wall. (90 U.S.) 420, 457.

2. The trite old aphorism, that "Honesty is the best policy," is true alike of individuals and communities. It is vital to their welfare.—Swayne: Farrington v. Tennessee, 5 Otto (95 U.S.) 679, 682.

3. A prudent regard to the maxim that honesty is the best policy is found by experience to be as little regarded by bodies of men as by individuals.—Douglas: *We the Judges,* 259.

4. Honesty seemed to be the best, even if the last, policy.—Jackson: Ashcraft v. Tennessee, 322 U.S. 143, 169.

5. His honesty was a deep, vital principle, not measured out by worldly rules.—Story: *Misc. Writings,* 205.

> Related subject: Dishonesty. *See also* Judgment 6; Religion 8.

HONOR

1. The power of honor to bind men's lives is not less now than it was in the Middle Ages. Now as then it is the breath of our nostrils; it is that for which we live, for which, if need be, we are willing to die. It is that which makes the man whose gift is the power to gain riches sacrifice health and even life to the pursuit. It is that which makes the scholar feel that he cannot afford to be rich.—Holmes: *Speeches,* 26.

2. Who of us could endure a world, although cut up into five-acre lots and having no man upon it who was not well fed and well housed, without the divine folly of honor, without the senseless passion for knowledge outreaching the flaming bounds of the possible, without ideals the essence of which is that they never can be achieved?—Holmes: *ibid.,* 59.

> *See also* Equity 3; Theft 4.

HOPE

Life teaches one to distinguish between hope and faith. — Jackson: Kunz v. New York, 340 U.S. 290, 314.

> Related subject: Aspiration. *See also* Covenant 1; Debtor 4; Insolvency 3; Litigant 3; Reform 10.

HOUSING

See Slum.

HUMANITY

And what is the decision of reason on the merits of these conflicting pretensions? Her first and favorite answer would be, that were the scales equally suspended between the parties the decision ought to be given in favor of humanity.—Johnson: The Nereide, 9 Cranch (13 U.S.) 388, 434.

> *See also* Public Welfare 3.

HUMAN NATURE

1. The passions of men stimulate them to avail themselves of the weak-

ness of others.—Marshall: Beveridge, *Life of Marshall,* I, 414.

2. Modern methods of doing business and modern complications resulting therefrom have not wrought any change in human nature itself.—Peckham: Crawford v. United States, 212 U.S. 183, 196.

3. It is the nature of the human mind to press a favorite hypothesis too far. — Johnson: Martin v. Hunter's Lessee, 1 Wheat. (14 U.S.) 305, 365.

4. Human nature, like human life, has complexities and diversities too many and too intricate to be compressed within a formula.—Cardozo: *Law and Literature,* 92.

5. Human nature is something whose action can never be ignored in the courts.—Brewer: Louisville Tr. Co. v. Louisville, N. A. & C. Ry., 174 U.S. 674, 688.

Related subjects: Character; Individual; Man. *See also* Defense; Desire; Faith 12; Government employee 1; Imitation 2; Law 36; Monopoly 10; Property 27; Virtue 3.

HUMOR
See Opinion (judicial) 21.

HUSBAND-WIFE

1. A husband without a wife, or a wife without a husband, is unknown to the law.—Gray: Atherton v. Atherton, 181 U.S. 155, 162.

2. A man does what is natural and reasonable when he makes provision for his wife.—Cardozo: In the Matter of Santrucek, 239 N.Y. 59, 63.

3. Not all marital flare-ups in which one spouse wants to hurt the other are permanent.—Black: Haw-

kins v. United States, 358 U.S. 74, 77-78.

4. You may have heard before this of the death of my wife, which not only takes away a half of my life but gives me notice. — Holmes: *Uncollected Letters,* 202.

Related subjects: Domestic relations and related subjects. *See also* Witness 18.

HYPOCRISY
See Imitation 3.

IDEA

1. A new and valid idea is worth more than a regiment and fewer men can furnish the former than can command the latter. — Holmes: *Uncollected Letters,* 181.

2. Ideas are not difficult . . . the trouble is in the words in which they are expressed.—Holmes: *ibid.,* 163.

3. When men have realized that time has upset many fighting faiths, they may come to believe even more than they believe the very foundations of their own conduct that the ultimate good desired is better reached by free trade in ideas.—Holmes: Abrams v. United States, 250 U.S. 616, 630.

4. Exposition of ideas readily merges into advocacy.—Frankfurter: Dennis v. United States, 341 U.S. 494, 545.

5. It is the aim of most ideas to shape conduct.—Douglas: Plumbers Union v. Graham, 345 U.S. 192, 202.

6. A man can be known by the ideas he spreads as well as by the company he keeps.—Stone: Schneiderman v. United States, 320 U.S. 118, 197.

7. Advocacy of an idea may be an

incitement too powerful for any resistance. — Douglas: *We the Judges,* 309.

8. Once the channels for communication are kept open, ideas will win on their merits.—Douglas: *ibid.,* 320.

9. Ideas are dangerous; and the traffic in them has been the concern of all dictators.—Douglas: *ibid.,* 353.

Related subjects: Thought and related subjects. *See also* Communism 6; Formula 7; Freedom 73; Incitement 3; Invention 4; Motion picture 1; Platitude 1; Power 1; Style 4; Symbol 10; Tax 94.

IDEAL, IDEALIST

1. It is an ideal, and without ideals what is life worth? They furnish us our perspectives and open glimpses of the infinite. It often is a merit of an ideal to be unattainable. Its being so keeps forever before us something more to be done, and saves us from the ennui of a monotonous perfection. At the least it glorifies dull details, and uplifts and sustains weary years of toil. — Holmes: "Law in Science and Science in Law," 12 Harv L. Rev. 462–63.

2. The trouble is that our ideals for the most part are inarticulate, and that even if we have made them definite we have very little experimental knowledge of the way to bring them about. — H o l m e s : "Ideals and Doubts," 10 Ill. L. Rev. 2.

3. With absolute truth I leave absolute ideals of conduct equally on one side.—Holmes: *ibid.*

4. The test of an ideal or rather of an idealist, is the power to hold to it and get one's inward inspiration from it under difficulties. When one is comfortable and well off, it is easy to talk high talk.—Holmes: *Uncollected Letters,* 164.

5. The elements necessary to determine the imaginary ideal are uncertain both in nature and degree of effect to the acutest commercial mind. —Holmes: International Harvester Co. v. Kentucky, 234 U.S. 216, 223.

6. The ideal being unattainable, we must not exaggerate the significance of deviations from the perfect norm. —Cardozo: Finsilver Still & Moss v. Goldberg, Maas & Co., 253 N.Y. 382, 392.

7. If ideals are developed locally the national ones will come pretty near taking care of themselves.—Brandeis: Mason, *Brandeis,* 602.

See also Honor 2; Tax 45.

IDENTITY

"This" book is one, though in its later editions words or phrases have been added, just as "this" body is one though its members may have grown. —Cardozo: Browne v. New York, 241 N.Y. 96, 111.

Related subject: Name. *See also* Corporation, identity; Master and servant; Principal and agent 1; Similarity; Whole-part 5.

IDIOM

See Construction 51; Word 6, 7.

IDLENESS

Related subjects: Inaction; Indolence. *See also* Freedom 96; Labor 4; Leisure.

IGNORANCE

1. Let us not waste our time in seeking for apologies for our ignorance,

where it exists, or in framing excuses to conceal it.—Story: *Misc. Writings,* 7.

2. It is no longer safe to be ignorant. Story: *Misc. Writings,* 122.

3. It will not do to remain wilfully ignorant of a thing readily ascertainable.—Davis: McQuiddy v. Ware, 20 Wall. (87 U.S.) 14, 19.

4. Ignorance and illiteracy are, of course, not synonymous; even illiterate masses can cast their ballots with intelligence, once they are informed. —Douglas: *We the Judges,* 320.

5. A man must find out at his peril things which a reasonable and prudent man would have inferred from the things actually known.—Holmes: *The Common Law,* 75.

6. When the ignorant are taught to doubt they do not know what they safely may believe.—Holmes: *Speeches,* 99.

——— (legal)

7. The rule that "ignorance of the law will not excuse" is deep in our law.—Douglas: Lambert v. California, 355 U.S. 225, 228.

8. To permit an ignorance of the law, to be alleged as the foundation of rights, or in excuse for omissions of duty, or for the privation of rights in others, would lead to the most serious mischief, and would disturb the entire fabric of social order.—Daniel: Magniac v. Thomson, 15 How. (56 U.S.) 281, 300.

9. The law is presumed to be equally within the knowledge of all parties.—Hunt: Upton v. Tribilcock, 1 Otto (91 U.S.) 45, 50.

10. It is precisely to those who are most likely to err by temperament, ignorance, or folly, that the threats of the law are the most dangerous.— Holmes: *The Common Law,* 51.

11. Where an individual acts in ignorance of his rights, he shall not be prejudiced by such acts.—McLean: Mayor v. United States, 10 Pet. (35 U.S.) 662, 735.

See also Defense (legal) 9; Disloyalty 1; Duty 9; Generality 12; Judge 34, 67; Judicial notice 2; Judicial process 15; Public official 14.

ILLEGALITY

1. There can be no civil right where there can be no legal remedy; and there can be no legal remedy for that which is itself illegal.—Johnson: Bank of U.S. v. Owens, 2 Pet. (27 U.S.) 527, 539.

2. Even generally lawful acts or conditions may become unlawful when done or imposed to accomplish an unlawful end. — Holmes: Frost v. Railroad Comm'n, 271 U.S. 583, 601.

Related subject: Legality. *See also* Conduct 14; Epithet 3; Liability 2; Means; Nuisance 3; Punishment 40; Subterfuge.

ILLEGITIMACY

All illegitimate children are the fruits of crime; differing, indeed, greatly in its degree of enormity.— Taney: Lessee of Brewer v. Blougher, 14 Pet. (39 U.S.) 178, 198–99.

Related subject: Legitimacy.

ILLITERACY

See Ignorance 4.

ILLUSION

Related subject: Imagination. *See also* Certainty 2; Expectation 2.

ILLUSTRATION

1. Illustrations are the mere language employed by the author to convey his ideas more clearly.—Bradley: Baker v. Selden, 11 Otto (101 U.S.) 99, 103.

2. I have chosen extreme illustrations as most likely to command assent.—Cardozo: *Law and Literature,* 52.

Related subjects: Analogy; Art; Picture. *See also* Design 1.

IMAGINATION

Related subject: Illusion. *See also* Corporation 6; Learning 5; Legislation 51; Will 7.

IMBECILE

See Sterilization.

IMITATION

1. Most of the things we do, we do for no better reason than that our fathers have done them or that our neighbors do them, and the same is true of a larger part than we suspect of what we think. The reason is a good one, because our short life gives us no time for a better, but it is not the best.—Holmes: "The Path of the Law," 10 Harv. L. Rev. 468.

2. Imitation is a necessity of human nature.—Holmes: *ibid.*

3. It is to be borne in mind that imitation is the sincerest form of flattery, and hypocrisy the tribute which vice pays to virtue.—Brandeis: Mason, *Brandeis,* 174.

4. We are living in an artificial age, and artificiality is ruining many of those just starting out in life. . . . Seeing others far better off in this world's good, enjoying the luxuries and good things of life, they deem it necessary to do likewise, for fear, I suppose, that they might be ridiculed for their thrift or sufficient strength of character to say no.—Brandeis: *ibid.,* 423–24.

See also Habit 1; Success 2.

IMMORAL, IMMORALITY

"Immoral" is a very comprehensive word. It means a dereliction of morals. In such sense it covers every form of vice, every form of conduct that is contrary to good order.—McKenna: Caminetti v. United States, 242 U.S. 470, 497.

See also Poverty 4; Usury 2.

IMMUNITY (legal)

Whether the good to be attained by procuring the testimony of criminals is greater or less than the evil to be wrought by exempting them forever from prosecution for their crimes is a question of high policy.—Cardozo: In the Matter of Doyle, 257 N.Y. 244, 261.

IMPARTIALITY

1. Impartiality is not a technical conception. It is a state of mind.—Hughes: United States v. Wood, 299 U.S. 123, 245.

2. Impartiality requires independence.—Frankfurter: Dennis v. United States, 339 U.S. 162, 182.

3. The appearance of impartiality is an essential manifestation of its reality.—Frankfurter: *ibid.*

See also Court 33; Judge 12, 13; Jury, challenge; Law 89.

IMPLICATION

Narrow at . . . times are the bounds of legitimate implication.—Cardozo: Browne v. New York, 241 N.Y. 96, 112.

Related subjects: Inference; Presumption. *See also* Legislation 71; Power 28, 29.

IMPOSSIBLE, IMPOSSIBILITY

Much which seems impossible is possible; and . . . most of the things worth doing in the world have been declared to be impossible, before they were done.—Brandeis: Mason, *Brandeis,* 309.

Related subject: Possible. *See also* Science 8.

IMPRESSION, IMPRESSIONISM

1. Impressions are often received without much reflection or examination.—Marshall: Marbury v. Madison, 1 Cranch (5 U.S.) 137, 169.

2. In case of doubt I have a leaning, which is not always shared by others, toward the impressionism that suggests and illumines without defining and imprisoning. — Cardozo: *Law and Literature,* 117.

See also Judgment 7.

IMPRISONMENT

1. No society is free where government makes one person's liberty depend upon the arbitrary will of another.—Black: Shaughnessy v. United States, 345 U.S. 206, 217.

2. Executive imprisonment has been considered oppressive and lawless since John, at Runnymede, pledged that no free man should be imprisoned, dispossessed, outlawed, or exiled save by the judgment of his peers or by the law of the land.—Jackson: *ibid.,* 218.

3. A man facing a prison term may, indeed, have as much at stake as life itself.—Douglas: Bute v. Illinois, 333 U.S. 640, 681.

4. The penitentiary is no sanctuary, and life in it does not confer immunity from capital punishment provided by law. He has no vested constitutional right to serve out his unexpired sentence. — Taft: Kelley v. Oregon, 273 U.S. 589, 593.

Related subject: Punishment. *See also* Bail 5; Debt 8; Punishment 38.

IMPROBABLE, IMPROBABILITY

Our daily experience apprises us that events are constantly occurring which would, *a priori,* be pronounced in the highest degree improbable.—Wayne: United States v. Castillero, 2 Black (67 U.S.) 1, 276.

IMPROVEMENT

Many modern improvements must be expected to take their toll of life.—Holmes: Nashville, C. & St. L. Ry. v. White, 278 U.S. 456, 459.

Related subjects: Reform; Utopia. *See also* Business 12; Effort 15; Invention 5; Mind 5; Reform 4; Virtue 4.

IMPULSE

1. The prey to sudden impulse, the fury of the fleeting moment.—Cardozo: People v. Zackowitz, 254 N.Y. 192, 195.

2. It matters not that some uncontrollable impulse, the product of mental disease, may have driven the de-

fendant to the commission of the murderous act. The law knows nothing of such excuses. — Cardozo: *Law and Literature*, 104.

3. When a woman sees a strange man, in plain clothes, prying up her bedroom window and climbing in, her natural impulse would be to shoot. —Jackson: McDonald v. United States, 335 U.S. 451, 460–61.

See also Insanity 9.

INACTION
Related subjects: Action and related subjects; Idleness; Indolence; Silence. *See also* Choice 1; Duty 11.

INCITEMENT
1. This is not the expression of philosophical abstraction, the mere prediction of future events; it is the language of direct incitement.—Sanford: Gitlow v. New York, 268 U.S. 652, 665.

2. The state cannot reasonably be required to measure the danger from every such utterance in the nice balance of a jeweler's scale. A single revolutionary spark may kindle a fire that, smoldering for a time, may burst into a sweeping and destructive conflagration.—Sanford: *ibid.*, 669.

3. Every idea is an incitement. It offers itself for belief, and if believed, it is acted on unless some other belief outweighs it, or some failure of energy stifles the movement at its birth. The only difference between the expression of an opinion and an incitement in the narrower sense is the speaker's enthusiasm for the result.— Holmes: *ibid.*, 673.

4. Every speech is indeed an incitement—sometimes an incitement to action, sometimes to meditation.— Douglas: *We the Judges*, 309.

5. Unity of purpose, passion and hatred, which merges the many minds of a crowd into the mindlessness of a mob, almost invariably is supplied by speeches. It is naive, or worse, to teach that oratory with this object or effect is a service to liberty.— Jackson: Terminiello v. Chicago, 337 U.S. 1, 32.

6. The most insulting words can be neutralized if the speaker will smile when he says them, but a belligerent personality and an aggressive manner may kindle a fight without use of words that in cold type shock us.— Jackson: *ibid.*, 35.

7. A little breath would be enough to kindle a flame. — Holmes: Frohwerk v. United States, 249 U.S. 204, 209.

See also Advocacy 3; Eloquence; Freedom 74, 75, 97; Idea 7; Speech 3, 4, 6.

INCLINATION
You will be yielding to the weakness of inclination, not governed by a clear, hard view of your opportunities and duty.—Holmes: *Uncollected Letters*, 199.

INCOME
1. It is of course true that the revenues derived from the working mines result to some extent in the exhaustion of the capital. But the same is true of the earnings of the human brain and hand when unaided by capital, yet such earnings are commonly dealt

with in legislation as income.—Pitney: Stratton's Ind. v. Howbert, 231 U.S. 399, 415.

2. Income within the meaning of the Sixteenth Amendment is the fruit that is born of capital, not the potency of fruition.—Cardozo: United States v. Safety Car Heat. & Light. Co., 297 U.S. 88, 99.

3. Congress cannot make a thing income which is not so in fact. — Brandeis: Burk-Waggoner Oil Assoc. v. Hopkins, 269 U.S. 110, 114.
> Related subjects: Investment and related subjects. *See also* Capital 2; Corporation 66, 67; Tax, income; Value 9.

INCOMPETENCE, INCOMPETENCY

One is not incompetent, within the meaning of the statute, to manage one's affairs because one is lacking in the sagacity that makes for success in business.—Cardozo: In the Matter of Case, 214 N.Y. 199, 203.
> Related subjects: Competence; Insanity; Mental disease. *See also* Distrust 1; Drunkard 1.

INDEFINITENESS
See Legislation 39.

INDEMNITY

There is a difference, not to be ignored, between profit and indemnity. —Cardozo: People v. Westchester Co. Nat'l Bank, 231 N.Y. 465, 491.
> *See also* Insurance 4.

INDEPENDENCE

1. The mutual dependence of the parties upon each other in fact does not affect the consequences of their independence of each other in law.—

Holmes: Denver v. Denver Union Water Co., 246 U.S. 178, 197–98.

2. He is bound hand and foot, . . . his freedom an illusion and his independence but a name.—Cardozo: In the Matter of Glielmi v. Netherland Dairy Co., 254 N.Y. 60–63.
> Related subject: Dependence. *See also* Author 1; Impartiality 2; Judge 9–11; Lawyer 48; Public official 11, 12; Supreme Court 19.

INDEPENDENCE (U.S.)

1. It is the doctrine of the American court, that the issue of the Revolutionary War settled the point that the American States were free and independent on the 4th of July, 1776.—Johnson: Shanks v. DuPont, 3 Pet. (28 U.S.) 242, 263.

2. Our independence was a great epoch in the history of freedom.—McLean: Dred Scott v. Sandford, 19 How. (60 U.S.) 393, 537.

3. Independence was the achievement, not of faction and ignorance, but of hearts as pure, and minds as enlightened, and judgments as sound, as ever graced the annals of mankind. —Story: *Misc. Writings,* 29.

4. Either our people will lose their political independence, or they will acquire industrial independence. We cannot exist half free and half slave.—Brandeis: Mason, *Brandeis,* 360–61.

INDIFFERENCE

The most formidable enemy to genius is not labor, but indolence; want of interest and excitement; want of motive to warm, and of object to accomplish; ignorance of means, leading to indifference to ends.—Story: *Misc. Writings,* 123.

INDIVIDUAL, INDIVIDUALISM

1. I wish I loved my fellow men more than I do, but to love one's neighbor as oneself, taken literally, would mean to realize all his impulses as one's own, which no one can, and which I humbly think would not be desirable if one could.—Holmes: *Uncollected Letters,* 178.

2. When I am told that under this or that regime selfishness would disappear, I cannot but reflect that my neighbor is better nourished by eating his own dinner than by my eating it for him.—Holmes: *ibid.,* 140.

3. Success in any democratic undertaking must proceed from the individual. It is possible only where the process of perfecting the individual is pursued. His development is attained mainly in the processes of common living. Hence the industrial struggle is essentially an affair of the Church and is its imperative task.—Brandeis: Mason, *Brandeis,* 585.

4. We can have intellectual individualism and the rich cultural diversities that we owe to exceptional minds only at the price of occasional eccentricity and abnormal attitudes.—Jackson: West Va. State Bd. of Educ. v. Barnette, 319 U.S. 624, 641–42.

5. Individual interests are aided only as the common interest is safeguarded.—Hughes: Cochran v. Louisiana State Bd. of Educ., 281 U.S. 370, 375.
Related subjects: Man and related subjects. *See also* Punishment 5, 24; Rights 1.

INDOLENCE
Related subjects: Inaction; Idleness. *See also* Generality 12; Indifference; Leisure.

INDUCEMENT

1. A man has at least as absolute a right to give his own money as he has to demand money from a party that has made no promise to him; yet if he gives it to induce another to steal or murder, the purpose of the act makes it a crime.—Holmes: American Bank & Tr. Co. v. Federal Res. Bank, 256 U.S. 350, 358.

2. The likelihood of mistake is multiplied when vigilance is thus disarmed.—Cardozo: South & Cent. Am. Com. Co. v. Panama R.R., 237 N.Y. 287, 292.
Related subject: Persuasion. *See also* Compulsion 1; Duress 3; Motive 9.

INDUCTION
In law, as in every other branch of knowledge, the truths given by induction tend to form the premises for new deductions.—Cardozo: *Nature of Judicial Process,* 47.
Related subjects: Deduction; Logic.

INDULGENCE
Liberality may well be greater when indulgence is craved in advance of the event.—Cardozo: Oliver v. Wells, 254 N.Y. 451, 460.
See also Progress 6.

INDUSTRIAL ACCIDENT
See Negligence, industrial accidents; Price 3.

INDUSTRY (business)
1. The time is not far distant, when the mechanic and manufacturing interest will form the great balancing

power, between the conflicting interests of commerce and agriculture; between the learned professions and the mere proprietors of capital; between the day laborer and the unoccupied man of ease.—Story: *Misc. Writings*, 126.

2. Leaders, not masters of industry, are needed.—Brandeis: Mason, *Brandeis*, 152.

Related subjects: Business and related subjects; Democracy (industrial). _See also_ Public welfare 20.

——— (effort)

3. Industry, talents and integrity, constitute a fund which is as confidently trusted as property itself.—Marshall: Sturges v. Crowninshield, 4 Wheat. (17 U.S.) 122, 198.

Related subjects: Diligence; Effort. *See also* Economy 1.

INEFFICIENCY

See Business (big) 4, 5; Competition 15; Scrutiny 1.

INEQUALITY

Related subject: Equality. *See also* Classification 5; Contract 7; Education 13, 14; Property 31, 33; Tax 69, 70, 103; Will (testament) 8; Woman.

INEVITABILITY

The inevitable is not wicked.—Holmes: *Holmes-Laski Letters*, I, 385. *See also* Effort 7.

INEXPERIENCE

Related subject: Experience. *See also* Fraud 4.

INFALLIBILITY

The persuasion that one's own infallibility is a myth leads by easy stages and with somewhat greater satisfaction to a refusal to ascribe infallibility to others. — Cardozo: *Nature of Judicial Process*, 30.

INFANT

It is evident in the beginning that there must be differences in the legal position of infants and adults. In the end we establish twenty-one as the dividing point. — Holmes: "Law in Science and Science in Law," 12 Harv. L. Rev. 456–57.

Related subjects: Child; Parent-child; Youth.

INFERENCE

1. Inference is capable of bridging many gaps.—Rutledge: Galloway v. United States, 319 U.S. 372, 386.

2. The line was not drawn between inference and conjecture, between legitimate deduction and unregulated suspicion.—Cardozo: People v. Van Aken, 217 N.Y. 532, 542.

3. We may multiply inferences at times, but in multiplying them, we must not refine and rarefy them beyond measure.—Cardozo: People v. Galbo, 218 N.Y. 283, 294.

4. It would be a long stride in dialectics . . . from this fact to the inference.—Swayne: Bechtel v. United States, 11 Otto (101 U.S.) 597, 600.

Related subjects: Implication; Presumption. *See also* Evidence, inferences; Knowledge 8; Premeditation; Self incrimination 14, 15; Silence; Trial 19.

INFERIORITY COMPLEX

I understand well the effort to help one's inner want of self-confidence by some outward show.—Holmes: *Uncollected Letters*, 202.

INFIDELITY

Infidelity to engagements causes loss of character to the individual; it entails reproach upon the State.—Field: Meriwether v. Garrett, 12 Otto (102 U.S.) 472, 520.

INFINITE, INFINITY

1. All mathematical distinctions vanish in presence of the infinite.— Holmes: "The Path of the Law," 10 Harv. L. Rev. 459.

2. Connect your subject with the universe and catch an echo of the infinite, a glimpse of its unfathomable process, a hint of the universal law.— Holmes: *ibid.,* 478.

3. We shall see that our little parish has its vistas that lie open to the infinite.—Cardozo: *Growth of the Law,* 142.

INFLATION

1. That the real dollar may represent property, and not the shadow of it.—Johnson: Craig v. Missouri, 4 Pet. (29 U.S.) 410, 443.

2. The war against inflation is a grim affair.—Douglas: Davies Warehouse Co. v. Bowles, 321 U.S. 144, 158.

3. Of all the consequences of war, except human slaughter, inflation is the most destructive. — Douglas: Hecht Co. v. Bowles, 321 U.S. 321, 331.

See also Tax 118.

INFLUENCE

See particular subjects; Trial unfair; Will (testament) 3.

INFORMER

1. Informers who disclose law vio-lations even for the worst of motives play an important part in making many laws effective. — Jackson: United States *ex rel.* Marcus v. Hess, 317 U.S. 537, 558.

2. The plea that evidence of guilt must be secret is abhorrent to free men, because it provides a cloak for the malevolent, the misinformed, the meddlesome, and the corrupt to play the role of informer undetected and uncorrected.—Jackson: United States v. Shaughnessey, 338 U.S. 537, 551.

3. When we relax our standards to accommodate the faceless informer, we violate our basic constitutional guarantees and ape the tactics of those we despise.—Douglas: Peters v. Hobby, 349 U.S. 331, 352.

4. The prejudices, the credibility, the passions, the perjury of the informer are never known. If they were exposed, the whole charge might wither under the cross-examination. —Douglas: United States v. Nugent, 346 U.S. 1, 14.

5. This is an age where faceless informers have been reintroduced into our society in alarming ways.— Douglas: Jones v. United States, 362 U.S. 257, 272.

INFRINGEMENT

Related subjects: Invention; Patent.

INGENUITY

No ingenuity can provide for every contingency. — McLean: Passenger Cases, 7 How. (48 U.S.) 283, 399–400.

INHERITANCE

1. The right to enjoy, transmit, and

inherit the fruits of our own labor, or that of our ancestors, stands on the same footing with the right to employ our industry wherever it can be best employed.—Johnson: Shanks v. DuPont, 3 Pet. (28 U.S.) 242, 261.

2. From the genius of our political institutions, as well as the habits of the people, there is every probability, that inheritances will continue to descend substantially in the same manner, as long as our free governments endure.—Story: *Misc. Writings,* 417.

3. The right to take property by devise or descent is a creature of the law, and not a natural right—a privilege.—McKenna: Magoun v. Illinois Tr. & Sav. Bank, 170 U.S. 283, 288.

4. The dead hand rules succession only by sufferance.—Jackson: Irving Tr. Co. v. Day, 314 U.S. 556, 562.

5. When the end comes, the power that property gives, no matter how absolutely it may have been held, also comes to an end—except in so far as the power to determine its succession and enjoyment may be projected beyond the grave.—Frankfurter: Whitney v. State Tax Comm'n, 309 U.S. 530, 538.

Related subject: Will (testament). *See also* Property 4; Tax, inheritance.

INIQUITY
Related subjects: Evil, Malevolence; Vice; Wickedness. *See also* Court 48; Equity court 3.

INITIAL (name)
See Name 2, 3.

INJUNCTION
See Labor 104.

INJURY
1. It is said that the pain cannot be shifted to another. Neither can the loss of a leg. But one can be paid for as well as the other.—Holmes: Arizona Copper Co. v. Hammer, 250 U.S. 400, 433.

2. A machine as well as a bullet may produce a wound, and the disabling effect may be the same.—Pitney: Mountain Timber Co. v. Washington, 243 U.S. 219, 240.

3. Death is the supreme personal injury.—Reed: American Stevedores v. Porello, 330 U.S. 446, 460.

Related subjects: Negligence and related subjects; Workmen's compensation. *See also* Crime 6; Liability 13; Motor vehicle 6–8; Price 3; Redress 2.

INJUSTICE
Related subject: Justice. *See also* Formula 11; Majority-minority 8; Political action; Socialism 2.

INNOCENCE, INNOCENT
1. Innocence will strangely multiply when the accuser is the paid defender.—Cardozo: Union Exch. Nat'l Bank v. Joseph, 231 N.Y. 250, 254.

2. A mind intent upon willful evasion is inconsistent with surprised innocence.—Black: United States v. Ragen, 314 U.S. 513, 524.

3. If the appellee had been indicted, and had gone to trial upon this record, God and his country would have given him a good deliverance.—Lamar: *In re* Neagle, 135 U.S. 1, 99.

See also Concealment 4; Constitution, Fifth Amendment 110; Legislature 15; Presumption; Trial 40.

INNOVATION

Innovations such as these may persist and become general. In course of time they may sink into common thought and common speech.—Cardozo: Van Vechten v. American Eagle Fire Ins. Co., 239 N.Y. 303, 306.

Related subject: Novelty. *See also* Reform 2, 3.

INQUIRY

1. The right to ask a question and the right to demand an answer are essential to the democratic processes.—Douglas: *We the Judges,* 160.

2. The subject the most innocent on the surface may turn out when it is probed to be charged with hidden fire.—Cardozo: *Law and Literature,* 130.

3. The extent to which inquiry must be pressed beyond appearance is a question of judgment, as to which opinions will often differ.—Cardozo: Ultramares Corp. v. Touche, 255 N.Y. 170, 179.

4. To probe into the past in the belief that discovery of its evils may bring correction in the future.—Cardozo: In the Matter of Edge Ho Holding Corp., 256 N.Y. 374, 380.

Related subjects: Hearing and related subjects: Question. *See also* Self incrimination 8; Teacher 4; Treason 5; Trial 37; Vendor 1.

INQUISITION

1. Secret inquisitions are dangerous things justly feared by free men everywhere. They are the breeding place for misuse of official power. They are often the beginning of tyranny as well as indispensable instru-

ments for its survival.—Black: *In re Groban,* 352 U.S. 330, 352–53.

2. Calling an interrogation an "inquisition" . . . adds to the problem only the emotions inherited from medieval experience.—Jackson: Stein v. New York, 346 U.S. 156, 184–85.

Related subjects: Hearing and related subjects; Informer. *See also* Freedom 31; Public official 27.

INSANITY

1. Insanity is a disease of the mind, which assumes as many and various forms as there are shades of difference in the human character.—Harlan: Connecticut Mut. Life Ins. Co. v. Lathrop, 111 U.S. 612, 620.

2. Whether an individual is insane, is not always best solved by abstruse metaphysical speculations, expressed in the technical language of medical science. The common sense and, we may add, the natural instincts of mankind, reject the supposition that only experts can approximate certainty upon such a subject.—Harlan: *ibid.,* 619.

3. The line between sanity and insanity is often shadowy and difficult to define.—Davis: Bigelow v. Berkshire Life Ins. Co., 3 Otto (93 U.S.) 284, 287.

4. Every one concedes that the present definition of insanity has little relation to the truths of mental life.—Cardozo: *Law and Literature,* 106.

5. Conceivably the twilight zone between sanity and insanity is so broad and so vague as to bid defiance to exact descriptions. I do not know, though I am reluctant to concede that

science is so impotent. — Cardozo: *ibid.,* 107.

6. Persons of most decided insanity often exhibit consistency of purpose, coolness, and even great ingenuity in the pursuit of some insane object to which they are impelled by the diseased condition of mind with which they are inflicted.—Bradley: Charter Oak Life Ins. Co. v. Rodel, 5 Otto (95 U.S.) 232, 241.

7. The inmates of lunatic asylums are largely governed, it has been remarked, by appeal to the same motives that govern other men.—Holmes: Drew v. Thaw, 235 U.S. 432, 440.

8. I am not unmindful of the difficulty of framing a definition of insanity that will not be so broad as to open wide the door to evasion and imposture. Conceivably the law will have to say that the risk is too great, that the insane must answer with their lives, lest under cover of their privilege the imposter shall escape.— Cardozo: *Law and Literature,* 107.

9. Many states . . . recognize the fact that insanity may find expression in an irresistible impulse, yet I am not aware that the administration of their criminal law has suffered as a consequence.—Cardozo: *ibid.,* 107–108.

10. If insanity is not to be a defense, let us say so frankly and even brutally, but let us not mock ourselves with a definition that palters with reality. Such a method is neither good morals nor good science nor good law.—Cardozo: *ibid.,* 108.

11. A lunatic needs more protection than a minor. — Strong: Dexter v. Hall, 15 Wall. (82 U.S.) 9, 25.

12. His darkened mind did not enable him to see or appreciate the moral consequences of his act, but still left him capacity enough to understand its physical nature.—Davis: Bigelow v. Berkshire Life Ins. Co., 3 Otto (93 U.S.) 284, 288.

13. A psychological disturbance, amounting to something more than worry but something less than insanity.—Jackson: Spies v. United States, 317 U.S. 492, 493.

Related subjects: Competence; Incompetence; Mental disease. *See also* Murder 4; Trial 34; Witness 10.

INSOLVENCY

1. Many find themselves, with ample means, good credit, large business, technically insolvent; that is, unable to meet their current obligations as fast as they mature.—Miller: Wilson v. City Bank, 17 Wall. (84 U.S.) 473, 486.

2. Insolvency is undoubtedly a casualty which is possible, but never expected. — Marshall: Ogden v. Saunders, 12 Wheat. (25 U.S.) 213, 343.

3. Expressions of hope of recovery indulged in by a person reduced to poverty by large losses must be taken with many grains of allowances.— Fuller: Crawford v. Neal, 144 U.S. 585, 598.

Related subject: Bankruptcy.

INSPIRATION

Method is much, technique is much, but inspiration is even more.—Cardozo: *Law and Literature,* 163.

INSTINCT

Related subject: Intuition. *See also* Opinion 24; Self-preservation.

INSTRUCTION

See Teacher 1.

INSULT

Related subjects: Defamation and related subjects. *See also* Flag 6; Incitement 6; Freedom, speech 100.

INSURANCE

1. Insurance is not production; nor manufacture; nor transportation; nor merchandise. — Lamar: German Alliance Ins. Co. v. Lewis, 233 U.S. 389, 420.

2. While life insurance is property, it is peculiar property. — Day: Burlingham v. Crouse, 228 U.S. 459, 472.

3. Annuity and insurance are opposites. . . . From the company's viewpoint, insurance looks to longevity, annuity to transiency.—Murphy: Helvering v. Le Gierse, 312 U.S. 531, 541.

4. Indemnity is the great object of the insured. — Clifford: Mercantile Ins. Co. v. Folsom, 18 Wall. (85 U.S.) 237, 247.

5. One may guess, or gamble on, or even insure against, any future event. The solicitor-general tells us that Lloyds of London will insure against having twins. — Brandeis: Humes v. United States, 276 U.S. 487, 494.

6. Historically and commonly insurance involves risk-shifting and risk-distributing. — Murphy: Helvering v. Le Gierse, 312 U.S. 531, 539.

7. Life insurance has become in our days one of the best recognized forms of investment and self-compelled saving.—Holmes: Grigsby v. Russell, 222 U.S. 149, 156.

8. The very meaning of an insurable interest is an interest in having the life continue, and so one that is opposed to crime.—Holmes: *ibid.,* 154.

9. The law has no universal cynic fear of the temptation opened by a pecuniary benefit accruing upon a death.—Holmes: *ibid.,* 155–56.

10. A contract of insurance upon a life in which the insured has no interest is a pure wager that gives the insured a sinister counter-interest in having the life come to an end.— Holmes: *ibid.,* 154.

11. The modern insurance business holds a commanding position in the trade and commerce of our nation. . . . Perhaps no modern commercial enterprise directly affects so many persons in all walks of life as does the insurance business. Insurance touches the home, the family, and the occupation or the business of almost every person in the United States.—Black: United States v. South-East. Underwriters Assoc., 322 U.S. 533, 539–40.

12. Insurance for dependents is today in the thought of many a pressing social duty. — Cardozo: Burnet v. Wells, 289 U.S. 670, 681.

13. Government has always had a special relation to insurance. The ways of safeguarding against the untoward manifestations of nature and other vicissitudes of life have long been withdrawn from the benefits and caprices of free competition.—Frank-

furter: Osborn v. Ozlin, 310 U.S. 53, 65.

14. The benefit to be gained by death has no periodicity. It is a substitution for money value for something permanently lost, either in a house, a ship, or a life.—Taft: United States v. Supplee-Biddle Hardware Co., 265 U.S. 189, 195.

15. The argument that to allow the owner to keep his insurance would encourage negligence and recklessness on his part can always be made in every case of insurance. It has been made and answered a hundred times. —Bradley: Place v. Norwich & N. Y. Transp. Co., 118 U.S. 468, 505.

16. The state might conceivably make itself a mutual insurance company against accidents, and distribute the burden of its citizens' mishaps among all its members. — Holmes: *The Common Law*, 96.

17. Universal insurance, if desired, can be better and more cheaply accomplished by private enterprise.— Holmes: *ibid*.

Related subject: Workmen's compensation. *See also* Depreciation 2; Negligence 12; Negligence, industrial accidents; Tort.

INTANGIBLE
See Fiction 11.

INTELLECT
See Freedom, thought 150.

INTELLIGENCE
Related subject: Wisdom. *See also* Fraud 4; Judgment 7; Literacy.

INTEMPERANCE
See Epithet 7; Speech 5, 7.

INTENT, INTENTION

1. The word "intent" as vaguely used in ordinary legal discussion means no more than knowledge at the time of the act that the consequences said to be intended will ensue. — Holmes: Abrams v. United States, 250 U.S. 616, 620.

2. Without the knowledge, the intent cannot exist.—Rutledge: Direct Sales Co. v. United States, 319 U.S. 703, 711.

3. An act, it is true, imports intention in a certain sense. It is a muscular contraction, and something more. A spasm is not an act. The contraction of the muscles must be willed. —Holmes: *The Common Law*, 54.

4. Attempt and intent, of course, are two distinct things. Intent to commit a crime is not itself criminal. There is no law against a man's intending to commit a murder the day after to-morrow. The law only deals with conduct. An attempt is an overt act.—Holmes: *ibid.*, 65.

5. A culpable state of mind is an element in most wrongs.—Holmes: *Uncollected Letters*, 51.

6. The law has nothing to do with the actual state of the parties' minds. In contract, as elsewhere, it must go by externals, and judge parties by their conduct.—Holmes: *The Common Law*, 309.

7. This shows the humbug of talking about the intention of the parties. It often happens that each party to a contract hopes and perhaps thinks that he had got this or that advantage which the Court may say he has not.

The dominant intention on each side is that the words used shall bind as they may be interpreted by the court in case of litigation, although the actual inducement may be the mistaken belief that the Court will say it means so and so.—Holmes: *Uncollected Letters,* 172.

8. The very inaccurate maxim, that every man is presumed to intend the natural consequences of his own acts. —Holmes: *The Common Law,* 147.

9. Intention not otherwise revealed may be presumed to hold in contemplation the reasonable and probable. —Cardozo: Jacob & Youngs v. Kent, 230 N.Y. 239, 242.

10. Triers of fact are constantly called upon to determine the intent with which a person acted. . . . Nearly three-quarters of a century ago, Bowen, Ld. J., made the classic statement that "the state of a man's mind is as much a fact as the state of his digestion." — Vinson: Commissioner of Int. Rev. v. Culbertson, 337 U.S. 733, 743 n.

11. I know that what we speak of as the intention of the testator is often, in reality, the intention of the draftsman of the will, if, indeed, the situation, afterwards arising, was within the range of thought at all.—Cardozo: In the Matter of Durant, 231 N.Y. 41, 50.

12. It would be in vain to administer justice . . . if mere statements of intention would outweigh the legal effects of the acts of the parties.— Story: The Nereide, 9 Cranch (13 U.S.) 388, 444.

13. It may be assumed that he intended not to break the law, but only to get as near to the line as he could, which he had a right to do, but if the conduct described crossed the line, the fact that he desired to keep within it will not help him.—Holmes: Horning v. Dist. of Columbia, 254 U.S. 135, 137.

14. Good intentions are no excuse for spreading slanders. — Holmes: Tasker v. Stanley, 153 Mass. 148, 150.

15. When one intends the acts to which the law attaches consequences, he must abide the consequences whether intended or not. — Stone: Texas v. Florida, 306 U.S. 398, 425.

16. The case is not relieved of its harsh features by the finding of the court that the claimant did not intend to aid the rebellion, but only to make money. It might as well be said that the man who would sell for a sum far beyond its value to a lunatic, a weapon with which he knew the latter would kill himself, only intended to make money and did not intend to aid the lunatic in his fatal purpose.— Miller: Sprott v. United States, 20 Wall. (87 U.S.) 459, 463.

17. A claim of guilelessness ill becomes those with evil intent.—Vinson: Dennis v. United States, 341 U.S. 494, 512.

18. The tokens of intention . . . have a force in combination that is denied to any one of them alone.— Cardozo: Norwegian Nitrogen Prod. Co. v. United States, 288 U.S. 294, 319.

19. So far as knowledge is the foun-

dation of intent, the latter thereby also becomes the more secure.—Rutledge: Direct Sales Co. v. United States, 319 U.S. 703, 712.

Related subjects: Mind; Will. *See also* Act 4, 5; Assault; Constitution (U.S.), construction; Construction; Contract 3; Crime; Guilt 1; Moral 2; Motive; Murder 3; Restraint of trade 16, 17; Right 1; Will 6–9.

INTEREST

1. The practice of regulating by legislation the interest receivable for the use of money ... is only the assertion of a right of the government to control the extent to which a privilege granted by it may be exercised and enjoyed. By the ancient common law it was unlawful to take any money for the use of money. ... Whilst the common law thus condemned all usury, Parliament interfered and made it lawful to take a limited amount of interest.—Field: Munn v. Illinois, 4 Otto (94 U.S.) 113, 153.

2. In equity, interest goes with the principal, as the fruit with the tree.—Johnson: Himely v. Rose, 5 Cranch (9 U.S.) 313, 319.

3. Interest is allowed by way of damages for failure to pay money when it is due.—Lamar: Consaul v. Cummings, 222 U.S. 262, 272.

4. It is common knowledge that interest rates vary not only according to the general use value of money but also according to the hazard of particular classes of loans. — Jackson: Meilink v. Unemployment Res. Comm'n, 314 U.S. 564, 567.

5. The punctual payment of interest has an importance to the lender as affecting his way of life, perhaps the very means of his support.—Cardozo: Graf v. Hope Bldg. Corp., 254 N.Y. 1, 10.

6. If it chose to keep the money, it should pay for what it kept.—Cardozo: Prager v. N.J. Fid. & Plate Glass Ins. Co., 245 N.Y. 1, 6.

Related subjects: Capital; Investment. *See also* Penalty 2; Tax 151.

INTERROGATION

Related subjects: Hearing and related subjects; Question. *See also* Criminal law, interrogation.

INTOLERANCE

1. The most common sign of our time, as it seems to me, is the indication of the growth of an intolerant spirit. It is the more dangerous when armed, as it usually is, with sincere conviction.—Hughes: Pusey, *Hughes*, 620.

2. I would not be understood as regarding intolerance as exclusively a vice of conservative minds. It is a fault of the radical as well.—Stone: Mason, *Stone*, 98.

3. The crowd mind is never tolerant of any idea which does not conform to its herd opinion. It does not want a tolerant effort at meeting of minds. It does not know the futility of trying to mob an idea.—Jackson: Terminiello v. Chicago, 337 U.S. 1, 33.

4. Courts must beware lest they become mere organs of popular intolerance.—Jackson, *ibid.*

5. As a people grow in capacity for

217

civilization and liberty their tolerance will grow, and they will endure, if not welcome discussion even on topics as to which they are committed. They regard conviction as tentative and know that time and events will make their own terms with theories, by whomever and by whatever majorities they are held, and many will be proved wrong.—Jackson, *ibid*.

6. History indicates that urges to do good have led to the burning of books and even to the burning of "witches." — Frankfurter: Beauharnais v. Illinois, 343 U.S. 250, 274.

7. The lesson of experience is that —with the passage of time and the interchange of ideas—organizations, once turbulent, perfervid and intolerant in their origin, mellow into intolerance and acceptance by the community, or else sink into oblivion.—Murphy: Martin v. Struthers, 319 U.S. 141, 149.

> Related subjects: Discrimination; Tolerance. *See also* Race, prejudice.

INTRUSION

1. Intrusion without privilege has certain liabilities and penalties.—Cardozo: People v. Defore, 242 N.Y. 13, 23.

2. For the high intruder and the low, the consequences become the same.—Cardozo: *ibid., 22.*

INTUITION

> Related subject: Instinct. *See also* Judgment 4; Law 50.

INVALID

Invalids are permitted to indulge in the hope of recovery, and are not called upon by reason of illness to retire at once from the affairs of this world and confine themselves to preparation for their passage into another.—Fuller: Briggs v. Spaulding, 141 U.S. 132, 155.

INVENTION

1. The act of invention ... consists neither in finding out the laws of nature, nor in fruitful research as to the operation of natural laws, but in discovering how those laws may be utilized or applied for some beneficial purpose, by a process, a device or a machine.—Roberts: United States v. Dubilier Condenser Corp., 289 U.S. 178, 188.

2. A machine is a thing. A process is an act, or a mode of acting. The one is visible to the eye—an object of perpetual observation. The other is a conception of the mind, seen only by its effects when being executed or performed. Either may be the means of producing a useful result.—Bradley: Tilghman v. Proctor, 12 Otto (102 U.S.) 707, 728.

3. Both discovery and invention, in the popular sense of those terms, were involved: discovery in finding the art, and invention in devising the means of making it useful.—White: Telephone Cases, 126 U.S. 1, 533.

4. It [invention] is the result of an inventive act, the birth of an idea and its reduction to practice; the product of original thought; a concept demonstrated to be true by practical application or embodiment in tangible

form.—Roberts: United States v. Dubilier Condenser Corp., 289 U.S. 178, 188.

5. All improvement is not invention.—Strong: Pearce v. Mulford, 12 Otto (102 U.S.) 112, 118.

6. The concept of invention is inherently elusive when applied to combination of old elements.—Jackson: Great A. & P. Tea Co. v. Supermarket Equip. Corp., 340 U.S. 147, 151.

7. When one notes the crude working of machines of famous pioneer inventions and discoveries, and compares them with the modern machines and processes exemplifying the principles of the pioneer discovery, one hesitates in the division of credit between the original inventor and the improvers.—Taft: Eibel Proc. Co. v. Minn. & Ont. Paper Co., 261 U.S. 45, 63.

8. The discoveries of science are the discoveries of the laws of nature, and like nature do not go by leaps. Even Newton and Einstein, Harvey and Darwin, built on the past and on their predecessors. Seldom indeed has a great discoverer or inventor wandered lonely as a cloud. Great inventions have always been parts of an evolution, the culmination at a particular moment of an antecedent process.—Frankfurter: Marconi Wireless Tel. Co. v. United States, 320 U.S. 1, 62.

9. The real question is how significant a jump is the new disclosure from the old knowledge. Reconstruction by hindsight, making obvious something that was not at all obvious to superior minds until someone pointed it out—this is too often a tempting exercise for astute minds.—Frankfurter: *ibid.*

10. A short step forward gives evidence of inventive power. For at that height a merely slight advance comes through insight only a first-rate mind can produce. This is so, whether it comes by years of hard work tracking down the sought secret or by intuition flashed from subconsciousness made fertile by long experience or shorter intensive concentration.—Rutledge: *ibid.*, 65.

11. As is often true with great inventions, the simplest and therefore generally the best solution is not obvious at the time, though it becomes so immediately it is seen and stated. Looking back now at Edison's light bulb one might think it absurd that highly useful and beneficial idea had not been worked out long before, by anyone who knew the elementary laws of resistance in the field of electric conduction.—Rutledge: *ibid.*, 74.

12. The invention was, so to speak, hovering in the general climate of science, momentarily awaiting birth. But just the right releasing touch had not been found. Marconi added it.—Rutledge: *ibid.*, 66.

13. We daily witness how the world has been benefited since by the patented inventions and discoveries in steam, in all its wonderful varieties and utilities and in cleaning, spinning, and weaving cotton by machinery for almost half the human race, and in myriads of other improvements in other things, shedding so benign a

219

light over the age in which we live, and most of them excited and matured only under the protection secured to their inventors by an enlightened government. — Woodbury: Wilson v. Rousseau, 4 How. (45 U.S.) 646, 708–709.

14. Now that it has succeeded it may seem very plain to any one that he could have done it as well. This is often the case with inventions of the greatest merit. — Bradley: Webster Loom Co. v. Higgins, 15 Otto (105 U.S.) 580, 591.

15. Experience has made it axiomatic to eschew dogmatism in predicting the impossibility of important developments in the realms of science and technology. Especially when the incentive is great, invention can rapidly upset prevailing opinions of feasibility.—Frankfurter: Radio Corp. v. United States, 341 U.S. 412, 427.

Related subjects: Inventor; Patent; Telephone.

INVENTOR

Inventors are a meritorious class. They are public benefactors. They add to the wealth and comfort of the community, and promote the progress of civilization.—Swayne: Consolidated Fruit-Jar Co. v. Wright, 4 Otto (94 U.S.) 92, 96.

Related subjects: Invention; Patent.

INVESTIGATION

1. The purpose of an investigation is the penetration of disguises.—McKenna: Smith v. ICC, 245 U.S. 33, 46.

2. An educational institution is not a constitutional sanctuary from inquiry into matters that may otherwise be within the constitutional legislative domain merely for the reason that inquiry is made of someone within its walls.—Harlan: Barenblatt v. United States, 360 U.S. 109, 112.

3. An investigation in which the processes of law-making and law-evaluating are submerged entirely in exposure of individual behavior—in adjudication, of a sort, through the exposure process—is outside the constitutional pale of congressional inquiry.—Brennan: *ibid.*, 165.

4. In America . . . the investigative function is sometimes turned to publicity purposes, with the aim of making political capital out of someone's misfortune or mistake. — Douglas: *We the Judges,* 160.

5. It is true that Communists are the current phobia in Washington. But always, since I can remember, some group or other is being investigated and castigated here. At various times it has been Bundists and Germans, Japanese, lobbyists, tax evaders, oil men, utility men, bankers, brokers, labor leaders, Silver Shirts and Fascists. — Jackson: Dennis v. United States, 339 U.S. 162, 175.

6. To reach down into the hidden wells of knowledge and the more hidden wells of motive.—Cardozo: Jones v. SEC, 298 U.S. 1, 32.

Related subjects: Hearing and related subjects. *See also* Freedom, belief 140; Freedom, thought 146, 147.

INVESTMENT, INVESTOR

1. For my own part, I can conceive of no surer plan to arrest all public improvements, founded on private capital and enterprise, than to make the outlay of that capital uncertain and unquestionable, both as to security and as to productiveness. No man will hazard his capital in any enterprise in which, if there be a loss, it must be borne exclusively by himself; and if there be success, he has not the slightest security of enjoying the rewards of that success for a single moment.—Story: Charles River Bridge v. Warren Bridge, 11 Pet. (36 U.S.) 420, 608.

2. It is common knowledge that nothing is more alluring than the expectation of receiving large returns on small investments.—Brewer: Durland v. United States, 161 U.S. 306, 313.

3. One who invests his money in a business of a somewhat hazardous character is very properly held to have the right of a larger return.—Peckham: Willcox v. Consol. Gas Co., 212 U.S. 19, 49.

4. In speculative enterprises the capital cost of money is always high; partly because the risks involved must be covered; partly because speculative enterprises appeal only to the relatively small number of investors who are unwilling to accept a low return on their capital. — Brandeis: Missouri *ex rel.* S. W. Bell Tel. Co. v. Public Serv. Comm'n, 262 U.S. 276, 307.

5. The less risk, the less right to any unusual returns upon the investments.—Peckham: Willcox v. Consol. Gas Co., 212 U.S. 19, 49.

6. He who buys bonds seeks primarily safety. If he can obtain it, he is content with a low rate of interest.—Brandeis: Missouri *ex rel.* S. W. Bell Tel. Co. v. Public Serv. Comm'n, 262 U.S. 276, 307.

7. My idea is . . . to treat investments as a necessary evil, indulging in the operation as rarely as possible. Buy only the thing you consider very good and stick to it—unless you have come to doubt the wisdom of the purchase. And when you buy, buy the thing which you think safe, and will yield a fair return, but don't try to make your money out of investments. Make it out of your business. Take in that all the risks you think it prudent to take, but risk only there.—Brandeis: Mason, *Brandeis,* 214.

Related subjects: Capital; Income; Interest; Profit; Securities; Speculation. *See also* Insurance 7; Motive 6; Public Utility.

INVITATION
See Temptation.

IRRATIONAL
Out of the domain of the rational into the land of whim and fantasy.—Cardozo: Binney v. Long., 299 U.S. 280, 299.

ISSUE

1. All human experience teaches us that a moral issue cannot be suppressed or settled by making its supporters martyrs. — Stone: Mason, *Stone,* 107.

2. The precise issue must be freed from all atmospheric innuendoes.—

Frankfurter: Thiel v. Southern Pac.
Co., 328 U.S. 217, 229.

Related subject: Question. *See also* Judicial process 16.

JAPANESE
See Race 19.

JEALOUSY
Unreasonable jealousies not only blight the pleasures, but dissolve the very texture of society.—Johnson: Anderson v. Dunn, 6 Wheat. (19 U.S.) 204, 232.

JUDGE, JUDICIARY
Qualifications 1–19; influences 20–33; disabilities 34–48; encomia 49–59; miscellaneous 60–72.

Related subjects: Constitutional adjudication; Court; Judicial notice; Judicial process; Jury, judge, functions; Opinion (judicial); Precedent; Supreme Court; Trial.

———, qualifications

1. Dismal would be the state of the world, and melancholy the office of a judge, if all the evils which the perfidy and injustice of power inflict on individual man were to be reflected from the tribunals which profess peace and good will to all mankind.—Johnson: The Nereide, 9 Cranch (13 U.S.) 388, 432.

2. To say, that, as a judge, he was wise, impartial, and honest, is but to attribute to him those qualifications, without which the honors of the bench are but the means of public disgrace, or contempt.—Story: *Misc. Writings,* 205.

3. He possessed the happy faculty of yielding just the proper weight to

authority; neither, on the one hand, surrendering himself blindfold to the dictates of other judges, nor, on the other hand, overruling settled doctrines upon his own private notion of policy or justice.—Story: *ibid.,* 206.

4. A judge of the United States is expected to be a man of ordinary firmness of character. — Holmes: Toledo Newspaper Co. v. United States, 247 U.S. 402, 424.

5. Judges are apt to be naif, simpleminded men, and they need something of Mephistopheles. — Holmes: *Speeches,* 102.

6. Judges commonly are elderly men, and are more likely to hate at sight any analysis to which they are not accustomed, and which disturbs repose of mind, than to fall in love with novelties.—Holmes: "Law in Science and Science in Law," 12 Harv. L. Rev. 455.

7. No man is desirous of becoming the peculiar subject of calumny. No man, might he let the bitter cup pass from him without self-reproach, would drain it to the bottom. But if he have no choice in the case, if there be no alternative presented to him but a dereliction of duty or of the opprobrium of those who are denominated the world, he merits the contempt as well as the indignation of his country who can hesitate which to embrace. —Marshall: Beveridge, *Life of Marshall,* III, 512–13.

8. A Judge ought to be responsible only to God and to his own conscience. Marshall: *ibid.,* IV, 496.

9. The independence of the judges

is the great bulwark of public liberty, and the great security of property.—Story: *Misc. Writings,* 414.

10. Independence in compensation, as well as in tenure of office, is essential to the permanent respectability of the judicial department.—Story: *ibid.,* 481.

11. The independence of all those who try causes between man and man, and between a man and his Government, can be maintained only by the tenure of their office.—Marshall: Beveridge, *Life of Marshall,* IV, 495.

12. No matter what the evidence was against him, he had the right to have an impartial judge.—Taft: Tumey v. Ohio, 273 U.S. 510, 535.

13. Courts lean backward to avoid suspicion of partiality to men of our own profession.—Jackson: Kingsland v. Dorsey, 338 U.S. 318, 326.

14. As judges we are neither Jew nor Gentile, neither Catholic nor agnostic.—Frankfurter: West Va. State Bd. of Educ. v. Barnette, 319 U.S. 624, 647.

15. The most important thing about a man is his philosophy. . . . This, if not true for everyone, is true at least for judges.—Cardozo: *Growth of the Law,* 59.

16. The lawyer cannot rise to the full measure of his power in persuading, nor the judge to the full measure of *his* power in deciding, without an understanding of the process which the one attempts to control and the other to pursue.—Cardozo: *ibid.,* 26.

17. Judges must be more than lawyers; they must be statesmen as well.—Douglas: *We the Judges,* 255.

18. All judges should be made to feel, as many judges already feel, that the things needed to protect liberty are radically different from what they were fifty years back.—Brandeis: Mason, *Brandeis,* 436.

19. We are oath-bound to defend the Constitution.—Warren: Trop v. Dulles, 356 U.S. 86, 103.

———, influences

20. The great tides and currents which engulf the rest of men, do not turn aside in their course, and pass the judges by.—Cardozo: *Nature of Judicial Process,* 168.

21. The ingenuity of casuists and linguists, the nice criticism of able counsel, the zeal which springs from a large pecuniary interest, and the appeal of injured parties against the bad faith of the Legislatures who violate the Constitution are easily invoked, and their influence persuasive with the courts, as they always must be.—Miller: Woodson v. Murdock, 22 Wall. (89 U.S.) 351, 381.

22. The angry vindictive passions of men have too often made their way into judicial tribunals, and we cannot hope forever to escape their baleful influence.—Johnson: Martin v. Hunter's Lessee, 1 Wheat. (14 U.S.) 305, 377.

23. I do not know whether it is the view of the Court that a judge must be thick-skinned or just thick-headed, but nothing in my experience confirms

the idea that he is insensitive to publicity.—Frankfurter: Craig v. Harney, 331 U.S. 367, 396.

24. The consequence of attacks may differ with the temperament of the judge. Some judges may take fright and yield while others become more set in their course if only to make clear that they will not be bullied.—Frankfurter: *ibid.*, 395–96.

25. To deny that bludgeoning or poisonous comment has power to influence, or at least to disturb, the task of judging is to play make-believe and to assume that men in gowns are angels. The psychological aspects of this problem become particularly pertinent in the case of elected judges with short tenure.—Frankfurter: Pennekamp v. Florida, 329 U.S. 331, 359.

26. If it is true of juries it is not wholly untrue of judges that they too may be "impregnated by the environing atmosphere."—F r a n k f u r t e r: Bridges v. California, 314 U.S. 252, 300.

27. Courts sit to determine questions on stormy as well as on calm days.—Douglas: *We the Judges*, 64.

28. Motives of commiseration, from whatever source they flow, must not mingle in the administration of justice.—Paterson: Penhallow v. Doane's Adm'r, 3 Dall. (3 U.S.), 507, 521.

29. It is a misfortune if a judge reads his conscious or unconscious sympathy with one side or the other prematurely into the law, and forgets that what seem to him to be first principles are believed by half his fellow

men to be w r o n g. — Holmes: *Speeches*, 101.

30. Like other mortals, judges, though unaware, may be in the grip of prepossessions.—Frankfurter: Haley v. Ohio, 332 U.S. 596, 602.

31. It is a matter of common observation, that judges and lawyers, even the most upright, able and learned, are sometimes too much influenced by technical rules.—Gray: Sparf v. United States, 156 U.S. 51, 174.

32. Judges are not essentially different from other government officials. Fortunately they remain human even after assuming their judicial duties. Like all the rest of mankind they may be affected from time to time by pride and passion, by pettiness and bruised feelings, by improper understanding or by excessive zeal.—Black: Green v. United States, 356 U.S., 165, 198.

33. Deep below consciousness are other forces, the likes and dislikes, the predilections and the prejudices, the complex of instinct and emotions and habits and convictions, which make the man, whether he be litigant or judge.—Cardozo: *Nature of Judicial Process*, 167.

———, disabilities

34. I have always thought, from my earliest youth till now, that the greatest scourge an angry Heaven ever inflicted upon an ungrateful and a sinning people, was an ignorant, a corrupt, or a dependent Judiciary.—Mar-

shall: quoted O'Donoghue v. United States, 289 U.S. 516, 532.

35. While "an overspeaking judge is no well-tuned cymbal," neither is an amorphous dummy, unspotted by human emotions, a becoming receptacle for judicial power. — McReynolds: Berger v. United States, 255 U.S. 22, 43.

36. Intemperate language does not become my age or office.—Marshall: Beveridge, *Life of Marshall,* IV, 464.

37. The egotism that displays itself in harsh and overbearing manners, in explosive vigor or voice. . . . Exuberances such as these are at times the result of infirmities of temper not unknown altogether to the bench though happily uncommon; more often they are the defensive appliances of weakness or incapacity, conscious of its failings, and hopeful to divert attention by what seems to be a manifestation of its strength.—Cardozo: *Law and Literature,* 185.

38. Weak characters ought not to be judges.—Frankfurter: Pennekamp v. Florida, 328 U.S. 331, 357.

39. It has not been unknown that judges persist in error to avoid giving the appearance of weakness and vacillation.—Frankfurter: Craig v. Harney, 331 U.S. 367, 392.

40. Men who make their way to the bench sometimes exhibit vanity, irascibility, narrowness, arrogance, and other weaknesses to which human flesh is heir.—Jackson: Sacher v. United States, 343 U.S. 1, 12.

41. A timid judge, like a biased judge, is intrinsically a lawless judge.

—Frankfurter: Wilkerson v. McCarthy, 336 U.S. 53, 65.

42. History proved that judges too were sometimes tyrants. — Douglas: Poulos v. New Hampshire, 345 U.S. 395, 426.

43. Those judges who are wholly or chiefly occupied in the administration of criminal justice are apt, not only to grow severe in their sentences, but to decide questions of law too unfavorably to the accused.—Gray: Sparf v. United States, 156 U.S. 151, 174.

44. The accuser should not be the judge of the accusation.—Field: *Ex parte* Wall, 107 U.S. 265, 295.

45. When the responsibilities of lawmaker, prosecutor, judge, jury and disciplinarian are thrust upon a judge he is obviously incapable of holding the scales of justice perfectly fair and true and reflecting impartially on the guilt or innocence of the accused. He truly becomes the judge of his own cause.—Black: Green v. United States, 365 U.S. 165, 199.

46. We must be ever on our guard, lest we erect our prejudices into legal principles.—Brandeis: New State Ice Co. v. Liebmann, 285 U.S. 262, 311.

47. Thinking only in phrases to which, as lawyers, the judges have become accustomed, instead of looking straight at things.—Holmes: Lorenzo v. Wirth, 170 Mass. 596, 600.

48. No one, no matter how exalted his public office or how righteous his private motive, can be judge in his own case. — Frankfurter: United States v. UMW, 330 U.S. 258, 308.

————, encomia

49. The misfortune of the profession is, that great judges and great lawyers cannot enjoy a wide-spread popular favor.—Story: *Misc. Writings,* 211.

50. I have another and strong motive—my profound reverence and affection for the dead. *Mr. Chief Justice* Marshall is not here to speak for himself, and knowing full well the grounds of his opinions, in which I concurred, that this act is unconstitutional, I have felt an earnest desire to vindicate his memory from the imputation of rashness, or want of deep reflection. Had he been living, he would have spoken in the joint names of both of us. I am sensible that I have not done that justice to his opinion which his own great mind and exalted talents would have done.—Story: Briscoe v. Bank of Kentucky, 11 Pet. (36 U.S.) 257, 350.

51. Perhaps the genius of Marshall never shone forth in greater power and lustre.—Swayne: Farrington v. Tennessee, 5 Otto (95 U.S.) 679, 685.

52. I do fully believe that if American law were to be represented by a single figure, sceptic and worshipper alike would agree without dispute that the figure, could be one alone, and that one John Marshall. — Holmes: *Speeches,* 90.

53. He [Holmes] has the soul of the artist and poet, a keen and incisive mind, enriched by a lifetime of reading, study, and experience, a keen sense of humor, as well as sparkling wit and a beautiful prose style, pe-

culiarly adapted to the revelation of the process of legal thought without . . . excessive definition. . . . In the unyielding fidelity to truth, to right conduct, to the tolerant treatment of his fellow men, he is essentially religious. Add to this the soul of the artist and you have the principal characteristics of the man.—Stone: Mason, *Stone,* 325, 326-27.

54. Here, as so often, the right word is said by Holmes.—Cardozo: *Growth of the Law,* 97.

55. Justices such as Holmes and Brandeis have not only furnished the highest expression but they have been the very source and the intellectual leaders of recent liberalism in the United States.—Jackson: *Struggle for Judicial Supremacy,* 12.

56. The most liberty-alert Justices of all times—Holmes and Brandeis.—Jackson: Terminiello v. Chicago, 337 U.S. 1, 29.

57. Such guardians of civil liberty as Mr. Justice Cardozo.—Frankfurter: Milk Wagon Drivers Union v. Meadowmoor Dairies, 312 U.S. 287, 298.

58. And nowhere can one find the philosophy of conservatism and opposition to the Administration's policy more intelligently or earnestly expressed than in the opinions of Justices Sutherland and Butler. — Jackson: *Struggle for Judicial Supremacy,* 312.

59. It is not invidious to single out Miller, Davis, Bradley, Waite, Matthews, Gray, Fuller, Holmes, Brandeis, Stone and Cardozo (to speak only of the dead) as judges who were alert in safeguarding and promoting

the interests of liberty and human dignity through law.—Frankfurter: Adamson v. California, 32 U.S. 46, 62.

See also Constitution 51.

———, miscellaneous

60. Codes and statutes do not render the judge superfluous.—Cardozo: *Nature of Judicial Process*, 14.

61. Federal judges are not referees at prize fights but functionaries of justice. — Frankfurter: Johnson v. United States, 333 U.S. 46, 54.

62. The master of the revels, if so, without disrespect, I may characterize the judge presiding on the bench.—Cardozo: *Law and Literature*, 150.

63. His authority to make determinations includes the power to make erroneous decisions as well as correct ones. — B r a n d e i s: Swift & Co. v. United States, 276 U.S. 311, 331–32.

64. Judges differ greatly in their reverence for the illustrations and comments and side-remarks of their predecessors, to make no mention of their own.—Cardozo: *Nature of Judicial Process*, 29.

65. I do not take it that an ambition of a judge to remain a judge is either unusual or dishonorable.—Frankfurter: Craig v. Harney, 331 U.S. 367, 397.

66. A judge is presumed to know the elements of law, but there is no presumption that he knows the facts.—Brandeis: Mason, *Brandeis*, 248–49.

67. I once remarked that ignorance was the best of law reformers. . . . The judges didn't know much history and used their wits with no bad effect.—

Holmes: *Holmes-Pollock Letters*, I, 43.

68. The law is administered by able and experienced men, who know too much to sacrifice good sense to a syllogism.—Holmes: *Uncollected Letters*, 10–11.

69. A judge can never do more than his duty and . . . he ought not to be publicly praised because he has not done less.—Stone: Mason, *Stone*, 708.

70. To say that "the law is an ass, an idiot" is not to impugn the character of those who must administer it.—Brennan: *In re* Sawyer, 360 U.S. 622, 634.

71. To say that prosecutors are corrupt is not to impugn the character of judges who might be unaware of it, or be able to find no method of restraining them.—Brennan: *ibid*.

72. The court that raises its hand against the mob may be temporarily unpopular; but it soon wins the confidence of the nation. The court that fails to stand before the mob is not worthy of the great tradition.—Douglas: *We the Judges*, 445.

See also Argument (in court) 2; Freedom, press 172; Justice 19; Law 6, 16; Public opinion 13; Tax court.

JUDGMENT (conclusion)

1. Judgment often involves prophecy, and all prophecy has an element of guesswork. But guessing can be less rather than more.—Frankfurter: Insurance Gr. Comm. v. Denver & R. G. W. R.R., 329 U.S. 607, 628.

2. We should have something surer for judgment than speculation—something more than a deduction equivocal

of itself, even though the facts it rests on or asserts were not contradicted.—McKenna: United States v. U. S. Steel Corp., 251 U.S. 417, 448.

3. Realities must dominate the judgment. — Hughes: Appalachian Coals v. United States, 288 U.S. 344, 360.

4. The action does not appear to have been arbitrary except in the sense in which many honest and sensible judgments are so. They express an intuition of experience which outruns impressions—impressions which may lie beneath consciousness without losing their worth.—Holmes: Chicago, B. & Q. Ry. v. Babcock, 204 U.S. 585, 598.

5. It might gather evidence from any source. It might seek advice in any quarter. None the less, the ultimate decision was to be its own; and in gathering evidence or seeking counsel, it was enlightening its own judgment, and guiding its own choice.—Cardozo: Tismer v. New York Edison Co., 228 N.Y. 156, 162.

6. To the exercise of good judgment, calmness is, in times of deep feeling and on subjects which excite passion, as essential as fearlessness and honesty.—Brandeis: Schaefer v. United States, 251 U.S. 466, 483.

7. Judgment, the play of impression and conviction along with intelligence, varies with judges and also with circumstance.—Rutledge: Kotteakos v. United States, 328 U.S. 750, 761.

8. Man is weak and his judgment is at best fallible.—Brandeis: New

State Ice Co. v. Liebmann, 285 U.S. 262, 310.

9. The future may judge us less leniently than we choose to judge ourselves.—Cardozo: *Law and Literature,* 93.

10. There is a zone of reasonableness within which judgment is at large.—Cardozo: Atlantic Coast Line R.R. v. Florida, 295 U.S. 301, 317.

11. The expression of a whim rather than an exercise of judgment.—Cardozo: American Tel. & Tel. Co. v. United States, 299 U.S. 232, 237.

Related subjects: Belief and related subjects. *See also* Prejudice 1; Thought 3; Understanding 3; Zeal 5.

——— (legal)

12. The remedy for enforcing a judgment is the life of the judgment, just as much as the remedy for enforcing a contract is the life of the contract.—Bradley: Louisiana v. Mayor, 109 U.S. 285, 291.

13. A money judgment which cannot be collected is of as little value as Pumpelly's farm was, when covered by water to such an extent that it could not be used for any of the purposes for which land is desired.—Harlan: *ibid.,* 295.

14. When this court gives a judgment by the opinion of a majority, it is the judgment, in a legal sense, of the whole court.—Paterson: Penhallow v. Doane's Adm'rs, 3 Dall. (3 U.S.) 507, 524.

15. Judgment ceases to be judicial if there is condemnation in advance of trial.—Cardozo: Escoe v. Zerbst, 295 U.S. 490, 494.

Related subjects: Decision (judicial) and related subjects. *See also* Constitutional adjudication, judgment; Heart 1; Supreme Court 61.

JUDICIAL NOTICE

1. What everybody knows the court must know. — Harlan: Jacobson v. Massachusetts, 197 U.S. 11, 30.

2. We cannot as judges be ignorant of that which is common knowledge to all men.—Frankfurter: Sherrer v. Sherrer, 334 U.S. 343, 366.

3. We are not to close our eyes as judges to what we must perceive as men.—Cardozo: People *ex rel*. Alpha Portland Cement Co. v. Knapp, 230 N.Y. 48, 63.

4. Courts are not to shut their eyes to the realities of business life.—Cardozo: Barkin Constr. Co. v. Goodman, 221 N.Y. 156, 161.

5. There are many things that courts would notice if brought before them that beforehand they do not know.—Holmes: Quong Wing v. Kirkendall, 223 U.S. 59, 64.

Related subject: Notice. *See also* Court 51.

JUDICIAL PROCESS

1. The judicial process demands that a judge move within the framework of relevant legal rules and the covenanted modes of thought for ascertaining them. He must think dispassionately and submerge private feeling on every aspect of a case.—Frankfurter: Public Util. Comm'n v. Pollak, 343 U.S. 451, 466.

2. Much must be left to that deftness in the use of tools which the practice of an art develops.—Cardozo: *Growth of the Law*, 36.

3. Those tentative gropings, those cautious experiments, those provisional hypotheses, that are part of the judicial process.—Cardozo: *Law and Literature*, 126.

4. Judges march at times to pitiless conclusions under the prod of a remorseless logic which is supposed to leave them no alternative. They deplore the sacrificial rite. They perform it, none the less, with averted gaze, convinced as they plunge the knife that they obey the bidding of their office. The victim is offered up to the gods of jurisprudence on the altar of regularity.—Cardozo: *Growth of the Law*, 66.

5. If I may borrow a metaphor from the law of waters, the process by which judges work is one of erosion rather than avulsion.—Cardozo: *Paradoxes*, 42.

6. We are to weigh the competing considerations in such scales as are available. — Cardozo: Hoadley v. Hoadley, 244 N.Y. 424, 434.

7. Benefit and hardship will be set off, the one against the other.—Cardozo: Landis v. North Am. Co., 299 U.S. 248, 259.

8. There is no good in railing at us. You should rail at the legislature. The judges have no option in the matter. They are bound, hand and foot, by the shackles of a statute. — Cardozo: *Law and Literature*, 106.

9. The question is now a new one in this court, and we are not fettered by an inveterate course of decisions upon it. We are at liberty ... to decide it upon reason and not by precedent.—

Matthews: Conner v. Long, 14 Otto (104 U.S.) 228, 243.

10. The judge interprets the social conscience, and gives effect to it in law, but in so doing he helps to form and modify the conscience he interprets. Discovery and creation react upon each other.—Cardozo: *Growth of the Law*, 96–97.

11. We have to divine which is likely to be the highroad and which a *cul de sac*. We may be wrong but we have to take the risks.—Holmes: *Uncollected Letters*, 173.

12. The truth, of course, is that every doubtful decision involves a choice between a nicely balanced alternative, and no matter how long we debate or how carefully we ponder, we shall never arrive at certitude.—Cardozo: *Growth of the Law*, 140.

13. We are balancing and compromising and adjusting every moment that we judge.—Cardozo: *Paradoxes*, 75.

14. That just in proportion as a case is new and therefore valuable, no one, not even the judges, can be trusted to state the *ratio decidendi*.—Holmes: *Uncollected Letters*, 121.

15. The court may reverse itself, and unsettle what seem settled. It may ignore or misapply established rules through carelessness or ignorance or in rare instances corruption. — Cardozo: *Growth of the Law*, 43.

16. It is one of the little understood characteristics of the judicial process that while small issues are in the spotlight great issues lurk in the background.—Jackson: *Struggle for Judicial Supremacy*, 144.

Related subjects: Constitutional adjudication; Decision (judicial); Discretion (judicial); Dissent; Opinion (judicial).

JURISDICTION

1. Jurisdiction, whatever else or more it may mean is *jurisdictio*, in its popular sense of authority to apply the law to the acts of men.—Holmes: Wedding v. Meyler, 192 U.S. 573, 584.

2. Jurisdiction is the right to put the wheels of justice in motion.—Brown: Illinois Cent. R.R. v. Adams, 180 U.S. 28, 34.

3. The foundation of jurisdiction is physical power.—Holmes: McDonald v. Mabee, 243 U.S. 90, 91.

4. Jurisdiction is a matter of power, and covers wrong as well as right decisions.—Holmes: Lamar v. United States, 240 U.S. 60, 64.

5. Jurisdiction rests ultimately on power, but there may be moral restraints upon its abstract scope. — Frankfurter: "Holmes and the Constitution," 41 Harv. L. Rev. 157.

6. Jurisdiction is not a matter of sympathy or favor.—Holmes: Reid v. United States, 211 U.S. 529, 539.

7. "Jurisdiction" c o m p e t e s with "right" as one of the most deceptive of legal pitfalls.—Frankfurter: Yonkers v. United States, 320 U.S. 685, 695.

8. States u s u a l l y confine their threats to those within the jurisdiction at the time of the act.—Holmes: Hyde v. United States, 225 U.S. 347, 386.

See also Court 32.

JURISPRUDENCE

Jurisprudence as I look at it, is simply law in its most generalized part.—Holmes: "The Path of the Law," 10 Harv. L. Rev. 474.

Related subject: Law. *See also* Legislation 38.

JUROR, JURY, JURY TRIAL

Importance 1–3; composition, qualities 4–10; function 11–16; challenge 17–19; influences 20–31; judge, functions 32, 33; functions, charge 34–40; verdict 41–45; miscellaneous 46–49.

Related subjects: Grand jury; Trial.

———, importance

1. When Magna Charta declared that no freeman should be deprived of life, etc., "but by the judgment of his peers or by the law of the land," it referred to a trial by twelve jurors. —Harlan: Thompson v. Utah, 170 U.S. 343, 349.

2. Where is to be found a nobler institution than the trial by jury, that impregnable bulwark of civil liberty. —Story: *Misc. Writings*, 19.

3. Jury trials, as indicated by its very name, as affirmed by the fathers of the law who have defined this institution and proclaimed it to be the ark of safety for life, liberty and property.—Daniel: Mitchell v. Harmony, 13 How. (54 U.S.) 115, 142.

———, composition, qualities

4. The very idea of a jury is a body of men composed of the peers or equals of the person whose rights it is selected or summoned to determine; that is, of his neighbors, fellow associates, persons having the same legal

status in society as that which he holds. —Strong: Strauder v. West Virginia, 10 Otto (100 U.S.) 303, 308.

5. Juries fairly chosen from different walks of life bring into the jury box a variety of different experiences, feelings, institutions and habits. — Black: United States v. Quarles, 350 U.S. 11, 18.

6. A jury reflects the attitudes and mores of the community from which it is drawn. It lives only for the day and does justice according to its limits. The group of twelve, who are drawn to hear a case, makes the decision and melts away. It is not present the next day to be criticised. It is the one governmental agency that has no ambition. It is as human as the people who make it up. It is sometimes the victim of passion. But it also takes the sharp edges off a law and uses conscience to ameliorate a hardship. Since it is of and from the community, it gives the law an acceptance which verdicts of judges could not do.— Douglas: *We the Judges*, 389.

7. The jury system needs citizens trained to the exercise of the responsibilities of jurors. In common-law countries centuries of tradition have prepared a conception of the impartial attitude jurors must assume.—Taft: Balzac v. Porto Rico, 258 U.S. 298, 310.

8. Whether right or wrong, the premise underlying the constitutional method for determining guilt or innocence in federal courts is that laymen are better than specialists to perform this task.—Black: United States v. Quarles, 350 U.S. 11, 18.

9. The defendant's right is a neutral jury. He has no constitutional right to friends on the jury.—Jackson: Fay v. New York, 332 U.S. 261, 289.

10. Jury competence is not limited to those who earn their livelihood on other than a daily basis.—Murphy: Thiel v. Southern Pac. Co., 328 U.S. 217, 223.

——, function

11. In our criminal courts the jury sits as the representative of the community; its voice is that of the society against which the crime was committed. — Murphy: Williams v. New York, 337 U.S. 241, 253.

12. In some regions of conduct of a special sort we have to be informed of facts which we do not know before we can draw our lines intelligently, and so, as we get near the dividing point, we call in the jury.—Holmes: "Law in Science and Science in Law," 12 Harv. L. Rev. 457.

13. I do not believe that the jury have any historic or *a priori* right to decide any standard of conduct. — Holmes: *ibid.*, 459.

14. Every time that a judge declines to rule whether certain conduct is negligent or not, he avows his inability to state the law, and . . . the meaning of leaving nice questions to the jury is that while if a question of law is pretty clear we can decide it, as it is our duty to do, if it is difficult it can be decided better by twelve men taken at random from the street.—Holmes: *ibid.*, 457.

15. As the teachings of experience are matters of fact, it is easy to see why the jury should be consulted with regard to them.—Holmes: *The Common Law*, 150.

16. With only the rough and ready tests supplied by their experience of life, the jurors were to look into the workings of another's mind, and discover its capacities and disabilities, its urges and inhibitions, in moments of intense excitement.—Cardozo: People v. Zackowitz, 254 N.Y. 192, 195.

——, challenge

17. Preservation of the opportunity to prove actual bias is a guarantee of a defendant's right to an impartial jury.—Minton: Dennis v. United States, 339 U.S. 162, 171–72.

18. The right to challenge is the right to reject, not to select a juror. —Field: Hayes v. Missouri, 120 U.S. 68, 71.

19. One of the features which has tended to discredit jury trials is interminable examination and rejection of prospective jurors.—Jackson: Fay v. New York, 332 U.S. 261, 271.

——, influences

20. I have not found juries specially inspired for the discovery of truth. I have not noticed that they could see further into things or form a saner judgment than a sensible and well trained judge. I have not found them freer from prejudice than an ordinary judge would be.—Holmes: "Law in Science and Science in Law," 12 Harv. L. Rev. 459.

21. One of their gravest defects from the point of view of their the-

oretical function: that they will introduce into their verdict a certain amount—a very large amount, so far as I have observed—of popular prejudice, and thus keep the administration of the law in accord with the wishes and feelings of the community. —Holmes: *ibid.,* 460.

22. The man who wants a jury has a bad case. . . . The use of it is to let a little popular prejudice into the administration of law—(in violation of their oath). — Holmes: *Holmes-Pollock Letters,* I, 74.

23. Any judge who has sat with juries knows that, in spite of forms, they are extremely likely to be impregnated by the environing atmosphere.—Holmes: Frank v. Mangum, 237 U.S. 309, 349.

24. It is our duty . . . to declare lynch law as little valid when practised by a regularly drawn jury as when administered by one elected by a mob intent on death.—Holmes: *ibid.,* 350.

25. The public trial can, of course, be an ominous affair. There have been times in this country when a tense, crowded courtroom turned the trial into a theatrical performance, diverting it from a calm, dispassionate search for the truth. At other times the hostility of the crowd inside the courtroom has deprived the jury of its impartiality.—Douglas: *We the Judges,* 381.

26. On many o c c a s i o n s, fully known to the Founders of this country, jurors—plain people—have manfully stood up in defense of liberty against the importunities of judges and despite prevailing hysteria and prejudices. The acquittal of William Penn is an illustrious example. Unfortunately, instances could also be cited where jurors have themselves betrayed the cause of justice by verdicts based on prejudice or pressures.— Black: United States v. Quarles, 350 U.S. 11, 18–19.

27. Impartiality cannot survive in the shadow of threats to a juror's reputation and livelihood.—Black: Dennis v. United States, 339 U.S. 162, 181.

28. The naive assumption that prejudicial effects can be overcome by instructions to the jury . . . all practicing lawyers know to be unmitigated fiction.—Jackson: Krulewitch v. United States, 336 U.S. 440, 453.

29. It is difficult to conceive of a more effective obstruction to the judicial process than a juror who has prejudged the case.—Black: In the Matter of Michael, 326 U.S. 224, 228.

30. On one proposition I should expect trial lawyers to be nearly unanimous: that a jury, every member of which is in the hire of one of the litigants, lacks something of being an impartial jury. — Jackson: Frazier v. United States, 335 U.S. 497, 514.

31. The general tendency among men . . . to look somewhat more favorably, though perhaps frequently unconsciously, upon the side of the person or corporation that employs them. —Peckham: C r a w f o r d v. United States, 212 U.S. 183, 196.

See also Freedom, speech 99.

———, judges, functions

32. In a trial by jury in a Federal court, the judge is not a mere moderator, but is the governor of the trial.—Hughes: Herron v. Southern Pac. Co., 283 U.S. 91, 95.

33. As on the one hand, it is presumed, that the juries are the best judges of facts, it is, on the other hand, presumably, that the court are the best judges of law.—Jay: Georgia v. Brailsford, 3 Dall. (3 U.S.) 483, 484.

———, functions, charge

34. Even under our unfortunate legislation, in his mode of presenting the different hypotheses and stating the law according to what the jury may find, a judge inevitably adopts such an order and such an emphasis as to bring to their attention what he deems the important elements of the case, and by so doing inevitably in some degree helps to lead them to what he thinks the proper result.—Holmes: *Uncollected Letters,* 129–30.

35. Charging a jury is not a matter of abracadabra.—Frankfurter: Andres v. United States, 333 U.S. 740, 765.

36. This disquisition of the court was calculated to darken the light cast . . . by the attendant circumstances.—Fuller: Allison v. United States, 160 U.S. 203, 212.

37. A jury, eager for light upon a point of crucial moment, avows itself in darkness, and for answer is confirmed in error.—Cardozo: People v. Dixon, 231 N.Y. 111, 129.

38. With such a charge, the jury stood in need of unusual poise of mind and power of analysis if it was to weigh the case . . . dispassionately.—Cardozo: In the Matter of Kaufmann, 245 N.Y. 423, 425.

39. The charge, pervasive and poisonous, even if insidious and covert.—Cardozo: People v. Zackowitz, 254 N.Y. 192, 199.

40. The instructions to the jury . . . consisted of threadbare generalities, a jumble of empty abstractions.—Frankfurter: Fisher v. United States, 328 U.S. 463, 487.

———, verdict

41. Justice is not there unless there is also understanding. — Cardozo: People v. Dixon, 231 N.Y. 111, 130.

42. The discretion of the jury does not mean the right to gratify a whim or a personal fancy.—Holmes: Jones v. United States, 258 U.S. 40, 49.

43. Courts uniformly disapprove compromise verdicts but are without other means than admonitions to ascertain or control the practice.—Jackson: Stein v. New York, 346 U.S. 156, 178.

44. Apart from the control exercised by the judge, it is to be hoped that juries would realize that unreasonable verdicts would tend to make the business impossible and thus injure those whom they might wish to help.—Holmes: Arizona Copper Co. v. Hammer, 250 U.S. 400, 433–34.

45. In the last resort, all verdicts involve presumptions of fact; as, for

example, that men in general speak the truth under oath.—Holmes: *Uncollected Letters*, 86.

——, miscellaneous

46. Jurors not unfrequently seek to excuse themselves on the ground of having formed an opinion, when, on examination, it turns out that no real disqualification exists. In such cases the manner of the juror while testifying is oftentimes more indicative of the real character of his opinion than his words.—Waite: Reynolds v. United States, 8 Otto (98 U.S.) 145, 156–57.

47. Juries are not bound by what seems inescapable logic to judges.—Jackson: Morissette v. United States, 342 U.S. 246, 276.

48. We do not know, we cannot know, what evidence was determinative of guilt in the jury room.—Murphy: Nye & Nissen v. United States, 336 U.S. 613, 629.

49. As the circumstances become more numerous and complex, the tendency to cut the knot with the jury becomes greater.—Holmes: *The Common Law*, 152.

See also Citizen 19; Judge 26; Lawyer 76; Public opinion 13; Woman 8.

JUSTICE

Defined 1–5; principles 6–13; miscellaneous 14–23.

Related subject: Injustice.

——, defined

1. Perfect justice belongs to one judgment-seat only, that which is linked to the throne of God.—Story: *Misc. Writings*, 82.

2. Justice is but truth in action, and we cannot hope to attain justice until we have the proper respect for truth.—Brandeis: Mason, *Brandeis*, 437.

3. Perhaps we shall even find at times that when talking about justice, the quality we have in mind is charity, and this though the one quality is often contrasted with the other.—Cardozo: *Growth of the Law*, 87.

4. Justice to which law in its making should conform. Justice in this sense is a concept by far more subtle and indefinite than any that is yielded by mere obedience to a rule. It remains to some extent, when all is said and done, the synonym of an aspiration, a mood of exaltation, a yearning for what is fine or high.—Cardozo: *ibid*.

5. Justice itself, which we are wont to appeal to as a test as well as an ideal, may mean different things to different minds and at different times.—Cardozo: *ibid.*, 86.

——, principles

6. There are certain great principles of justice, whose authority is universally acknowledged. — Marshall: Fletcher v. Peck, 6 Cranch (10 U.S.) 87, 133.

7. As there are unchangeable principles of right and morality, without which society would be impossible, and men would be but wild beasts preying upon each other, so there are fundamental principles of eternal justice, upon the existence of which all constitutional government is founded, and without which government would be an intolerable and hateful

tyranny.—Field: Legal Tender Cases, 12 Wall. (79 U.S.) 457, 670.

8. The ideas of natural justice are regulated by no fixed standard; the ablest and purest men have differed upon the subject.—Iredell: Calder v. Bull, 3 Dall. (3 U.S.) 648, 654.

9. Nations differ from each other in condition, and that of the same nation may change by the revolutions of time, but the principles of justice are the same. They rest upon a base which will remain beyond the endurance of time.—Marshall: Worcester v. Georgia, 6 Pet. (31 U.S.) 515, 582.

10. There are certain principles of natural justice inherent in the Anglo-Saxon character, which need no expression in constitutions or statutes to give them effect.—Brown: Downes v. Bidwell, 182 U.S. 244, 280.

11. This fundamental principle flows from the very nature of our free Republican governments, that no man should be compelled to do what the laws do not require; nor to refrain from acts which the laws permit.—Chase: Calder v. Bull, 3 Dall. (3 U.S.) 648, 649.

12. Causes and not parties to causes, are weighed by justice in her equal scales: On the former solely, her attention is fixed: To the latter, she is as she is painted, blind.—Wilson: Chisholm v. Georgia, 2 Dall. (2 U.S.) 419, 466.

13. This great moral truth, that justice is the same whether due from one man or a million, or from a million to one man.—Jay: *ibid.,* 479.

——, miscellaneous

14. The sovereign does not create justice in an ethical sense . . . and there may be cases in which it would not dare to deny that justice for fear of war or revolution.—Holmes: United States v. Thompson, 257 U.S. 419, 432.

15. Judges may die, and courts be at an end; but justice still lives, and though she may sleep for a while, will eventually awake and must be satisfied.—Paterson: Penhallow v. Doane's Adm'rs, 3 Dall. (3 U.S.) 507, 520.

16. Out of the attempt to enforce individual justice grew the attempt to do social justice.—Brandeis: New York Cent. R.R. v. Winfield, 244 U.S. 147, 165.

17. Justice is not to be taken by storm. She is wooed by slow advances. —Cardozo: *Growth of the Law,* 133.

18. The edifice of justice stands, in its symmetry, to many, greater than before.—Cardozo: Palko v. Connecticut, 302 U.S. 319, 328.

19. There is no guaranty of justice except the personality of the judge.— Cardozo: *Nature of Judicial Process,* 17.

20. Justice must be tempered by compassion rather than by vengeance. —Murphy: In the Matter of Yamashita, 327 U.S. 1, 29.

21. Justice must satisfy the appearance of justice.—Frankfurter: Offutt v. United States, 348 U.S. 11, 14.

22. Those who undertake the search for justice are members of a universal priesthood. The search is world-wide.

No race is excluded.—Douglas: *We the Judges,* 16–17.

23. The justice of the case is most manifestly on the same side with the law.—Taney: Bank of U.S. v. United States, 2 How. (43 U.S.) 711, 761.

> See also Fiction 1; Form 12; Fraud 12; Freedom 38; Government (U.S.) 19; Legislation 19; Litigation 6, 27; Oppression 2; Remedy 16; Rule 3; Sovereignty 17; Tax 48.

KNOWLEDGE

1. If curiosity does not stimulate us to knowledge, we are almost compelled to ask it for safety.—Story: *Misc. Writings,* 141.

2. It is one of the wise dispensations of Providence, that knowledge should not only confer power, but should also confer happiness.—Story: *ibid.,* 124.

3. Knowledge is essential to understanding. — Brandeis: Burns Baking Co. v. Bryan, 264 U.S. 504, 520.

4. The first essential of wise and just action is knowledge.—Brandeis: Mason, *Brandeis,* 403.

5. There is nothing new in charging a party with knowledge of what it is his duty to know.—Holmes: Ferry v. Ramsey, 277 U.S. 88, 95.

6. When a man does the series of acts called walking, it is assumed for purposes of responsibility that he knows the earth is under his feet.—Holmes: *The Common Law,* 152–53.

7. The impossibility of nicely measuring a man's powers and limitations is far clearer than that of ascertaining his knowledge of law.—Holmes: *ibid.,* 108.

8. Knowledge that an act is forbidden by law will in most cases permit the inference of knowledge that, according to the accepted standards of mankind, it is also condemned as an offense against good morals.—Cardozo: People v. Schmidt, 216 N.Y. 324, 340.

> Related subjects: Education and related subjects; Judicial notice. *See also* Citizen 13, 14; Corporation 18, 52, 53; Fraud 2; Freedom, learning; Freedom, press; Generality 7; Honor 2; Intent 1, 2, 19; Investigation 6; Law 10; Liability 9; Litigation 6; Patent 3; Prophecy 3; Tax 95; Virtue 4; Waiver 1, 2.

LABEL

1. We must be on guard against being misled by labels.—Cardozo: Techt v. Hughes, 229 N.Y. 222, 246.

2. Catchwords and labels, such as the words "protective tariff," are subject to the dangers that lurk in metaphors and symbols, and must be watched with circumspection lest they put us off our guard.—Cardozo: Henneford v. Silas Mason Co., 300 U.S. 577, 586.

3. To take the name of a well understood concept and assign that name as a label to something which in ordinary understanding never fell within such concept. By this process any exaction can be tortured into something else and then justified under an assumed name.—Roberts: Wisconsin v. J. C. Penney Co., 311 U.S. 435, 449.

> Related subjects: Catch phrase; symbol. *See also* Form 17; Misbranding; Tax 75.

——, commercial

4. Every labeling is in a sense an advertisement. — Douglas: Kordel v.

United States, 335 U.S. 345, 351.

5. Few purchasers read long labels, many cannot read them at all. — Clarke: Houston v. St. Louis Ind. Pack. Co., 249 U.S. 479, 487.

See also Trade-mark 2.

LABOR (work, workingman)

General 1–4; employment 5–9; employer 10–15; employee 16–22; labor-management relations 23–27; public interest 28–38; union, defined 39, 40, history 41–44, need for 45, right to organize 46–49, value 50–56, power 57–59; union purposes 60–62, collective bargaining 63–74, closed shop 75–82; union, abuses 83–93, labor disputes, communication 94–98, strikes 99–104, picketing 105–107, violence 108–110; miscellaneous 111–113.

Related subjects: Child labor; Democracy (industrial); Foreman; Unemployment; Wage; Work.

———, general

1. Labor is property, and as such merits protection. The right to make it available is next in importance to the rights of life and liberty. It lies to a large extent at the foundation of most other forms of property, and of all solid individual and national prosperity. — Swayne: S l a u g h t e r House Cases, 16 Wall. (83 U.S.) 36, 127.

2. The rewards of labor will give an irresistible impulse to enterprise which must secure to our country a prosperity unequalled in history. — McLean: Pennsylvania v. Wheeling & Belmont Bridge Co., 13 How. (54 U.S.) 518, 576.

3. What c o n s t i t u t e s work for which payment is to be made varies with customs and practices in differ-

ent industries or businesses. — Roberts: Tennessee Coal, Iron & R.R. v. Muscoda Local, 321 U.S. 590, 608.

4. Refraining from other activity often is a factor of instant readiness to serve, and idleness plays a part in all employments in a stand-by capacity.—Jackson: Armour & Co. v. Wantock, 323 U.S. 126, 133.

———, employment

5. Employment is a business relation, if not itself a business.—Cardozo: Steward Mach. Co. v. Davis, 301 U.S. 548, 581.

6. Employment, like any other contract, presupposes understanding.—Cardozo: Murray v. Union Ry., 229 N.Y. 110, 113.

7. The right to employ and the right to labor are correlative—neither can be destroyed nor unduly hindered without impairing the other. — McReynolds: Arizona Copper Co. v. Hammer, 250 U.S. 400, 451–52.

8. The one has as much right to purchase as the other to sell labor.—Peckham: Lochner v. New York, 198 U.S. 45, 56.

9. One of the eternal conflicts out of which life is made up is that between the effort of every man to get the most he can for his services, and that of society, disguised under the name of capital, to get his services for the least possible return. — Holmes: Vegelahn v. Guntner, 167 Mass. 92, 108.

———, employer

10. Employers are as necessary to production as employees.—McKenna:

Arizona Copper Co. v. Hammer, 250 U.S. 400, 435.

11. Consider what the employer does: he invests his money in productive enterprise — mining, smelting, manufacturing, railroading; he engages employees at their request and pays them the wages they demand; he takes all the risks of the adventure. —McKenna: *ibid.*, 436.

12. The difference between the position of the employer and the employee, simply considering the latter as economically weaker, is not a justification for the violation of the rights of the former.—McKenna: *ibid.*, 437.

13. There is no more certain way of securing attention to the safety of the men—an unquestionably constitutional object of legislation—than by holding the employer liable for accidents. . . . They probably will happen a good deal less often when the employer knows that he must answer for them if they do.—Holmes: *ibid.*, 432–33.

14. There are few things so interesting in life as work, under proper conditions; and the way that employers generally work establishes the truth of this. They complain because their employees do not work similarly, do not feel the responsibility of the business. Let them give the employees a chance to bear responsibility and the response will come.—Brandeis: Mason, *Brandeis,* 432.

15. No employer has such a property in his workmen, or in their services, that he can . . . maintain a suit, as for a nuisance, against the keeper of a house at which they voluntarily buy intoxicating liquors, and thereby get so drunk as to be unfit for work. —Gray: Northern Pac. R.R. v. Whalen, 149 U.S. 157, 162.

———, employee

16. The right to work, I had assumed, was the most precious liberty that man possesses. Man has indeed as much right to work as he has to live, to be free, to own property. . . . It does many men little good to stay alive and free and own properties, if they cannot work. To work means to eat. It also means to live. For many it would be better to work in jail, than to sit idle on the curb. The great values of freedom are in the opportunities afforded man to press to new horizons, to pit his strength against the forces of nature, to match skills with his fellow man.—Frankfurter: Barsky v. Board of Regts., 347 U.S. 442, 472.

17. The assertion of the right to regularity in employment—a moral right, in a civilized community, superior to the right to dividends and equal, at least, to the right to regularity in the receipt of income from rents or interest.—Brandeis: Mason, *Brandeis,* 587.

18. I think the time is here when regularity of employment should be made an insistent fundamental demand of labor to take its place beside living wages, shorter hours, proper working conditions.—Brandeis: *ibid.*, 586.

19. What we want is to have the

workingman free; not to have him the beneficiary of a benevolent employer; and freedom demands a development in the employees of that self-control which results in thrift and in adequate provision for the future.—Brandeis: *ibid.*, 164.

20. Unrest means ordinarily unused facilities and there will be labor unrest until the faculties of the laboring man are fully utilized, and they cannot be without a share in the responsibility for the results of the business in which they are engaged.—Brandeis: *ibid.*, 432.

21. The coming of the machine age tended to despoil human personality. It turned men and women into "hands."—Frankfurter: AFL v. Am. Sash & Door Co., 335 U.S. 538, 542.

22. There is no more elemental cause for discharge of an employee than disloyalty to his employer.—Burton: NLRB v. Elec. Workers Union, 346 U.S. 464, 472.

———, labor-management relations

23. The problems of a trade should be no longer the problems of the employer alone. The problems of his business . . . are the problems of all in it. The union cannot shift upon the employer the responsibility for conditions, nor can the employer insist upon determining, according to his will, the conditions which shall exist. . . . There must be a division not only of profits, but a division also of responsibilities. — Brandeis: Mason, *Brandeis,* 430–31.

24. The relations between labor and industry are one of the crucial problems of the era. Their solution will doubtless entail many methods—education of labor leaders and business executives; the encouragement of mediation and conciliation by the President and the use of his great office in the cause of industrial peace; and the passage of laws.—Douglas: Youngstown Sheet & Tube Co. v. Sawyer, 343 U.S. 579, 630.

25. The ingredients of industrial peace and stabilized labor-management relations are numerous and complex. They may well vary from age to age and from industry to industry. What would be needful one decade might be anathema the next.—Douglas: Railway Emp. Dept. v. Hanson, 351 U.S. 225, 234.

26. Substantive rights and duties in the field of labor-management do not depend on verbal ritual reminiscent of medieval real property law.—Jackson: NLRB v. Rockaway News Supp. Co., 345 U.S. 71, 75.

27. Don't assume that the interests of employer and employee are necessarily hostile—that what is good for one is necessarily bad for the other. The opposite is more apt to be the case. While they have different interests, they are likely to prosper or suffer together. — Brandeis: Mason, *Brandeis,* 141.

———, public interest

28. The exploitation of a class of workers who are in an unequal position with respect to bargaining power

and are thus relatively defenceless against the denial of a living wage is not only detrimental to their health and well-being but casts a direct burden for their support upon the community. What these workers lose in wages the taxpayers are called upon to pay.—Hughes: West Coast Hotel Co. v. Parrish, 300 U.S. 379, 399.

29. No one doubts that the presence in the community of a large number of those compelled by economic necessity to accept a wage less than is needful for subsistence is a matter of grave public concern, the more so when, as has been demonstrated here, it tends to produce ill health, immorality and deterioration of the race. — Stone: Morehead v. New York, 298 U.S. 587, 633.

30. To protect labor is the highest office of our laws.—Field: *Ex parte Newman*, 9 Cal. 502, 521.

31. The drift of opinion and legislation now is to set labor apart and to withdraw it from its conditions and from the action of economic forces and their consequences—give it immunity from the pitilessness of life.— McKenna: Arizona Copper Co. v. Hammer, 250 U.S. 400, 438.

32. All men are entitled to the equal protection of the law in their right to work for the support of themselves and families.—Lamar: Smith v. Texas, 233 U.S. 630, 641.

33. The state must in some way come to the aid of the workingman if democratization is to be secured.— Brandeis: Mason, *Brandeis,* 431.

34. What can be closer to the pub-

lic interest than the health of women and their protection from unscrupulous and overreaching employers?— Hughes: West Coast Hotel Co. v. Parrish, 300 U.S. 379, 398.

35. The law should be as zealous to protect the constitutional liberty of the employee as it is to guard that of the employer.—Holmes: Coppage v. Kansas, 236 U.S. 1, 40.

36. Espousal of the cause of labor is entitled to no higher constitutional protection than the espousal of any other lawful cause. It is entitled to the same protection.—Rutledge: Thomas v. Collins, 323 U.S. 516, 538.

37. Labor relations are not matters of mere local or private concern.— Murphy: Thornhill v. Alabama, 310 U.S. 88, 103.

38. The peaceable settlement of labor controversies, especially where they may seriously impair the ability of an interstate rail carrier to perform its service to the public, is a matter of public concern.—Stone: Virginian Ry. v. System Fed., 300 U.S. 515, 552.

———, union, defined

39. Labor unions are business associations; their object is generally business dealings and relationships as is manifest from the financial statements of some of the national unions. Men are persuaded to join them for business reasons, as employers are persuaded to join trade associations for like reasons. — Roberts: Thomas v. Collins, 323 U.S. 516, 556.

40. Structurally and functionally, a labor union is an institution which

involves more than the private or personal interests of its members. It represents organized, institutional activity as contrasted with wholly individual activity.—Murphy: United States v. White, 322 U.S. 694, 701.

———, union, history

41. The history of trade unions. At first the law held them anathema. They were combinations in restraint of trade, pernicious, it was thought, in so far as they were effective, and, in the long run, as futile as they were pernicious, since economic "laws," then supposed to be inexorable, would nullify the gains of victory, and restore the pre-existing level. The result belied the prophecy. The urge to associate and unify was too spontaneous and persistent for any interdict to stifle it. The courts perceived and yielded. —Cardozo: *Paradoxes,* 133.

42. The industrial history of the early Nineteenth Century demonstrated the helplessness of the individual employee to achieve human dignity in a society so largely affected by technological advances. Hence the trade union made itself increasingly felt, not only as an indispensable weapon of self-defense on the part of workers but as an aid to the wellbeing of a society in which work is an expression of life and not merely the means of earning subsistence.—Frankfurter: AFL v. Am. Sash & Door Co., 335 U.S. 538, 542–43.

43. The labor movement in the United States is passing into a new phase. The struggle of the unions for recognition and rights to bargain, and of workmen for the right to join without interference, seems to be culminating in a victory for labor forces. We appear now to be entering the phase of struggle to reconcile the rights of individuals and minorities with the power of those who control collective bargaining groups. — J a c k s o n : Wallace Corp. v. NLRB, 323 U.S. 248, 271.

44. With this decision, the labor movement has come full circle. The workman has struggled long, the fight has been filled with hatred, and conflict has been dangerous, but now workers may not be deprived of their livelihood merely because their employers oppose and they favor unions. ... This Court now sustains the claim of a union to the right to deny participation in the economic world to an employer simply because the union dislikes him. — Jackson: Hunt v. Crumboch, 325 U.S. 821, 830–31.

———, union, need for

45. Long ago we stated the reason for labor organizations. We said that they were organized out of the necessities of the situation; that a single employee was helpless in dealing with an employer; that he was dependent ordinarily on his daily wage for the maintenance of himself and family; that if the employer refused to pay him the wages that he thought fair, he was nevertheless unable to leave the employ and resist arbitrary and unfair treatment; that union was essential to give laborers opportunity

to deal on equality with their employer.—Hughes: NLRB v. Jones & Laughlin Steel Corp., 301 U.S. 1, 33.

———, union, right to organize

46. I think that unity of organization is necessary to make the contest of labor effectual, and that societies of laborers lawfully may employ in their preparation the means which they might use in the final contest.—Holmes: Plant v. Woods, 176 Mass. 492, 505.

47. If it be true that workingmen may combine with a view, among other things, to getting as much as they can for their labor, just as capital may combine with a view to getting the greatest possible return, it must be true that when combined they have the same liberty that combined capital has to support their interests by argument, persuasion, and the bestowal or refusal of those advantages which they otherwise lawfully control.—Holmes: Vegelahn v. Guntner, 167 Mass. 92, 108.

48. Society itself is an organization, and does not object to organizations for social, religious, business, and all legal purposes. The law, therefore, recognizes the right of workingmen to unite and to invite others to join their ranks, thereby making available the strength, influence, and power that comes from such association. By virtue of this right powerful labor unions have been organized. — L a m a r : Gompers v. Bucks Stove & Range Co., 221 U.S. 418, 439.

49. In a free country every person,

be he an employer or an employee, be he in the public or in private service, should have an opportunity to combine with any other person or persons for the purpose of improving his condition. The right to combine is absolute; but the action of a combination must necessarily be confined to such action as is lawful, and should be confined to such action as is reasonable.—Brandeis: Mason, *Brandeis,* 150.

———, union, value

50. I could not pronounce it unwarranted if Congress should decide that to foster a strong union was for the best interest, not only of the men, but of the railroads and the country at large. — H o l m e s: Adair v. United States, 208 U.S. 161, 192.

51. The question what and how much good labor unions do, is one on which intelligent people may differ; I think that laboring men sometimes attribute to them advantages, as many attribute to combinations of capital advantages, that really are due to economic conditions of a far wider and deeper kind.—Holmes: *ibid.,* 191–92.

52. If ability, the qualities of efficient and faithful workmanship, can be found outside of labor associations, surely they may be found inside of them.—McKenna: *ibid.,* 186.

53. In present conditions a workman not unnaturally may believe that only by belonging to a union can he secure a contract that shall be fair to him.—Holmes: Coppage v. Kansas, 236 U.S. 1, 26–27.

54. The trade unions also stand as a strong bulwark against the great wave of socialism. They for the most part stand out for individualism as against the great rising of socialism on the one hand and of the accumulation of great fortunes on the other.—Brandeis: Mason, *Brandeis,* 149.

55. One would have to be blind to history to assert that trade unionism did not enhance and strengthen the right to work. — Douglas: Railway Emp. Dept. v. Hanson, 351 U.S. 225, 235.

56. Protection of the workers' right to self-organization does not curtail the appropriate sphere of managerial freedom; it furthers the wholesome conduct of business e n t e r p r i s e.— Frankfurter: Phelps Dodge Corp. v. NLRB, 313 U.S. 177, 182.

———, union, power

57. The very fact that it is lawful to form these bodies, with multitudes of members, means that they have thereby acquired a vast power, in the presence of which the individual may be helpless. — Lamar: Gompers v. Bucks Stove & Range Co., 221 U.S. 418, 439.

58. Unions are powers within the State.—Frankfurter: AFL v. American Sash & Door Co., 335 U.S. 538, 544.

59. The need for unprecedented economic mobilization propelled by World War II enormously stimulated the power of organized labor and soon aroused consciousness of its power outside its ranks.—Frankfurt-er: United States v. UAW, 352 U.S. 567, 578.

———, union purposes

60. The ethical right of every worker, man or woman, to a living wage, may be conceded. One of the declared and important purposes of trade organizations is to secure it.—Sutherland: Adkins v. Children's Hosp., 261 U.S. 525, 556.

61. Unions obviously are concerned not to have union standards undermined by non-union shops. This interest penetrates into self-employer shops. — Frankfurter: Teamsters Union v. Hanke, 339 U.S. 470, 475.

62. Unions should strive to make the earnings of any business as large as possible.
Unions should not limit the production of individuals.
Should be so faithful and diligent that espionage will not be needed.
Should demand steady work.
Should adapt their demands to the conditions of a particular business.
Labor unions should strive to make labor share all the earnings of a business except what is required for capital and management.—Brandeis: Mason, *Brandeis,* 151.

———, union purposes, collective bargaining

63. Collective bargaining between powerful combinations of employers and employees in an entire industry, each group conscious of what it seeks and having not merely responsibility for its membership but resourceful experience in discharging it, is a form

of industrial government whereby self-imposed law supplants force.—Frankfurter: Bay Ridge Oper. Co. v. Aaron, 334 U.S. 446, 492.

64. No time is a good time needlessly to sap the principle of collective bargaining or to disturb harmonious and fruitful relations between employers and employees brought about by collective bargaining.—Frankfurter: *ibid.*, 477–78.

65. Whatever may be the advantages of "collective bargaining," it is not bargaining at all, in any just sense, unless it is voluntary on both sides.—Pitney: Hitchman Coal & Coke Co. v. Mitchell, 245 U.S. 229, 250.

66. Good-faith bargaining necessarily requires that claims made by either bargainer should be honest claims.—Black: NLRB v. Truitt Mfg. Co., 351 U.S. 149, 152.

67. "Good faith" means more than merely going through the motions of negotiating; it is inconsistent with a predetermined resolve not to budge from an initial position. But it is not necessarily incompatible with stubbornness or even with what to an outsider may seem unreasonableness. A determination of good faith or of want of good faith normally can rest only on an inference based upon more or less persuasive manifestations of another's state of mind.—Frankfurter: *ibid.*, 154–55.

68. A business man who entered into negotiations with another for an agreement having numerous provisions, with the reservation that he would not reduce it to writing or sign

it, could hardly be thought to have bargained in good faith. — Stone: Heinz Co. v. NLRB, 311 U.S. 514, 526.

69. The bargaining representative, whoever it may be, is responsible to, and owes complete loyalty to, the interests of all whom it represents.—Burton: Ford Mot. Co. v. Huffman, 345 U.S. 330, 338.

70. The practice and philosophy of collective bargaining looks with suspicion on . . . individual advantages. —Jackson: J. I. Case Co. v. NLRB, 321 U.S. 332, 338.

71. E x p e r i e n c e has abundantly demonstrated that the recognition of the right of employees to self-organization and to have representatives of their own choosing for the purpose of collective bargaining is often an essential condition of industrial peace.—Hughes: NLRB v. Jones & Laughlin Steel Corp., 301 U.S. 1, 42.

72. It is of the essence of collective bargaining that it is a continuous process. Neither the conditions to which it addresses itself nor the benefits to be secured by it remain static. — Frankfurter: Aeronautical Ind. Dist. Lodge v. Campbell, 337 U.S. 521, 525.

73. It is too late now to argue that employees can have no collective voice to influence railroads to act in a way that will preserve the interests of the employees as well as the interests of the railroad and the public at large.—Black: Railroad Teleg'rs v. Chicago & N. W. Ry., 362 U.S. 330, 338.

74. A collective bargaining agree-

ment is an effort to erect a system of industrial self-government. — Douglas: United Steelworkers v. Warrior & Gulf Nav. Co., 363 U.S. 574, 580.

———, union purposes, closed shop

75. The closed shop is well known in labor relations. Its essential philosophy is that once the employees have chosen their representative union, it is entitled to bargain for the employer's help to maintain its control. . . . A closed shop is the ultimate goal of most union endeavor.—Jackson: Wallace Corp. v. NLRB, 323 U.S. 248, 267.

76. The cause of industrial liberty will ordinarily be best subserved by an open shop in which a strong union has a predominating influence. But it is not true that the closed shop— that is, the shop open to all willing to become union men, and to such only—"will never give us peace with liberty." The union shop is not necessarily prejudicial to industrial liberty; its adoption may, at times, be indispensable to the attainment or preservation of liberty . . . ; e.g., where the employer, while pretending to run an open shop, is actually and insidiously discriminating against union men. . . . In such cases, adoption of the union shop becomes a proper war measure.—Brandeis: Mason, *Brandeis*, 150–51.

77. The American people should not, and will not, accept unionism if it involves a closed shop. They will not consent to the exchange of the tyranny of the employer for the tyran-

ny of the employee. Unionism therefore cannot make a great advance until it abandons the closed shop; and it cannot accept the open shop as an alternative. The "open shop means the destruction of the union."—Brandeis, *ibid.,* 303.

78. The objections, legal, economic, and social, against the closed shop are so strong, and the ideas of the closed shop so antagonistic to the American spirit, that the insistence upon it has been a serious obstacle to union progress. On the other hand, the open shop, as ordinarily practiced, has tended to disintegrate union membership, and has in it inherent injustice—namely, that the burden of obtaining satisfactory wages, hours, and conditions is borne by but a fraction of those who enjoy the benefits. The preferential union shop seems to offer a solution consistent with American spirit and traditions as well as with justice and with the necessity of strengthening the unions.—Brandeis: *ibid.,* 301.

79. One of the oldest techniques in the art of collective bargaining is the closed shop. It protects the integrity of the union and provides stability of labor relations.—Minton: Colgate-Palmolive-Peet Co. v. NLRB, 338 U.S. 355, 362.

80. The same liberty, which enables men to form unions, and through the union to enter into agreements with employers willing to agree, entitles other men to remain independent of the union, and other employers to agree with them to employ no man who owes any allegiance to the union.

—Pitney: Hitchman Coal & Coke Co. v. Mitchell, 245 U.S. 229, 250–51.

81. There cannot be wrung from a constitutional right of workers to assemble to discuss improvement of their own working standards, a further constitutional right to drive from remunerative employment all other persons who will not or can not, participate in union assemblies.—Black: Lincoln Fed. Lab. Union v. Northwestern Iron & Metal Co., 335 U.S. 525, 531.

82. An appreciable number of men who are non-unionist. . . . Such a nucleus of unorganized labor will check oppression by the union as the union checks oppression by the employer.—Brandeis: Mason, *Brandeis,* 150.

————, union, abuses

83. A bad act is no worse, as it is no better, because it has been done by a labor union and not by a partnership or a business corporation. If unions are lawless, restrain and punish their lawlessness; if they are arbitrary, repress their arbitrariness; if their demands are unreasonable or unjust, resist them; but do not oppose unions as such.—Brandeis: *ibid.,* 142.

84. I think there is no man or body of men whose character will stand absolute power, and I should no more think of giving absolute power to unions than I should of giving it to capital monopoly power.—Brandeis: *ibid.,* 360.

85. The maintenance of a "company union" dominated by the em-

ployer, may be a ready and effective means of obstructing self-organization of employees and their choice of their own representatives for the purpose of collective bargaining.—Stone: NLRB v. Pennsylvania Greyhound Lines, 303 U.S. 261, 266.

86. Management control over company sponsored employee organizations runs the entire scale of intensity. It may be slight or complete.—Reed: NLRB v. Southern Bell Tel. & Tel. Co., 319 U.S. 50, 60.

87. The denial of jobs to men because of union affiliations is an old and familiar aspect of American industrial relations.—F r a n k f u r t e r: Phelps Dodge Corp. v. NLRB, 313 U.S. 177, 182.

88. Discrimination against union labor in the hiring of men is a dam to self-organization at the source of supply. The effect of such discrimination is not confined to the actual denial of employment; it inevitably operates against the whole idea of the legitimacy of organization. In a word, it undermines the principle which, as we have seen, is recognized as basic to the attainment of industrial peace. —Frankfurter: *ibid.,* 185.

89. Discrimination in hiring is twin to discrimination in firing.—Frankfurter: *ibid.,* 187.

90. Race discrimination by an employer may reasonably be deemed more unfair and less excusable than discrimination against workers on the ground of union affiliation.—Roberts: New Negro Alliance v. Sanitary Grocery Co., 303 U.S. 552, 561.

91. The desire for fair and equitable conditions of employment on the part of persons of any race, color, or persuasion, and the removal of discriminations against them by reason of their race or religious beliefs is quite as important to those concerned as fairness and equity in terms and conditions of employment can be to trade or craft unions or any form of labor organization or association.—Roberts: *ibid*.

92. The right of association, like any other right carried to its extreme, encounters limiting principles. . . . At the point where the mutual advantage of association demands too much individual disadvantage, a compromise must be struck.—Frankfurter: AFL v. Am. Sash & Door Co., 335 U.S. 538, 546.

93. However desirable the elimination of all industrial featherbedding practices may have appeared to Congress, the legislative history of the Taft-Hartley Act demonstrates that when the legislation was put in final form Congress decided to limit the practice but little by law.—Burton: American Newspaper Pub. Assoc. v. NLRB, 345 U.S. 100, 106.

———, union, labor disputes, communication

94. Members of a union might, without special statutory authorization by a State, make known the facts of a labor dispute, for freedom of speech is guaranteed by the Federal Constitution.—Brandeis: Senn v. Tile Layers Union, 301 U.S. 468, 478.

95. The publication unaccompanied by violence, of a notice that the employer is unfair to organized labor and requesting the public not to patronize him is an exercise of the right of free speech guaranteed by the First Amendment which cannot be made unlawful by act of Congress.—Stone: United States v. Hutcheson, 312 U.S. 219, 243.

96. Free speech on both sides and for every faction on any side of the labor relation is to me a constitutional and useful right. Labor is free to turn its publicity on any labor oppression, substandard wages, employer unfairness, or objectionable working conditions. The employer, too, should be free to answer, and to turn publicity on the records of the leaders or the unions which seek the confidence of his men.—Jackson: Thomas v. Collins, 323 U.S. 516, 547.

97. This conduct is the stuff out of which labor-management strife has been made, ever since trade unionism began its growth. For years the law of the jungle applied, victory going to the strongest. The emergence of more civilized methods of settling these disputes is familiar history. At first, the law was mostly on the side of management. The courts, as well as the legislatures, shaped the rules against the interests of labor. Gradually the human rights in industry were recognized until they finally received more generous recognition under the Wagner Act.—Douglas: United Constr. Workers v. Laburnum Constr. Corp., 347 U.S. 656, 670.

98. The processing of disputes through the grievance machinery is actually a vehicle by which meaning and content are given to the collective bargaining agreement. — Douglas: United Steelworkers v. Warrior & Gulf Nav. Co., 363 U.S. 574, 581.

———, union, strikes

99. I can remember when many people thought that, apart from violence or breach of contract, strikes were wicked, as organized refusals to work. I suppose that intelligent economists and legislators have given up that notion today. I feel pretty confident that they equally will abandon the idea that an organized refusal by workmen of social intercourse with a man who shall enter their antagonists employ is wrong, if it is disassociated from any threat of violence, and is made for the sole object of prevailing if possible in a contest with their employer about the rate of wages. — Holmes: Vegelahn v. Guntner, 167 Mass. 92, 108–109.

100. I cherish no illusions as to the meaning and effect of strikes. While I think the strike a lawful instrument in the universal struggle of life, I think it pure phantasy to suppose that there is a body of capital of which labor as a whole secures a larger share by that means. The annual produce, subject to an infinitesimal deduction for the luxuries of the few, is directed to consumption by the multitude, and is consumed by the multitude, always. Organization and strikes may get a larger share for the members of an organization, but, if they do, they get it at the expense of the less organized and less powerful portion of the laboring mass.—Holmes: Plant v. Woods, 176 Mass. 492, 505.

101. The change in the law by which strikes once illegal and even criminal are now recognized as lawful was effected in America largely without the intervention of legislation. This . . . was . . . due . . . to a better realization of the facts of industrial life.—Brandeis: Duplex P. P. Co. v. Deering, 254 U.S. 443, 481.

102. Neither the common law, nor the 14th Amendment, confers the absolute right to strike.—Brandeis: Dorchy v. Kansas, 272 U.S. 306, 311.

103. The ultimately desirable social policy is to make it a matter of industrial habit to rely for a remedy for such grievances not on stoppage of work or on lawsuits but on the grievance procedure within an industry.—Burton, Minton: Association v. Westinghouse Elec. Co., 348 U.S. 437, 458.

104. Labor injunctions were long used as cudgels—so broad in scope, so indiscriminate in application as once to be dubbed "a 'scarecrow' device for curbing the economic pressure of the strike."—Douglas: United Steelworkers v. United States, 361 U.S. 39, 73.

———, union, picketing

105. Peaceful picketing is the workingman's means of communication.—Frankfurter: Milk Wagon Drivers Union v. Meadowmoor Dairies, 312 U.S. 287, 293.

106. In declaring . . . picketing per-

missible Wisconsin has put this means of publicity on a par with advertisements in the press.—Brandeis: Senn v. Tile Layers Union, 301 U.S. 468, 479.

107. Picketing by an organized group is more than free speech since it involves patrol of a particular locality and since the very presence of a picket line may induce action of one kind or another, quite irrespective of the nature of the ideas which are being disseminated.—Douglas: Bakery & Pastry Drivers v. Wohl, 315 U.S. 769, 776.

———, union, violence

108. From the standpoint of the state, industrial controversy may not overstep the bounds of an appeal to reason and sympathy.—Reed: Milk Wagon Drivers Union v. Meadowmoor Dairies, 312 U.S. 287, 319.

109. It cannot be doubted that attempts to persuade others by the application of physical force and violence as a substitute for persuasion by reason and peaceable argument is contrary to the first principles of our government.—Black: *ibid.,* 301.

110. "Right to free speech in the future cannot be forfeited because of dissociated acts of past violence." . . . Still less can the right to picket itself be taken away merely because there may have been isolated incidents of abuse falling far short of violence occurring in the course of that picketing.—Frankfurter: Cafeteria Emp. Union v. Angelos, 320 U.S. 293, 296.

———, miscellaneous

111. Few tasks of leadership are more difficult than those which confront those who represent labor. If they are gentle, they are often unheeded; and if they are blunt, they are often held up as menacing.—Jackson: NLRB v. Indiana & Mich. Elec. Co., 318 U.S. 9, 27–28.

112. Strife between competing unions has been an obdurate conflict in the evolution of so-called craft unionism and has undoubtedly been one of the potent forces in the modern development of industrial unions.—Frankfurter: United States v. Hutcheson, 312 U.S. 219, 232.

113. The history of the rules governing contests between employer and employed in the several English-speaking countries illustrates both the susceptibility of such rules to change and the variety of contemporary opinion as to what rules will best serve the public interest.—Brandeis: Truax v. Corrigan, 257 U.S. 312, 357.

See also Constitution 88; Foreman; Fraud 11; Monopoly 16; Occupation; Property 5; Real property 3; Restraint of trade 18, 19; Rights 3; Seaman; Sunday 2; Transportation; Unemployment 6; Veteran 5; Wage.

LACHES (legal)

1. The lapse of time . . . gradually shapes the mind to expect and demand the continuance of what it actually and long has enjoyed, even if without right, and dissociates it from a like demand of even a right which long

has been denied.—Holmes: Davis v. Mills, 194 U.S. 451, 457.

2. From the earliest ages, courts of equity have refused their aid to those who have neglected for an unreasonable length of time, to assert their claims.—Marshall: Elmendorf v. Taylor, 10 Wheat. (23 U.S.) 152, 168.

3. The hour-glass must supply the ravages of the scythe, and those who have slept upon their rights must be remitted to the repose from which they should not have been aroused.—Fuller: Hammond v. Hopkins, 143 U.S. 224, 274.

4. Sometimes it is said that, if a man neglects to enforce his rights, he cannot complain if, after a while, the law follows his example. — Holmes: "The Path of the Law," 10 Harv. L. Rev. 476.

Related subjects: Limitations; Limitations, statute of; Prescription.

LAND

Related subject: Real property. See also Air (aviation); Ownership 5.

LANDLORD

See Rent law 1.

LANGUAGE

1. It is desirable that all the citizens of the United States should speak a common tongue.—Holmes: Meyer v. Nebraska, 262 U.S. 390, 412.

2. Among the respectable there are some who regard me as a dangerous radical! If I had seen fit to clothe my views in different language, I dare say I could have been a pet of the proletariat—whereas they care nothing for me and some of the others distrust

me. — Holmes: *Holmes-Pollock Letters,* I, 50.

Related subjects: Catch phrase; Construction and related subjects; Speech; Word. *See also* Constitution, construction; Construction, technical terms; Construction, penal; Doubt 1; Education 6; Illustration 1; Incitement; Judge 36; Mind 7; opinion 22, 23; Prohibition 4; Purpose 3; Symbol 7.

LARCENY

The stealing of one cent is larceny as truly as the stealing of a thousand dollars.—Brewer: Frisbie v. United States, 157 U.S. 160, 167.

Related subjects: Conversion; Theft. *See also* Dishonesty 2.

LAW

Defined 1–14; basis 15–24; development 25–52; importance, obedience 53–60; function 61–72; standards 73–76; operation, general 77–84, certainty, consistency 85–93; enforcement 94–107; miscellaneous 108–111.

Related subjects: Admiralty; Constitution (general); Constitution (U.S.) Constitutional adjudication; Constitutional law; Court; Criminal law; Equal protection; Equity; Equity court; Government (U.S.); Judge; Justice; Legislation; Military law; Precedent.

——, defined

1. Law is a statement of the circumstances, in which the public force will be brought to bear upon men through the courts.—Holmes: American Banana Co. v. United Fruit Co., 213 U.S. 347, 356.

2. The prophecies of what the courts will do in fact, and nothing more pretentious, are what I mean by the law.—Holmes: "The Path of the Law," 10 Harv. L. Rev. 460–61.

3. Law is a word used with different meanings, but law in the sense in which courts speak of it today, does not exist without some definite authority behind it.—Holmes: Black & White Taxi. Transfer Co. v. Brown & Yellow Taxi. Transfer Co., 276 U.S. 518, 533.

4. Pretty much all law consists in forbidding men to do some things that they want to do.—Holmes: Adkins v. Children's Hosp., 261 U.S. 525, 568.

5. It is not every Act, legislative in form, that is law. Law is something more than mere will exerted as an act of power. . . . Arbitrary power, enforcing its edicts to the injury of the person and property of its subjects, is not law, whether manifested as the decree of a personal monarch or of an impersonal multitude.—Matthews: Hurtado v. People of Calif., 110 U.S. 516, 531.

6. What has been termed the general law of the country—is often little less than what the judge advancing the doctrine thinks at the time should be the general law on a particular subject.—Field: Baltimore & O. R. R. v. Baugh, 149 U.S. 368, 401.

7. A use of the term law strengthens the analogy between the law which is the concern of jurisprudence, and those principles of order, the natural or moral laws, which are the concern of natural or moral science. —Cardozo: *Growth of the Law*, 34.

8. As in the processes of nature, we give the name of law to uniformity of succession.—Cardozo: *ibid.*, 40.

9. Law, by the very terms of the hypothesis, is the expression of the convictions of the present, not the convictions of the past.—Cardozo: *ibid.*, 104.

10. Law is the expression of a principle of order to which men must conform in their conduct and relations as members of society, if friction and waste are to be avoided among the units of the aggregate, the atoms of the mass.—Cardozo: *ibid.*, 140–41.

11. Law is neither formal logic nor the embodiment of inexorable scientific laws. It is a human institution, created by human agents to serve human ends.—Stone: Mason, *Stone,* 140.

12. Law has the mandate of man's striving for reason and justice; but explicitly it is the voice of some defined organ of government.—Frankfurter: "Holmes and the Constitution," 41 Harv. L. Rev. 157.

13. Deeply embedded traditional ways of carrying out state policy . . . are often tougher and truer law than the dead words of the written text.— Frankfurter: Nashville, C. & St. L. Ry v. Browning, 310 U.S. 362, 369.

14. The law, so far as it depends on learning, is indeed, as it has been called, the government of the living by the dead. To a very considerable extent no doubt it is inevitable that the living should be so governed.— Holmes: *Speeches,* 67.

———, basis

15. The basis of sound and genuine jurisprudence: laws derived from the

pure source of equality and justice must be founded on the consent of those, whose obedience they require. The sovereign, when traced to his source, must be found in the man.—Wilson: Chisholm v. Georgia, 2 Dall. (2 U.S.) 419, 458.

16. In a civilized state it is not the will of the sovereign that makes lawyers' law, even when that is its source, but what a body of subjects, namely, the judges, by whom it is enforced *say* is his will.—Holmes: *Uncollected Letters*, 25.

17. The first requirement of a sound body of law is, that it should correspond with the actual feelings and demands of the community, whether right or wrong.—Holmes: *The Common Law*, 41.

18. The substance of the law at any given time pretty nearly corresponds, so far as it goes, with what is then understood to be c o n v e n i e n t.—Holmes: *ibid.*, 1–2.

19. The law, if not a part of morality, is limited by it. But this limit of power is not coextensive with any system of morals. For the most part it falls far within the lines of any such system, and in some cases may extend beyond them, for reasons drawn from the habits of a particular people at a particular time.—Holmes: "The Path of the Law," 10 Harv. L. Rev. 460.

20. Theory is the most important part of the dogma of the law, as the architect is the most important man who takes part in the building of a house.—Holmes: *ibid.*, 477.

21. I am so sceptical as to our knowledge about the goodness or badness of laws that I have no practical criticism except what the crowd wants. Personally I bet that the crowd if it knew more wouldn't want what it does—but that is i m m a t e r i a l.—Holmes: *Holmes-Pollock Letters*, I, 163.

22. It is not the words of the law but the internal sense of it that makes the law; the letter of the law is the body; the sense and reason of the law is the soul.—Harlan: Civil Rights Cases, 109 U.S. 3, 26.

23. Life casts the moulds of conduct, which will some day become fixed as laws. Law preserves the moulds, which have taken form and shape from life. — Cardozo: *Nature of Judicial Process*, 64.

24. We are told by a great master that law is civilized to the extent that it is purposefully conscious.—Frankfurter: Mitchell v. Trawler Racer, 362 U.S. 539, 551.
See also Custom 1.

———, development

25. The life of the law has not been logic; it has been experience. — Holmes: *The Common Law*, 1.

26. The process of justice is never finished, but reproduces itself, generation after generation, in ever-changing forms.—Cardozo: *Law and Literature*, 167.

27. Nothing is stable. Nothing absolute. All is fluid and changeable. There is an endless "becoming."—Cardozo: *Nature of Judicial Process*, 28.

28. This court has not failed to recognize the fact that the law is to a certain extent a progressive science.—Brown: Holden v. Hardy, 169 U.S. 366, 385.

29. Law is not a science, but is essentially empirical.—Holmes: *Uncollected Letters*, 66–67.

30. It will be remembered that the earliest appearance of law was as a substitute for the private feuds between families or clans. — Holmes: *The Common Law*, 248.

31. In substance the growth of the law is legislative.—Holmes: *ibid.*, 35.

32. The development of our law has gone on for nearly a thousand years, like the development of a plant, each generation taking the inevitable next step, mind, like matter, simply obeying a law of spontaneous growth.—Holmes: "The Path of the Law," 10 Harv. L. Rev. 468.

33. The law is the witness and external deposit of our moral life. Its history is the history of the moral development of the race.—Holmes: *ibid.*, 459.

34. We do not realize how large a part of our law is open to reconsideration upon a slight change in the habit of the public mind.—Holmes: *ibid.*, 466.

35. It cannot be helped. It is as it should be, that the law is behind the times. . . . It means that the law is growing. As law embodies beliefs that have triumphed in the battle of ideas and then have translated themselves into action, while there still is doubt, while opposite convictions still keep a battle-front against each other, the time for law has not come; the notion destined to prevail is not yet entitled to the field. — H o l m e s: *Speeches,* 101.

36. The law has grown, and even if historical mistakes have contributed to its growth, it has tended in the direction of rules consistent with human nature. — Holmes: Brown v. United States, 256 U.S. 335, 343.

37. If I haven't done my share in the way of putting in new and remodeling old thoughts for the last twenty years then I delude myself.—Holmes: *Holmes-Pollock Letters,* I, 106.

38. It is obvious, that the law must fashion itself to the wants, and, in some sort, to the spirit of the age. Its stubborn rules, if they are not broken down, must bend to the demands of society.—Story: *Misc. Writings,* 307.

39. The new generations bring with them their new problems which call for new rules, to be patterned, indeed, after the rules of the past, and yet adapted to the needs and the justice of another day and hour.—Cardozo: *Law and Literature,* 166.

40. We do not pick our rules of law full-blossomed from the trees.—Cardozo: *Nature of Judicial Process,* 103.

41. The law which is the resulting product is not found but made.—Cardozo: *ibid.,* 115.

42. Logic, and history, and custom, and utility, and the accepted standards of right conduct, are the forces

which singly or in combination shape the progress of the law.—Cardozo: *ibid.,* 112.

43. The old forms remain, but they are filled with a new content.—Cardozo: *ibid.,* 101.

44. The judge in shaping the rules of law must heed the mores of the day. —Cardozo: *ibid.,* 104.

45. Responsibility must rest primarily on those who undertake to blaze a new path in the law, to say how far it shall go.—Stone: First Nat'l Bank v. Maine, 284 U.S. 312, 331.

46. Jurisprudence will be the gainer in the long run by fanning the fires of mental insurrection instead of smothering them with platitudes.—Cardozo: *Paradoxes,* 3.

47. "Laissez Faire" in law is going or has gone the way of "laissez faire" in economics.—Cardozo: *Law and Literature,* 121.

48. Law is a social organism, and evolution operates in the sociological domain no less than in the biological. The vitality and therefore validity of law is not arrested by the circumstances of its origin. — Frankfurter: Green v. United States, 356 U.S. 165, 189.

49. The eternal struggle in the law between constancy and change is largely a struggle between history and reason, between past reason and present needs.—Frankfurter: "Holmes and the Constitution," 41 Harv. L. Rev. 160.

50. The truth, of course, is that in the development of law, as in other fields of thought, we can never rid ourselves of our dependence upon intentions or flashes of insight, transcending and transforming contributions of mere experience.—Cardozo: *Growth of the Law,* 89–90.

51. Our law, and particularly our procedural law, does not stick fast in the past.—Frankfurter: Rios v. United States, 364 U.S. at p. 233.

52. The evolution of judge-made law is a process of accretion and erosion.—Frankfurter: Mitchell v. Trawler Racer, 362 U.S. 539, 550.
See also Common law.

——, importance, obedience

53. The supremacy of the law is the foundation rock upon which our institutions rest.—Harlan: Northern Sec. Co. v. United States, 193 U.S. 197, 350.

54. Rigorous laws, when necessary, will be cheerfully observed by a patriotic people, struggling to preserve the rich blessings of a free government. —Davis: *Ex parte* Milligan, 4 Wall. (71 U.S.) 2, 130.

55. Law and obedience to law are facts confirmed every day to us in all our experience of life.—Cardozo: *Nature of Judicial Process,* 127.

56. The "cultivation of respect for the law and the dignity of the courts" will not come until the administration of the law and its creation are made deserving of respect. The present lack of respect for the law and criticism of the judiciary is due largely to the inefficiency of the system.—Brandeis: Mason, *Brandeis,* 436–37.

57. If one man can be allowed to

determine for himself what is law, every man can. That means first chaos, then tyranny. — Frankfurter: United States v. UMW, 330 U.S. 258, 312.

58. The contrast between morality professed by society and immorality practiced on its behalf makes for contempt of law. Respect for law cannot be turned off and on as though it were a hot-water faucet.—Frankfurter: On Lee v. United States, 343 U.S. 747, 758–59.

59. Preserving and enhancing respect for law is always more important than sustaining the infliction of punishment in a particular case.—Frankfurter: Sacher v. United States, 343 U.S. 1, 33.

60. I know of no way that we can have equal justice under law except we have some law.—Jackson: Brown v. Allen, 344 U.S. 443, 546.

See also Citizen 11; Duty 3; Freedom, conscience 141; Majority-minority 1, 3; Martyr; Public official 2; Success 3; Supreme Court 25.

————, function

61. Civilization involves subjection of force to reason, and the agency of this subjection is law."—Frankfurter: United States v. UMW, 330 U.S. 258, 308 (quot. Roscoe Pound).

62. The law was designed to remedy existing evils. — Davis: United States v. Lane, 8 Wall. (75 U.S.) 185, 198.

63. The object of all law is to repress vice and to promote the general welfare of society.—Wayne: Harris v. Runnels, 12 How. (53 U.S.) 79, 83.

64. The final cause of law is the welfare of society.—Cardozo: *Nature of Judicial Process,* 66.

65. The object of the law is to accomplish an external result.—Holmes: *Uncollected Letters,* 27.

66. All law is directed to conditions of things manifest to the senses.—Holmes: *The Common Law,* 49.

67. The law does all that is needed when it does all that it can.—Holmes: Buck v. Bell, 274 U.S. 200, 208.

68. The law does not attempt to equalize fortune, opportunities, or abilities.—Holmes: ICC v. Diffenbaugh, 222 U.S. 42, 46.

69. We are coming to realize more completely that law is not an end, but a means to an end—the adequate control and protection of those interests social and economic, which are the special concern of government and hence of law.—Stone: Mason, *Stone,* 435.

70. Law is concerned with external behavior and not with the inner life of man. It rests in large measure upon compulsion. Socrates lives in history partly because he gave his life for the conviction that duty of obedience to secular law does not presuppose consent to its enactment or belief in its virtue.—Frankfurter: West Va. State Bd. of Educ. v. Barnette, 319 U.S. 624, 655.

71. Law addresses itself to actualities.—Frankfurter: Griffin v. Illinois, 351 U.S. 12, 23.

72. Law, no doubt, is concerned with "practical and substantial rights, not to maintain theories." — Frankfurter: United States v. Scophony

Corp., 333 U.S. 795, 819–20 (quot. 194 U.S. 451, 457).

——, standards

73. The law embodies the story of a nation's development through many centuries, and it cannot be dealt with as if it contained only the axioms and corollaries of a book of mathematics. —Holmes: *The Common Law*, 1.

74. The standards of the law are standards of general application. The law takes no account of the infinite varieties of temperament, intellect, and education which make the internal character of a given act so different in different men. It does not attempt to see men as God sees them. —Holmes: *ibid.*, 108.

75. Law contents herself for the most part with those tests and standards of identity that are accepted by the average mind, untrained in metaphysics.—Cardozo: *Growth of the Law*, 128.

76. As political economy has its economic man, so jurisprudence has its reasonable man, its negligent man, and . . . its moral man.—Cardozo: *Paradoxes*, 34.

——, operation, general

77. Upon the actual administration of justice in all governments, and especially in free governments, must depend the welfare of the whole community.—Story: *Misc. Writings*, 453.

78. The administration of justice is filled with perplexities, that strain the human mind to its utmost bearings. —Story: *ibid.*, 428.

79. No man or group is above the law. Nor is any beyond its protection. —Rutledge: United States v. UMW, 330 U.S. 258, 343.

80. The law never requires an idle thing to be done.—Swayne: Brooklyn Life Ins. Co. v. Dutcher, 5 Otto (95 U.S.) 269, 272.

81. I have no thought to paint the failings of our law in lurid colors of detraction. I have little doubt that its body is for the most part sound and pure. Not even its most zealous advocate, however, will assert that it is perfect.—Cardozo: *Law and Literature*, 48–49.

82. The law does not perfectly accomplish its ends.—Holmes: *The Common Law*, 111.

83. With any rule of law which attempts to reconcile fundamentally antagonistic social policies, there may be occasional instances of actual injustice which will go unredressed, but we think that price a necessary one to pay for the greater good.—Harlan: Barr v. Matteo, 360 U.S. 564, 576.

84. While justice should be administered with dispatch, the essential ingredient is orderly expedition and not mere speed.—Warren: Smith v. United States, 360 U.S. 1, 10.
See also Conscience 2; Wrongdoer 6.

——, operation, certainty, consistency

85. The law requires, not conjecture, but certainty.—Swayne: Coffin v. Ogden, 18 Wall. (85 U.S.) 120, 124.

86. To a certain extent, law must for ever be subject to uncertainty and doubt; not from the obscurity and

fluctuation of decisions, as the vulgar erroneously suppose, but from the endless complexity and variety of human actions.—Story: *Misc. Writings*, 226.

87. The truth is, that the law is always approaching, and never reaching, consistency. It is forever adopting new principles from life at one end, and it always retains old ones from history at the other, which have not yet been absorbed or sloughed off. It will become entirely consistent only when it ceases to grow.—Holmes: *The Common Law*, 36.

88. The tendency of the law must always be to narrow the field of uncertainty.—Holmes: *ibid.*, 127.

89. One of the most fundamental social interests is that law shall be uniform and impartial. — Cardozo: *Nature of Judicial Process*, 112.

90. Uniformity ceases to be a good when it becomes uniformity of oppression. The social interest served by symmetry or certainty must then be balanced against the social interest served by equity and fairness or other elements of social welfare.—Cardozo: *ibid.*, 113.

91. Overemphasis of certainty may carry us to the worship of an intolerable rigidity.—Cardozo: *Growth of the Law*, 19.

92. The delusive hope of certainty satisfies the conscience, only too ready to approve what inertia suggests.—Cardozo: *ibid.*, 139.

93. Opinion and counter-opinion bewilder the citizen who wants to obey the law but who does not know what to do when one judicial star differeth from another. — Jackson: *Struggle for Judicial Supremacy*, 303.

————, operation, enforcement

94. Only in the exact administration of the law will justice in the long run be done.—Brewer: Clyatt v. United States, 197 U.S. 207, 222.

95. To enforce popular laws is easy.—Curtis: United States v. Morris, 1 Curt. 62, 63.

96. The bite of law is in its enforcement.—Frankfurter: Fisher v. United States, 328 U.S. 463, 484.

97. A failure to enforce the law does not change it. — Hughes: Louisville & N. R.R. v. United States, 282 U.S. 740, 759.

98. The public conscience must be satisfied that fairness dominates the administration of justice.—Frankfurter: Adams v. United States, 317 U.S. 269, 279.

99. Respect for law will not be advanced by resort, in its enforcement, to means which shock the common man's sense of decency and fair play.—Brandeis: Burdeau v. McDowell, 256 U.S. 465, 477.

100. Law, like social institutions generally, attains its aim as a device for promoting order and reducing waste at the price of occasional hardship when its mandate is disregarded or forgotten. — Cardozo: *Paradoxes*, 69.

101. The law is not so primitive that it sanctions every injustice except brute force and downright fraud.—Frankfurter: United States v. Beth-

lehem Steel Corp., 315 U.S. 289, 326.

102. We do not speak of evasion, because, when the law draws a line, a case is on one side of it or the other, and if on the safe side is none the worse legally that a party has availed himself to the full of what the law permits. When an act is condemned as an evasion, what is meant is that it is on the wrong side of the line indicated by the policy if not by the mere letter of the law.—Hughes: Bullen v. Wisconsin, 240 U.S. 625, 630–31.

103. Law is at its loftiest when it examines claimed injustice even at the instance of one to whom the public is bitterly hostile.—Murphy: Eisler v. United States, 338 U.S. 189, 194.

104. Providing equal justice for poor and rich, weak and powerful alike is an age-old problem. People have never ceased to hope and strive to move closer to that goal.—Douglas, Clark: Griffin v. Illinois, 351 U.S. 12, 16.

105. Effort to find a way out from the rigors of a severe statute has alluring appeal.—Harlan: Rowoldt v. Perfetto, 355 U.S. 115, 145.

106. The use of force to further obedience to law is in any event a last resort and one not congenial to the spirit of our Nation. — Frankfurter: Cooper v. Aaron, 358 U.S. 20, 21.

107. Cases of notorious criminals—like cases of small, miserable ones—are apt to make bad law.—When guilt permeates a record, even judges sometimes relax and let the police take shortcuts not sanctioned by constitutional procedures.—Douglas: Abel v. United States, 362 U.S. 217, 241–42. *See also* Entrapment; Freedom, conscience 141.

———, miscellaneous

108. Every denunciation of existing law tends in some measure to increase the probability that there will be a violation of it. Condonation of a breach enhances the probability. Expressions of approval add to the probability.—Brandeis: Whitney v. California, 274 U.S. 357, 376.

109. Even habitual disobedience in some things is consistent with the rule of law; it is certain that only a minority of motorists observe the statutory speed limit on a clear road.—Holmes: *Holmes-Pollock Letters,* II, 26.

110. Federal laws grow like mushrooms without Congress passing a bill. — Douglas: United States v. Sharpnack, 355 U.S. 286, 291.

111. What I fear and would avoid is the law that maintains a noxious life when the soil of habit and custom and conviction and utility has been washed away beneath it.—Cardozo: *Law and Literature,* 116.

See also Admiralty 1, 2; Certainty; Common sense; Constitution 8, 90; Court; Democracy; Equality 19, 20; Freedom, limitations; Freedom, speech, limitations and other subdivisions; Force; Fraud 15; Ignorance (legal); Judge 68; Jurisprudence; Law reports; Lawyer; Maritime law; Prophecy 5; Public opinion 12; Real property 6, 7; Sovereignty 2, 6; Supreme Court; Tax 126; War 36, 37; Woman 1.

LAWLESSNESS

1. Few sociological generalizations are more valid than that lawlessness

begets lawlessness.—Frankfurter: On Lee v. United States, 343 U.S. 747, 760.

2. Lawlessness if not checked is the percursor of anarchy. — Frankfurter: Cooper v. Aaron, 358 U.S. 20, 22.

See also Law 57; Liquor 6; Prosecutor 7.

LAW OF THE LAND

1. "Perhaps no definition," says Judge Cooley, "is more often quoted than that given by Mr. Webster in the *Dartmouth College Case*: 'By the law of the land is most clearly intended the general law; a law which hears before it condemns; which proceeds upon inquiry and renders judgment only after trial. The meaning is that every citizen shall hold his life, liberty, property and immunities, under the protection of the general rules which govern society.' " — Bradley: *Ex parte* Wall, 107 U.S. 265, 289.

2. It is easy to see that when the great Barons of England wrung from King John, at the point of the sword, the concession that neither their lives nor their property should be disposed of by the Crown, except as provided by the law of the land, they meant by "law of the land" the ancient and customary laws of the English people, or laws enacted by the Parliament of which those Barons were a controlling element.—Miller: Davidson v. Board of Adm'rs, 6 Otto (96 U.S.) 97, 102.

Related subjects: Due process; Magna Charta.

LAW REPORTS

1. The mass of the law is, to be sure, accumulating with an almost incredible rapidity. . . . It is impossible not to look without some discouragement upon the ponderous volumes, which the next half century will add to the groaning shelves of our jurists. —Story: *Misc. Writings,* 436.

2. It is a great mistake to be frightened by the ever increasing number of reports. The reports of a given jurisdiction in the course of a generation take up pretty much the whole body of the law, and restate it from the present point of view.—Holmes: "The Path of the Law," 10 Harv. L. Rev. 458.

3. The fecundity of our case law would make Malthus stand aghast.— Cardozo: *Growth of the Law,* 4.

See also Opinion 13; Precedent 23.

LAWS (statutes)
See Legislation.

LAW SCHOOL
Related subject: Lawyer, education. *See also* Lawyer 19, 20.

LAWSUIT
See Litigation.

LAWYER
Status 1–6; education 7–20; importance 21–36; qualifications 37–49; functions, obligations 50–59; characteristics 60–76; compensation 77–83; criticism 84–92; misconduct 93–96; disbarment 97–104; miscellaneous 105–108.

Related subjects: Bar association; Law school.

———, status

1. Attorneys and counsellors are not officers of the United States. . . . They are officers of the court.—Field: *Ex parte* Garland, 4 Wall. (71 U.S.) 333, 378.

2. They are officers of the law, as well as the agents of those by whom they are employed. Their fidelity is guaranteed by the highest considerations of honor and good faith, and to those is superadded the sanction of an oath. The slightest divergence from rectitude involves the breach of all these obligations. None are more honored or more deserving than those of the brotherhood who, uniting ability with integrity, prove faithful to their trusts and worthy of the confidence reposed in them.—Swayne: Baker v. Humphrey, 11 Otto (101 U.S.) 494, 502.

3. Historically, a lawyer is an officer of the court and is bound to work for the advancement of justice while faithfully protecting the rightful interests of his clients.—Murphy: Hickman v. Taylor, 329 U.S. 495, 510.

4. The practice of law is not a matter of the State's grace. — Black: Schware v. Bd. of Bar Exam'rs, 353 U.S. 232, 239 n.

5. A lawyer is engaged in a private profession, important though it be to our system of justice. In general he makes his own decisions, follows his own best judgment, collects his own fees and runs his own business. The word "officer" as it has always been applied to lawyers conveys quite a different meaning from the word "officer" as applied within the conventional meaning of that term.—Black: Cammer v. United States, 350 U.S. 399, 405.

6. An attorney of an individual, retained for a single suit, is not his employe. It is true, he has engaged to render services; but his engagement is rather that of a contractor than that of an employe.—Brewer: Louisville, E. & St. L. R.R. v. Wilson, 138 U.S. 501, 505–506.

———, education

7. To be a sound lawyer, he must not merely taste, but drink deep at the ancient fountains of the law.—Story: *Misc. Writings,* 228.

8. The history of what the law has been is necessary to the knowledge of what the law is.—Holmes: *The Common Law,* 37.

9. If we are to speak of the law as our mistress, we who are here know that she is a mistress only to be wooed with sustained and lonely passion—only to be won by straining all the faculties by which man is likest to a god.—Holmes: *Speeches,* 17.

10. If you want to know the law and nothing else, you must look at it as a bad man, who cares only for the material consequences which such knowledge enables him to predict, not as a good one, who finds his reasons for conduct, whether inside the law or outside of it, in the vaguer sanctions of conscience.—Holmes: "The Path of the Law," 10 Harv. L. Rev. 459.

11. The rational study of law is still to a large extent the study of history. History must be a part of the study, because without it we cannot know the precise scope of rules which it is our business to know. It is a part of the rational study, because it is the

first step toward an enlightened scepticism, that is, toward a deliberate reconsideration of the worth of those rules.—Holmes: *ibid.*, 469.

12. The training of lawyers is a training in logic. The processes of analogy, discrimination, and deduction are those in which they are most at home. The language of judicial decision is mainly the language of logic. And the logical method and form flatter that longing for certainty and for repose which is in every human mind. —Holmes: *ibid.*, 465.

13. Every lawyer ought to seek an understanding of e c o n o m i c s . — Holmes: *ibid.*, 474.

14. The man of science in the law is not merely a bookworm. To a microscopic eye for detail he must unite an insight which tells him what details are significant.—Holmes: "Law in Science and Science in Law," 12 Harv. L. Rev. 451.

15. Lawyers who are unwilling to study the law as it is, may discover, as they think, that study is unnecessary; sentiment or benevolence or some vague notion of social welfare becomes the only equipment needed. I hardly need to say that this it not my point of view.—Cardozo: *Growth of the Law*, 59–60.

16. You will study the precepts of justice, for these are the truths that through you shall come to their hour of triumph.—Cardozo: *Law and Literature*, 175.

17. You will study the life of mankind, for this is the life you must or-der, and, to order with wisdom, must know.—Cardozo: *ibid*.

18. You will study the wisdom of the past, for in a wilderness of conflicting counsels, a trail has there been blazed.—Cardozo: *ibid*.

19. I am a vestigial remnant of the system which permitted one to come to the bar by way of apprenticeship in a law office. Except for one term at law school, I availed myself of that method of preparation which already was causing uneasiness — to which feeling I must have added, for the system was almost immediately abolished. You may be comforted to realize that I am the last relic of that method likely to find a niche on the Supreme Court.—Jackson: "Address," 3 Stan. L. Rev. 48.

20. The law school, the proving ground for legal learning and practice, cannot be effective in isolation from the individuals and institutions with which the law interacts. Few students and no one who has practiced law would choose to study in an academic vacuum, removed from the interplay of ideas and the exchange of views with which the law is concerned — Vinson: Sweatt v. Painter, 339 U.S. 629, 634.

———, importance

21. The legal profession is found wherever Christian civilization exists. Without it, society could not well go on. But, like all other great instrumentalities, it may be potent for evil as well as for good. Hence the im-

portance of keeping it on the high plane it ought to occupy.—Swayne: Baker v. Humphrey, 11 Otto (101 U.S.) 494, 502.

22. Notwithstanding the sneers of ignorance, and the gibes of wit, no men are so constantly called upon in their practice to exemplify the duties of good faith, incorruptible virtue, and chivalric honor, as lawyers. To them is often entrusted the peace and repose, as well as the property, of whole families; and the slightest departure from professional secrecy, or professional integrity, might involve their clients in ruin.—Story: *Misc. Writings,* 452.

23. The history of the Anglo-Saxon race shows that, for ages past, the members of the legal profession have been powerful for good and evil to the government. They are, by the nature of their duties, the molders of public sentiment on questions of government, and are every day engaged in aiding in the construction and enforcement of the laws. From among their numbers are necessarily selected the judges who expound the laws and the Constitution. — Miller: *Ex parte* Garland, 4 Wall. (71 U.S.) 333, 385–86.

24. No instance is known of a court of law without a bar.—Miller: *ibid.,* 384.

25. Lawyers predominate in American legislatures.—Frankfurter: AFL v. Am. Sash & Door Co., 335 U.S. 538, 555.

26. The profession of law, because of its public and political character,

must not be allowed to become the monopoly of any social or economic class.—Stone: Mason, *Stone,* 95.

27. The march of economic events has substituted for the leadership of the advocate and the legal scholar the leadership of the business lawyer and specialist.—Stone: *ibid.,* 97.

28. One does not have to inhale the self-adulatory bombast of after-dinner speeches to affirm that all the interests of man that are comprised under the constitutional guarantees given to "life, liberty and property" are in the professional keeping of lawyers.—Frankfurter: Schware v. Bd. of Bar Exam'rs, 353 U.S. 232, 247.

29. The guiding hand of counsel is needed lest the unwary concede that which only bewilderment or ignorance could justify or pay a penalty which is greater than the law of the State exacts for the offense which they in fact and in law committed.—Douglas: Tomkins v. Missouri, 323 U.S. 423, 489.

30. The right to be heard would be, in many cases, of little avail if it did not comprehend the right to be heard by counsel.—Sutherland: Powell v. Alabama, 287 U.S. 48, 68–69.

31. Our Constitution guarantees the assistance of counsel to a man on trial for his life in an orderly courtroom, presided over by a judge, open to the public, and protected by all the procedural safeguards of the law. Surely a Constitution which promises that much can vouchsafe no less to the same man under midnight inquisition in the squad room of a po-

lice station.—Stewart: Spano v. New York, 360 U.S. 315, 327.

32. Nor does he suggest how a lawyer might have helped him unless he picked the lock on the jail house door.—Minton: United States v. Morgan, 346 U.S. 502, 517.

33. A layman is usually no match for the skilled prosecutor whom he confronts in the courtroom. He needs the aid of counsel. — Douglas: Williams v. Kaiser, 323 U.S. 471, 476.

34. The need of counsel is the same, whatever the economic status of the accused. — Douglas: McNeal v. Culver, 365 U.S. 109, 118.

35. If due process requires that a rich man who wants a lawyer be allowed the opportunity to obtain one before he is tried, why should not due process give the same protection to the accused who is indigent? Even penniless vagrants are at times caught in a tangle of laws that only an astute lawyer can resolve.—Douglas: *ibid*.

36. Even in the most routine-appearing proceedings the assistance of able counsel may be of inestimable value.—Black: Reynolds v. Cochran, 365 U.S. 525, 532–33.

———, qualifications

37. It cannot be denied, indeed, that there have been great lawyers, who were not orators; as there have been great orators, who were not great lawyers. But it must be admitted at the same time, that, when both characters are united in the same person, human genius has approached as near perfection, as it may. They are kindred arts, and flourish best in the neighborhood of each other.—Story: *Misc. Writings*, 461.

38. He possessed, in a remarkable degree, the faculty of analyzing a complicated case into its elements, and of throwing out at once all its accidental and unimportant ingredients. He easily separated the gold from the dross, and refined and polished the former with an exquisite skill.—Story: *ibid.*, 110.

39. That fidelity to the government under which he lives, a true and loyal attachment to it, and a sincere desire for its preservation, are among the most essential qualifications which should be required in a lawyer.—Miller: *Ex parte* Garland, 4 Wall. (71 U.S.) 333, 385.

40. The law is not the place for the artist or the poet. The law is the calling of thinkers.—Holmes: *Speeches*, 22–23.

41. If a man goes into law it pays to be a master of it, and to be a master of it means to look straight through all the dramatic incidents and to discern the true basis for prophecy.—Holmes: "The Path of the Law," 10 Harv. L. Rev., 474–75.

42. One mark of a great lawyer is that he sees the application of the broadest rules.—Holmes: *ibid.*, 474.

43. I cannot but believe that if the training of lawyers led them habitually to consider more definitely and explicitly the social advantage on which the rule they lay down must be justified, they sometimes would hesitate where now they are confident, and see

that really they were taking sides upon debatable and often burning questions.—Holmes: *ibid.*, 467–68.

44. The perfect lawyer is he who commands all the ties between a given case and all others. But few lawyers are perfect, and all have to learn their business.—Holmes: *Uncollected Letters,* 66.

45. Membership in the bar is a privilege burdened with conditions. A fair private and professional character is one of them.—Cardozo: In the Matter of Rouss, 221 N.Y. 81, 84.

46. There is more in membership in the bar than a license to sign a brief or intone a prosy argument. — Cardozo: *Law and Literature,* 145–46.

47. This is no life of cloistered ease to which you dedicate your powers. This is a life that touches your fellow men at every angle of their being, a life that you must live in the crowd, and yet apart from it, man of the world and philosopher by turns.—Cardozo: *ibid.,* 175.

48. It is . . . important both to society and the bar itself that lawyers be unintimidated — free to think, speak, and act as members of an Independent Bar — Black: Konigsberg v. State Bar, 353 U.S. 252, 273.

49. The most persuasive counsel may not be able to speak for a defendant as the defendant might, with halting eloquence, speak for himself.—Frankfurter: Green v. United States, 365 U.S. 301, 304.

———, functions, obligations

50. He [the lawyer] may be re-quired to defend against the arm of the government a party standing charged with some odious crime, real or imaginary. He is not at liberty to desert even the guilty wretch in his lowest estate; but he is bound to take care, that even here the law shall not be bent or broken to bring him to punishment. He will, at such times, from love of the law, as well as from compassion, freely give his talents to the cause, and never surrender the victim, until the judgment of his peers has convicted him upon legal evidence.—Story: *Misc. Writings,* 354.

51. There are few of the business relations of life involving a higher trust and confidence than that of attorney and client, or, generally speaking, one more honorably or faithfully discharged; few more anxiously guarded by the law, or governed by sterner principles of morality and justice. — Nelson: Stockton v. Ford, 11 How. (52 U.S.) 232, 247.

52. It is a fair characterization of the lawyer's responsibility in our society that he stands "as a shield," to quote Devlin, J., in defense of right and to ward off wrong.—Frankfurter: Schware v. Bd. of Bar Exam'rs, 353 U.S. 232, 247.

53. The confidence manifested by the client gave him the right to expect a corresponding return of zeal, diligence and good faith on the part of the attorney. — Swayne: Baker v. Humphrey, 11 Otto (101 U.S.) 494, 500.

54. The appellant was received into that ancient fellowship for something

more than private gain.—Cardozo: People *ex rel*. Karlin v. Culkin, 248 N.Y. 465, 470.

55. Lawyers owe a large, but not an obsequious duty of respect to the court in its presence.—Rutledge: Fisher v. Pace, 336 U.S. 155, 168.

56. To bring in a lawyer means a real peril to solution of the crime because, under our adversary system, he deems that his sole duty is to protect his client—guilty or innocent—and that in such a capacity he owes no duty whatever to help society solve its crime problem. — Jackson: Watts v. Indiana, 338 U.S. 49, 59.

57. The right to counsel guaranteed by the Constitution contemplates the services of an attorney devoted solely to the interests of his client.—Black: Von Moltke v. Gillies, 332 U.S. 708, 725.

58. An attorney actively engaged in the conduct of a trial is not merely another citizen. He is an intimate and trusted and essential part of the machinery of justice, an "officer of the court" in the most compelling sense. —Frankfurter: *In re* Sawyer, 360 U.S. 622, 668.

59. A lawyer belongs to a profession with inherited standards of propriety and honor, which experience has shown necessary in a calling dedicated to the accomplishment of justice. He who would follow that calling must conform to those standards.— Stewart: *ibid.*, 646.

———, characteristics

60. I am happy to think that . . .

now it is the rule that a lawyer will try his case like a gentleman without giving up any portion of his energy and force.—Holmes: *Uncollected Letters*, 128–29.

61. Undivided allegiance and faithful devoted service to a client are prized traditions of the American lawyer.—Black: Von Moltke v. Gillies, 332 U.S. 708, 725–26.

62. To encourage the hope that is eternal in the breast of losing counsel. —Frankfurter, Jackson: NLRB v. Mexia Textile Mills, 339 U.S. 563, 573.

63. The average lawyer wants the absolute. — Holmes: *Holmes-Pollock Letters*, I, 216.

64. When a lawyer sees a rule of law in force he is very apt to invent, if he does not find, some ground of policy for its base.—Holmes: "Law in Science and Science in Law," 12 Harv. L. Rev. 452.

65. While I was in practice at the bar, I tried to find the pertinent authority, and fit it to the case at hand. I was not much concerned whether it was right if I was sure it was pertinent.—Cardozo: *Growth of the Law,* 57.

66. So well read a lawyer would not have advanced so bold a doctrine, without attempting to find some shadow of authority for it.—Johnson: Ramsay v. Allegre, 12 Wheat. (25 U.S.) 611, 638.

67. I yield to the lawyer's impulse to prove my point by citing a precedent.—Jackson: *Struggle for Judicial Supremacy*, 324.

68. It is certain, therefore, that no

averment has been omitted from the pleadings, no fact from the testimony, that has any bearing on the case; the industry of counsel has neglected no statute or citation, and their ability no comment or reason that can elucidate or persuade.... It is not the fault of counsel if we have misunderstood them.—McKenna: Oregon & C. R.R. v. United States, 238 U.S. 393, 412.

69. The lawyer's habit of caution which so often protects his client from consequences of rash action is a real conservative force in the community which should not be lightly valued.—Stone: Mason, *Stone,* 98.

70. That which is simple, orderly and necessary to the lawyer—to the untrained layman may appear intricate, complex and mysterious. — Black: Johnson v. Zerbst, 304 U.S. 458, 463.

71. One illustration of the lag of reform because of the opposition of lawyers who resist change of the familiar, particularly when they have thriven under some outworn doctrine of law. —Frankfurter: Ferguson v Moore-McCormack Lines, 352 U.S. 521, 539.

72. Advocates ... are like managers of pugilistic and election contestants in that they have a propensity for claiming everything. — Frankfurter: First Iowa Hydro-Elec. Co-op. v. Fed. Power Comm'n, 328 U.S. 152, 187.

73. The minds of lawyers and judges are boundless in their abilities to raise serious jurisdictional objections.—Murphy: United States v. UMW, 330 U.S. 258, 340.

74. Precise use of words is part of the lawyer's craft.—Murphy: Nye & Nissen v. United States, 336 U.S. 613, 629.

75. The tendency of lawyers to carry arguments to the extreme of empty formal logic.—Frankfurter: Kedroff v. St. Nicholas Cathedral, 344 U.S. 94, 123.

76. The familiar kind of jury play which a good trial lawyer sometimes uses to affect an appearance of unconcern towards damaging evidence which he knows he cannot keep out of the case.—Harlan: Lawn v. United States, 355 U.S. 321, 355.

———, compensation

77. The law, though a profession, must also be a means of livelihood.—Cardozo: *Law and Literature,* 169.

78. Although the law is a highly learned profession, we are well aware that it is an intensely practical one.—Vinson: Sweatt v. Painter, 339 U.S. 629, 634.

79. Free competition prevails at the bar as well as elsewhere, and different men command different rates of compensation, and some of them much in excess of any official salaries. Thus far the experience of the commonwealth has been that this freedom has not operated to keep citizens from the courts, or to shut the poor off from justice. — Holmes: Hyde v. Moxie Nerve-food Co., 160 Mass. 559, 560-61.

80. The well known difficulties and delays in obtaining payment of just claims which are not within the ordinary course of procedure of the auditing officers of the government,

justifies a liberal compensation in successful cases, where none is to be received in case of failure.—Miller: Taylor v. Bemiss, 110 U.S. 42, 45.

81. While fifty per cent seems to be more than a fair proportion in the division between client and attorney in an ordinary case, we are not prepared to assume that it is extortionate for that reason alone.—Miller: *ibid.*

82. The bargain must exhibit a measurable degree of providence in the adjustment of reward to service.—Cardozo: In the Matter of Reisfeld, 227 N.Y. 137, 140.

83. The employment of a lawyer to serve for a contingent fee does not make it the client's duty to continue the lawsuit and thus increase the lawyer's profit. The lawsuit is his own. He may drop it when he will.—Cardozo: Andrewes v. Haas, 214 N.Y. 255, 258.

———, criticism

84. I think the legal profession, as a whole, presents a very sad spectacle. I fear that it has become so legalized and commercialized in its higher strata and has so little professional and public spirit throughout that it is lagging behind the other professions.—Stone: Mason, *Stone,* 210.

85. There is a limited number of the entire membership of the bar, found principally in the larger cities, who are counted as its leaders. They are men of high character, distinct intellectual power, great skill, and devoted to the practice of their profession. Their success is measured by

the profession and the public very largely in terms of their professional income. . . . You rarely find their services enlisted in any case which does not involve substantial professional remuneration, and almost never on the unpopular side of a case involving human rights and personal liberty.—Stone: *ibid., 376.*

86. Great number of members of the bar who, though personally honest, regard their profession in the light of a business or trade. They do not even make an ideal of good workmanship; any kind of professional training which will secure admission to the bar is good enough to be submitted to the court.—Stone: *ibid., 376.*

87. The leading lawyers of the United States have been engaged mainly in supporting the claims of the corporations; often in endeavoring to evade or nullify the extremely crude laws by which legislators sought to regulate the power or curb the excesses of corporations. . . . Instead of holding a position of independence, between the wealthy and the people, prepared to curb the excesses of either, able lawyers have, to a large extent, allowed themselves to become adjuncts of great corporations and have neglected the obligation to use their powers for the protection of the people.—Brandeis: Mason, *Brandeis,* 103.

88. We hear much of the "corporation lawyer" and far too little of the "people's lawyer."—Brandeis: *ibid.*

89. It cannot be successfully controverted that the law has been, in the last fifty years, a singularly unprogres-

sive profession.—Brandeis: *ibid.*, 436.

90. The legal profession, like many another, tends to become over-professionalized. We forget that law is the rule for simple and untaught people to live by. We complicate and over-refine it as a weapon in legal combat until we take it off the ground where people live and into the thin atmosphere of sheer fiction. — Jackson: *Struggle for Judicial Supremacy*, 292.

91. The entire philosophy, interest, and training of the legal profession tend toward conservatism. . . . it is much concerned with precedents, authorities, existing customs, usages, vested rights and established relationships. Its method of thinking, accepted by no other profession, cultivates a supreme respect for the past, and its order.—Jackson: *ibid.*, 313–14.

92. Lawyers are free to criticize the state of the law.—Brennan: *In re* Sawyer, 360 U.S. 622, 631.

———, misconduct

93. Of all classes and professions, the lawyer is most sacredly bound to uphold the laws. He is their sworn servant; and for him, of all men in the world, to repudiate and override the laws, to trample them under foot and to ignore the very bands of society, argues recreancy to his position and office and sets a pernicious example to the insubordinate and dangerous elements of the body politic. It manifests a want of fidelity to the system of lawful government which he has sworn to uphold and preserve.

—Bradley: *Ex parte* Wall, 107 U.S. 265, 274.

94. He was not sufficiently mindful of the restraints imposed, by prudence, upon lawyers in making engagements with their clients, which cannot be disregarded without subjecting them to misconception and suspicion, and the profession to the already too prevalent impression that it is not practiced with all the forbearances of the strictest honesty, or of the highest moral principle. — Wayne: Laflin v. Herrington, 1 Black (66 U.S.) 326, 338–39.

95. There have always been obscure attorneys, whose industry, or cunning, or patronage has given them the command of that portion of business, which is not without profit, if it be not attended with honor. — Story: *Misc. Writings,* 234.

96. It is always dangerous for counsel to undertake to act, in regard to the same thing, for parties whose interests are diverse. Such a case requires care and circumspection on his part.— Swayne: Baker v. Humphrey, 11 Otto (101 U.S.) 494, 501–502.

———, disbarment

97. The profession of an attorney is of great importance to an individual, and the prosperity of his whole life may depend on its exercise. The right to exercise it ought not to be lightly or capriciously taken from him.—Marshall: *Ex parte* Burr, 9 Wheat. (22 U.S.) 529, 530.

98. The attorney and counsellor, be-

ing, by the solemn judicial act of the court, clothed with his office, does not hold it as a matter of grace and favor. The right which it confers upon him to appear for suitors, and to argue causes, is something more than a mere indulgence, revocable at the pleasure of the Court, or at the command of the Legislature. It is a right of which he can only be deprived by the judgment of the court, for moral or professional delinquency. — Field: *Ex parte* Garland, 4 Wall. (71 U.S.) 333, 379.

99. A conviction of a felony or a misdemeanor involving moral turpitude implies the absence of qualities which fit one for an office of trust, where the rights and property of others are concerned. — Field: *Ex parte* Wall, 107 U.S. 265, 307.

100. It is not for every moral offense which may leave a stain upon character, that courts can summon an attorney to account. Many persons, eminent at the bar, have been chargeable with moral delinquencies which were justly a cause of reproach to them. . . . It is only for that moral delinquency which consists in a want of integrity and trustworthiness, and renders him an unsafe person to manage the legal business of others, that the courts can interfere and summon him before them.—Field: *ibid.*, 306–307.

101. There are . . . many forms of professional misconduct that do not amount to crime. Cardozo: People *ex rel.* Karlin v. Culkin, 248 N.Y. 465, 470.

102. There is no vested right in an individual to practice law. Rather there is a right in the Court to protect itself, and hence society, as an instrument of justice. That to the individual disbarred there is a loss of status is incidental to the purpose of the Court.—Vinson: *In re* Isserman, 345 U.S. 286, 289.

103. To strike the unworthy lawyer from the roll is not to add to the pains and penalties of crime.—Cardozo: In the Matter of Rouss, 221 N.Y. 81, 85.

104. The honor of the profession does not demand the sacrifice of the innocent.—Cardozo: In the Matter of Kaufmann, 245 N.Y. 423, 429.

—————— miscellaneous

105. The defendant was a member of the bar, and the charges struck at his honor as well as at his judgment. —Jackson: Boone v. Lightner, 319 U.S. 561, 575.

106. From the thirteenth century to this day, in England the profession itself has determined who should enter it. In the United States the courts exercise ultimate control. — Frankfurter: Schware v. Bd. of Bar Exam'rs, 353 U.S. 232, 248.

107. To prohibit solicitation is to regulate the business, not to prohibit it. . . . Regulation which aims to bring the conduct of the business into harmony with ethical practice of the legal profession, to which it is necessarily related, is obviously reasonable.— Brandeis: McCloskey v. Tobin, 252 U.S. 107, 108.

108. The defendant needs counsel

and counsel needs time. — Reed: Hawk v. Olson, 326 U.S. 271, 278.

See also Appeal 7; Englishmen 1; Equality 21; Form 3; Happiness 2; Judge 16; Prolixity 2; Public opinion; Reputation 6; Supreme Court 11; Witness 3, 17.

LEADERSHIP

1. They talk about our leading the procession—we only follow it ahead like little boys. If we turn down a side street it doesn't. — Holmes: *Holmes-Pollock Letters,* I, 124 (quot.).

2. Our society grows increasingly complex, and our need for trained leaders increases correspondingly.— Vinson: McLaurin v. Oklahoma St. Regts. 339 U.S. 637, 641.

See also Industry 2; Labor 111; Politician 3; President 9.

LEARNING

1. We must guide our footsteps by those stars, which have shone, and still continue to shine, with inextinguishable light in the firmament of learning.—Story: *Misc. Writings,* 26.

2. He read to learn, and not to quote; to digest and master, and not merely to display.—Story: *ibid.,* 206.

3. Learning . . . is a very good thing. I should be the last to undervalue it. . . . But it is liable to lead us astray.— Holmes: *Speeches,* 67.

4. The book, the speech, the pamphlet open new horizons for people.— Douglas: *We the Judges,* 321–32.

5. Vast erudition is no substitute for creative imagination.—Frankfurter: "Holmes and the Constitution," 41 Harv. L. Rev. 127.

Related subjects: Education and related subjects. *See also* Dogma 3; Freedom, learning; Reputation 1.

LEASE

See Rent law 2.

LEGALITY

Related subject: Illegality. *See also* Motive 1; Power 23 .

LEGISLATION

Defined 1–4; origin 5–11; authority 12–16; function, purpose 17–27; content, form 28–39; effectiveness 40–47; inadequacies, infirmities 48–53; new, experimental 54–59; discriminatory 60–63; amendment 64–68; repeal 69–72; miscellaneous 73–76.

Related subjects: Constitution (U.S.); Constitutional adjudication; Construction; Legislature; Lobbying.

————, defined

1. The sovereign will is made known to us by legislative enactment. —McLean: Wheeler v. Smith, 9 How. (50 U.S.) 55, 78.

2. Legislation consists in laying down laws or rules for the future.— Pitney: Mitchell Coal & Coke Co. v. Pennsylvania R.R., 230 U.S. 247, 272.

3. We think it plain that the expression, "a law of the United States," . . . means just what the similar expression means all through the Constitution—and that is, a *statute* of the United States.—Lamar: *In re* Neagle, 135 U.S. 1, 93.

4. Statutes, including penal enactments, are not inert exercises in literary composition. They are instruments of government.—Frankfurter: United States v. Shirey, 359 U.S. 255, 260.

——, origin

5. All history demonstrates that legislation intervenes only when a definite abuse has disclosed itself, through the excess of which public feeling has finally been aroused.—Cardozo: *Nature of Judicial Process*, 144.

6. The laws of the people correspond with their habits. — Miller: Miles v. Caldwell, 2 Wall. (69 U.S.) 35, 44.

7. It is oftener the existence of necessity rather than the prescience of it which dictates legislation. — McKenna: German Alliance Ins. Co. v. Lewis, 233 U.S. 389, 416.

8. Time with its tides brings new conditions which must be cared for by new laws.—Cardozo: Williams v. Baltimore, 289 U.S. 36, 46.

9. In the eternal struggle that exists between the avarice, enterprise and combinations of individuals on the one hand, and the power charged with the administration of the laws on the other, severe laws are rendered necessary to enable the executive to carry into effect the measures of policy adopted by the legislature.—Johnson: United States v. 1960 Bags, 8 Cranch (12 U.S.) 398, 405.

10. In the last resort a man rightly prefers his own interest to that of his neighbors, and this is as true in legislation as in any other form of corporate action. All that can be expected from modern improvements is that legislation should easily and quickly, yet not too quickly, modify itself in accordance with the will of the *de facto* supreme power in the community, and that the spread of an educated sympathy should reduce the sacrifice of minorities to minimum.—Holmes: *Uncollected Letters*, 107.

11. Whatever body may possess the supreme power for the moment is certain to have interests inconsistent with others which have competed unsuccessfully. The powerful interests must be more or less reflected in legislation; which, like every other device of man or beast, must tend in the long run to aid the survival of the fittest.—Holmes: *ibid.*, 107–108.

——, authority

12. The only reason, I believe, why a freeman is bound by human laws, is, that he binds himself.—Wilson: Chisholm v. Georgia, 2 Dall. (2 U.S.) 419, 456.

13. The constitution overrides a statute, but a statute, if consistent with the constitution, overrides the law of judges.—Cardozo: *Nature of Judicial Process*, 14.

14. Statutes do not cease to be law because the power to fix their meaning in case of doubt or ambiguity has been confided to the courts. — Cardozo: *ibid.*, 127.

15. Substitute statute for decision, and you shift the center of authority, but add no quota of inspired wisdom. —Cardozo: *Growth of the Law*, 133.

16. A void act is neither a law nor a command. It is a nullity. It confers no authority. If affords no protection. —Lamar: Hopkins v. Clemson, 221 U.S. 636, 644.

———, function, purpose

17. The great truth, that *action*, not *opinion*, is the proper object of human legislation. — Story: *Misc. Writings*, 61.

18. The wretch beneath the gallows may repine at the fate which awaits him, and yet it is no less certain, that the laws under which he suffers were made for his security.—Johnson: Anderson v. Dunn, 6 Wheat. (19 U.S.) 204, 227.

19. There is a general principle of justice pervading our laws, and the laws of all free governments.—Bradley: Newport & Cincinnati Bridge Co. v. United States, 15 Otto (105 U.S.) 470, 503.

20. Legislation is impelled and addressed to concrete conditions deemed or demonstrated to be obstacles to something better.—McKenna: Lower Vein Coal Co. v. Indust. Bd., 255 U.S. 144, 148.

21. I can understand better legislation that aims rather to improve the quality than to increase the quantity of the population.—Holmes: *Uncollected Letters*, 140.

22. Laws are made to protect the trusting as well as the suspicious.—Black: Federal Trade Comm'n v. Standard Educ. Soc., 302 U.S. 112, 116.

23. Laws are intended for all of our people to live by; and the people go to law offices to learn what their rights under those laws are. — Jackson: Schwegmann Bros. v. Calvert Dist. Corp., 341 U.S. 384, 396.

24. Through . . . statutes t h a t change the law, organized government expresses the social purposes that motivate its legislation.—Reed: Dalehite v. United States, 346 U.S. 15, 30–31.

25. Nearly all legislation involves a weighing of public needs as against private desires; and likewise a weighing of relative social values.—Brandeis: Traux v. Corrigan, 257 U.S. 312, 357.

26. As to what extent legislation should interfere in affairs political philosophers have always disputed and always will dispute.—McKenna: Tanner v. Little, 240 U.S. 369, 385.

27. The clash of fact and opinion should be resolved by the democratic process and not by the judicial sword.—Frankfurter: Teamsters Union v. Hanke, 339 U.S. 470, 478.

———, content, form

28. The drawing of a legislative act requires exceptional training, experience and skill.—Stone: Mason, *Stone*, 119.

29. A wide range of discretion . . . is necessary in legislation to make it practical.—McKenna: District of Columbia v. Brooke, 214 U.S. 138, 150.

30. The state must adapt its legislation to evils as they appear.—McKenna: Merrick v. Halsey, 242 U.S. 568, 588.

31. Legislation looks to probabilities.—Cardozo: People *ex rel*. Alpha Portland Cement Co. v. Knapp, 230 N.Y. 48, 61.

32. Our faith in legislation as the universal panacea for all the irregularities in human conduct tends con-

stantly to carry legislation across the boundaries of that considerable area of human conduct which lies outside the province of positive law because it can only be suitably regulated and controlled by the conscience of the individual or the moral sanctions of public opinion. — Stone: Mason, *Stone,* 99.

33. It is not unknown, when opinion is divided, that qualifications sometimes are inserted into an act that are hoped to make it ineffective.—Holmes: United States v. Plowman, 216 U.S. 372, 375.

34. A proviso has not infrequently been the means of introducing into a law independent legislation, notwithstanding it is the true office of a proviso to restrict the sense or make clear that which has gone before.—Day: American Exp. Co. v. United States, 212 U.S. 522, 534.

35. Statutory law need not profess to be consistent with itself.—Holmes: *The Common Law,* 63.

36. A statute expressive of such large public policy as that on which the National Labor Relations Board is based must be broadly phrased and necessarily carries with it the task of administrative application. — Frankfurter: Phelps Dodge Corp v. NLRB, 313 U.S. 177, 194.

37. Congress could not catalogue all the devices and stratagems for circumventing the policies of the Act.—Frankfurter: *ibid.*

38. It would be a narrow conception of jurisprudence to confine the notion of "laws" to what is found written on the statute books, and to disregard the gloss which life has written upon it.—Frankfurter: Nashville, C. & St. L. Ry. v. Browning, 310 U.S. 362, 369.

39. It is true also of a statute that it cannot lift itself up by its bootstraps. — Roberts, Frankfurter, Jackson: Screws v. United States, 325 U.S. 91, 154.

——, effectiveness

40. Legislation can eradicate a cancer, right some hoary wrong, correct some definitely established evil, which defies the feebler remedies, the distinctions and the fictions, familiar to the judicial process. — Cardozo: *Growth of the Law,* 134.

41. Do not pin too much faith in legislation. Remedial institutions are apt to fall under the control of the enemy and to become instruments of oppression.—Brandeis: Mason, *Brandeis,* 585.

42. Laws enacted with good intention, when put to the test, frequently, and to the surprise of the law maker himself, turn out to be mischievous, absurd or otherwise objectionable.—Sutherland: Crooks v. Harrelson, 282 U.S. 55, 60.

43. It is the operation of the statute which determines its character.—McKenna: Winfree v. Northern Pac. Ry., 227 U.S. 296, 302.

44. Few persons, indeed, are sufficiently aware, how forcible, though silent, is the operation of laws upon our manners, habits, and feelings.—Story: *Misc. Writings,* 223.

274

45. It is not unusual for a legislative act to involve consequences which are not expressed.—Marshall: Osborn v. Bank of U. S., 9 Wheat. (22 U.S.) 738, 865.

46. All legislation is not simple, nor its consequences obvious, or to be controlled, even if obvious.—McKenna: Pirie v. Chicago Title & Tr. Co., 182 U.S. 438, 451–52.

47. Few laws are of universal application.—Brandeis: Truax v. Corrigan, 257 U.S. 312, 355.

———, inadequacies, infirmities

48. More doubts arise in the administration of justice from the imperfections of positive legislation, than from any other source.—Story: *Misc. Writings,* 449.

49. Human transactions are dividing and subdividing themselves into such innumerable varieties, that they cannot be adjusted or bounded by any written or positive legislation.—Story: *ibid.,* 308.

50. Legislatures and courts generally have recognized that the natural evolutions of a complex society are to be touched only with a very cautious hand, and that such coarse attempts at a remedy for the waste incident to every social function as a simple prohibition and laws to stop its being are harmful and vain.—Holmes: Board of Trade v. Christie Grain & Stock Co., 198 U.S. 236, 247–48.

51. Legislation by even the most competent hands, like other forms of composition, is subject to the frailties of the imagination.—Frankfurter: *Ex*

parte Republic of Peru, 318 U.S. 578, 596.

52. The dominant conditions of the Reconstruction Period were not conducive to the enactment of carefully considered and coherent legislation. Strong post-war feeling caused inadequate deliberation and led to loose and careless phrasing of laws relating to the new political issues.—Frankfurter: United States v. Williams, 341 U.S. 70, 74.

53. Our national free intercourse is never in danger of being suddenly stifled by dramatic and sweeping acts of restraint. That would produce its own antidote. Our danger, as the forefathers well knew, is from the aggregate strangling effect of a multiplicity of individually petty and diverse and local regulations. — Jackson: Duckworth v. Arkansas, 314 U.S. 390, 401.

———, new, experimental

54. Statutes are addressed to the future, not to the past. They usually constitute a new factor in the affairs and relations of men. — McKenna: Winfree v. Northern Pac. Ry., 227 U.S. 296, 301.

55. Every new statute is individual and presents its own problem.—McKenna: Nicholas & Co. v. United States, 249 U.S. 34, 38.

56. Legislation is often tentative, beginning with the most obvious case, and not going beyond it, or to the full length of the principle on which its act must be justified. — Holmes: Beard v. Boston, 151 Mass. 96, 97.

57. The fact is that legislation in

this country, as well as elsewhere, is empirical. It is necessarily made a means by which a body, having the power, put burdens which are disagreeable to them on the shoulders of somebody else. Communism would no more get rid of the difficulty than any other system, unless it limited or put a stop to the propagation of the species. And it may be doubted whether that solution would not be as disagreeable as any other. — Holmes: *Uncollected Letters*, 108–109.

58. New legislation is often disturbing to those who are being subjected to regulation. — Douglas: *We the Judges*, 54.

59. A *casus omissus* is not unusual, particularly in legislation introducing a new system. — Brandeis: United States v. Weitzel, 246 U.S. 533, 543.

———, discriminatory

60. Where size is not an index to an admitted evil, the law cannot discriminate between the great and small. —Holmes: Engel v. O'Malley, 219 U.S. 128, 138.

61. It is no sufficient condemnation of legislation that it favors one class at the expense of another; for much or all legislation does that; and none the less when the *bona fide* object is the greatest good of the greatest number. Why should the greatest number be preferred? Why not the greatest good of the most intelligent and most highly developed?—Holmes: *Uncollected Letters*, 108.

62. The greatest good of a minority of our generation may be the greatest good of the greatest number in the long run. But if the welfare of all future ages is to be considered, legislation may as well be abandoned for the present. If the welfare of the living majority is paramount, it can only be on the ground that the majority have the power in their hands.—Holmes: *ibid*.

63. Legislation essential to the protection of individuals of limited or no means is not invalidated by the circumstance that other individuals are financially able to protect themselves. —Brandeis: New State Ice Co. v. Liebmann, 285 U.S. 262, 290.

———, amendment

64. Legislatures may alter or change their laws, without injury, as they affect the future only.—Grier: Minnesota Min. Co. v. National Min. Co., 3 Wall. (70 U.S.) 332, 334.

65. Statutes are designed to meet the fugitive exigencies of the hour. Amendment is easy as the exigencies change.—Cardozo: *Nature of Judicial Process*, 83.

66. But even if a law is found wanting on trial, it is better that its defects should be demonstrated and removed than that the law should be aborted by judicial fiat.—Frankfurter: AFL v. Am. Sash & Door Co., 335 U.S. 538, 553.

67. Legislation whose basis in economic wisdom is uncertain can be redressed by the processes of the ballot box or the pressures of opinion. But when the channels of opinion and of peaceful persuasion are corrupted or

clogged, these political correctives can no longer be relied on, and the democratic system is threatened at its most vital point.—Jackson: *Struggle for Judicial Supremacy,* 285.

68. An amendment is not a repeal. —Frankfurter: Massachusetts Bond. & Ins. Co. v. United States, 352 U.S. 128, 139.

———, repeal
69. A law, absolutely repugnant to another, as entirely repeals that other as if express terms of repeal were used. —Marshall: McCulloch v. Maryland, 4 Wheat. (17 U.S.) 316, 425–26.

70. One obvious effect of the repeal of a statute is that it no longer exists. Its life is at an end.—Miller: Greenwood v. Union Fr. R.R., 15 Otto (105 U.S.) 13, 18.

71. Implied repeals are not favored. —Taft: United States v. Noce, 268 U.S. 613, 619.

72. Conditions change; and . . . the rules evolved, being merely experiments in government, must be discarded when they prove to be failures. —Brandeis: Truax v. Corrigan, 257 U.S. 312, 354–55.

———, miscellaneous
73. With laws; their power floats on the atmosphere we breathe. Necessity, or convention, or power, has given them a legal ubiquity co-extensive with the legislative power of the government that enacts them.—Johnson: The Mary & Susan, 1 Wheat. (14 U.S.) 46, 58.

74. That which purports to be a law of the State is a law or it is not

a law, according as the truth of the fact may be, and not according to the shifting circumstances of the parties. —Bradley: South Ottawa v. Perkins, 4 Otto (94 U.S.) 260, 267.

75. There is no constitutional inhibition against retrospective laws. Though generally distrusted, they are often beneficial, and sometimes necessary. — Miller: Blount v. Windley, 5 Otto (95 U.S.) 173, 180.

76. It was a contest of large sallies and small retreats in which as much ground was occupied, at any time, as the temporary coalescences of forces strong enough to enroll a prevailing vote could agree upon.—Frankfurter: Monroe v. Pape, 365 U.S. 167, 248.

See also Accident 2; Court 4; Despotism 2, 3; Divorce; Equality 19; Freedom, speech 105; Government (U.S.), federal-state, authority; Judicial process 8; Majority-minority 12; Marriage 2; Prolixity 1; Public opinion 6; Reform 11; Remedy 4; Seaman 7, 10; Tax 39; Treaty 1; Tyranny 1; Unemployment 5.

LEGISLATOR, LEGISLATURE
Authority 1–3; duties, functions 4–9; power, limitations 10–16 qualifications 17–19; influences 20–23; miscellaneous 24.

Related subjects: Congress; Legislation and related subjects.

———, authority
1. The Legislature is in no just sense sovereign. It is but the agent, with limited authority, of the State sovereignty. — Story: Charles River Bridge v. Warren Bridge, 11 Pet. (36 U.S.) 420, 643.

2. The Legislature speaks; its offi-

cers act. The voice and act are equally those of the State. — Hunt: United States v. Reese, 2 Otto (92 U.S.) 214, 252.

3. The doctrine of legislative absolutism is foreign to free government as it exists in this country.—Harlan: Taylor v. Beckham, 178 U.S. 548, 609.

———, duties, functions

4. It is the province of the legislature to make the laws and of the courts to enforce them.—Day: Barrett v. Indiana, 229 U.S. 26, 30.

5. It falls to the lot of legislative bodies and administrative officials to find practical solutions within the frame of our decisions.—Frankfurter: Niemotko v. Maryland, 340 U.S. 268, 276.

6. Legislators should act with a single eye to the true interest of the whole people.—Grier: Marshall v. Baltimore & O. R.R., 16 How. (57 U.S.) 314, 335.

7. The legislature is the proper guardian of the public faith.—Brown: Yazoo & Miss. Val. Ry. v. Adams, 180 U.S. 1, 25.

8. Legislature as well as court is an interpreter and a guardian of constitutional immunities.—Cardozo: *Paradoxes,* 121.

9. It is for the legislature to declare when conscience is disturbed.—Cardozo: People v. Westchester Co. Nat'l Bank, 231 N.Y. 465, 489.

———, power, limitations

10. All the legislative powers are concessions of sovereignty from the people of the States.—Wayne: Dodge v. Woolsey, 18 How. (59 U.S.) 331, 349.

11. In my opinion the Legislature has the whole lawmaking power except so far as the words of the Constitution expressly or impliedly withhold it.—Holmes: Opinions of the Justices, 160 Mass. 586, 594.

12. Many things that a legislature may do if it does them with no ulterior purpose, it cannot do as a means to reach what is beyond its constitutional power.—Holmes: Maxwell v. Bugbee, 250 U.S. 525, 543.

13. A legislature is subject to no laws in the selection of the course to be pursued.—Johnson: United States v. Palmer, 3 Wheat. (16 U.S.) 610, 639.

14. The Legislature cannot bargain away the police power of a State.— Waite: Stone v. Mississippi, 11 Otto (101 U.S.) 814, 817.

15. The Legislature may enjoin, permit, forbid and punish; they may declare new crimes, and establish rules of conduct for all its citizens in future cases; they may command what is right and prohibit what is wrong, but they cannot change innocence into guilt, or punish innocence as a crime, or violate the rights of an antecedent lawful private contract, or the right of private property. — Field: Legal Tender Cases, 12 Wall. (79 U.S.) 457, 670.

16. A legislature cannot by mere legislative fiat convert a business into a public utility.—Brandeis: New State Ice Co. v. Liebmann, 285 U.S. 262, 283–84.

———, qualifications

17. We are apt to think, that men are born legislators; that no qualifications beyond plain sense and common honesty are necessary for the management of the intricate machine of government; and, above all, of that most delicate and interesting of all machines, a republican government. To adjust its various parts requires the skill of the wisest, and often baffles the judgment of the best.—Story: *Misc. Writings,* 448.

18. It would be too much to expect the construction of a philosophic system from Congress.—Holmes: *Uncollected Letters,* 110.

19. One must not expect uncommon courage even in legislators.—Frankfurter: Tenney v. Brandhove, 341 U.S. 367, 377.

———, influences

20. Unfortunately, it is true that legislative assemblies, born to defend the liberty of the people, have at times violated their sacred trusts and become the instruments of oppression.—Black: *ibid.,* 380.

21. In times of political passion, dishonest or vindictive motives are readily attributed to legislative conduct and as readily believed.—Frankfurter: *ibid.,* 378.

22. The sly and stealthy arts to which state Legislatures are exposed, and the greedy appetites of adventurers, for monopolies and immunities from the state right of government.—Campbell: State Bank v. Knoop, 16 How. (57 U.S.) 369, 412.

23. The conservatism of legislators is moderated by elimination and by expediency, just as liberalism among them is restrained by the average opinion of electors.—Jackson: *Struggle for Judicial Supremacy,* 320.

———, miscellaneous

24. Tact, respect, and generosity toward variant views will always commend themselves to those charged with the duties of legislation so as to achieve a maximum of good will and to require a minimum of unwilling submission to a general law.—Frankfurter: West Va. State Bd. of Educ. v. Barnette, 319 U.S. 624, 651.
See also Lawyer 25; Legislation; Name 14, 15; Property 18; Public expenditure; Public welfare; Supreme Court; Tax 90.

LEGITIMACY
Related subject: Illegitimacy. *See also* Marriage 6; Polygamy.

LEISURE
The welfare of our country demands that leisure be provided for. This is not a plea for indolence. Leisure does not imply idleness. The provision for leisure does not contemplate working less hard. It means ability to work not less, but more—ability to work at something besides breadwinning. We need leisure, among other reasons, because with us every man is of the ruling class. Our education and condition of life must be such as become a ruler.—Brandeis: Mason, *Brandeis,* 151.

LENDER
Related subjects: Borrowing; Loan. *See also* Interest 5; Usury 1.

LESS
See Greater-less.

LETTER (communication)

Notwithstanding all modern inventions, letters still are the principal means of speech with those who are not before our face.—Holmes: Leach v. Carlile, 258 U.S. 138, 140.

LETTER (literalness)
See Construction, literal; Literalism.

LIABILITY

1. Liability exists as a duty imposed by law. — Cardozo: New Georgia Nat'l Bank v. Lippman, 249 N.Y. 307, 312.

2. Illegality established, liability ensues.—Cardozo: Schubert v. Schubert Wagon Co., 249 N.Y. 253, 256.

3. It set its hand to the task, and must answer for the doing. — Cardozo: Murtha v. N.Y. Homeopathic Med. Col. & Flower Hospital, 228 N.Y. 183, 186.

4. The various forms of liability known to modern law spring from the common ground of revenge.— Holmes: *The Common Law*, 37.

5. Civil liability, in its immediate working, is simply a redistribution of an existing loss between two individuals. . . . Sound policy lets losses lie where they fall, except where a special reason can be shown for interference. The most frequent of such reasons is, that the party who is charged has been to blame.—Holmes: *ibid.*, 50.

6. What the law really forbids, and the only thing it forbids, is the act on the wrong side of the line, be that act blameworthy or otherwise.—Holmes: *ibid.*, 110.

7. The rule that the law does, in general, determine liability by blameworthiness, is subject to the limitation that minute differences of character are not allowed for. The law considers, in other words, what would be blameworthy in the average man, the man of ordinary intelligence and prudence, and determines liability by that. If we fall below the level in those gifts, it is our misfortune.—Holmes: *ibid.*, 108.

8. That the condition of a man's heart or conscience ought to be more considered in determining criminal than civil liability, it might almost be said . . . is the very opposite of truth. —Holmes: *ibid.*, 50.

9. A man may have to pay damages, may be sent to prison, at common law might be hanged, if at the time of his act he knew facts from which common experience showed that the consequences would follow, whether he individually could foresee them or not. —Holmes: Abrams v. United States, 250 U.S. 616, 626–27.

10. Liability without fault is not a novelty in the law.—Pitney: New York Cent. R.R. v. White, 243 U.S. 188, 204.

11. The whole philosophy of liability without fault is that losses which are incidental to socially desirable conduct should be placed on those best able to bear them.—Stone: Seas Shipping Co. v. Sieracki, 328 U.S. 85, 108.

12. It seems to me to be the very foundation of right—of the essence

of liberty as it is of morals, to be free from liability if one is free from fault. It has heretofore been the sense of the law and the sense of the world, pervading the regulations of both, that there can be no punishment where there is no blame.—McKenna: Arizona Copper Co. v. Hammer, 250 U.S. 400, 436.

13. Whatever may be the injury that casually results to an individual from the act of another while pursuing the reasonable exercise of an established right, it is his misfortune.—Johnson: The Eleanor, 2 Wheat (15 U.S.) 345, 358.

14. The general principle of our law is that loss from accident must lie where it falls, and this principle is not affected by the fact that a human being is the instrument of misfortune. — Holmes: *The Common Law*, 94.

15. Unless my act is of a nature to threaten others, unless under the circumstances a prudent man would have foreseen the possibility of harm, it is no more justifiable to make me indemnify my neighbor against the consequences, than to make me do the same thing if I had fallen upon him in a fit, or to compel me to insure him against lightning.—Holmes: *ibid.*, 96.

16. There is no individual liability for an act which ordinary human care and foresight could not guard against. —Lurton: Chicago v. Sturges, 222 U.S. 313, 322.

17. The law recognizes the fact that the measure of liability originally applied to a carter's wain or a waterman's hoy may often be illy adapted to the exigencies of modern commerce.—Brown: The Queen of the Pacific, 180 U.S. 49, 57.

Related subjects: Negligence and related subjects. *See also* Error 5; Intrusion 1; Principal, agent 1; Tax 5, 152; Wrong.

LIAR

Liar ordinarily is a fighting word spoken in anger to express bitter personal hostility against another. — Black: Sacher v. United States, 343 U.S. 1, 16.

LIBEL

1. The spoken word dissolves, but the written one abides and "perpetuates the scandal."—Cardozo: Ostrowe v. Lee, 256 N.Y. 36, 39.

2. Criminal libel laws are consistent with the concept of ordered liberty only when applied with safeguards evolved to prevent their invasion of freedom of expression.—Jackson: Beauharnais v. Illinois, 343 U.S. 250, 295.

3. Group libel statutes represent a commendable desire to reduce sinister abuses of our freedoms of expression —abuses which I have had occasion to learn can tear apart a society, brutalize its dominant elements, and persecute, even to extermination, its minorities.—Jackson: *ibid.*, 304.

Related subjects: Defamation and related subjects. *See also* Press 5; Public official 37.

LIBERALISM

Professions of extreme liberalism always come round to holding that of course every right-minded person will freely come to my conclusions.—Holmes: *Holmes-Pollock Letters,* I, 140.

See also Construction; Legislature 23.

LIBERALITY
See Generosity; indulgence.

LIBERTY
We can afford no liberties with liberty itself.—Jackson: United States v. Spector, 343 U.S. 169, 180.

See also Freedom.

LICENSE
The valid requirements of license are for the good of the applicants and the public.—Reed: Poulos v. New Hampshire, 345 U.S. 395, 409.

Related subject: Restraint. *See also* Citizen 32; Freedom 24, 86; Occupation 7, 8; Tax 92.

LIEN
See Maritime lien.

LIFE
1. Life is the gift of God, and the right to preserve it is the most sacred of the rights of man. — Swayne: Slaughter House Cases, 16 Wall. (83 U.S.) 36, 127.

2. To live is to function. That is all there is to living.—Holmes: Radio Address, 1931.

3. From the point of view of the world the end of life is life. Life is action, the use of one's powers. As to use them to their height is our joy and duty, so it is the one end that justifies itself.—Holmes: *Speeches,* 85.

4. If a man gets a year's life out of a year, he can ask no more.—Holmes: *Holmes-Pollock Letters,* I, 24.

5. When I hear that one of the builders has ceased his toil, I do not ask what statue he has placed upon some conspicuous pedestal, but I think of the mighty whole, and say to myself, he has done his part to help the mysterious growth of the world along its inevitable lines towards its unknown end.—Holmes: *Speeches,* 47-48.

6. The changes on the bench show the uncertainty of life, and the emptiness of human hopes. — McLean: United States v. Bank of U. S., 5 How. (46 U.S.) 382, 401.

7. Life is never static. — Cardozo: United States v. Swift & Co., 286 U.S. 106, 119.

8. Life has relations not capable of division into inflexible compartments. The moulds expand and shrink.—Cardozo: Glanzer v. Shepard, 233 N.Y. 236, 241.

9. He lived, as a wise man would aspire to live. He died, as a good man would desire to die.—Story: *Misc. Writings,* 111.

10. If any one thing . . . has been settled . . . by unison of opinion, it is the State-wide extension of the interest in the maintenance of life and health.—Cardozo: Adler v. Deegan, 251 N.Y. 467, 485.

11. The classic tradition that the life of a free human being . . . did not admit of valuation—which no longer is true sentimentally, as is shown by the statutes, and which economically is false.—Holmes: Panama R.R. v. Rock, 266 U.S. 209, 216.

12. An undue regard for a man's

life when it is adequately proved to have been forfeited under the law.—Clarke: Valdez v. United States, 244 U.S. 432, 455.

See also Constitution 122; Effort; Equality 23; Law 25; Lawyer 47; Nation 5; Rights 4; Science 4; Struggle.

LIMITATION (legal)

1. Length of time necessarily obscures all human evidence, and deprives parties of the means of ascertaining the nature of original transactions.—Grier: Wagner v. Baird, 7 How. (48 U.S.) 234, 258.

2. Raids by the unscrupulous will multiply apace if claims may be postponed till the injury is stale.—Cardozo: Thomann v. Rochester, 256 N.Y. 165, 170.

3. The right to be free of stale claims in time comes to prevail over the right to prosecute them.—Jackson: Telegraphers v. Railway Exp. Agency, 321 U.S. 343, 349.

Related subjects: Laches; Prescription; Statute of Limitations. See also Constitution (U.S.), construction, limitations; Definition 1; Discretion 10; Freedom, limitations; Freedom, speech, limitations; Privilege 1; Property, limitations; Sherman Antitrust Law 3; Sovereignty, limitations; Supreme Court, functions, limitations; Tax, power, scope, limitations.

LIQUOR

1. From the first settlement of this country, and in most other nations, ancient or modern, civilized or savage, it has been found useful to discountenance excesses in the use of intoxicating liquor.—Woodbury: License Cases, 5 How. (46 U.S.) 504, 627.

2. By the general concurrence of opinion of every civilized and Christian community, there are few sources of crime and misery to society equal to the dram shop, where intoxicating liquors, in small quantities, to be drunk at the time, are sold indiscriminately to all parties applying. The statistics of every State show a greater amount of crime and misery attributable to the use of ardent spirits obtained at these retail liquor saloons than to any other source. — Field: Crowley v. Christensen, 137 U.S. 86, 91.

3. We cannot shut out of view the fact, within the knowledge of all, that the public health, the public morals, and the public safety, may be endangered by the general use of intoxicating drinks; nor the fact, accessible to everyone, that the idleness, disorder, pauperism, and crime existing in the country are, in some degree at least, traceable to this evil.—Harlan: Mugler v. Kansas, 123 U.S. 623, 662.

4. Liquor drinking is not a wrong; but excessive drinking is.

Liquor will be sold; hence the sale should be licensed.

Liquor is dangerous; hence the business should be regulated.

No regulation can be enforced which is not reasonable.

The better the men who sell liquor, the less the harm done by it.

Hence, strive to secure for the business those who are respectable.

Self-respect and prosperity are the most effective guardian of morals.

Unenforceable or harassing laws tend to make criminals.

—Brandeis: Mason, *Brandeis,* 90.

5. I cannot for a moment believe that apart from the Eighteenth Amendment special constitutional principles exist against strong drink. The fathers of the Constitution so far as I know approved it.—Holmes: Knickerbocker Ice Co. v. Stewart, 253 U.S. 149, 169.

6. The people of the United States knew that liquor is a lawlessness unto itself.—Jackson: Duckworth v. Arkansas, 314 U.S. 390, 398.

7. We are, to be sure, dealing with a historic calling. We meet the alewife, sprightly and ribald, in Shakespeare, but centuries before him she played a role in the social life of England.—Frankfurter: Goessert v. Cleary, 335 U.S. 464, 465.

> Related subjects: Constitution, Eighteenth Amendment; Drunkard. *See also* Punishment 33.

LITERACY

1. Illiterate people may be intelligent voters.—Douglas: Lassiter v. Northampton Co., 360 U.S. 45, 52.

2. Literacy and intelligence are obviously not synonymous. — Douglas: *ibid.*

3. Literacy and illiteracy are neutral on race, creed, color and sex, as reports around the world show.—Douglas: *ibid.,* 51–52.

LITERALISM

A false and hollow sound; a dead and polluting letter; a letter which killeth, when the spirit would make alive.—Story: *Misc. Writings,* 430.

> *See also* Construction, literal.

LITERATURE

> Related subject: Book. *See also* Censor; Classic.

LITIGANT

1. One does not have to be an easy generalizer of national characteristics to believe that litigiousness is one of our besetting sins. — Frankfurter, Jackson: NLRB v. Mexia Textile Mills, 339 U.S. 563, 573.

2. Litigants usually have selfish purposes. — Douglas: Casey v. United States, 343 U.S. 808, 809.

3. Hope springs eternal in a litigant's breast.—Frankfurter: Elgin, J. & E. Ry. v. Burley, 327 U.S. 661, 668.

4. All parties to a litigation tend to become partisans.—Jackson: United States v. Nat'l City Lines, 334 U.S. 573, 601.

5. It is not easy to satisfy interested parties, and defeated litigants, no matter how fairly treated, do not always have the feeling they have received justice.—Frankfurter: NLRB v. Donnelly Co., 330 U.S. 219, 237.

6. The litigious tendency of our people and the unwillingness of litigants to rest content with adverse decisions after their cause has been litigated in two and often in three courts, lead to attempts to get a final review by the Supreme Court.—Frankfurter: Dick v. New York Life Ins. Co., 359 U.S. 437, 459.

7. Citizens generally go through life subject to the risk that they may, though in the right, be subject to liti-

gation and the possibility of a miscarriage of justice.—Warren: Barr v. Matteo, 360 U.S. 564, 589.

8. Lawsuits frequently engender in defeated litigants sharp resentments and hostilities against adverse witnesses.—Black: Weiler v. United States, 323 U.S. 606, 609.

9. The natural selfishness of litigants to exploit the law's weaknesses. —Frankfurter: Lumbermen's Mut. Cas. Co. v. Elbert, 348 U.S. 48, 57.

10. The long history of Anglo-American litigation, whereby unsuccessful litigants and lawyers give vent to their disappointment in tavern or press.—Frankfurter: United States v. Morgan, 313 U.S. 409, 421.

11. Litigants . . . have a right to have their lawsuits decided without unreasonable and unnecessary delay or expense.—Black: Clay v. Sun Ins. Off., 363 U.S. 207, 224.

12. Some litigants have long purses. Many, however, can hardly afford one lawsuit, let alone two.—Douglas: *ibid.,* 228.

13. To a litigant, there is no greater injury than to lose a case.—Harlan: United States v. American-Foreign S.S. Corp., 363 U.S. 685, 696.

LITIGATION

————, definition

1. What is a suit? We understand it to be the prosecution, or pursuit, of some claim, demand, or request. In law language, it is the prosecution of some demand in a court of justice. —Marshall: Cohens v. Virginia, 6 Wheat. (19 U.S.) 264, 407.

2. To maintain a suit is to uphold, continue on foot and keep from collapse a suit already begun.—Holmes: Smallwood v. Gallardo, 275 U.S. 56, 61.

3. The right to sue and defend in the courts is the alternative of force. In an organized society it is the right conservative of all other rights, and lies at the foundation of orderly government. It is one of the highest and most essential privileges of citizenship. —Moody: Chambers v. Baltimore & O. R.R., 207 U.S. 142 148.

4. A lawsuit is one of the ultimates of a grievance.—Douglas: Association v. Westinghouse Elec. Co., 348 U.S. 437, 467.

————, commencement

5. A contest begins when the contestants, satisfied no longer with minatory gestures, are at grips with each other in the arena of the fight. When the fight is a civil controversy, the arena is the court.—Cardozo: Killian v. Metropolitan Life Ins. Co., 251 N.Y. 44, 50.

————, function, purpose

6. The end of litigation is justice. Knowledge of the truth is essential thereto.—Brewer: Union Pac. Ry. v. Botsford, 141 U.S. 250, 258.

7. The civil damage action, prosecuted and adjusted by private initiative, neither burdening our overworked criminal processes nor confined by the limits of criminal liability, is one of the law's most effective inducements to the watchfulness and prudence necessary to avoid calamity from hazardous operations in the midst of an unshielded populace. —Jackson: Dalehite v. United States, 346 U.S. 15, 49.

8. Litigation is not the cure-all, the solution for every conflict.—Douglas: *We the Judges,* 56.

———, parties

9. A plaintiff sometimes is under temptation to resort to a strategy of forcing the trial at a most inconvenient place for an adversary, even at some inconvenience to himself.—Jackson: Gulf Oil Corp. v. Gilbert, 330 U.S. 501, 507.

10. Every man is liable to be sued wrongfully or without cause, but he is, by the very genius of our laws, bound to submit to this evil and make defense.—Miller: Dow v. Johnson, 10 Otto (100 U.S.) 158, 193.

11. Imposition on the public is not a ground on which the plaintiff can come into court, but it is a very good ground for keeping him out of it.— Holmes: Ubeda v. Zialcita, 226 U.S. 452, 454.

12. The plaintiffs are not the champions of any rights except their own. —Cardozo: Henneford v. Silas Mason Co., 300 U.S. 577, 583.

13. He is not given a remedy, but only a lawsuit.—Jackson: Miles v. Illinois Cent. R.R., 315 U.S. 698, 707.

———, characteristics

14. The facts are less complicated than the proceedings that have grown out of them.—Holmes: Kansas City Southern Ry. v. Guardian Tr. Co., 240 U.S. 166, 172–73.

15. Look at the dockets. You will find them crowded with suits which the life of man will not see determined.—Marshall: Beveridge, *Life of Marshall,* I, 453.

16. Ages will probably elapse, before the litigations founded on it will be closed.—Story: *Misc. Writings,* 423.

17. Delay is unfortunate, but the expense and annoyance of litigation is a price citizens must pay for life in an orderly society.—Reed: Poulos v. New Hampshire, 345 U.S. 395, 409.

18. Delay, cost, and uncertainty . . . take their toll of both the successful, the just and the unjust litigant.—Jackson: Western Pac. R. Corp. v. Western Pac. R. Co., 345 U.S. 247, 273.

19. Litigation procedures are clumsy and narrow, at best; technical and tricky, at their worst.—Jackson: *Struggle for Judicial Supremacy,* 288.

———, consequences

20. Litigation without limit produces ruinous consequences to individuals.—McLean: Lewis v. Marshall, 5 Pet. (30 U.S.) 470, 478.

21. No one wishes to buy anything if with it he must buy a law suit.— Moody: Kessler v. Eldred, 206 U.S. 285, 289.

22. Lawsuits are rare and catas-

trophic experiences for the vast majority of men.—Cardozo: *Nature of Judicial Process,* 128.

23. If a large amount is in controversy, the claimant can afford to litigate. But he cannot well do so when there is but the trifle of a dollar or two in dispute.—Brewer: Seaboard Air Line Ry. v. Seegers, 207 U.S. 73, 78.

24. It is no concern of ours that the controversy at the root of this lawsuit seems to be trivial. That fact supplies, indeed, the greater reason why the jury should not have been misled into the belief that justice might therefore be denied to the suitor.—Cardozo: Morningstar v. Lafayette Hotel Co., 211 N.Y. 465, 468.

25. The advantage of prolonged litigation lies with the party able to bear heavy expenses.—Brandeis: Crowell v. Benson, 285 U.S. 22, 94.

26. There is always in litigation a margin of error, representing error in fact-finding. — Brennan: Speiser v. Randall, 357 U.S. 513, 525.

————, miscellaneous

27. To know "the justice of the particular case" . . . one must know the case in its particulars.—Cardozo: Lowden v. Northwestern Nat'l Bank & Tr. Co., 298 U.S. 160, 165.

28. It will not do to decide the same question one way between one set of litigants and the opposite way between another.—Cardozo: *Nature of Judicial Process,* 33.

29. I do not suppose that civilization will come to an end whichever way this case is decided.—Holmes: Haddock v. Haddock, 201 U.S. 562, 628.

30. It is desirable to terminate every cause upon its real merits, if those merits are fairly before the court, and to put an end to litigation where it is in the power of the court to do so. —Marshall: Church v. Hubbart, 2 Cranch (6 U.S.) 187, 232.

31. It is just as important that there should be a place to end as that there should be a place to begin litigation. —Reed: Stoll v. Gottlieb, 305 U.S. 165, 172.

See also Defense 8; Divorce; Execution 1; Lawyer 83; Patent 14, 16; Real property 5; Supreme Court, function, litigation; Tax 34, 124, 129; Turpitude 1.

LOAN
Related subjects: Borrowing; Lender. See also Interest; Pawnshop.

LOBBYING, LOBBYIST
1. Our constitutional system is to allow the greatest freedom of access to Congress, so that the people may press for their selfish interests, with Congress acting as arbiter of their demands and conflicts.—Jackson: United States v. Harriss, 347 U.S. 612, 635.

2. Congress . . . should know from experience both the good in the right of petition and the evils of professional lobbying.—Jackson: *ibid.,* 636.

3. Present-day legislative complexities are such that individual members of Congress cannot be expected to explore the myriad pressures to which they are regularly subjected. Yet full realization of the American ideal of government by elected representatives depends to no small extent

on their ability to properly evaluate such pressures. Otherwise the voice of the people may all too easily be drowned out by the voice of special interest groups seeking favored treatment while masquerading as proponents of the public weal.—Warren: *ibid.*, 625.

4. Where persons act as counsel or agents, or in any representative capacity, it is due to those before whom they plead or solicit, that they should honestly appear in their true characters, so that their arguments and representations, open and candidly made, may receive their just weight and consideration.—Grier: Marshall v. Baltimore & O. R.R., 16 How. (57 U.S.) 314, 335.

See also Freedom, petition 160, 161.

LOGIC
1. The logic of words should yield to the logic of realities.—Brandeis: De Santo v. Pennsylvania, 273 U.S. 34, 43.

2. The logic is inexorable if the premises are accepted.—Stone: First Bank Stock Corp. v. Minnesota, 301 U.S. 234, 239.

3. Is there weakness in the logic, or do the consequences repel.—McKenna: De Lima v. Bidwell, 182 U.S. 1, 201.

4. The misuse of logic or philosophy begins when its method and its ends are treated as supreme and final. —Cardozo: *Nature of Judicial Process,* 46.

Related subjects: Deduction; Induction. *See also* History 1; Judge 68; Judicial process 4; Juror 47; Law 25; Lawyer 12; Tax 47; Understanding 2.

LOGOMACHY
Excessive nicety in terminology tends to degenerate into logomachy. —Stone: Mason, *Stone,* 98.

LOSS
See Liability 5, 11, 14; Penalty 5; Profit 2; Suffering 4; Value 7, 10; War 35; Wrongdoer 1.

LOTTERY
1. Experience has shown that the common forms of gambling are comparatively innocuous when placed in contrast with the widespread pestilence of lotteries. The former are confined to a few persons and places, but the latter infests the whole community; it enters every dwelling; it reaches every class; it preys upon the hard earnings of the poor; it plunders the ignorant and simple.—Grier: Phalen v. Virginia, 8 How. (49 U.S.) 163, 168.

2. They (lotteries) are a species of gambling, and wrong in their influences. They disturb the checks and balances of a well ordered community. Society built on such a foundation would almost of necessity bring forth a population of speculators and gamblers, living on the expectation of what, "by the casting of lots, or by lot, chance or otherwise," might be "awarded to them from the accumulations of others."—Waite: Stone v. Mississippi, 11 Otto (101 U.S.) 814, 821.

3. If lotteries are to be tolerated at all, it is, no doubt, better that they should be regulated by law, so that the people may be protected as far as

possible against the inherent vices of the system; but that they are demoralizing in their effects, no matter how carefully regulated, cannot admit of a doubt.—Waite: *ibid.,* 818.

4. Whatever may be the factual differences between a "lottery," a "gift enterprise," and a "similar scheme," the traditional tests of chance, prize, and consideration are applicable to each. — Warren: F e d e r a l Com. Comm'n v. Am. Broadcasting Co., 347 U.S. 284, 290n.

5. Law enforcement officers, federal and state, have been plagued with as many types of lotteries as the seemingly inexhaustible ingenuity of their promoters could devise in their efforts to circumvent the law.—Warren: *ibid.,* 292.

Related subjects: Gamble and related subject. *See also* Numbers racket; Theater 2.

LOYALTY

See Allegiance and related subjects; Disloyalty; Fiduciary; Lawyer 39; Loyalty oath 1.

LOYALTY OATH

1. I am certain that loyalty to the United States can never be secured by the endless proliferation of "loyalty" oaths; loyalty must arise spontaneously from the hearts of people who love their country and respect their government.—Black: Speiser v. Randall, 357 U.S. 513, 532.

2. Loyalty oaths, as well as other contemporary "security measures," tend to stifle all forms of unorthodox or unpopular thinking or expression —the kind of thought and expression

which has played such a vital and beneficial role in the history of this Nation.—Black: *ibid.*

Related subjects: Oath; Test oath.

LUNATIC

See Insanity.

LYNCHING

It [lynching] is not a mere crime against the law; it is much more than that. It is the prostration of all law and government; a defiance of the laws; a resort to the methods of vengeance of those who recognize no law, no society, no government.— Bradley: *Ex parte* Wall, 107 U.S. 265, 274.

MACHINES

1. Mere manual skill and dexterity are nothing, when put in competition with the regularity, rapidity, and economy of machinery, working under the guidance of science.—Story: *Misc. Writings,* 126.

2. The old instrumentalities exist for all who are content with them and who care not for the better ones which inventive genius creates.—McKenna: United States v. United Shoe Mach. Co., 247 U.S. 32, 57.

Related subjects: Automation; Invention; Patent. *See also* Depreciation 3; Injury 2.

MAGNA CHARTA

As to the words from Magna Charta . . . , after volumes spoken and written with a view to their exposition, the good sense of mankind has at length settled down to this: that they were intended to secure the individual from the arbitrary exercise of the powers of government, unrestrained by the established principles of private rights and distributive justice.—Johnson: Bank of Columbia v. Okely, 4 Wheat. (17 U.S.) 235, 244.

> Related subject: Law of the Land. *See also* Constitution 109; Due process 3, 9 Jury 1.

MAIL

1. The postal service is by no means an indispensable adjunct to a civil government, and for hundreds, if not for thousands, of years the transmission of private letters was either intrusted to the hands of friends or to private enterprise. Indeed, it is only within the last three hundred years that governments have undertaken the work. . . . While it has been known in this country since colonial times . . . it was not until 1845 . . . that it assumed anything of the importance it now possesses.—Brown: Public Clearing House v. Coyne, 194 U.S. 497, 506.

2. The United States may give up the Postoffice when it sees fit; but while it carries it on, the use of the mails is almost as much a part of free speech as the right to use our tongues. —Holmes: United States *ex rel.* Milwaukee Soc. Dem. Pub. Co. v. Burleson, 255 U.S. 407, 437.

MAJORITY-MINORITY

> Majority rule 1–6; minorities, rights, protection 7–15; minorities, abuses 16, 17; miscellaneous 18.
>
> Related subject: Minority.

———, majority rule

1. The best rule for freemen . . .

in the opinion of our ancestors, was . . . that . . . of obedience to laws enacted by a majority.—Marshall: Beveridge, *Life of Marshall,* II, 402.

2. Organized society . . . must function by majorities. It contemplates that minorities who are against all war or a particular war may vote and speak against it, but it cannot admit of the right of minorities to resist it, and remain o r g a n i z e d society.— Stone: Mason, *Stone,* 105.

3. I believe that inasmuch as I must live in and be a part of organized society, the majority must rule, and that consequently I must obey some laws of which I do not approve, and even participate in a war which I may think ill-advised.—Stone: *ibid.*

4. To assume that political power is a function exclusively of numbers is to disregard the practicalities of government.—Per curiam: MacDougall v. Green, 335 U.S. 281, 283.

5. The more silent and unobtrusive influence of *popular* dependence, though less striking to the vulgar eye, is not less subversive of the great purposes of justice. It is, indeed, more dangerous to the liberty and property of the people; since it assumes the attractive appearance of obedience to the will of the majority; and thus, without exciting jealousy or alarm, it tramples under foot all those, who refuse to obey the idol of the day.— Story: *Misc. Writings,* 415.

6. It is to be feared, that the experience of mankind has never shown, that the despotism of numbers has been more mild or equitable than that

swayed by a single hand.—Story:*ibid.*, 428.

———, minorities, rights, protection

7. To take appropriate measures in order to avert injustice even towards a member of a despised group is to enforce justice. It is not to play favorites.—Frankfurter: Dennis v. United States, 339 U.S. 162, 184.

8. But while one of an unpopular minority group must be accorded that solicitude w h i c h properly accompanies an accused person, he is not entitled to unusual protection or exception.—Minton: *ibid.*, 168.

9. The treatment of its minorities, especially their legal position, is among the most searching tests of the level of civilization attained by a society.—Frankfurter: Dennis v. United States, 341 U.S. 494, 548–49.

10. We have deemed it more costly to liberty to suppress a despised minority than to let them vent their spleen. We have above all else feared the political censor.—Douglas: *ibid.*, 585.

11. Since prejudice manifests itself in much the same way in every age and country and since what has happened before can happen again, it surely should not be amiss to call attention to what has occurred when dominant governmental groups have been left free to give uncontrolled rein to their prejudices against unorthodox minorities.—Black: Joint Anti-Fascist Ref. Comm. v. McGrath, 341 U.S. 123, 145.

12. Centuries of experience testify that laws aimed at one political or religious group, however rational these laws may be in their beginnings, generate hatreds and prejudices which rapidly spread beyond control. — Black: American Com. Assoc. v. Douds, 339 U.S. 382, 448.

13. Restrictions imposed on proscribed groups are seldom static, even though the rate of expansion may not move in geometric progression from discrimination to arm-band to ghetto and worse.—Black: *ibid.*, 449.

14. History should teach us . . . that in times of high emotional excitement minority parties and groups which advocate extremely unpopular social or governmental innovations will always be typed as criminal gangs and attempts will always be made to drive them out.—Black: Barenblatt v. United States, 360 U.S. 109, 151.

15. It may be doubted whether the Constitution which, of course, protects the right to dissent can be construed also to protect one from the embarrassment that always attends nonconformity, whether in religion, politics, behavior or dress.—Jackson: Illinois v. Bd. of Educ., 333 U.S. 203, 233.

———, minorities, abuses

16. The experience of the past one hundred and fifty years has revealed the danger that, through judicial interpretation, the constitutional device for the protection of minorities from oppressive majority action, may be made the means by which the ma-

jority is subjected to the tyranny of the minority.—Stone: Mason, *Stone,* 331.

17. The First Amendment grew out of an experience which taught that society cannot trust the conscience of a majority to keep its religious zeal within the limits that a free society can tolerate. It do not think it any more intended to leave the conscience of a minority to fix its limits. Civil government cannot let any group ride rough-shod over others simply because their "consciences" tell them to do so.—Jackson: Douglas v. Jeannette, 319 U.S. 157, 179.

———, miscellaneous

18. There is a wide difference between claiming the benefit of a privilege conferred upon a few to the prejudice of the many, and resisting exclusion from privileges conferred upon the many, and denied only to a few.—Cardozo: Postal Tel. Cable Co. v. Assoc. Press, 228 N.Y. 370, 380.

See also Contribution 1; Corporation 35, 38; Legislation 61, 62; Sterilization 4.

MALEVOLENCE

Related subjects: Evil; Iniquity; Vice; Wickedness. *See also* Purpose 2.

MAN

1. A state I cheerfully admit, is the noblest work of man; but man himself, free and honest, is, I speak as to this world, the noblest work of God. —Wilson: Chisholm v. Georgia, 2 Dall. (2 U.S.) 419, 462–63.

2. It seems to be probable that the only cosmic significance of man is that he is part of the cosmos. —

Holmes: *Holmes-Pollock Letters,* II, 13.

Related subjects: Character; Human nature; Individual; Person. *See also* Age (years); Judgment 8; Life; Moral 5; State.

MANDATE (legal)

1. Each order carried in its bosom a court of chancery.—Marshall: Tucker v. Oxley, 5 Cranch (9 U.S.) 34, 44.

2. If it is clear enough to be understood, it is clear enough to be obeyed. —Cardozo: Cooper v. Dasher, 290 U.S. 106, 109.

3. Though professing adherence to this mandate, honored it . . . with lip service only. — Cardozo: Federal Trade Comm'n v. Alcoma Lumber Co., 291 U.S. 67, 73.

Related subject: Judgment (legal).

MANNERS

See Custom 1, 2.

MANSLAUGHTER

See Murder 1.

MANUFACTURE

1. No distinction is more popular to the common mind, or more clearly expressed in economic and political literature, than that between manufactures and commerce. Manufacture is transformation—the fashioning of raw materials into a change of form for use. The functions of commerce are different. The buying and selling and transportation incidental thereto constitutes commerce.—Lamar: Kidd v. Pearson, 128 U.S. 1, 20.

2. Manufacture implies a change, but every change is not manufacture.

—McKenna: Anheuser-Busch Assoc. v. United States, 207 U.S. 556, 562.

3. To say that one who makes, and then gives form and shape to the product made, is not engaged in manufacturing because he makes his product and gives it form and shape in the place where it is to remain, is too narrow a construction.—Lurton: Friday v. Hall & Kaul Co., 216 U.S. 449, 456.
See also Negligence 8.

MARITIME LAW
The law of the sea is in a peculiar sense an international law.—Jackson: Farrell v. United States, 336 U.S. 511, 517.
Related subjects: Admiralty; Maritime lien; Seaman.

MARITIME LIEN
The origin of the maritime lien is the need of the ship. — Hughes: Dampskibsselskabet Dannebrog v. Signal Oil & Gas Co., 310 U.S. 268, 280.

MARKET
A sale at an exchange differs from a sale made at a man's private office, or on his farm . . . because, although the subject matter . . . may be the same . . . there are at an exchange certain advantages in the way of finding a market, obtaining a price, the saving of time, and in the security of payment, and other matters which are more easily obtained there. . . . The market is there.—Peckham: Nicol v. Ames, 173 U.S. 509, 522.
See also Value 5.

MARRIAGE
1. Marriage, while from its very nature a sacred obligation, is, nevertheless, in most civilized nations, a civil contract and usually regulated by law. Upon it society may be said to be built, and out of its fruits spring social relations and social obligations and duties, with which government is necessarily required to deal.—Waite: Reynolds v. United States, 8 Otto (98 U.S.) 145, 165.

2. No legislation can be supposed more wholesome and necessary in the founding of a free, self-governing commonwealth, fit to take rank as one of the co-ordinate States of the Union, than that which seeks to establish it on the basis of the idea of the family, as consisting in and springing from the union for life of one man and one woman in the holy estate of matrimony; the sure foundation of all that is stable and noble in our civilization. — Matthews: Murphy v. Ramsey, 114 U.S. 15, 45.

3. The great basis of human society throughout the civilized world is founded on marriages and legitimate offspring.—Catron: Gaines v. Relf, 12 How. (53 U.S.) 472, 534.

4. Marriage and procreation are fundamental to the very existence and survival of the race.—Douglas: Skinner v. Oklahoma, 316 U.S. 535, 541.

5. Cohabitation is but one of the many incidents to the marriage relation. It is not essential to it.—Matthews: Murphy v. Ramsey, 114 U.S. 15, 42.

6. Legitimacy is the lawful consequence of lawful marriage.—Wayne:

Gaines v. Relf, 12 How. (53 U.S.) 472, 595.

7. A marriage is unreal if procured by force or fraud.—Cardozo: Sleicher v. Sleicher, 251 N.Y. 366, 369.

8. Marriages of convenience are not uncommon.—Jackson: Lutwak v. United States, 344 U.S. 604, 621.

Related subjects: Divorce; Domestic relations; Husband and wife; Polygamy; Polygyny.

MARTIAL LAW
See Military.

MARTYR, MARTYRDOM
One who is a martyr to a principle —which may turn out in the end to be a delusion or an error—does not prove by his martyrdom that he has kept within the law.—Cardozo: Hamilton v. University of Calif., 293 U.S. 245, 268.

See also Issue 1; Parent-child 7; Prophet.

MASTER AND SERVANT
1. Master and servant are "fained to be all one person."—Holmes: Byington v. Simpson, 134 Mass. 169, 170.

2. On the one side there is an intimacy of control and on the other a fullness of submission that imports the presence of a "sovereign," as the master, we are reminded, was sometimes called in the old books.—Cardozo: In the Matter of Glielmi v. Netherland Dairy Co., 254 N.Y. 60, 63–64.

3. The inference is legitimate that it was not the comradeship of friends, but the tacit sanctions of a relation of power and dependence, which prompted the master's request and the servant's acquiescence.—Cardozo: In the Matter of Grieb v. Hammerle, 222 N.Y. 382, 387.

Related subject: Principal and agent.

MAXIM
1. General maxims are oftener an excuse for the want of accurate analysis than a help.—Holmes: Ryalls v. Mechanics Mills, 150 Mass. 190, 194.

2. Great maxims, if they may be violated with impunity, are honored often with lip-service, which passes easily into irreverence. — Cardozo: *Nature of Judicial Process,* 94.

3. Kant's categorical imperative, "Act on a maxim which thou canst will to be law universal."—Cardozo: *ibid.,* 139.

Related subjects: Adage; Axiom. See also Caveat emptor; Democracy 1; Equity 1; Equity court; Form 10; Hearing 7; Honesty 2, 3; Ignorance (legal); Imitation 3; Incitement 7; Intent 8; Profit 5; Public official 17; Rule 15; Search and seizure 8; Tax 129; Theft 3; Treason 8; Tyranny 3, 4; War 18, 39; Whole-part 2–4; Wisdom 5; Witness 15; Word 4.

MEANING
Related subjects: Construction; Definition; Word. See also Act 4, 5; Cliche 1; Constitution, construction; Symbol 9; Virtue 1; Will 9.

MEANS
Means unlawful in their inception do not become lawful by relation when suspicion ripens into discovery.—Cardozo: People v. Defore, 242 N.Y. 13, 19.

Related subject: End-means. See also Law 69; Rule 8.

MEDIATION

The concept of mediation is the antithesis of justiciability. — Douglas: General Comm. v. Missouri, K. & T. R.R., 320 U.S. 323, 337.

MEDICINE

Related subjects: Disease; Physician; Proprietary medicine. *See also* Experiment 6.

MEMORIAL

1. I think it is a noble and pious thing to do whatever we may by written word and moulded bronze and sculptured stone to keep our memories, our reverence and our love alive and to hand them on to new generations all too ready to forget.— Holmes: *Speeches,* 92.

2. The longing for posthumous remembrance is an emotion not so weak as to justify us in saying that its gratification is a negligible good. —Cardozo: Allegheny Col. v. Nat'l Chautauqua Co. Bank, 246 N.Y. 369, 377.

MEMORY

1. Long-range retroactive diagnosis, however competent the physician, becomes hazardous by progression as the passing years add distortions of the past and destroy its perspective.— Rutledge: Marconi Wireless Tel. Co. v. United States, 320 U.S. 1, 66.

2. Dates are easily confused with the passing of the years.—Cardozo: Title Guar. & Tr. Co. v. Pam, 232 N.Y. 441, 455.

Related subjects: Forgetfulness; Mind. *See also* Representation; Testimony 4; Witness 7.

MENTAL DISEASE

Related subjects: Competence; Incompetence; Insanity; Mental healing. *See also* Impulse.

MENTAL HEALING

1. There can be no doubt that the influence of the mind upon the physical condition of the body is very powerful, and that a hopeful mental state goes far, in many cases, not only to alleviate, but even to aid very largely in the cure of an illness from which the body may suffer. . . . Just exactly to what extent the mental condition affects the body, no one can accurately and definitely say . . . surely it cannot be said that it is a fraud for one person to contend that the mind has an effect upon the body . . . greater than even a vast majority of intelligent people admit or believe.—Peckham: American School of Magnetic Healing v. McAnnulty, 187 U.S. 94, 104.

2. While the healer inculcates the faith of the church as a method of healing, he is immune. When he goes beyond that, puts his spiritual agencies aside and takes up the agencies of the flesh, his immunity ceases.—Cardozo: People v. Vogelgesand, 221 N.Y. 290, 293.

Related subject: Mental disease.

MERCHANT

The question, how far merchants are responsible for the character they give each other, is one of much delicacy, and of great importance to the commercial world. — Marshall: Russell v. Clarks Ex'rs, 7 Cranch (11 U.S.) 69, 92.

METAPHOR

1. Metaphors in law are to be narrowly watched, for starting as devices to liberate thought, they end often by enslaving it.—Cardozo: Berkey v. Third Ave. Ry., 244 N.Y. 84, 94.

2. Attribution of legal rights and duties to a juristic person other than man is necessarily a metaphorical process. And none the worse for it.—Frankfurter: United States v. Scophony Corp., 333 U.S. 795, 820.

METHOD

We must learn that all methods are to be viewed not as idols but as tools.—Cardozo: *Growth of the Law,* 103.

See also Opinion 16, Tax, power, method; Tax, standards; Test oath 2; Zeal 4.

MIGRATION

The spectacle of large segments of our population constantly on the move has given rise to urgent demands upon the ingenuity of government.—Byrnes: Edwards v. California, 314 U.S. 160, 173.

See also Nation 16, 17; Pension 2.

MILITARY

General 1–5; law (martial law) 6–11; military tribunals (courts-martial) 12–17.

Related subjects: Army; Conscientious objector and related subjects; Selective service (military); Veteran; War.

———, general

1. The military should always be kept in subjection to the laws of the country to which it belongs, and . . . he is no friend to the Republic who advocates the contrary. The established principle of every free people

is, that the law shall alone govern; and to it the military must always yield.—Field: Dow v. Johnson, 10 Otto (100 U.S.) 158, 169.

2. A free people are naturally jealous of the exercise of military power.—Story: Martin v. Mott, 12 Wheat. (25 U.S.) 19, 29.

3. Abhorrence of military rule is ingrained in our form of government.—Murphy: Duncan v. Kahanamoku, 327 U.S. 304, 325.

4. Supremacy of the civil over the military is one of our great heritages.—Murphy: *ibid.*

5. Civil liberties and military expediency are often irreconcilable.—Murphy: *ibid.,* 331.

See also Citizen 16, 29.

———, law (martial law)

6. By it [martial law], every citizen, instead of reposing under the shield of known and fixed laws as to his liberty, property, and life, exists with a rope round his neck, subject to be hung up by a military despot at the next lamp post, under the sentence of some drum-head court-martial.—Woodbury: Luther v. Borden, 7 How. (48 U.S.) 1, 62.

7. Martial law is the law of military necessity in the actual presence of war.—Waite: United States v. Diekelman, 2 Otto (92 U.S.) 520, 526.

8. Martial rule can never exist where the courts are open, and in the proper and unobstructed exercise of their jurisdiction.—Davis: *Ex parte Milligan,* 4 Wall. (71 U.S.) 2, 127.

9. Military decisions must be made

without the benefit of hindsight.—
D o u g l a s: Hirabayashi v. United
States, 320 U.S. 81, 107.

10. The military forces ... act upon
appearances, not upon testimony.—
Waite: LaMar v. Browne, 2 Otto (92
U.S.) 187, 196.

11. In the very nature of things
military decisions are not susceptible
of intelligent judicial appraisal. They
do not pretend to rest on evidence,
but are made on information that
often would not be admissible and
on assumptions that could not be
proved.—Jackson: Korematsu v. United States, 323 U.S. 214, 245.

See also Peace 2.

————, military tribunals
(courts-martial)

12. Military tribunals are as necessary to secure subordination and discipline in the army as courts are to
maintain law and order in civil life;
and the experience of our government
for now more than a century and a
quarter, and of the English government for a century more, proves that
a much more expeditious procedure
is necessary in military than is thought
tolerable in civil affairs. — Clarke:
United States *ex rel.* Creary v. Weeks,
259 U.S. 336, 343.

13. Courts-martial are deeply rooted in history.—Reed: United States
v. Quarles, 350 U.S. 11, 29.

14. Military tribunals have not been
and probably never can be constituted
in such way that they can have the
same kind of qualifications that the
Constitution has deemed essential to

fair trials of civilians in federal courts.
—Black: *ibid.,* 17.

15. The swift trial and punishment
which the military desires is precisely
what the Bill of Rights outlaws.—
Murphy: Duncan v. Kahanamoku,
327 U.S. 304, 331.

16. Trial of soldiers to maintain discipline is merely incidental to an
army's primary fighting function.—
Black: United States v. Quarles, 350
U.S. 11, 17.

17. The idea of a civilian being tried
by military authorities is repulsive to
the American scheme of justice.—
Douglas: *We the Judges,* 70.

MIND

1. The human mind not unfrequently passes from one extreme to
another; from one of implicit faith,
to one of absolute incredulity.—Story:
Misc. Writings, 18.

2. We all know, that nothing is
more distracting to the mind than a
variety of pursuits. A steady devotion
to one gives great accuracy and acute-
ness, and keeps the whole current of
thought fresh and transparent.—
Story: *ibid.,* 285.

3. Few minds are accustomed to the
same habit of thinking, and our conclusions are most satisfactory to ourselves when arrived at in our own
way.—Johnson: Martin v. Hunter's
Lessee, 1 Wheat. (14 U.S.) 305, 362.

4. Sometimes if we would guide by
the light of reason, we must let our
minds be bold.—Brandeis: Burns Baking Co. v. Bryan, 264 U.S. 504, 520.

5. You talk about improving your

mind, you only exercise it on the subjects with which you are familiar.—Holmes: *Holmes-Pollock Letters,* II, 13 (quot. Brandeis).

6. I doubt if there is any more exalted form of life than that of a great abstract thinker, wrapt in the successful study of problems to which he devotes himself, for an end which is neither unselfish nor selfish in the common sense of those words, but is simply to feed the deepest hunger and to use the greatest gifts of his soul.—Holmes: "Law in Science and Science in Law," 12 Harv. L. Rev. 452–53.

7. Every living sentence which shows a mind at work for itself is to be welcomed.—Holmes: *ibid.,* 455.

8. There is a tendency of a certain type of mind to become closed the moment it has formed a conclusion and announced it.—Stone: Mason, *Stone,* 319.

9. The conservative mind is subject to two great dangers—the danger of intolerance and the danger of its becoming a "closed mind."—Stone: *ibid.,* 98.

10. Without open minds there can be no open society. — Frankfurter: Dennis v. United States, 341 U.S. 494, 556.

11. There is to be the peace of mind that is born of definiteness and certainty.—Cardozo: Killian v. Metropolitan Life Ins. Co., 251 N.Y. 44, 49.

12. The sphygmograph records with graphic certainty the fluctuations of the pulse. There is no instrument yet invented that records with equal certainty the fluctuations of the mind.—Cardozo: People v. Zackowitz, 254 N.Y. 192, 195.

13. The variable word is seen as the reflection of the variable mind.—Cardozo: In the Matter of Durant, 231 N.Y. 41, 50.

14. The state of a man's mind must be inferred from the things he says or does.—Vinson: American Com. Assoc. v. Douds, 339 U.S. 382, 411.

15. The courts cannot "ascertain the thought that has had no outward manifestation."—Vinson: *ibid.*

16. The minds of the parties . . . moved on parallel not on concentric lines.—Swayne: First Nat'l Bank v. Hall, 11 Otto (101 U.S.) 43, 49.

Related subjects: Freedom, belief, conscience, thought; Idea; Intent; Memory; Reason; Thought; Will. *See also* Civilization 4; Fraud 8; Freedom, belief; Freedom, thought; Freedom, learning; Heart 1; Human nature 2; Impartiality 1; Intent 6, 10; Jury 16; Mental healing 1; Moral 2, 4; Pain 1; Political party; Reason 3; Rights 49; Self-interest 1; Solution 1; Suffering 2, 3; Symbol 1; Vagary.

MINIMUM WAGE
See Wage 6.

MINING
Mining brings the subject matter of commerce into existence. Commerce disposes of it.—Sutherland: Carter v. Carter Coal Co., 298 U.S. 238, 304.

MINORITY
See Majority-minority. *See also* Association; Constitution (U.S.) 98; Democracy 24, 26; Election 18; Freedom 33, 39, 44, 59; Legislation 10; Negro 8; Opposition 3; Persecution 2, 3; Supreme Court 48; Vote 3.

MISBEHAVIOR
Related subjects: Behavior and related subjects. *See also* Citizen 32; Conduct 15; Contempt (of court) 2.

MISBRANDING
Misbranding in its crude manifestations, what would colloquially be d e e m e d a false representation.—Frankfurter: Cases of Jam v. United States, 340 U.S. 593, 596.

MISCONDUCT
Related subjects: Behavior and related subjects. *See also* Lawyer, misconduct; Lawyer, disbarment; Lawyer 105, 107.

MISREPRESENTATION
See Falsities and related subjects.

MISTAKE
1. Mistake may be considered a corollary of accident. — McKenna: Levinson v. United States, 258 U.S. 198, 203–204.

2. A sort of misspeech to which the human mind is perversely addicted. It is done every day, even by painstaking people.—Bradley: Patch v. White, 117 U.S. 210, 216.

3. So palpable a slip of the pen, that its use, although furnishing an opportunity for cavil, could not be said to create an ambiguity on the face of the instrument, or leave any doubt as to its true intent in the mind of any one who will read the whole of it together, and has no intent or desire to pervert it.—Grier: Randon v. Toby, 11 How. (52 U.S.) 493, 519.

4. No mistake can be corrected until it is discovered.—Miller: Mahn v. Harwood, 112 U.S. 354, 366.

5. Mistakes may occur and some-times do occur, but it is better that they should be endured than that, in a vain search for infallibility, questions shall remain open indefinitely.—Moody: Tilt v. Kelsey, 207 U.S. 43, 56.
Related subjects: Error; Omission. *See also* Claim 1; Inducement 2; Repetition 2; Verdict.

MOB
1. Released from the sense of personal responsibility that would restrain even the worst individuals in it if alone and brave with the courage of numbers, both radical and reactionary mobs endanger liberty as well as order.—Jackson: Terminiello v. Chicago, 357 U.S. 1, 33–34.

2. Few are the mobs that have not had their immediate origin in harangue. — Jackson: Kunz v. New York, 340 U.S. 290, 307.

3. No mob has ever protected any liberty, even its own.—Jackson: Terminiello v. Chicago, 357 U.S. 1, 32.
Related subjects: Force; Violence. *See also* Incitement; Intolerance 3; Judge 72; Redress 1; Trial 21, 22.

MONEY
1. From the earliest period in the history of civilized Nations, we find pieces of gold and silver used as money. . . . They have . . . naturally, if not necessarily, become throughout the world a standard of value. In exchange for pieces of them, products requiring an equal amount of labor, are readily given. When the produce and the piece of metal represent the same labor, or an approximation of it, they are freely exchanged. There can be no adequate substitute for

these metals.—Field: Legal Tender Cases, 110 U.S. 421, 463.

2. Money is not only a medium of exchange, but it is a standard of value. Nothing can be such standard which has not intrinsic value, or which is subject to frequent changes in value. —Field: *ibid.,* 462–63.

3. A sound currency should be a desirable object to every government; and this in our country is secured generally through the instrumentality of a well-regulated system of banking.— McLean State Bank v. Knoop, 16 How. (57 U.S.) 369, 384.

4. Money is certainly property.— McKenna: Pirie v. Chicago Title & Tr. Co., 182 U.S. 438, 443.

5. Money is money and is a medium of exchange which does not deflate or inflate according to the owner's use of it.—Jackson: Railway Exp. Agency v. Virginia, 347 U.S. 359, 365.

6. Appeals for money . . . has a cooling effect on many persons.— Jackson: Beauharnais v. Illinois, 343 U.S. 250, 304.

See also Interest; Power 1; Value 2, 3, 27; War 7, 8; Wealth 3.

MONOPOLY

1. What is a monopoly, as understood in law? It is an exclusive right granted to a few of something which was before of common right.—Story: Charles River Bridge v. Warren Bridge, 11 Pet. (36 U.S.) 420, 607.

2. The granting of monopolies, or exclusive privileges to individuals or corporations, is an invasion of the right of others to choose a lawful calling, and an infringement of personal liberty. — Bradley: Slaughter House Cases, 16 Wall. (83 U.S.) 36, 120.

3. The idea of monopoly is not now confined to a grant of privileges.— McKenna: National Cotton Oil Co. v. Texas, 197 U.S. 115, 129.

4. Nor is it for the substantial interests of the country that any one commodity should be within the sole power and subject to the sole will of one powerful combination of capital. —Peckham: United States v. Trans-Missouri Fr. Assoc., 166 U.S. 290, 324.

5. Monopoly power is the power to control prices or exclude competition.—Reed: United States v. Du Pont, 351 U.S. 377, 391–92.

6. Monopoly is a protean threat to fair prices.—Reed: United States v. Line Material Co., 333 U.S. 287, 309.

7. The law does not visit with its reprobation a fair competition in trade; its tendency is rather to discourage monopolies, except where protected by statute, and to build up new enterprises from which the public is likely to derive a benefit.—Brown: Brown Chem. Co. v. Meyer, 139 U.S. 540, 544.

8. The trust problem can never be settled right for the American people by looking at it through the spectacles of bonds and stocks. You must study it through the spectacles of people's rights and people's interests; must consider the effect upon the development of the American democracy. When you do that you will realize the extraordinary perils to our

institutions which attend the trusts; you will realize the danger of letting the people learn that our sacred Constitution protects not only vested rights but vested wrongs.—Brandeis: Mason, *Brandeis,* 357.

9. The employment of one's wealth to construct or purchase facilities for one's business greater than others possess constitutes no monopoly that does not appertain to all property. Such facilities may give advantages, and, it may be, power; so does all property and in proportion to its extent. — McKenna: United States v. Ohio Oil Co., 234 U.S. 548, 571–72.

10. Human nature is such that monopolies, h o w e v e r well intentioned, and however well regulated, inevitably become, in course of time, oppressive, arbitrary, unprogressive, and inefficient. — Brandeis: Mason, *Brandeis,* 181.

11. That trusts, that monopoly, is not only not more efficient than competitive business, but that monopoly is inefficient as compared with competition; inefficient both economically and socially. There used to be a certain glamour about big things. Anything big, simply because it was big, seemed to be good and great. We are now coming to see that big things may be very bad and mean.—Brandeis: *ibid.,* 354.

12. In certain things we have got to have a monopoly. We have to have a monopoly in electric light, we have to have a monopoly in gas, we have to have monopolies in telephones.—Brandeis, *ibid.,* 216.

13. There is for a community, a general limit where efficiency can be reached by consolidation. To that point I am in favor of it, but I am now, and always have been directly opposed to distinct monopoly.—Brandeis: *ibid.,* 180.

14. The economic theories which the Court has read into the Anti-Trust Laws have favored rather than discouraged monopoly. As a result . . . big business has become bigger. Monopoly has flourished. Cartels have increased their hold on the nation. The trusts wax strong. There is less and less place for the independent.—Douglas: Standard Oil Co. v. United States, 337 U.S. 293, 315.

15. Under the law, agreements are forbidden which "tend to create a monopoly," and it is immaterial that the tendency is a creeping one rather than one that proceeds at full gallop; nor does the law await arrival at the goal before condemning the direction of the movement.—Jackson: International Salt Co. v. United States, 332 U.S. 392, 396.

16. A business monopoly is no less such because a union participates.—Black: Allen Bradley Co. v. Electric Workers Union, 325 U.S. 797, 811.

Related subjects: Business (big); Competition; Corporation; Restraint of trade; Sherman Antitrust Law; Trust. *See also* Capitalist 3; Lawyer 26; Patent 10, 11, 16.

MORAL, MORALITY

1. I do not mean to say that the same moral rule which should regulate the affairs of private life should not be regarded by communities or

nations. — Marshall: Worcester v. Georgia, 6 Pet. (31 U.S.) 515, 593.

2. Morals deal with the actual internal state of the individual's mind, what he actually intends.—Holmes: "The Path of the Law," 10 Harv. L. Rev. 463.

3. Our system of morality is a body of imperfect social generalizations expressed in terms of emotion. To get at its truth, it is useful to omit the emotion and ask ourselves what those generalizations are and how far they are confirmed by fact accurately ascertained. — Holmes: "Ideals and Doubts," 10 Ill. L. Rev. 3.

4. Moral predilections must not be allowed to influence our minds in settling legal distinctions.—Holmes: *The Common Law,* 148.

5. I don't believe that it is an absolute principle or even a human ultimate that man always is an end in himself—that his dignity must be respected, etc. We march up a conscript with bayonets behind to die for a cause he doesn't believe in. And I feel no scruples about it. Our morality seems to me only a check on the ultimate domination of force, just as our politeness is a check on the impulse of every pig to put his feet in the trough.—Holmes: *Uncollected Letters,* 187.

6. Morality is not merely different in different communities. Its level is not the same for all the component groups within the same community. —Cardozo: *Paradoxes,* 37.

See also Custom 2; Law 19, 33; Obliga-

tion (duty); Rights, moral; Rule 7; State 11; Wire tapping 11.

MORAL TURPITUDE

1. The term "moral turpitude" has deep roots in the law.—Vinson: Jordan v. De George, 341 U.S. 223, 227.

2. Fraud has consistently been regarded as such a contaminating component in any crime that American courts have, without exception, included such crimes within the scope of moral turpitude. — Vinson: *ibid.,* 229.

MORES

The customary forms and methods of business and of fellowship, the prevalent conviction of equity and justice, the complex of belief and practice which we style the *mores* of the day.—Cardozo: *Growth of the Law,* 53.

Related subjects: Custom and related subjects. *See also* Duty 2; Imitation 4; Law 38, 44; Precedent 36; Prejudice 2.

MOTION PICTURES

1. It cannot be doubted that motion pictures are a significant medium for the communication of ideas. They may affect public attitudes and behavior in a variety of ways, ranging from direct espousal of a political or social doctrine to the subtle shaping of thought which characterizes all artistic expression. The importance of motion pictures as an organ of public opinion is not lessened by the fact that they are designed to entertain as well as to inform.—Clark: Burstyn v. Wilson, 343 U.S. 495, 501.

2. Motion pictures are of course a different medium of expression than the public speech, the radio, the stage, the novel, or the magazine. But the First Amendment draws no distinction between the various methods of communicating ideas.—Douglas: Superior Films v. Dept. of Educ., 346 U.S. 587, 589.

See also Freedom 64.

MOTIVE

1. If the act of an individual is within the terms of the law, whatever may be the reason which governs him, or whatever may be the result, it cannot be impeached.—Hunt: Doyle v. Continental Ins. Co., 4 Otto (94 U.S.) 535, 538.

2. The intentions of the mind, lying dormant in the brain, had long since ceased to be subjects for which Legislatures prescribed punishment. —Field: Henderson's Distilled Spirits, 14 Wall. (81 U.S.) 44, 65.

3. We have no right, unless there is clear proof it is so, to ascribe a bad motive for a good act.—Davis: Gaines v. New Orleans, 6 Wall. (73 U.S.) 642, 708.

4. With possible irrelevant exceptions the motive has a bearing only when there is an issue open on the intent. — Holmes: Williamson v. Osenton, 232 U.S. 619, 625.

5. Motive may be very material when it is sought to justify what until justified is a wrong. — Holmes: United States v. American Livestock Comm'n, 279 U.S. 435, 437-38.

6. I don't readily give up the belief that Washington and the rest had for their dominant motive a patriotic desire to see a powerful nation take the place of squabbling states. If the change helped their investments, I should suppose that it was because they invested in the belief that what they thought best would come to pass, not that they talked patriotism because they had invested. — Holmes: *Uncollected Letters,* 197.

7. Motive is a persuasive interpreter of equivocal conduct. — Hughes: Texas & N. O. R.R. v. Railway Clerks, 281 U.S. 548, 559.

8. No such motive could exist, for the whole conduct of the party is at war with the supposition. — Story: The Apollon, 9 Wheat. (22 U.S.) 362, 443.

9. Motives and inducements may not be easily estimated. — McKenna: Standard Sanitary Mfg. Co. v. United States, 226 U.S. 20, 42.

10. It confuses motive with coercion.—Cardozo: Steward Mach. Co. v. Davis, 301 U.S. 548, 589.

11. It is not to be expected that they should lay bare all the motives and promptings, some avowed and conscious, some perhaps half-conscious and inarticulate, which swayed their conduct. — Cardozo: De Cicco v. Schweizer, 221 N.Y. 431, 437.

12. The difficulty of searching the motives and purposes of one who is dead. — Stone: Heiner v. Donnan, 285 U.S. 312, 343.

Related subjects: Intent and related subjects. *See also* Investigation 6; Punishment.

MOTOR VEHICLE

1. It is known of all men that the radical change in transportation of persons and goods effected by the introduction of the automobile, the speed with which it moves, and the ease with which evil-minded persons can avoid capture, have greatly encouraged and increased crimes. — Taft: Brooks v. United States, 267 U.S. 432, 438.

2. The horse has yielded to the motor car as an instrument of pursuit and flight.—Cardozo: In the Matter of Barrington v. Yellow Taxi Corp., 250 N.Y. 14, 17.

3. With the increase in number and size of the vehicles used on a highway, both the danger and the wear and tear grow. To exclude unnecessary vehicles — particularly the large ones commonly used by carriers for hire—promotes both safety and economy.—Brandeis: Buck v. Kuykendall, 267 U.S. 307, 315.

4. The problems arising out of the sudden increase of motor vehicles present extraordinary difficulties. As yet nobody definitely knows what should be done.—McReynolds: Bush v. Maloy, 267 U.S. 317, 325.

5. An automobile is, potentially, a dangerous instrumentality, as the appalling number of fatalities brought about every day by its operation bear distressing witness.—Sutherland: District of Columbia v. Colts, 282 U.S. 63, 73.

6. The increasing slaughter on our highways, most of which should be avoidable, now reaches the astounding figures only heard of on the battlefield. — Clark: Breithaupt v. Abram, 352 U.S. 432, 439.

7. The potentialities of damage by a motorist, in a population as mobile as ours, are such that those whom he injures must have opportunities of redress against him provided only that he is afforded an opportunity to defend himself. — Frankfurter: Olberding v. Illinois Cent. R.R., 346 U.S. 338, 341.

8. Highway accidents with their train of property and personal injuries are notoriously important problems in every community. Clearing the highways of irresponsible drivers, devising ways and means for making sure that compensation is awarded the innocent victims, and yet managing a scheme which leaves the highways open for the livelihood of the deserving are problems that have taxed the ingenuity of law makers and administrators.—Douglas: California Auto. Assoc. v. Maloney, 341 U.S. 105, 110.

9. The supreme rule of the road is the rule of mutual forbearance.—Cardozo: Ward v. Clark, 232 N.Y. 195, 198.

See also Negligence 12; Street, 2.

MUNICIPALITY

1. The city is a miniature state, the council is its legislature, the charter is its constitution.—Brewer: Paulsen v. Portland, 149 U.S. 30, 38.

2. A municipality is merely a department of the state, and the state may withhold, grant or withdraw

powers and privileges, as it sees fit.—Butler: Trenton v. New Jersey, 262 U.S. 182, 187.

3. A municipality without the power of taxation would be a body without life, incapable of acting, and serving no useful purpose.—Field: United States v. New Orleans, 8 Otto (98 U.S.) 381, 393.

4. Taxation by municipal or public corporations must be for a corporate purpose.—Waite: Weightman v. Clark, 13 Otto (103 U.S.) 256, 260.

5. Many welfare measures are city affairs solely. — Cardozo: Adler v. Deegan, 251 N.Y. 467, 484.

6. A city is presumptively the more populous and better organized community.—Lurton: Chicago v. Sturges, 222 U.S. 313, 324.

7. The City of Asbury Park is a seashore resort with a resident population of 15,000. It presents a familiar picture of optimistic and extravagant municipal expansion caught in the destructive grip of general economic depression: elaborate beach front improvements, costs in excess of estimates, deficits not annually met by taxation, declining real estate values, inability to refinance a disproportionately heavy load of short-term obligations, and inevitably default.—Frankfurter: Faitoute Iron & Steel Co. v. Asbury Park, 316 U.S. 502, 503.

8. A city cannot be taken over and operated for the benefit of its creditors, nor can its creditors take over the taxing power.—Frankfurter: *ibid.,* 509.

Related Subjects: City; Municipal planning. *See also* Sovereignty 14; Tax 29; Water 1, 2.

MUNICIPAL PLANNING

1. Chalcedon was called the city of the blind, because its founders rejected the nobler site of Byzantium lying at their feet. The need for vision of the future in the governance of cities has not lessened with the years. The dweller within the gates, even more than the stranger from afar, will pay the price of blindness. — Cardozo: Hesse v. Rath, 249 N.Y. 436, 438.

2. The city that is without the foresight to build the ports for the new traffic may soon be left behind in the race of competition.—Cardozo: *ibid.*

Related subjects: City; Municipality.

MURDER

1. The crimes of murder and of manslaughter, it has been truly said, are kindred crimes. — Marshall: United States v. Wiltberger, 5 Wheat. (18 U.S.) 76, 97.

2. The division of murder into degrees arose from the steadily weakened hold of capital punishment on the conscience of mankind.—Frankfurter: Fisher v. United States, 328 U.S. 463, 482–83.

3. Behind a muscular contraction resulting in another's death there must be culpability to turn homicide into murder. — Frankfurter: Leland v. Oregon, 343 U.S. 790, 803.

4. Ever since our ancestral common law emerged out of the darkness of its early barbaric days, it has been a postulate of Western civilization that the taking of life by the hand of

an insane person is not murder.—
Frankfurter: United States v. Baldi,
344 U.S. 561, 570.

5. Murder is not an offense against
the United States, except when committed on the high seas or in some port
or harbor without the jurisdiction of
the State . . . or at other places where
the national government has exclusive jurisdiction.—Lamar: *In re* Neagle, 135 U.S. 1, 98–99.

6. Where counsel contended that
there should be no conviction for murder, unless the body was actually
found—namely, that in the cases of
murder upon the high seas, the body
is rarely if ever found; and a more
complete encouragement and protection for the worst offenses of this sort
could not be invented, than a rule of
this strictness. It would amount to a
universal condonation of all murders
committed on the high seas.—Story:
United States v. Gibert, 2 Sumner,
19, 27.

7. What disposition shall we now
make of the prisoner, who is entitled
to his discharge from the custody of
the warden . . . because . . . he is in
custody in violation of the Constitution . . . but who is, nevertheless,
guilty, as the record before us shows,
of the crime of murder in the first degree?—Miller: Medley Pet'r, 134 U.S.
160, 174.

See also Impulse 2; Public official 15;
Punishment 8; Railroad 2; Self-defense 3,
4; Wrongdoer 8.

MUSICAL COMPOSITION

1. A musical composition is a rational collocation of sounds apart
from concepts, reduced to a tangible
expression from which the collocation
can be reproduced either with or without continuous human intervention.—
Holmes: White-Smith Music Pub.
Co. v. Apollo Co., 209 U.S. 1, 19–20.

2. A musical composition is an intellectual creation which first exists in
the mind of the composer; he may
play it for the first time upon an instrument.—Day: *ibid.,* 17.

MYSTERY

Men do not usually employ so much
labor for nothing. If they use mystery
without an object, they must expect
to excite suspicion. To do away with
that suspicion they ought to show an
object. — Marshall: Locke v. United
States, 7 Cranch (11 U.S.) 339, 347.

NAME (nomenclature)

Persons 1–3; things 4–12; miscellaneous
13–16.

———, persons

1. A proper name always purports
to designate one person and no other,
and although through the imperfec-
tion of our system of naming, the
same combination of letters and
sounds may be applied to two or more,
the name of each, in theory of law,
is distinct, although there is no way
of finding out which person was
named but by inquiring which was
meant. — Holmes: Hanson v. Globe
News Co., 159 Mass. 293, 305.

2. Initials are no legal part of a
name, the authorities holding the full
Christian name to be essential. —
Brown: Monroe Cattle Co. v. Becker,
147 U.S. 47, 58.

3. Some men have a well-known and constantly used Christian name; others are addressed by an abbreviation for the Christian name; others by initials for the Christian name; others are known by nickname. Some men use one name in business and another among their acquaintances. Some men, while personally addressed by their full Christian name, use initials in signing letters, notes, checks, and other papers.—Lamar: Kreitlein v. Ferger, 238 U.S. 21, 29.

———, things

4. A proper name, when used in business or in pleading means one individual thing, and no other, as every one knows, and therefore one to whom such a name is used must find out at his peril what the object designated is. — Holmes: *The Common Law,* 309.

5. Calling them by the same name does not obliterate the differences between them.—Matthews: Cincinnati, N. O. & T. P. R.R. v. Kentucky, 115 U.S. 321, 337.

6. When things are called by the same name it is easy for the mind to slide into an assumption that the verbal identity is accompanied in all its sequences by identity of meaning.—Cardozo: Lowden v. Northwestern Nat'l Bank & Tr. Co., 298 U.S. 160, 165.

7. A distinctive name is a name that distinguishes. — Hughes: U n i t e d States v. Forty Barrels, 241 U.S. 265, 286.

8. Refinements of nomenclature adopted for the sake of decency in speech may not be used to conjure up doubts and distinctions. — Butler: Hansen v. Haff, 291 U.S. 559, 565.

9. As names of things are considered significant of their attributes, the names, it may be assumed, announce a difference in attributes, and, as dependent upon it, a difference in uses. —McKenna: Heisler v. Thomas Colliery Co., 260 U.S. 245, 256.

10. One cannot intelligently discuss things or actions except by using the names commonly employed to describe them.—Roberts: Wisconsin v. J. C. Penney Co., 311 U.S. 435, 447.

11. We may not clarify a subject when we give it a special name, but perhaps, in the eyes of some, we give it added dignity, if the name selected is a hard one.—Cardozo: *Growth of the Law,* 94.

12. Could hickory logs be called "wooden toothpicks," because when cut up into little pieces they may be used as such; or would ivory fall under the designation of piano keys, because when sawed into proper shape it is used for that purpose?—Brewer: Hartranft v. Meyer, 149 U.S. 544, 550.

———, miscellaneous

13. I don't know that I should call anything a monad, the nomenclature is not natural to me.—Holmes: *Uncollected Letters,* 160.

14. Mere names and definitions, however important as aids to understanding, do not conclude the law-

maker, who is free to ignore them and adopt his own.—Sutherland: Tyler v. United States, 281 U.S. 497, 502.

15. The Legislature may affix to new combinations of events the name of an old crime. — Cardozo: Van Vechten v. American Eagle Fire Ins. Co., 239 N.Y. 303, 305.

16. It would hardly be too much to say that the drink characterizes the name as much as the name the drink. —Holmes: Coca-Cola Co. v. Koke Co., 254 U.S. 143, 146.

See also Corporation 11.

NATION

1. No principle of general law is more universally acknowledged than the perfect equality of nations. Russia and Geneva have equal rights.— Marshall: The Antelope, 10 Wheat. (23 U.S.) 66, 122.

2. A nation, whose citizens are habitually attentive to the principles and workings of government, may sometimes be betrayed; but it can scarcely be ruined. — Story: *Misc. Writings,* 165.

3. No nation can be so vain as to imagine, that she possesses all wisdom and all excellence.—Story: *ibid.,* 308.

4. There is a growing aspiration that the time will come when nations will not do as they please and bid their wills avouch it.—McKenna: Grogan v. Walker & Co., 259 U.S. 80, 97.

5. A hundred years is a brief space in the life of a nation.—Pitney: Economy Light & Power Co. v. United States, 256 U.S. 113, 124.

6. Great nations, like great men, should keep their word. — Black: Federal Power Comm'n v. Tuscarora Ind. Nat., 362 U.S. 99, 142.

7. This country was not built by men who were afraid and it cannot be preserved by such men.—Black: Wilkinson v. United States, 365 U.S. 399, 422.

See also Race 15, 16; War 3, 16; Consequence.

―――― (U.S.), people

8. Such as we are, we have been from the beginning; simple, hardy, intelligent, accustomed to self-government and self-respect.—Story: *Misc. Writings,* 86.

9. We are indulged by a kind Providence with the blessings of civil, political, and religious liberty—blessings of inestimable value, without which life loses half its charms, property all its security, and patriotism itself sinks back from a virtue into a gross and venal prejudice.—Story: *ibid.,* 347.

10. Though the people might sometimes be deceived, to their intelligence and virtue we might safely trust, to equalize all the eccentricities and perturbations of the political system.—Story, *ibid.,* 182.

11. We are a heterogeneous people. In some of our larger cities a majority of the school children are the offspring of parents only one generation, if that far, removed from the steerage of the immigrant ship, children of those who sought refuge in the new world from the cruelty and oppression of the old, where men have been burned at the stake, imprisoned, and

driven into exile in countless numbers for their political and religious beliefs. Here they have hoped to achieve a political status as citizens in a free world in which men are privileged to think and act and speak according to their convictions, without fear of punishment or further exile so long as they keep the peace and obey the law.—Murphy; Schneiderman v. United States, 320 U.S. 118, 120.

12. Gregariousness and friendliness are among the most characteristic of American attitudes. Throughout our history they have been manifested in "joining." — Frankfurter: Garner v. Board of Pub. Works, 341 U.S. 716, 728.

13. We of this nation are one people undivided in ability or freedom by differences in race, color or creed.—Murphy: Akins v. Texas, 325 U.S. 398, 410.

14. We are a religious people whose institutions presuppose a Supreme Being. We guarantee the freedom to worship as one chooses. We make room for as wide a variety of beliefs and creeds as the spiritual needs of man deem necessary. We sponsor an attitude on the part of government that shows no partiality to any one group and that lets each flourish according to the zeal of its adherents and the appeal of its dogma.—Douglas: Zorach v. Clauson, 343 U.S. 306, 313–14.

15. The power of the nation . . . enabled to move with strength and dignity and effect among the other nations of the earth to such purpose as it may undertake or to such destiny as it may be called.—McKenna: De Lima v. Bidwell, 182 U.S. 1, 220.

16. This has become a nation of transient people.—Murphy: Williams v. North Carolina, 325 U.S. 226, 252.

17. We are a mobile people, historically on the move, and perhaps the rigid concept of domicile derived by common law from feudal attachment to the land is too rigid for a society so restless as ours.—Jackson: May v. Anderson, 345 U.S. 528, 539.

18. The fundamental constitutional principle that our people, adequately informed, may be trusted to distinguish between the true and the false. — Black: Viereck v. United States, 318 U.S. 236, 251.

19. Before we may expect international responsibility among nations, might not it be well to require individual responsibility at home? — Clark: Talley v. California, 362 U.S. 60, 71.

See also Conscientious objector 2; Constitution (U.S.), First Amendment, 104; Democracy 4; Fetter 1; Flag; Freedom 50, 65; Government (U.S.), state 2; Independence (U.S.) 4; Law, bases; Legislation, purpose; Litigant 1; Migration; Murder 5; Patriotism; Political party; Progress; Slavery 4; Society; Sovereignty 1; Supreme Court 6; Unemployment 6; Wealth 4.

NATIONAL DEFENSE

1. A defenseless country cannot be secure.—Marshall: Beveridge, *Life of Marshall*, I, 414.

2. The United States will only arm to defend their own rights; neither their policy nor their interests permit

them to arm, in order to compel a surrender of the rights of others.—Marshall: *ibid.*, II, 305.

3. The whole world is in arms and no rights are respected but those that [are] maintained by force. In such a state of things we dare not be totally unmindful of ourselves or totally neglectful of that military position to which, in spite of the prudence and pacific disposition of our government, we may be driven for the preservation of our liberty and national independence.—Marshall: *ibid.*, 479.

4. Every resource within the ambit of sovereign power is subject to use for the national defense. . . . Reasonable preparation for the storm of war is a proper exercise of the war power. —Reed: Silesian Am. Corp. v. Clark, 332 U.S. 469, 476.

See also War 12.

NATIONALISM

1. I do not pin my dreams for the future to my country or even to my race.—Holmes: *Speeches*, 103.

2. The new nationalism adopted by America proclaims that each race or people, like each individual, has the right and duty to develop, and that only through such differentiated development will high civilization be attained. — Brandeis: Mason, *Brandeis*, 439.

3. Struggles to coerce uniformity of sentiment in support of some end thought essential to their time and country have been waged by many good as well as by evil men. Nationalism is a relatively recent phenomenon but at other times and places the ends have been racial or territorial security, support of a dynasty or regime, and particular plans for saving souls.— Jackson: West Va. State Bd. of Educ. v. Barnette, 319 U.S. 624, 640.

4. Any credo of nationalism is likely to include what some disapprove or to omit what others think essential, and to give off different overtones as it takes on different accents or interpretations.—Jackson: *ibid.*, 634.

5. In the belief of many thoughtful people nationalism is the seed-bed of war.—Frankfurter: *ibid.*, 660.

6. One who is without any sense of nationalism is not well bound or held by the ties of affection to any nation or government. — Butler: United States v. Schwimmer, 279 U.S. 644, 652.

Related subject: Patriotism.

NATIONALITY

The great weight of modern opinion, and we believe the practice of most nations, is in favor of making parentage and not place the test of nationality by birth. In our days, when citizenship and allegiance are a matter of choice and not of compulsion, if a party is too young to choose, it seems most proper to fix his nationality *pro tempore,* either by the wishes of those having authority over him, or else by what it may be presumed would have been his own wishes, if he had been capable of having any. By such criteria the country of the child would, in general, be that to which the parents acknowledge their allegiance to be due, rather than that in which the child happened to be born.—Holmes: *Uncollected Letters,* 243-44.

Related subject: Citizen.

NATIONAL RESOURCES

Altho' we ought never to make a loan if it be avoidable, yet when forc'd to it much real consolation is to be deriv'd from the future resources of America. These resources, if we do not throw them away by dissolving the union, are invaluable. . . . It is the plain and certain consequence of our increasing population and our increasing wealth. — Marshall: Beveridge, *Life of Marshall,* II, 479.

NATIONAL UNITY

1. National unity is the basis of national security.—Frankfurter: Minersville School Dist. v. Gobitis, 310 U.S. 586, 595.

2. The ultimate foundation of a free society is the binding tie of cohesive sentiment. Such a sentiment is fostered by all those agencies of the mind and spirit which may serve to gather up the traditions of a people, transmit them from generation to generation, and thereby create that continuity of a treasured common life which constitutes a civilization.— Frankfurter: *ibid.,* 596.

3. The influences which help toward a common feeling for the common country are manifold. Some may seem harsh and others no doubt are foolish. Surely, however, the end is legitimate.—Frankfurter: *ibid.,* 598.

NATURAL GAS

1. The wealth of Midas and the wit of man cannot produce or reproduce a natural gas field.—Jackson: Federal Power Comm'n v. Hope Nat. Gas Co., 320 U.S. 591, 629.

2. The service one renders to society in the gas business is measured by what he gets out of the ground, not by what he puts into it, and there is little more relation between the investment and the results than in a game of poker.—Jackson: *ibid.,* 649.

3. Natural gas is a wasting resource and . . . the necessity for conserving it is paramount. — Warren: Federal Power Comm'n v. Transcontinental Gas Pipe Line Corp., 365 U.S. 1, 8.

See also Public utility 10.

NATURALIZATION

1. Naturalization is the act of adopting a foreigner, and clothing him with the privileges of a native citizen.—Fuller: Boyd v. Nebraska, 143 U.S. 135, 162.

2. The opportunity to become a citizen of the United States is said to be merely a privilege and not a right. —Brandeis: Tutun v. United States, 270 U.S. 568, 578.

3. There is abundant room for enforcing the requisite authority of law as it is enacted and requires obedience, and for maintaining the conception of the supremacy of law as essential to orderly government, without demanding that either citizens or applicants for citizenship shall assume by oath an obligation to regard alle-

giance to God as subordinate to allegiance to civil power. — Hughes: United States v. Macintosh, 283 U.S. 605, 634.

4. It [the oath] relates to a state of mind and is a promise of future conduct. It is the final act by which an alien acquires the status of citizen. It requires forswearing of allegiance in good faith and with no mental reservations.—Douglas: Knauer v. United States, 328 U.S. 654, 671.

5. It is not within the province of the courts to make bargains with those who seek naturalization. — Sutherland: United States v. Macintosh, 283 U.S. 605, 626.

6. A foreigner by naturalization enters into new obligations. More than that, he thereby changes his status, he ceases to be an alien, and becomes a citizen, and when that change is once accomplished, no disloyalty on his part, no breach of the obligations of citizenship, of itself destroys his citizenship.—Brewer: *In re* Grimley, 137 U.S. 147, 152.

See also Freedom 83.

NAVY (U.S.)

There is constant demand . . . for those who have an honorable discharge from the Navy for employment in civil life. The qualities of obedience, of daring, of fidelity, of the capacity for quick adaptation of insufficient means to the end which may be desired—all the result of training upon the sea—are qualities which are needed in many stations of civil life.

—Moody: Ellis v. United States, 206 U.S. 246, 265.

NECESSARY

1. The word "necessary" . . . has not a fixed character peculiar to itself. It admits of all degrees of comparison. —Marshall: McCulloch v. Maryland, 4 Wheat. (17 U.S.) 316, 414.

2. The word "necessary" . . . has always been recognized as a word to be harmonized with its context.—Jackson: Armour & Co. v. Wantock, 323 U.S. 126, 129–30.

3. The legal conception of the necessary is apt to be confined to somewhat rudimentary wants. — Holmes: Hudson Co. v. McCarter, 209 U.S. 349, 357.

Related subjects: Necessity; Need.

NECESSITY

1. Necessity, the never to be worn out apology for violence, is alleg'd.—Marshall: Beveridge, *Life of Marshall*, II, 243.

2. Stark necessity is an impressive and often compelling thing.—Black: Green v. United States, 356 U.S. 165, 213.

Related subjects: Necessary; Need. *See also* Obligation (duty) 3; River 1; Rule 6; Tax, power, need for.

NEED

Related subjects: Necessary; Necessity. *See also* Duty 10; Legislation 7; Power 31; Wants.

NEGATION

1. The present time is experimenting in negations—an amusing sport if it is remembered that while it takes

but a few minutes to cut down a tree it takes a century for a tree to grow.— Holmes: *Uncollected Letters,* 139.

2. As a practical matter, it is never easy to prove a negative.—Stewart: Elkins v. United States, 364 U.S. 206, 218.

NEGLIGENCE (legal)

Defined 1–6; standards 7–12; industrial accidents 13–17; miscellaneous 18–19.

Related subjects: Act; Conduct; Fault; Liability; Standard; Tort.

————, defined

1. Negligence, like ownership, is a complex conception.—Holmes: *The Common Law,* 115.

2. Negligence is all degree. — Holmes: LeRoy Fibre Co. v. St. Paul Ry., 232 U.S. 340, 354.

3. Negligence consists in conduct which common experience or the special knowledge of the actor shows to be so likely to produce the result complained of, under the circumstances known to the actor, that he is held answerable for that result, although it was not certain, intended, or foreseen.—Holmes: Schlemmer v. Buffalo, R. & P. Ry., 205 U.S. 1, 12.

4. Negligence as a term of legal art is, strictly speaking, a misnomer, for negligence connotes to the ordinary man the notion of lack of care, and yet one can be negligent in the view of the law though one has taken what one has supposed to be extraordinary care, and not negligent though one has taken no care at all.—Cardozo: *Paradoxes,* 72–73.

5. Surveyors can measure an acre.

But measuring negligence is different. The definitions of negligence are not definitions at all, strictly speaking.— Black: Schulz v. Pennsylvania R.R., 350 U.S. 523, 525.

6. No human inquiry, no possible precaution, is sufficient to absolutely determine in advance whether a party under certain exigencies will or will not do a negligent act.—Brewer: Baltimore & O. R.R. v. Baugh, 149 U.S. 368, 385.

————, standards

7. The terms "ordinary care," "reasonable prudence," and such like terms, as applied to the conduct and affairs of men, have a relative significance, and cannot be arbitrarily defined.—Lamar: Grand Trunk Ry. v. Ives, 144 U.S. 408, 417.

8. If the nature of a thing is such that it is reasonably certain to place life and limb in peril when negligently made, it is then a thing of danger. Its nature gives warning of the consequences to be expected.—Cardozo: MacPherson v. Buick Motor Co., 217 N.Y. 382, 389.

9. The more probable the danger, the greater the need of caution.— Cardozo: *ibid.,* 395.

10. The size of the catastrophe does not excuse liability.—Jackson: Dalehite v. United States, 346 U.S. 15, 54.

11. Confused as the law is with cross-lights of tradition, and hard as we may find it to arrive at any perfectly satisfactory general theory, it does distinguish in a pretty sensible way, according to the nature and de-

gree of the different perils incident to a given situation. — Holmes: *The Common Law,* 153.

12. The capricious capers of that "reasonably prudent man" who is the fictional standard of conduct in negligence trials is now creating a demand for automobile accident compensation.—Jackson: *Struggle for Judicial Supremacy,* 294.

——, industrial accidents

13. To apply the concepts of "negligence" and "proximate cause" to the infinite complexities of modern industry is like catching butterflies without a net.—Frankfurter: Carter v. Atlanta & St. A. B. Ry., 338 U.S. 430, 437–38.

14. The difficulties in these cases derive largely from the outmoded concept of "negligence" as a working principle for the adjustments of injuries inevitable under the technological circumstances of modern industry. This cruel and wasteful mode of dealing with industrial injuries has long been displaced in industry generally by the insurance principle that underlies workmen's compensation laws.—Frankfurter: Wilkerson v. McCarthy, 336 U.S. 53, 65.

15. The remedy for an obsolete and uncivilized system of compensation for loss of life or limb of crews on ships and trains . . . is an adequate and effective system of workmen's compensation. — Frankfurter: McAllister v. United States, 348 U.S. 19, 23–24.

16. The functioning of this back-

ward system of dealing with industrial accidents in interstate commerce burdens it with perhaps two dollars of judgment for every dollar that actually reaches those who have been damaged.—Jackson: Miles v. Illinois Cent. R.R., 315 U.S. 698, 707.

17. Attention should be directed, not to the employer's fault, but to the employee's misfortune. — Brandeis: New York Cent. R.R. v. Winfield, 244 U.S. 147, 165.

——, miscellaneous

18. Perhaps no field of the law comes closer to the lives of so many families in this country than does the law of negligence. — Frankfurter: Tiller v. Atlantic Coast Line R.R., 318 U.S. 54, 73.

19. One traveler run down through the negligence of another is not concerned to inquire whether the offender has gone forth on the highway for the love of man or of money—Cardozo: Murtha v. New York Homeopathic Med. Col. & Flower Hosp., 228 N.Y. 183, 186.

See also Error 5; Experience 3; Foresight 3; Ignorance 5; Jury 14; Litigation 7; Motor vehicle; Physician; Risk 4.

NEGOTIATOR

There is a tact and skill and a happy manner with some persons, which render them successful as negotiators; while others of equal learning, attainments, and intellectual ability, fail for the want of those qualities.—Field: Forsyth v. Doolittle, 120 U.S. 73, 74.

NEGRO

1. Merely striking off the fetters of

the slave, without removing the incidents and consequences of slavery, would hardly have been a boon to the colored race.—Bradley: Blyew v. United States, 13 Wall. (80 U.S.) 581, 601.

2. It was not deemed enough "to help the feeble up, but to support him after." The one underlying purpose of congressional legislation has been to enable the black race to take the rank of mere citizens. . . . At every step in this direction, the Nation has been confronted with class tyranny, which a contemporary English historian says is, of all tyrannies, the most intolerable. — Harlan: Civil Rights Cases, 109 U.S. 3, 61.

3. In the argument, it was said that a colored citizen would not be an agreeable member of society. This is more a matter of taste than of law.—McLean: Dred Scott v. Sandford, 19 How. (60 U.S.) 393, 533.

4. It would never occur to anyone that the presence of a colored citizen in a courthouse, or court room, was an invasion of the social rights of white persons who may frequent such places. And yet, such a suggestion would be quite as sound in law . . . as is the suggestion that the claim of a colored citizen to use, upon the same terms as is permitted to white citizens the accommodations of public highways, or public inns, or places of public amusement, established under the license of the law, is an invasion of the social rights of the white race.—Harlan: Civil Rights Cases, 109 U.S. 3, 62.

5. Today . . . many Negroes have achieved outstanding success in the arts and sciences as well as in the business and professional world.—Warren: Brown v. Bd. of Educ., 347 U.S. 483, 490.

6. Their right to equality of treatment has at last been realized. No minority in any country has progressed so far in the same length of time as the American Negro. Today he sits in our legislatures, on our school boards, on many of the administrative agencies, and on our courts. He is present in every profession and calling; he is an honored member of the American community. — Douglas: *We the Judges,* 19.

7. Political action is, doubtless, the main reason for the tremendous advancement of the Negro during the last ninety years. His political action was made possible by a liberal and vigorous enforcement by the Supreme Court of the Negro's political rights under the Fifteenth Amendment.—Douglas: *ibid.,* 413.

8. Too often unpopular minorities, such as Negroes, are unable to find effective refuge from the cruelties of bigoted and ruthless authority.—Murphy: Screws v. United States, 325 U.S. 91, 138.

See also Education 13, 14; Race; Vote 4.

NEWS

1. News is information about matters of general interest. The term has been defined as "a report of a recent event."—Roberts: Associated Press v. United States, 326 U.S. 1, 29.

2. Information respecting current events . . . is not the creation of the writer, but is a report of matters that ordinarily are *publici juris;* it is the history of the day.—Pitney: International News Serv. v. Assoc. Press, 248 U.S. 215, 234.

3. The peculiar value of news is in the spreading of it while it is fresh.—Pitney: *ibid.,* 235.

4. Fresh news is got only by enterprise and expense. — Holmes: *ibid.,* 247.

NOTICE

1. Nothing can be more unjust than that a person should have his rights passed upon, and finally decided by a tribunal, without some process being served upon him by which he will have notice, which will enable him to appear and defend himself.—Barbour: Toland v. Sprague, 12 Pet. (37 U.S.) 300, 329.

2. Friendship, however close, is not the equivalent of notice.—Cardozo: Title Guar. & Tr. Co. v. Pam, 232 N.Y. 441, 453.

3. Everyone has notice of the force of gravitation. — Holmes: Quinn v. Crimmings, 171 Mass. 255, 258.

4. Notice is required before property interests are disturbed.—Douglas: Lambert v. California, 355 U.S. 225, 228.

5. It is an absurdity to hold that every farmer who insures his crops knows what the Federal Register contains or even knows that there is such a publication. If he were to peruse this voluminous and dry publication . . . he would never need crop insurance, for he would never get time to plant any crops. Nor am I convinced that a reading of technically-worded regulations would enlighten him much in any event.—Jackson: Federal Crop Ins. Corp. v. Merrill, 332 U.S. 380, 387.

Related subject: Judicial notice.

NOVELTY

The bait of novelty suffices at the outset.—Cardozo: Broadway Photoplay Co. v. World Film Co., 225 N.Y. 104, 107.

Related subject: Innovation. *See also* Constitutional adjudication, novelty; Reform 2.

NUISANCE

1. Nuisance may be merely a right thing in a wrong place—like a pig in the parlor instead of in the barnyard. — Sutherland: Euclid v. Ambler Realty Co., 272 U.S. 365, 388.

2. There are many lawful and necessary occupations which, by the odors they engender, or the noise they create, are nuisances when carried on in the heart of a city.—Field: Baltimore & P. R.R. v. Fifth Bapt. Church, 108 U.S. 317, 334.

3. Many articles, such, for instance, as cards, dice, and other articles used for gambling purposes, are perfectly harmless in themselves, but may become nuisances by being put to an illegal use.—Brown: Lawton v. Steele, 152 U.S. 133, 142.

4. The organs of smell and hearing, assailed by sounds and odors too pungent to be borne, have been ever fa-

vored of the law . . . more conspicuously, it seems, than sight, which perhaps is more inured to what is ugly or disfigured.—Cardozo: People v. Rubenfeld, 254 N.Y. 245, 248.

5. Here is tumult so great . . . as to be a plague to a whole neighborhood.—Cardozo: *ibid.*, 249.

6. The judicial power to enjoin public nuisance at the instance of the Government has been a commonplace of jurisdiction in American judicial history. — Douglas: U n i t e d Steelworkers v. United States, 361 U.S. 39, 61.

NUMBER

It is only a difference in numbers which marks the moment when day ends and night begins, when the disabilities of infancy terminate and the status of legal competency is assumed. It separates large incomes which are taxed from the smaller ones which are exempt. — Stone: Carmichael v. Southern Coal & Coke Co., 301 U.S. 495, 510–11.

See also Witness 14.

NUMBERS RACKET

Conduct of the numbers racket is not a solitary vice, practised in secrecy and discoverable only by crashing into dwelling houses. The real difficulty is that it is so little condemned by other law-abiding people that it flourishes widely and involves multitudes of people. — Jackson: McDonald v. United States, 335 U.S. 451, 459.

See also Search and seizure 17.

OATH

1. It is melancholy truth, that forces itself upon the observation of everyone who is conversant with courts of admiralty, that positive oaths are too often the most unsatisfactory evidence that can be resorted to. A species of casuistry or moral sophistry seems to have acquired too great an ascendancy over the witnesses.—Johnson: The St. Nicholas, 1 Wheat. (14 U.S.) 417, 426.

2. The oath of a witness has no effect unless it is believed.—Holmes: *The Common Law*, 255.

Related subject: Loyalty oath; Test oath. *See also* Naturalization 4; Trial 17.

OBEDIENCE

1. It is only by obedience that affection and reverence can be shown to a superior having a right to command.—Field: Legal Tender Cases, 12 Wall. (79 U.S.) 457, 680–81.

2. The obedience thus due is not a blind obedience.—Field: In the Matter of Howard, 9 Wall. (76 U.S.), 175, 183.

Related subject: Disobedience; Law, obedience. *See also* Army 1; Citizen 11; Request.

OBJECTION

The failure to make the objection is persuasive that the facts do not justify the making.—Cardozo: Lawrey v. Hines, 237 N.Y. 174, 177.

See also Lawyer 73.

OBLIGATION

1. Moral obligations are those arising from the admonitions of conscience, and accountability to the Supreme Being. No human law-giver can impair them.—Trimble: Ogden

v. Saunders, 12 Wheat (25 U.S.) 213, 318.

2. Obligations purely moral, are to be enforced by the operation of internal and invisible agents, not by the agency of human laws. — Marshall: *ibid.*, 337-38.

3. The word "obligation" . . . certainly imports an existing moral or physical necessity.—Johnson: Fletcher v. Peck, 6 Cranch (10 U.S.) 87, 144-45.

4. The moral obligations never die. If broken by states and nations, though the terms of reproach are not the same with which we are accustomed to designate the faithlessness of individuals, the violation of justice is not the less. — Wayne: Dodge v. Woolsey, 18 How. (59 U.S.) 331, 360.

5. We are considering political, not moral obligations. The latter are universal and immutable, but the former must frequently vary according to political circumstances. — Johnson: Shanks v. DuPont, 3 Pet. (28 U.S.) 242, 258.

6. What is meant by honorary, so far as I can understand it, is that the obligations may or may not be fulfilled; . . . in other words, that they are matters of convenience and not of duty, to be performed if the caprice of the hour approve, to be disregarded if the caprice of a subsequent hour disapprove. — Field: Louisiana v. Jumel, 107 U.S. 711, 739.

7. Legal obligations that exist but cannot be enforced are ghosts that are seen in the law, but that are elusive to the grasp.—Holmes: United States v. Thompson, 257 U.S. 419, 433.

8. A personal obligation goes with the person.—Holmes: Fall v. Eastin, 215 U.S. 1, 15.

9. Impairment of an obligation means refusal to pay an honest debt. —Frankfurter: Faitoute Iron & Steel Co. v. Asbury Park, 316 U.S. 502, 511.
Related subject: Duty. *See also* Brevity; Confusion 1; Style 3.

OBSCENITY

1. One may run afoul of the law if he uses obscene language; but obscenity may not be put beyond the pale of debate. — Douglas: *We the Judges,* 309.

2. In 1890 Tolstoi's Kreutzer Sonata had been excluded from the mails as indecent.—Brandeis: United States *ex rel.* Milwaukee Soc. Dem. Pub. Co. v. Burleson, 255 U.S. 407, 422.

OBSCURITY

1. The question in the case is made obscure by an attempt at its simplification.—McKenna: United States v. New River Co., 265 U.S. 533, 545.

2. It has not said so with the simplicity and clearness through which a halting impression ripens into reasonable certitude.—Cardozo: United States v. Chicago, M., St. P. & P. R.R., 294 U.S. 499, 510.

3. Accepting the risk of obscuring the obvious by discussing it.—Clarke: United States v. Reading Co., 253 U.S. 26, 61.
See also Brevity; Confusion 1; Style 3.

OBSTACLE

The step on which it "must fall down or else o'erleap." — McKenna:

United States v. Woo Jan, 245 U.S. 552, 556.

OCCUPATION

1. The power of the individual to earn a living for himself and those dependent upon him is in the nature of a personal liberty quite as much as if not more than it is a property right. To preserve its free exercise is of the utmost importance, not only because it is a fundamental private necessity, but because it is a matter of great public concern. — Sutherland: Local Loan Co. v. Hunt, 292 U.S. 234, 245.

2. This right to choose one's calling is an essential part of that liberty which it is the object of government to protect; and a calling, when chosen, is a man's property and right. Liberty and property are not protected where these rights are arbitrarily assailed.— Bradley: Slaughter House Cases, 16 Wall. (83 U.S.) 36, 116.

3. The abolition of slavery and involuntary servitude was intended to make everyone born in this country a freeman, and as such to give to him the right to pursue the ordinary avocations of life without other restraint than such as affects everyone, and to enjoy equally with others the fruits of his labor.—Field: *ibid.,* 90.

4. Occupations, however important, which cannot be conducted without necessary danger to life, body, or limb should not be prosecuted at all without all reasonable precautions against such dangers afforded by science.— Field: Mather v. Rillston, 156 U.S. 391, 399.

5. To argue that an occupation is hazardous because someone engaged therein has received personal injuries is not helpful. Many have suffered fatal accidents while eating, but eating could hardly be called hazardous. —McReynolds: Ward v. Krinsky, 259 U.S. 503, 528–29.

6. In the nature of things, it is not every citizen of every age, sex and condition that is qualified for every calling and position.—Bradley: Bradwell v. The State, 16 Wall. (83 U.S.) 130, 141.

7. A man has no affirmative right to any particular job or skill or occupation. The Bill of Rights does not say who shall be doctors or lawyers or policemen. — Frankfurter: Barsky v. Board of Regts., 347 U.S. 442, 472–73.

8. The modern state owes and attempts to perform a duty to protect the public from those who seek for one purpose or another to obtain its money. When one does so through the practice of a calling, the state may have an interest in shielding the public against the untrustworthy, the incompetent, or the irresponsible.— Jackson: Thomas v. Collins, 323 U.S. 516, 545.

9. Every calling is great when greatly pursued.—Holmes: *Speeches,* 16.

10. Certainly there is no profession, possibly no business, which does not offer peculiar opportunities for reprehensible practices. — McReynolds: Adams v. Tanner, 244 U.S. 590, 594.

11. He is accredited by his calling in the minds of the inexperienced or the ignorant with a knowledge greater

than their own.—Cardozo: Roman v. Lobe, 243 N.Y. 51, 55.

> *See also* Freedom 96; Nuisance 2; Woman 1.

OCEAN

1. Upon the ocean, . . . in time of peace, all possess an entire equality. It is the common highway of all appropriated to the use of all.—Story: The Marianna Flora, 11 Wheat. (24 U.S.) 1, 42.

2. Ocean waters are the highways of the world. They are no less such because they happen to lap the shores of different nations that border them.—Black: Alabama v. Texas, 347 U.S. 272, 278.

3. We should not forget that the ocean "belongs to no one nation, but is the common property of all."—Black: *ibid.*, 279 (quot. 12 Otto [102 U.S.] 541, 544).

4. Freedom of the seas everywhere is essential to trade, commerce, travel and communication among the nations.—Black: *ibid.*, 278.

5. The marginal sea is a national not a state concern. National interests, national responsibilities, national concerns are involved. The problems of commerce, national defense, relations with other powers, war and peace focus there.—Douglas: United States v. Louisiana, 339 U.S. 699, 704.

6. Once low-water mark is passed the international domain is reached.—Douglas: United States v. Louisiana, 339 U.S. 707, 719.

> Related subjects: Admiralty; Maritime law; Seaman; Ship. *See also* Ship 4.

OFFENSIVENESS

Degrees of offensiveness, perhaps, lie largely in the eye of the person offended. — Frankfurter: Monroe v. Pape, 365 U.S. 167, 254.

OFFICER

"Officers" normally means those who hold defined offices. It does not mean the boys in the back room or other agencies of invisible government, whether in politics or in the trade-union movement. — Frankfurter: NLRB v. Coca-Cola Co., 350 U.S. 264, 269.

> Related subject: Public official. *See also* Lawyer, status.

OIL WELLS

Perhaps some land may be discovered which, like the widow's curse, will afford an inexhaustible supply of oil. But the common experience of man has been that oil wells, and the territory in which they are sunk, become exhausted in time. — Brandeis: United States v. Ludey, 274 U.S. 295, 303.

OLIGARCHIC, OLIGARCHY

> Related subjects: Absolutism, Despotism. *See also* Democracy (industrial) 3; Supreme Court 17, 19.

OMISSION

> Related subjects: Mistake; Error. *See also* Construction 13, 14; Generality 1; Legislation 59.

OPINION

1. The questions . . . are among those on which any two minds may differ, without incurring the imputation of wilful, or precipitate error.—

Johnson: Green v. Biddle, 8 Wheat. (21 U.S.) 1, 94.

2. We are all too prone, perhaps, to impute either weakness of intellect or corrupt motives to those who differ with us in opinion.—Grier: Burchell v. Marsh, 17 How. (58 U.S.) 344, 350.

3. The tendency that is distinctive good to some is to some distinctive error.—Cardozo: *Growth of the Law,* 144.

4. Opinions in science, in physics, in philosophy, in morals, in religion, in literature have been subjected to the severest scrutiny; and many, which had grown hoary under the authority of ages, have been quietly conveyed to their last home, with scarcely a solitary mourner to grace their obsequies.—Story: *Misc. Writings,* 13.

5. Opinion has a significance proportioned to the sources that sustain it.—Cardozo: Petrogradsky M. K. Bank v. Nat'l City Bank, 253 N.Y. 23, 35.

6. If opinion be nearer to or farther from persuasion than belief, both are of influence, and universally regarded as of influence, in the affairs of men, and determinative of their conduct.—McKenna: Berger v. United States, 255 U.S. 22, 34.

7. Magnanimity will always be ready to sacrifice the pride of opinion to public welfare.—Johnson: Martin v. Hunter's Lessee, 1 Wheat (14 U.S.) 305, 365.

8. The law does not hold one responsible for the extravagant notions he may entertain of the value of the property, dependent upon its future successful exploitation, or the result of future enterprises; nor for expressing them to one acquainted with its general character and condition. . . . Whenever property of any kind depends for its value upon contingencies which may never occur, or developments which may never be made, opinion as to its value must, necessarily, be more or less of a speculative character.—Field: Gordon v. Butler, 15 Otto (105 U.S.) 553, 557.

9. The law does not fasten responsibility upon one for expressions of opinion as to matters in their nature contingent and uncertain. Such opinions will probably be as variant as the individuals who give them utterance. —Field: *ibid.*

10. The law does not exact good faith from a seller in those vague commendations of his wares which are manifestly open to difference of opinion, which do not imply untrue assertions concerning matters of direct observations and as to which "it has always been understood the world over, that such statements are to be distrusted."—Holmes: Deming v. Darling, 148 Mass. 504, 505.

11. Such a statement . . . is shown to be false only in its commendatory and prophetic aspect. — Holmes: United States v. Johnson, 221 U.S. 488, 498.

Related subjects: Belief and related subjects; Expert. *See also* Age (years) 3; Dissent 5; Evidence 40; Freedom 51, 94; Freedom, belief; Legislation 17; Persecution 1; Radio 2; Trial 19.

————, judicial

12. The power over our opinions and the records of our Court we shall exercise at all times while we have the honor to sit on the bench, against all encroachments from any source, but in a manner, we trust, befitting the highest tribunal in the state. We cannot possibly have any interest in the opinions except that they shall embody the results of our most mature deliberation, and be presented to the public in an authentic form, after they have been subjected to the most careful revision.—Field: Houston v. Williams, 13 Cal. 24, 28.

13. The whole work done by the judges constitutes the authentic exposition and interpretation of the law, which, binding every citizen, is free for publication to all. — Blatchford: Banks v. Manchester, 128 U.S. 244, 253.

14. Opinions are required in our legal system in order that the reasoning which justifies a conclusion may be made manifest. — Frankfurter: Darr v. Burford, 229 U.S. 200, 225.

15. To be writing an opinion in a case affecting two lives after the curtain has been rung down upon them has the appearance of pathetic futility. But history also has its claims.—Frankfurter: Rosenberg v. United States, 346 U.S. 271, 310.

16. I seem to discern six types or methods which divide themselves from one another with measurable distinctness. There is the type magisterial or imperative; the type laconic or sententious; the type conversational or homely; the type refined or artificial, the type demonstrative or persuasive; and finally the type tonsorial or agglutinative, so called from the shears and the pastepot which are its implements and emblem.—Cardozo: *Law and Literature,* 10.

17. We hear the voice of the law speaking by its consecrated ministers with the calmness and assurance that are born of a sense of mastery and power.—Cardozo: *ibid.*

18. It is thus men speak when they are conscious of their power. One does not need to justify oneself if one is the mouthpiece of divinity. The style will fit the mood.—Cardozo: *ibid.,* 14.

19. In matters of literary style the sovereign virtue for the judge is clearness.—Cardozo: *ibid.,* 7.

20. One must permit oneself, and that quite advisedly and deliberately, a certain margin of misstatement.—Cardozo: *ibid.*

21. The form of opinion which aims at humor from beginning to end is a perilous adventure, which can be justified only by success, and even then is likely to find its critics almost as many as its eulogists.—Cardozo: *ibid.,* 26–27.

22. This court always speaks in respectful terms of the decisions it reviews, but the implication of the most courteous language may be as certain as a direct charge.—Brewer: Schlemmer v. Buffalo R.R., 205 U.S. 1, 19.

23. Language alters, and there is a fashion in judicial writing as in other things. — Frankfurter: Freeman v. Hewit, 329 U.S. 249, 254.

24. The opinion is instinct with a ruling.—Cardozo: In the Matter of Richardson, 247 N.Y. 401, 418.

25. The best draughtsman that ever lived can feel a ground of decision more accurately than he can state it.—Holmes: *Uncollected Letters,* 61–62.

26. Chief Justice Marshall, for the court, delivered one of those opinions which are among the chief ornaments of American jurisprudence.—Lamar: *In re* Neagle, 135 U.S. 1, 87.

27. For quotable good things, for pregnant aphorisms, for touchstones of ready application, the opinions of the English judges are a mine of instruction and a treasury of joy.—Cardozo: *Law and Literature,* 20–21.

28. Such qualities on the whole are rarer close at home, yet we have one judge even now who can vie with the best of his English brethren, past as well as present, in the art of packing within a sentence the phosphorescence of a page. If I begin to quote from the opinions of Mr. Justice Holmes, I hardly know where I shall end, yet fealty to a master makes me reluctant to hold back. The sheaf will be a tiny one, made up haphazard, the barest sample of the riches which the gleaner may gather where he will.—Cardozo: *ibid.,* 21.

29. In the main I have been listening to arguments and turning out decisions — one or two involving interesting points of theory—the average having no more than the interest that every decision has, but that is considerable to the one who writes them.—Holmes: *Uncollected Letters,* 191.

Related subjects: Decision and related subjects. *See also* Copyright 3; Dictum 4; Res judicata 7; Supreme Court, functions, limitations.

OPIUM

By universal sentiment and settled policy, as evidenced by state and local legislation for more than half a century, opium is an illegitimate commodity, the use of which, except as a medicinal agent, is rigidly condemned.—Sutherland: Yee Hem v. United States, 268 U.S. 178, 184.

OPPORTUNITY

1. There is a tide in the affairs of nations, of parties, and of individuals.—Marshall: Beveridge, *Life of Marshall,* II, 515.

2. The richest man among us may be brought down to the humblest level; and the child, with scarcely clothes to cover his nakedness, may rise to the highest office in our government. And the poor man, while he rocks his infant on his knees, may justly indulge the consolation, that, if he possess talents and virtue, there is no office beyond the reach of his honorable ambition.—Story: *Misc. Writings,* 515.

3. Equal opportunity for all people as for all individuals—that is the essential of international as well as of national justice upon which a peace which is to be permanent must rest.—Brandeis: Mason, *Brandeis,* 440.

4. What America needs is not that

we do anything for these our fellow-citizens, but that we keep open the path of opportunity to enable them to do for themselves.—Brandeis: *ibid.*, 177.

5. Every new community is potentially a new centre of economic opportunity.—Cardozo: Liggett Co. v. Lee, 288 U.S. 517, 582.

See also Freedom 45.

OPPOSITION

1. Opposition, whether disguised or real, is the same thing. — Johnson: Houston v. Moore, 5 Wheat. (18 U.S.) 1, 35.

2. To allow opposition by speech seems to indicate that you think the speech impotent, as when a man says that he has squared the circle.—Holmes: Abrams v. United States, 250 U.S. 616, 630.

3. The factious opposition of an intransigeant minority.—Cardozo: People v. Teuscher, 248 N.Y. 454, 462.

See also Political party 9; Freedom, speech 101.

OPPRESSION

1. The plaintiff's privilege is the defendant's oppression.—Baldwin: Livingston's Ex'r v. Story, 11 Pet. (36 U.S. 351, 416.

2. The most odious of all oppressions are those which mask as justice.—Jackson: Krulewitch v. United States, 336 U.S. 440, 458.

3. The poor were oppressed and the ignorant overreached. — Cardozo: People *ex rel.* Karlin v. Culkin, 248 N.Y. 465, 468.

Related subjects: Bigotry; Persecution. *See also* Citizen 28; Freedom, religion

131; Legislature 20; Majority-minority 10, 14; Power 13; Radio 4; Tax 24; Unrest.

OPTOMETRY

We see no constitutional reason why a State may not treat all who deal with the human eye as members of a profession who should use no merchandising methods for obtaining customers.—Douglas: Williamson v. Lee Optical, 348 U.S. 483, 490.

ORATOR

See Freedom 62; Lawyer 37.

ORDER

Related subject: Conduct. *See also* Freedom 25–27; Law 7, 10; Mob 1.

ORDINARY

1. Ordinary has the connotation of normal, usual, or customary.—Douglas: Deputy v. Du Pont, 308 U.S. 488, 495.

2. What is ordinary, though there must always be a strain of constancy within it, is none the less a variable affected by time and place and circumstance.—Cardozo: Welch v. Helvering, 290 U.S. 113, 114.

3. In the complexities of modern life, one does not know where the ordinary ends and the extraordinary begins.—Cardozo: Kerr S.S. Co. v. Radio Corp., 245 N.Y. 284, 290.

ORGANIZATION

Related subject: Association. *See also* Intolerance 7; Labor union; Nation (U.S.) 14.

ORIGINAL COST

Original cost is well termed the "false standard of the past" where . . .

present market value in no way reflects that cost.—Clark: United States v. Toronto, H. & B. Nav. Co., 338 U.S. 396, 403.

ORTHODOXY
The "party line" of the orthodox view, of the conventional thought, of the accepted approach. — Douglas: Adler v. Board of Educ., 342 U.S. 485, 510.
Related subjects: Conservatism; Unorthodox.

OWNERSHIP
1. Ownership itself . . . is only a bundle of rights and privileges invested with a single name.—Cardozo: Steward Mach. Co. v. Davis, 301 U.S. 495, 581.

2. The bundle of power and privileges to which we give the name of ownership is not constant through the ages. The faggots must be put together and rebound from time to time.—Cardozo: *Paradoxes,* 129.

3. Possession is the beginning of ownership. — Holmes: Missouri v. Holland, 252 U.S. 416, 434.

4. Ownership does not always mean absolute dominion. The more an owner, for his advantage, opens up his property for use by the public in general, the more do his rights become circumscribed by the statutory and constitutional rights of those who use it.—Black: Marsh v. Alabama, 326 U.S. 501, 506.

5. Ownership implies acquisition in the various ways in which land is acquired—by conquest, by discovery and claim, by cession, by prescription, by purchase, by condemnation.—Reed: United States v. California, 332 U.S. 19, 44.

6. Ownership of property implies two things: first, attention to it; second, a discharge of all obligations, of taxation or otherwise, to the State which protects it.—Brewer: Underwood v. Dugan, 139 U.S. 380, 384.
See also Corporation, control; Debt 1; Negligence 1; Property 8, 9; Tax 27.

PAIN
1. Pain of mind, though induced by terror, remains pain, and nothing more.—Cardozo: Bishop v. New York Times Co., 233 N.Y. 446, 462-63.

2. Impulsive people with little intelligence or foresight may be expected to lay hold of anything that affords a relief from present pain, even though it will cause greater trouble by and by.—Holmes: United States v. Reynolds, 235 U.S. 133, 150.

PAMPHLET
See Freedom, press 174.

PANACEA
I have no belief in panaceas and almost none in sudden ruin. — Holmes: *Speeches,* 102.
See also Legislation 32.

PANIC
See Freedom 95.

PAPACY
See Pope; Roman Catholic Church.

PARDON (legal)
1. The pardon not merely releases the offender from the punishment prescribed for the offense, but . . . obliterates in legal contemplation the of-

fense itself.—Field: Carlisle v. United States, 16 Wall. (83 U.S.) 147, 151.

2. A pardon of an offense removes the offending act out of sight; but, if there is no offense in the eye of the law, there can be no pardon. Consequently, the acts which are not extinguished by a pardon remain to confront the actor.—White: Young v. United States, 7 Otto (97 U.S.) 39, 62.

3. A pardon may be conditional, and the condition may be more objectionable than the punishment inflicted.—Marshall: United States v. Wilson, 7 Pet. (32 U.S.) 150, 161.

4. The pardoning power, committed to the executive, should be exercised as free from any improper bias or influence as the trial of the convict before the court.—Grier: Marshall v. Baltimore & O. R.R., 16 How. (57 U.S.) 314, 334.

Related subject: Clemency.

PARENT (corporation)

See Corporation, holding companies.

PARENT-CHILD

1. In the course of nature, man has need of protection and improvement long before he is able to reciprocate these benefits. These are purchased by the submission and services of our parents. — Johnson: Shanks v. Du Pont, 3 Pet. (28 U.S.) 242, 263.

2. Right or wrong, it is to be expected that a parent will favor the child who stands by him.—Brewer: Mackall v. Mackall, 135 U.S. 167, 172.

3. The child is not the mere creature of the state; those who nurture him and direct his destiny have the right, coupled with the high duty, to recognize and prepare him for additional obligations. — McReynolds: Pierce v. Society, 268 U.S. 510, 535.

4. Corresponding to the right of control, it is the natural duty of the parent to give his children education suitable to their station in life.—McReynolds: Meyer v. Nebraska, 262 U.S. 390, 400.

5. That the son had the misfortune of being a chip off the old block—a tree inclined as the twig had been bent — metaphors which express the common sense observation that parents are as likely to influence the character of their children as are children to shape that of their parents.—Jackson: Haupt v. United States, 330 U.S. 631, 642.

6. The natural father, as well as the natural mother, remains a parent no matter how estranged parent and child may become. A stranger may by conduct become a foster parent; but no conduct can transmute a natural parent into a stranger. — Douglas: Baumet v. United States, 344 U.S. 82, 85.

7. Parents may be free to become martyrs themselves. But it does not follow they are free, in identical cirsumstances, to make martyrs of their children before they have reached the age of full and legal discretion when they can make that choice for themselves.—Rutledge: Prince v. Massachusetts, 321 U.S. 158, 170.

Related subject: Child; Infant; Youth.

PARK

In the case of many of the older cities and towns, there were commons or public grounds, but the purpose of these was not to provide places for exercise and recreation, but places on which the owners of domestic animals might pasture them in common. . . . The Central Park of New York was the first place deliberately provided for the inhabitants of any city or town in the United States for exclusive use as a pleasure ground for rest and exercise in the open air.—Shiras: Shoemaker v. United States, 147 U.S. 282, 297.

See also Street 3.

PAROLE (legal)

Parole is intended to be a means of restoring offenders who are good social risks to society; to afford the unfortunate another opportunity by clemency.—Black: Zerbst v. Kidwell, 304 U.S. 359, 363.

Related subject: Clemency.

PART

See Whole-part.

PARTIALITY

Related subjects: Favor; Impartiality. See also Disclosure 1.

PARTISAN

See Litigant 4; Witness 2.

PASSION

Related subject: Emotion. See also Human nature 1; Judge, influences; Reason 4; Treason 4, 5, 9; War 17.

PAST

The past cannot be recalled by the most absolute power. — Marshall: Fletcher v. Peck, 6 Cranch (10 U.S.) 87, 135.

See also Future; Tax 119; Time; Tradition.

PATENT, PATENTEE

1. A patent is property carried to the highest degree of abstraction—a right in rem to exclude, without a physical object or content.—Holmes: Holmes-Pollock Letters, I, 53.

2. Every patent is the grant of a privilege of exacting tolls from the public.—Douglas: Great A. & P. Tea Co. v. Supermarket Equip. Corp., 340 U.S. 147, 154.

3. The function of a patent is to add to the sum of useful knowledge.—Jackson: ibid., 152.

4. The policy of the law is to encourage useful discoveries by securing their fruits to those who make them.—Fuller: Fowle v. Park, 131 U.S. 88, 97.

5. The public interest in patents comes first, reward to the inventor second.—Douglas: Automatic Radio Mfg. Co. v. Hazeltine Research, 339 U.S. 827, 837.

6. The public purpose is "to promote the progress of science and useful arts." The exclusive right of the inventor is but the means to that end.—Douglas: Special Equip. Co. v. Coe, 324 U.S. 370, 382.

7. Courts have not been reluctant to sustain a patent to the man who has taken the final step which has turned a failure into a success.—Brown: Washburn & Moen Mfg. Co. v. Beat 'Em Co., 143 U.S. 275, 282-83.

8. Patents cannot issue for the discovery of the phenomena of nature. . . . He who discovers a hitherto unknown phenomenon of nature has no claim to a monopoly of it which the law recognizes. — Douglas: Funk Bros. v. Kalo Co., 333 U.S. 127, 130.

9. The Constitution never sanctioned the patenting of gadgets. Patents serve a higher end—the advancement of science.—Douglas: Great A. & P. Tea Co. v. Supermarket Equip. Corp., 340 U.S. 147, 155.

10. Patent Monopoly? The word is descriptive and must be used, but it does not imply oppression.—McKenna: United States v. United Shoe Mach. Co., 247 U.S. 32, 57.

11. A patent is an exception to the general rule against monopolies and to the right to access to a free and open market.—Murphy: Precision Instr. Mfg. Co. v. Automotive Maint. Mach. Co., 324 U.S. 806, 816.

12. A patentee is given rights to his device, but he is given no power to force it on the world. If the world buy it or use it, the world will do so upon a voluntary judgment of its utility.— McKenna: United States v. United Shoe Mach. Co., 247 U.S. 32, 65.

13. That the extent to which a patented device has gone into use is an unsafe criterion even of its actual utility, is evident from the fact that the general introduction of manufactured articles is as often effected by extensive and judicious advertising, activity in putting the goods upon the market, and large commissions to dealers, as by the intrinsic merit of the articles

themselves. — Brown: McClain v. Ortmayer, 141 U.S. 419, 428.

14. The very fact, which courts as well as the public have not failed to recognize, that almost every important patent, from the cotton gin of Whitney to the one under consideration, has been attacked by the testimony of witnesses who imagined they had made similar discoveries long before the patentee had claimed to have invented his device, has tended to throw a certain amount of discredit upon all that class of evidence.— Brown: Washburn & Moen Mfg. Co. v. Beat 'Em Co., 143 U.S. 275, 284-85.

15. One who seeks to pirate an invention, like one who seeks to pirate a copyrighted book or play, may be expected to introduce minor variations to conceal and shelter the piracy. Outright and forthright duplication is a dull and very rare type of infringement.—Jackson: Graver Tank Mfg. Co. v. Linde Air Prod. Co., 339 U.S. 605, 607.

16. Where the patent owner has ample resources to bear the costs of repeated litigation, the power of the infringement suit to stifle competition is increased. And where potential competitors are weak and few, it may afford a practically complete protection for the preservation of undeserved monopoly.—Black: Williams Mfg. Co. v. United Shoe Mach. Co., 316 U.S. 364, 381.

17. Suppression of patents has become commonplace. Patents are multiplied to protect an economic barony or empire, not to put new discoveries

to use for the common good.—Douglas: Special Equip. Co. v. Coe, 324 U.S. 370, 382.

18. Ridding the public of stale or specious patents is one way of serving the end of the progress of science.—Douglas: Automatic Radio Mfg. Co. v. Hazeltine Research, 339 U.S. 827, 840.

19. Patents would be valueless to their owner without the organized societies constituted by the states.—Holmes: Long v. Rockwood, 277 U.S. 149–50.

Related subject: Invention. *See also* Copyright 1; Success 1.

PATRIOTISM

1. We still believe, that love of country, is not yet an idle name.—Holmes: *Speeches,* 64.

2. There are many, poor and rich, who think that love of country is an old wife's tale, to be replaced by interest in a labor union, or, under the name of cosmopolitanism, by a rootless self-seeking search for a place where the most enjoyment may be had at the least cost.—Holmes: *ibid.,* 57.

3. I do not deny, that the poor man may possess as much patriotism as the rich; but it is unjust to suppose, that he necessarily possesses more.—Story: *Misc. Writings,* 512.

4. A state may exert its power to strengthen the bonds of the Union, and therefore, to that end, may encourage patriotism and love of country among its people. When, by its legislation, the state encourages a feeling of patriotism towards the nation,

it necessarily encourages a like feeling towards the state. One who loves the Union will love the state in which he resides. — Harlan: Halter v. Nebraska, 205 U.S. 33, 42.

5. To believe that patriotism will not flourish if patriotic ceremonies are voluntary and spontaneous instead of a compulsory routine is to make an unflattering estimate of the appeal of our institutions to free minds.—Jackson: West Va. State Bd. of Educ. v. Barnette, 319 U.S. 624, 641.

6. Love of country must spring from willing hearts and free minds, inspired by a fair administration of wise laws enacted by the people's elected representatives within the bounds of express constitutional prohibitions.—Black and Douglas: *ibid.,* 644.

7. We might be tempted to say that the deepest patriotism is best engendered by giving unfettered scope to the most crochety beliefs.—Frankfurter: Minersville School Dist. v. Gobitis, 310 U.S. 586, 598.

Related subjects: Allegiance and related subjects. *See also* Motive 6; Sincerity; Wealth 1.

PAUPER

It is due to the cause of humanity, as well as the public economy of the state, that the maintenance of paupers, whether of foreign or domestic origin should be well provided for. Instead of being whipped or carted back to their places of abode or settlement, as was once the practice in England and this country in respect to them; or, if aliens, instead of being reshipped over a desolate waste of ocean, they are to be treated with kindness and relieved or maintained. — Woodbury: Passenger Cases, 7 How. (48 U.S.) 283, 520.

Related subject: Poverty. *See also* Public expenditure 4.

PAWNSHOP

In England, as in the United States, the private pledge system prevails. In this country, the practice of pledging personal property for loans dates back to early colonial times, and pawnshops have been regulated by state laws for more than a century.—Butler: Askura v. Seattle, 265 U.S. 332, 343.

PAYMENT

The chance of double payment is a common risk of life.—Cardozo: Coler v. Corn Exch. Bank, 250 N.Y. 136, 145.

Related subject: Debt. *See also* Promise 5; Sacrifice; Veteran 4, 5.

PEACE

1. Our terms remain the same: we still pursue peace. We still embrace it, if it can be obtained without violating our national honor or our national faith; but we will reject without hesitation all propositions which may compromise the one or the other.— Marshall: Beveridge, *Life of Marshall,* II, 509.

2. Where peace exists the laws of peace must prevail.—Chase: *Ex parte* Milligan, 4 Wall. (71 U.S.) 2, 140.

3. Peace is a sweet and holy thing, and war is a hateful and an abominable thing to be avoided by any sacrifice or concession that a free people

can make. But thus far mankind has been unable to devise any method of indefinitely prolonging the one or of entirely abolishing the other.—Sutherland: United States v. Macintosh, 283 U.S. 605, 621.

4. Unfortunately, there is nothing which seems to afford positive ground for thinking that the near future will witness the beginning of the reign of perpetual peace for which good men and women everywhere never cease to pray.—Sutherland: *ibid.,* 621–22.

5. No peace which is lasting can ever come until the nations, great and small, accept the democratic principle that there is and shall be no supernation to rise through subjection of others, and the truth that each people has in it something of peculiar value which it can contribute to that civilization for which we are all striving.— Brandeis: Mason, *Brandeis,* 440.

6. Agreements for the renunciation of war presuppose a preponderant public sentiment against wars of aggression.—Hughes: United States v. Macintosh, 283 U.S. 605, 635.

7. In the peace of the state, most men past their lives, and find repose in its protection.—Cardozo: Holmes Elec. Prot. Co. v. Williams, 228 N.Y. 407, 442.

Related subjects: Foreign affairs; War. *See also* Opportunity 3; War 11.

PENAL, PENOLOGY

Related subjects: Crime, Criminal law. *See also* Construction, penal; Punishment 41.

PENALTY

1. "Penalty" is a term of varying

and uncertain meaning. There are penalties recoverable in vindication of the public justice of the state. There are other penalties designed as reparation to sufferers from wrongs.—Cardozo: Life & Cas. Ins. Co. v. McCray, 291 U.S. 566, 574.

2. A penalty is a means of punishment; interest a means of compensation.—McKenna: United States v. Childs, 266 U.S. 304, 307.

3. The penalty is a deterrent, not compensation. — Holmes: Missouri, K. & T. R.R. v. United States, 231 U.S. 112, 119.

4. Liability to pay the fair price or value of an enjoyment, or to be compelled to restore or give up property belonging to another, is not a penalty. —Holmes: *Uncollected Letters*, 27.

5. The penalty may be no more than the fair price of the adventure. In that event, the litigant must pay for his experience, like others who have tried and lost.—Cardozo: Life & Cas. Ins. Co. v. McCray, 291 U.S. 566, 575.

See also Tax 4; Wrongdoer 2.

PEONAGE
Compulsory work for no private master in a jail is not peonage.— Holmes: Bailey v. Alabama, 219 U.S. 219, 247.

PERFORMANCE
See Promise 6, 9; Question 2.

PERJURY
1. Perjury is one thing; testimonial recalcitrance another. — Frankfurter: Brown v. United States, 356 U.S. 148, 153.

2. The special rule which bars conviction for perjury solely upon the evidence of a single witness is deeply rooted in past centuries. — Black: Weiler v. United States, 323 U.S. 606, 608–609.

Related subjects: Evidence; Testimony; Witness. *See also* Divorce 4; Informer 4; Promise 4; Self incrimination 13; Testimony 3.

PERMISSION
Permission, like sufferance, connotes something less than consent. Sufferance, like permission, connotes some opportunity for knowledge.— Cardozo: People *ex rel.* Price v. Sheffield Farms Co., 225 N.Y. 25, 31.

PERPETUITY
From our point in history 969 years hence is perpetuity. — Frankfurter: Palmer v. Connecticut Ry. & Light. Co., 311 U.S. 544, 564.

PERSECUTION
1. Persecution for the expression of opinions seems to me perfectly logical. If you have no doubt of your premises or your power and want a certain result with all your heart you naturally express your wishes in law and sweep away all o p p o s i t i o n. — Holmes: Abrams v. United States, 250 U.S. 616, 630.

2. The law knows no finer hour than when it cuts through formal concepts and transitory emotions to protect unpopular citizens against discrimination and persecution.—Murphy: Falbo v. United States, 320 U.S. 549, 561.

3. Those who have suffered most

from secret and dictatorial proceedings have almost always been the poor, the ignorant, the numerically weak, the friendless, and the powerless.—Black: Chambers v. Florida, 309 U.S. 227, 238.

Related subject: Oppression.

PERSON

1. No right is held more sacred, or is more carefully guarded by the common law, than the right of every individual to the possession and control of his own person, free from all restraint or interference of others, unless by clear or unquestionable authority of law.—Gray: Union Pac. Ry. v. Botsford, 141 U.S. 250, 251.

2. The inviolability of the person is as much invaded by a compulsory stripping and exposure, as by a blow. To compel anyone, and especially a woman, to lay bare the body, or to submit it to the touch of a stranger, without lawful authority, is an indignity, an assault and a trespass.—Gray: *ibid.,* 252.

Related subjects: Man and related subjects. *See also* Age (years) 1; Safeguard 2; Ship (personality).

PERSUASION

Related subject: Inducement. *See also* Freedom 73; Proof 1; Repetition 1.

PERVERSION

See Constitution, perversion; Construction, perversion; Religion 17; Remedy 19; Rights 28; Zeal 6.

PHILANTHROPIST, PHILANTHROPY

This glorious march of philanthropy, under the banners of the meek sect, which does good by stealth, and blushes to find it fame.—Story: *Misc. Writings,* 14.

PHILOSOPHER, PHILOSOPHIC, PHILOSOPHY

1. The theorist has a hard time to make his way in an ungrateful world. He is supposed to be indifferent to realities; yet his life is spent in the exposure of realities which, till illumined by his searchlight, were hidden and unknown. He is contrasted, and to his great disfavor, with the strenuous man of action, who ploughs or builds or navigates or trades, yet, in moments of meditation he takes the consoling knowledge to his heart that the action of his favored brothers would be futile unless informed and inspired by thoughts that came from him. Of the lot of all theorists, that of the philosopher is the sorriest.—Cardozo: *Growth of the Law,* 21–22.

2. A troublesome lot, these men who are searching always for the ultimate.—Cardozo: *ibid.,* 22.

3. The philosophers were hired by the comfortable class to prove that everything is all right. — Holmes: *Holmes-Pollock Letters,* I, 139.

4. Philosophy does not furnish motives, but it shows men that they are not fools for doing what they already want to do. It opens to the forlorn hopes on which we throw ourselves away, the vista of the farthest stretch of human thought, the chords of a harmony that breathes from the unknown.—Holmes: "Natural Law," 32 Harv. L. Rev. 44.

5. Philosophy has her feuds that heed no truce of God. For several thousand years she has been trying to compose them, yet it is only with indifferent success that she has kept the peace within her borders.—Cardozo: *Growth of the Law,* 28.

6. You think perhaps of philosophy as dwelling in the clouds. I hope you may see that she is able to descend to earth. You think that in stopping to pay court to her, when you should be hastening forward on your journey, you are loitering in bypaths and wasting precious hours. I hope you may share my faith that you are on the highway to the goal. Here you will find the key for the unlocking of bolts and combinations that shall never be pried open by clumsier or grosser tools. — Cardozo: *ibid.,* 23.

See also Judge 15; Logic 4; Supreme Court 18; Vanity.

PHYSICIAN

The doctor apparently made a wrong diagnosis but that does not prove that it was a negligent one.—Jackson: De Zon v. American Pres. Lines, 318 U.S. 660, 671.

Related subjects: Disease; Medicine. *See also* Disease 3.

PICTURE

Related subjects: Art; Illustration. *See also* Advertising 2; Distortion; Symbol 2.

PIONEER

1. The adventurous pioneer, who is found in advance of our settlements, encounters many hardships, and not unfrequently dangers from savage incursions. He is generally poor, and it is fit that his enterprise should be rewarded by the privilege of purchasing the favorite spot selected by him.—McLean: Lytle v. Arkansas, 9 How. (50 U.S.) 314, 333-34.

2. These western pioneers, emulating the spirit of so many others who had gone before them in similar ventures, faced the difficult problem of wresting a living and creating homes from the raw elements about them, and threw down the gage of battle to the forces of nature.—Sutherland: California, Ore. Power Co. v. Beaver Portland Cement Co., 295 U.S. 142, 157.

3. Each day was an anticipation of attack, and when the night came repose was only taken with the rifle ready to repel it.—Wayne: Howard v. Ingersoll, 13 How. (54 U.S.) 381, 410.

4. Empire was given a path westward and prosperous commonwealths took the place of a wilderness.—McKenna: Oregon & C. R.R. v. United States, 238 U.S. 393, 416.

PLATITUDE

1. Any idea that has been in the world for twenty years and has not perished has become a platitude although it was a revelation twenty years ago.—Holmes: *Uncollected Letters,* 139.

2. The elect representatives of western culture are continually getting hold of words excellent in themselves but running them so hard that they become banal.—Holmes: *ibid.,* 203.

PLEASURE

The rough and boisterous joke, the horseplay of the crowd, evokes its own guffaws, but they are not the pleasures of tranquility.—Cardozo: Murphy v. Steeplechase Amuse. Co., 250 N.Y. 479, 483.

PLEDGE

No man can be pledged but by himself.—Marshall: Winship v. Bank of U. S., 5 Pet. (30 U.S.) 529, 561.

Related subject: Pawnshop.

POET, POETRY

Poetry requires a special adaptation not possessed by the "mob of gentlemen who write with ease."—Holmes: *Uncollected Letters,* 174.

See also Lawyer 40.

POLICE

1. Criminal activity is such that stealth and strategy are necessary weapons in the arsenal of the police officer.—Warren: Sherman v. United States, 356 U.S. 369, 372.

2. In my opinion, locally established and controlled police can never develop into the menace to general civil liberties that is inherent in a federal police.—Jackson: Terminiello v. Chicago, 337 U.S. 1, 35.

3. Though the police are honest and their aims worthy, history shows they are not appropriate guardians of the privacy which the Fourth Amendment protects. — Douglas: Jones v. United States, 362 U.S. 257, 273.

Related subject: Third degree. *See also* Arrest 4; Criminal law, interrogation; Freedom 84, 85, 96; Lottery 5; Privacy 7;

Prosecutor 7; Search and seizure; Wire tapping.

POLICE POWER (legal)

1. The police power . . . is the most absolute of the sovereign powers of the state. . . . It "extends to so dealing with the conditions which exist in a state as to bring out of them the greatest welfare of its people."—McKenna: Louisville & N. R.R. v. Central Stock Yards Co., 212 U.S. 132, 150 (quot. 204 U.S. 311).

2. In a sense, the police power is but another name for the power of government. — McKenna: Mutual Loan Co. v. Martell, 222 U.S. 225, 233.

3. Police power often is used in a wide sense to cover . . . and . . . to apologize for the general power of the legislature to make a part of the community uncomfortable by a change.— Holmes: Tyson v. Banton, 273 U.S. 418, 446.

4. One of the difficult social problems of the day is what shall be done in respect to those vocations which minister to and feed upon human weaknesses, appetites, and passions. The management of these vocations comes directly within the scope of what is known as the police power.— Brewer: L'Hote v. New Orleans, 177 U.S. 587, 596.

Related subject: Eminent domain. *See also* Legislature 14.

POLICY

New policies are usually tentative in their beginnings, advance in firmness as they advance in acceptance. . . . Time may be necessary to fashion them to precedent customs and conditions.—McKenna: Bunting v. Oregon, 243 U.S. 426, 438.

See also Law 13; Public policy; Tax 37, 102, 104.

POLITICAL ACTION

Political action is, indeed, a versatile remedy for the correction of injustices. — Douglas: *We the Judges,* 56.

POLITICAL BELIEF

See Freedom, belief 135.

POLITICAL CONTRIBUTION

See Public official, political contributions.

POLITICAL ECONOMY

There are few, if any questions in political economy about which entire certainty may be predicated. — Harlan: Lochner v. New York, 198 U.S. 45, 72.

POLITICAL PARTY

1. Political parties in the modern sense were not born with the Republic. They were created by necessity, by the need to organize the rapidly increasing population, scattered over our Land, so as to coordinate efforts to secure needed legislation and oppose that deemed undesirable.—Reed: Ray v. Blair, 343 U.S. 214, 220–21.

2. It is a matter of common knowledge that the great mass of the American electorate is grouped into political parties, to one or the other of which voters adhere with tenacity, due to their divergent views on questions of public policy, their interest, their environment, and various other influences, sentimental and historical. So strong with the great majority of voters are party associations, so potent the party slogan, so effective the party organization, that the likelihood of a candidate succeeding in an election without a party nomination is practically negligible.—Pitney: Newberry v. United States, 256 U.S. 232, 285–86.

3. Political parties must almost necessarily exist under a republican form of government, and when public employment depends to any considerable extent on party success, those in office will naturally be desirous of keeping the party to which they belong in power.—Waite: *Ex parte* Curtis, 106 U.S. 371, 375.

4. Nothing I believe more debases or pollutes the human mind than faction [party]. — Marshall: Beveridge, *Life of Marshall,* II, 410.

5. Factions are the natural, nay, perhaps, the necessary growth of all free governments; and they must prevail with more activity and influence, just in proportion, as they enlist in their ranks the interest and power of numbers.—Story: *Misc. Writings,* 157.

6. No system, that aims *merely* at temporary, or party, or local objects, or, that bends the great interests of the whole to the partial benefit of the few, ever was, or ever can be salutary. Such a system is not only unworthy of a free and enlightened people; but brings disgrace and ruin, wherever it is established. It is the harbinger of faction and discontent; and leads to animosities, from which the people can derive nothing, but bad laws, bad

morals, and bad government.—Story: *ibid.,* 348–49.

7. Men in adhering to a political party or other organization notoriously do not subscribe unqualifiedly to all of its platforms or asserted principles. — Murphy: Schneiderman v. United States, 320 U.S. 118, 136.

8. We would deny our experience as men if we did not recognize that official party programs are unfortunately often opportunistic devices as much honored in the breach as in the observance.—Murphy: *ibid.,* 154–55.

9. All parties, when in opposition, strive to discredit and embarrass the Government of the day by spreading exaggerations and untruths and by inciting prejudiced or unreasoning discontent, not even hesitating to injure the Nation's prestige among the family of nations.—Jackson: American Com. Assoc. v. Douds, 339 U.S. 382, 423.

10. Parties, whether in office or out, are often irresponsible in their use and abuse of freedoms of speech and press. They all make scapegoats of unpopular persons or classes and make promises of dubious sincerity or feasibility in order to win votes.—Jackson: *ibid.*

See also Communism; Election 24; Politician 1, 3; President 3.

POLITICAL PRACTICE

A political practice which has its origin in custom must rely upon custom for its sanctions.—Jackson: Ray v. Blair, 343 U.S. 214, 233.

POLITICAL WRITING

Political writings are often over-exaggerated polemics bearing the imprint of the period and the place in which written.—Murphy: Schneiderman v. United States, 320 U.S. 118, 154.

POLITICIAN

1. There are men who will hold power by any means rather than not hold it; and who would prefer a dissolution of the union to a continuance of an administration not of their own party. They will risk all ills . . . rather than permit that happiness which is dispensed by other hands than their own. — Marshall: Beveridge, *Life of Marshall,* 11, 407.

2. Politicians, even if their motives are not of the purest, come much nearer performing their duties than the so-called "good" citizens who stay at home.—Brandeis: Mason, *Brandeis,* 123.

3. Every utterance of party leaders is not taken as party gospel.—Murphy: Schneiderman v. United States, 320 U.S. 118, 154.

POLITICS

1. Our political tempests will long, very long, exist, after those who are now toss'd about by them shall be at rest. — Marshall: Beveridge, *Life of Marshall,* III, 104.

2. In the science of politics there has very frequently been a strong current against the natural order of things, and an inconsiderate or an interested disposition to sacrifice the end to the means.—Wilson: Chisholm v. Georgia, 2 Dall. (2 U.S.) 419, 455.

3. The alternations of our national

moods are such that a cycle of liberal government seldom exceeds eight years.—Jackson: *Struggle for Judicial Supremacy,* 187.

See also Freedom 96; Supreme Court 40–42.

POLYGAMY

1. Polygamy has always been odious among the Northern and Western Nations of Europe and, until the establishment of the Mormon Church, was almost exclusively a feature of the life of Asiatic and African people. . . . There has never been a time in any State of the Union when polygamy has not been an offense against society, cognizable by the civil courts and punishable with more or less severity.—Waite: Reynolds v. United States, 8 Otto (98 U.S.) 145, 164.

2. Legislation for the protection of children born in polygamy is not necessarily legislation favorable to polygamy. There is no inconsistency in shielding the one and in denouncing the other as a crime. — Brown: Cope v. Cope, 137 U.S. 682, 687.

3. The organization of a community for the spread and practice of polygamy is, in a measure, a return to barbarism. It is contrary to the spirit of Christianity and of the civilization which Christianity has produced in the Western World.—Bradley: Late Corp. of Latter Day Saints v. United States, 136 U.S. 1, 49.

4. The establishment or maintenance of polygamous households is a notorious example of promiscuity.—Douglas: Cleveland v. United States, 329 U.S. 14, 19.

5. Society also has an interest in the avoidance of polygamous marriages and in the protection of innocent offspring of marriages.—Douglas: Williams v. North Carolina, 317 U.S. 287, 303.

POLYGYNY

We are dealing here with polygyny, one of the basic forms of marriage. Historically, its use has far exceeded that of any other form. It was quite common among ancient civilizations and was referred to many times by the writers of the Old Testament; even today it is to be found frequently among certain pagan and non-Christian peoples of the world. We must recognize, then, that polygyny, like other forms of marriage, is basically a cultural institution rooted deeply in the religious beliefs and social mores of those societies in which it appears. — Murphy: Cleveland v. United States, 329 U.S. 14, 26.

POPE

Related subjects: Papacy; Roman Catholic Church. *See also* Power 3.

POSSESSION

1. Possession has always been a means of acquiring title to property. It was the earliest mode recognized by mankind of the appropriation of anything tangible by one person to his own use, to the exclusion of others. —Miller: Campbell v. Holt, 115 U.S. 620, 623.

2. A state of the law . . . where possession apparently is not merely nine points of the law but all of them and self-help the ultimate authority, has

little to commend it in legal logic or as a principle of order in a federal system.—Jackson: May v. Anderson, 345 U.S. 528, 539.

See also Guilt 9; Ownership 3; Property 7.

POSSIBLE, POSSIBILITY

1. Possibilities are the enemies of truth.—Wayne: Patterson v. Gaines, 6 How. (47 U.S.) 550, 599.

2. At most there has been made out, not likelihood, but possibility.—Cardozo: Brooklyn Pub. Lib. v. City of New York, 240 N.Y. 465, 469.

3. A possibility that hardly rises to the level of an expectancy.—Harlan: Society for Savings v. Bowers, 349 U.S. 143, 150.

Related subject: Impossible.

POVERTY

1. Poverty leads to temptation, and temptation often leads to vice.—Story: *Misc. Writings,* 514.

2. A man's mere property status, without more, cannot be used by a state to test, qualify or limit his rights as a citizen of the United States.—Jackson: Edwards v. California, 314 U.S. 160, 184.

3. "Indigence" in itself is neither a source of rights nor a basis for denying them.—Jackson: *ibid.*

4. Poverty and immorality are not synonymous.—Byrnes: *ibid.,* 177.

5. The mere state of being without funds is a neutral fact—constitutionally an irrelevance, like race, creed, or color.—Jackson: *ibid.,* 185.

Related subject: Pauper. See also Bail 2; Freedom, contract 180; Patriotism 3; Public welfare 7, 9, 22; Trial 29–31; Unemployment 1; Wealth 1.

POWER

1. To an imagination of any scope the most far-reaching form of power is not money, it is the command of ideas. — Holmes: "The Path of the Law," 10 Harv. L. Rev. 478.

2. If there were only one other man in the world, and he was safe under lock and key in jail, the person having the key would not possess the swallows that flew over the prison.—Holmes: *The Common Law,* 216.

3. The Pope can't repeal the Decalogue. — Holmes: *Holmes-Pollock Letters,* II, 6 (quot. Cardinal Merry del Val).

4. The only prize much cared for by the powerful is power. The prize of the general is not a bigger tent, but command.—Holmes: *Speeches,* 100.

5. If the world were my dream, I should be God in the only universe I know. — Holmes: "I d e a l s and Doubts," 10 Ill. L. Rev. 2.

6. We fear power and are unwilling to recognize it when it exists.—Holmes: Tyson v. Banton, 273 U.S. 418, 445.

7. Power begets wealth; and added wealth opens ever new opportunities for the acquisition of wealth and power. — Brandeis: *Other People's Money,* 16.

8. I should not rely upon the goodness of heart of anybody. Nobody ought to be absolute; everybody ought to be protected from arbitrariness and wrong decisions by the representations of others who are being affected.—Brandeis: Mason, *Brandeis,* 149.

9. Any who wield a large amount

of power should always feel the check of power. The very principle on which the nation exists is that no person shall rise above power. — Brandeis: *ibid.,* 140.

10. All our human experience shows that no one with absolute power can be trusted to give it up even in part.—Brandeis: *ibid.,* 431.

11. Power is more satisfying to some than wealth.—Douglas: *We the Judges,* 30.

12. Power is, indeed, a heady thing —whether it be a King, a President, a Legislature, a Court, or an Administrative agency that is concerned.— Douglas: *ibid.*

13. All power needs some restraint, some check, lest it become an instrument of oppression.—Douglas: *ibid.*

14. Those in power need checks and restraints lest they come to identify the common good with their own tastes and desires, and their continuation in office as essential to the preservation of the nation.—Douglas: *ibid.,* 256.

15. All executive power—from the reign of ancient kings to the rule of modern dictators—has the outward appearance of efficiency.—Douglas: Youngstown Sheet & Tube Co. v. Sawyer, 343 U.S. 579, 629.

16. Evil men are rarely given power; they take it over from better men to whom it had been entrusted.—Roberts, Frankfurter, Jackson: Screws v. United States, 325 U.S. 91, 160.

17. Power might be exercised with brutal indifference to the many when society was organized on a basis of special privilege for the few. Democracy has brought in its wake a new outlook, and with the new outlook a new law.—Cardozo: *Paradoxes,* 19.

18. In a democracy, power implies responsibility. — Frankfurter: United States v. UMW, 330 U.S. 258, 312.

19. Superior strength may give the power, but cannot give the right.— Marshall: Ogden v. Saunders, 12 Wheat. (25 U.S.) 213, 345.

20. Power is not synonymous with right.—Roberts: Poe v. Seaborn, 282 U.S. 101, 113.

21. Power should answer to reason none the less because its fiat is beyond appeal.—Jackson: Jewell Ridge Coal Corp. v. UMW, 325 U.S. 161, 196.

22. Power ... must exist somewhere; else society will be at the mercy of the few, who, regarding only their own appetites or passions, may be willing to imperil the peace and security of the many, provided only they are permitted to do as they please. —Harlan: Mugler v. Kansas, 123 U.S. 623, 660–61.

23. The legality of power must be estimated not by what it will do, but by what it can do.—McKenna: Block v. Hirsh, 256 U.S. 135, 162.

24. A power is given to be exercised.—McKenna: Rhode Island v. Palmer, 253 U.S. 350, 403.

25. Power granted is seldom neglected.—Douglas: United States v. Wunderlich, 342 U.S. 98, 101.

26. The possession of power is one thing; the propriety of its exercise in particular circumstances is quite a different thing. — Van Devanter: John-

son v. Manhattan Ry., 289 U.S. 479, 504.

27. The exercise of a power for the first time may be called upon to justify itself.—Moody: Howard v. Illinois Cent. R.R., 207 U.S. 463, 522.

28. A power to create implies a power to preserve. — Marshall: McCulloch v. Maryland, 4 Wheat. (17 U.S.) 316, 426.

29. The end being required, it has been deemed a just and necessary implication that the means to accomplish it are given also.—Story: Prigg v. Pennsylvania, 16 Pet. (41 U.S.) 539, 619.

30. The greater power includes the less. — McReynolds: Seaboard Air Line Ry. v. North Carolina, 245 U.S. 298, 304.

31. The power is as broad as the need that evokes it.—Cardozo: Carter v. Carter Coal Co., 298 U.S. 238, 328.

32. The question is, where does the power reside? not, how far will it probably be a b u s e d . — Marshall: Brown v. Maryland, 12 Wheat. (25 U.S.) 419, 447.

33. From the very nature of things, the absolute right of decision, in the last resort, must rest somewhere—wherever it may be vested it is susceptible of abuse.—Story: Martin v. Hunter's Lessee, 1 Wheat. (14 U.S.) 305, 345.

34. It is not sufficient to urge, that the power may be abused, for, such is the nature of all power—such is the tendency of every human institution. —Iredell: Calder v. Bull, 3 Dall. (3 U.S.) 648, 654.

35. We must be content to limit power where we can, and where we cannot, consistently with its use, we must be content to repose a salutary confidence.—Iredell: *ibid*.

36. It is impossible to guard an investiture of power so that it may not, in some form, be abused.—Marshall: Worcester v. Georgia, 6 Pet. (31 U.S.) 515, 572.

37. The most absolute tyranny could not subsist where men could not be trusted with power because they might abuse it.—Johnson: Anderson v. Dunn, 6 Wheat. (19 U.S.) 204, 232.

38. Power is not abused because the shock of its impact is equitably distributed.—Roberts: United States v. Constantine, 296 U.S. 287, 298.

39. They are exhibitions of power. They are not pronouncements of authority.—Cardozo: Petrogradsky M. K. Bank v. National City Bank, 253 N.Y. 23, 28.

40. Arbitrary and tyrannical power has no place in our system.—Field: Fong Yue Ting v. United States, 149 U.S. 698, 755.

41. Acquiescence in or silence under unauthorized power can never give legality to its exercise under our form of government.—Field: Baltimore & O. R.R. v. Baugh, 149 U.S. 368, 399.

42. The accretion of dangerous power does not come in a day. It does come, however slowly, from the generative force of unchecked disregard of the restrictions that fence in even the most disinterested assertion of au-

thority. — Frankfurter: Youngstown Sheet & Tube Co. v. Sawyer, 343 U.S. 579, 594.

43. Power can never be delegated which the authority said to delegate itself never possessed. — Daniel: New Jersey Steam Nav. Co. v. Merchants' Bank, 6 How. (47 U.S.) 344, 407.

Related subject: Police power and particular subjects. *See also* Business (big) 2, 3; Citizen 28; Congress; Constitution, powers; Constitutional adjudication, power; Contempt (of court); Contempt (of Congress); Democracy 8, 9, 19; Emergency; Equity court, powers; Error 2; Government (general); Government (U.S.), various subdivisions; Inheritance 5; Jurisdiction; Knowledge 2; Labor, various subdivisions; Law 5; Legislation 10, 11; Legislature, powers; President; Public official, power; Restraint of trade 5; Right 13; Sherman Antitrust Law 5; Slavery 2; Sovereignty 4, 12; State, power; Sunday 6; Supreme Court; Tax, power; Tax 85, 142; Thought 4; War, powers; Wealth 5; Wrongdoer 6.

PRACTICAL, PRACTICALITY

1. There is, in the public mind, a strong disposition to turn everything to a practical account, to deal less with learning, and more with experiment; to seek the solid comforts of opulence, rather than the indulgence of mere intellectual luxury. — Story: *Misc. Writings,* 19–20.

2. The practical is disagreeable, a mean and stony soil, but from that it is that all valuable theory comes.— Holmes: *Uncollected Letters,* 184.

3. Probably the true solution is to be found in practical considerations. —Holmes: *The Common Law,* 332.

4. This is eminently a practical age;

. . . courts must recognize things as they are.—Brewer: Adams Exp. Co. v. Ohio St. Auditor, 166 U.S. 185, 225.

Related subject: Common sense. *See also* Construction, practical; Tax 143.

PRACTICE

1. Such a practice, begun so early and continued so long, would be in the highest degree persuasive if not absolutely controlling, in its effect.— Waite: United States v. Graham, 110 U.S. 219, 221.

2. The practice is so inveterate that it may be ranked as rudimentary.— Cardozo: Hopkins Fed. Sav. & Loan Assoc. v. Cleary, 296 U.S. 315, 339.

3. The endeavor to put a stop to illicit practices must not itself become illicit.—Hughes: Sugar Inst. v. United States, 297 U.S. 553, 599.

4. It has long been recognized that a socially undesirable practice may seek acceptance under the guise of conventional moral symbols.—Black: Mercoid Corp. v. Mid-Cont. Inv. Co., 320 U.S. 661, 673.

5. History shows that some repulsive practices have masqueraded under the guise of religion or otherwise sought its protection and blessing. — Douglas: *We the Judges,* 342.

6. My abhorrence of the odious practices of the town gossip, the peeping Tom, and the private eavesdropper is quite as strong as that of any of my brethren.—Sutherland: Nardone v. United States, 302 U.S. 379, 387.

Related subjects: Conduct; Custom and related subjects. *See also* Freedom, religion 126; Thought 5.

PRAGMATISM

Pragmatism is at least a working rule by which truth is to be tested, and its attainment known.—Cardozo: *Growth of the Law,* 46–47.

PRAYER

Related subject: Sermon.

PREACHER, PREACHING

1. It is not uncommon for ordained ministers of more orthodox religions to work a full day in secular occupations, especially in rural communities.—Douglas: Cox v. United States, 332 U.S. 442, 456–57.

2. Freedom of religion is not merely reserved for those with a long purse. Preachers of the more orthodox faiths are not engaged in commercial undertakings because they are dependent on their calling for a living. Whether needy or affluent, they avail themselves of the constitutional privilege of a "free exercise" of their religion when they enter the pulpit to proclaim their faith. The priest or preacher is as fully protected in his function as the parishioners are in their worship. — Douglas: Follett v. McCormick, 321 U.S. 573, 576–77.

3. Many preachers, including those in the more traditional and orthodox sects, may not be blessed with congregations or parishes capable of paying them a living wage. — Clark: Dickinson v. United States, 346 U.S. 389, 395.

4. Preaching from house to house is an age-old method of proselyting.—Murphy: Martin v. Struthers, 319 U.S. 141, 150.

Related subject: Clergyman. *See also* Tax 79.

PRECAUTION

Precautions must be seasonable in order to be effectual.—Clifford: The Teutonia, 23 Wall. (90 U.S.) 77, 85.

Related subjects: Care; Vigilance.

PRECEDENT (legal)

Creation 1–6; importance 7–13; use 14–23; extension 24–27; lack 28–33; inapplicable, obsolete 34–43; danger 44–47; miscellaneous 48–51.

Related subjects: Decision and related subjects; Res judicata.

———, creation

1. Every opinion tends to become a law.—Holmes: Lochner v. New York, 198 U.S. 45, 76.

2. The sordid controversies of litigants are the stuff out of which great and shining truths will ultimately be shaped.—Cardozo: *Nature of Judicial Process,* 35.

3. The sentence of today will make the right and wrong of tomorrow.—Cardozo: *ibid.,* 21.

4. In the life of the mind as in life elsewhere, there is a tendency toward the reproduction of kind.—Cardozo: *ibid.*

5. Not all the progeny of principles begotten of a judgment survive . . . to maturity.—Cardozo: *ibid.,* 22.

6. The power of precedent, when analyzed, is the power of the beaten track.—Cardozo: *Growth of the Law,* 62.

———, importance

7. We must respect the solemn decisions of our predecessors and associ-

342

ates, as we may wish that those who succeed us should respect ours, or the supreme law of the land, so far as depends on judicial interpretation, will change with the change of judges. —Baldwin: *Ex parte* Crane, 5 Pet. (30 U.S.) 189, 202.

8. In questions which respect the rights of property, it is better to adhere to principles once fixed, though, originally, they might not have been perfectly free from all objection, than to unsettle the law, in order to render it more consistent with the dictates of sound reason.—Washington: Marine Ins. Co. v. Tucker, 3 Cranch (7 U.S.) 357, 388.

9. Those of us who have borne our part in the case will pass away. The case will live. Years hence, as well as now, the profession will look to it for what has been ruled.—Wayne: Gaines v. Relf, 12 How. (53 U.S.) 472, 596.

10. It is almost as important that the law should be settled permanently, as that it should be settled correctly. —Swayne: Gilman v. Philadelphia, 3 Wall. (70 U.S.) 713, 724.

11. If the other departments of the government must look to the judicial for light, that light should burn steadily. It should not, like the exhalations of a marsh, shine to mislead.—McKenna: De Lima v. Bidwell, 182 U.S. 1, 205.

12. Adherence to precedent must . . . be the rule rather than the exception if litigants are to have faith in the even-handed administration of justice in the courts.—Cardozo: *Nature of Judicial Process,* 34.

13. Decisions affecting the business interests of the country should not be disturbed except for the most cogent reasons.—Sanford: United States v. Flannery, 268 U.S. 98, 105.

——, use

14. Precedents have so covered the ground that they fix the point of departure from which the labor of the judge begins.—Cardozo: *Nature of Judicial Process,* 20.

15. It is easier to follow the beaten track than it is to clear another.—Cardozo: *Growth of the Law,* 62.

16. While I was in practice at the bar, I tried to find the pertinent authority, and fit it to the case at hand. I was not much concerned whether it was right if I was sure that it was pertinent, and I had a blind faith which persisted in the face of reverses and discouragements, that if its pertinency was established, if it fitted well and truly, the courts would follow it inexorably to the limit of its logic.—Cardozo: *ibid.,* 57.

17. Citation of precedent is tending to count for less, and appeal to an informing principle is tending to count for more.—Cardozo: *ibid.,* 5.

18. The judge who can take refuge in a precedent does not need to justify his decision to the reason. He may "reluctantly feel himself bound" by a doctrine, supported by a respected historical name, that he would not be able to justify to contemporary opinion or under modern conditions.— Jackson: *Struggle for Judicial Supremacy,* 295.

19. Before overruling a precedent in any case it is the duty of the court to make certain that more harm will not be done in rejecting than in retaining a rule of even dubious validity.—Stone: United States v. Southeast Underwriters Assoc., 322 U.S. 533, 580.

20. To fortify principle with precedent.—Holmes: *The Common Law*, 209.

21. The direction in which the law moves is often a guide for decision of particular cases.—Frankfurter: Universal Camera Corp. v. NLRB, 340 U.S. 474, 497.

22. We do not write on a clean slate.—Jackson: United States v. Buffalo Ry., 333 U.S. 771, 774.

23. Cases hold only what they decide, not what slipshod or ignorant headnote writers state them to decide; ... decisions are one thing, gratuitous remarks another.—Frankfurter: Bisso v. Inland Waterways Corp., 349 U.S. 85, 100.

———, extension

24. A court, by announcing that its decision is confined to the facts before it, does not decide in advance that logic will not drive it further when new facts arise.—Holmes: Haddock v. Haddock, 201 U.S. 562, 631.

25. Acquiescence in a precedent does not require approval of its extension. — Frankfurter: Dennis v. United States, 339 U.S. 162, 181.

26. It is unsafe to go much beyond what we find in the books.—Holmes: Ker & Co. v. Couden, 223 U.S. 268, 276.

27. The ruling in that case marks the high water line beyond which courts have been unwilling to go.—Cardozo: Shepard v. United States, 290 U.S. 96, 105.

———, lack

28. It is so unique that it is without precedent and is likely to be without progeny.—Jackson: Western Pac. R.R. Corp. v. Western Pac. R.R. Co., 345 U.S. 247, 275.

29. The decision on all fours which counsel love to produce with a latent note of triumph, cowing with authority the sceptic on the bench, this buried treasure of the law books, refuses to come forth.—Cardozo: *Growth of the Law*, 98–99.

30. The vigils and the quest yield at most a few remote analogies, which can be turned as easily to the service of one side as to the service of the other.—Cardozo: *ibid.*, 99.

31. A new situation which could not force itself without mutilation into any of the existing moulds.—Cardozo: *ibid.*, 100–101.

32. We stand at the threshold of a previously unopened door. We should pause long before opening it.—Murphy: Associated Press v. United States, 326 U.S. 1, 59.

33. Except for the establishment of general principles, very little aid can be procured from adjudged cases in the construction of wills. It seldom happens that two cases can be found precisely alike. — Washington: Lambert's Lessee v. Paine, 3 Cranch (7 U.S.) 97, 131.

————, inapplicable, obsolete

34. Precedents should be overruled when they become inconsistent with present conditions.—Holmes: *The Common Law*, 126.

35. The official theory is that each new decision follows syllogistically from existing precedents. But just as the clavicle in the cat only tells of the existence of some earlier creature to which a collar-bone was useful, precedents survive in the law long after the use they once served is at an end and the reason for them has been forgotten.—Holmes: *ibid.*, 35.

36. If judges have woefully misinterpreted the *mores* of their day or if the *mores* of their day are no longer those of ours, they ought not to tie, in helpless submission, the hands of their successors.—Cardozo: *Nature of Judicial Process*, 152.

37. Precedents drawn from the days of travel by stage coach do not fit the conditions of travel today.—Cardozo: McPherson v. Buick Mot. Co., 217 N.Y. 382, 391.

38. It is often the practice in Anglo-American jurisprudence to distinguish and qualify precedents, not to overrule them. They slowly become mere ghosts of their former selves, barely clinging to existence.—Douglas: *We the Judges*, 199.

39. Precedent . . . is not lacking for ways by which a judge may recede from a prior opinion that has proven untenable and perhaps misled others. —Jackson: McGrath v. Kristensen, 340 U.S. 162, 177.

40. Their interment is tactfully accomplished, without ceremony, eulogy, or report of their demise. The ground beneath them has been deftly excavated by a soothing process which limits them to their facts, their precise facts, their plain requirements. — Black: Hood v. DuMond, 336 U.S. 525, 555.

41. Overruling a precedent always introduces some confusion and the necessity for it may be unfortunate. But it is as nothing to keeping on our books utterances to which we ourselves will give full faith and credit only if the outcome pleases us.—Jackson: Magnolia Pet. Co. v. Hunt, 320 U.S. 430, 447.

42. The precedent ignored was as mouldy as the grave from which counsel had brought it forth to face the light of a new age.—Cardozo: *Growth of the Law*, 132.

43. Indeed, precisely because I believe that the world would be just as well off if it lived under laws that differed from ours in many ways, and because I believe that the claim of our especial code to respect is simply that it exists, that it is the one to which we have become accustomed, and not that it represents an eternal principle, I am slow to consent to overruling a precedent. — Holmes: "Law in Science and Science in Law," 12 Harv. L. Rev. 460.

————, danger

44. A wrong decision does not end with itself; it is a precedent, and, with the swing of sentiment, its bad influence may run from one extremity

of the arc to the other.—Sutherland: Adkins v. Children's Hosp., 261 U.S. 525, 561.

45. The successive neglect of a series of small distinctions, in the effort to follow precedent, is very liable to end in perverting instruments from their plain meaning.—Holmes: Merrill v. Preston, 135 Mass. 451, 455.

46. There is no more certainty that a last opinion is more correct than the first.—Baldwin: Livingston's Ex'rx v. Story, 11 Pet. (36 U.S.) 351, 400.

47. Anything *bound* might be cited, though wrought through no process more intellectual than the use of paste pot and scissors.—Cardozo: *Growth of the Law*, 13–14.

———, miscellaneous

48. The extent to which judges should feel in duty bound not to innovate is a perennial problem, and the pull of the past is different among different judges as it is in the same judge about different aspects of the past.—Frankfurter: Commissioner of Int. Rev. v. Church, 335 U.S. 632, 677.

49. Today's new decision becomes a coveted anchorage for new vested interests. The former proponents of change acquire an acute conservatism in their new *status quo*. It then takes an oncoming group from a new generation to catch the broader vision which may require the undoing of the work of their predecessors.—Douglas: *We the Judges*, 433.

50. The weights are constantly shifted to restore the equilibrium between precedent and justice. — Cardozo: *Paradoxes*, 30.

51. This is not an area of commercial law in which, presumably individuals may have arranged their affairs in reliance on the expected stability of decision.—Frankfurter: Monroe v. Pape, 365 U.S. 167, 221–22.

See also Constitutional adjudication, stare decisis; Decision 10; Judicial process 9, 14; Law 8, 14; Lawyer 65–67; Supreme Court 67, 68; Tradition 7.

PREFERENCE

Deep-seated preferences can not be argued about. — Holmes: "Natural Law," 32 Harv. L. Rev. 41.

Related subject: Discrimination.

PREJUDICE

1. It is one of many matters on which one must be governed by prejudices—preliminary judgments based on a knowledge admitted not to be exhaustive but on which at the peril of one's soul one has to act as life is short. If we have eternity I suppose it might be our duty to have an articulate answer to every imbecility that can be found from the words in the dictionary. — Holmes: *Uncollected Letters*, 173.

2. The spirit of the age, as it is revealed to each of us, is too often only the spirit of the group in which the accidents of birth or education or occupation or fellowship have given us a place. No effort or revolution of the mind will overthrow utterly and at all times the empire of these subconscious loyalties.—Cardozo: *Nature of Judicial Process*, 175.

346

Related subjects: Bias; Bigotry. *See also* Judge 46; Jury, influences; Majority-minority 11; Race.

PREMEDITATION

The swiftness with which some of the changes followed, permits the inference that they were premeditated. — Cardozo: Globe Woolen Co. v. Utica Gas & Elec. Co., 224 N.Y. 483, 491.

See also Purpose 1.

PREMIUM SYSTEM

The "premium system" is not one of advertising merely. It has other, and, it may be deleterious, consequences.—McKenna: Tanner v. Little, 240 U.S. 369, 384.

PRESCRIPTION (legal)

1. In this country there are few rights founded on prescription. The settlement of our country is comparatively recent, and its rapid growth in population and advance in improvements have prevented, in a great degree, interests from being acquired by i m m e m o r i a l usage. — McLean: Charles River Bridge v. Warren Bridge, 11 Pet. (36 U.S.) 420, 563.

2. Prescription is a thing of policy, growing out of the experience of its necessity.—Fuller: Metcalf v. Watertown, 153 U.S. 671, 674.

Related subjects: Laches; Limitation. *See also* Real Property 1.

PRESIDENT (U.S.)

1. By the Constitution of the United States, the President is invested with certain important political powers, in the exercise of which he is to use his own discretion, and is accountable only to his country in his political character and to his own conscience. —Marshall: Marbury v. Madison, 1 Cranch (5 U.S.) 137, 165–66.

2. The Founders in their wisdom made him [the President] not only the Commander-in-Chief but also the guiding organ in the conduct of our foreign affairs. — Frankfurter: Ludecke v. Watkins, 335 U.S. 160, 173.

3. He heads a political system as well as a legal system. Party loyalties and interests, sometimes more binding than law, extend his effective control into branches of government other than his own and he often may win, as a political leader, what he cannot command under the Constitution. —Jackson: Youngstown Sheet & Tube Co. v. Sawyer, 343 U.S. 579, 654.

4. Executive power has the advantage of concentration in a single head in whose choice the whole Nation has a part, making him the focus of public hopes and expectations. In drama, magnitude and finality his decisions so far overshadow any others that almost alone he fills the public eye and ear. No other personality in public life can begin to compete with him in access to the public mind through modern methods of communications. By his prestige as head of state and his influence upon public opinion he exerts a leverage upon those who are supposed to check and balance his power which often cancels their effectiveness.—Jackson: *ibid.,* 653–54.

5. When the President acts pursuant to an express or implied authori-

zation of Congress, his authority is at its maximum. . . . In these circumstances, and in these only, may he be said (for what it may be worth) to personify the federal sovereignty. —Jackson: *ibid.*, 635–36.

6. In the framework of our Constitution, the President's power to see that the laws are faithfully executed refutes the idea that he is to be a lawmaker. The Constitution limits his functions in the law-making process to the recommending of laws he thinks wise and the vetoing of laws he thinks bad.—Black: *ibid.*, 587.

7. No penance would ever expiate the sin against free government of holding that a President can escape control of executive powers by law through assuming his military role. —Jackson: *ibid.*, 646.

8. The limits of presidential power are obscure.—Clark: *ibid.*, 661.

9. The great office of President is not a weak and powerless one. The President represents the people and is their spokesman in domestic and foreign affairs. The office is respected more than any other in the land. It gives a position of leadership that is unique. The power to formulate policies and mould opinion inheres in the presidency and conditions our national life. — Douglas: *ibid.*, 633.

10. The duty of the President to see that the laws be executed is a duty that does not go beyond the laws.— Holmes: Myers v. United States, 272 U.S. 108, 177.

See also Foreign affairs 2.

PRESS

1. The press in its historic connotation comprehends every sort of publication which affords a vehicle of information and opinion. — Hughes: Lovell v. Griffin, 303 U.S. 444, 452.

2. The daily press first instructed men in their wants, and soon found, that the eagerness of curiosity outstripped the power of gratifying it. —Story: *Misc. Writings*, 7.

3. Nothing can be more notorious than the calumnies and invectives with which the wisest measures and most virtuous characters of the United States have been pursued and traduced [by American newspapers]. — Marshall: Beveridge, *Life of Marshall*, II, 330.

4. You say the papers "have made a great farce" of some of your decisions. I hope that does not mean that they laugh at them, but only that they report them stupidly, which is common.—Holmes: *Uncollected Letters*, 192.

5. Considering the wide circulation of present day newspapers and their power for doing injury to reputation, it is highly important that the ancient doctrine "Whatever a man publishes he publishes at his peril," should be strictly enforced. — McReynolds: Williams v. Vreeland, 250 U.S. 290, 294.

6. Newspapers are conducted by men who are laymen to the law. With too rare exceptions their capacity for misunderstanding the significance of legal events and procedures, not to speak of opinions, is great. But this is

neither remarkable nor peculiar to newsmen. For the law, as lawyers best know, is full of perplexities.—Rutledge: Pennekamp v. Florida, 328 U.S. 331, 371.

7. As the press has business aspects it has no special immunity from laws applicable to business in general.—Douglas: Mabee v. White Plains Pub. Co., 327 U.S. 178, 184.

See also Freedom, press; Trial, influences.

PRESSURE

1. Human nature has not put an impassable barrier between subjection and subserviency, particularly when job security is at stake.—Black: Marcello v. Bonds, 349 U.S. 302, 319.

2. Pressure so effective is equivalent to a command to yield.—Cardozo: People v. Teuscher, 248 N.Y. 454, 463.

Related subjects: Compulsion; Coercion.

See also Supreme Court 53; Tax 33; Trial, influences 24.

PRESUMPTION (legal)

1. A presumption is an inference as to the existence of a fact not actually known, arising from its usual connection with another which is known.—Davis: Home Ins. Co. v. Weide, 11 Wall. (78 U.S.) 438, 441–42.

2. Presumptions are founded upon the experience of human conduct in the course of trade and business, under the promptings of interest or public responsibility. — Bradley: Knickerbocker Life Ins. Co. v. Pendleton, 115 U.S. 339, 345.

3. A presumption is the expression of a process of reasoning.—McKenna: Illinois Cent. R.R. v. ICC, 206 U.S. 441, 459.

4. The inevitable tendency to obscure the result of a truth, when the truth itself is forgotten or ignored, admonishes that the protection of so vital and fundamental a principle as the presumption of innocence be not denied, when requested, to any one accused of crime.—White: Coffin v. United States, 156 U.S. 432, 460.

5. Probable cause cannot be found from submissiveness, and the presumption of innocence is not lost or impaired by neglect to argue with a policeman.—Jackson: United States v. Di Re, 332 U.S. 581, 595.

6. Presumptions of guilt are not lightly to be indulged from mere meetings.—Jackson: *ibid.*, 593.

7. Once the thumbscrew, and the following confession, made conviction easy; but that method was crude and, I suppose, now would be declared unlawful upon some ground. Hereafter, presumption is to lighten the burden of the prosecutor. The victim will be spared the trouble of confessing, and will go to his cell without mutilation or disquieting outcry.—McReynolds: Casey v. United States, 276 U.S. 413, 420.

8. Whilst Rome and the Mediaevalists taught that whenever doubt existed in a criminal case, acquittal must follow, the expounders of the common law, in their devotion to human liberty and individual rights, traced this doctrine of doubt to its true origin, the presumption of innocence, and rested it upon this enduring basis. —White: Coffin v. United States, 156 U.S. 432, 460.

9. The presumption of innocence, deep in our criminal law, has been one of our most important safeguards against oppression. — Douglas: McPhaul v. United States, 364 U.S. 372, 384.

Related subjects: Implication; Inference. *See also* Bail 1; Constitutional adjudication, presumptions; Ignorance 9; Intent 9; Judge 66; Jury 45; Knowledge 6; Principal agent 2; Public official 6, 19; Trial 40.

PRICE

1. The point of most profitable returns marks the equilibrium of social desires, and determines the fair price in the only sense in which I can find meaning in those words.—Holmes: Dr. Miles Medical Co. v. John Park & Sons Co., 220 U.S. 373, 412.

2. We, none of us, can have as much as we want of all the things that we want. Therefore, we have to choose. As soon as the price of something that we want goes above the point at which we are willing to give up other things to have that, we cease to buy it and buy something else. Of course, I am speaking of things that we can get along without.—Holmes: *ibid*.

3. It is reasonable that the public should pay the whole cost of producing what it wants, and a part of that cost is the pain and mutilation incident to production. By throwing that loss upon the employer in the first instance we throw it upon the public in the long run, and that is just. — Holmes: Arizona Copper Co. v. Hammer, 250 U.S. 400, 433.

4. Any change in price of a service or commodity reacts to encourage or discourage its use.—Jackson: Federal Power Comm'n v. Hope Nat. Gas Co., 320 U.S. 591, 653.

Related subjects: Monopoly and related subjects; Public utility; Restraint of trade, price fixing. *See also* Competition 6, 16; Economics 2; Monopoly; Penalty 4, 5; Public utility 3; Reform 8; Tax 17, 18; Value, defined; War, consequences.

PRINCIPAL-AGENT

1. The fiction of identity between principal and agent is used to work out certain liabilities, which it is deemed politic to impose upon the former; but it remains a fiction.—Holmes: Commonwealth v. Mulrey, 170 Mass. 103, 106.

2. Certainly it cannot be laid down as a rule that there is an invariable presumption of rascality as to one's agents in business transactions, and that the degree of watchfulness must be proportioned to that presumption.—Fuller: Briggs v. Spaulding, 141 U.S. 132, 162.

3. Others may divert profits from the business of the principal. He [the agent] may not.—Cardozo: Beatty v. Guggenheim Explor. Co., 225 N.Y. 380, 384.

4. He must stand or fall with those whom he selects to act for him.—Cardozo: People *ex rel*. Price v. Sheffield Farms Co., 225 N.Y. 25, 30.

5. His duty being imperative, he is protected by the command of his superior.—Cardozo: Moore Ice Cream Co. v. Rose, 289 U.S. 373, 381.

Related subject: Master and servant.

PRINCIPLE

1. That the people have an original right to establish, for their future government, such principles, as, in their opinion, shall most conduce to their own happiness is the basis on which the whole American fabric has been erected.—Marshall: Marbury v. Madison, 1 Cranch (5 U.S.) 137, 176.

2. The States are bound by all of those principles of justice which bind individuals to their contracts. — Wayne: Dodge v. Woolsey, 18 How. (59 U.S.) 331, 351.

3. Everywhere the basis of principle is tradition, to such an extent that we even are in danger of making the role of history more important than it is.—Holmes: "The Path of the Law," 10 Harv. L. Rev. 472.

4. No single principle can answer all of life's complexities.—Frankfurter: Minersville School Dist. v. Gobitis, 310 U.S. 586, 594.

5. The natural reluctance of the mind to follow an erroneous principle to its necessary conclusion, and thus to give effect to a grievous wrong arising from the erroneous principle, is an admonition that the principle itself is wrong.—White: Northern Sec. Co. v. United States, 193 U.S. 197, 372.

6. Principles and conduct bear a relation, one to the other.—White: *ibid.*, 397.

Related subjects: Formula; Rule; Standard. *See also* Precedent 8, 17, 20; Technicality 4.

PRIVACY

1. The principles that embody the essence of constitutional liberty and security forbid all invasions on the part of the government and its employees of the sanctity of a man's home, and the privacies of his life.—Harlan: ICC v. Brimson, 154 U.S. 447, 479.

2. The exigencies of trade are not ordinarily expected to have a higher rating constitutionally than the tranquillity of the fireside.—Reed: Breard v. Alexandria, 341 U.S. 622, 627.

3. Surely there is not a constitutional right to force unwilling people to listen.—Frankfurter: Saia v. New York, 334 U.S. 558, 563.

4. The unwilling listener is not like the passer-by who may be offered a pamphlet in the street but cannot be made to take it. In his home or on the street he is practically helpless to escape this interference with his privacy by loud speakers except through the protection of the municipality.—Reed: Kovacs v. Cooper, 336 U.S. 77, 86–87.

5. Science has perfected amplifying and recording devices to become frightening instruments of surveillance and invasion of privacy, whether by the policeman, the blackmailer, or the busybody.—Warren, Reed, Minton: Irvin v. California, 347 U.S. 128, 132.

6. Once privacy is invaded, privacy is gone. — Douglas: Public Util. Comm'n v. Pollak, 343 U.S. 451, 469.

7. The dignity and privacy of the individual were worth more to society than an all-powerful police.—Douglas: United States v. Carignan, 342 U.S. 36, 46.

Related subjects: Constitution (U.S.), Fourth Amendment; Freedom, privacy; Search and seizure; Sound truck; Wire tapping. *See also* Association.

PRIVATE DETECTIVE

1. Private detective agencies are not organs of government. The state is still the primary guardian of the peace and order of its members.—Cardozo: Holmes Elec. Power Co. v. Williams, 228 N.Y. 407, 442.

2. The most exemplary resent having their footsteps dogged by private detectives. All know that men who accept such employment commonly lack fine scruples, often wilfully misrepresent innocent conduct and manufacture charges. — McReynolds: Sinclair v. United States, 279 U.S. 749, 765.

3. Private detectives may use methods to obtain evidence not open to officers of the law.—Warren, Reed, Minton: Irvine v. California, 347 U.S. 128, 136.

PRIVILEGE

1. The privilege must be taken with the limitations placed upon the manner of its exercise.—Day: Stilson v. United States, 250 U.S. 583, 587.

2. The recognition of a privilege does not mean that it is without conditions or exceptions. — C a r d o z o: Clark v. United States, 289 U.S. 1, 13.

3. The privilege takes flight if the relation is abused.—Cardozo: *ibid.*, 15.

4. Being a privilege, it may be lost. —Frankfurter: Nierbo Co. v. Bethlehem Steel Corp., 308 U.S. 165, 168.

5. Whenever the condition is broken, the privilege is lost.—Cardozo: In the Matter of Rouss, 221 N.Y. 81, 84–85.

Related subjects: Constitution, Fifth Amendment; Immunity; Self incrimination. *See also* Citizen; Majority-minority 18; Monopoly 2, 4; Oppression 1; Ownership; Property, attributes; Silence 9; Tax 22, 131.

PROBABLE CAUSE

1. Probable cause does not mean sufficient cause.—Holmes: Burt v. Smith, 293 U.S. 129, 134.

2. One does not speak of probable cause when justification is complete. —Cardozo: Moore Ice Cream Co. v. Rose, 289 U.S. 373, 382.

See also Presumption 5.

PROBATION (legal)

1. Probation is the attempted saving of a man who has taken one wrong step and whom the judge thinks to be a brand who can be plucked from the burning.—Taft: United States v. Murray, 275 U.S. 347, 538.

2. Probation is a system of tutelage. —Roberts: Frad v. Kelly, 302 U.S. 312, 318.

3. Probation or suspension of sentence "comes as an act of grace to one convicted of a crime."—Hughes: Berman v. United States, 302 U.S. 211, 213.

4. Probation is concerned with rehabilitation, not with the determination of guilt.—Hughes: *ibid.*

Related subject: Clemency.

PROCEDURE

See Criminal law; Due process 5; Fiction 2; Litigant 19.

PROCLAMATION

What is a proclamation? It is to cry aloud, publicly to make known. One may proclaim, as of old, by the sound of trumpet, or by voice, or by print or by posting; but not by silence.—Hunt: Lapayre v. United States, 17 Wall. (84 U.S.) 191, 201.

PRODUCTION

1. In an economic sense, production includes all activity directed to increasing the number of scarce economic goods. It is not simply the manual, physical labor involved in changing the form or utility of a tangible article. Such labor is but an integral part of the coordinated productive pattern of modern industrial organizations. Equally a part of that pattern are the administration, management and control of the various physical processes together with the accompanying accounting and clerical activities. — Murphy: Borden Co. v. Borella, 325 U.S. 679, 683.

2. It seems to me that we are so far away in this country, and probably in any country, from satisfying the possible wants of the community, that there is no fear of over-production in its proper sense. It all comes to the question of what people can afford to buy.—Brandeis, Mason, *Brandeis,* 428.

3. A condition might well arise where it might be to my individual benefit to restrict production, but the benefit to labor as a whole would be immensely advanced by increasing production.—Brandeis: *ibid.,* 429.

4. Overproduction was at a point

where free competition had been degraded into anarchy.—Cardozo: Carter v. Carter Coal Co., 298 U.S. 238, 330.

See also Restraint of trade 15; Vendor 2.

PROFIT

1. Popularly speaking, the net receipts of a business are its profits.—Waite: Eyster v. Centennial Bd., 4 Otto (94 U.S.) 500, 503.

2. It is by the average of the year that business commonly reckons its losses and its gains. On the other hand, there may be times when the average must be distributed over periods still longer.—Cardozo: Municipal Gas Co. v. Public Serv. Comm'n, 225 N.Y. 89, 98.

3. Many factors enter to make one kind of enterprise more gainful than another. — Cardozo: S t e w a r t Dry Goods Co. v. Lewis, 294 U.S. 550, 573.

4. When a people is largely engaged in the expansion of business and the accumulation of wealth, attention must be more and more directed to the procedures by which profits may be made and conserved.—Stone: Mason, *Stone,* 209.

5. The goose that lays golden eggs has been considered a most valuable possession. But even more profitable is the privilege of taking the golden eggs laid by somebody else's goose.—Brandeis: *Other People's Money,* 12.

Related subjects: Investment and related subjects. *See also* Conduct 17; Fiduciary 21; Indemnity; Labor 23; Value 30; War 27, 28.

PROGRESS

1. The spirit of internal improve-

ment pervades the whole country.—McLean: Charles River Bridge v. Warren Bridge, 11 Pet. (36 U.S.) 420, 583.

2. The powers thus granted . . . keep pace with the progress of the country, and adapt themselves to the new developments of time and circumstances. They extend from the horse with its rider to the stagecoach, from the sailing vessel to the steamboat, from the coach and the steamboat to the railroad, and from the railroad to the telegraph, as these new agencies are successfully brought into use to meet the demands of increasing population and wealth.—Waite: Pensacola Tel. Co. v. Western Union Tel. Co., 6 Otto (96 U.S.) 1, 9.

3. There must be progress, and if in its march private interests are in the way, they must yield to the good of the community.—McKenna: Hadacheck v. Sebastian, 239 U.S. 394, 410.

4. We read on with a deepening impression of movement from the ancient moorings.—Cardozo: Van Vechten v. American Eagle Fire Ins. Co., 239 N.Y. 303, 306.

5. We must shape our path and our progress by such light as we have.—Cardozo: People ex rel. Alpha Portland Cement Co. v. Knapp, 230 N.Y. 48, 55.

6. In the progress of population, of wealth, and of civilization, new and vicious indulgences spring up, which require restraints that can only be imposed by the legislative power.—McLean: License Cases, 5 How. (46 U.S.) 504, 592.

7. Progress generally begins in skepticism about accepted truths.—Jackson: American Com. Assoc. v. Douds, 339 U.S. 382, 442.

8. When the seas are so boisterous and their perils so insidious, one creeps from cape to cape.—Cardozo: *Law and Literature,* 118.

9. The point of view seems obvious, yet it wins its way slowly, and with hesitant avowal.—Cardozo: *Growth of the Law,* 112.

10. When a college head can seriously suggest, not by way of irony, that soon there will be no need of people being able to read—that illiteracy will be the saving of wasteful labor—one gets an idea of the possibilities of the new barbarism parading as scientific progress.—Frankfurter: Radio Corp. v. United States, 341 U.S. 412, 425.

See also Civilization 5; Commerce 3; Conservatism 1; Democracy 21; Effort 13; Law 42, 43; Patent 6, 18; Science 1, 3; Supreme Court 8; Telegraph; Truth, progress.

PROHIBITION

1. Prohibition stays what is about to be done, but which ought not to be done without it.—Fuller: *Ex parte Cooper,* 143 U.S. 472, 504.

2. The notion that prohibition is any less prohibition when applied to things now thought evil I do not understand.—Holmes: Hammer v. Dagenhart, 247 U.S. 251, 280.

3. A prohibition so indefinite as to be unintelligible is not a prohibition by which conduct can be governed. It is not a rule at all; it is merely

exhortation and entreaty.—Cardozo: Standard Chem. & Metal Corp. v. Waugh Chem. Corp., 231 N.Y. 51, 54.

4. The prohibition must be kept within the limits of common speech and understanding. — Cardozo: City of Rochester v. Rochester Gas & Elec. Corp., 233 N.Y. 39, 53.

5. The command "thou shalt not" is usually rendered as to forbid.—Jackson: Connecticut Light & Power Co. v. Federal Power Comm'n, 324 U.S. 515, 529.

See also Law 4.

PROHIBITION (liquor)

See Constitution, Eighteenth Amendment; Liquor.

PROLIXITY

1. In statutes, as is sometimes the case in legal documents, more words are occasionally used than are necessary to convey the meaning and it may happen that this very excess of verbiage tends to confuse rather than to enlighten. — Peckham: Phoenix Fire & Marine Ins. Co. v. Tennessee, 161 U.S. 174, 176–77.

2. Inveterate, too, has been the habit of inordinate prolixity. From time immemorial judges have struggled fruitlessly against it, offering rewards to brevity and laying burdens on garrulity, but all to small avail.—Cardozo: *Law and Literature,* 151.

See also Lawyer 68.

PROMISE

1. To explain how mankind first learned to promise, we must go to metaphysics, and find out how it ever came to frame a future tense.— —Holmes: *The Common Law,* 251.

2. Our law does not enforce every promise which a man may make.—Holmes: *ibid.,* 253.

3. There is confusion between promise and condition. — Cardozo: Steward Mach. Co. v. Davis, 301 U.S. 548, 595.

4. The peril of perjury and error is latent in the spoken promise.—Cardozo: Burns v. McCormick, 233 N.Y. 230, 234.

5. A promise is not payment unless it would naturally be so regarded in the common speech of men. — Cardozo: Realty Assoc. Sec. Corp. v. O'Connor, 295 U.S. 295, 300.

6. It is a case frequent in all our experience in life, where the promise and the performance are sadly at variance, and suggest those many sayings, some serious and some jocular, which are used to picture the grotesque incongruity so often manifested between the beginning and the end, the proclamation and the act.—Brewer: Chicago, B. & Q. R.R. v. Chicago, 166 U.S. 226, 259.

7. A promise to the ear to be broken to the hope, a teasing illusion like a munificent bequest in a pauper's will. —Jackson: Edwards v. California, 314 U.S. 160, 186.

See also Falsity 10.

PROOF

1. Proof implies persuasion.—Brandeis: St. Louis & O. Ry. v. United States, 279 U.S. 461, 493.

2. But although I cannot prove that

I am awake, I believe that my neighbors exist in the same sense that I do, and if I admit that, it is easy to admit also that I am in the universe, not it in me. — H o l m e s: "Ideals and Doubts," 10 Ill. L. Rev. 2.

3. Persons of speculative minds may in almost every . . . case suggest possibilities of the truth being different from that established by the most convincing proof. — Field: Hopt v. Utah, 120 U.S. 439, 440.

4. The most convincing proof that one believes his statements is to show that they have been true in his experience. Likewise, that one knowingly falsified is best proved by showing that what he said happened never did happen.—Jackson: United States v. Ballard, 322 U.S. 78, 92–93.

See also Conviction; Crime 2; Self incrimination 3; Trial, requirements.

PROPAGANDA

Giving propaganda actually circulated by a party in interest the appearance of being spontaneous declarations of independent groups . . . , though in widespread use among practitioners of the art of public relations, is one which falls far short of the ethical standards generally approved in this country.—Black: Eastern R.R. Pres. Conf. v. Noerr Motor Fr., 365 U.S. 127, 140.

See also Public opinion 8; Teacher 9.

PROPAGATION

See Reform 9; Socialism 3.

PROPERTY

Defined, attributes 1–10; limitations 11–17; regulations 18–23; protection 24–30; miscellaneous 31–36.

Related subjects: Community of property; Community property.

———, defined, attributes

1. What is property? What is the common understanding of the term? It is . . . whatever a person can possess and enjoy by right, and the person who has that right has the property. —Strong: Central Pac. R.R. v. Gallatin, 9 Otto (99 U.S.) 727, 738.

2. Property is everything which has an exchangeable value, and the right of property includes the power to dispose of it according to the will of the owner. — Swayne: Slaughter House Cases, 16 Wall. (83 U.S.) 36, 127.

3. The legal conception of property is of right.—McKenna: Leroy Fibre Co. v. Chicago, M. & St. P. Ry. 232 U.S. 340, 350.

4. Property, which is at first held at the mere pleasure of the chief, acquires a permanency in its tenure, and soon becomes transmissible to the descendants of those, whose enterprise or good fortune has accumulated it. —Story: Misc. Writings, 406.

5. Where a subject, animate or inanimate, which otherwise could not be brought under the control or use of man, is reduced to such control or use by individual labor, a right of property in it is acquired by such labor.—Field: Spring Valley Water Works v. Schottler, 110 U.S. 347, 374.

6. All that is beneficial in property arises from its use, and the fruits of

that use.—Field: Munn v. Illinois, 4 Otto (94 U.S.) 113, 141.

7. The notion of property starts, I suppose, from confirmed possession of a tangible object, and consists in the right to exclude others from interference with the more or less free doing with it as one wills.—Holmes: White-Smith Mus. Pub. Co. v. Apollo Co., 209 U.S. 1, 19.

8. The power of disposition of property is the equivalent of ownership. —Stone: Graves v. Elliott, 307 U.S. 383, 386.

9. The privilege of use is only one attribute, among many, of the bundle of privileges that make up property or ownership.—Cardozo: Henneford v. Silas Mason Co., 300 U.S. 577, 582.

10. All property not public is private.—McLean: West River Bridge v. Dix, 6 How. (47 U.S.) 507, 538.

———, limitations

11. An essential element of individual property is the legal right to exclude others from enjoying it. If the property is private, the right of exclusion may be absolute; if the property is affected with a public interest, the right of exclusion is qualified.—Brandeis: International News Serv. v. Assoc. Press, 248 U.S. 235, 250.

12. Not all economic interests are "property rights"; only those economic advantages are "rights" which have the law back of them.—Jackson: United States v. Willow River Power Co., 324 U.S. 499, 502.

13. Property like every other social institution has a social function to fulfill.—Cardozo: *Nature of Judicial Process,* 87.

14. Depart from the simple requirement of law, that everyone must use his property so as not to injure others, and you pass to refinements and confusing considerations. — McKenna: Leroy Fibre Co. v. Chicago, M. & St. P. Ry., 232 U.S. 340, 350.

15. The rights of one man in the use of his property cannot be limited by the wrongs of another.—McKenna: *ibid.*

16. The property rights of the individual we are to respect, yet we are not to press them to the point at which they threaten the welfare of the security of the many.—Cardozo: *Paradoxes,* 5.

17. All property and all rights, even those of liberty and life, are held to the fundamental condition of being liable to be impaired by providential calamities and national vicissitudes. —Bradley: Legal Tender Cases, 12 Wall. (79 U.S.) 457, 564.

———, regulation

18. It is the province of the legislature to declare, in explicit terms, how far the citizen shall be restrained in the exercise of that power over property which ownership gives.—Marshall: Schooner Paulina's Cargo v. United States, 7 Cranch (11 U.S.) 52, 61.

19. We know that, in the concept of property, there are the rights of its acquisition, disposition, and enjoyment—in a word, dominion over it. Yet all of these rights may be regu-

lated.—McKenna: Hall v. Geiger-Jones Co., 242 U.S. 539, 549.

20. When regulation is transcended and becomes a taking of property may, at times, be a close question; but the power of regulation must not be overlooked or underestimated.—McKenna: Louisville & N. R.R. v. Central Stock Yards Co., 212 U.S. 132, 150.

21. No man liveth unto himself alone, and no man's property is beyond the touch of another's welfare.—Brewer: Budd v. New York, 143 U.S. 517, 549.

22. When property is used to interfere with that fundamental freedom of life for which property is *only a means,* then property must be controlled. . . . It has been a frequent error of our courts that they have made the means an end.—Brandeis: Mason, *Brandeis,* 436.

23. Property, like liberty, though immune under the Constitution from destruction, is not immune from regulation essential for the common good. What that regulation shall be, every generation must work out for itself.—Cardozo: *Nature of Judicial Process,* 87.

———, protection

24. That government can scarcely be deemed to be free where the rights of property are left solely dependent upon the will of a legislative body without any restraint.—Story: Wilkinson v. Leland, 2 Pet. (27 U.S.) 627, 657.

25. Due protection of the rights of property has been regarded as a vital principle of republican institutions.—Harlan: Chicago, B. & Q. R.R. v. Chicago, 166 U.S. 226, 235.

26. Our social system rests largely upon the sanctity of private property; and that state or community which seeks to invade it will soon discover the error in the disaster which follows.—Moody: Mayor of Knoxville v. Knoxville Water Co., 212 U.S. 1, 18.

27. Property is protected because such protection answers a demand of human nature and therefore takes the place of a right.—Holmes: Davis v. Mills, 194 U.S. 451, 457.

28. The security of property, next to personal security against the exactions of government, is of the essence of liberty.—McKenna: Block v. Hirsh, 256 U.S. 135, 165.

29. The conception of property is exclusiveness, the rights of exclusive possession, enjoyment, and disposition. Take away these rights and you take all that there is of property. Take away any of them, force a participation in any of them, and you take property to that extent.—McKenna: United States v. Ohio Oil Co., 234 U.S. 548, 571.

30. One does not lose what is one's own because its utility would be greater if it were awarded to some one else.—Cardozo: Golde Clothes Shop v. Loews Buffalo Theatres, 236 N.Y. 465, 470.

———, miscellaneous

31. Unless all things are held in common, some persons must have

more property than others, it is from the nature of things impossible to uphold freedom of contract and the right of private property without at the same time recognizing as legitimate those inequalities of fortune that are the necessary result of the exercise of those rights.—Pitney: Coppage v. Kansas, 236 U.S. 1, 17.

32. Property has adversaries in this world and different forms excite different degrees of antagonism.—McKenna: United States v. New River Co., 265 U.S. 533, 544.

33. Property can have no more dangerous, even if unwitting, enemy than one who would make its possession a pretext for unequal or exclusive civil rights. — Jackson: Edwards v. California, 314 U.S. 160, 185.

34. The realization of the benefits of property must always depend in large degree on the ability and sagacity of those who employ it.—Hughes: Simpson v. Shepard, 230 U.S. 352, 458.

35. The function of private ownership is to divine in advance the equilibrium of social desires.—Holmes: *Speeches,* 100.

36. It must always be a question of the highest moment, how the property-holding part of the community may be sustained against the inroads of poverty and vice. — Story: *Misc. Writings,* 514.

See also Covenant 3; Insurance 2; Labor 1; Legislature 15; Money 4; Notice 4; Ownership; Patent 1; Possession 1; Rights 7, 19, 40; Roman Catholic Church; Tax 70; Value 6, 9; War 32, 34,

36; Wealth; Will (testament); Wrongdoer 5.

PROPHECY

1. Prophecy, however honest, is generally a poor substitute for experience.—Cardozo: West Ohio Gas Co. v. Public Util. Comm'n, 294 U.S. 79, 82.

2. There are times . . . when resort to prophecy becomes inevitable in default of methods more precise.—Cardozo: *ibid.*

3. Every year if not every day we have to wager our salvation upon some prophecy based upon imperfect knowledge. — Holmes: Abrams v. United States, 250 U.S. 616, 630.

4. The prophecies of evil may be the vain forebodings of timidity.—Cardozo: Municipal Gas Co. v. Public Serv. Comm'n, 225 N.Y. 89, 99.

5. Every dogmatic statement of the law is prophetic of what will happen in a certain event.—Holmes: Druggan v. Anderson, 269 U.S. 36, 39.

6. It was not an unsupported prophecy . . . but rather an endeavor to perform the essential duty of making "an honest and intelligent forecast."—Hughes: St. Joseph Stock Yards Co. v. United States, 298 U.S. 38, 71.

Related subjects: Forecast; Foresight. *See also* Danger 1; Dissent 13; Experience 5; Invention 15; Judgment 1; Law 2; Rights 46; Value 26.

PROPHET

The prophet and the martyr do not see the hooting throng. Their eyes are fixed on the eternities.—Cardozo: *Law and Literature,* 36.

PROPOSITION

1. No concrete proposition is self-evident, no matter how ready we may be to accept it, not even Mr. Herbert Spencer's.—Holmes: "The Path of the Law," 10 Harv. L. Rev. 70.

2. One might also venture on the paradox that by the time that a proposition becomes generally articulate it ceases to be true — because things change about as fast as they are realized.—Holmes: *Uncollected Letters*, 139.

3. It is hard to exhaust the possibilities of a general proposition.—Holmes: Jaster v. Currie, 198 U.S. 144, 148.

4. A proposition may be generally applicable and yet involve embarrassment when pushed to a logical extreme.—McKenna: Davis v. Cleveland, C. & St. L. Ry., 217 U.S. 157, 177.
Related subject: Question. *See also* Extreme 2.

PROPRIETARY MEDICINE

The popularity of a proprietary medicine ... would be an unsafe criterion of its real value, since it is a notorious fact that the extent to which such preparations are sold is very largely dependent upon the liberality with which they are advertised and the attractive manner in which they are put up and exposed to the eye of the purchaser.—Brown: McClain v. Ortmayer, 141 U.S. 419, 428.
Related subject: Medicine.

PROSECUTION

See Criminal law, prosecution; Self incrimination 2, 4, 6.

PROSECUTOR

1. A prosecutor must draw a careful line. On the one hand, he should be fair; he should not seek to arouse passion or engender prejudice. On the other hand, earnestness or even a stirring eloquence cannot convict him of hitting foul blows. — Black: Viereck v. United States, 318 U.S. 236, 253.

2. Our system of criminal justice necessarily depends on "conscience and circumspection in prosecuting officers." — Frankfurter: United States v. Dotterweich, 320 U.S. 277, 285.

3. The United States Attorney is the representative not of an ordinary party in controversy, but of a sovereignty whose obligation to govern impartially is as compelling as its obligation to govern at all; and whose interest, therefore, in a criminal prosecution is not that it shall win a case, but that justice shall be done. While he may strike hard blows, he is not at liberty to strike foul ones.—Sutherland: Berger v. United States, 295 U.S. 78, 88.

4. He is to act impartially, neither presenting from malice nor concealing from favor. One might say the same of any prosecutor.—Cardozo: In the Matter of Richardson, 247 U.S. 401, 412.

5. He is to follow trails of suspicion, to uncover hidden wrongs, to build up a case as a prosecutor builds one. —Cardozo: *ibid.,* 411.

6. Prosecutors seldom fail to stress, if not to exaggerate, the importance of the case before them, to the whole social, if not the cosmic, order.—Jack-

son: Frazier v. United States, 335 U.S. 497, 515.

7. A sturdy, self-respecting democratic community should not put up with lawless police and prosecutors. —Frankfurter: Irvine v. California, 347 U.S. 128, 149.
See also Trial 16, 32.

PROSTITUTE, PROSTITUTION

Prostitution . . . normally suggests sexual relations for hire. But debauchery has no such implied limitation. In common understanding the indulgence which that term suggests may be motivated solely by lust.— Douglas: Cleveland v. United States, 329 U.S. 14, 17.
See also Concubine.

PROTECTION

Protection does not imply the destruction of the protected.—Marshall: Worcester v. Georgia, 6 Pet. (31 U.S.) 515, 552.
Related subjects: Equal protection and related subjects; Freedom, various subdivisions; particular subjects. *See also* Army 2; Citizen; Commerce 5; Constitution, protections; Due process; Freedom 2; Labor 30; Majority-minority, rights; Principal-agent 5; Property, protection; Punishment 12; Redress 4; Rights, protection; Search and seizure 6; Self-defense; Supreme Court, functions; Supreme Court, duty; Tax 61, 147; Trademark 4, 5; Unemployment 5; Vendor 2.

PROTEST

Pious protestations and smug preambles but intensify distrust when men are found busy with schemes to enrich themselves through circumvention. — McKenna: Maple Floor Mfg. Assoc. v. United States, 268 U.S. 563, 587.

PROTESTANT
See Public school 2.

PRUDENCE
Related subjects: Conduct; Negligence; Standard. *See also* Wisdom 2.

PUBLIC (open)
See Trial, requirements; Trial 27.

PUBLIC ACCOUNTANT
Public accountants are public only in the sense that their services are offered to anyone who chooses to employ them. — Cardozo: Ultramares Corp. v. Touche, 255 N.Y. 170, 188.

PUBLIC BUILDING
The necessity of complete jurisdiction over the place which should be selected as the seat of government was obvious to the framers of the Constitution. Unless it were conferred, the deliberations of Congress might in times of excitement be exposed to interruptions without adequate means of protection; its members and the officers of the government be subjected to insult and intimidation, and the public archives be in danger of destruction.—Field: Fort Leavenworth R.R. v. Lowe, 114 U.S. 525, 528–29.

PUBLIC DEBT
No one can be selected which is of more vital interest to the community than this of borrowing money on the credit of the United States. No power has been conferred by the American people on their government, the free and unburdened exercise of which

361

more deeply affects every member of our Republic.—Marshall: Weston v. Charleston, 2 Pet. (27 U.S.) 449, 465.

PUBLIC DOMAIN

The United States is the owner of millions of acres of valuable public land, and has been the owner of much more which it has sold. Some of these lands owe a large part of their value to the forests which grow upon them. These forests are liable to depredations by people living in the neighborhood, known as timber thieves, who make a living by cutting and selling such timber. — Miller: *In re* Neagle, 135 U.S. 1, 65.

PUBLIC EMERGENCY

1. The purge of nation-wide calamity that began in 1929 has taught us many lessons. Not the least is the solidarity of interests that may once have seemed to be divided. Unemployment spreads from state to state, the hinterland now settled that in pioneer days gave an avenue of escape. . . . Spreading from state to state, unemployment is an ill not particular but general, which may be checked, if Congress so determines, by the resources of the nation.—Cardozo: Helvering v. Davis, 301 U.S. 619, 641.

2. The economic emergencies of the past were incidents of scarcity.—Brandeis: New State Ice Co. v. Liebmann, 285 U.S. 262, 305.

> Related subjects: Depression. *See also* Public welfare; Unemployment 4.

PUBLIC EMPLOYMENT

The Constitution does not guarantee public employment.—Frankfurt-

er: Garner v. Board of Pub. Works, 341 U.S. 716, 724.

PUBLIC EXPENDITURE

1. There have been great statesmen in our history who have stood for other views. We will not resurrect the contest. It is now settled by decision. . . . The conception of the spending power advocated by Hamilton and strongly reinforced by Story has prevailed over that of Madison, which has not been lacking in adherents.—Cardozo: Helvering v. Davis, 301 U.S. 619, 640.

2. Public moneys are not appropriated as mere gifts. They are appropriated in recognition and reward of merit or in recompense for service, or reparation for injustice done. — McKenna: McLean v. United States, 226 U.S. 374, 380–81.

3. The responsibility of Congress is to utilize the assets that come into its hands as sovereign in the way it decides is best for the future of the Nation.—Reed: Alabama v. Texas, 347 U.S. 272, 277.

4. The state may pay out tax-raised funds to relieve pauperism, but it may not under our Constitution do so to induce or reward piety. It may spend funds to secure old age against want, but it may not spend funds to secure religion against skepticism. It may compensate individuals for loss of employment, but it cannot compensate them for adherence to a creed.—Jackson: Everson v. Board of Educ., 330 U.S., 1, 25.

5. Many groups have sought aid

from tax funds only to find that it carried political controls with it. — Jackson: *ibid.*, 27–28.

6. The power of the sovereign to attach conditions to its bounty is firmly established.—Clark: Speiser v. Randall, 357 U.S. 513, 541.

See also Public emergency 1; Public welfare; Tax 23.

PUBLIC HEALTH

1. The preservation of public health is a matter of grave and primary concern to the states and the nation at all times, but even more so in time of war. Then indeed a healthy citizenry is essential to national survival.—Murphy: Penn Dairies v. Milk Control Comm'n, 318 U.S. 261, 279.

2. In this country with its heterogeneous population living under diverse conditions in widely separated areas, state and local authorities are best qualified to determine what measures are most appropriate and necessary to promote the health and well-being of the people within their borders.—Murphy: *ibid.*, 280.

Related subject: Health. See also Public use.

PUBLIC INTEREST

1. It must be recognized that public interest is much more likely to be kindled by a controversial event of the day than by a generalization, however penetrating, of the historian or scientist.—Black: Bridges v. California, 314 U.S. 252, 268.

2. With the increasing complexity of society, the public interest tends to become omnipresent; and the prob-

lems presented by new demands for justice cease to be simple.—Brandeis: International News Serv. v. Assoc. Press, 248 U.S. 235, 262.

3. In some degree the public interest is concerned in every transaction between men, the sum of the transactions constituting the activities of life.—McKenna: German Alliance Ins. Co. v. Lewis, 233 U.S. 389, 406.

4. The public interest is a texture of multiple strands. It includes more than contemporary investors and contemporary consumers. The needs to be served are not restricted to immediacy, and social as well as economic costs must be counted.—Frankfurter: Federal Power Comm'n v. Hope Nat. Gas Co., 320 U.S. 591, 627.

5. We are not unmindful of the public interests, of the insistent hope and need that the ways of bribers and corruptionists shall be exposed to an indignant world. — Cardozo: In the Matter of Doyle, 257 N.Y. 244, 268.

———, business

6. In a sense, the public is concerned about all lawful business because it contributes to the prosperity and well-being of the people. . . . But the expression "clothed with a public interest," as applied to a business, means more than that the public welfare is affected by continuity or by the price at which a commodity is sold or a service rendered.—Taft: Wolff Packing Co. v. Court of Ind. Rel., 262 U.S. 522, 536.

7. To say that a business is clothed with a public interest is not to im-

port that the public may take over its entire management and run it at the expense of the owner. The extent to which regulation may reasonably go varies with different kinds of business.—Taft: *ibid.*, 539.

8. The notion that a business is clothed with a public interest and has been devoted to the public use is little more than a fiction intended to beautify what is disagreeable to the sufferers.—Holmes: Tyson v. Banton 273 U.S. 418, 446.

9. The phrase "affected with a public interest" can, in the nature of things, mean no more than that an industry, for adequate reason, is subject to control for the public good.—Roberts: Nebbia v. New York, 291 U.S. 502, 536.

> Related subjects: Labor, public interest; Public welfare. *See also* Court 30; Legislature 6, 7; Life 10; Litigation 11, 12; Patent 5; Property 13; Public utility 8; Railroad 3, 4; State 12; Witness 15.

PUBLICITY

1. The moment publicity is given to affairs of state, they excite everywhere an irresistible interest.—Story: *Misc. Writings, 7.*

2. Publicity is justly commended as a remedy for social and industrial diseases. Sunlight is said to be the best of disinfectants; electric light the most efficient policeman.—Brandeis: *Other People's Money,* 62.

3. Publicity alone may give effective remedy to abuses.—Reed: Valvoline Oil Co. v. United States, 308 U.S. 141, 146.

> *See also* Investigation 4; Judge 23.

PUBLIC OFFICE

1. In this country . . . offices of honor and emolument are commonly more eagerly sought after than shunned. — Bradley: Edwards v. United States, 13 Otto (103 U.S.) 471, 474.

2. Of course, no one has a constitutional right to a government job.—Douglas: J o i n t Anti-Fascist Ref. Comm. v. McGrath, 341 U.S. 123, 182.

3. There can be no dispute about the consequences visited upon a person excluded from public employment on disloyalty grounds. In the view of the community, the stain is a deep one; indeed, it has become a badge of infamy.—Clark: Wieman v. Updegraff, 344 U.S. 183, 190–91.

> Related subject: Public official.

PUBLIC OFFICIAL

> Authority, obligations 1–6; qualifications 7–16; functions, powers 17–20; functions, powers, limitations, 21–24, abuse 25–32; compensation 33–34; criticism 35–37; political contributions 38–39; miscellaneous 40–41.

> Related subjects: Officer; Public office.

———, authority, obligations

1. The genius of the Constitution, and the opinions of the people of the United States, cannot be overruled by those who administer the Government.—Marshall: Beveridge, *Life of Marshall,* II, 329.

2. No man in this country is so high that he is above the law. No officer of the law may set that law at defiance, with impunity. All the officers of the Government, from the highest to the lowest, are creatures of

the law and are bound to obey it. It is the only supreme power in our system of government. — Miller: United States v. Lee, 106 U.S. 196, 220.

3. I have yet to learn that any office is so exalted that its incumbent may be deprived of the privileges or released from the duties of citizenship. —Field: Swisher, *Field,* 315.

4. No man ceases to be a citizen of the United States by being an officer under the State Government.—Bradley: Buffington v. Day, 11 Wall. (78 U.S.) 113, 128.

5. Decency, security, and liberty alike demand that government officials shall be subjected to the same rules of conduct that are commands to the citizen.—Brandeis: Olmstead v. United States, 277 U.S. 438, 485.

6. Every public officer is presumed to act in obedience to his duty, until the contrary is shown.—Story: Martin v. Mott, 12 Wheat (25 U.S.) 19, 32.

————, qualifications

7. All systems of government suppose they are to be administered by men of common sense and common honesty. In our country, as all ultimately depends on the voice of the people, they have it in their power, and it is to be presumed they generally will choose men of this description; but if they will not, the case, to be sure, is without remedy.—Iredell: Fries Case, 9 Fed. Cas. 827 (No. 5126).

8. It is the interest of the State that all places of public trust should be filled by men of capacity and integrity,

and that the appointing power should be shielded from influences which may prevent the best selection; hence the law annuls every contract for procuring the appointment or election of any person to an office.—Grier: Marshall v. Baltimore & O. R.R., 16 How. (57 U.S.) 314, 334.

9. Those should hold office who believe in order and law and property, and the great institutions of society upon which progress and civilization depend.—Field: Swisher, *Field,* 315.

10. The theory of our government is, that all public stations are trusts, and that those clothed with them are to be animated in the discharge of their duties solely by considerations of right, justice and the p u b l i c good. — Swayne: Trist v. Child, 21 Wall. (88 U.S.) 441, 450.

11. A feeling of independence under the law conduces to faithful public service, and nothing tends more to take away this feeling than a dread of dismissal.—Waite: *Ex parte* Curtis, 106 U.S. 371, 373–74.

12. One who holds his office only during the pleasure of another cannot be depended upon to maintain an attitude of independence against the latter's will.—Sutherland: Rathbun v. United States, 295 U.S. 602, 629.

13. Officialdom, however it displays itself, is the husk and that what is precious is the man within.—Cardozo: *Law and Literature,* 189–90.

14. Ignorance of the law is no excuse for men in general. It is less an excuse for men whose special duty is

to apply it, and therefore to know and observe.—Rutledge: Screws v. United States, 325 U. S. 91, 129.

15. Knowledge of a comprehensive law library is unnecessary for officers of the law to know that the right to murder individuals in the course of their duties is unrecognized in this nation.—Murphy: *ibid.,* 136–37.

16. Cabinet officers charged by Congress with adjudicatory functions are not assumed to be flabby creatures any more than judges are. . . . Both are assumed to be men of conscience and intellectual discipline, capable of judging a particular controversy fairly on the basis of its own circumstances.—Frankfurter: United States v. Morgan, 313 U.S. 409, 421.

—————, functions, powers

17. If there is one maxim which necessarily rides over all others, in the practical application of government, it is, that the public functionaries must be left at liberty to exercise the powers which the people have intrusted to them.—Johnson: Anderson v. Dunn, 6 Wheat (19 U.S.) 204, 226.

18. Executive officers who are required to act under the laws, of necessity must give a construction to them. But their construction is not final.—McLean: Cary v. Curtis: 3 How. (44 U.S.) 236, 264.

19. Official bodies would be of no use as instruments of government if they could be prevented from action by the supposition of wrongful action.—McKenna: Lehmann v. State Bd. of Pub. Accts., 263 U.S. 394, 398.

20. The responsibility of those who exercise power in a democratic government is not to reflect inflamed public feeling but to help form its understanding. — Frankfurter: Cooper v. Aaron, 358 U.S. 1, 26.

—————, functions, powers, limitations

21. If there is any fixed star in our constitutional constellation, it is that no official, high or petty, can prescribe what shall be orthodox in politics, nationalism, religion, or other matters of opinion or force citizens to confess by word or act their faith therein.—Jackson: West Va. State Bd. of Educ. v. Barnette, 319 U.S. 624, 642.

22. The philosophy that constitutional limitations and legal restraints upon official action may be brushed aside upon the plea that good, perchance, may follow, finds no countenance in the American system of government.—Sutherland: Jones v. SEC, 298 U.S. 1, 27.

23. The Constitution creates no executive prerogative to dispose of the liberty of the individual. — Hughes: Valentine v. United States, 299 U.S. 5, 9.

24. The Attorney General is certainly not immune from the historic requirements of fairness merely because he acts, however conscientiously, in the name of security.—Frankfurter: Joint Anti-Fascist Ref. Comm. v. McGrath, 341 U.S. 123, 173–74.

———, functions, powers, abuse

25. To the precise extent that the mere will of an official or an official body is permitted to take the place of allowable official discretion or to supplant the standing law as a rule of human conduct, the government ceases to be one of laws and becomes an autocracy. — Sutherland: Jones v. SEC, 298 U.S. 1, 23–24.

26. The larger interests of public justice will not tolerate, under any circumstances, that a public official shall retain any profit or advantage which he may realize through the acquirement of an interest in conflict with his fidelity as an agent.—Lurton: United States v. Carter, 217 U.S. 286, 306.

27. In times gone by, officialdom had arrogated to itself a privilege of indiscriminate inquisition.—Cardozo: People v. Defore, 242 N.Y. 13, 22.

28. The slumbering beast is in us, and may be waked to life and fury if we feed him overmuch. The ravening official will seek to swallow up the man.—Cardozo: *Law and Literature,* 188.

29. One can have an outlook on the law itself which will be the outlook of the drill-master rather than the genuine strategist, the official rather than the man.—Cardozo: *ibid.,* 186.

30. There are village tyrants as well as village Hampdens, but none who acts under color of law is beyond reach of the Constitution.—Jackson: West Va. State Bd. of Educ. v. Barnette, 319 U.S. 624, 638.

31. History shows that all officers tend to be officious.—Douglas: Frank v. Maryland, 359 U.S. 360, 382.

32. We live in an era "when politically controlled officials have grown powerful through an ever increasing series of minor infractions of civil liberties."—Douglas: *ibid.*

———, compensation

33. That we do pay our public servants is not at all inconsistent with the fact that public service in a large measure represents an honest expression of the social conscience. Nor does individual dependence upon remuneration for such services detract at all from the high and uncompromising standards of those who perform public duties.—Black: McDonald v. Comm'r of Int. Rev., 323 U.S. 57, 69–70.

34. Without m o n e t a r y rewards office-holding would necessarily be limited to one class only—the independently wealthy. Proposals to accomplish such a purpose were deliberately rejected at the very beginning of the Nation's history.—Black: *ibid.,* 70.

———, criticism

35. The effective functioning of a free government like ours depends largely on the force of an informed public opinion. This calls for the widest possible understanding of the quality of government service rendered by all elective or appointed public officials or employees. Such an informed understanding depends, of course, on the freedom people have to applaud or to criticize the way public employees do their jobs, from

the least to the most important.—Black: Barr v. Matteo, 360 U.S. 564, 577.

36. Presidents and governors and legislators are political officials traditionally subject to political influence and the rough and tumble of the hustings, who have open to them traditional m e a n s of self-defense.—Frankfurter: Bridges v. California, 314 U.S. 252, 292.

37. Public officers, whose character and conduct remain open to debate and free discussion in the press, find their remedies for false accusations in actions under libel laws.—Hughes: Near v. Minnesota, 283 U.S. 697, 718–19.

See also Communism 9.

————, political contributions

38. If contributions from those in public employment may be solicited by others in official authority, it is easy to see that what begins as a request may end as a demand.... Contributions secured under such circumstances will quite as likely be made to avoid the consequences of the personal displeasure of a superior, as to promote the political views of the contributor; to avoid a discharge from service, not to exercise a political privilege.—Waite: Ex parte Curtis, 106 U.S. 371, 374.

39. If persons in public employ may be called on by those in authority to contribute from their personal income to the expenses of political campaigns, and a refusal may lead to putting good men out of the service, liberal payments may be made the ground of keeping poor ones in.—Waite: ibid., 375.

————, miscellaneous

40. Those to whom the people have committed high trusts, are entitled at least to common courtesy, and are not bound to submit to the insolence or ill temper of those who disregard the decencies of social intercourse.—Grier: Boyden v. Burke, 14 How. (55 U.S.) 575, 583.

41. The serious evils which followed the practice of dismissing civil officers as caprice or interest dictated ... are known to all. It brought the public service to a low estate and caused insistent demand for reform.— McReynolds: Myers v. United States, 272 U.S. 108, 179.

See also Constitution 30; Corruption 2; Freedom 69; Holiday 3; Political party 3; power 14; President; Prosecutor; Punishment 2; Trial 48.

PUBLIC OPINION

1. The good opinion of the people at large must be consulted by their representatives—otherwise mischiefs would be produced which would shake the government to its foundations.—Marshall: Beveridge, Life of Marshall, I, 459.

2. Nothing here can resist the will of the people; and nothing, certainly, ought to resist their deliberate will.—Story: Misc. Writings, 157.

3. Changes may be wrought by public opinion, wherever it shall lead us. They may be sudden, or they may be slow; they may be for the worse, as

well as for the better; they may be the solid growth of a sober review of public principles, and a more enlightened philosophy; or they may be the spurious product of a hasty and ill advised excitement, flying from evils, which it knows and feels, to those far greater, which it sees not, and may never be able to redress.—Story: *ibid*.

4. We need not be told, how often the popular delusions of the day are seized upon, to deprive the best patriots of their just reward, and to secure the triumph of the selfish, the cunning, and the timeserving.—Story: *ibid.,* 158.

5. Since government is not an exact science, prevailing public opinion concerning the evils and the remedy is among the important facts deserving consideration; particularly, when the public conviction is both deep-seated and wide-spread, and has been reached after deliberation. What, at any particular time, is the paramount public need is, necessarily, largely a matter of judgment.—Brandeis: Truax v. Corrigan, 257 U.S. 312, 357.

6. The truth is that public opinion is oftentimes like a pendulum, swinging backward and forward to extreme lengths. We are not unfrequently in danger of becoming purists, instead of wise reformers, in particular directions; and hastily pass inconsiderate laws which overreach the mark they are aimed at, or conflict with rights and privileges that a sober mind would regard as indisputable.—Brad-

ley: *Ex parte* Curtis, 106 U.S. 371, 377-78.

7. The universal sense of a people cannot be accidental; its persistence saves it from the charge of unconsidered impulse. — McKenna: German Alliance Ins. Co. v. Lewis, 233 U.S. 389, 412.

8. Most of the world is in more or less a hypnotic state, and it is comparatively easy to make people believe anything, particularly the right. — Brandeis: Mason, *Brandeis,* 108.

9. The taste of any public is not to be treated with contempt. It is an ultimate fact for the moment, whatever may be our hopes for a change.— Holmes: Bleistein v. Donaldson Co., 188 U.S. 239, 252.

10. That our democracy ultimately rests on public opinion is a platitude of speech but not a commonplace in action. Public opinion is the ultimate reliance of our society only if it be disciplined and responsible. It can be disciplined and responsible only if habits of open-mindedness and of critical inquiry are required in the formative years of our citizens. The process of education has naturally enough been the basis of hope for the endurance of our democracy on the part of all our great leaders, from Thomas Jefferson onwards. — Frankfurter: Wieman v. Updegraff, 344 U.S. 183, 196.

11. The vital test of self-government is not so much its satisfactoriness weighed in the scales of outsiders as it is its satisfactoriness weighed in the scales of "the governed."—Burton: Bute v. Illinois, 333 U.S. 640, 652.

369

12. All the law is a dead letter without public opinion behind it, but law and public opinion interact and they are both capable of being made.— Brandeis: Mason, *Brandeis,* 108.

13. Large and important issues which divide people and heavily implicate their emotions also affect the bench and bar. For judges, lawyers, and jurors are also human.—Douglas: *We the Judges,* 425.

> See also Constitutional adjudication 43; Court, influences; Freedom, press; Government (U.S.) 1; Judge 72; Juror, influences; Law, basis; Law 34; Motion picture 1; President 4; Public official 1, 20, 35; Punishment 32; Supreme Court, operation; Supreme Court, public opinion; War, public opinion.

PUBLIC POLICY

1. The very meaning of public policy is the interest of others than the parties.—Holmes: Beasley v. Texas & Pac. Ry., 191 U.S. 492, 498.

2. The public policy of this state when the legislature acts is what the legislature says that it shall be.—Cardozo: Messersmith v. American Fid. Co., 232 N.Y. 161, 163.

3. The public policy of one generation may not, under changed conditions, be the public policy of another. —Sutherland: Patton v. United States, 281 U.S. 276, 306.

4. The needs of successive generations may make restrictions imperative today which were vain and capricious to the vision of times past.— Cardozo: Klein v. Maravelas, 219 N.Y. 383, 386.

5. The very considerations which the courts most rarely mention, and always with an apology, are the secret root from which the law draws all the juices of life. We mean, of course, considerations of what is expedient for the community concerned. — Holmes: *Uncollected Letters,* 10.

6. Public policy sacrifices the individual to the general good.—Holmes: *The Common Law,* 48.

7. The public policy of the United States is shaped with a view to the benefit of the nation as a whole.— Holmes: Hammer v. Dagenhart, 247 U.S. 251, 281.

> Related subject: Policy. See also Foreign affairs; Legislation, purpose; Progress 2; Res judicata 1; Restraint of trade 2; Rights 27; Supreme Court 52; Trust 3.

PUBLIC SCHOOL

1. The public school is at once the symbol of our democracy and the most pervasive means for promoting our common destiny.—Frankfurter: Illinois v. Board of Educ., 333 U.S. 203, 231.

2. Our public school, if not a product of Protestantism, at least is more consistent with it than with the Catholic culture and scheme of values. It is a relatively recent development dating from about 1840. It is organized on the premises that secular education can be isolated from all religious teaching so that the school can inculcate all needed temporal knowledge and also maintain a strict and lofty neutrality as to religion. — Jackson: Everson v. Board of Educ., 330 U.S. 1, 23–24.

3. The public school was the true

melting pot; and the public school teacher was the leading architect of the new America that was being fashioned.—Douglas: *We the Judges,* 18.

4. The youngsters who came to maturity through our public school system lost their racial identity and became plain Americans, standing on their merits before their fellow men, and winning or losing according to their abilities.—Douglas: *ibid.,* 19.

Related subjects: Education and related subjects.

PUBLIC USE

Public uses are not limited, in the modern view, to matters of mere business necessity and ordinary convenience, but may extend to matters of public health, recreation and enjoyment.—Sanford: Rindge Co. v. Los Angeles Co., 262 U.S. 700, 707.

Related subject: Eminent domain. *See also* Ownership 4; Public interest, business; Public utility; Theater 1.

PUBLIC UTILITY

1. For our society the needs that are met by public utilities are as truly public services as the traditional governmental functions of police and justice. They are not less so when these services are rendered by private enterprise under governmental regulation. — Frankfurter: Federal Power Comm'n v. Hope Nat. Gas Co., 320 U.S. 591, 625.

2. The devotion of their property to the public use does not give to the public an interest in the property, but only in its use.—Pitney: Wilson v. New, 243 U.S. 332, 386.

3. The investor agrees, by embarking capital in a utility, that its charges to the public shall be reasonable. His company is the substitute for the state in the performance of the public service, thus becoming a public servant. —Brandeis: Missouri *ex rel.* S. W. Bell Tel. Co. v. Public Serv. Comm'n, 262 U.S. 276, 290–91.

4. Profits of the past cannot be used to sustain confiscatory rates for the future.—Butler: Board of Pub. Util. Comm'rs v. New York Tel. Co., 271 U.S. 23, 32.

5. Present confiscation is not atoned for by merely holding out the hope of a better life to come.—Cardozo: West Ohio Gas Co. v. Public Util. Comm'n, 294 U.S. 79, 83.

6. Property may be as effectively taken by long-continued and unreasonable delay in putting an end to confiscatory rates as by an express affirmance of them.—Sutherland: Smith v. Illinois Bell Tel. Co., 270 U.S. 587, 591.

7. A public utility (subjected to maximum rates that do not yield a fair return) . . . has no outlet of escape. If it is running its business with reasonable economy, it must break the law or bleed to death.—Cardozo: Hegeman Farms Corp. v. Baldwin, 293 U.S. 163, 171.

8. Controversy with utilities is obviously injurious . . . to the public interest. . . . The community can get efficient service . . . only if managers of the utility are free to devote themselves to problems of operation and of development. It can get ample service through private companies only if in-

vestors may be assured of receiving continuously a fair return upon the investment. — Brandeis: Missouri *ex rel.* S. W. Bell Tel. Co. v. Public Serv. Comm'n, 262 U.S. 276, 308.

9. The slight gain to the consumer, which he would obtain from a reduction in rates charged by public service corporations, is as nothing compared with his share in the ruin which would be brought about by denying to private property its just reward, thus unsettling values and destroying confidence.—Moody: Mayor of Knoxville v. Knoxville Water Co., 212 U.S. 1, 18.

10. If natural gas rates are intelligently to be regulated we must fit our legal principles to the economy of the industry and not try to fit the industry to our books.—Jackson: Federal Power Comm'n v. Hope Nat. Gas Co., 329 U.S. 591, 650.

Related subjects: Depreciation; Going concern; Original cost; Railroad; Valuation.

PUBLIC WELFARE

Concept 1–10; government powers 11–24.

Related subjects: Labor, public interest; Public interest.

———, concept

1. The public welfare is a broad and inclusive concept. The moral, social, economic and physical well-being of the community is one part of it; the political well-being another.—Douglas: Day-Brite Light. v. Missouri, 342 U.S. 421, 424–25.

2. When we consult the common good, we consult our own.—Marshall:

Beveridge, *Life of Marshall,* I, 417.

3. It is among the duties of society to enforce the rights of humanity.—Johnson: Ogden v. Saunders, 12 Wheat. (25 U.S.) 213, 283.

4. Society has an interest in preserving every member of the community from despondency—in relieving him from a hopeless state of prostration, in which he would be useless to himself, his family, and the community.—Johnson: *ibid.*

5. The state still retains an interest in his welfare, however reckless he may be. The whole is no greater than the sum of all the parts, and when the individual health, safety, and welfare are sacrificed, or neglected, the State must suffer. — Brown: Holden v. Hardy, 169 U.S. 366, 397.

6. Justice to the individual is rightly outweighed by the larger interests on the other side of the scales.—Holmes: *The Common Law,* 48.

7. Upon the state falls directly the . . . burden of the demoralization of its citizenry and of the social unrest which attend destitution and the denial of opportunity.—Brandeis: New York Cent. R.R. v. Winfield, 244 U.S. 147, 166.

8. Society needs such a protection as much as the individual; because ultimately society must bear the burden.—Brandeis: *ibid.,* 165.

9. Among the benefits sought by relief is the avoidance of destitution, and of the gathering cloud of evils which beset the worker, his family and the community after wages cease and before destitution begins. —

Stone: Carmichael v. Southern Coal & Coke Co., 301 U.S. 495, 519.

10. The end to be achieved is the quality of men and women.—Cardozo: Adler v. Deegan, 251 N.Y. 467, 484.

————, government powers

11. Peculiar privileges are sometimes vested in the body politic, with the view of advancing convenience and interests of the public.—McLean: West River Bridge v. Dix, 6 How. (47 U.S.) 507, 537.

12. Congress may spend money in aid of the "general welfare." — Cardozo: Helvering v. Davis, 301 U.S. 619, 640.

13. It is too late today for the argument to be heard with tolerance that in a crisis so extreme the use of the moneys of the nation to relieve the unemployed and their dependents is a use for any purpose narrower than the promotion of the general welfare.—Cardozo: Steward Mach. Co. v. Davis, 301 U.S. 548, 586–87.

14. The public welfare cannot override constitutional privileges. — Harlan: Patterson v. Colorado, 205 U.S. 454, 465.

15. We are in danger of forgetting that a strong public welfare to improve the public condition is not enough to warrant achieving the desire by a shorter cut than the constitutional way of paying for the change. —Holmes: Pennsylvania Coal Co. v. Mahon, 260 U.S. 393, 416.

16. The end—to remove conditions leading to ill health, immorality and the deterioration of the race—no one would deny to be within the scope of constitutional legislation. — Holmes: Adkins v. Children's Hosp., 261 U.S. 525, 567.

17. Against that conservatism of the mind which puts to question every new act of regulating legislation, and regards the legislation invalid or dangerous until it has become familiar, government—state and national—has pressed on in the general welfare.— McKenna: German Alliance Ins. Co. v. Lewis, 233 U.S. 389, 409.

18. There has been a growing appreciation of public needs and of the necessity of finding ground for a rational compromise between individual rights and public welfare. — Hughes: Home Build. & Loan Assoc. v. Blaisdell, 290 U.S. 398, 442.

19. Nor is the concept of the general welfare static. Needs that were narrow or parochial a century ago may be interwoven in our day with the well-being of the nation. What is critical or urgent changes with the times.—Cardozo: Helvering v. Davis, 301 U.S. 619, 641.

20. More and more, in its social engineering, the law is looking to cooperative effort by those within an industry as a force for social good. It is harnessing the power that is latent within groups as it is harnessing the power in wind and fall and stream. —Cardozo: People v. Teuscher, 248 N.Y. 454, 463.

21. The good of one generation is not always the good of its successor. —Cardozo: *Growth of the Law*, 84.

22. The theory of the Elizabethan poor laws no longer fits the facts. Recent years, and particularly the past decade, have been marked by a growing recognition that in an industrial society the task of providing assistance to the needy has ceased to be local in character.—Byrnes: Edwards v. California, 314 U.S. 160, 174–75.

23. The community is not bound to provide what is in effect a subsidy for unconscionable employers. The community may direct its lawmaking power to correct the abuse which springs from their selfish disregard of the public interest. — Hughes: West Coast Hotel Co. v. Parrish, 300 U.S. 399, 400.

24. In matters relating to business, finance, industrial and labor conditions, health and the public welfare, great leeway is now granted the legislature, for there is no guarantee in the Constitution that the *status quo* will be preserved against regulation by government.—Douglas: Beauharnais v. Illinois, 343 U.S. 250, 286.

> See also Law 63, 64, 77; Legislation, purpose; Liquor 3; Municipality 5; Opinion 7; Police power 1; Progress 3; Property 16, 19, 23; Public expenditure 3, 4; Public health 2; Real property 2; Rights 32; Sterilization 2; Trust 4.

PUBLIC WORKS

1. The public character of such works cannot be doubted. Where they go they animate the sources of prosperity, and minister to the growth of the cities and towns within the sphere of their influence. — Swayne: Pine Grove Township v. Talcott, 19 Wall. (86 U.S.) 666, 676.

2. Public works usually are of a permanent nature, and that fact leads to a certain degree of association between the notion of permanence and the phrase. But the association is only empirical, not one of logic. Whether a work is public or not does not depend upon its being attached to the soil; if it belongs to the representative of the public, it is public.—Holmes: Title Guar. & Tr. Co. v. Crane Co., 219 U.S. 24, 33.

PUNCTUATION
See Construction, punctuation.

PUNISHMENT
Standards 1–10; purpose 11–18; measure 19–27; cruel and unusual 28–34; dual 35, 36; miscellaneous 37–41.

Related subjects: Constitution, Eighth Amendment; Criminal law; Imprisonment.

———, standards

1. Punishment presupposes an offense, not necessarily an act previously declared criminal, but an act for which retribution is exacted.—Frankfurter: United States v. Lovett, 328 U.S. 303, 324.

2. No one can be allowed to undertake the punishment of wrong-doers according to his own notions; ... the administration of punitive justice for all offenses is confided by the law to certain public officers.—Field: Beckwith v. Bean, 8 Otto (98 U.S.) 266, 301–302.

3. Punishment is not in our days inflicted for the motives for which

lawful acts are done.—Field: Evans v. United States, 153 U.S. 584, 601.

4. A law which punished conduct which would not be blameworthy in the average member of the community would be too severe for that community to bear.—Holmes: *The Common Law,* 50.

5. Theory and fact agree in frequently punishing those who have been guilty of no moral wrong, and who could not be condemned by any standard that did not avowedly disregard the personal peculiarities of the individuals concerned.—Holmes: *ibid.,* 44–45.

6. A man sometimes may be punished where he has brought consequences to pass, although he was not there in person. — Holmes: United States v. Thayer, 209 U.S. 39, 44.

7. The defendants are to be made to suffer not for what the indictment alleges, but for the creed that they avow—a creed that I believe to be the creed of ignorance and immaturity when h o n e s t l y held. — Holmes: Abrams v. United States, 250 U.S. 616, 629.

8. There is certainly nothing anomalous in punishing the crime of murder differently in different jurisdictions.—McKenna: Johnson v. United States, 225 U.S. 405, 417.

9. While the State has the power to punish, the [Eighth] Amendment stands to assure that this power be exercised within the limits of civilized standards. ... The Amendment must draw its meaning from the evolving standards of decency that mark the progress of a maturing society.—Warren: Trop v. Dulles, 356 U.S. 86, 100–101.

10. It is the protection from arbitrary punishments through the right to a judicial trial with all these safeguards which over the years has distinguished America from lands where drum-head courts and other similar "tribunals" deprive the weak and the unorthodox of life, liberty and property without due process of law.—Black: Barenblatt v. United States, 360 U.S. 109, 162.

————, purpose

11. The object of prosecution and punishment is to prevent crime, as well as to vindicate public justice. The fear of it, the anticipation of it, stands between the assassin and his victim like a vindictive shade. It arrests his arm and loosens the dagger from his grasp. — Bradley: Blyew v. United States, 13 Wall. (80 U.S.) 581, 600.

12. Punishment is the means; protection is the end.—Hunt: United States v. Reese, 2 Otto (92 U.S.) 214, 254.

13. The aim of the law is not to punish sins, but is to prevent certain external results.—Holmes: Commonwealth v. Kennedy, 170 Mass. 18, 20.

14. If the typical criminal is a degenerate, bound to swindle or to murder by as deep-seated an organic necessity as that which makes the rattlesnake bite, it is idle to talk of deterring him by the classical method of imprisonment. He must be got rid of; he cannot be improved, or frightened

out of his structural reaction. If, on the other hand, crime, like normal human conduct, is mainly a matter of imitation, punishment fairly may be expected to help to keep it out of fashion. — Holmes: "The Path of the Law," 10 Harv. L. Rev. 470.

15. The punishment of the wrongdoer is not designed as atonement for a crime; it is solace to the individual who has suffered a private wrong.— Cardozo: Loucks v. Standard Oil Co., 224 N.Y. 99, 105.

16. Even if vengeance be forgotten and the social consequences alone considered, there are inhibitions in the threat of punishment that society cannot afford to withdraw from any capable of feeling them. . . . If the ignominy were withdrawn, the horror might be dimmed. — Cardozo: *Law and Literature,* 88, 89.

17. Retribution is no longer the dominant objective of the criminal law. Reformation and rehabilitation of offenders have become important goals of criminal jurisprudence. — Black: Williams v. New York, 337 U.S. 241, 248.

18. The punishment imposed is generally punishment by humiliation and public shame. There is nothing strange or novel about this kind of punishment. It is in fact one of the oldest forms of governmental punishment known to mankind; branding, the pillory, ostracism and subjection to public hatred being but a few examples of it.—Black: Barenblatt v. United States, 360 U.S. 109, 153–54.

———, measure

19. The sanguinary codes, over which humanity wept and philosophy shuddered, have felt the potent energy of reform, and substituted for agonizing terror the gentle spirit of mercy.—Story: *Misc. Writings,* 14.

20. The purpose of punishment is fulfilled, crime is repressed by penalties of just, not tormenting, severity, its repetition is prevented, and hope is given for the reformation of the criminal.—McKenna: Weems v. United States, 217 U.S. 349, 381.

21. All punitive legislation contemplates some relation between guilt and punishment. To inflict the latter where the former does not exist would shock the sense of justice of everyone.— Field: Felton v. United States, 6 Otto (96 U.S.) 699, 703.

22. The punishment adheres to the offense.—Brown: Peoria Gas & Elec. Co. v. Peoria, 200 U.S. 48, 56.

23. The lesser punishments are just as fit for the lesser crimes as the greater for the greater. — Holmes: *The Common Law,* 46.

24. Liability to punishment cannot be finally and absolutely determined by considering the actual personal unworthiness of the criminal alone. That consideration will govern only so far as the public welfare permits or demands.—Holmes: *ibid.,* 49.

25. The deprivation of any rights, civil or political, previously enjoyed, may be punishment.—Field: Cummings v. Missouri, 4 Wall. (71 U.S.) 277, 320.

26. Neither in punishment nor in any form of judging shall we ever rid ourselves altogether of the heartbreaking burden of individual adjustment. —Cardozo: *Law and Literature,* 92.

27. A prevalent modern philosophy of penology that the punishment should fit the offender and not merely the crime. . . . The belief no longer prevails that every offense in a like legal category calls for an identical punishment without regard to the past life and habits of a particular offender.—Black: Williams v. New York, 337 U.S. 241, 247.

———, cruel and unusual

28. Harsh and vindictive punishments have been discountenanced or abolished.—Story: *Misc. Writings,* 14.

29. What constitutes a cruel and unusual punishment has not been exactly decided. It has been said that ordinarily the terms imply something inhuman and barbarous.—McKenna: Weems v. United States, 217 U.S. 349, 368.

30. Undue leniency in one case does not transform a reasonable punishment in another case to a cruel one. —Brewer: Howard v. Fleming, 191 U.S. 126, 136.

31. The word "unusual" must be construed with the word "cruel" and cannot be taken so broadly as to prohibit every humane improvement not previously known.—Holmes: Storti v. Commonwealth, 178 Mass. 549, 553.

32. What punishments shall be considered as infamous may be affected by the changes of public opinion from one age to another.—Gray: *Ex parte* Wilson, 114 U.S. 417, 427.

33. The State may, indeed, make the drinking of one drop of liquor an offense to be punished by imprisonment, but it would be an unheard-of cruelty if it should count the drops in a single glass and make thereby a thousand offenses, and thus extend the punishment for drinking the single glass of liquor to any imprisonment of almost indefinite duration. —Field: O'Neil v. Vermont, 144 U.S. 323, 340.

34. A convict is not to be scourged until the flesh fall from his body and he die under the lash, though he may have committed a hundred offenses, for each of which, separately, a whipping of twenty stripes might be inflicted.—Field: *ibid.,* 364.

———, dual

35. Nothing can be more repugnant or contradictory than two punishments for the same act. It would be a mockery of justice and a reproach to civilization. It would bring our system of government into merited contempt.—McLean: Fox v. Ohio, 5 How. (46 U.S.) 410, 440.

36. To punish the same act by the two governments would violate, not only the common principles of humanity, but would be repugnant to the nature of both governments.—McLean: *ibid.,* 439.

———, miscellaneous

37. The punishment of crimes, at first arbitrary, is gradually moulded into a system, and moderated in its

severity.—Story: *Misc. Writings,* 406.

38. The prisoner pays with his body. —Holmes: *The Common Law,* 41.

39. It is probably true that very often punishment does more harm than good; but the way to remedy that evil is not to set up a lottery in which the party indicated may draw an escape by mere luck.—Holmes: *Uncollected Letters,* 111.

40. Whatever his desert of punishment may be, it is more important to the country and to every citizen that he should not be punished under an illegal sentence, . . . than that he should be punished at all.—Chase: *Ex parte* Milligan, 4 Wall. (71 U.S.) 2, 132.

41. This does not detract from the fullness of my belief that at a day not far remote the teachings of bio-chemists and behaviorists, of psychiatrists and penologists, will transform our whole system of punishment for crime. Vain is the attempt to forecast here and now the lines of the transfigured structure. — Cardozo: *Law and Literature,* 86.

See also Citizen 30, 31, 33; Clemency; Death penalty; Debt 8; Deportation 2; Freedom, thought 155; Lawyer 103; Liability 12; Pardon; Parole; Penalty; Remedy 9.

PURITAN

1. These men and their fellows . . . planted something mightier even than institutions. Whether they knew it or not, they planted the democratic spirit in the heart of man.—Holmes: *Speeches,* 20.

2. Time, the purifier, has burned away what was particular to them and individual, and has left only the type of courage, constancy, devotion —the august figure of the Puritan.— Holmes: *ibid.*

PURPOSE

1. Premeditation implies purpose and purpose is excluded by instantaneous action.—Frankfurter: Fisher v. United States, 328 U.S. 463, 481.

2. If without a word of falsehood, but acting from what we have called disinterested malevolence, a man, by persuasion, should organize and carry into effect a run upon a bank, and ruin it, we cannot doubt that an action would lie.—Holmes: American Bank & Tr. Co. v. Federal Res. Bank, 256 U.S. 350, 358.

3. A change of language is some evidence of purpose. — McKenna: Johnson v. United States, 225 U.S. 405, 415.

4. The sequence of events may help to fix the limits of a purpose that would be obscure if viewed alone.— Cardozo: De Haen v. Rockwood Spr. Co., 258 N.Y. 350, 355.

5. People not of good moral character like others, travel from place to place and change their residence. But to say that because they indulge in illegal or immoral acts, they travel for that purpose, is to emphasize that which is incidental and ignore what is of primary significance.—Roberts: Hansen v. Haff, 291 U.S. 559, 562–63.

See also Coincidence 2; Constitution (U.S.), purpose; Construction, purpose; Zeal 3.

QUAKER

I would suggest that the Quakers have done their share to make the country what it is . . . and I had not supposed hitherto that we regretted our inability to expel them because they believe more than some of us do in the teachings of the Sermon on the Mount. — Holmes: United States v. Schwimmer, 279 U.S. 644, 655.

QUALIFICATION (fitness)

See Citizen 12, 13; Corporation, directors; Judge, qualifications; Jury, qualities; Lawyer, qualifications; Legislature, qualifications; Occupation 6–8, 11; Public official, qualifications.

QUASI

The mere retreat to the qualifying "quasi" is implicit with confession that all recognized classifications have broken down, and "quasi" is a smooth cover which we draw over our confusion as we might use a counterpane to conceal a disordered bed.—Jackson: Federal Trade Comm'n v. Ruberoid Co., 343 U.S. 470, 487–88.

QUESTION

1. To state the question often is to decide it. And it may do this by failure to reveal fully what is at stake.—Rutledge: Yakus v. United States, 321 U.S. 414, 482.

2. When the question is, whether a thing can be done or not, it is always easy to find persons ready to show how not to do it.—Bradley: Webster Loan Co. v. Higgins, 15 Otto (105 U.S.) 580, 586.

3. So-called constitutional questions seem to exercise a mesmeric influ-ence over the popular mind.—Frankfurter: Youngstown Sheet & Tube Co. v. Sawyer, 343 U.S. 579, 594.

4. On the question you ask depends the answer you get. If the problem is conceived of merely as a matter of arithmetic you get an arithmetical answer. — Frankfurter: Bay Ridge Oper. Co. v. Aaron, 334 U.S. 446, 484.

5. Putting the wrong questions is not likely to beget right answers even in law.—Frankfurter: Vanston Bondholders Prot. Comm. v. Green, 329 U.S. 156, 170.

6. Subtle question-begging is nevertheless question-begging. — Frankfurter: Shapiro v. United States, 335 U.S. 1, 51.

Related subjects: Inquiry; Issue; Proposition. *See also* Answer 1; Inquiry 1.

RACE, RACISM

General 1–3; equality 4–16; prejudice 17–22; miscellaneous 23, 24.

Related subjects: Chinese; Japanese; Negro; White person.

———, general

1. The Aryan theory as a racial basis seems to be discredited by most, if not all, modern writers. . . . The term "Aryan" has to do with linguistic, and not at all with physical, characteristics.—Sutherland: United States v. Bhag at Singh Thind, 261 U.S. 204, 210.

2. Manifestly, the test afforded by the mere color of the skin of each individual is impracticable, as that differs greatly among persons of the same race, even among Anglo-Saxons, ranging by imperceptible gradations from

the fair blond to the swarthy brunette, the latter being darker than many of the lighter hued persons of the brown or yellow races.—Sutherland: Ozawa v. United States, 260 U.S. 178, 197.

3. One whose racial origins are so blended as to be not discoverable at sight will often be unaware of them. —Cardozo: Morrison v. California, 291 U.S. 82, 94.

————, equality

4. The supreme law of the land has decreed that no authority shall be exercised in this country upon the basis of discrimination, in respect of civil rights, against freemen and citizens because of their race, color or previous condition of servitude. To that decree . . . every one must bow, whatever may have been, or whatever now are, his individual views as to the wisdom or policy. — Harlan: Civil Rights Cases, 109 U.S. 3, 62.

5. If the Constitutional Amendments be enforced, according to the intent with which, as I conceive, they were adopted, there cannot be in this Republic, any class of human beings in practical subjection to another class, with power in the latter to dole out to the former just such privileges as they may choose to grant.—Harlan: *ibid.,* 62.

6. Today, it is the colored race which is denied, by corporations and individuals wielding public authority, rights fundamental in their freedom and citizenship. At some future time, it may be that some other race will

fall under the ban of race discrimination.—Harlan: *ibid.*

7. Government has nothing to do with social, as distinguished from technically legal, rights of individuals. No government ever has brought or ever can bring its people into social intercourse against their wishes. . . . If one citizen chooses not to hold social intercourse with another, he is not and cannot be made amenable to the law for his conduct in that regard; for even upon grounds of race, no legal right of a citizen is violated by the refusal of others to maintain merely social relations with him.—Harlan: *ibid.,* 59.

8. The Constitution voices its disapproval whenever economic discrimination is applied under authority of law against any race, creed or color. A sound democracy cannot allow such discrimination to go unchallenged.— Murphy: Steele v. Louisville & N. R.R., 323 U.S. 192, 209.

9. That there exists a serious and difficult problem arising from a feeling of race hostility which the law is powerless to control, and to which it must give a measure of consideration, may be freely admitted. But its solution cannot be promoted by depriving citizens of their constitutional rights and privileges.—Day: Buchanan v. Warley, 245 U.S. 60, 80–81.

10. Pressing public necessity may sometimes justify the existence of . . . restrictions; racial antagonism never can. — Black: Korematsu v. United States, 323 U.S. 214, 216.

11. The operation of the Constitu-

tion and laws is not limited by their language or effects to one race. They reach weak and vicious white men as well as weak and vicious black men, and whatever is sinister in their intention, if anything, can be prevented by both races by the exertion of that duty which voluntarily pays taxes and refrains from crime.—McKenna: Williams v. Mississippi, 170 U.S. 213, 222.

12. The denial to appellant of equality of accommodations because of his race would be an invasion of a fundamental individual right which is guaranteed against state action by the Fourteenth Amendment. — Hughes: Mitchell v. United States, 313 U.S. 80, 94.

13. Distinctions between citizens solely because of their ancestry are by their very nature odious to a free people whose institutions are founded upon the doctrine of equality. — Stone: Hirabayashi v. United States, 320 U.S. 81, 100.

14. Local tradition cannot justify failure to comply with the constitutional mandate requiring equal protection of the laws.—Black: Eubanks v. Louisiana, 356 U.S. 584, 588.

15. America today is a multi-racial community. By and large it extends to all lawful inhabitants the same privileges.—Douglas: We the Judges, 412.

16. A nation without race hatred is singularly strong in spirit.—Douglas: ibid., 427.

———, prejudice

17. Persons [Negro and white] be-

tween whom distinctions and prejudices exist to be subdued only by the grave.—Marshall: Beveridge, Life of Marshall, II, 21.

18. The removal of state restrictions will not necessarily abate individual and group predilections, prejudices and choices.—Vinson: McLaurin v. Oklahoma St. Regts., 339 U.S. 637, 641.

19. The anti-Japanese fever which has been evident in California in varying degrees since the turn of the century. . . . That fever, of course, is traceable to the refusal or the inability of certain groups to adjust themselves economically and socially relative to residents of Japanese ancestry.—Murphy: Takahashi v. Fish & Game Comm'n, 334 U.S. 410, 422–23.

20. Racism in America has not been completely eradicated. It is a sturdy pestilence. Racism and intolerance raise their heads repeatedly, not only in America but in every land.—Douglas: We the Judges, 20.

21. Only those lacking responsible humility will have a confident solution for problems as intractable as the frictions attributable to differences of race, color or religion.—Frankfurter: Beauharnais v. Illinois, 343 U.S. 250, 262.

22. If any two subjects are intrinsically incendiary and divisive, they are race and religion.—Jackson: Kunz v. New York, 340 U.S. 290, 313.

———, miscellaneous

23. When any naturally cohesive or artificially organized group possesses a racial or sectarian solidarity which

is or may be exploited to influence public affairs, that group becomes a legitimate subject for public comment.—Jackson: Beauharnais v. Illinois, 343 U.S. 250, 301.

24. In time of war residents having ethnic affiliations with an invading enemy may be a greater source of danger than those of a different ancestry. —Stone: Hirabayashi v. United States, 320 U.S. 81, 101.

> See also Constitution (U.S.), Thirteenth Amendment, Fourteenth Amendment, Fifteenth Amendment; Corporation 15; Deportation 1; Election 14; Equality 12, 13.

RADICAL
See Intolerance 2.

RADIO
1. Wireless is so unconscious a part of us, like the automobile to the modern child, that it is almost impossible to imagine ourselves back into the time when Marconi gave to the world what for us is part of the order of our universe.—Frankfurter: Marconi Wireless Tel. Co. v. United States, 320 U.S. 1, 63.

2. In the dissemination of information and opinion, radio has assumed a position of commanding importance, rivaling the press and the pulpit.—Murphy: National Broadcasting Co. v. United States, 319 U.S. 190, 228.

3. Although radio broadcasting, like the press, is generally conducted on a commercial basis, it is not an ordinary business activity.—Murphy: *ibid.*

4. Radio may readily be a weapon of authority and misrepresentation, instead of a means of entertainment and enlightenment. It may even be an instrument of oppression. — Murphy: *ibid.*

5. Unlike other modes of expression, radio inherently is not available to all. That is its unique characteristic, and that is why, unlike other modes of expression, it is subject to governmental regulation. — Frankfurter: *ibid.*, 226.

6. The right of free speech does not include, however, the right to use the facilities of radio without a license.—Frankfurter: *ibid.*, 227.

7. No doubt the radio enlarges man's horizon. But by making him a captive listener it may make for a spiritual impoverishment. Indiscriminate use of the radio denies him the opportunities for reflection and for satisfying those needs of withdrawal of which silent prayer is only one manifestation. — Frankfurter: Radio Corp. v. United States, 341 U.S. 412, 425.

> See also Freedom 64.

RAILROAD
1. The presence of railroads, and especially of their *termini,* are beneficial to cities by increasing their business and promoting their growth. Such works animate all the sources of local prosperity.—Swayne: James v. Milwaukee, 16 Wall. (83 U.S.) 159, 161.

2. When a railroad is built, it is practically certain that some deaths will ensue, but the builders are not

murderers on that account when the foreseen comes to pass. — Holmes: Southern Pac. Co. v. Berkshire, 254 U.S. 415, 418.

3. A railroad, from its nature and public responsibilities, must be kept a going concern. This is the supreme necessity.—Holmes: Gregg v. Metropolitan Tr. Co., 197 U.S. 183, 196.

4. The state has an interest in seeing to it that railroads shall be run, but an interest also in how they shall be run.—Cardozo: Williams v. Baltimore, 289 U.S. 36, 45.

5. Science has wrought her wonders but the time is not yet here when trains will run under the impulsion of duty without more.—Cardozo: *ibid.,* 44–45

6. The enterprise that is necessary, and is exhibited in the conduct of great railroad systems where traffic is concerned with a continent, is not induced by the altruistic—it is, and naturally must be, prompted by interest.—McKenna: United States v. Southern Pac. Co., 259 U.S. 214, 246.
    Related subjects: Public utility and related subjects. *See also* Labor 73.

RATE REGULATION
Related subjects: Depreciation; Going concern; Original cost; Public utility. *See also* Railroad 5, 6.

REALITY
1. The reality that is absolute and unconditioned may exist, but man must know it, if at all, through its manifestations in the conditioned and relative.—Cardozo: *Growth of the Law,* 46.

2. An old proverb warns us to take heed lest we "walk into a well from looking at the stars."—Jackson: Terminiello v. Chicago, 337 U.S. 1, 14.
    Related subjects: Actuality; Fact. *See also* Court 52; Fate 1; Form 6, 17; Judgment 3; Judicial notice 4; Logic 1; Rule 10; Sentiment 1; Symbol 3; Trial 2.

REAL PROPERTY
1. No class of laws is more universally sanctioned by the practice of nations and the consent of mankind, than laws which give peace and confidence to the actual possessor and tiller of the soil.—Johnson: Hawkins v. Barney's Lessee, 5 Pet. (30 U.S.) 457, 466.

2. The general welfare of society is involved in the security of the titles to real estate and in the public registry of such titles. — White: American Land Co. v. Zeiss, 219 U.S. 47, 60.

3. Nothing so much retards the growth and prosperity of a country as insecurity of titles to real estate. Labor is paralyzed where the enjoyment of its fruits is uncertain.—McLean: Lewis v. Marshall, 5 Pet. (30 U.S.) 470, 477.

4. The situation and productiveness of the soil constitutes the value of the land. — McLean: West River Bridge v. Dix, 6 How. (47 U.S.) 507, 537.

5. A prudent man will not purchase a lawsuit, or risk the loss of his money and labor upon a litigious title. — Grier: Parker v. Overman, 18 How. (59 U.S.) 137, 140.

6. Deep into the soil go the roots of the words in which the rights of the owners of the soil find expression

in the law. — C a r d o z o: Techt v. Hughes, 229 N.Y. 222, 240.

7. Concepts of real property are deeply rooted in state traditions, customs, habits and laws.—Black: Reconstruction Fin. Corp. v. Beaver Co., 328 U.S. 204, 210.

8. Acquisitiveness, which develops a law of real property, is an accomplishment only of the "civilized."—Jackson: Northwestern Shoshone Indians v. United States, 324 U.S. 335, 357.

9. It does not follow that because small parcels of land in the suburbs of a city may be made profitable by cultivation and improvement, therefore the whole suburbs can be turned to account in the same way. . . . Large outlying tracts have to abide the natural growth and spread of the city. They may lie unproductive in the hands of the most provident man for years.—Bradley: New Orleans v. Christmas, 131 U.S. 191, 217.

10. In all ages and climes those who are settled in strategic localities have made the moving world pay dearly. —Black: Northwest Airlines v. Minnesota, 322 U.S. 292, 307.

Related subject: Land.

REASON, REASONING

1. Reason means truth and those who are not governed by it take the chances that some day the sunken fact will rip the bottom out of their boat.—Holmes: *Uncollected Letters,* 140.

2. To reason upon what is reasonable is always uncertain and often mis-

leading. — Clarke: Northern Ohio Trac. & Light Co. v. Ohio, 245 U.S. 574, 592.

3. If we would guide by the light of reason, we must let our minds be bold.—Brandeis: New State Ice Co. v. Liebmann, 285 U.S. 262, 311.

4. While the ramparts of reason have been found to be more fragile than the Age of Enlightenment had supposed, the means for arousing passion and confusing judgment have been reinforced.—Frankfurter: Pennekamp v. Florida, 328 U.S. 331, 357.

5. The balance is swayed, not by gusts of fancy, but by reason.—Cardozo: Growth of the Law, 58.

6. When, by a train of abstract reasoning, we are brought to an absurd conclusion, it behooves us carefully to reconsider the steps by which we have been led up to it.—Bradley: Chicago v. Tebbetts, 14 Otto (104 U.S.) 120, 124.

Related subjects: Mind and related subjects. See also Dictum 2, 3; Freedom 55; Generality 5; Law 22; Power 21; Presumption 3; Rule 14; Test 4; Thought 6; Tradition 8; Whole-part 2.

REASONABLE

1. What is reasonable is a question of practical details, into which fiction cannot enter. — Holmes: Kido v. Alabama, 188 U.S. 730, 733.

2. What would be reasonable in one class of cases would be entirely unreasonable in another. — Bradley: McGahey v. Virginia (*In re* Brown), 135 U.S. 662, 707.

3. Questions of reasonableness are necessarily questions of relation and

degree. — Hughes: Sugar Inst. v. United States, 297 U.S. 553, 600.

4. There is no formula for the determination of reasonableness.—Butler: Go-Bart Imp. Co. v. United States, 282 U.S. 344, 357.

5. "Reasonable"—that irrepressible, vague and delusive standard which at times threatens to engulf the entire law, including the Constitution itself, in a sea of judicial discretion.—Black: Green v. United States, 356 U.S. 165, 197.

See also Art 3.

RECKLESSNESS
See Conduct 10; Deceit 2.

RECRUITING
See Selective service (military).

REDRESS

1. No wrong, real or fancied, carries with it legal warrant to invite as a means of redress the co-operation of a mob, with its accompanying acts of violence.—Brewer: *In re* Debs, 158 U.S. 564, 599.

2. The law will afford redress to a litigant only for injuries which invade his own legal rights.—Sutherland: Baltimore & O. R.R. v. United States, 264 U.S. 258, 273.

3. Redress for public grievances must be sought by public agents, not by private intervention.—Sutherland: *ibid.,* 272.

4. The right to seek redress . . . extends to all whom there was a purpose to protect. — Cardozo: Altz v. Leiberson, 233 N.Y. 16, 19.

Related subject: Remedy. *See also* Litigation, parties; Rights 41.

REFLECTION

Reflection is a slow process. Wisdom, like good wine, requires maturing.—Frankfurter: Kinsella v. Krueger, 351 U.S. 470, 485.

REFORM, REFORMER

1. Under the pressure of temporary evils, or the misguided impulses of party, or plausible alarms for public liberty, it is not difficult to persuade ourselves, that what is established is wrong; that what bounds the popular wishes is oppressive; and that what is untried will give permanent relief and safety. — Story: *Misc. Writings,* 429–30.

2. Innovation is not necessarily improvement; . . . novelty is not necessarily excellence; . . . what was deemed wisdom in former times, is not necessarily folly in ours.—Story: *ibid.,* 18.

3. This very facility of introducing changes should make us more scrupulous in adopting innovations; since they often bring permanent evils in their train, and compensate us only by accidental and temporary good. — Story: *ibid.,* 157.

4. Many were ardently devoted to the cause of reform; but wished to touch gross abuses only, and thus to pave the way for gradual, but solid improvements.—Story: *ibid.,* 53.

5. Behind every scheme to make the world over, lies the question, what kind of a world do you want? — Holmes: *Speeches,* 58.

6. It has become popular to believe that society advantageously may take

its destiny into its own hands—may give a conscious direction to much that heretofore has rested on the assumption that the familiar is the best, or that has been left to the mechanically determined outcome of the co-operation and clash of private effort.— Holmes: *Uncollected Letters*, 138.

7. A first step toward such social control is to take an account of stock and to set a valuation upon what we have.—Holmes: *ibid.*

8. I can understand a man's saying in any case, I want this or that and I am willing to pay the price, if he realizes what the price is. What I most fear is saying the same thing when those who say it do not know and have made no serious effort to find out what it will cost, as I think we in this country are rather inclined to do.— Holmes: *ibid.*, 141.

9. I think it a manifest humbug to suppose that even relative universal bliss is to be reached by tinkering with property or changing forms of government so long as every social improvement is expended in increased and unchecked p r o p a g a t i o n. — Holmes: *ibid.*, 181.

10. Perhaps more is to be apprehended from ungrounded hopes than from criticisms without a fulcrum.— Holmes: *ibid.*, 139.

11. The social reformers of today seem to me so far to forget that we no more can get something for nothing by legislation than we can by mechanics as to be satisfied if the bill to be paid for their improvements is not presented in a lump sum. —

Holmes: "Ideals and Doubts," 10 Ill. L. Rev. 2–3.

12. I think the crowd now has substantially all there is, that the luxuries of the few are a drop in the bucket, and that unless you make war on moderate comfort there is no general economic question. — Holmes: *Holmes-Pollock Letters*, I, 123.

13. Concentration on the basic aims of a reform . . . inevitably overlooks lacunae and the ambiguities which the future reveals and which the future must correct.—Frankfurter: *Ex parte* Republic of Peru, 318 U.S. 578, 596–97.

14. Most even of the enlightened reformers that I hear or read seem to me not to have considered with accuracy the means at our disposal and to become rhetorical just where I want figures. — Holmes: *Uncollected Letters*, 140.

Related subjects: Improvement; Utopia. *See also* Book 3; Criticism 1; Lawyer 71; Punishment 17, 19; Socialism 4–6.

REGULATION

1. Covenants formed and promulgated by a divine wisdom and foresight can have the attribute of immutability, and their language may be used and interpreted to express it. Human regulations are for the most part occasional and temporary.—McKenna: Osborne v. San Diego Land & Town Co., 178 U.S. 22, 38.

2. Regulation and suppression are not the same, either in purpose or result.—Reed: Poulos v. New Hampshire, 345 U.S. 395, 408.

3. The power to regulate implies

the existence, and not the destruction, of the thing to be controlled.—Lamar: Grand T. W. Ry v. South Bend, 227 U.S. 544, 555.

4. Favors from government often carry with them an enhanced measure of regulation.—Jackson: United States v. Morton Salt Co., 338 U.S. 632, 652.

5. The habits and security of life in sparsely settled rural communities, or even in those few cities which a hundred and fifty years ago had a population of a few thousand, cannot be made the basis of a judgment for determining the area of allowable self-protection by present-day industrial communities. — Murphy: Martin v. Struthers, 319 U.S. 141, 152.

> Related subjects: Restraint; Restriction. *See also* Administration; Business 4–6; Competition 7; Conduct 11, 12; Contract 16; Exoneration 1; Freedom, limitations; Freedom, speech, limitations; Legislation 53, 58; Liquor 1, 4; Lottery 3; Occupation 7, 8; Optometry; Police power; Progress 6; Property, regulation; Public utility; Radio 5; Rights 31; Sermon; Tax 2, 10, 144.

RELIGION

Defined 1, 2; belief 3–10; influence 11–14; discrimination 15–17; miscellaneous 18, 19.

> Related subjects: Church; Freedom, religion, belief; Papacy; Pope; Quaker; Roman Catholic Church; Sunday.

———, defined

1. The term "religion" has reference to one's views of his relations to his Creator, and to the obligations they impose of reverence for his being and character, and of obedience to his will.

—Field: Davis v. Beason, 133 U.S. 333, 342.

2. The essence of religion is belief in a relation to God involving duties superior to those arising from any human relation.—Hughes: United States v. Macintosh, 283 U.S. 605, 633–34.

———, belief

3. When dealing with religious scruples we are dealing with an almost numberless variety of doctrines and beliefs entertained with equal sincerity by the particular groups for which they satisfy man's needs in his relation to the mysteries of the universe.—Frankfurter: West Va. State Bd. of Educ. v. Barnette, 319 U.S. 624, 658.

4. If a religious belief has substance, it can survive criticism heated and abusive though it may be, with the aid of truth and reason alone. By the same method those who follow false prophets are exposed.—Murphy: Martin v. Struthers, 319 U.S. 141, 149–50.

5. It is possible to hold a faith with enough confidence to believe that what should be rendered to God does not need to be decided and collected by Caesar.—Jackson: Zorach v. Clauson, 343 U.S. 306, 324–25.

6. All schools of religious thought make enormous assumptions, generally on the basis of revelations authenticated by some sign or miracle. The appeal in such matters is to a very different plane of credulity than is evoked by representations of secular fact in commerce. Some who profess

belief in the Bible read literally what others read as allegory or metaphor, as they read Aesop's fables. Religious symbolism is even used by some with the same mental reservations one has in teaching of Santa Claus or Uncle Sam or Easter bunnies or dispassionate judges.—Jackson: United States v. Ballard, 322 U.S. 78, 94.

7. Scores of sects flourish in this country by teaching what to me are queer notions. It is plain that there is a wide variety in American religious taste.—Jackson: *ibid.*

8. Any inquiry into intellectual honesty in religion raises profound psychological problems. — Jackson: *ibid., 93.*

9. Heresy trials are foreign to our Constitution. Men may believe what they cannot prove. They may not be put to the proof of their religious doctrines or beliefs. Religious experiences which are as real as life to some may be incomprehensible to others. Yet the fact that they may be beyond the ken of mortals does not mean that they can be made suspect before the law.—Douglas: *ibid., 86–87.*

10. A striking picture of a holiness which one loves none the less for disbelieving what it was founded on in the way of beliefs.—Holmes: *Holmes-Pollock Letters,* I ,62.

———, influence

11. The influence of religion upon the human character is one of the most interesting studies in the history of our race.—Story: *Misc. Writings,* 51.

12. Music without sacred music, architecture minus the cathedral, or painting without the scriptural themes would be eccentric and incomplete, even from a secular point of view. Yet the inspirational appeal of religion in these guises is often stronger than a forthright s e r m o n. Certainly a course in English literature that omitted the Bible and other powerful uses of our mother tongue for religious ends would be pretty barren.—Jackson: Illinois v. Board of Educ., 333 U.S. 203, 236.

13. I should suppose it is a proper, if not an indispensable, part of preparation for a worldly life to know the roles that religion and religions have played in the tragic story of mankind. The fact is that, for good or for ill, nearly everything in our culture worth transmitting, everything which gives meaning to life, is saturated with religious influences.—Jackson: *ibid.*

14. It is not theology and ceremonies which keep religion going. Its vitality is in the religious experiences of many people.—Jackson: United States v. Ballard, 322 U.S. 78, 93.

———, discrimination

15. Habits of living or of thought which tend to keep alive differences of origin or to classify men according to their religious beliefs are inconsistent with the American ideal of brotherhood, and are disloyal.—Brandeis: Mason, *Brandeis,* 442.

16. It never occurs to me until after the event that a man I like is a Jew, nor do I care, when I realize it. If I

had to choose I think I would rather see power in the hands of the Jews than in the Catholics—not that I wish to be run by either. — Holmes: *Holmes-Pollock Letters,* II, 8.

17. How it is possible to imagine, that a religion, breathing the spirit of mercy and benevolence, teaching the forgiveness of injuries, the exercise of charity, and the return of good for evil; how it is possible, I say, for such a religion to be so perverted, as to breathe the spirit of slaughter and persecution, of discord and vengeance, for differences of opinion, is a most unaccountable and extraordinary moral phenomenon. — Story: *Misc. Writings,* 61.

———, miscellaneous
18. The hand distribution of religious tracts is an age-old form of missionary evangelism—as old as the history of printing presses. It has been a potent force in various religious movements down through the years. . . . It is more than preaching; it is more than distribution of religious literature. It is a combination of both. Its purpose is as evangelical as the revival meeting.—Douglas: Murdock v. Pennsylvania, 319 U.S. 105, 108–109.

19. Neither at law nor in equity is it written that a license has been granted to religious corporations, by reason of the high purpose of their being, to set covenants at naught. Indeed, if in such matters there can be degrees of obligation, one would suppose that a more sensitive adherence to the demands of plighted faith might

be expected of them than would be looked for of the world at large.—Cardozo: Evangelical Luth. Church v. Sahlem, 254 N.Y. 161, 168.

See also Censor 10; Election 17; Fraud 9; Holiday; Majority-minority 17; Mental healing 2; Nation 14; Practice 5; Public school 2; Race 8, 21, 22; Sermon; Symbol 8; Tax 92; Zealot 2.

REMEDY (legal)
Defined 1–4; function 5, 6; need for 7–10; adaptation, change 11–15; inadequacy 16–20; miscellaneous 21–24.

Related subject: Redress.

———, defined
1. Remedies are the life of rights.—Bradley: Campbell v. Holt, 115 U.S. 620, 631.

2. Inquiry is one thing; remedy another. Adjudication is of no value unless enforcement follows. — Waite: Memphis & C. R.R. v. Tennessee, 11 Otto (101 U.S.) 337, 339.

3. A remedy is only wanted after entreaty is ended. Consequently, that is not a remedy, in the legal sense of the term, which can only be carried into effect by entreaty.—Waite: *ibid.,* 340.

4. Statutory remedies . . . are what the state creating them declares that they shall be.—Cardozo: Sanders v. Armour, 292 U.S. 190, 208.

———, function
5. The remedies of the law are substitutes for violence, not supplements to violence.—Jackson: NLRB v. Indiana & Mich. Elec. Co., 318 U.S. 9, 29.

6. To state the function of the rem-

389

edy is to give the password to its use. —Cardozo: Sinclair Ref. Co. v. Jenkins Pet. Proc. Co., 289 U.S. 689, 693.

———, need for

7. Once a wrong is brought to light. There can be no stopping after that until justice has been done.—Cardozo: Bemis Bro. Bag Co. v. United States, 289 U.S. 28, 36.

8. To assert that he has a right, and yet admit that he has no remedy, appears to me rather paradoxical.—Johnson: Fairfax's Devisee v. Hunter's Lessee, 7 Cranch (11 U.S.) 603, 629.

9. There will be only partial attainment of the ends of public justice unless retribution for the past is added to prevention for the future.—Cardozo: Jones v. SEC, 298 U.S. 1, 30.

10. The effect of the postponement of a remedy would be equivalent to a denial of justice altogether.—Cardozo: Thomann v. Rochester, 256 N.Y. 165, 174.

———, adaptation, change

11. Remedies are necessarily modified by the wants and manners of the community; and processes, which from habit are thought useful and inconvenient in one state of society are rejected as burdensome and injurious in another. — Story: *Misc. Writings,* 419–20.

12. New situations call for new adaptation of judicial remedies. — Frankfurter: Radio Station WOW v. Johnson, 326 U.S. 120, 132.

13. A remedy may . . . be shaped to meet the evil.—Sutherland: Chicago, R. I. & P. Ry. v. United States, 284 U.S. 80, 121.

14. The quality of the remedy is to be determined by the end to be achieved, and not by any label. — Cardozo: Reed v. Allen, 286 U.S. 191, 209.

15. Changes in the form of remedies . . . are retrospective if viewed in relation to the wrongs. They are prospective if viewed in relation to the means of reparation.—Cardozo: In the Matter of Berkovitz v. Arbib & H., 230 N.Y. 261, 270.

———, inadequacy

16. There are many cases, in which the parties are without remedy at law, or in which the remedy is wholly inadequate to the attainment of justice.—Story: *Misc. Writings,* 281.

17. The remedy might bring evils worse than the present disease.— Brandeis: New State Ice Co. v. Liebmann, 285 U.S. 262, 309–10.

18. "The principle of judicial parsimony," if nothing more, condemns a useless remedy.—Cardozo: Sinclair Ref. Co. v. Jenkins Pet. Proc. Co., 289 U.S. 689, 694.

19. The use of a legal remedy devised for a simple situation might in a totally different environment become a perversion of that remedy.— Frankfurter: Mayo v. Lakeland Highlands Can. Co., 309 U.S. 310, 322.

20. Adequate remedies are not likely to be fashioned by those who are not hostile to evils to be remedied.— Frankfurter: United States v. Paramount Pictures, 334 U.S. 131, 180.

———, miscellaneous

21. The first remedy for this situation is to go backward to the place where you lost your way and start on again from that point.—Brandeis: Mason, *Brandeis,* 204.

22. The average and not the exceptional case determines the fitness of the remedy.—Cardozo: In the Matter of Sweeting v. American Knife Co., 226 N.Y. 199, 201.

23. Extraordinary conditions may call for extraordinary remedies.— Hughes: Schechter v. United States, 295 U.S. 495, 528.

24. We are not so provincial as to say that every solution of a problem is wrong because we deal with it otherwise at home.—Cardozo: Loucks v. Standard Oil Co., 224 N.Y. 99, 111.

See also Equity court 25, 26; Force 3; Illegality 1; Judgment 12; Legislation, effectiveness, inadequacies; Litigation 13; Promise 2; Property 12; Publicity 2, 3; Rights 41, 43; Tax 122.

RENT LAW

1. Its [rent law's] only basis is that tenants are more numerous than landlords, and that, in some way, this disproportion, it is assumed, makes a tyranny in the landlord and an oppression to the tenant.—McKenna: Block v. Hirsh, 256 U.S. 135, 161.

2. If the public interest can extend a lease, it can compel a lease; the difference is only in degree and boldness.—McKenna: *ibid.,* 162.

3. If the statute keeps a tenant in, it keeps a tenant out.—McKenna: *ibid.,* 161.

RENUNCIATION
See Rights 22, 23.

REORGANIZATION
See Corporation, reorganization.

REPEAL
See Legislation, repeal; Legislation 68.

REPETITION

1. There is persuasion in the repetition.—McKenna: Standard Parts Co. v. Peck, 264 U.S. 52, 59.

2. Repetition reduces the likelihood of mistake or mere coincidence. —Cardozo: People v. Gerks, 243 N.Y. 166, 170.

3. Judges and lawyers have told each other the contrary so often that they have come to accept it as the gospel truth.—Black: Reina v. United States, 364 U.S. 507, 516.

4. The claim of a dogma solely through reiteration. — Frankfurter: Monroe v. Pape, 365 U.S. 167, 221.

See also Dictum 6; History 8; Word 5.

REPRESENTATION

How easily and insensibly words of hope or expectation are converted by an interested memory into statements of quality and value, when the expectation has b e e n disappointed. — Holmes: Deming v. Darling, 148 Mass. 504, 506.

Related subjects: Falsity and related subjects. See also Tax 49, 50.

REPUBLIC

The foundation of a republic is the virtue of its citizens. They are at once sovereigns and subjects. As the foundation is undermined, the structure is weakened. When it is destroyed the fabric must fall. Such is the voice of universal history.—Swayne: Burke v. Child, 21 Wall. (88 U.S.) 441, 450.

Related subject: Democracy.

REPUTATION

1. Reputation and learning are akin to capital assets, like the good-will of an old partnership. For many, they are the only tools with which to hew a pathway to success. The money spent in acquiring them is well and wisely spent.—Cardozo: Welch v. Helvering, 290 U.S. 111, 115–16.

2. Reputation and character are quite tangible attributes, but there can be no legislative definition of them that can automatically attach to or identify individuals possessing them. —McKenna: Hall v. Geiger-Jones Co., 242 U.S. 539, 553.

3. From time immemorial, one's reputation has been determined in part by the company he keeps.—Minton: Adler v. Board of Educ., 342 U.S. 485, 493.

4. May warrantably believe that a man's job and his educational opportunities and the dignity accorded him may depend as much on the reputation of the racial and religious group to which he willy-nilly belongs, as on his own merits.—Frankfurter: Beauharnais v. Illinois, 343 U.S. 250, 263.

5. Men of good general repute may not deserve it.—Rutledge: Michelson v. United States, 335 U.S. 469, 490.

6. The fair fame of a lawyer, however innocent, is at the mercy of the tongue of ignorance or malice. . . .

Reputation in such a calling is a plant of tender growth, and its bloom, once lost, is not easily restored.—Cardozo: People *ex rel.* Karlin v. Culkin, 248 N.Y. 465, 478.

7. The common law has not grown in the tradition of convicting a man and sending him to prison because he is generally a bad man or generally regarded as one. General bad character, much less general bad reputation, has not yet become a criminal offense in our scheme.—Rutledge: Michelson v. United States, 335 U.S. 469, 489.

8. The record of a conviction for a serious crime is often a lifelong handicap. There are a dozen ways in which even a person who has reformed, never offended again, and constantly endeavored to lead an upright life may be prejudiced thereby. The stain on his reputation may at any time threaten his social standing or affect his job opportunities.—Minton: United States v. Morgan, 346 U.S. 502, 519.

9. A conviction . . . may be accepted as a misfortune or an injustice, and even enhance the standing of one who mends his ways and lives it down.—Jackson: Michelson v. United States, 335 U.S. 469, 481.

10. Even to be acquitted may damage one's good name if the community receives the verdict with a wink and chooses to remember defendant as one who ought to have been convicted.—Jackson: *ibid.*

11. Arrest without more may . . . impair or cloud one's reputation.—

False arrest may do that.—Jackson: *ibid*.

Related subjects: Character; Evidence, character. *See also* Self incrimination 10.

REQUEST

It is an error to suppose that the word "request" necessarily imports an option to refuse, and excludes the idea of obedience as corresponding duty.—Matthews: Colton v. Colton, 127 U.S. 300, 319.

REQUIREMENTS

See particular subjects.

RESCUE

1. Danger invites rescue. The cry of distress is the summons to relief. —Cardozo: Wagner v. International Ry., 252 N.Y. 176, 180.

2. The risk of rescue, if only it be not wanton, is born of the occasion. —Cardozo: *ibid*.

RESISTANCE

See Defense; Duty 4; Supreme Court 66; Violence 1.

RES JUDICATA (legal)

1. This doctrine of res judicata is not a mere matter of practice or procedure inherited from a more technical time than ours. It is a rule of fundamental and substantial justice, "of public policy and of private peace," which should be cordially regarded and enforced.—Clarke: Hart Steel Co. v. Railroad Supply Co., 244 U.S. 294, 299.

2. The doctrine of res judicata demands that a decision made by the highest court, whether it be a determination of a fact or a declaration of a rule of law, shall be accepted as a final disposition of the particular controversy, even if confessedly wrong. — Brandeis: Burnet v. Coronado Oil & Gas Co., 285 U.S. 393, 412.

3. So deeply is this principle implanted in her [Louisiana's] jurisprudence, that commentators upon it have said, the *res judicata* renders white that which is black, and straight that which is crooked. — Campbell: Jeter v. Hewitt, 22 How. (63 U.S.) 352, 364.

4. The weariness of the courts should lead them finally to speak res judicata.—Rutledge: Schneiderman v. United States, 320 U.S. 118, 167.

5. Unless we can say that they were an adjudication of the merits, the doctrine of estoppel by judgment would serve an unjust cause: it would become a device by which a decision not shown to be on the merits would forever foreclose inquiry into the merits.—Douglas: United States v. International Bldg. Co., 345 U.S. 502, 506.

6. It is grounded in the policy that unless a litigant gets a real bite at the apple of discord he should not be foreclosed from another attempt. — Rutledge: Angel v. Bullington, 330 U.S. 183, 207.

7. What was said by the judge in the course of his opinion may be significant as a precedent; it is ineffective as a bar.—Cardozo: Hill v. United States, 298 U.S. 460, 467.

Related subject: Precedent.

RESPECT

RESPONSIBILITY

RESTRAINT

RESTRAINT OF TRADE

———, defined

1. Contracts in restraint of trade are dealt with and defined by the common law. They are contracts with a stranger to the contractor's business (although, in some cases, carrying on a similar one), which wholly or partially restrict the freedom of the contractor in carrying on that business as otherwise he would. . . . Combinations or conspiracies in restraint of trade, on the other hand, were combinations to keep strangers to the agreement out of the business. —Holmes: Northern Sec. Co. v. United States, 193 U.S. 197, 404.

2. There are two principal grounds on which the doctrine is founded, that a contract in restraint of trade is void as against public policy. One is, the injury to the public by being deprived of the restricted party's industry; the other is, the injury to the party himself by being precluded from pursuing his occupation and thus being prevented from supporting himself and his family. — Bradley:

Oregon Steam Nav. Co. v. Winsor, 20 Wall. (87 U.S.) 64, 68.

3. Every exclusive arrangement in the business or commercial field may produce a restraint of trade.—Douglas: Associated Press v. United States, 326 U.S. 1, 23.

4. Monopoly and the acts which produce the same result as monopoly, that is, an undue restraint of the course of trade, all came to be spoken of as, and to be indeed synonymous with, restraint of trade. — White: Standard Oil Co. v. United States, 221 U.S. 1, 61.

5. Restraint may be exerted through force or fraud or agreement. It may be exerted through moral or through legal obligations; through fear or through hope. It may exist although it is not manifested in any overt act, and even though there is no intent to restrain. Words of advice, seemingly innocent and perhaps benevolent, may restrain, when uttered under circumstances that make advice equivalent to command. For the essence of restraint is power; and power may arise merely out of position.—Brandeis: American C. & L. Co. v. United States, 257 U.S. 377, 414.

6. A combination in unreasonable restraint of trade imports an attempt to override normal market conditions.—Holmes: *ibid.,* 412.

7. The evil is in the combination. —Lurton: United States v. Reading Co., 226 U.S. 324, 353.

8. Neither the letter of the law nor its purpose "distinguishes between strangling of commerce which has

been born and preventing the birth of a commerce which does not exist." — McKenna: United States v. United Shoe Mach. Co., 247 U.S. 32, 53.

9. Arrangements or combinations designed to stifle competition cannot be immunized by adopting a membership device accomplishing that purpose.—Black: Associated Press v. United States, 326 U.S. 1, 19.

———, price-fixing

10. The aim and result of every price-fixing agreement, if effective, is the elimination of one form of competition.—Stone: United States v. Trenton Potteries Co., 273 U.S. 392, 397.

11. Ruinous competition, financial disaster, evils of price cutting and the like appear throughout our history as ostensible justifications for price-fixing.—Douglas: United States v. Socony-Vac. Oil Co., 310 U.S. 150, 221.

12. The power to fix prices, whether reasonably exercised or not, involves power to control the market and to fix arbitrary and unreasonable prices.—Stone: United States v. Trenton Potteries Co., 273 U.S. 392, 397.

13. The reasonable price fixed today may through economic and business changes become the unreasonable price of tomorrow.—Stone: *ibid*.

14. Any combination which tampers with price structures is engaged in an unlawful acticity.—Douglas: United States v. Socony-Vac. Oil Co., 310 U.S. 150, 221.

———, miscellaneous

15. General knowledge that there is an accumulation of surplus of any market commodity would undoubtedly tend to diminish production, but the dissemination of that information cannot, in itself, be said to be restraint upon commerce in any legal sense. The manufacturer is free to produce, but prudence and business foresight based on that knowledge influences free choice in favor of more limited production. — Stone: Maple Floor. Mfgrs. Assoc. v. United States, 268 U.S. 563, 583.

16. It is too late in the day to assert against statutes which forbid combinations of competing companies that a particular combination was induced by good intentions and has had some good effect.—McKenna: International Harvester Co. v. Missouri, 234 U.S. 199, 209.

17. If the necessary result is materially to restrain trade between the states, the intent with which the thing was done is of no consequence. But when there is only a probability, the intent to produce consequences may become important.—Lurton: United States v. Reading Co., 226 U.S. 324, 370.

18. To exalt all labor union conduct in restraint of trade above all state control would greatly reduce the traditional powers of states over their domestic economy and might conceivably make it impossible for them to enforce their anti-trade restraint laws.—Black: Giboney v. Em-

pire Storage & Ice Co., 336 U.S. 490, 497.

19. Benefits to organized labor cannot be utilized as a cat's-paw to pull employers' chestnuts out of the antitrust fires.—Jackson: United States v. Women's Sportswear Assoc., 336 U.S. 460, 464.

RESTRICTION
Related subjects: Regulation; Restraint. *See also* Freedom, limitations; Freedom, speech, limitations; Majority-minority 13; Public policy 4; Race 10, 18.

RESULT
1. The result speaks for itself, irrespective of the motive.—Cardozo: Allegheny Col. v. National Chautauqua Co. Bank, 246 N.Y. 369, 375.

2. Of course results are not to be despised. But they are not the only evidence. They are often deceptive—and their absence is by no means conclusive.—Brandeis: Mason, *Brandeis,* 94.
Related subject: Consequence. *See also* Search and seizure 13.

RETIREMENT
When a man has made one outlet his only channel of experience for so many years, and when it is too late to expect to master a new subject and to produce results from it, it seems wise until one is ready for idleness to try to do as much as one can in one's chosen way.—Holmes: *Holmes-Pollock Letters,* I, 205.
See also Liability 4; Vengeance.

REVENUE
Revenue is indispensable to meet the public necessities.—Swayne: Cher-

okee Tobacco v. United States, 11 Wall. (78 U.S.) 616, 627.
See also Fraud 17.

REVOLUTION
1. Our own Government originated in revolution and is legitimate only if overthrow by force may sometimes be justified.—Jackson: American Com. Assoc. v. Douds, 339 U.S. 382, 439.

2. The men who led the struggle forcibly to overthrow lawfully constituted British authority found moral support by asserting a natural law under which their revolution was justified, and they broadly proclaimed these beliefs in the document basic to our freedom.—Jackson: *ibid.*
See also Election 4, 6; Incitement.

RIGHT
1. There can be no more uncertain rule of action than that which is furnished by an intention to do right. How or by whom is the right to be ascertained? What is right in a particular case? ... What is or what may be right depends upon many circumstances. — Hunt: Allen v. Ferguson, 18 Wall. (85 U.S.) 1, 4–5.

2. Right must ... be done as right would be conceived of by men of character and feeling. — Cardozo: Yome v. Gorman, 242 N.Y. 395, 404.
Related subjects: Truth; Wrong. *See also* Distinction 2; Fact 12; Self-righteousness; Settlement; Usage 2.

RIGHTS
Natural 1–5; absolute 6–8; moral 9–11; legal 12–18; constitutional 19–23; vested 24–28; special 29, 30; limitations 31–40;

enforcement 41–44; protection 45–49; miscellaneous 50, 51.

———, natural

1. Individuals are not the creatures of the State, but constitute it. They come into society with rights which cannot be invaded without injustice. —Campbell: Dodge v. Woolsey, 18 How. (59 U.S.) 331, 368.

2. It must be conceded that there are such rights in every free government beyond the control of the State. A government which recognized no such rights, which held the lives, the liberty and the property of its citizens subject at all times to the absolute disposition and unlimited control of even the most democratic depository of power, is after all but a despotism. It is true it is a despotism of the many, of the majority, if you choose to call it so, but it is none the less a despotism. —Miller: Savings & Loan Assoc. v. Topeka, 20 Wall. (87 U.S.) 655, 662.

3. That it [slavery] is contrary to the law of nature will scarcely be denied. That every man has a natural right to the fruits of his own labor, is generally admitted; and that no other person can rightfully deprive him of those fruits and appropriate them against his will, seems to be the necessary result of this admission. —Marshall: The Antelope, 10 Wheat. (23 U.S.) 66, 120.

4. I have always supposed that the gift of life was accompanied with the right to seek and produce food, by which life can be preserved and enjoyed, in all ways not encroaching upon the equal rights of others. I have supposed that the right to take all measures for the support of life, which are innocent in themselves, is an element of that freedom which every American citizen claims as his birthright.—Field: Powell v. Pennsylvania, 127 U.S. 678, 690.

5. There is, of course, a sphere within which the individual may assert the supremacy of his own will, and rightfully dispute the authority of any human government—especially of any free government existing under a written constitution — to interfere with the exercise of that will.—Harlan: Jacobson v. Massachusetts, 197 U.S. 11, 29.

———, absolute

6. It would be idle and trite to say that no right is absolute.—McKenna: Orient Ins. Co. v. Daggs, 172 U.S. 557, 566.

7. Rights, property or otherwise, which are absolute against all the world are certainly rare. — Jackson: United States v. Willow River Power Co., 324 U.S. 499, 510.

8. If different rights are of different extent, if they stand on different grounds of policy and have different histories, it does not follow that because one right is absolute another is. —Holmes: "Law in Science and Science in Law," 12 Harv. L. Rev. 462.

———, moral

9. The true mode of ascertaining a moral right, is to inquire whether it is such as the reason, the cultivated reason of mankind, must necessarily

assent to. — Johnson: Wheaton v. Peters, 8 Pet. (33 U.S.) 591, 672.

10. It is only tautologous to say that the law knows nothing of moral rights unless they are also legal rights.—Holmes: Heard v. Sturgis, 146 Mass. 545, 548.

11. Nothing but confusion of thought can result from assuming that the rights of man in a moral sense are equally rights in the sense of the Constitution and the law.—Holmes: "The Path of the Law," 10 Harv. L. Rev. 460.

———, legal

12. Every right is consequence attached by the law to one or more facts which the law defines.—Holmes: *The Common Law,* 214.

13. A legal right is nothing but a permission to exercise certain natural powers, and upon certain conditions to obtain protection, restitution, or compensation by the aid of the public force. Just so far as the aid of the public force is given a man, he has a legal right, and this right is the same whether his claim is founded in righteousness or iniquity.—Holmes: *ibid.*

14. While there are in some cases legal duties without corresponding rights, we never see a legal right without either a corresponding duty or a compulsion stronger than duty.— Holmes: *Uncollected Letters,* 66.

15. Right and obligation are considered by all ethical writers as correlative terms. — Johnson: Ogden v.

Saunders, 12 Wheat. (25 U.S.) 213, 281–82.

16. A prospective right is not yet a right. It is only an expectation having a certain intensity of reasonableness.—Holmes: Southern Pac. R.R. v. United States, 189 U.S. 447, 450.

17. The matter of amount does not determine the question of right.— Brewer: Gulf, C. & S. F. Ry. v. Ellis, 165 U.S. 150, 153–54.

18. Such words as "right" are a constant solicitation to fallacy.—Holmes: Jackman v. Rosenbaum Co., 260 U.S. 22, 31.

———, constitutional

19. I am yet to learn that the right of liberty of the citizen is not as dear to him, and entitled to be guarded with equal care by the Constitution and laws, as the right of property.— Nelson: *In re* Kaine, 14 How. (55 U.S.) 103, 135.

20. Constitutional rights like others are matters of degree.—Holmes: Martin v. Dist. of Columbia, 205 U.S. 135, 139.

21. Constitutional rights, if they are to be available in time of greatest need, cannot give way to an emergency, however immediate, or justify the sacrifice of private rights secured by the Constitution.—Day: Wilson v. New, 243 U.S. 332, 372.

22. In order to enter into most of the relations of life people have to give up some of their constitutional rights. . . . Some rights, no doubt, a person is not allowed to renounce, but

very many he may.—Holmes: Power Mfg. Co. v. Saunders, 274 U.S. 490, 497.

23. A man may not barter away his life or his freedom, or his substantial rights.—Hunt: Home Ins. Co. v. Morse, 20 Wall. (87 U.S.) 445, 451.

————, vested

24. When I say that a right is vested in a citizen, I mean, that he has the power to do certain actions; or to possess certain things, according to the law of the land.—Chase: Calder v. Bull, 3 Dall. (3 U.S.) 648, 652.

25. There is no technicality about vested rights. Most of them grow out of contracts and, no matter how they arise, they are all equally sacred, equally beyond the reach of legislative interference. — Strong: Sinking Fund Cases, 9 Otto (99 U.S.) 727, 733.

26. A right . . . which is vested in all by the consent of all, can be devested only by consent. — Marshall: The Antelope, 10 Wheat. (23 U.S.) 66, 122.

27. The fundamental public policy is perceived to be that rights lawfully vested shall be everywhere maintained. At least, that is so among the States of the union. Cardozo: Loucks v. Standard Oil Co., 224 N.Y. 99, 113.

28. There is no such thing as a vested right to do wrong. — Pitney: Johannessen v. United States, 225 U.S. 227, 242 (quot. 16 Mass. 273).

————, special

29. Wherever the law gives any one special rights not shared by the body of the people, it does so on the ground that certain special facts, not true of the rest of the world, are true of him. —Holmes: *The Common Law,* 214.

30. A large part of the advantages enjoyed by one who has a right are not created by the law. . . . What the law does is simply to prevent other men to a greater or less extent from interfering with my use or abuse.—Holmes: *ibid.,* 220.

————, limitations

31. When men form a social compact, and organize a civil government, they necessarily surrender the regulation and control of these natural rights and obligations into the hands of the government.—Trimble: Ogden v. Saunders, 12 Wheat. (25 U.S.) 213, 319.

32. The rights of all must be held and enjoyed in subserviency to the good of the whole.—Johnson: *ibid.,* 282.

33. Society based on the rule that each one is a law unto himself would soon be confronted with disorder and anarchy. Real liberty for all could not exist under the operation of a principle which recognizes the right of each individual person to use his own, whether in respect of his person or his property, regardless of the injury that may be done to others.—Harlan: Jacobson v. Massachusetts, 197 U.S. 11, 26.

34. Every member of a political community must necessarily part with some of the rights which, as an individual, not affected by his relation to

others, he might have retained. Such concessions make up the consideration he gives for the obligation of the body politic to protect him in life, liberty, and property. — Waite: Canada Southern Ry. v. Gebhard, 109 U.S. 527, 536.

35. While the rights of private property are sacredly guarded, we must not forget that the community also have rights, and that the happiness and well being of every citizen depends on their faithful preservation. —Taney: Charles River Bridge v. Warren Bridge, 11 Pet. (36 U.S.) 420, 548.

36. All rights are derived from the purposes of the society in which they exist; above all rights rises duty to the community. — Brandeis: Duplex P. P. Co. v. Deering, 254 U.S. 443, 488.

37. Every man has a right to do what he wills, provided he interferes not with a like right on the part of his neighbor.—Holmes: "The Path of the Law," 10 Harv. L. Rev. 466.

38. No civilized government sacrifices the citizen more than it can help, but still sacrificing his will and his welfare to that of the rest. — Holmes: *The Common Law*, 43.

39. Those correlative rights, that of the citizen to exercise exclusive dominion over property and freely to contract about his affairs, and that of the state to regulate the use of property and the conduct of business, are always in collision.—Roberts: Nebbia v. New York, 291 U.S. 502, 524.

40. When we balance the Constitutional rights of owners of property against those of the people to enjoy freedom of press and religion, . . . we remain mindful of the fact that the latter occupy a preferred position. —Black: Marsh v. Alabama, 326 U.S. 501, 509.

——, enforcement

41. The distinction between rights and remedies is fundamental. A right is a well-founded or acknowledged claim; a remedy is the means employed to enforce a right or redress an injury. — McReynolds: Chelentis v. Luckenbach S.S. Co., 247 U.S. 372, 384.

42. Religious animosities, political controversies, antagonisms of race and a multitude of other causes will always operate, in a greater or less degree, as impediments to the full enjoyment and enforcement of civil rights.—Field: Virginia v. Rives, 10 Otto (100 U.S.) 313, 332–33.

43. To take away all remedy for the enforcement of a right is to take away the right itself.—Matthews: Virginia Coupon Cases, 114 U.S. 270, 303.

44. To enforce one's rights when they are violated is never a legal wrong, and may often be a moral duty. It happens in many instances that the violation passes with no effort to redress it—sometimes from mere inertia. But the law, which creates a right, can certainly not concede that an insistence upon its enforcement is evidence of a wrong.—Cardozo Morningstar v. Lafayette Hotel Co., 211 N.Y. 465, 468.

———, protection

45. By the protection of the law human rights are secured; withdraw that protection, and they are at the mercy of wicked rulers, or the clamor of an excited people.—Davis: *Ex parte Milligan*, 4 Wall. (71 U.S.) 2, 119.

46. For legal purposes a right is only the hypostasis of a prophecy— the imagination of a substance supporting the fact that the public force will be brought to bear upon those who do things said to contravene it. —Holmes: "Natural Law," 32 Harv. L. Rev. 42.

47. Under a constitutional system of government, all rights, in their last analysis, are referable to the safeguards of the Constitution.—White: Apapas v. United States, 233 U.S. 587, 591.

48. The strength and vitality of civil rights . . . is perhaps the tenacity with which the community defends them, the care with which local governments foster and protect them.—Douglas: *We the Judges*, 425.

49. The less legal rights depend on someone's state of mind, the better. —Jackson: Mercoid Corp. v. Mid-Cont. Inv. Co., 320 U.S. 661, 680.

———, miscellaneous

50. Rights must be judged in their context and not *in vacuo*.—Frankfurter: Bridges v. California, 314 U.S. 252, 303.

51. That a government cannot be too liberal in extending to individuals the right of using their talents and seeking their fortunes wherever their judgments may lead them, I readily agree.—Johnson: Shanks v. Dupont, 3 Pet. (28 U.S.) 242, 258.

See also Corporation, rights; Duty 14; Equality 22; Equal protection 8; Equity 6; Fiction 6; Formula 6, 10; Ignorance 11; Illegality 1; Labor, employee; Law 72; Legislature 15; Life 1; Litigation 12; Majority-minority, rights; Monopoly 1; Ownership; Power 19, 20; Property, defined; Race; Remedy 1, 8; Rule 9; Tax 28, 76; Trial 10; Value 27; Whole-part 4; Wrongdoer 3; Zeal 2, 4.

RISK

1. We may say, that that, which generally works well, should rarely be hazarded upon the chances of a better.—Story: *Misc. Writings*, 448.

2. He takes the risk of the dispute. He must abide by the outcome.— Cardozo: Title Guar. Tr. Co. v. Pam, 232 N.Y. 441, 458.

3. Casual and irregular is the risk of the belated traveler, hurrying to his home.—Cardozo: In the Matter of Heidemann v. Am. Dist. Tel. Co., 230 N.Y. 305, 308.

4. The risk reasonably to be perceived defines the duty to be obeyed, —Cardozo: Palsgraf v. Long Island Ry., 248 N.Y. 339, 344.

Related subjects: Gamble and related subjects. See also Contract 14; Insurance 6; Rescue 2; Seaman 11; Standard 6; Vigilance 2.

RIVER

1. A river is more than an amenity, it is a treasure. It offers a necessity of life that must be rationed among those who have power over it.—Holmes: New Jersey v. New York, 283 U.S. 336, 342.

2. There are benefits from a great river that might escape a lawyer's view.—Holmes: Hudson Co. Water Co. v. McCarter, 209 U.S. 349, 357.

ROMAN CATHOLIC CHURCH

1. The corporate existence of the Roman Catholic Church, as well as the position occupied by the papacy, have always been recognized by the government of the United States.— Fuller: Municipality of Ponce v. Roman Catholic Church, 210 U.S. 296, 318.

2. The Roman Catholic Church has been recognized as possessing a legal personality and the capacity to take and acquire property since the time of the Emperor Constantine.—Fuller: *ibid.*, 311.

3. It is no exaggeration to say that the whole historic conflict in temporal policy between the Catholic Church and non-Catholics comes to a focus in their respective school policies. — Jackson: Everson v. Board of Educ., 330 U.S. 1, 23.

Related subjects: Papacy; Pope.

RULE (legal)

1. Every system of law has within it artificial devices which are deemed in the main and on the average to promote convenience or security or other forms of public good. These devices take the form of rules or standards to which the individual though he be careless or ignorant, must at his peril conform.—Cardozo: *Paradoxes,* 68.

2. The suspension of all principle and rule and the substitution of senti-

ment or unregulated benevolence . . . pushed to an extreme, is the negation of all law.—Cardozo: *ibid.*

3. The mind submits reluctantly to the rule of law, and laboriously searches for something which shall reconcile that rule with what would seem to be the dictate of abstract justice.—Marshall: Hannay v. Eve, 3 Cranch (7 U.S.) 242, 247.

4. The rules . . . of all substantial law, must widen with the wants of society; . . . they must have flexibility, as well as strength; . . . they must accomplish the ends of justice, and not bury it beneath the pressure of their own weight.—Story: *Misc. Writings,* 210.

5. Precision and certainty are often of more importance to the rules of law than their abstract justice.—Johnson: M'Gruder v. Bank of Washington, 9 Wheat. (22 U.S.) 598, 602.

6. As necessity creates the rule, so it limits its duration.—Davis: *Ex parte* Milligan, 4 Wall. (71 U.S.) 2, 127.

7. As the rules of law are or should be based upon a morality which is generally accepted, no rule founded on a theory of absolute unselfishness can be laid down without a breach between law and working beliefs.— Holmes: *The Common Law,* 44.

8. Few rules in our time are so well established that they may not be called upon any day to justify their existence as means adapted to an end. If they do not function, they are diseased. If they are diseased, they must not propagate their kind.—Cardozo: *Nature of Judicial Process,* 98.

9. At times, the rule, though wrong, has become the cornerstone of past transactions. Men have accepted it as law, and have acted on the faith of it. At least, the possibility that some have done so, makes change unjust, if it were practicable, without saving vested rights.—Cardozo: *Law and Literature, 53.*

10. The rule that is rooted in identities or analogies of customary belief and practice is felt and rightly felt to be rooted in reality. — Cardozo: *ibid.,* 19.

11. My experience as a judge in other fields of law has made me distrustful of rules of thumb generally. They are a lazy man's expedient for ridding himself of the trouble of thinking and deciding. — Cardozo: *ibid.,* 92.

12. The operation of a general rule will seldom be the same for every one.—Cardozo: Fox v. Standard Oil Co., 294 U.S. 79, 102.

13. Rules are not made solely for the easiest cases they govern.—Frankfurter: Staub v. Bailey, 355 U.S. 313, 333.

14. The reason for the rule is not clarified much by the Latin phrases in which it is sometimes clothed.—Moody: Standard Oil Co. v. Anderson, 212 U.S. 215, 220.

See also Conduct 13; Construction, rules; Definition 3; Evidence, rules; Freedom 89; Government (U.S.) 5; Labor 113; Law 39, 40; Lawyer 42, 43; Motor Vehicle 9; Res judicata; Right 1; Tax 38; War, rules.

————, exception

15. An exception to a rule is said to prove the existence of the rule.— McLean: Groves v. Slaughter, 15 Pet. (40 U.S.) 449, 505.

16. There is the exception, almost as well settled as the rule, and courts and lawyers finding the law to be established proceed to account for it by consulting their wits. — Holmes: "Law in Science and Science in Law," 12 Harv. L. Rev. 453.

17. It is not a case where an exception can prove the rule; it is one where the exception destroys the rule. —McKenna: De Lima v. Bidwell, 182 U.S. 1, 211.

18. The exception which exhausts the principal rule must be incorrect, if the rule itself be admitted as a correct one.—Johnson: The Atalanta, 3 Wheat. (16 U.S.) 409, 426.

RULE OF THUMB
See Rule 11.

SACRIFICE
Others may think that high and unselfish sacrifice is cheapened when repaid in money.—Cardozo: People v. Westchester Co. Nat'l Bank, 231 N.Y. 465, 489.
See also Sale; War, consequences.

SACRILEGIOUS
See Censor 6.

SAFEGUARD
1. Safeguards . . . have at times an aspect of triviality when our scrutiny is narrowed to one instance or another. Their value is perceived when

the outlook is extended to something wider than particulars. — Cardozo: People *ex rel.* Fordham M. R. Church v. Walsh, 244 N.Y. 280, 290–91.

2. It cannot be that the safeguards of the person, so often and so rightly mentioned with solemn reverence, are less than those that protect from a liability in debt. — Holmes: United States v. Oppenheimer, 242 U.S. 85, 87.

See also Self incrimination 9; Zealot 1.

SAFETY

1. What is safe, is not always expedient.—Story: *Misc. Writings,* 157.

2. Somewhere between worship of the past and exaltation of the present, the path of safety will be found.— Cardozo: *Nature of Judicial Process,* 160.

See also Ignorance; Virtue 4.

SAGACITY

See Incompetence.

SALE

In business life, forced sales for cash are such a last resort for obtaining money that a sale "under the hammer" is synonymous with a sale at a sacrifice. — Clarke: Geddes v. Anaconda Copper Min. Co., 254 U.S. 590, 602.

See also Competition 9; Market; Tax 6.

SALUTE

See Flag 8.

SCEPTICISM

See Progress 7; Science 5; Speculation (conjecture).

SCHOOL

1. A school system producing stu-

dents trained as robots threatens to rob a generation of the versatility that has been perhaps our greatest distinction. — Douglas: Adler v. Board of Educ., 342 U.S. 485, 511.

2. The vigilant protection of constitutional freedoms is nowhere more vital than in the community of American schools. — Stewart: Shelton v. Tucker, 364 U.S. 479, 487.

Related subjects: Education and related subjects. *See also* Investigation 2; Roman Catholic Church; Tax, school.

SCIENCE

1. It is in physical science, and especially in its adaptation to the arts of life, that the present age may claim precedence of all others. — Story: *Misc. Writings,* 15.

2. Science may be said to foster and nourish genius; to administer to its wants, and soothe its disquietudes, and animate its inquiries. — Story: *ibid.,* 127.

3. The pursuit of practical science is not only a source of inexhaustible pleasure, opening new avenues to rank and reputation; but it is, at the same time, one of the surest foundations of opulence.—Story: *ibid.,* 126.

4. I can imagine a future in which science shall have passed from the combative to the dogmatic stage, and shall have gained such catholic acceptance that it shall take control of life, and condemn at once with instant execution what now is left for nature to destroy. — H o l m e s: *Speeches,* 58.

5. Science has taught the world scepticism and has made it legitimate

to put everything to the test of proof.
—Holmes: *ibid.,* 98.

6. If we have satisfied ourselves that our pursuits are good for society, or at least not bad for it, I think that science, like art, may be pursued for the pleasure of the pursuit and of its fruits, as an end in itself.—Holmes: "Law in Science and Science in Law," 12 Harv. L. Rev. 444.

7. It is finally for science to determine, so far as it can, the relative worth of our different social ends.—Holmes: *ibid.,* 462.

8. The advances in the exact sciences and the achievements in invention remind us that the seemingly impossible sometimes happens. — Brandeis: New State Ice Co. v. Liebmann, 285 U.S. 262, 310.

9. The economic and social sciences are largely uncharted seas. — Brandeis, *ibid.*

See also Construction 48; Expert 2; Fashion 2; Government, general; Law 28, 29; Patent; Progress 10.

SCRUTINY

1. What, at the first glance, seems beneficial and plausible, is, upon more mature examination, often found to be mischievous or inefficient. — Story: *Misc. Writings,* 157.

2. Scrutiny becomes futile with the lapse of the obscuring years.—Cardozo: Thomann v. Rochester, 256 N.Y. 165, 172.

SEA

Related subject: Ocean. *See also* Admiralty; Maritime law; Maritime lien; Murder 6; Seaman; Ship.

SEAMAN

1. In a broad sense, a seaman is a mariner of any degree, one who lives his life upon the sea.—Cardozo: Warner v. Goltra, 293 U.S. 155, 157.

2. He is a "ward of the admiralty," often ignorant and helpless, and so in need of protection against himself as well as others.—Cardozo: *ibid.,* 162.

3. From the earliest historical period the contract of the sailor has been treated as an exceptional one and involving, to a certain extent, the surrender of his personal liberty during the life of the contract. — Brown: Robertson v. Baldwin, 165 U.S. 275, 282–83.

4. As a class, particularly those serving as common sailors, they are proverbially improvident, and frequently the prey of unscrupulous landsmen. Soon stripped when in port of their hard earnings, they are generally willing to accept employment on almost any terms. Their necessitous condition often compelled them to submit to harsh contracts which placed them completely in the power of the masters of vessels.—Field: Young v. American S.S. Co., 15 Otto (105 U.S.) 41, 44.

5. During the period of his tenure the vessel is not merely his place of employment; it is the framework of his existence.—Rutledge: Aguilar v. Standard Oil Co., 318 U.S. 724, 732.

6. Men cannot live for long cooped up aboard ship without substantial impairment of their efficiency, if not also serious danger to discipline. Relaxation beyond the confines of the

ship is necessary if the work is to go on, more so that it may move smoothly. . . . Even more for the seaman than for the landsman, therefore, "the superfluous is the necessary . . . to make life livable" and to get work done. In short, shore leave is an elemental necessity in the sailing of ships, a part of the business as old as the art, not merely a personal diversion.—Rutledge: *ibid.,* 733–34.

7. Workers at sea have been the beneficiaries of extraordinary legislative solicitude, undoubtedly prompted by the limits upon their ability to help themselves. — Byrnes: Southern S.S. Co. v. NLRB, 316 U.S. 31, 39.

8. He [the seaman] is subject to the rigorous discipline of the sea, and all the conditions of his service constrain him to accept, without critical examination and without protest, working conditions and appliances as commanded by his superior officers.—Stone: Mahnich v. Southern S.S. Co., 321 U.S. 96, 103.

9. A seaman takes his employment, like his fun, where he finds it; a ship takes on crew in any port where it needs them.—Jackson: Lauritzen v. Larsen, 345 U.S. 571, 588.

10. From ancient times admiralty has given to seamen rights which the common law did not give to landsmen, because the conditions of sea service were different from conditions of any other service, even harbor service. . . . While his lot has been ameliorated, even under modern conditions the seagoing laborer suffers an entirely different discipline and risk

than does the harbor worker. His fate is still tied to that of the ship. His freedom is restricted. He is under an unusual discipline and is dependent for his food, medicine, care and welfare upon the supplies of the ship.—Jackson: Pope & Talbot v. Hawn, 346 U.S. 406, 423–24.

11. A seaman with a proclivity for assaulting people may, indeed, be a more deadly risk, than a rope with a weak strand or a hull with a latent defect. The problem, as with many aspects of the law, is one of degree. If the seaman has a savage and vicious nature, then the ship becomes a perilous place. A vessel bursting at the seams might well be a safer place than one with a homicidal maniac as a crew member.—Douglas: Boudoin v. Lykes Bros. S.S. Co., 348 U.S. 336, 339–40.

See also Admiralty; Maritime law; Ocean; Ship.

SEARCH AND SEIZURE

1. It is said, "A search implies a quest by an officer of the law; a seizure contemplates a forcible dispossession of the owner." — McKenna: Hale v. Henkel, 201 U.S. 43, 80.

2. Search and seizure incident to lawful arrest is a practice of ancient origin and has long been an integral part of the law-enforcement procedures of the United States and of the individual states.—Vinson: Harris v. United States, 331 U.S. 145, 150–51.

3. The right goes back beyond doubt to the days of the hue and cry, when there was short shrift for the

thief who was caught "with the mainour" still "in seisen of his crime."—Cardozo: People v. Chiagles, 237 N.Y. 193, 196.

4. The genius of our liberties holds in abhorrence all irregular inroads upon the dwelling-houses and persons of the citizens.—Woodbury: Luther v. Borden, 7 How. (48 U.S.) 1, 66.

5. Uncontrolled search and seizure is one of the first and most effective weapons in the arsenal of every arbitrary government. And one need only briefly to have dwelt and worked among a people possessed of many admirable qualities but deprived of these rights to know that the human personality deteriorates and dignity and self-reliance disappear where homes, persons and possessions are subject at any hour to unheralded search and seizure by the police. — Jackson: Brinegar v. United States, 338 U.S. 160, 180–81.

6. The protection of the Fourth Amendment extends to all equally—to those justly suspected or accused, as well as to the innocent.—Butler: Agnello v. United States, 269 U.S. 20, 32.

7. The framers of the Constitution ... only intended to restrain the abuse, while they did not abolish the power. —Miller: Boyd v. United States, 116 U.S. 616, 641.

8. An Englishman's home, though a hovel, is his castle, precisely because the law secures freedom from fear of intrusion by the people except under carefully safeguarded authorization by a magistrate.—Frankfurter: Harris v. United States, 331 U.S. 145, 164–65.

9. Security against unlawful searches is more likely to be attained by resort to search warrants than by reliance upon the caution and sagacity of petty officers while acting under the excitement that attends the capture of persons accused of crime. —Butler: United States v. Lefkowitz, 285 U.S. 452, 464.

10. The right of privacy was deemed too precious to entrust to the discretion of those whose job is the detection of crime and the arrest of criminals. — Douglas: McDonald v. United States 335 U.S. 451, 455–56.

11. The American Colonists had ... also experienced the lash of subservient judges, who did the bidding of the Crown in crucial matters, including the use of unconscionable search warrants.—Douglas: *We the Judges,* 257.

12. The presence of a search warrant serves a high function. Absent some grave emergency, the Fourth Amendment has interposed a magistrate between the citizen and the police. This was done not to shield criminals nor to make the home a safe haven for illegal activities. It was done so that an objective mind might weigh the need to invade that privacy in order to enforce the law.—Douglas: McDonald v. United States, 335 U.S. 451, 455.

13. A search is not to be made legal by what it turns up. In law it is good or bad when it starts and does not

change character from its success. —
Jackson: United States v. Di Re., 332
U.S. 581, 595.

14. Search would be mere futility
if what is found could not be used.—
Cardozo: People v. Chiagles, 237 N.Y.
193, 198.

15. The prohibition against unreasonable search and seizure is normally invoked by those accused of
crime, and criminals have few friends.
— Frankfurter: Harris v. United
States, 331 U.S. 145, 156.

16. The criminal is to go free because the constable has blundered.—
Cardozo: People v. Defore, 242 N.Y.
13, 21.

17. While the enterprise of parting
fools from their money by the "numbers" lottery is one that ought to be
suppressed, I do not think its suppression is more important to society
than the security of the people against
unreasonable searches and seizures.—
Jackson: McDonald v. United States,
335 U.S. 451, 460.

18. It must always be remembered
that what the Constitution forbids is
not all searches and seizures, but unreasonable searches and seizures. —
Stewart: Elkins v. United States, 364
U.S. 206, 222.

Related subjects: Constitution, Fourth
Amendment; Privacy and related subjects. See also Arrest 5.

SECRECY

Secrecy is not congenial to truth
seeking. — Frankfurter: Joint Anti-
Fascist Ref. Comm. v. McGrath, 341
U.S. 123, 171.

See also Third degree 3; Trial, public.

SECURITIES

Bonds 1–5; miscellaneous 6–8.

Related subjects: Bond; Investment and
related subjects.

————, bonds

1. A bond implies an obligor bound
to do what it is agreed shall be done.
—Waite: Davenport v. Dodge Co.,
15 Otto (105 U.S.) 1018, 1020.

2. It is not primitive tradition alone
that gives their peculiarities to bonds,
but a tradition laid hold of, modified
and adapted to the convenience and
understanding of business men. —
Holmes: Wheeler v. Schmer, 233 U.S.
434, 439.

3. The market value of a bond security depends chiefly upon the confidence or want of confidence in its
ultimate payment.—Hunt: Memphis
v. Brown, 20 Wall. (87 U.S.) 289,
316.

4. An unsecured municipal security is . . . merely a draft on the good
faith of a municipality in exercising
its taxing power.—Frankfurter: Faitoute Iron & Steel Co. v. Asbury Park,
316 U.S. 502, 509.

5. The value of the notes of the
government in the market, and in the
commercial world generally, depends
upon their convertibility on demand
into coin. — Field: Legal Tender
Cases, 110 U.S. 421, 464.

————, miscellaneous

6. A very large part of the country's
wealth is invested in negotiable securities whose protection against discrimination, unjust and oppressive
taxation is matter of the greatest mo-

ment.—McReynolds: Farmers Loan & Tr. Co. v. Minnesota, 280 U.S. 204, 212.

7. The value of securities consists in what they represent, and to determine such value is a complex problem even to the most skillful and informed.—McKenna: Hall v. Geiger-Jones Co., 242 U.S. 539, 552.

8. The integrity of . . . securities can only be assured by the probity of the dealers in them and the information which may be given of them.—McKenna: *ibid*.

See also Falsity 4.

SECURITY (safety)

1. Security is like liberty in that many are the crimes committed in its name.—Jackson: United States v. Shaughnessy, 338 U.S. 537, 551.

2. The problems of security are real. So are the problems of freedom. The paramount issue of the age is to reconcile the two. — Douglas: Joint Anti-Fascist Ref. Comm. v. McGrath, 341 U.S. 123, 174.

See also Virtue 5.

SEGREGATION

Related subjects: Discrimination; Negro; Prejudice; Race. *See also* Education 13, 14.

SELECTIVE SERVICE
(military)

The philosophy of the Act is that the obligations and privileges of serving in the armed forces should be shared generally in accordance with a system of selection which is fair and just.—Jackson: Dickinson v. United States, 346 U.S. 389, 399.

Related subjects: Conscientious objector and related subjects.

SELF-DEFENSE

1. The powers used for self-defense and protection against harm cannot be perverted into weapons of offense and aggression upon the rights of others.—Grier: Passenger Cases, 7 How. (48 U.S.) 283, 463.

2. Both parties to a mutual combat are wrongdoers, and the law of self-defense cannot be invoked by either, so long as he continues in the combat.—Harlan: Rowe v. United States, 164 U.S. 546, 556.

3. Detached reflection cannot be demanded in the presence of an uplifted knife. Therefore, in this court, at least, it is not a condition of immunity that one in that situation should pause to consider whether a reasonable man might not think it possible to fly with safety, or to disable his assailant rather than to kill him.—Holmes: Brown v. United States, 256 U.S. 335, 343.

4. Many respectable writers agree that if a man reasonably believes that he is in immediate danger of death or grievous bodily harm from his assailant, he may stand his ground, and that if he kills him, he has not exceeded the bounds of lawful self-defense.—Holmes: *ibid*.

5. It is not now, and never has been the law that a man assailed in his own dwelling, is bound to retreat. If assailed there, he may stand his ground, and resist the attack. He is under no duty to take to the fields and the high-

ways, a fugitive from his own home. —Cardozo: People v. Tomlins, 213 N.Y. 240, 243.

Related subject: Defense.

SELF-DISCIPLINE

Related subject: Discipline.

SELF INCRIMINATION,
privilege against

Purpose 1–4; importance, value 5–8; miscellaneous 9–17.

Related subjects: Confession and related subjects; Constitution (U.S.), Fifth Amendment; Immunity.

————, purpose

1. The constitutional p r i v i l e g e against self-incrimination . . . grows out of the high sentiment and regard of our jurisprudence for conducting criminal trials and investigatory proceedings upon a plane of dignity, humanity and impartiality. — Murphy: United States v. White, 322 U.S. 694, 698.

2. The immediate and potential evils of compulsory self-disclosure transcend any difficulties that the exercise of the privilege may impose on society in the detection and prosecution of crime. While the privilege is subject to abuse and misuse, it is firmly embedded in our constitutional and legal framework as a bulwark against iniquitous methods of prosecution.— Murphy: ibid., 698–99.

3. Under our system society carries the burden of proving its charge against the accused not out of his own mouth. It must establish its case, not by interrogation of the accused

even under judicial safeguards, but by evidence independently s e c u r e d t h r o u g h skillful investigation.— Frankfurter: Watts v. Indiana, 338 U.S. 49, 54.

4. A witness may have a reasonable fear of prosecution and yet be innocent of any wrongdoing. The privilege serves to protect the innocent who otherwise might be ensnared by ambiguous circumstances. — Clark: Slochower v. Board of Educ., 350 U.S. 551, 557–58.

————, importance, value

5. The right of an accused person to refuse to testify . . . has been recognized as "one of the most valuable prerogatives of the citizen."—Clark: ibid., 557 (quot. 161 U.S. 591, 610).

6. The privilege against self-incrimination is a right that was hard-earned by our forefathers. . . . The privilege, the Court has stated, "was generally regarded then, as now, as a privilege of great value, a protection to the innocent though a shelter to the guilty, and a safeguard against heedless, unfounded or tyrannical prosecutions." — Warren: Quinn v. United States, 349 U.S. 155, 161–62 (quot. 341 U.S. 479, 486).

7. Today as in the past there are students of our penal system who look upon the immunity as a mischief rather than a benefit, and who would limit its scope or destroy it altogether.—Cardozo: Palko v. Connecticut, 302 U.S. 319, 325–26.

8. Justice . . . would not perish if

the accused were subject to a duty to respond to orderly inquiry. — Cardozo: *ibid.*, 326.

——, miscellaneous

9. The safeguards against self-incrimination are for the benefit of those who do not wish to become witnesses in their own behalf and not for those who do.—Stone: Raffel v. United States, 271 U.S. 494, 499.

10. A person who commits a criminal act is bound to contemplate the consequences of exposure to his good name and reputation, and ought not to call upon the courts to protect that which he has himself esteemed to be of such little value. . . . The design of the constitutional privilege is not to aid the witness in vindicating his character.—Brown: Brown v. Walker, 161 U.S. 591, 605.

11. The Constitution safeguards the right of a defendant to remain silent; it does not assure him that he may remain silent and still enjoy the advantages that might have resulted from testifying.—Jackson: Stein v. New York, 346 U.S. 156, 177.

12. This constitutional protection must not be interpreted in a hostile or niggardly spirit. — Frankfurter: Ullmann v. United States, 350 U.S. 422, 426.

13. Too many, even those who should be better advised, view this privilege as a shelter for wrongdoers. They too readily assume that those who invoke it are either guilty of crime or commit perjury in claiming the privilege.—*ibid.*

14. At the outset we must condemn the practice of imputing a sinister meaning to the exercise of a person's constitutional right under the Fifth Amendment. — Clark: Slochower v. Board of Educ., 350 U.S. 551, 557.

15. I would allow no inference of wrongdoing to flow from the invocation of any constitutional right. I would not let that principle bow to popular passions.—Douglas: Beilan v. Board of Educ., 357 U.S. 399, 414.

16. No ritualistic formula is necessary in order to invoke the privilege. — Warren: Quinn v. United States, 349 U.S. 155, 164.

17. Under our system of government, police cannot compel people to furnish the evidence necessary to send them to prison.—Douglas: Breithaupt v. Abram, 352 U.S. 432, 443.

See also Tax 135; Wire tapping.

SELF-INTEREST

1. Self-interest stimulates the mind to activity, and sharpens its perspicacity. Parties in such cases often claim more, but rarely less, than they are entitled to. The probabilities are largely in the direction of the former. —Swayne: Brooklyn Life Ins. Co. v. Dutcher, 5 Otto (95 U.S.) 269, 273.

2. Enlightenment sometimes comes through self-interest. — Frankfurter: United States v. ICC, 337 U.S. 426, 445.

3. Self-interest is often an unsafe guide.—Brown: Holden v. Hardy, 169 U.S. 366, 397.

4. At the bottom of all private relations, however tempered by sympathy

and all the social feelings, is a justifiable self-preference.—Holmes: *The Common Law,* 44.

See also Coercion 3; Contract 15; Criminal law 25; Fiduciary; Individual 5; Witness 8, 9.

SELFISHNESS

Related subject: Unselfishness. *See also* Individual 2; Litigant 2, 9.

SELF-PRESERVATION

We know of no more universal instinct than that of self-preservation—none that so insistently urges to care against injury. It has its motives to exercise in the fear of pain, maiming, and death.—McKenna: Baltimore & P. R.R. v. Landrigan, 191 U.S. 461, 474.

SELF-PURIFICATION

If the house is to be cleaned, it is for those who occupy and govern it, rather than for strangers, to do the noisome work.—Cardozo: People *ex rel.* Karlin v. Culkin, 248 N.Y. 465, 480.

SELF-RELIANCE

Each of us has to work out his salvation in his own way. The most that another can help is to be able to give a helping hand.—Holmes: *Uncollected Letters,* 205–206.

SELF-RESTRAINT

1. Self-restraint belongs in the domain of will and not of judgment.—Sutherland: West Coast Hotel Co. v. Parrish, 300 U.S. 379, 402.

2. Every day's experience admonishes us, that life is short, and art is long, furnishing motives at once to excite our diligence, and to restrain an undue ardor in any human pursuit. —Story: *Misc. Writings,* 438.

SELF-RIGHTEOUSNESS

Self-righteousness gives too slender an assurance of rightness.—Frankfurter: Joint Anti-Fascist Ref. Comm. v. McGrath, 341 U.S. 123, 171.

SELLER

Related subjects: Vendor and related subjects. *See also Falsity* 5, 6, 11; Fiduciary 3; Opinion 10, 11.

SENATE (U.S.)

The senate of the United States is a representation of sovereignties, coordinate and coequal. — Story: *Misc. Writings,* 521.

SENTIMENT

1. The facts of the world . . . are the best answer to magnified sentiment.—McKenna: Grogan v. Walker & Sons, 259 U.S. 80, 94.

2. Even without contract, sentiments and usages, devoutly held as sacred, may not be flouted for caprice. —Cardozo: Yome v. Gorman, 242 N.Y. 395, 403.

See also Rule 2.

SERMON

Sermons are as much a part of a religious service as prayers. They cover a wide range and have as great a diversity as the Bible or other Holy Book from which they commonly take their texts. To call the words which one minister speaks to his congregation a sermon, immune from regulation, and the words of another minister an address, subject to regulation, is merely an indirect way of preferring one religion over another. —Douglas: Fowler v. Rhode Island, 345 U.S. 67, 70.

Related subject: Prayer.

SETTLEMENT

The inexorable law that nothing is settled until it is settled right.—Brandeis: Mason, *Brandeis,* 204.

Related subject: Compromise.

SEX, SEXES

The two sexes are not fungible; a community made exclusively of one is different from a community composed of both; the subtle interplay of influence one on the other is among the imponderables. — Douglas: Ballard v. United States, 329 U.S. 187, 193–94.

See also Classification 3; Woman.

SHERMAN ANTITRUST LAW

1. The concentration of wealth consequent upon the industrial expansion in the post-Civil War era had profound implications for American life. The impact of the abuses resulting from this concentration gradually made itself felt by a rising tide of reform protest in the last decade of the nineteenth century. The Sherman Law was a response to the felt threat to economic freedom created by enormous industrial combines. — Frankfurter: United States v. UAW, 352 U.S. 567, 570.

2. The Sherman Act was intended to secure equality of opportunity and to protect the public against evils commonly incident to monopolies and those abnormal contracts and combi-

nations which tend directly to suppress the conflict for advantage called "competition"—the play of contending forces ordinarily engendered by an honest desire for gain.—McReynolds: United States v. American Linseed Oil Co., 262 U.S. 371, 388.

3. The Sherman Law ... "is a limitation of rights ... which may be pushed to evil consequences."—Stone: United States v. Trenton Potteries, 273 U.S. 392, 398.

4. It was not the purpose or the intent of the Sherman Anti-Trust Law to prohibit the intelligent conduct of business operations. — Stone: Maple Floor. Mfgrs. Assoc. v. United States, 268 U.S. 563, 583.

5. The philosophy and the command of the Sherman Act ... is founded on a theory of hostility to the concentration in private hands of power so great that only a government of the people should have it. — Douglas: United States v. Columbia Steel Co., 334 U.S. 495, 536.

6. The vagueness of the Sherman Law was saved by imparting to it the gloss of history.—Frankfurter: Federal Trade Comm'n v. Motion Pict. Adv. Co., 344 U.S. 392, 405.

Related subjects: Monopoly and related subjects.

SHIP

1. A ship is born when she is launched, and lives so long as her identity is preserved. Prior to her launching she is a mere congeries of wood and iron. . . . In the baptism of launching she receives her name, and

from the moment her keel touches the water she is transformed. . . . She acquires a personality of her own.—Brown: Tucker v. Alexandroff, 183 U.S. 424, 438.

2. A ship is the most living of inanimate things.—Holmes: *The Common Law,* 26.

3. That a merchant ship is part of the territory of the country whose flag she flies . . . is a figure of speech —a metaphor.—Van Devanter: Cunard S.S. Co. v. Mellon, 262 U.S. 101, 123.

4. Every vessel undoubtedly has a right to the use of so much of the ocean as she occupies, and as is essential to her own movements.—Story: The Marianna Flora, 11 Wheat. (24 U.S.) 1, 43.

See also Admiralty; Maritime law; Maritime lien; Ocean; Seaman.

SIGN
See Symbol 3; Word 2.

SIGNIFICANCE
See Business (big) 1; Opinion 5; Silence 1, 6, 8; Symbol 6; Understanding 1.

SILENCE
1. In an instrument well drawn, as in a poem well composed, silence is sometimes most expressive.—Wilson: Chisholm v. Georgia, 2 Dall. (2 U.S.) 419, 454.

2. Mere silence is quite different from concealment.—Gray: Stewart v. Wyoming Cattle Ranche Co., 128 U.S. 383, 388.

3. Inferences from silence should be cautiously drawn.—Stone: United States *ex rel.* Vajtauer v. Commission-er of Immigration, 273 U.S. 103, 112.

4. If silence is induced by a person's doubts of his rights, by a belief that his security will be best promoted by his silence, then no inference of assent can be drawn from that silence. — Stone: *ibid.*

5. Silence must not be taken as importing acquiescence.—Cardozo: Carter v. Carter Coal Co., 298 U.S. 238, 325–26.

6. Silence and inaction are not significant of surrender till notice of invasion becomes a challenge to resistance.—Cardozo: O'Connor v. Collins, 239 N.Y. 457, 462.

7. He who is silent when he should speak must be silent when he would speak, if he cannot do so without a violation of law and injustice to others.—Swayne: Consolidated Fruit-Jar Co. v. Wright, 4 Otto (94 U.S.) 92, 96.

8. Sensible and just-minded men, in important affairs of life, deem it significant that a man remains silent when confronted with serious and responsible evidence against himself which it is within his power to contradict.—Frankfurter: Adamson v. California, 332 U.S. 46, 60.

9. There is no privilege of silence when reticence, if tolerated, would thwart the public good.—Cardozo: In the Matter of Edge Ho Holding Co., 256 N.Y. 374, 380.

See also Answer 2; Congress 5; Construction 127, 128; Evidence, inferences; Power 41; Self incrimination 1.

SIMILARITY
Similarity is not identity, but re-

semblance between different things. —Black: United States v. Raynor, 302 U.S. 540, 547.

SIMPLICITY
The simplest statement is the best. —Chase: United States v. Klein, 13 Wall. (80 U.S.) 128, 148.
> See also Description 3; Obscurity 1; Style 1, 2; Theory 1.

SINCERITY
Sincerity and patriotism do not, unfortunately, insure against unconstitutional acts. Indeed some of the most lamentable and tragic deaths of history were instigated by able, patriotic and sincere men.—Black: Barenblatt v. United States, 360 U.S. 109, 159n.

SKILL
Skill is not won by chance. Growth is not the sport of circumstance. Skill comes by training; and training, persistent and unceasing, is transmuted into habit. The reaction is adjusted ever to the action. What goes out of us as effort comes back to us as character. The alchemy never fails. — Cardozo: *Law and Literature,* 172.
> See also Character 1; Legislator 17.

SLANDER
> Related subjects: Defamation and related subjects. *See also* Intent 14; Libel 1; Reputation 6.

SLAVERY
1. The existence of slavery, under any shape, is so repugnant to the natural rights of man and the dictates of justice, that it seems difficult to find for it any adequate justification. — Story: *Misc. Writings,* 358.

2. All slavery has its origin in power, and is against right.—McLean: Dred Scott v. Sandford, 19 How. (60 U.S.) 393, 538.

3. It is a well-known fact that a belief was cherished by the leading men, South as well as North, that the institution of slavery would gradually decline, until it would become extinct. —McLean: *ibid.*

4. Slavery exists wherever the law recognizes a right of property in a human being; but slavery cannot exist in any form within the United States. —Harlan: Robertson v. Baldwin, 165 U.S. 275, 292.
> Related subject: Constitution (U.S.), Thirteenth, Fourteenth, Fifteenth Amendments. *See also* Freedom 3, 181; Race; Rights 3; War 30.

SLUM
Miserable and disreputable housing conditions may do more than spread disease and crime and immorality. They may also suffocate the spirit by reducing the people who live there to the status of cattle. They may indeed make living an almost insufferable burden. They may also be an ugly sore, a blight on the community which robs it of charm, which makes it a place from which men turn. The misery of housing may despoil a community as an open sewer may ruin a river.—Douglas: Berman v. Parker, 348 U.S. 26, 32–33.

SMITHSONIAN INSTITUTION
Congress long ago established the Smithsonian Institution to question which would be to lay hands on the

Ark of the Covenant. — Holmes: Springer v. Philippine Islands, 277 U.S. 189, 211.

SOCIALISM

1. The talk of the agitator alone does not advance socialism a step. . . . The great captains of industry and of finance, who profess the greatest horror of the extension of governmental functions, are the chief makers of socialism.—Brandeis: Mason, *Brandeis,* 160.

2. The only way to meet the socialistic and restless spirit of the times is to meet and remove each individual case of injustice.—Brandeis: *ibid.,* 165.

3. I shall think socialism begins to be entitled to serious treatment when and not before it takes life in hand and prevents the continuance of the unfit.—Holmes: *Uncollected Letters,* 181.

4. The notion that with socialized property we should have women free and a piano for everybody seems to me an empty humbug. — Holmes: "Ideals and Doubts," 10 Ill. L. Rev. 3.

5. There is quite a body of opinion which considers the individual ownership of property economically and politically wrong and insists upon a community of all that is profit-bearing. This opinion has its cause, among other causes, in the power—may I say the duress—of wealth.—McKenna: United States v. Ohio Oil Co., 234 U.S. 548, 573.

6. Have conditions come . . . that are not amenable to passing palliatives, and that socialism, or some form of socialism, is the only permanent corrective or accommodation?—McKenna: Black v. Hirsh, 256 U.S. 135, 162.

See also Labor 64; Reform 6, 7.

SOCIAL SECURITY

The Social Security program . . . was designed to function into the indefinite future, and its specific provisions rest on predictions as to expected economic conditions which must inevitably prove less than wholly accurate, and on judgments and preferences as to the proper allocation of the Nation's resources which evolving economic and social conditions will of necessity in some degree modify.—Harlan: Fleming v. Nestor, 363 U.S. 603, 610.

SOCIETY

Related subjects: Nation (U.S.), people; State. *See also* Evidence 41; Property 26; Public welfare; Rights, limitations; Rights 48; Rule 4; Science 9; Sovereignty 8; Supreme Court 22, 25; Tax 4; Tradition 2; Utopia 2.

SOLUTION

1. There are as many solutions as there are minds.—McKenna: Rhode Island v. Palmer, 253 U.S. 350, 398–99.

2. The way specific problems are approached naturally has much to do with the decisions reached.—Black: Graver Tank Mfg. Co. v. Linde Air Prod. Co., 339 U.S. 605, 617.

SOUND TRUCK

Loud-speakers are today indispensable instruments of effective public speech. The sound truck has become an accepted method of political campaigning. It is the way people are reached. — Douglas: Saia v. New York, 334 U.S. 558, 561.

Related subject: Speech.

SOVEREIGNTY

Defined 1–7; importance 8–10; limitations 11–15; miscellaneous 16, 17.

Related subjects: Constitution (general); Constitution (U.S.); Democracy; Government (U.S.).

———, defined

1. Sovereignty is the right to govern; ... here it rests with the people; ... our governors are the agents of the people.—Jay: Chisholm v. Georgia, 2 Dall. (2 U.S.) 419, 472.

2. The very meaning of sovereignty is that the decree of the sovereign makes law.—Holmes: American Banana Co. v. United Fruit Co., 213 U.S. 347, 358.

3. When theory is left on one side, sovereignty is a question of strength, and may vary in degree.—Holmes: Carino v. Insular Gov't, 212 U.S. 449, 458.

4. Exclusive legislative power is in essence complete sovereignty.—Reed: S. R. A., Inc. v. Minnesota, 327 U.S. 558, 562.

5. Boundary means sovereignty, since, in modern times, sovereignty is mainly territorial.—Holmes: Central R.R. v. Mayor of Jersey City, 209 U.S. 473, 479.

6. The authority that makes the law is itself superior to it.—Holmes: United States v. Thompson, 257 U.S. 419, 432.

7. The creature cannot rule the creator.—Brewer: Kansas v. Colorado, 206 U.S. 46, 83.

———, importance

8. A political society cannot endure without a supreme will somewhere. —Sutherland: United States v. Curtiss-Wright Corp., 299 U.S. 304, 316–17.

9. Rulers come and go; governments end and forms of government change; but sovereignty survives. — Sutherland: *ibid.*, 316.

10. The right of a government to maintain its existence—self-preservation—is the most pervasive aspect of sovereignty.—Frankfurter: Dennis v. United States, 341 U.S. 494, 519.

———, limitations

11. However extensive the prerogatives and attributes of sovereignty may theoretically be, in free governments they are universally held to be restrained within some limits.—Story: Charles River Bridge v. Warren Bridge, 11 Pet. (36 U.S.) 420, 642.

12. Sovereignty is a question of power, and no human power is unlimited. — Holmes: United States v. Thompson, 257 U.S. 419, 432.

13. When a government becomes a partner in any trading company ... it descends to a level with those with whom it associates itself.—Marshall: Bank of U. S. v. Planters Bank, 9 Wheat. (22 U.S.) 904, 907.

14. States and cities, when they borrow money and contract to repay it with interest, are not acting as sovereignties. They come down to the level of ordinary individuals. —

Strong: Murray v. Charleston, 6 Otto (96 U.S.) 432, 445.

15. Sovereigns may contract without derogating from their sovereignty. —Cardozo: Steward Mach. Co. v. Davis, 301 U.S. 548, 597.

———, miscellaneous

16. Sovereignty is derived from a feudal source; and like many other parts of that system so degrading to man, still retains its influence over our sentiments and conduct. — Wilson: Chisholm v. Georgia, 2 Dall. (2 U.S.) 419, 457.

17. In the exercise of sovereign right, the sovereign is sole arbiter of his own justice. The penalty of wrong is war and subjugation. — Johnson: Cherokee Nation v. Georgia, 5 Pet. (30 U.S.) 1, 29.

> *See also* Citizen 20; Constitution (U.S.) 1; Constitution (U.S.), authority; Good will; Government (general); Legislation 1; Legislature 1, 10; Master and servant 2.

SPECTATOR
See Fencer 1.

SPECULATION (conjecture)
The unavoidable tendency of free speculation is to lead to occasional extravagances. When once the reverence for authority is shaken, there is apt to grow in its stead a cold skepticism respecting established opinions. Their very antiquity, under such circumstances, betrays us into suspicion of their truth.—Story: *Misc. Writings,* 18.

> Related subject: Conjecture. *See also* Judgment 2; Value 29.

SPECULATION (financial)
1. The spirit of speculation was pushed to a most extravagant extent, and . . . the spirit of fraud, as is but too common, followed close upon the heels of speculation.—Story: *ibid.,* 422.

2. There is no doubt that purchases on margin may be and frequently are used as a means of gambling for a great gain or a loss of all one has.— Holmes: Otis v. Parker, 187 U.S. 606, 610.

3. California is a mining state, and mines offer the most striking temptations to people in a hurry to get rich. Mines generally are represented by stocks. Stock is convenient for purposes of speculation, because of the ease with which it is transferred from hand to hand, as well as for other reasons.—Holmes: *ibid.*

4. Speculation of this kind [in futures] by competent men is the self-adjustment of society to the probable. Its value is well known as a means of avoiding or mitigating catastrophes, equalizing prices, and providing for periods of want.—Holmes: Board of Trade v. Christie Grain & Stock Co., 198 U.S. 236, 247.

> Related subjects: Gamble and related subjects; Profit.

SPEECH
1. Articulate speech . . . is an "uttered sound" produced by the "human voice."—Waite: T e l e p h o n e Cases, 126 U.S. 1, 532.

2. What people say is what others reasonably hear and are meant to hear.

—Frankfurter: *In re* Sawyer, 360 U.S. 622, 653.

3. The purpose of speech is not only to inform but to incite to action.—Douglas: United States v. UAW, 352 U.S. 567, 595.

4. Written words are less apt to incite or provoke to mass action than spoken words, speech being the primitive and direct communication with the emotions.—Jackson: Kunz v. New York, 340 U.S. 290, 307.

5. When a speaker mounts a platform it is not unusual to find him resorting to exaggeration, to vilification of ideas and men, to the making of false charges.—Douglas: Feiner v. New York, 340 U.S. 315, 331.

6. Words can readily be so coupled with conduct as to provoke violence.—Burton: Youngdahl v. Rainfair, 355 U.S. 151, 156.

7. Intemperate speech is a distinctive characteristic of man. Hot heads blow off and release destructive energy in the process. They shout and rave, exaggerating weaknesses, magnifying error, viewing with alarm. So it has been from the beginning; and so it will be throughout time.—Douglas: Beauharnais v. Illinois, 343 U.S. 250, 287.

8. It takes no master of psychology to know that if the speaker does not discriminate neither will the audience.—Frankfurter: *In re* Sawyer, 360 U.S. 622, 660.

Related subjects: Freedom, speech; Word and related subjects. *See also* Constitution, First Amendment; Defamation; Force 4; Freedom, thought; Incitement; Letter; Loyalty oath 2; Mind 15; Mistake 2; Mob 2; Opposition 2; Privacy 3–5; Proclamation; R a d i o 6; Simplicity; Sound truck.

SPEED

A speed too great at other times is proper in emergencies.—Cardozo: In the Matter of Barington v. Yellow Taxi. Corp., 250 N.Y. 14, 18.

SPIRIT (human)

The widest scope of freedom is to be given to the adventurous and imaginative exercise of the human spirit.—Frankfurter: Kingsley Co. v. Regents, 360 U.S. 684, 695.

Related subject: Effort. *See also* Freedom, belief 139; Heart 1.

STANDARD

1. We are tending more and more toward an appreciation of the truth that, after all, there are few rules; there are chiefly standards and degrees.—Cardozo: *Nature of Judicial Process,* 161.

2. New times and new manners may call for new standards and new rules.—Cardozo: *ibid.,* 88.

3. The standard set for men of good will is even more useful to the venal.—Douglas: New York v. United States, 342 U.S. 882, 884.

4. Standards must be enforced to be respected. If they are merely left as something on paper, they might as well be written on water.—Frankfurter: Ferguson v. Moore-McCormack, 352 U.S. 521, 537.

5. The standards of conscionable conduct are established by the State for those contracting within its bor-

ders. — Cardozo: Rivara v. Stewart, 241 N.Y. 259, 266.

6. If the individual falls short of the standards of the group, he does so at his peril.—Cardozo: *Paradoxes,* 73.

7. What is generally called the "ethics" of the profession is but the consensus of expert opinion as to the necessity of . . . standards.—Hughes: Semler v. Oregon Bd. of Dental Exam'rs, 294 U.S. 608, 612.

8. The standard of conduct . . . is an external standard, and takes no account of the personal equation of the man concerned. — Holmes: The Germanic, 196 U.S. 589, 596.

9. Standards of prudent conduct are declared at times by courts, but they are taken over from the facts of life.—Cardozo: Pokora v. Wabash Ry., 292 U.S. 98, 104.

> Related subjects: Formula; Rule; Principle. *See also* Competition 12; Constitutional adjudication, standards; Corporation, directors; Equity court, standards; Fault 1; Jury 13; Law, standards; Lawyer, functions; Money 1, 2; Negligence, standards; Punishment, standards; Tax, standards.

STARE DECISIS

> Related subjects: Constitutional adjudication, stare decisis; Precedent.

STATE

> Defined 1–5; acts 6–8; obligations 9–11; powers 12–14.

> Related subjects: Government (general); Government (U.S.), state; Society.

———, defined

1. By a state I mean, a complete body of free persons united together for their common benefit, to enjoy peaceably what is their own, and to do justice to others.—Wilson: Chisholm v. Georgia, 2 Dall. (2 U.S.) 419, 455.

2. States and governments were made for man. — Wilson: *ibid.*

3. Let a state be considered as subordinate to the people: But let everything else be subordinate to the state. —Wilson: *ibid.*

4. A state, useful and valuable as the contrivance is, is the inferior contrivance of man. . . . It is a contrivance inferior only to that, which is divine. Of all human contrivances, it is certainly most transcendantly excellent.—Wilson: *ibid.*

5. A state is not a citizen. — Gray: Postal Tel. Cable Co. v. Alabama, 155 U.S. 482, 487.

———, acts

6. In all our contemplations . . . concerning this feigned and artificial person [the state], we should never forget that, in truth and nature, those who think and speak and act, are men.—Wilson: Chisholm v. Georgia, 2 Dall. (2 U.S.) 419, 456.

7. Even in almost every nation, which has been denominated free, the state has assumed a supercilious pre-eminence above the people who have formed it.—Wilson: *ibid.,* 461.

8. States act through men, and, of course, cannot have a greater appreciation or prophecy of things than men. —McKenna: Citizens' Bank v. Parker, 192 U.S. 73, 80.

———, obligations

9. The moral duty of a state to keep its word, in spirit as well as in letter, is no less than that of an individual. —Sutherland: Pacific Co. v. Johnson, 285 U.S. 480, 501.

10. A state, like a merchant, makes a contract: A dishonest state, like a dishonest merchant, wilfully refuses to discharge it.—Wilson: Chisholm v. Georgia, 2 Dall. (2 U.S.) 419, 456.

11. We naturally look to the action of a sovereign state, to be characterized by a more scrupulous regard to justice, and a higher morality, than belong to the ordinary transactions of individuals. — McLean: Woodruff v. Trapnell, 10 How. (51 U.S.) 190, 207.

———, powers

12. The State continues to possess authority to safeguard the vital interests of its people.—Hughes: Home Build. & Loan Assoc. v. Blaisdell, 290 U.S. 398, 434.

13. The range of the state's discretion is large.—Holmes: Bain Peanut Co. v. Pinson, 282 U.S. 499, 501.

14. Who can doubt the power of the state to prohibit her citizens from running into debt altogether?—Johnson: Ogden v. Saunders, 12 Wheat. (25 U.S.) 213, 290.

See also Man 1; Municipality 2; Sovereignty 14; Symbol 8; Veteran 2.

STATECRAFT
See Constitutional adjudication.

STATESMAN, STATESMANSHIP
See Judge 17; Tax 31; War 41.

STATUS QUO
He cannot of his own volition throw off the garments he has once put on.—Brewer: United States v. Grimley, 137 U.S. 147, 152.
See also Reform 1.

STATUTE
See Legislation.

STATUTE OF LIMITATIONS
Related subject: Limitations. *See also* Estoppel 2.

STENOGRAPHER
Very often a stenographer does not grasp the meaning of dictated words till the dictation is over and the symbols have been read.—Cardozo: Ostrowe v. Lee, 256 N.Y. 36, 39.

STERILIZATION
1. The principle that sustains compulsory vaccination is broad enough to cover cutting the Fallopian tubes. ... Three generations of imbeciles are enough.—Holmes: Buck v. Bell, 274 U.S. 200, 207.

2. We have seen more than once that the public welfare may call upon the best citizens for their lives. It would be strange if it could not call upon those who already sap the strength of the state for these lesser sacrifices, in order to prevent our being swamped with incompetence. It is better for all the world, if instead of waiting to execute degenerate offspring for crime, or to let them starve for their imbecility, society can prevent those who are manifestly unfit from c o n t i n u i n g their kind. — Holmes: *ibid.*

3. The power to sterilize, if exercised, may have subtle, far-reaching and devastating effects. In evil or reckless hands it can cause races or types which are inimical to the dominant group to wither and disappear.—Douglas: Skinner v. Oklahoma, 316 U.S. 535, 541.

4. There are limits to the extent to which a legislatively represented majority may conduct biological experiments at the expense of the dignity and personality and natural powers of a minority—even those who have been guilty of what the majority define as crimes.—Jackson: *ibid., 546.*

STOCK
Related subject: Corporation. *See also* Corporation 65, 69; Speculation (financial) 3; Tax 43.

STOCKBROKER
The business of a stockbroker is ordinarily distinct from the business of a banker. . . . A stockbroker may do some of the kinds of business that are usually done by bankers, and many banks and bankers do business which, as a general rule, is only done by stockbrokers.—Harlan: Richmond v. Blake, 132 U.S. 592, 598.

STOCK DIVIDENDS
See Corporation, stock dividends.

STOCKHOLDER
See Corporation, control; Corporation, stockholder; Tax 117.

STRATAGEM
A stratagem so transparent does not cast a shadow of substance.—Vinson:

United States v. Fleischman, 339 U.S. 349, 364.
Related subject: Subterfuge.

STREET
1. In earlier and simpler times the surface of the streets was enough to accommodate all travel. But under the more complex conditions of modern urban life, with its high and populous buildings, and its rapid interurban transportation, the requirements of public travel are largely increased. Sometimes the increased demands may be met by subways and sometimes by viaducts.—Moody: Sauer v. New York City, 206 U.S. 536, 555.

2. We all know what serious problems the automobile has introduced. The difficulties of keeping the streets reasonably clear for travel and for traffic are very great. . . . I see nothing to prevent its [the state's] going to the point of requiring a license and bringing the whole business under . . . control . . . so far as to determine the number, character and conduct of transportation companies and so as to prevent the streets from being made useless and dangerous by the number and lawlessness of those who seek to use them.—Holmes: Frost Truck Co. v. R.R. Comm'n, 271 U.S. 583, 601.

STRENGTH
See Power 19; Sovereignty 3; Style 1; Testimony 1.

STRIKE
See Labor, disputes, strike.

STRUGGLE
1. For my own part, I believe that

the struggle for life is the order of the world, at which it is vain to repine. I can imagine the burden changed in the way in which it is to be borne, but I cannot imagine that it ever will be lifted from men's backs.—Holmes: *Speeches,* 58.

2. Although it might seem that the day of trial was over, in fact it is renewed each day.—Holmes: *ibid.,* 86.

See also Legislation 9.

STYLE

1. I have . . . learned that one is never so strong as when he is calm, and never writes so forcibly as when he uses the simplest language.—Field: Swisher, *Field,* 50.

2. The best style that a man can hope for is a free, unconscious expression of his own spontaneity, not an echo of some one else. Therefore, although one can learn by reading, the help is only indirect.—Holmes: *Uncollected Letters,* 168.

3. He seems to me to have more of our cosmos in his head than any philosopher I ever read, but he does his best to disguise it by obscure writing.—Holmes: *ibid.,* 192.

4. Most things can be said in untechnical English and it is a great help to most readers to have them put so. When you write about law the technical phrases of the law are all right, as legal readers will understand them, but if you bring in even very familiar philosophical words, you hamper many legal readers. As I probably have said before now, the trouble generally is not with ideas. Few ideas are hard to understand, but with words, every group has its own slang but outsiders are bothered by it.—Holmes: *Uncollected Letters,* 170–71.

Related subjects: Word and related subjects. *See also* Opinion (judicial).

SUBSIDIARY

See Corporation, holding companies.

SUBSTANCE

See Form (substance); Formula 10; Stratagem; Tax 83, 84.

SUBTERFUGE

Subterfuge—illegal purpose liveried in legal forms to give color or right to illegal practices.—McKenna: Standard San. Mfg. Co. v. United States, 226 U.S. 20, 39.

Related subject: Stratagem.

SUCCESS

1. Now that it has succeeded, it may seem very plain to anyone, that he could have done it as well.—Bradley: Webster Loom Co. v. Higgins, 15 Otto (105 U.S.) 580, 591.

2. It is true that the success of the strong induces imitation by the weak.—Holmes: Board of Trade v. Christie Grain & Stock Co., 198 U.S. 236, 247.

3. A moral, a lesson worth remembering, that observance of law and the truth are necessary to lasting financial success.—Brandeis: Mason, *Brandeis,* 211.

4. Worldly success is pleasant in itself, and that it is also for many in the world the badge of all success.—Cardozo: *Law and Literature,* 169.

See also Accounting; Business 10; Competition 11; Happiness 1, 2; Individual 3; Negro 5–7.

SUFFERING

1. From societies for the prevention of cruelty to animals up to socialism, we express in numberless ways the notion that suffering is a wrong which can be and ought to be prevented.—Holmes: *Speeches,* 57.

2. I cannot say there is an equity in unrequited wounds, and none in other suffering of body or of mind.—Cardozo: People v. Westchester Co. Nat'l Bank, 231 N.Y. 465, 488.

3. The catalogue of pain and suffering does not end with pain of mind and body.—Cardozo: *ibid.,* 485.

4. I cannot say, if there is an equity in suffering of body or of mind, that there is none in economic suffering, the loss of money or money's worth.—Cardozo: *ibid.,* 488.

See also Death penalty 1, 3.

SUNDAY

1. The law relating to the observance of Sunday defines a duty of a citizen to the State, and to the State only.—Grier: Philadelphia, W. & B. R.R. v. Philadelphia & Havre de Grace Steam Towboat Co., 23 How. (64 U.S.) 209, 218.

2. Laws setting aside Sunday as a day of rest are upheld, not from any right of the Government to legislate for the promotion of religious observances, but from its right to protect all persons from the physical and moral debasement which comes from uninterrupted labor. Such laws have always been deemed beneficent and merciful laws, especially to the poor and dependent, to the laborers in our factories and workshops and in the heated rooms of our cities.—Field: Soon Hing v. Crowley, 113 U.S. 703, 710.

3. Upon no subject is there such a concurrence of opinion, among philosophers, moralists, and statesmen of all nations, as on the necessity of periodical cessations from labor. One day in seven is the rule, founded in experience, and sustained by science.—Fuller: Petit v. Minnesota, 177 U.S. 164, 165.

4. The ground upon which courts have refused to maintain actions on contracts made in contravention of statutes for the observance of the Lord's Day is the elementary principle that one who has himself participated in a violation of law cannot be permitted to assert in a court of justice any right founded upon or growing out of the illegal transaction.—Woods: Gibbs & Sterrett Mfg. Co. v. Brucker, 111 U.S. 597, 601.

5. At common law Sunday was *dies non juridicus,* and no strictly judicial act could be performed on that day.—Fuller: Town of Danville v. Brown, 128 U.S. 503, 505.

6. A power that may be exercised up to and including a given day of the month may generally, when that day happens to be Sunday, be exercised on the succeeding day.—Brewer: Street v. United States, 133 U.S. 299, 306.

SUPPRESSION

See Freedom 29, 43; Freedom, speech 103; Regulation 2; Will 4.

SUPREME COURT

————, authority

1. The Supreme Court of the United States, a creature of the Constitution, and possessing no greater capacity to receive jurisdiction or power than the Constitution gives it. — Johnson: *Ex parte* Bollman, 4 Cranch (8 U.S.) 75, 107.

2. It was to prevent an appeal to the sword and a dissolution of the compact that this Court, by the organic law, was made equal in origin and equal in title to the legislative and executive branches of the government.—Taney: Gordon v. United States, 117 U.S. 697, 701.

3. Even this Court has the last say only for a time. Being composed of fallible men, it may err. But revision of its errors must be by orderly process of law.—Frankfurter: United States v. UMW, 330 U.S. 258, 308.

————, importance

4. The existence of this Court is . . . as essential to the organization of the government established by the Constitution as the election of a president or members of Congress. — Taney: Gordon v. United States, 117 U.S. 697, 700.

5. So long . . . as this Constitution shall endure, this tribunal must exist with it, deciding in the peaceful forms of judicial proceeding the angry and irritating controversies between sovereignties, which in other countries have been determined by the arbitrament of force.—Taney: Ableman v. Booth, 21 How. (62 U.S.) 506, 521.

6. As I look back over the more than a third of a century that I have sat on this bench, I am more and more impressed with the immeasurable importance of this court. Now and then we hear it spoken of as an aristocratic feature of a republican government. But it is the most democratic of all. Senators represent their states and representatives their constituents, but this court stands for the whole country, and as such it is truly "of the people, by the people, and for the people."—Field: Letter of resignation, October 12, 1897, 42 L. Ed. 1219.

7. On the whole, the Supreme Court has written highly responsible treatises on the legal issues coming to it. Today it is one of the great cohesive forces in America. — Douglas: *We the Judges,* 82.

8. Perhaps even more than by interpretation of its written word, this Court has advanced the solidarity and prosperity of this Nation by the meaning it has given to these great silences of the Constitution.—Jackson: Hood v. Du Mond, 336 U.S. 525, 535.

————, composition

9. We pretend not to more infalli-

---

bility than other courts composed of the same frail materials which compose this.—Johnson: Martin v. Hunter's Lessee, 1 Wheat (14 U.S.) 305, 364.

10. In this court, every state in the Union is represented; we are constituted by the voice of the Union, and when decisions take place, which nothing but a spirit to give ground and harmonize can reconcile, ours is the superior claim upon the comity of the state tribunals.—Johnson: *ibid.*, 365.

11. Custom decrees that the Supreme Court shall be composed only of lawyers, though the Constitution does not say so.—Jackson: *Struggle for Judicial Supremacy,* 291.

12. The Court . . . is almost never a really contemporary institution. The operation of life tenure in the judicial department as against elections at short intervals of the Congress, usually keeps the average viewpoint of the two institutions a generation apart. The judiciary is thus the check of a preceding generation on the present one; a check of conservative legal philosophy upon a dynamic people, and nearly always the check of a rejected regime on the one in being.—Jackson: *ibid.,* 315.

———, characteristics

13. We are very quiet there, but it is the quiet of a storm centre, as we all know.—Holmes: *Collected Legal Papers,* 292.

14. Not anointed priests, but men with proved grasp of affairs, who have developed resilience and spaciousness of mind through seasoned and diversified experience in a work-a-day world, usually in public life, are the judges who have wrought abidingly on the Supreme Court.—Frankfurter: "Holmes and the Constitution," 41 Harv. L. Rev. 127.

15. There is no doubt that if there were a super-Supreme Court, a substantial proportion of our reversals of state courts would also be reversed. We are not final because we are infallible, but we are infallible only because we are final.—Jackson: Brown v. Allen, 344 U.S. 443, 540.

16. Because the Court is without power to shape measures for dealing with the problems of society but has merely the power of negation over measures shaped by others, the indispensable judicial requisite is intellectual humility, and such humility presupposes complete disinterestedness. And so, in the end, it is right that the Court should be indifferent to public temper and popular wishes.—Frankfurter: AFL v. Am. Sash & Door Co., 335 U.S. 538, 557.

17. The powers exercised by this Court are inherently oligarchic. . . . The Court is not saved from being oligarchic because it professes to act in the service of humane ends.—Frankfurter: *ibid.,* 555–56.

18. The Constitution, in making the balance between different parts of our government a legal rather than a political question, casts the Court as the most philosophical of our political departments. It keeps the most fun-

damental equilibriums of our society, such as that between liberty and authority, and between stability and progress. These issues underlie nearly every movement in organized society. Jackson: *Struggle for Judicial Supremacy,* 312–13.

19. The Supreme Court ... is an institution of distinctive characteristics which were intended to give it independence and detachment, but which also tend to make it anti-democratic. —Jackson: *ibid.,* 311.

20. Never in its entire history can the Supreme Court be said to have for a single hour been representative of anything except the relatively conservative forces of its day.—Jackson: *ibid.,* 187.

———, functions, general

21. We have nothing to do but to expound the law as we find it; the defects of the system must be remedied by another department of the government.—Story: Gelston v. Hoyt, 3 Wheat. (16 U.S.) 246, 309.

22. The ultimate function of the Supreme Court is nothing less than the arbitration between fundamental and everpresent rival forces or trends in our organized society. — Jackson: *Struggle for Judicial Supremacy,* 311.

23. Adjudication is, of course, the most exacting and most time-consuming of the Court's labors.—Frankfurter: Dick v. New York Life Ins. Co., 359 U.S. 437, 459.

24. While the Supreme Court is thus in the perilous realm of government, it is itself freed from the ter-

rible burdens of governing wisely. The Court is merely the brake on other men's conduct, the judge of other men's decisions. Responsibility for action rests with legislators. — Frankfurter: "Holmes and the Constitution," 41 Harv. L. Rev. 131.

25. As the Nation's ultimate judicial tribunal, this Court, beyond any other organ of society, is the trustee of law and charged with the duty of securing obedience to it. — Frankfurter: United States v. UMW, 330 U.S. 258, 312.

26. This is a court of review, not a tribunal unbounded by rules. We do not sit like a kadi under a tree dispensing justice according to considerations of individual expediency. —Frankfurter: Terminiello v. Chicago, 337 U.S. 1, 11.

———, functions, constitutional

27. The power of this court is not to amend but only to expound the Constitution as an agency of the sovereign people who made it and who alone have authority to alter or unmake it.—Hughes: Worthen Co. v. Thomas, 292 U.S. 426, 435.

28. Sitting here, we are not at liberty to add one jot of power to the national government beyond what the people have granted by the Constitution.—Story: Houston v. Moore, 5 Wheat. (18 U.S.) 1, 48.

29. We may declare defects in the constitution, without being justly chargeable with creating them; but if they exist, it is not for us to correct them.—Johnson: *ibid.,* 36.

30. This court has no alternative . . . but to stand by the Constitution and laws with fidelity to their duties and their oaths. Their path is a straight and narrow one, to go where that Constitution and the laws lead, and not to break both, by traveling without or beyond them. — Woodbury: Jones v. Van Zandt, 5 How. (46 U.S.) 215, 231.

———, functions, litigation

31. Our exclusive business is litigation. — Frankfurter: Coleman v. Miller, 307 U.S. 433, 462.

32. This is the Nation's ultimate judicial tribunal, not a super-legal-aid bureau.—Frankfurter: Uveges v. Pennsylvania, 335 U.S. 437, 449–50.

33. This court does not sit to redress every apparent error committed by competent and responsible courts whose judgments we are empowered to review.—Roberts: Bailey v. Central Vermont Ry., 319 U.S. 350, 358.

34. Not every judgment by which a man gets less than he ought, and in that sense is deprived of his property, can come to this court.—Holmes: Mc-Govern v. New York, 229 U.S. 363, 370.

35. The Supreme Court ought to devote itself to the consideration of cases involving important public questions, that its time and energy ought not to be absorbed in hearing and deciding cases merely to provide an unsuccessful litigant with further opportunity for delay, or to give him another chance, or where the issue is not doubtful or has plainly been consid-

ered and adequately dealt with by a competent appellate tribunal. — Stone: Mason, *Stone*, 448.

———, functions, limitations

36. The duty of not going beyond the necessities of a case is not a lifeless technicality. The experience of centuries is behind the wisdom of not deciding, whether explicitly or by atmospheric pressure, matters that do not come to the Court with the impact of necessity.—Frankfurter: Mercoid Corp. v. Mid-Cont. Inv. Co., 320 U.S. 661, 678.

37. Opinions in the nature of advice concerning legislative action—a function never conferred upon it by the Constitution, and against the exercise of which this court has steadily set its face from the beginning. — Day: Muskrat v. United States, 219 U.S. 346, 362.

38. It is not our function, and it is beyond our power, to write legal essays or to give legal opinions, however solemnly requested and however great the national emergency.—Frankfurter: Coleman v. Miller, 307 U.S. 433, 462.

39. The Court itself took the position early in the life of the nation that it would not aid public officers in answering legal questions, but would only express its opinion in rendering judgment in justiciable controversies between litigating parties. — Jackson: *Struggle for Judicial Supremacy,* 288–89.

40. It is not for us [the court] to depart from the beaten track pre-

scribed for us, and to tread the devious and intricate path of politics.—Marshall: The Nereide, 9 Cranch (13 U.S.) 388, 422–23.

41. Questions of political expediency belong to the legislative halls, not to the judicial forum.—Bradley: Legal Tender Cases, 12 Wall. (79 U.S.) 457, 562.

42. We have no supervising control over the political branch of the government in its action within the limits of the Constitution.—Brewer: Wilson v. Shaw, 204 U.S. 24, 32.

———, duty

43. It is most true that this court will not take jurisdiction if it should not; but it is equally true, that it must take jurisdiction if it should. . . . We have no more right to decline the exercise of jurisdiction which is given, than to usurp that which is not given. The one or the other would be treason to the constitution. — Marshall: Cohens v. Virginia, 6 Wheat. (19 U.S.) 264, 404.

44. Should Congress, in the execution of its powers, adopt measures which are prohibited by the constitution; or should Congress, under the pretext of executing its powers, pass laws for the accomplishment of objects not entrusted to the government, it would become the painful duty of this tribunal, should a case requiring such a decision come before it, to say that such an act was not the law of the land. — Marshall: McCulloch v. Maryland, 4 Wheat. (17 U.S.) 316, 423.

45. It is the duty of this court, by decisions, to preserve the supremacy of the laws of the United States, which they cannot do without disregarding all State Laws and State decisions which conflict with the laws of the United States.—McKinley: Amis v. Smith, 16 Pet. (41 U.S.) 303, 313.

46. It is the unenvied province of this court to be directed by the head, and not the heart. In deciding upon principles that must define the rights and duties of the citizen and direct the future decisions of justice, no latitude is left for the exercise of feeling. Johnson: The Rapid, 8 Cranch (12 U.S.) 155, 164.

47. While this Court sits, it has the inescapable duty of seeing that the mandates of the Constitution are obeyed. — Murphy: Hirabayashi v. United States, 320 U.S. 81, 113.

48. No higher duty, no more solemn responsibility, rests upon this Court, than that of translating into living law and maintaining this constitutional shield deliberately planned and inscribed for the benefit of every human being subject to our Constitution—of whatever race, creed or persuasion.—Black: Chambers v. Florida, 309 U.S. 227, 241.

49. This court has the duty of alertness in safeguarding rights guaranteed by the Constitution of the United States against infringement by the States even in their difficult task of repressing crime and dealing with transgressors. — Frankfurter: Uveges v. Pennsylvania, 335 U.S. 437, 449.

50. It is no less our duty to recog-

nize and protect the powers reserved to the state under the Constitution than the immunities granted to the federal government.—Stone: Missouri v. Gebner, 281 U.S. 313, 328.

51. This Court is under no duty to make law less than sound logic and good sense.—Frankfurter: New York v. United States, 326 U.S. 572, 577.

————, operation

52. Nowhere, than in this court, ought the will of the nation . . . to be more liberally construed or more cordially executed.—Swayne: Slaughter House Cases, 16 Wall. (83 U.S.) 36, 129.

53. The Court has no reason for existence if it merely reflects the pressures of the day. Our system is built on the faith that men set apart for this special function, freed from the influences of immediacy and from the deflections of worldly ambition, will become able to take a view of longer range than the period of responsibility entrusted to Congress and legislatures.—Frankfurter: West Va. State Bd. of Educ. v. Barnette, 319 U.S. 624, 665.

54. The task of this Court to maintain a balance between liberty and authority is never done, because new conditions today upset the equilibrium of yesterday. The seesaw between freedom and power makes up most of the history of governments. — Jackson: American Com. Assoc. v. Douds, 339 U.S. 382, 445.

55. Certainly our own Supreme Court has erred, sometimes grievous-

ly. But in the main it has stood high above the storms.—Douglas: *We the Judges,* 81.

56. To the extent that the courts can serve to vindicate civil liberties, the recent decisions of the Supreme Court show how the job can be done.—Jackson: *Struggle for Judicial Supremacy,* 285.

57. There is danger that, if the Court does not temper its doctrinaire logic with a little practical wisdom, it will convert the constitutional Bill of Rights into a suicide pact. — Jackson: Terminiello v. Chicago, 337 U.S. 1, 37.

58. Mr. Dooley's "th' Supreme Coort follows th' iliction returns" expressed the wit of cynicism, not the demand of principle.—Frankfurter: AFL v. Am. Sash & Door Co., 335 U.S. 538, 557.

59. Many a decision of this Court rests on some inarticulate major premise and is none the worse for it. — Frankfurter: Niemotko v. Maryland, 340 U.S. 268, 285.

60. Intervention by this Court in the administration of the criminal justice of a State has all the disadvantages of interference from without.—Frankfurter: Uveges v. Pennsylvania, 335 U.S. 437, 449.

61. The judgments of this Court are collective judgments. Such judgments presuppose ample time and freshness of mind for private study and reflection in preparation for discussion at Conference. Without adequate study there cannot be adequate reflection; without adequate reflection

there cannot be adequate discussion; without adequate discussion there cannot be that fruitful interchange of minds which is indispensable to thoughtful, unhurried decision and its formulation in learned and impressive opinions. — Frankfurter: Dick v. New York Life Ins. Co., 359 U.S. 437, 458–59.

——, public opinion

62. The opinion of this court is of high authority in itself; and the judge who delivers it has a support as strong in moral influence over public opinion as any human tribunal can impart. —Baldwin: Cherokee Nation v. Georgia, 5 Pet. (30 U.S.) 1, 32.

63. This court has contributed its share to that stability which results from a respect for things adjudicated. —Campbell: Beauregard v. New Orleans, 18 How. (59 U.S.) 497, 502.

64. It is a mistake to suppose that the Supreme Court is either honored or helped by being spoken of as beyond criticism. On the contrary the life and character of its justices should be the objects of constant watchfulness by all, and its judgments subject to the freest criticism. The time is past in the history of the world when any living man or body of men can be set on a pedestal and decorated with a halo.—Brewer: Government by Injunction, 15 Nat. Corp. Rep. 849.

65. Our people often criticize the Court and disagree with it; but they have a respect and reverence for it, born of decades of experience.—Douglas: *We the Judges,* 82.

66. The duty to abstain from resistance to "the supreme Law of the Land," . . . as declared by the organ of our Government for ascertaining it, does not require immediate approval of it nor does it deny the right of dissent. Criticism need not be stilled. Active obstruction or defiance is barred. — Frankfurter: Cooper v. Aaron, 358 U.S. 1, 24.

67. It is regrettable that in an era marked by doubt and confusion, an era whose greatest need is steadfastness of thought and purpose, this court, which has been looked to as exhibiting consistency in adjudication, and a steadiness which would hold the balance even in the face of temporary ebbs and flows of opinion, should now itself become the breeder of fresh doubt and confusion in the public mind as to the stability of our institutions.—Roberts: Smith v. Allwright, 321 U.S. 649, 670.

68. Rightly or wrongly, the belief is widely held by the practicing profession that this Court no longer respects impersonal rules of law but is guided in these matters by personal impressions which from time to time may be shared by a majority of Justices. Whatever has been intended, this Court also has generated an impression in much of the judiciary that regard for precedents and authorities is obsolete, that words no longer mean what they have always meant to the profession, that the law knows no fixed principles.—Jackson: Brown v. Allen, 344 U.S. 443, 535.

69. Our Court is . . . an institution

that has created in our people a confidence that the humblest and the most powerful will receive the same treatment.—Douglas: *We the Judges,* 82.

70. Like all human institutions, the Supreme Court must earn reverence through the test of truth. — Frankfurter: "Holmes and the Constitution," 41 Harv. L. Rev. 164.

SUSPICION
When suspicion is suggested, it is easily entertained.—Holmes: United States v. Clark, 200 U.S. 601, 609.

> Related subject: Conjecture. *See also* Arrest 1, 4; Discovery 1; Faith 11; Inference 2; Teacher 12; Treason 9.

SYMBOL, SYMBOLISM
1. We live by symbols, and what shall be symbolized by any image of the sight depends upon the mind of him who sees it.—Holmes: *Speeches,* 90.

2. Any symbol suffices — pictures, hieroglyphics, shorthand notes—if only what is written is intelligible to him who reads.—Cardozo: Ostrowe v. Lee, 256 N.Y. 36, 40.

3. "Signs and Symbols" must be turned "into their equivalent realities." — Cardozo: In the Matter of Rausch, 258 N.Y. 327, 332.

4. In social and economic life the grooves of thought and action are not always those of logic, and ... symbols may mean as much as conduct has put into them.—Cardozo: Liggett Co. v. Lee, 288 U.S. 517, 586.

5. The will of Congress is expressed in abbreviated signs and symbols, but none the less it is expressed.—Cardozo: Ward v. Erie R.R., 230 N.Y. 230, 234.

6. The significance of a symbol lies in what it represents.—Frankfurter: West Va. State Bd. of Educ. v. Barnette, 319 U.S. 624, 662.

7. The language of all people is merely a symbol of thought.—Frankfurter: Baltimore & O. R.R. v. Kepner, 314 U.S. 44, 60.

8. Symbols of State often convey political ideas just as religious symbols come to convey theological ones. —Jackson: West Va. State Bd. of Educ. v. Barnette, 319 U.S. 624, 632.

9. A person gets from a symbol the meaning he puts into it, and what is one man's comfort and inspiration is another's jest and scorn. — Jackson: *ibid.,* 632–33.

10. Symbolism is a primitive but effective way of communicating ideas. —Jackson: *ibid.,* 632.

11. Symbolism is inescapable. Even the most sophisticated live by symbols. Frankfuter: *ibid.,* 662.

12. Our quest for certitude is so ardent that we pay an irrational reverence to a technique which uses symbols of certainty, even though experience again and again warns us that they are delusive.—Jackson: Federal Power Comm'n v. Hope Nat. Gas Co., 320 U.S. 591, 643 n.

13. Few words possess the precision of mathematical symbols. — Clark: Boyce Motor Lines v. United States, 342 U.S. 337, 340.

See also Bookkeeping; Construction 67, 83; Corporation 11; Flag; Trade-mark.

SYMPATHY

See Judge 28, 29; Jurisdiction 6.

SYSTEM

See Tax 125, 127, 149.

TALENT

See Industry 3; Rights 51.

TARIFF

A tariff is not an abstraction.—Harlan: United States v. Western Pac. R.R., 352 U.S. 59, 66.

TASTE

1. One should not allow taste to blind one to great qualities, as it is apt to.—Holmes. *Holmes-Pollock Letters,* I, 160.

2. What is good literature, what has educational value, what is refined public information, what is good art, varies with individuals as it does from one generation to another.—Douglas: Hannegan v. Esquire, 327 U.S. 146, 157.

TAX, TAXATION, TAXPAYER

Defined, distinguished 1–8; power 9–12, need for 13–18; power, scope 19–23, limitations 24–30; power, exercise, difficulties 31–36, methods 37–43; standards, general 44–48, fairness 49–53, uniformity 54–55, equality, equity 56–71; bases 72–81; validity 82–84; abuse 85–95; double taxation 96–100; exemption 101–110; avoidance 111–117; history 118–121; judicial review 122–130; income taxes 131–137; inheritance taxes 138, 139; school taxes 140; tax court 141; miscellaneous 142–152.

———, defined, distinguished

1. A tax is an exaction.—Frankfurter: Wisconsin v. J. C. Penney Co., 311 U.S. 435, 443.

2. Any tax is a discouragement and therefore a regulation so far as it goes. —Holmes: Pacific Am. Fisheries v. Alaska, 269 U.S. 269, 277.

3. Taxes are not debts in the sense that having once been established and paid all further liability of the individual to the government has ceased. . . . The obligation of the individual to the state is continuous and proportioned to the extent of the public wants. No human wisdom can always foresee what may be the exigencies of the future.—Brewer: Patton v. Brady, 184 U.S. 608, 619.

4. Taxes are what we pay for civilized society, including the chance to insure. A penalty on the other hand is intended altogether to prevent the thing punished. — Holmes: Compañía Gen. de Tabacos v. Collector, 275 U.S. 87, 100.

5. Crime had to be committed before liability for the imposition arose. Taxes are not so conditioned.—Butler: United States v. One Ford Coupe Auto., 272 U.S. 321, 350.

6. A sales tax is a tax on the freedom of purchase.—Frankfurter: McLeod v. Dilworth Co., 322 U.S. 327, 330.

7. A use tax is a tax on the enjoyment of that which was purchased.— Frankfurter: *ibid.*

8. A tax is not an assessment of benefits.—Stone: Carmichael v. Southern Coal & Coke Co., 301 U.S. 495, 522.

———, power

9. In every free country the power

of laying taxes is considered a legislative power over the property and persons of the citizens. — Chase: Ware v. Hylton, 3 Dall. (3 U.S.) 199, 232.

10. The power to tax is indeed one of the most effective forms of regulation. And no more powerful instrument for centralization of government could be devised. — Douglas: New York v. United States, 326 U.S. 572, 594.

11. A state's power to tax property is plenary. — Roberts: Coolidge v. Long, 282 U.S. 582, 633.

12. The power to tax is . . . the strongest, the most pervading of all the powers of government reaching directly or indirectly to all classes of the people. — Miller: Savings & Loan Assoc. v. Topeka, 20 Wall. (87 U.S.) 655, 663.

———, power, need for

13. The power of taxing the people and their property is essential to the very existence of government.—Marshall: McCulloch v. Maryland, 4 Wheat. (17 U.S.) 316, 428.

14. The foundation of the obligation to pay taxes is not the privileges enjoyed or the protection given to a citizen by government. . . . The necessity of money for the support of States in times of peace or war, fixes the obligation upon their citizens.— Wayne: Dobbins v. Commissioners, 16 Pet. (41 U.S.) 435, 445–46.

15. No civilized government has ever existed that did not depend upon taxation in some form for the con-

tinuance of . . . existence. — Miller: Washington Univ. v. Rouse, 8 Wall. (75 U.S.) 439, 443.

16. Taxes are the life-blood of government, and their prompt and certain availability an imperious need.— Roberts: Bull v. United States, 295 U.S. 247, 259.

17. It costs something to be governed.—McKenna: Merrick v. Halsey, 242 U.S. 568, 587.

18. Taxes owing to the Government . . . are the price that business has to pay for protection and security. —Cardozo: Michigan v. Michigan Tr. Co., 286 U.S. 334, 344.

———, power, scope

19. They [the people] prescribe no limits to the exercise of this right [taxation], resting confidently on the interest of the legislator, and on the influence of the constituents over their representative, to guard them against its abuse.—Marshall: McCulloch v. Maryland, 4 Wheat. (17 U.S.) 316, 428.

20. The right to tax "in its nature acknowledges no limits." — Holmes: Pullman Co. v. Kansas, 216 U.S. 56, 77.

21. The arm of the tax-gatherer reaches far.—Rutledge: Commissioner of Int. Rev. v. Flowers, 326 U.S. 465, 480.

22. The power to tax the exercise of a privilege is the power to control or suppress its enjoyment. — Douglas: Murdock v. Pennsylvania, 319 U.S. 105, 112.

23. Taxation may run *pari passu*

with expenditure. The constituted authorities may rightfully make one equal the other.—Brewer: Patton v. Brady, 184 U.S. 608, 620.

———, power, scope, limitations

24. The great correction of excessive taxation is its oppression on the constituent, which causes a reaction to reduce it. — Woodbury: Passenger Cases, 7 How. (48 U.S.) 283, 532.

25. The powers of taxation are broad but the distinction between taxation and confiscation must still be observed. — Sutherland: Burnet v. Wells, 289 U.S. 670, 683.

26. A State cannot tax a stranger for something that it has not given him. —Frankfurter: Tax Comm'n v. Aldrich, 316 U.S. 174, 183.

27. Orthodox concepts of ownership fail to reflect the outer boundaries of taxation.—Murphy: Commissioner of Int. Rev. v. Wilcox, 327 U.S. 404, 407.

28. A state may not impose a charge for the enjoyment of a right granted by the federal constitution.—Douglas: Murdock v. Pennsylvania, 319 U.S. 105, 113.

29. The notion that a city has unlimited taxing power, is, of course, an illusion. — Frankfurter: Faitoute Iron & Steel Co. v. Asbury Park, 316 U.S. 502, 509.

30. Due process requires some definite link, some minimum connection, between a state and the person, property or transaction it seeks to tax.—Jackson: Miller Bros. Co. v. Maryland, 347 U.S. 340, 344-45.

———, power, exercise, difficulties

31. The task of devising means for distributing the burdens of taxation equitably has always challenged the wisdom of the wisest financial statesmen.—Reed: Newark Fire Ins. Co. v. State Bd., 307 U.S. 313, 323.

32. If we enjoyed the freedom of the framers it is possible that we might, in the light of experience, devise a more equitable system of taxation than that which they gave us.—Stone: Curry v. McCanless, 307 U.S. 357, 373.

33. As pressures for new revenues become more and more insistent, ways and means of meeting them present to a state not only the baffling task of tapping fresh sources of revenue but of doing so with due regard to a state's existing taxing system.—Frankfurter: Wisconsin v. J. C. Penney Co., 311 U.S. 435, 442.

34. It is of course idle to expect that the complexities of our economic life permit revenue measures to be drawn with such simplicity and particularity as to avoid much litigation.—Frankfurter: Burton-Sutton Oil Co. v. Comm'r of Int. Rev., 328 U.S. 25, 37.

35. It is impossible to escape nice distinctions in the application of complicated tax legislation. — Frankfurter: *ibid*.

36. Elaborate machinery, designed to bring about a perfect equilibrium between benefit and burden, may at times defeat its aim through its own elaboration.—Cardozo: Stewart Dry Goods Co. v. Lewis, 294 U.S. 550, 576.

———, power, exercise, methods

37. The methods and subjects of taxation are matters of governmental policy.—Cardozo: People *ex rel.* Clark v. Gilchrist, 243 N.Y. 173, 185.

38. Taxes must be laid by general rules.—Stone: Fernandez v. Wiener, 326 U.S. 340, 360.

39. Tax statutes and tax regulations never have been static. Experience, changing needs, changing philosophies inevitably produce constant change in each.—Douglas: Helvering v. Wilshire Oil Co., 308 U.S. 90, 97.

40. The power to make distinctions exists with full vigor in the field of taxation.—Reed: New York Rapid Transit Corp. v. New York, 303 U.S. 573, 578.

41. Distinctions which originated under a feudal economy when land dominated social relations are peculiarly irrelevant in the application of tax measures now so largely directed toward intangible wealth. — Frankfurter: Helvering v. Hallock, 309 U.S. 106, 118.

42. The net worth method, it seems, has evolved from the final volley to the first shot in the Government's battle for revenue.—Clark: Holland v. United States, 348 U.S. 121, 126–27.

43. A distinction between bonds and stocks for the essentially practical purposes of taxation is more fanciful than real. — Sutherland: First Nat'l Bank v. Maine, 284 U.S. 312, 328.

———, standards, general

44. There is nothing in the Con-stitution which requires a state to adopt the best possible system of taxation.—Stone: New York v. Latrobe, 279 U.S. 421, 427.

45. Systems of taxation need not achieve the ideal. But the fact that the Constitution does not demand pure reason and is satisfied by practical reason does not justify unreason. — Frankfurter: Capitol Greyhound Lines v. Brice, 339 U.S. 542, 552.

46. Might does not make right even in taxation. — Jackson: International Harvester Co. v. Wisconsin Dept. of Tax., 322 U.S. 435, 450.

47. Taxation . . . in most communities, is a long way off from a logical and coherent theory.—Holmes: Paddell v. City of New York, 211 U.S. 446, 450.

48. There is no abstract justice in any system of taxation.—Roberts: Helvering v. New York Tr. Co., 292 U.S. 455, 471.

———, standards, fairness

49. Representation is the ordinary guaranty of fairness in taxation.—Jackson: International Harvester Co. v. Wisconsin Dept. of Tax., 322 U.S. 435, 451.

50. The soundest principles of republicanism do sanction some relation between representation and taxation. . . . The two ought to be connected. . . . This was the principle of the revolution.—Marshall: Beveridge, *Life of Marshall,* IV, 503.

51. Even tax administration does not as a matter of principle preclude considerations of fairness. — Frank-

furter: Angelus Milling Co. v. Comm'r of Int. Rev., 325 U.S. 293, 297.

52. Revenue laws are notoriously not expressions of an ordered system of reason and fairness. There has probably never been a revenue statute which, by design or oversight, has not favored some groups and laid the basis for a claim of unfairness to others similarly situated. — Frankfurter: Lewyt Corp. v. Comm'r of Int. Rev., 349 U.S. 237, 249.

53. Nothing is more familiar in taxation than the imposition of a tax upon a class or upon individuals who enjoy no direct benefit from its expenditure, and who are not responsible for the condition to be remedied.— Stone: Carmichael v. Southern Coal & Coke Co., 301 U.S. 495, 521–22.

———, standards, uniformity

54. The Constitution does not require uniformity in the manner of collection. Uniformity in the assessment is all it demands.—Waite: Tappan v. Merchants Nat'l Bank, 19 Wall. (86 U.S.) 490, 505.

55. Uniform taxation upon those equally able to bear their fair shares of the burdens of government is the objective of every just government.— Black: Helvering v. Gerhardt, 304 U.S. 405, 427.

———, standards, equality, equity

56. Perfect equality and perfect uniformity of taxation as regards individuals or corporations, or the different classes of property subject to taxation, is a dream unrealized. It may be admitted that the system which most nearly attains this is the best.— Miller: Taylor v. Secor, 2 Otto (92 U.S.) 575, 612.

57. There is . . . no constitutional guaranty of equality of taxation. — Stone: Stebbins v. Riley, 268 U.S. 137, 141.

58. Mathematical equality . . . cannot be reached in any system of taxation, and it is useless and idle to attempt it.—Peckham: First Nat'l Bank v. Chapman, 173 U.S. 205, 216.

59. The real friends of property are not those who would exempt the wealth of the country from bearing its fair share of the burdens of taxation, but rather those who seek to have every one, without reference to his locality, contribute from his substance, upon terms of equality with all others, to the support of the government.— Harlan: Pollock v. Farmers Loan & Tr. Co., 158 U.S. 601, 676.

60. Those who are subject to be taxed cannot complain that they are denied the equal protection of the laws because those who cannot legally be taxed are not taxed.—McKenna: Cahen v. Brewster, 203 U.S. 543, 553.

61. Protection and taxation are not necessarily correlative obligations, nor precise equality of burden attainable, however desirable. — Lurton: Southern Pac. Co. v. Kentucky, 222 U.S. 63, 76.

62. A desire for equality among taxpayers is to be attributed to Congress, rather than the reverse. — Reed: Colgate-Palmolive-Peet Co. v. United States, 320 U.S. 422, 425.

63. Eccentricities of incidence are common, and perhaps inevitable, in every system of taxation.—Cardozo: Binney v. Long, 299 U.S. 280, 299.

64. Systems of taxation are not framed, nor is it possible to frame them, with perfect distribution of benefit and burden. Their authors must be satisfied with a rough and ready form of justice.—Cardozo: Liggett Co. v. Lee, 288 U.S. 517, 586.

65. It may be true that plaintiff does not receive the same amount of benefit from some of these taxes, or from any of them, as do citizens living in the heart of the City. . . . But who can undertake to adjust with precise accuracy the amount which each individual in an organized civil community shall contribute to sustain the organization?—Miller: Kelly v. Pittsburgh, 14 Otto (104 U.S.) 78, 82.

66. One might as well compare the federal income tax of a banker whose net earnings are in the millions with that of a thousand clerks who by reason of exemptions are to pay no tax whatever. The comparison proves nothing unless it be the obvious fact that taxpayers are few when the count is at the highest level.—Cardozo: Stewart Dry Goods Co. v. Lewis, 294 U.S. 550, 571.

67. The state is not called upon to explain the reasons for taxing the members of the one class more heavily than it does the members of the other.—Cardozo: Concordia Fire Ins. Co. v. Illinois, 292 U.S. 535, 558.

68. If Congress may tax one citizen to the point of discouragement for making an honest living, it is hard to say that it may not do the same to another just because he makes a sinister living. If the law-abiding must tell all to the tax collector, it is difficult to excuse one because his business is lawbreaking.—Jackson: United States v. Kahriger, 345 U.S. 22, 35.

69. Gross inequalities may not be ignored for the sake of ease of collection. — Roberts: Stewart Dry Goods Co. v. Lewis, 294 U.S. 550, 560.

70. Many inequities are inherent in the income tax. We multiply them needlessly by nice distinctions which have no place in the practical administration of the law.—Douglas: United States v. Lewis, 340 U.S. 590, 592.

71. A State must not play favorites in the operation of its taxing system between business confined within its borders and the common interests of the nation expressed through business conducted across State lines.—Frankfurter: Capitol Greyhound Lines v. Brice, 339 U.S. 542, 556.

———, bases

72. Property is made the constitutional basis of taxation. This is not unreasonable. Governments are organized for the protection of persons and property and the expenses of the protection may very properly be apportioned among the persons protected according to the value of their property protected. — Waite: Tappan v. Merchants Nat'l Bank, 19 Wall. (86 U.S.) 490, 501.

73. Taxes generally are imposed upon persons for the general advan-

tages of living within the jurisdiction, not upon property, although generally measured more or less by reference to the riches of the person taxed.—Holmes: Safe Dep. & Tr. Co. v. Virginia, 280 U.S. 83, 97.

74. Wealth has long been accepted as a fair measure of a tax assessment.—Reed: Greenough v. Tax Assessors, 331 U.S. 486, 492.

75. The law of taxation is more concerned with the substance of economic opportunity than with classifying legal concepts, and tagging them with names and labels.—Cardozo: Freuler v. Helvering, 291 U.S. 35, 49.

76. Natural rights, so called, are as much subject to taxation as rights of less importance. — Cardozo: Steward Mach. Co. v. Davis, 301 U.S. 495, 580.

77. What the individual does in the operation of a business is amenable to taxation just as much as what he owns, at all events if the classification is not tyrannical or arbitrary.—Cardozo: *ibid.,* 581.

78. Moral turpitude is not a touchstone of taxability.—Murphy: Commissioner of Int. Rev. v. Wilcox, 327 U.S. 404, 408.

79. It is one thing to impose a tax on the income or property of a preacher. It is quite another thing to exact a tax from him for the privilege of delivering a sermon.—Douglas: Murdock v. Pennsylvania, 319 U.S. 105, 112.

80. The encouragement or discouragement of competition is an end for which the power of taxation may be exerted. — Brandeis: Liggett Co. v. Lee, 288 U.S. 517, 572.

81. In the last twenty years, revenue needs have come to exceed the demands that legislatures feel it expedient to make upon accumulated wealth or property with fixed location within the state. The states therefore have turned to taxing activities connected with the movement of commerce, such as exchange and consumption.—Jackson: Miller Bros. Co. v. Maryland, 347 U.S. 340, 342–43.

———, validity

82. The validity of a tax depends upon its nature, and not upon its name.—Cardozo: Concordia Fire Ins. Co. v. Illinois, 292 U.S. 535, 550.

83. In determining whether the tax is in truth a tax on property, we are to consider, not its form or label, but its practical operation.—Cardozo: People *ex rel.* Alpha Portland Cement Co. v. Knapp, 230 N.Y. 48, 56.

84. The incidence of taxation depends upon the substance of a transaction.—Black: Commissioner of Int. Rev. v. Court Holding Co., 324 U.S. 331, 334.

———, abuse

85. That the power to tax involves the power to destroy; that the power to destroy may defeat and render useless the power to create . . . are propositions not to be denied.—Marshall: McCulloch v. Maryland, 4 Wheat. (17 U.S.) 316. 431.

86. No one imagines . . . that a law professing to tax, will be permitted

to destroy.—Marshall: Weston v. City Council, 2 Pet. (27 U.S.) 449, 473.

87. The power to tax is the power to destroy only in the sense that those who have power can misuse it.—Reed: Murdock v. Pennsylvania, 319 U.S. 105, 137.

88. The power to tax is not the power to destroy while this court sits. —Holmes: Panhandle Oil Co. v. Mississippi, 277 U.S. 218, 223.

89. Of all burdens imposed upon mankind that of grinding taxation is the most cruel.—Hunt: United States v. Baltimore & O. R.R., 17 Wall. (84 U.S.) 322, 326.

90. The power to tax may be exercised oppressively upon persons, but the responsibility of the legislature is not to the courts, but to the people by whom its members are elected. — Chase: Veazie Bank v. Fenno, 8 Wall. (75 U.S.) 533, 548.

91. Of all the powers conferred upon government that of taxation is most liable to abuse. . . . This power can as readily be employed against one class of individuals and in favor of another, so as to ruin the one class and give unlimited wealth and prosperity to the other, if there is no implied limitation of the uses for which the power may be exercised.—Miller: Savings & Loan Assoc. v. Topeka, 20 Wall. (87 U.S.) 655, 663.

92. It is wise to remember that the taxing and licensing power is a dangerous and potent weapon which, in the hands of unscrupulous or bigoted men, could be used to suppress freedoms and destroy religion unless it is kept within appropriate bounds. — Murphy: Follett v. McCormick, 321 U.S. 573, 579.

93. One of our basic rights is to be free of taxation to support a transgression of the constitutional command that the authorities "shall make no law respecting an establishment of religion, or prohibiting the free exercise thereof." — Jackson: Everson v. Board of Educ., 330 U.S. 1, 22.

94. Taxes on the circulation of ideas have a long history of misuse against freedom of thought.—Murphy: Jones v. Opelika, 316 U.S. 584, 616.

95. The taxes that have an invidious incidence are those which historically were known in America as "taxes on knowledge." — Douglas: *We, the Judges,* 328.

———, double taxation

96. That the power of taxation is one of vital importance; that it is retained by the States; that it is not abridged by the grant of a similar power to the government of the Union; that it is to be concurrently exercised by the two governments: are truths which have never been denied. —Marshall: McCulloch v. Maryland, 4 Wheat (17 U.S.) 316, 425.

97. Justice requires that the burdens of government shall as far as is practicable be laid equally on all; and if property is taxed once in one way, it would ordinarily be wrong to tax it again in another way, when the burden of both taxes falls on the same person.—Waite: Tennessee v. Whitworth, 117 U.S. 129, 137.

98. The objection to double taxation by a single sovereign is no more potent under the objection that a tax otherwise valid has been doubled.—Stone: Senior v. Braden, 295 U.S. 422, 439.

99. The burden of Federal taxation necessarily sets an economic limit to the practical operation of the taxing power of the States, and vice versa.—Stone: Metcalf v. Mitchell, 269 U.S. 514, 523.

100. Modern enterprise often brings different parts of an organic commercial transaction within the taxing power of more than one State, as well as of the nation. It does so because the transaction in its entirety may receive the benefits of more than one government.—Frankfurter: Tax Comm'n v. Aldrich, 316 U.S. 174, 183.

———, exemption

101. Why should one who enjoys all the advantages of a society purchased at a heavy expense, and lives in affluence upon an income derived exclusively from interest on government stock, be exempted from taxation? — Marshall: Weston v. City Council, 2 Pet. (27 U.S.) 449, 473.

102. The exemption of property from taxation is a question of policy and not of power.—McLean: Piqua Branch v. Knoop, 16 How. (57 U.S.) 369, 384.

103. Exemptions from the operation of a tax always create inequalities. Those not exempted must, in the end, bear an additional burden or pay more than their share.—Field: Pollock v. Farmers Loan & Tr. Co., 157 U.S. 429, 595.

104. Strong considerations of fiscal and social policy view tax exemptions with a hostile eye.—Murphy: Oklahoma Tax Comm'n v. United States, 319 U.S. 598, 612.

105. Whether the property of the United States shall be taxed under the laws of a State depends upon the will of its owner, the United States, and no State can tax the property of the United States without their consent. —Gray: Van Brocklin v. Anderson, 117 U.S. 151, 175.

106. Just what instrumentalities of either a state or the Federal government are exempt from taxation by the other cannot be stated in terms of universal application.—Stone: Metcalf v. Mitchell, 269 U.S. 514, 522.

107. A grant of exemption is never to be considered as a mere gratuity— a simple gift from the legislature. . . . A consideration is presumed to exist. The recipient of the exemption may be supposed to be doing part of the work which the state would otherwise be under obligations to do. A college, or an academy, furnishes education to the young, which it is a part of the state's duty to furnish. — Brewer: Illinois Cent. R.R. v. Decatur, 147 U.S. 190, 201.

108. The legislative reasons for granting immunity from taxes to . . . charitable institutions . . . prominent among which would doubtless be the fact, that the support and maintenance extended to the objects of the charity relieves the State from a burden which

would involve a much larger amount of taxation than that which it waives by granting the exemption. — Bradley: St. Ann's Asylum v. New Orleans, 15 Otto (105 U.S.) 362, 368.

109. Looking backward it is easy to see that the line between the taxable and the immune has been drawn by an unsteady hand.—Jackson: United States v. Allegheny, 322 U.S. 174, 176.

110. The tax-exempt privilege is a feature always reflected in the market price of bonds. The investor pays for it.—Brandeis: National Life Ins. Co. v. United States, 277 U.S. 508, 528.

————, avoidance

111. The legal right of a taxpayer to decrease the amount of what otherwise would be his taxes, or altogether avoid them, by means which the law permits, cannot be doubted.—Sutherland: Gregory v. Helvering, 293 U.S. 465, 469.

112. Business may pass on taxes.—Reed: New York Rapid Transit Corp. v. New York, 303 U.S. 573, 581.

113. True, of course, it is that in a system of taxation so intricate and cast as ours there are many other loopholes unsuspected by the framers of the statute, many other devices whereby burdens can be lowered.—Cardozo: Woolford Realty Co. v. Rose, 286 U.S. 319, 330.

114. Taxes cannot be escaped "by anticipatory arrangements and contracts however skillfully devised . . . by which the fruits are attributed to a different tree from that on which

they grew."—Frankfurter: Griffiths v. Helvering, 308 U.S. 355, 358 (quot. 281 U.S. 111, 115).

115. The fact that the incidences of income taxation may have been taken into account by arranging matters one way rather than another, so long as the way chosen was the way the law allows, does not make a transaction something else than it truly is. —Frankfurter: Commissioner of Int. Rev. v. Wodehouse, 337 U.S. 369, 410.

116. Those who have large estates and watchful lawyers will find ways of minimizing these tax burdens. — Jackson: Tax Comm'n v. Aldrich, 316 U.S. 174, 195.

117. The many small stockholders cannot afford professional counsel or evasion devices.—Jackson: *ibid.,* 195–96.

————, history

118. Taxes rise with inflation, however caused or to whatever extent, whether temporary or permanent; and depression, be it ever so great, and whether caused by imaginary difficulties or by war or famine, lessens the demand for contribution in a corresponding ratio. — Clifford: Hamilton Mfg. Co. v. Massachusetts, 6 Wall. (32 U.S.) 623, 641.

119. Objects and means of taxation were not in the years past sought for with the same avidity as at present. The demand for revenue was not so great. — Brewer: Citizens' Bank v. Parker, 192 U.S. 73, 93.

120. Our modern income tax experience began with the Revenue Act

of 1913. The World War soon brought high rates. — Jackson: Dobson v. Comm'r of Int. Rev., 320 U.S. 489, 496.

121. Our colonial forbears knew more about the ways of taxing than some of their descendants seem to be willing to concede. — Cardozo: Steward Mach. Co. v. Davis, 301 U.S. 495, 580.

―――, judicial review

122. It is reasonable that a man who denies the legality of a tax should have a clear and certain remedy.— Holmes: Atchison, T. & S. F. Ry. v. O'Connor, 223 U.S. 280, 285.

123. Courts sometimes, perhaps, have been a little too slow to recognize the implied duress under which payment is made.—Holmes: *ibid.,* 286.

124. No government could exist, that permitted the collection of its revenue to be delayed by every litigious man or every embarrassed man, to whom delay was more important than the payment of costs. — Hunt: Tennessee v. Sneed, 6 Otto (96 U.S.) 69, 75.

125. Judicial efforts to mold tax policy by isolated decisions make a national tax system difficult to develop, administer or observe. — Jackson: Commissioner of Int. Rev. v. Church, 335 U.S. 632, 653.

126. No other branch of the law touches human activities at so many points. It can never be made simple, but we can try to avoid making it needlessly complex. — Jackson: Dob-

son v. Comm'r of Int. Rev,. 320 U.S. 489, 494–95.

127. Students of federal taxation agree that the tax system suffers from delay in getting the final word in judicial review, from retroactivity of the decision when it is obtained, and from the lack of a roundly tax-informed viewpoint of judges. — Jackson: *ibid.,* 500.

128. Conflicts are multiplied by treating as questions of law what really are disputes over proper accounting. The mere number of such questions and the mass of decisions they call forth becomes a menace to the certainty and good administration of the law.—Jackson: *ibid.,* 499.

129. There was wisdom as well as wit in a cynical wag's remark that the lawyers had transformed the ancient principle of "no taxation without representation" into a doctrine of "no taxation without litigation."—Jackson: *Struggle for Judicial Supremacy,* 141.

130. Solicitude for the revenues is a plausible but treacherous basis upon which to decide a particular tax case. —Jackson: Arrowsmith v. Comm'r. of Int. Rev., 344 U.S. 6, 11.

―――, income tax

131. In form, the tax is one upon the value of a privilege, and income is nothing but the measure. — Cardozo: People *ex rel.* Alpha Portland Cement Co. v. Knapp, 230 N.Y. 48, 62.

132. The income tax laws do not profess to embody perfect economic

theory. — Holmes: Weiss v. Wiener, 279 U.S. 333, 335.

133. There is no tax which, in its essence, is more just and equitable than an income tax.—Harlan: Pollock v. Farmers Loan & Tr. Co., 158 U.S. 601, 676.

134. In every civilized country there is an exemption of small incomes which it would be manifest cruelty to tax. — Brown: *ibid.,* 694.

135. It would be an extreme if not an extravagant application of the Fifth Amendment to say that it authorized a man to refuse to state the amount of his income because it had been made in crime. — Holmes: United States v. Sullivan, 274 U.S. 259, 264.

136. The question where an income is earned is always a matter of doubt when the business is begun in one country and ended in another. — McKenna: Barclay & Co. v. Edwards, 276 U.S. 442, 450.

137. The taxpayer has equally enjoyed the fruits of his labor or investment and obtained the satisfaction of his desires whether he collects and uses the income to procure those satisfactions, or whether he disposes of his right to collect it as the means of procuring them.—Stone: Helvering v. Horst, 311 U.S. 112, 117.

——, inheritance tax

138. The taking of possession of inherited property is one of the most ancient subjects of taxation known to the law.—Stone: Fernandez v. Wiener, 326 U.S. 340, 353.

139. The policy behind estate tax legislation . . . is the diversion to the purposes of the community of a portion of the total current of wealth released by death. — Frankfurter: Whitney v. State Tax Comm'n, 309 U.S. 530, 538.

——, school tax

140. General taxation to maintain public schools is an appropriation of property to a use in which the taxpayer may have no private interest, and, it may be, against his will. It has been condemned by theorists on that ground. Yet no one denies its constitutionality. People are accustomed to it and accept it without doubt. — Holmes: Interstate Consol. St. Ry. v. Massachusetts, 207 U.S. 79, 87.

——, tax court

141. The court is independent, and its neutrality is not clouded by prosecuting duties. Its procedures assure fair hearings. Its deliberations are evidenced by careful opinions. All guides to judgment available to judges are habitually consulted and respected. It has established a tradition of freedom from bias and pressures. It deals with a subject that is highly specialized and so complex as to be the despair of judges. It is relatively better staffed for its task than is the judiciary. — Jackson: Dobson v. Comm'r of Int. Rev., 320 U.S. 489, 498.

——, miscellaneous

142. I know of no power, indeed, of which a free people ought to be more jealous, than of that of levying taxes

444

and duties.—Story: Cary v. Curtis, 3 How. (44 U.S.) 236, 253.

143. Taxation is eminently practical, and is in fact brought to every man's door. — Peckham: Nicol v. Ames, 173 U.S. 509, 516.

144. The tight net which the Treasury Regulations fashion is for the protection of the revenue.—Frankfurter: Angelus Milling Co. v. Comm'r of Int. Rev., 325 U.S. 293, 297.

145. Trade being a sensitive plant, a direct tax upon it to some extent at least deters trade even if its effect is not precisely calculable.—Frankfurter: Freeman v. Hewit, 329 U.S. 249, 257.

146. The payment of taxes is an obvious and insistent duty, and its sanction is usually punitive. — McKenna: Bankers Tr. Co. v. Blodgett, 260 U.S. 647, 651.

147. The payment of taxes gives a right to protection. — Wayne: Dobbins v. Comm'rs, 16 Pet. (41 U.S.) 435, 445–46.

148. When a revenue agent confronts the taxpayer with an apparent deficiency, the latter may be more concerned with a quick settlement than an honest search for the truth.—Clark: Holland v. United States, 348 U.S. 121, 128.

149. The United States has a system of taxation by confession. That a people so numerous, scattered and individualistic annually assesses itself with a tax liability, often in highly burdensome amounts, is a reassuring sign of the stability and vitality of our system of self-government. What sur-prised me in once trying to help administer these laws was not to discover examples of recalcitrance, fraud or self-serving mistakes in reporting, but to discover that such derelictions were so few. — Jackson: United States v. Kahriger, 345 U.S. 22, 36.

150. Delinquent taxpayers as a class are a poor credit risk; tax default, unless an incident of legitimate tax litigation, is, to the eye sensitive to credit indications, a signal of distress. —Jackson: Meilink v. Unemployment Res. Comm'n, 314 U.S. 564, 567.

151. A rate of interest on tax delinquencies which is low in comparison to the taxpayer's borrowing rate—if he can borrow at all—is a temptation to use the state as a convenient, if involuntary, banker by the simple practice of deferring the payment of taxes.—Jackson: *ibid*.

152. [Tax] liability is one of the notorious incidents of social life. — Holmes: Seattle v. Kelleher, 195 U.S. 351, 360.

See also Construction 30, 47; Freedom, speech 108; Municipality 3, 4; Securities 4, 6.

TEACHER, TEACHING

1. The capacity to impart instruction to others is given by the Almighty for beneficent purposes; and its use may not be interfered with by government—certainly not, unless such instruction is, in its nature, harmful. —Harlan: Berea Col. v. Kentucky, 211 U.S. 45, 67.

2. No one would doubt that a teacher might be forbidden to teach many

things.—Holmes: Meyer v. Nebraska, 262 U.S. 390, 412.

3. I don't doubt you do more than half in setting your class on fire. When you do that you do the best and rarest thing that a teacher can do. I used to say that Emerson's great gift was that of imparting a ferment. — Holmes: *Uncollected Letters,* 176.

4. Teachers must fulfill their function by precept and practice, by the very atmosphere which they generate; they must be exemplars of open-mindedness and free inquiry. They cannot carry out their noble task if the conditions for the practice of a responsible and critical mind are denied to them. They must have the freedom of responsible inquiry, by thought and action, into the meaning of social and economic ideas, into the checkered history of social and economic dogma.— Frankfurter: Wieman v. Updegraff, 344 U.S. 183, 196.

5. A teacher works in a sensitive area in a schoolroom. There he shapes the attitude of young minds towards the society in which they live. In this, the state has a vital concern. It must preserve the integrity of the schools. —Minton: Adler v. Board of Educ., 342 U.S. 485, 493.

6. Spying and surveillance with its accompanying reports and trials cannot go hand in hand with academic freedom. It produces standardized thought, not the pursuit of truth. — Douglas: *ibid.,* 510–11.

7. A problem can no longer be pursued with impunity to its edges. Fear stalks the classroom. The teacher is no longer a stimulant to adventurous thinking; she becomes instead a pipe line for safe and sound information. A deadening dogma takes the place of free inquiry. Instruction tends to become sterile; pursuit of knowledge is discouraged; discussion often leaves off where it should begin. This, I think, is what happens when a censor looks over a teacher's shoulder. — Douglas: *ibid.,* 510.

8. He [the university professor] must be and remain free, free to form and hold his opinions and free to express them without incurring the risk of loss of the privileges and emoluments of his position. Restraints upon the intellectual freedom of the university teacher, whatever their form and however plausible their justification, will inevitably impair confidence in its teaching and ultimately undermine and destroy its influence.— Stone: Mason, *Stone,* 110.

9. The university professor should voluntarily renounce the role of propagandist and agitator. The university stands for scientific truth. Its attitude, if it would preserve its influence, must never be that of the partisan, but rather that of the judicially minded. Stone: *ibid.*

10. By engaging in teaching in the public schools, petitioner did not give up his right to freedom of belief, speech, or association.—Burton: Beilan v. Board of Educ., 357 U.S. 399, 405.

11. Competent teachers of law are

born, not made exclusively by training or environment.—Stone: Mason, *Stone*, 86.

12. Scholarship cannot flourish in an atmosphere of suspicion and distrust. Teachers and students must always remain free to inquire, to study and to evaluate.—Warren: Sweezy v. New Hampshire, 354 U.S. 234, 250.

13. Fitness for teaching depends on a broad range of factors. — Burton: Beilan v. Board of Educ., 357 U.S. 399, 406.

Related subjects: Education and related subjects. *See also* Experience 1; Freedom, learning 159; History 6; Public school 3.

TECHNICALITY (legal)

1. Technical niceties . . . the days for such subtilties in a great measure passed away.—Story: Bottomly v. United States, 1 Story 152.

2. The law has outgrown its primitive stage of formalism when the precise word was the sovereign talisman, and every slip was fatal.—Cardozo: Wood v. Duff-Gordon, 222 N.Y. 88, 91.

3. The law does not stand upon punctilios if there is a starving wife at home.—Cardozo: Coler v. Corn Exch. Bank, 250 N.Y. 136, 143.

4. In some cases, good sense is sacrificed to technical nicety, and a sound principle carried to an extravagant extent.—Hunt: United States v. Reese, 2 Otto (92 U.S.) 214, 243.

5. Lawyers know, if others do not, that what may seem technical may embody a great tradition of justice.—Rutledge: Kotteakos v. United States, 328 U.S. 750, 761.

6. To the laity such matters may seem technicalities in a derogatory sense of the term. But this is only one phase of an attitude of mind that thinks ill of law which does not accord with private wishes. When informed by a legal adviser that to carry out his desires would encounter "technical legal difficulties," a strenuous President of the United States impatiently observed that "all law is technicality."—Frankfurter: United States v. Storer Broadcast Co., 351 U.S. 192, 214.

7. Legal refinements are not always the worse for eluding the quick understanding of a layman.—Frankfurter: Pacific Coast Dairy v. Dep't of Agriculture, 318 U.S. 285, 298.

Related subjects: Form (substance); Formalism. *See also* Common sense 2; Criminal law, technicalities; Form 14; Judge 31; Will 5; Witness 5.

TELEGRAPH

The electric telegraph marks an epoch in the progress of time. In a little more than a quarter of a century it has changed the habits of business, and become one of the necessities of commerce. — Waite: Pensacola Tel. Co. v. Western Union Tel. Co., 6 Otto (96 U.S.) 1, 9.

TELEPHONE

1. It is quite true that when Bell applied for his patent he had never actually transmitted telegraphically spoken words so that they could be distinctly heard and understood at the receiving end of his line. . . . The particular instrument which he had

and which he used in his experiments did not, under the circumstances in which it was tried, reproduce the words spoken, so that they could be clearly understood. — Waite: Telephone Cases, 126 U.S. 1, 535.

2. We do not question Mr. Bell's merits. He appreciated the importance of the invention, and brought it before the public in such a manner as to attract to it the attention of the scientific world. His professional experience and attainments enabled him to see, at a glance, that it was one of the great discoveries of the century. —Bradley: *ibid., 575.*

TELEVISION

Doubtless, television may find a place among the devices of education; but much long-headed thought and patient experimentation are demanded lest uncritical use may lead to hasty jettisoning of hard-won gains of civilization.—Frankfurter: Radio Corp. v. United States, 341 U.S. 412, 425.

See also Freedom 64.

TEMPTATION

Temptation is not always invitation. —Holmes: Erie R.R. v. Hilt, 247 U.S. 97, 101.

See also Hazard 2; Poverty 1.

TENANT

See Rent law 1, 3.

TERMINOLOGY

See Logomachy; Word 7.

TEST

1. We shall hardly go astray if we prefer the test of conduct.—Cardozo:

Dayton Power & Light Co. v. Public Util. Comm'n, 292 U.S. 290, 312.

2. Extraordinary situations may not wisely or fairly be subjected to tests or regulations that are fitting for the common-place or normal.—Cardozo: Pokora v. Wabash Ry., 292 U.S. 98, 105–106.

3. The tests to be applied are those of common understanding as revealed by common speech.—Cardozo: In the Matter of Connelly v. Hunt Furn. Co., 240 N.Y. 83, 85.

4. Difficulties in applying the test of reason do not justify abandonment of reason. — Frankfurter: Capitol Greyhound Lines v. Brice, 339 U.S. 542, 556.

See also Character 3; Experience 3; Form 3; Truth, test; Usage 1.

TESTIMONY (legal)

1. If a defendant asserts a fact which is not and cannot be within his own knowledge, the nature of his testimony cannot be changed by the positiveness of his assertion. The strength of his belief may have betrayed him into a mode of expression of which he was not fully apprised.— Marshall: Clark's Ex'rs v. Van Riemseyk, 9 Cranch (13 U.S.) 153, 160.

2. These cases . . . have generally been supported by the same species of testimony, it cannot be wondered at if this court shall receive, with considerable jealousy and caution, evidence which is so perpetually recurring, and which if compared will be found to present the same uniform statements of facts, with very few

shades of difference. — Livingston: Brig Struggle, 9 Cranch (13 U.S.) 71, 74.

3. It is true that the court does not find that the witnesses have sworn falsely, but that is not essential when that is its belief. To say that the testimony is not satisfactory is more polite and less offensive, and at the same time equally sufficient. — Brewer: Stone v. United States, 164 U.S. 380, 382.

4. When words are to be proved by witnesses who depend on their memory alone, the precise terms employed by the parties will seldom be recollected, and courts and juries must form their opinions upon the substance and upon all the circumstances.—Marshall: Pawling v. United States, 4 Cranch (8 U.S.) 219, 223.

5. The testimony of women is weighed with caution and allowance for them differently from that of men, but never with the slightest suspicion that they are not as truthful.—Wayne: Gaines v. Relf, 12 How. (53 U.S.) 472, 551.

6. Negative testimony is often as compelling as bits of affirmative evidence.—Frankfurter: Romero v. International Term. Oper. Co., 358 U.S. 354, 370.

Related subjects: Confession and related subjects; Expert; Immunity; Self incrimination; Witness. *See also* Common law 12; Conviction (crime) 4; Hearing 6; Informer; Patent 14; Perjury.

TEST OATH

1. Test oaths are notorious tools of tyranny. When used to shackle the mind they are, or at least they should be, unspeakably odious to a free people.—Black: Wieman v. Updegraff, 344 U.S. 183, 193.

2. It is asking more than rightfully may be asked of ordinary men to take oath that a method is not "unconstitutional" or "illegal" when constitutionality or legality is frequently determined by this Court by the chance of a single vote. — Frankfurter: American Com. Assoc. v. Douds, 339 U.S. 382, 420.

Related subjects: Oath; Loyalty oath.

THEATER

1. If we are to yield to fashionable conventions, it seems to me that theaters are as much devoted to public use as anything well can be.—Holmes: Tyson v. Banton, 273 U.S. 418, 447.

2. Lotteries were thought useful adjuncts of the state a century or so ago; now they are believed to be immoral and they have been stopped. Wine has been thought good for man from the time of the Apostles until recent years. What has happened to lotteries and wine might happen to theaters in some moral storm of the future, not because theaters were devoted to a public use, but because people had come to think that way. — Holmes: *ibid.,* 446–47.

3. It may be true, as asserted, that, among the Greeks, amusement and instruction of the people through the drama was one of the duties of government.—Sutherland: *ibid.,* 441.

THEFT, THIEF

1. "Theft," though often used as

synonymous with "larceny," the proper term of art in the penal statutes of New York, is none the less a looser term, and one more colloquial or popular. — Cardozo: Van Vechten v. American Eagle Fire Ins. Co., 239 N.Y. 303, 305.

2. The crimes [theft and larceny] are one today in the common speech of men as they are in moral quality.—Cardozo: *ibid.,* 306.

3. Thieves do not remain at the scene of their crime. — Black: Bollenbach v. United States, 326 U.S. 607, 618–19.

4. Even such honor as exists among thieves is not too precious to be sacrificed for a chance at liberty.—Jackson: Price v. Johnston, 334 U.S. 266, 297.

5. A thief cannot be charged with committing two offenses — that is, stealing and receiving the goods he has stolen. . . . And this is so for the commonsensical, if not obvious, reason that a man who takes property does not at the same time give himself the property he has taken. — Frankfurter: Milanovich v. United States, 365 U.S. 551, 558.

Related subjects: Conversion; Larceny. *See also* Flight 1.

THEORIST, THEORY

1. Nothing is so fascinating, and so delusive, as the simplicity of theory, in the earlier stages of life. — Story: *Misc. Writings,* 164.

2. Mere theories are not entitled to consideration, unless they find some support in the evidence. — Clifford:

Wiggins v. People, 3 Otto (93 U.S.) 465, 480.

3. I know no reason why theory should disagree with the facts. — Holmes: "Theory of Legal Interpretation," 12 Harv. L. Rev. 417.

See also Law 20; Philosopher 1; Practical 2; Tax 132; Truth 9.

THIRD DEGREE

1. "The third degree" is not unjustly called "the American method." —Frankfurter: Pennekamp v. Florida, 328 U.S. 331, 360.

2. Third-degree violence has been too often denounced by courts for anything useful to come out of mere repetition of invectives.—Jackson: Stein v. New York, 346 U.S. 156, 196.

3. The third degree flourishes only in secrecy.—Douglas: Crocker v. California, 357 U.S. 433, 443.

Related subjects: Confession and related subjects. *See also* Arrest 2; Criminal law, interrogation.

THOUGHT

1. Most men think dramatically, quantitatively, a fact that the rich would be wise to remember more than they do. — Holmes: *Speeches,* 99–100.

2. We must think things not words, or at least we must constantly translate our words into facts for which they stand, if we are to keep to the real and the true. — Holmes: "Law in Science and Science in Law," 12 Harv. L. Rev. 460.

3. The men whom I should be tempted to commemorate would be the o r i g i n a t o r s of transforming

thought. They often are half obscure, because what the world pays for is judgment, not the original mind. — Holmes: *Speeches,* 90.

4. All thought is social, is on its way to action; that, to borrow the expression of a French writer, every idea tends to become first a catechism and then a code; and that according to its worth his unhelped meditation may one day mount a throne, and without armies, or even with them, may shoot across the world the electric despotism of an unresisted power. — Holmes: *ibid.,* 91.

5. A man is bound to be parochial in his practice—to give his life, and if necessary his death, for the place where he has his roots. But his thinking should be cosmopolitan and detached. He should be able to criticize what he reveres and loves.—Holmes: *ibid.,* 89.

6. All i n s t r u m e n t s of thought should be narrowly watched lest they be abused and fail in their service to reason.—Frankfurter: United States v. Scophony Corp., 333 U.S. 795, 820.
Related subjects: Freedom, belief, conscience, thought; Idea; Mind; Reason. *See also* Freedom 57, 159; Heart 1; Judge 47; Loyalty oath 2; Metaphor 1; Tradition 6; Truth 14; Value 3; Word 1, 7.

THREAT
As a general rule, even if subject to some exceptions, what you may do in a certain event you may threaten to do, that is, give warning of your intention to do in that event, and thus allow the other person the chance of avoiding the consequence.—Holmes:

Vegelahn v. Guntner, 167 Mass. 92, 107.

TIME
Related subject: Past. *See also* Change 1; Court 46; Perpetuity.

TIMIDITY
See Judge 41; Prophecy 4.

TIPPING
In businesses where tipping is customary, the tips, in the absence of an explicit contrary understanding, belong to the recipient.—Reed: William v. Jacksonville Terminal Co., 315 U.S. 386, 397.

TITLE
See Real property 2, 3, 5; War 32.

TOBACCO
From the first settlement of the colony of Virginia to the present day tobacco has been one of the most profitable and important products of agriculture and commerce, and while its effects may be injurious to some, its extensive use over practically the entire globe is a remarkable tribute to its popularity and value. — Brown: Austin v. Tennessee, 179 U.S. 343, 345.
Related subject: Cigarette.

TOLERANCE
By working together, by sharing in a common effort, men of different minds and tempers, even if they do not reach agreement, acquire understanding and thereby tolerance of their differences.—Frankfurter: Cooper v. Aaron, 358 U.S. 1, 20.
Related subjects: Discrimination; Intolerance. *See also* Patriotism 7.

451

TORT

The torts with which our courts are kept busy today are mainly the incidents of certain well known businesses. They are injuries to persons or property by railroads, factories, and the like. The liability for them is estimated, and sooner or later goes into the price paid by the public. The public really pays the damages, and the question of liability, if pressed far enough, is really the question how far it is desirable that the public should insure the safety of those whose work it uses.—Holmes: "The Path of the Law," 10 Harv. L. Rev. 467.

Related subjects: Litigation; Negligence and related subjects. *See also* Damages 2; Litigation 7.

TRADE, TRADING

Related subject: Business. *See also* Speculation 2; Tax 145; Trade-mark.

TRADE-MARK

1. A trade-mark is not only a symbol of an existing good will . . . Primarily it is a distinguishable token devised or picked out . . . with the hope that it will come to symbolize good will. — Holmes: Beech-Nut P. Co. v. P. Lorillard Co., 273 U.S. 629, 632.

2. A trade-mark may sometimes, it is true, in form serve as a label, but it differs from a mere label in such cases in that . . . by its words or design [it] is a symbol or device which, affixed to a product of one's manufacture, distinguishes it from articles of the same general nature manufactured or sold by others.—Field: Higgins v. Keuffel, 140 U.S. 428, 433.

3. A trade-mark is a merchandising short-cut which induces a purchaser to select what he wants, or what he has been led to believe he wants.—Frankfurter: Mishawaka Rubber & Wool Mfg. Co. v. S. S. Kresge Co., 316 U.S. 203, 205.

4. Wherever the trade goes, attended by the use of the mark, the right of the trader to be protected against the sale by others of their wares in the place of his wares will be protected.—Pitney: United Drug Co. v. Rectanus Co., 248 U.S. 90, 98.

5. The protection of trade-marks is the law's recognition of the psychological function of symbols. If it is true that we live by symbols, it is no less true that we purchase goods by them. — Frankfurter: Mishawaka Rubber & Wool Mfg. Co. v. S. S. Kresge Co., 316 U.S. 203, 205.

6. The creation of a market through an established symbol implies that people float on a psychological current engendered by the various advertising devices which give a trade-mark its potency.—Frankfurter: *ibid.*, 208.

TRADITION

1. Tradition and the habits of the community count for more than logic.—Holmes: Laurel Hill Cem. v. San Francisco, 216 U.S. 358, 366.

2. The traditions of a society, the habits of obedience to law, the effectiveness of the law-enforcing agencies, are all peculiarly matters of time and place.—Frankfurter: Tigner v. Texas, 310 U.S. 141, 149.

3. We do not save our traditions, in this country.—Holmes: *Speeches,* 63.

4. We must beware of the pitfall of antiquarianism, and must remember that for our purposes our only interest in the past is for the light it throws upon the present. — Holmes: "The Path of the Law," 10 Harv. L. Rev. 474.

5. Continuity with the past is only a necessity and not a duty.—Holmes: "Law in Science and Science in Law," 12 Harv. L. Rev. 444.

6. Continuity simply limits the possibilities of our imagination, and settles the terms in which we shall be compelled to think.—Holmes: *ibid.*

7. The justification of a law for us cannot be found in the fact that our fathers always have followed it. It must be found in some help which the law brings toward reaching a social end which the governing power of the community has made up its mind that it wants. — Holmes: *ibid.,* 452.

8. Whether the past has controlling claims or its wisdom be outworn can be ascertained only by the critical pursuit of reason.—Frankfurter: "Holmes and the Constitution," 41 Harv. L. Rev. 161.

9. Family traditions are not always well preserved, especially when the descendants are men and women of humble origin, remote from kith and kin.—Cardozo: Morrison v. California, 291 U.S. 82, 95.

Related subjects: Custom and related subjects. *See also* Principle 3; Race 14; Securities 2; Technicality 5.

TRANSPORTATION

The business of transportation is not an abstraction. It is the labor of men. . . . In every form of transportation, from the simplest to the most complex, whether the man carries the burden on his back, or drives an animal which carries it, or a locomotive which draws a car which carries it, the one and only constant factor is the labor of mankind.—Moody: Howard v. Illinois Cent. R.R., 207 U.S. 463, 525–26.

Related subjects: Railroad; Ship. *See also* Education 12; Street 1, 2.

TRAVEL

The right to travel is a part of the "liberty" of which the citizen cannot be deprived without due process of law. . . . Freedom of movement is basic in our scheme of values.—Douglas: Kent v. Dulles, 357 U.S. 116, 125.

TREASON

1. Treason is a breach of allegiance, and can be committed by him only who owes allegiance either perpetual or temporary. — Marshall: United States v. Wiltberger, 5 Wheat. (18 U.S.) 76, 97.

2. There may be aid and comfort [to the enemy] without treason. — Waite: Young v. United States, 7 Otto (97 U.S.) 39, 62.

3. In treason all are principals. — Marshall: Beveridge, *Life of Marshall,* III, 621.

4. As this is the most atrocious of-

fence which can be committed against the political body, so it is the charge which is most capable of being employed as the instrument of those malignant and vindictive passions which may rage in the bosoms of contending parties struggling for power. — Marshall: *ibid.,* 377.

5. There is no crime which can more excite and agitate the passions of men than treason, no charge demands more from the tribunal before which it is made a deliberate and temperate inquiry. — Marshall: *Ex parte* Bollman, 4 Cranch (8 U.S.) 75, 125.

6. A man who voluntarily assists one known or believed to be an enemy agent may not defend on the ground that he betrayed his country for only thirty pieces of silver.—Jackson: Cramer v. United States, 325 U.S. 1, 55.

7. Treason—insidious and dangerous treason—is the work of the shrewd and crafty more often than of the simple and impulsive.—Jackson: *ibid.,* 32.

8. The innovations made by the forefathers in the law of treason were conceived in a faith such as Paine put in the maxim that "He that would make his own liberty secure must guard even his enemy from oppression; for if he violates this duty he establishes a precedent that will reach himself." We still put trust in it.—Jackson: *ibid.,* 48.

9. Time has not made the accusation of treachery less poisonous, nor the task of judging one charged with betraying the country, including his

triers, less susceptible to the influence of suspicion and rancor. — Jackson: *ibid*.

Related subjects: Allegiance and related subjects.

TREATY

1. Under the Constitution, a treaty between the United States and a foreign Nation is to be considered in two aspects—as a compact between the two Nations, and as a law of our country.—Field: Baldwin v. Franks, 120 U.S. 678, 702.

2. No Nation treats with a citizen of another Nation, except through his government. The treaty, when made, represents a compact between the governments and each government holds the other responsible for everything done by their respective citizens under it.—Waite: Frelinghuysen v. Key, 110 U.S. 63, 71.

3. The general purpose of treaties of amity and commerce is to avoid injurious discrimination in either country against the citizens of the other.—Hughes: Todok v. Union St. Bank, 281 U.S. 449, 455.

Related subject: Foreign affairs.

TRIAL (legal)

Function 1; requirements, general 2–6, fair trial 7–10, public trial 11–13, judge 14–16, cross-examination 17–19, proof 20; unfair, atmosphere 21–22, influences 23–27, other grounds 28–36; miscellaneous 37–49.

Related subjects: Appeal; Confession and related subjects; Court; Defense (legal); Double jeopardy; Hearing; Inquiry; Inquisition; Investigation; Jury; Litigation; Military tribunals.

——, function

1. The function of trial is to sift the truth from a mass of contradictory evidence, and to do so the fact finding tribunal must hear both truthful and false witnesses.—Black: In the Matter of Michael, 326 U.S. 224, 227–28.

——, requirements, general

2. The trial, of course, must be a reality, not the shadow of a name. —Cardozo: United States v. Mack, 295 U.S. 480, 489.

3. Because a State may dispense with a jury trial, it does not follow that it may substitute trial by ordeal. The rack and torture chamber may not be substituted for the witness stand. — Hughes: Brown v. Mississippi, 297 U.S. 278, 285–86.

4. It is the right of the accused to be tried by a legally constituted court, not by a kangaroo court. — Douglas: Williams v. United States, 341 U.S. 97, 101.

5. A trial is not a game of blind man's buff.—Frankfurter: Johnson v. United States, 333 U.S. 46, 54.

6. Legal trials are not like elections, to be won through the use of the meeting-hall, the radio, and the newspaper.—Black: Bridges v. California, 314 U.S. 252, 271.

——, requirements, fair trial

7. A defendant is entitled to a fair trial but not a perfect one. — Minton: Lutwak v. United States, 344 U.S. 604, 619–20.

8. When we deny even the most degraded person the rudiments of a fair trial, we endanger the liberties of everyone. We set a pattern of conduct that is dangerously expansive and is adaptable to the needs of any minority bent on suppressing opposition or dissension. — Douglas: Joint Anti-Fascist Ref. Comm. v. McGrath, 341 U.S. 123, 179.

9. Nothing is a more fundamental characteristic of a civilized society than those securities which safeguard a fair trial for one accused of crime. —Frankfurter: Williams v. Kaiser, 323 U.S. 471, 482.

10. The right to fair trial is the right that stands guardian over all other rights. — Jackson: Dennis v. United States, 339 U.S. 162, 173.

——, requirements, public trial

11. It is desirable that the trial of causes should take place under the public eye, not because the controversies of one citizen with another are of public concern, but because it is of the highest moment that those who administer justice should always act under the sense of public responsibility, and that every citizen should be able to satisfy himself with his own eyes as to the mode in which a public duty is performed. — Holmes: Cowley v. Pulsifer, 137 Mass. 392, 394.

12. A trial is a public event. What transpires in the court room is public property.—Douglas: Craig v. Harney, 331 U.S. 367, 374.

13. A secret trial would, indeed, be anathema to us. It would be unthinkable that in America a person could be spirited away, held *incom-*

municado, tried in secret, and executed.—Douglas: *We the Judges,* 380.

————, requirements, judge

14. The fair conduct of a trial depends largely on the wisdom and understanding of the trial judge. . . .
He may guide a defendant without
a lawyer past the errors that make
fair trials unfair.— Reed: Gibbs v.
Burke, 337 U.S. 773, 781.

15. Criminal justice is concerned
with the pathology of the body politic. In administering the criminal law,
judges wield the most awesome surgi-
cal instruments of society. A criminal
trial, it has been well said, should have
the atmosphere of the operating room.
The presiding judge determines the
atmosphere. He is not an umpire who
enforces the rules of a game, or merely
a moderator between contestants. If
he is adequate to his functions, the
moral authority which he radiates will
impose the indispensable standards of
dignity and austerity upon all those
who participate in a criminal trial.—
Frankfurter: Sacher v. United States,
343 U.S. 1, 37–38.

16. The rights and immunities of
accused persons would be exposed to
serious and obvious abuse if the trial
bench did not possess and frequently
exert power to curb prejudicial and
excessive zeal of prosecutors. The interests of society in the preservation
of courtroom control by the judges are
no more to be frustrated through unchecked improprieties by defenders.
—Jackson: *ibid.,* 8.

————, requirements,
cross-examination

17. Confrontation and cross-examination under oath are essential, if the
American ideal of due process is to
remain a vital force in our public life.
—Douglas: Peters v. Hobby, 349 U.S.
331, 351.

18. The oral examination of witnesses before the court, with a stringent cross-examination by skillful
counsel, is almost the only method of
eliciting truth.—Grier: Walsh v. Rogers, 13 How. (54 U.S.) 283, 284.

19. Cross-examination is the right
of the party against whom the witness
is called and the right is a valuable
one as a means of separating hearsay
from knowledge, error from truth,
truth, opinion from fact, and inference from recollection. — Clifford:
The Ottawa v. Stewart, 3 Wall. (70
U.S.) 269, 271.

————, requirements, proof

20. It is for the prosecution to make
out its case. — Holmes: Rearick v.
Pennsylvania, 203 U.S. 507, 511.

————, unfair, atmosphere

21. Such a trial is only a farce. It
gives no fair opportunity to defend.
Passion, rather than reason, rules. The
courtroom is not a place of quiet dignity, where the evidence is weighed
carefully and dispassionately. The
courtroom is dominated by a mob.
Hysteria takes the place of calm deliberation. The court has become an
instrument of public passion. A person tried in those circumstances is

not granted that procedural due process which the American Constitution guarantees.—Douglas: *We the Judges,* 362.

22. Mob law does not become due process of law by securing the assent of a terrorized jury.—Holmes: Frank v. Mangum, 237 U.S. 309, 346.

————, unfair, influences

23. The theory of our system is that the conclusions to be reached in a case will be induced only by evidence and argument in open court, and not by any outside influence, whether of private talk or public print.—Holmes: Patterson v. Colorado, 205 U.S. 454, 462.

24. It is difficult enough to seal the court-room, as it were, against outside pressures. The delicate scales of justice ought not to be wilfully agitated from without by any of the participants responsible for the fair conduct of the trial.—Frankfurter: *In re* Sawyer, 360 U.S. 622, 667.

25. The atmosphere in a courtroom may be subtly influenced from without. — Frankfurter: Pennekamp v. Florida, 328 U.S. 331, 361.

26. "Trial by newspaper," like all catch phrases, may be loosely used but it summarizes an evil influence upon the administration of criminal justice in this country.—Frankfurter: *ibid.,* 359.

27. Of course trials must be public and the public have a deep interest in trials. The public's legitimate interest, however, precludes distortion of what goes on inside the courtroom,

dissemination of matters that do not come before the court, or other trafficking with truth intended to influence proceedings or inevitably calculated to disturb the course of justice. —Frankfurter: *ibid.,* 361.

————, unfair, other grounds

28. The crude injustices of a trial so conducted that it becomes bent on fixing guilt by dispensing with rudimentary fairness rather than finding truth through adherence to those basic guarantees which have long been recognized and honored. — Reed: Burton, Clark: Burns v. Wilson, 346 U.S. 137, 142–43.

29. In criminal trials a State can no more discriminate on account of poverty than on account of religion, race, or color.—Douglas, Clark: Griffin v. Illinois, 351 U.S. 12, 17.

30. There can be no equal justice where the kind of trial a man gets depends on the amount of money he has.—Douglas, Clark: *ibid.,* 19.

31. A defendant may be at an unfair disadvantage if he is unable because of poverty to parry by his own witnesses the thrusts of those against him.—Cardozo: In the Matter of Reilly v. Berry, 250 N.Y. 456, 461.

32. The idea of letting a prosecutor judge the very case he prosecutes or supervise and control the job of the judge before whom his case is presented is wholly inconsistent with our concepts of justice.—Black: Marcello v. Bonds, 349 U.S. 302, 318.

33. Evidence and truth are of no avail unless they can be adequately

presented.—Frankfurter: Adams v. United States, 317 U.S. 269, 279.

34. No trial can be fair that leaves the defense to a man who is insane, unaided by counsel, and who by reason of his mental condition stands helpless and alone before the court.—Douglas: Massey v. Moore, 348 U.S. 105, 108.

35. A revolting crime . . . requires unusual circumspection for its trial, so that dispassionate judgment may have sway over the inevitable tendency of the facts to introduce prejudice or passion into the judgment.—Murphy: Fisher v. United States, 328 U.S. 463, 494.

36. To summon a lawyer before the bench and pronounce him guilty of contempt is not unlikely to prejudice his client.—Jackson: Sacher v. United States, 343 U.S. 1, 10.

————, miscellaneous

37. There is a limit to the nicety of inquiry which is possible in a trial.—Holmes: *The Common Law,* 117.

38. Surely, it cannot be deemed a denial of justice, that a man shall not be permitted to try his cause two or three times over. If he has one opportunity for the trial of all the parts of his case, justice is satisfied.—Wilson: Wiscart v. Dauchy, 3 Dall. (3 U.S.) 619, 623.

39. An exception was taken at every step of the trial in the hope that some shot might hit the mark.—Holmes: Francis v. United States, 188 U.S. 375, 376.

40. Every accused person, of course, enters upon his trial clothed with the presumption of innocence.—Sutherland: Yee Hem v. United States, 268 U.S. 178, 184.

41. The right of a speedy trial is necessarily relative. It is consistent with delays and depends upon circumstances.—McKenna: Beavers v. Haubert, 198 U.S. 77, 87.

42. The venue of his trial is . . . made by the criminal himself.—McKenna: Brown v. Elliott, 225 U.S. 392, 402.

43. The state is not attempting to wear the accused out by a multitude of cases with accumulated trials. It asks no more than this, that the case against him shall go on until there shall be a trial free from the corrosion of substantial legal error.—Cardozo: Palko v. Connecticut, 302 U.S. 319, 328.

44. The doom of mere sterility was on the trial from the beginning. — Cardozo: Clark v. United States, 289 U.S. 1, 11.

45. In a very real sense a defendant starts his life afresh when he stands before a jury, a prisoner at the bar.—Cardozo: People v. Zackowitz, 254 N.Y. 192, 197.

46. The Constitution does not compel an accused who admits his guilt to stand trial against his own wishes. — Frankfurter: A d a m s v. United States, 317 U.S. 269, 276.

47. As once stated by Mr. Justice Holmes, one objection to the introduction of collateral issues is a "purely practical one, a concession to the shortness of life."—Douglas: United States

v. Socony-Vac. Oil Co., 319 U.S. 150, 230.

48. A disloyalty trial is the most crucial event in the life of a public servant. If condemned, he is branded for life as a person unworthy of trust or confidence.—Douglas: Joint Anti-Fascist Ref. Com. v. McGrath, 341 U.S. 123, 180.

49. As lawyers not without experience in the practicalities of law-enforcement, we know that the trial of a criminal case can be wrecked by pretrial of the issues on the civil side of the court, particularly if the civil trial is conducted by those not interested in the criminal prosecution. — Jackson: United States *ex rel*. Marcus v. Hess, 317 U.S. 537, 560–61.

> See also Crime 41; Freedom 58; Judgment 15; Lawyer 3; Punishment 1.

TRIAL AND ERROR

> Related subject: Experiment. *See also* Experience 4; Legislation, experimental, amendment, repeal.

TRUST (legal)

1. The trust is not a metaphysical entity or a Prince Rupert's drop which flies to pieces if broken in any part. —Holmes: Landram v. Jordan, 203 U.S. 56, 63.

2. The doctrine of trusts is deemed to be "the most efficient instrument in the hands of a chancellor for maintaining justice, good faith, and good conscience."—Butler: Alexander v. Hillman, 296 U.S. 222, 239 (quot. 182 U.S. 461, 479).

3. From an early date, public policy has been opposed to the private interest which impelled men to withdraw property from the channels of trade and tie it up with limitations intended, among other things, to secure to the beneficiary the use of the property, while at the same time removing it, to some extent, from liability for his debts.—Lamar: Keeney v. New York, 222 U.S. 525, 535.

4. The welfare of society, it is thought, does not tolerate limitations that will last throughout the ages. The living may not dictate, without restriction, the forms of ownership for posterity. — Cardozo: Carrier v. Carrier, 226 N.Y. 114, 122.

TRUST (monopoly)

Here we have the pattern of the evolution of the great trusts. Little, independent units are gobbled up by the bigger ones. At times the independent is driven to the wall and surrenders. At other times any number of "sound business reasons" appear why the sale to or merger with the trust should be made. If the acquisition were the result of predatory practices or restraints of trade, the trust could be required to disgorge. . . . But the impact on future competition and on the economy is the same though the trust was built in more gentlemanly ways.—Douglas: United States v. Columbia Steel Co., 334 U.S. 495, 534–35.

> Related subjects: Business (big); Monopoly and related subjects.

TRUSTEE

1. The office of a trustee is important to the community at large, and

frequently most so to those least able to take care of themselves. It is one of confidence. The law regards the incumbent with jealous scrutiny, and frowns sternly at the slightest attempt to pervert his powers and duties for his own benefit.—Swayne: Union Pac. R.R. v. Durant, 5 Otto (95 U.S.) 576, 579.

2. A trustee is not an agent. . . . A trustee may be defined generally as a person in whom some estate, interest or power in or affecting property is vested for the benefit of another.—Woods: Taylor v. Davis, 110 U.S. 330, 334–35.

3. Who can doubt that courts of equity in enforcing the great principle that a trustee shall not profit by his trust nor even place himself in a position where his private interest may collide with his fiduciary duty, have raised the level of business honor, and kept awake a conscience that might otherwise have slumbered? — Cardozo: *Growth of the Law,* 96 .

Related subject: Fiduciary.

TRUTH

Defined 1–5; general 6–7; degree 8–10; progress 11–13; test 14–20; miscellaneous 21–22

Related subjects: Falsity and related subjects; Right (verity).

———, defined

1. In one sense, that only is true which is conformable to the actual state of things. In that sense, a statement is untrue which does not express things exactly as they are. But in another and broader sense, the word

"true" is often used as a synonym of honest, sincere, not fraudulent.—Harlan: Moulor v. American Life Ins. Co., 111 U.S. 335, 345.

2. All I mean by truth is what I can't help thinking. — H o l m e s: *Holmes-Pollock Letters,* I, 126.

3. I used to say, when I was young, that truth was the majority vote of that nation that could lick all others. —Holmes: "Natural Law," 32 Harv. L. Rev. 40.

4. I define the truth as the system of my limitations, and leave absolute truth for those who are better equipped.—Holmes: "Ideals and Doubts," 10 Ill. L. Rev. 2.

5. Truth and understanding are not wares like peanuts or potatoes.—Frankfurter: Associated Press v. United States, 326 U.S. 1, 28.

———, general

6. General truths are hard to grasp. Most of us have all we can do in accumulating by dint of toil the knowledge of a few particulars.—Cardozo: *Growth of the Law,* 22.

7. One of those general truths which become untrue by being inaccurately expressed. — Holmes: Damon v. Hawaii, 194 U.S. 154, 160.

———, degree

8. I don't believe or know anything about absolute truth.—Holmes: *Uncollected Letters,* 165.

9. What is theoretically true, is often practically false, or doubtful.—Story: *Misc. Writings,* 157.

10. In these "a hair perhaps divides

the false and true." — Jackson: Pollock v. Williams, 322 U.S. 4, 21.

———, progress

11. The progress, however, even of the most salutary truths is slow, when there are no artificial obstacles in the way.—Story: *Misc. Writings,* 115.

12. So slowly does truth make its way, even among the most gifted minds, in opposition to preconceived opinions and prejudices.—Story: *ibid.,* 63.

13. If truth were not often suggested by error, if old implements could not be adjusted to new uses, human progress would be slow. — Holmes: *The Common Law,* 37.

———, test

14. The best test of truth is the power of the thought to get itself accepted in the competition of the market. — Holmes: Abrams v. United States, 250 U.S. 616, 630.

15. Truth from the lips is often felt with double sway; but truth, confirmed by experiment, is not only irresistible in its conviction, but in its permanent impression on the memory.—Story: *Misc. Writings,* 137.

16. That which is true does not always present the appearance of truth. —Wayne: United States v. Castillero, 2 Black (67 U.S.) 1, 276.

17. Rather . . . the *"deshabille* of truth," than that meretricious ostentation of consistency, which falsehood would not have neglected to display. —Wayne: *ibid.,* 275.

18. The outstanding truths of life, the great and unquestioned phenomena of society, are not to be argued away as myths and vagaries when they do not fit within our little moulds.— Cardozo: *Nature of Judicial Process,* 127.

19. The truth is not always to be reached by looking back to the beginning and deducing from the source. The end may be frustrated unless we look forward to the goal.—Cardozo: *Growth of the Law,* 73–74.

20. Truth needs no disguise. — Black: Hazel-Atlas Glass Co. v. Hartford-Emp. Co., 322 U.S. 238, 247.

———, miscellaneous

21. We believe that truth and justice are more sacred than any personal consideration.—Brewer: Union Pac. Ry. v. Botsford, 141 U.S. 250, 259.

22. The half truths of one generation tend at times to perpetuate themselves in the law as the whole truths of another, when constant repetition brings it about that qualifications, taken once for granted, are disregarded or forgotten.—Cardozo: Allegheny Col. v. National Chautauqua Co. Bank, 246 N.Y. 369, 373.

TURPITUDE

1. No man can be permitted, in a court of justice, to allege his own tur-

pitude as a ground of recovery in a suit.—Story: Columbia Ins. Co. v. Lawrence, 10 Pet. (35 U.S.) 507, 518.

2. Where there is turpitude, the law will help neither party.—Swayne: Trist v. Child, 21 Wall. (88 U.S.) 441, 451.

3. It lacks the element of wickedness necessary to constitute moral turpitude. — Brown: McIntire v. Pryor, 173 U.S. 38, 58.

Related subject: Immorality. *See also* Defense (legal) 6; Tax 78.

TYRANNY, TYRANT

1. Whenever legislation renders the possession or enjoyment of property precarious; whenever it cuts down the obligation and security of contracts; whenever it breaks in upon personal liberty, or compels a surrender of personal privileges, upon any pretext, plausible or otherwise, it matters little, whether it be the act of many, or the few, of the solitary despot, or the assembled multitude; it is still in its essence tyranny. — Story: *Misc. Writings,* 447.

2. The history of every country in Europe will furnish flagrant instance of tyranny exercised under the pretext of penal dispensations. Rival factions, in their efforts to crush each other, have superseded all the forms, and suppressed all the sentiments of justice; while attainders, on the principle of retaliation and proscription, have marked all the vicissitudes of party triumph. The temptation to such abuses of power is unfortunately too alluring for human virtue.—Iredell:

Calder v. Bull, 3 Dall. (3 U.S.) 648, 654.

3. It has been said, with much truth, "Where the law ends, tyranny begins."—Bradley: Merritt v. Welsh, 14 Otto (104 U.S.) 694, 702.

4. Tyranny . . . seldom boldly bids its will avouch its acts.—McKenna: Arizona Copper Co. v. Hammer, 250 U.S. 400, 437.

5. It is from petty tyrannies that large ones take root and grow. . . . Seedlings planted in that soil grow great and, growing, break down the foundations of liberty. — Rutledge: Thomas v. Collins, 323 U.S. 516, 543.

6. Democracy has its own capacity for tyranny. Some of the most menacing encroachments upon liberty invoke the democratic principle and assert the right of the majority to rule. —Hughes: Pusey, *Hughes,* 620.

Related subjects: Despotism and related subjects. *See also* Cruelty 2; Freedom 186; Judge 42; Majority-minority 16; Power 40; Test oath 1; War 34.

UNCERTAINTY

Related subjects: Certainty; Doubt. *See also* Commerce 6; Construction, uncertainty; Doubt 3; Law, certainty; Life 6; Valuation, uncertainty; Venture.

UNDERSTANDING

1. If we think of our existence not as that of a little god outside, but as that of a ganglion within, we have the infinite behind us. It gives us our only but our adequate significance. A grain of sand has the same, but what competent person supposes that he understands a grain of sand? That is as much beyond our grasp as man.—

Holmes: "Natural Law," 32 Harv. L. Rev. 44.

2. When common understanding and practice have established a way it is a waste of time to wander in by-paths of logic.—Holmes: Ruddy v. Rossi, 248 U.S. 104, 111.

3. Understanding should precede judging.—Brandeis: Burns Bak. Co. v. Bryan, 264 U.S. 504, 520.

Related subjects: Knowledge and related subjects. *See also* Judge 16; Jury 41; Knowledge 3; Labor 6; Speech 2; Technicality 7; Test 3; Tolerance; Truth 5.

UNEMPLOYMENT

1. Poverty is one, but not the only evil consequence of unemployment. —Stone: Carmichael v. Southern Coal & Coke Co., 301 U.S. 495, 519.

2. We are responsible for unemployment because we have tolerated the idea that an employer is free with impunity to decrease or increase his force. — Brandeis: Mason, *Brandeis,* 621–22.

3. About ten years ago we began to recognize the right to have the business assume the risk of accidents. They should now assume the risk of unemployment. — Brandeis: *ibid.,* 586.

4. During the years 1929 to 1936, when the country was passing through a cyclical depression, the number of the unemployed mounted to unprecedented heights. Often the average was more than 10 million; at times a peak was attained of 16 million or more. — Cardozo: Steward Mach. Co. v. Davis, 301 U.S. 495, 586.

5. An unemployment law framed in such a way that the unemployed who look to it will be deprived of reasonable protection is one in name and nothing more.—Cardozo: *ibid.,* 593.

6. The number of persons in the United States 65 years of age or over is increasing proportionately as well as absolutely. What is even more important, the number of such persons unable to take care of themselves is growing at a threatening pace. More and more our population is becoming urban and industrial instead of rural and agricultural. The evidence is impressive that among industrial workers the younger men and women are preferred over the older. In times of retrenchment the older are commonly the first to go, and even if retained, their wages are likely to be lowered. The plight of men and women at so low an age as 40 is hard, almost helpless, when they are driven to seek for re-employment. — Cardozo: Helvering v. Davis, 301 U.S. 619, 642.

7. The ill is all one or at least not greatly different whether men are thrown out of work because there is no longer work to do or because the disabilities of age make them incapable of doing it. Rescue becomes necessary irrespective of the cause. The hope behind this statute is to save men and women from the rigors of the poorhouse as well as from the haunting fear that such a lot awaits them when journey's end is near.— Cardozo: *ibid.,* 641.

8. With the loss of savings inevita-

ble in periods of idleness, the fate of workers over 65, when thrown out of work, is little less than desperate. —Cardozo: *ibid.*, 642–43.

Related subjects: Labor; Wage. *See also* Public expenditure 4; Public welfare 9, 13.

UNIFORMITY

Related subject: Consistency. *See also* Law 90; Tax, uniformity; Testimony 2.

UNITED STATES

The term "United States" may be used in any one of several senses. It may be merely the name of a sovereign occupying the position analogous to that of other sovereigns in the family of nations. It may designate the territory over which the sovereignty of the United States extends, or it may be the collective name of the states which are united by and under the Constitution. — Stone: Hooven & Allison Co. v. Evatt, 324 U.S. 652, 671–72.

Related subject: Nation (U.S.), people.

UNORTHODOX

Related subject: Orthodoxy. *See also* Freedom, religion 116, 131; Zealot 2.

UNREST

Social unrest is largely caused by industrial oppression on one side and ostentatious extravagance on the other. — Brandeis: Mason, *Brandeis,* 361.

UNSELFISHNESS

Related subject: Selfishness. *See also* Rule 7.

USAGE

1. The test of general usage. That which has received the assent of all, must be the law of all. — Marshall: The Antelope, 10 Wheat. (23 U.S.) 66, 120–21.

2. A long uninterrupted usage in the affirmative establishes nothing but its being rightful.—Story: *Misc. Writings,* 402.

Related subjects: Custom and related subjects. *See also* Construction, usage; Prescription 1; Sentiment 2.

USE

Related subject: Useless. *See also* Property 6, 8, 14, 15; Remedy 6; Tax 7, 137; Value 6.

USELESS

Related subject: Use. *See also* Remedy 18.

USURY

1. The ingenuity of lenders has devised many contrivances, by which, under forms sanctioned by law, the [usury] statute may be evaded. — Marshall: Scott v. Lloyd, 9 Pet. (34 U.S.) 418, 446.

2. The act of usury has long since lost that deep moral stain which was formerly attached to it; and is now generally considered only as an illegal or immoral act, because it is prohibited by law.—McLean: Lloyd v. Scott, 4 Pet. (29 U.S.) 205, 224.

Related subject: Interest.

UTOPIA

1. When everything is all right, it will be about time to die.—Holmes: *Holmes-Pollock Letters,* I, 144.

2. While enthusiasts may picture to us an ideal state of society where neither riches nor poverty shall exist, wherein all shall be comfortably

housed and clad . . . such a Utopia is utterly inconsistent with human character as at present constituted. . . . Rich men are essential even to the well-being of the poor. . . . One has but to consider for a moment the immediate consequences of the abolition of large private fortunes to appreciate the danger which lurks in any radical disturbance of the present social system.—Brown: Report, American Bar Association, 16: 225

Related subjects: Improvement; Reform.

VAGARY

The output of a multitude of minds must be expected to contain its proportion of vagaries. — Cardozo: *Growth of the Law,* 5.

VALUATION, VALUE

Defined, basis 1–19; uncertainties 20–26; miscellaneous 27–32.

Related subjects: Depreciation; Going concern; Eminent domain; Original cost; Price; Public utility; Rate regulation.

———, defined, basis

1. Value has been defined as the ability to command the price. — Brandeis: St. Louis & O. Ry. v. United States, 279 U.S. 461, 504.

2. The value of property at a given time depends upon the relative intensity of the social desire for it at that time, expressed in the money that it would bring in the market.—Holmes: Ithaca Tr. Co. v. United States, 279 U.S. 151, 155.

3. It is hard to answer the proposition that value expressed in money depends on what people think at the time. That determines what they will give for the thing, and whether they think rightly or wrongly, if they or some of them will give a certain price for it, that is its value then.—Holmes: San Diego Land & Town Co. v. Jasper, 189 U.S. 439, 444.

4. It is commonplace to say that we only know the value of a thing by that which makes its worth. — McKenna: Fink v. Muskogee County, 248 U.S. 399, 404.

5. Position of property is as much a constituent of its value as its composition. A market for its products is as necessary as its products. — McKenna: United States v. New River Co., 265 U.S. 533, 543.

6. Property is not to be deemed worthless because the owner allows it to go to waste, or to be regarded as valueless because he is unable to put it to any use. Others may be able to use it, and make it subserve the necessities or conveniences of life. — Field: Mississippi & Rum River Boom Co. v. Patterson, 8 Otto (98 U.S.) 403, 408.

7. Past losses obviously do not tend to prove present values. — Brandeis: Galveston Elec. Co. v. Galveston, 258 U.S. 388, 395.

8. In determining the value of a business, as between buyer and seller, the good will and earning power due to effective organization are often more important elements than tangible property.—Brandeis: *ibid.,* 396.

9. The commercial value of property consists in the expectation of income from it. — Holmes: Galveston,

H. & S. A. Ry. v. Texas, 210 U.S. 217, 226.

10. Substantial prices are not paid for the privilege of conducting a business at a loss.—Cardozo: Roberts v. City of New York, 295 U.S. 264, 282.

11. Past earnings are significant only when they tend to reflect future returns.—Clark: United States v. Toronto, H. & B. Nav. Co., 338 U.S. 396, 403.

12. The law sensibly recognizes that market price reflects fair dealing by men who are freely engaged in it. —Frankfurter: United States v. Commodities Trad. Corp., 339 U.S. 121, 137.

13. As fixed by the market, value is no more than a summary expression of forecasts that the needs and attitudes which made up demand in the past will have their counterparts in the future.—Frankfurter: Kimball Laundry Co. v. United States, 338 U.S. 1, 10.

14. Cost in and of itself, though far from conclusive, is still evidence of value . . . especially where there is no market value in the strict or proper sense.—Cardozo: McCandless v. Furlaud, 296 U.S. 140, 158.

15. The low market value of the stock was due in part to the ignorance of the public as to the assets of the company. On this concession the market value of the stock was not a test of the value of the business.—Holmes: Fargo v. Hart, 193 U.S. 490, 497.

16. The absence of market price is no barrier to valuation. — Douglas:

Guggenheim v. Rasquin, 312 U.S. 254, 258.

17. The difference between a dead plant and a live one is real value.— Lurton: Omaha v. Omaha Water Co., 218 U.S. 180, 202.

18. Going value is not something to be read into every balance sheet as a perfunctory addition. "It calls for consideration of the history and circumstances of the particular enterprise."—Cardozo: Dayton Power & Light Co. v. Public Util. Comm'n, 292 U.S. 290, 309 (quot. 289 U.S. 313, 314).

19. A live horse is worth more than a dead one, though the physical object may be the same, and a smooth-going automobile is worth more than an unassembled collection of all its parts. The physical facilities used in carrying on a prosperous business are worth more than the same assets in bankruptcy liquidation or on sale by the sheriff. —Jackson: R a i l w a y Exp. Agency v. Virginia, 347 U.S. 359, 364.

———, uncertainties

20. Values are relative. — Brandeis: Pennsylvania Coal Co. v. Mahon, 260 U.S. 393, 419.

21. Intelligent men differ as to the value of even the most common objects before them—of animals, houses and lands in constant use. — Field: Stanley v. Board of Supervisors, 121 U.S. 535, 550.

22. An intelligent estimate of probable future values, and even indeed of present ones, is at best an approxima-

tion.—Cardozo: Dayton Power & Light Co. v. Public Util. Comm'n, 292 U.S. 290, 310.

23. Many are the degrees of value. —Cardozo: In the Matter of Brown, 242 N.Y. 1, 6.

24. All values are anticipations of the future.—Holmes: Lincoln v. Commonwealth, 164 Mass., 368, 378.

25. Unpredictable v i c i s s i t u d e s might reduce it [value] to a nullity. Cardozo: United States v. Safety Car Heat. & Light. Co., 297 U.S. 88, 100.

26. Like all values, as the word is used by the law, it depends largely on more or less certain prophecies of the future, and the value is no less real at the time if later the prophecy turns out false than when it comes out true. —Holmes: Ithaca Tr. Co. v. United States, 279 U.S. 151, 155.

———, miscellaneous

27. There are many rights and immunities secured by the Constitution, of which freedom of speech and assembly are conspicuous examples, which are not capable of money valuation. — Stone: Hague v. Committee for Indust. Org., 307 U.S. 496, 529.

28. A contested claim is rarely appraised at face value.—Cardozo: General Rubber Co. v. Benedict, 215 N.Y. 18, 24.

29. The enhanced value reflects speculation as to what the government can be compelled to pay. That is a hold-up value, not a fair market value. — Douglas: United States v. Cors, 337 U.S. 325, 334.

30. What makes the right to mine

coal valuable is that it can be exercised with profit.—Holmes: Pennsylvania Coal Co. v. Mahon, 260 U.S. 393, 414.

31. Against counterfeits of value the law can give protection.—McKenna: Hall v. Geiger-Jones Co., 242 U.S. 539, 555.

32. Some things are worth more than money and the costs of a new enterprise.—Black: Federal Power Comm'n v. Tuscarora Ind. Nat., 362 U.S. 99, 142.

See also Book 1; Corporation 69; Freedom 184; Life 11, 12; Opinion 8–10; Real Property 4, 9, 10; Science 7; Securities 3, 5, 7, 8; Widowhood.

VANITY

1. Let us not discredit our just honors by exaggerating little attainments. —Story: *Misc. Writings*, 27.

2. Vanity is the most philosophical of those feelings that we are taught to despise. For vanity recognizes that if a man is in a minority of one we lock him up, and therefore longs for assurance from others that one's work has not been in vain. — Holmes: *Speeches*, 98.

VENDOR-VENDEE

1. No rule of law protects a purchaser who wilfully closes his ears to information, or refuses to make inquiry when circumstances of grave suspicion imperatively demand it. — Brown: Lytle v. Lansing, 147 U.S. 59, 72.

2. This is a day of synthetic living, when to an ever-increasing extent our population is dependent upon mass

producers for its food and drink, its cures and complexions, its apparel and gadgets. These no longer are natural or simple products but complex ones whose composition and qualities are often secret. . . . Where experiment or research is necessary to determine the presence or the degree of danger, the product must not be tried out on the public, nor must the public be expected to possess the facilities or the technical knowledge to learn for itself of inherent but latent dangers. The claim that a hazard was not foreseen is not available to one who did not use foresight appropriate to his enterprise. — Jackson: Dalehite v. United States, 346 U.S. 15, 51–52.

Related subjects: Buyer; Seller.

VENGEANCE

The thirst for vengeance is a very real, even if it be a hideous, thing; and states may not ignore it till humanity has been raised to greater heights than any that have yet been scaled in all the long ages of struggle and ascent.—Cardozo: *Law and Literature,* 87–88.

Related subject: Revenge.

VENTURE

No man can determine whether his venture will enrich him, or make him a bankrupt.—Hunt: Arthur v. Morrison, 6 Otto (96 U.S.) 108, 110.

Related subjects: Gamble and related subjects. *See also* Capitalist 2.

VERDICT

The mistake is sanctified by the verdict, so that none may name it a mistake, however, visible the truth.—Car-

dozo: In the Matter of Kaufmann, 245 N.Y. 423, 429.

Related subjects: Decision (judicial) and related subjects; Judgment.

VETERAN

1. No thoughtful person questions the obligations which the nation is under to those who have done faithful service in its army or navy. — Brewer: Keim v. United States, 177 U.S. 290, 295.

2. The service that preserved the life and safety of the nation preserved at the same time the life and safety of the states.—Cardozo: People v. Westchester Co. Nat'l Bank, 231 N.Y. 465, 484.

3. The parent does not listen unmoved to the necessities of her sons who have fought in her defense.—Cardozo: *ibid.,* 484–85.

4. The perils of battle, the hardships of camp and trench, may be poorly paid at any price.—Cardozo: *ibid.,* 485.

5. Labor in the market was paid with no such modest stipend as these men received for labor in submarine and trench.—Cardozo: *ibid.*

6. The relation of the government . . . if not paternal, was at least avuncular. It was a relation of benevolence. —Holmes: White v. United States, 270 U.S. 175, 180.

Related subjects: Army; Military; Pension.

VICE

Related subjects: Evil, Iniquity; Malevolence; Wickedness. *See also* Character 2; Immoral; Law 63; Poverty 1.

VIGILANCE

1. The vigilance that is due will vary with the place and the occasion. —Cardozo: Hinz v. Eighth Avenue R.R., 243 N.Y. 90, 94.

2. There is a duty of reasonable vigilance in proportion to the risk.— Cardozo: McFarlane v. Niagara Falls, 247 N.Y. 340, 350.

Related subjects: Care; Precaution; Standard and related subjects.

VIOLENCE

1. Violent resistance to law cannot be made a legal reason for its suspension without loosening the fabric of our society.—Frankfurter: Cooper v. Aaron, 358 U.S. 1, 22.

2. The momentum of fear generated by past violence.—Frankfurter: Milk Wagon Drivers Union v. Meadowmoor Dairies, 312 U.S. 287, 294.

Related subjects: Force; Mob. *See also* Crime 15; Criminal 7, 29; Freedom 93; Labor, disputes; Picketing, violence; Necessity 1; Redress 1; Remedy 5; Third degree 2.

VIRTUE, VIRTUOUS

1. Philosophers and poets, thinkers of high and low degree from every age and race have sought to expound the meaning of virtue, but each teaches his own conception of the moral excellence that satisfies standards of good conduct. Are the tests of the Puritan or the Cavalier to be applied, those of the city or the farm, the Christian or non-Christian, the old or the young?—Reed: Beauharnais v. Illinois, 343 U.S. 250, 284.

2. Virtues are important in the inverse order to the credit that is due to those who cultivate and practice them. — Cardozo: *Law and Literature,* 188–89.

3. The very modest virtue of being merely a human being. — Cardozo: *ibid.,* 189.

4. The first great lesson of human improvement has been taught, that knowledge is power; and the last great lesson of human experience felt, that without virtue there is neither happiness nor safety. — Story: *Misc. Writings,* 73.

5. Where there is not private virtue, there cannot be public security and happiness.—Story: *ibid.,* 517.

6. The good are always more tardy. They neglect the beginning of things, and are roused only in the last necessity.—Story: *ibid.,* 156.

See also Character 2; Classification 2.

VOTE, VOTER

1. The citizen of this country, where nearly everything is submitted to the popular test and where office is eagerly sought, who possesses the right to vote, holds a powerful instrument for his own advantage. — Hunt: United States v. Reese, 2 Otto (92 U.S.) 214, 248.

2. The right to vote is personal.— McReynolds: United States v. Bathgate, 246 U.S. 220, 227.

3. Equality in voting has given every minority in America an opportunity to protect its interests through political action. — Douglas: *We the Judges,* 413.

4. The Negro's right to vote is be-

ing capitalized on more and more.—
Douglas: *ibid.,* 416.

Related subjects: Election; Elector. *See
also* Corporation, stockholder, control;
Ignorance 4; Legislation 67; Literacy 1;
Freedom, speech 99.

WAGES

1. Mere mechanical labor, from the
perpetual competition arising from an
increasing population, has a natural
tendency to descend in the scale of
compensation. — Story: *Misc. Writings,* 126.

2. No proposition in economics is
better established than that low wages
are not cheap wages. On the contrary,
the best in wages is the cheapest. . . .
Why should the proposition be doubted, that wages insufficient to sustain
the worker properly are uneconomical? Does anybody doubt that the
only way you can get work out of a
horse is to feed the horse properly?—
Brandeis: Mason, *Brandeis,* 660.

3. When we once get to a point
where workingmen are paid throughout the year, as the officers of a corporation are paid throughout the year,
and the higher employees are paid
throughout the year, everyone will
recognize that a business can not be
run profitably unless you keep it running, because if you have to pay,
whether your men are working or
not, your men will work.—Brandeis:
ibid., 429.

4. We have had opportunity to
learn that a wage is not always the
resultant of free bargaining between
employers and employees; that it may
be one forced upon employees by their

economic necessities and upon employers by the most ruthless of their
competitors. — Stone: Morehead v.
New York, 298 U.S. 587, 635.

5. There can be no real estimate
of the wages one receives until it is
understood what time one has worked
to receive them.—McKenna: Wilson
v. New, 243 U.S. 332, 361–62.

6. If women require a minimum
wage to preserve their morals, men require it to preserve their honesty.—
Sutherland: Adkins v. Children's
Hosp., 261 U.S. 525, 556.

Related subjects: Labor; Unemployment.
See also Public welfare.

WAIVER

1. "Waiver" is a vague term used
for a great variety of purposes, good
and bad, in the law. In any normal
sense, however, it connotes some kind
of voluntary knowing relinquishment
of a right.—Black: Green v. United
States, 355 U.S. 184, 191.

2. One cannot waive or acquiesce in
a wrong while ignorant that it has
been committed. Current suspicion
and rumor are not enough.—Swayne:
Pence v. Langdon, 9 Otto (99 U.S.)
578, 581.

WANTS

If we have but a just sense of our
wants, we have gained half the victory.—Story: *Misc. Writings,* 27.

WAR

Defined 1–3; causes 4–6; requirements
7–9; powers 10–14; consequences 15–29;
rules 30–37; public opinion 38–41; miscellaneous 42–44.

Related subjects: Army; Conscientious

objector and related subjects; Military; National defense; Peace; Selective service (military); Veteran.

———, defined

1. War is a suit prosecuted by the sword.—Johnson: Harcourt v. Gaillard, 12 Wheat. (25 U.S.) 523, 528.

2. War is the business of youth and early middle age.—Holmes: *Speeches,* 62.

3. War between nations is war between their individual citizens. — Sutherland: Sutherland v. Mayer, 271 U.S. 272, 287.

———, causes

4. Until mankind shall cease to have ambition and avarice, wars will arise. —Marshall: Beveridge, *Life of Marshall,* I, 414.

5. If the different desires of different peoples come in conflict in a region that each wishes to occupy (especially if it is a physical region) and each wishes it strongly enough, what is there to do except to remove the other if you can?—Holmes: *Uncollected Letters,* 153.

6. The cause of a war—as of most human action—is not single. War is ordinarily the result of many different conditions, acts, and motives. Historians rarely agree in their judgment as to what was the determining factor in a particular war, even when they write under circumstances where detachment and the availability of evidence from all sources minimizes both prejudice and other sources of error.—Brandeis: Pierce v. United States, 252 U.S. 239, 267.

———, requirements

7. Money and wealth, the products of agriculture and commerce, are said to be the sinews of war, and as necessary in its conduct as numbers and physical force.—Grier: Prize Cases, 2 Black (67 U.S.) 635, 671–72.

8. Never were the industrial, commercial and financial resources of belligerent nations so vital to the success of war as now. It is not extravagant to affirm that the effective organization of these resources is more likely to determine the result of the present conflict than armies and navies.— Taft: Swiss Nat'l Ins. Co. v. Miller, 267 U.S. 42, 58.

9. War brooks no delay. — Reed: Silesian Am. Corp. v. Clark, 332 U.S. 469, 477.

———, powers

10. The war power of the national government is "the power to wage war successfully." . . . The power is not restricted to the winning of victories in the field and the repulse of enemy forces.—Stone: Hirabayashi v. United States, 320 U.S. 81, 93.

11. Preparation for war may be made in peace.—Clifford: Legal Tender Cases, 12 Wall. (79 U.S.) 457, 631.

12. One of the best means to repel invasion is to provide the requisite force for action before the invader himself has reached the soil.—Story: Martin v. Mott, 12 Wheat. (25 U.S.) 19, 29.

13. The war power is not a blank check to be used in blind disregard of all the individual rights which we

have struggled so long to recognize and preserve. It must be used with discretion and with a sense of proportionate values. — Murphy: Estep v. United States, 327 U.S. 114, 132.

14. This power is the most dangerous one to free government in the whole catalogue of powers. It usually is invoked in haste and excitement when calm legislative consideration of constitutional limitation is difficult. It is executed in a time of patriotic fervor that makes moderation unpopular. And, worst of all, it is interpreted by the Judges under the influence of the same passions and pressures.—Frankfurter: Woods v. Miller, 333 U.S. 138, 146.

————, consequences

15. War strips man of his social nature; it demands of him the suppression of those sympathies which claim man for a brother; and accustoms the ear of humanity to hear with indifference, perhaps exultation, "that thousands have been slain." — Johnson: The Rapid, 8 Wheat. (21 U.S.) 155, 161.

16. In the state of war, nation is known to nation only by their armed exterior; each threatening the other with conquest or annihilation. The individuals who compose the belligerent states, exist, as to each other, in a state of utter occlusion. If they meet, it is only in combat.—Johnson: ibid., 160–61.

17. My complaint against war is not that it kills men but that it kills

the wrong ones.—Holmes: Holmes-Pollock Letters, II, 49.

18. The maxim about the law becoming silent in the noise of arms applies.—Rutledge: In the Matter of Yamashita, 327 U.S. 1, 47.

19. War breeds atrocities. From the earliest conflicts of recorded history to the global struggles of modern times inhumanities, lust, and pillage have been the inevitable by-products of man's resort to force and arms.—Murphy: ibid., 29.

20. The citizen of necessity has few rights when he faces the war machine.—Jackson: Bowles v. United States, 319 U.S. 33, 37.

21. War such as we now fight calls into play the full power of government in extreme emergency. It compels invention of legal, as of martial tools adequate for the times' necessity. Inevitably some will be strange, if also life-saving, instruments for a people accustomed to peace and the normal working of constitutional limitations. Citizens must surrender or forego exercising rights which in other times could not be impaired. — Rutledge: Yakus v. United States, 321 U.S. 414, 461.

22. The price he [the citizen], with all others, must pay for living in a nation which ordinarily gives him so much of protection but in a world which has not been organized to give it security against events so disruptive of democratic procedures.—Rutledge: ibid., 465.

23. War is a grim business, requir-

ing sacrifice of ease, opportunity, freedom from restraint, and liberty of action. — Reed: U n i t e d States v. Quarles, 350 U.S. 11, 29.

24. War means burdens, and there is no calculus by which they can be fairly distributed. From any point of view the ultimate sacrifices are uncompensable. — Frankfurter: United States v. Commodities Trading Corp., 339 U.S. 121, 134.

25. The conditions engendered by the war may linger for months or years, or may vanish with the coming peace.—Cardozo: Municipal Gas Co. v. Public Serv. Comm'n, 225 N. Y. 89, 99.

26. All of the mobilization and all of the war effort will have been in vain if, when all is finished, we discover that in the process we have destroyed the very freedoms for which we fought.—Murphy: Estep v. United States, 327 U.S. 114, 132.

27. The problem of war profits is not new. In this country, every war we have engaged in has provided opportunities for profiteering and they have been too often scandalously seized.—Black: United States v. Bethlehem Steel Corp., 315 U.S. 289, 309.

28. No man or set of men should want to make excessive profits out of the travail of the nation at war. — Murphy: *ibid.,* 310.

29. War requires much of the citizen. He surrenders rights for the time being to secure their more permanent establishment. Most men do so freely. According to our plan others must do so also, as far as the nation's safety

requires. But the surrender is neither permanent nor total. The great liberties of speech and the press are curtailed but not denied. Religious freedom remains a living thing. With these, in our system, rank the elemental protections thrown about the citizen charged with crime, more especially those forged on history's anvil in great crises.—Rutledge: Yakus v. United States, 321 U.S. 414, 487–88.

———, rules

30. Throughout Christendom, this harsh rule has been exploded, and war is no longer considered as giving a right to enslave captives. But this triumph of humanity has not been universal.—Marshall: The Antelope, 10 Wheat. (23 U.S.) 66, 121.

31. Property captured in war is not taken to punish its owner, any more than the life of a soldier slain in battle is taken to punish him. The property, as well as the life, is taken only as a means of lessening the warlike strength of the enemy.—Waite: Kirk v. Lynd, 106 U.S. 315, 317–18.

32. The title by conquest is acquired and maintained by force. The conqueror prescribes its limits. Humanity, however, acting on public opinion, has established, as a general rule, that the conquered shall not be wantonly oppressed.—Marshall: Johnson v. M'Intosh, 8 Wheat (21 U.S.), 543, 589.

33. Property taken on a field of battle is not usually collected until after resistance has ceased; but it is none the less on that account captured

property.—Waite: Lamar v. Browne, 2 Otto (92 U.S.) 187, 193–94.

34. Conquest by the United States, unlike conquest by many other nations, does not mean tyranny. For our people "choose to maintain their greatness by justice rather than violence."—Black: Johnson v. Eisentrager, 339 U.S. 763, 798.

35. The destruction or injury of private property in battle, or in the bombardment of cities and towns, and in many other ways, in the war, had to be borne by the sufferers alone as one of its consequences.—Field: United States v. Pacific R.R., 120 U.S. 227, 234.

36. We do not make the laws of war but we respect them so far as they do not conflict with the commands of Congress or the Constitution.—Stone: In the Matter of Yamashita, 327 U.S. 1, 16.

37. The whole tendency of modern law and practice is to soften the "ancient severities of war."—Sutherland: Sutherland v. Mayer, 271 U.S. 272, 287.

———, public opinion

38. Already is the aspect of the world sufficiently darkened by the horrors of war. It is time to listen to the desponding claims of man engaged in the peaceful pursuits of life.—Johnson: The Nereide, 9 Wheat. (22 U.S.) 388, 434.

39. Nor do I think that a philosophic view of the world would regard war as absurd. But most people who have known it regard it with horror, as a last resort, and, even if not yet ready for cosmopolitan efforts, would welcome any practicable combinations that would increase the power on the side of peace.—Holmes: United States v. Schwimmer, 279 U.S. 644, 654.

40. Have we come to the realization of the observation that "war, unless it be fought for liberty, is the most deadly enemy of liberty"?—McKenna: Block v. Hirsch, 256 U.S. 135, 163.

41. Among the most eminent statesmen here and abroad have been those who condemned the action of their country in entering into wars they thought to be unjustified.—Hughes: United States v. Macintosh, 283 U.S. 605, 635.

———, miscellaneous

42. Now, at least, and perhaps as long as man dwells upon the globe, his destiny is battle, and he has to take the chances of war. — Holmes: *Speeches,* 58.

43. War, when you are at it, is horrible and dull. It is only when time has passed that you see that its message was divine.—Holmes: *ibid.,* 62.

44. Even for those who did not reach the firing line, there were the pangs of separation from home and kindred, the anxieties and the strain of a new and hazardous adventure.—Cardozo: People v. Westchester Co. Nat'l Bank, 231 N.Y. 465, 485.

See also Freedom, speech 80, 81, 102; Nationalism; Race 24.

WARNING

The thoughtless will be checked, though the recklessly indifferent will be free to go their way.—Cardozo: De Haen v. Rockwood Spr. Co., 258 N.Y. 350, 354.

Related subject: Alarm. *See also* Threat.

WATER

1. No higher police duty rests upon municipal authority than that of furnishing an ample supply of pure and wholesome water for public and domestic uses.—Lurton: Columbus v. Mercantile Tr. & Dep. Co., 218 U.S. 645, 658.

2. The public interest in the conservation and distribution of water for a great variety of purposes—ranging from ordinary agricultural, domestic and sanitary uses, to the preservation of health and of life itself—is obvious and well settled. For the modern city, such conservation and distribution of water in sufficient quantity and in a state of purity is as vital as air.—Sutherland: Brush v. Comm'r of Int. Rev., 300 U.S. 352, 366.

WEAK, WEAKNESS

Related subjects: Majority-minority and related subjects. *See also* Court 11, 29; Grand jury; Human nature 1; Inclination; Judge, disabilities; Judgment 8.

WEALTH

1. Patriotism and poverty do not necessarily march hand in hand; nor is wealth that monster, which some imaginations have depicted, with a heart of adamant, and a sceptre of iron, surrounded with scorpions, stinging every one within its reach, and planting its feet of oppression upon the needy and the dependent.— Story: *Misc. Writings*, 512–13.

2. Nor does wealth here form a permanent distinction of families. Those, who are wealthy to-day, pass to the tomb, and their children divide their estates. Property is thus divided quite as fast as it accumulates. No family can, without its own exertions, stand erect for a long time under our statute of descents and distributions, the only true and legitimate agrarian law. It silently and quietly dissolves the mass, heaped up by the toil and diligence of a long life of enterprise and industry. Property is continually changing, like the waves of the sea.—Story: *ibid.*, 514–15.

3. The object of ambition, power, generally presents itself nowadays in the form of money alone. Money is the most immediate form, and is a proper object of desire. — Holmes: "The Path of the Law," 10 Harv. L. Rev. 477–78.

4. That portion of the American people upon whom rests the larger part of the burdens of the government . . . ought not to be subjected to the dominion of aggregated wealth any more than the property of the country should be at the mercy of the lawless.—Harlan: Pollock v. Farmers Loan & Tr. Co., 158 U.S. 601, 685.

5. Wealth, power, the struggle for ephemeral social and political prestige, which so absorb our attention and energy, are but the passing phase of every age; ninety-day wonders which pass from man's recollection almost before the actors who have striven for them have passed from the stage.—Stone: Mason, *Stone*, 209.

Related subjects: Investment and related subjects. *See also* Capitalist; Equity 24; Ideal 4; Monopoly 9; Patriotism 3; Power 7, 11; Securities 6; Socialism 5; Tax 74, 101, 116, 139; Thought 1; Utopia 2; War 7, 8.

WHITE PERSON

The words "white persons" . . . are words of common speech, and not of scientific origin.—Sutherland: United States v. Bhagat Singh Thind, 261 U.S. 204, 208

Related subject: Race.

WHITE-SLAVE TRAFFIC

The designation "white slave traffic" has the sufficiency of an axiom.—McKenna: Caminetti v. United States, 242 U.S. 470, 497.

WHOLE-PART

1. The difference is that which always exists, and always must exist, between the action of the whole on a part, and the action of a part on the whole.—Marshall: McCulloch v. Maryland, 4 Wheat (17 U.S.) 316, 435–36.

2. It is as well a maxim of political law as of reason, that the whole must necessarily contain all the parts. — Trimble: Ogden v. Saunders, 12 Wheat. (25 U.S.) 213, 323.

3. The part can not swallow the whole—that our categories are not, or may not be, adequate to formulate what we can not know.—Holmes: "Natural Law," 32 Harv. L. Rev. 43.

4. The sum of the rights in the parts cannot be greater than the rights in the whole. — Brandeis: Pennsylvania Coal Co. v. Mahon, 260 U.S. 393, 419.

5. The whole, though larger than any of its parts, does not necessarily obscure their separate identities. — Douglas: United States v. Powers, 307 U.S. 214, 218.

Related subject: Greater-less.

WICKEDNESS

Related subjects: Evil; Iniquity; Malevolence; Vice. *See also* Deceit 1; Inevitability; Turpitude 3; Wrongdoer 9.

WIDOWHOOD

How can any calculation be made in regard to the continuance of widowhood? . . . How can a valuation of a probable continuance of widowhood be made? Who can say what the probability of remarrying is in regard to any particular widow? We know what some of the factors may be in the question: inclination, age, health, property, attractiveness, children. . . . Yet there are no statistics which can be gathered which would tend in the slightest degree to aid in the solving of the question.—Peckham: Dunbar v. Dunbar, 190 U.S. 340, 345–46.

WILL (mind)

1. We see how force of will has carried g i f t s to achievement. — Holmes: *Uncollected Letters,* 202.

2. A man once broken in will does not readily, if ever, recover from the breaking. — Rutledge: Malinski v. New York, 324 U.S. 401, 428.

Related subjects: Intent; Mind and related subjects; *See also* Freedom 182; Rights 5; Self-restraint 1.

WILL (testament)

1. The disposition of property to

476

take effect after death is one of the most solemn acts in the life of a man. —Davis: Gaines v. New Orleans, 6 Wall. (73 U.S.) 642, 710.

2. In the case of a will. It is true that the testator is a despot, within limits, over his property. — Holmes: "Theory of Legal Interpretations," 12 Harv. L. Rev. 420.

3. Influence obtained by flattery, importunity, threats, superiority of will, mind or character, or by what art soever that human thought, ingenuity or cunning might employ, which would give dominion over the will of the deceased to such an extent as to destroy free agency or constrain him against his will to do what he was unable to refuse, was such influence as the law condemned as undue. —Harlan: Ormsby v. Webb, 134 U.S. 47, 66.

4. Surely the probate of a fraudulent or forged paper is a fraud on the living as much as the suppression of the last Will.—Catron: Gaines v. Chew, 2 How. (43 U.S.) 619, 651.

5. Experience has shown that often after the death of a testator unexpected difficulties arise, technical rules of law are found to have been trespassed upon, contests are commenced wherein not infrequently are brought to light matters of private life that ought never to be made public. — Brewer: Smithsonian Inst. v. Meech, 169 U.S. 398, 415,

6. The first and great rule in the exposition of wills (to which all other rules must bend) is that the intention of the testator expressed in his will shall prevail, provided it be consistent with the rules of law. — Marshall: Smith v. Bell, 6 Pet. (31 U.S.) 68, 75.

7. The English courts are especially and wisely careful not to substitute a lively imagination of what a testatrix would have said if her attention had been directed to a particular point, for what she has said in fact. — Holmes: Eaton v. Brown, 193 U.S. 411, 414.

8. As to the inequalities in case of a will, they must be taken to be contemplated by the testator. — Holmes: New York Tr. Co. v. Eisner, 256 U.S. 345, 349.

9. The meaning of a testator is not required to be found in law lexicons; the usages of popular speech may furnish a guide to it.—McKenna: Taylor v. George Washington Univ., 226 U.S. 126, 136.

10. One of the objects of a residuary clause is to gather up unremembered as well as uncertain rights. — Holmes: Mayor v. American Sec. & Tr. Co., 222 U.S. 295, 300.

Related subject: Inheritance. *See also* Intent 12; Precedent 33.

WIRE TAPPING

1. For years controversy has raged with respect to the morality of the practice of wire-tapping by officers to obtain evidence. — Roberts: Nardon v. United States, 302 U.S. 379, 384.

2. It is desirable that criminals should be detected, and to that end all available evidence should be used. It is also desirable that the Government should not itself foster and pay

for other crimes, when they are the means by which the evidence is to be obtained. — H o l m e s: Olmstead v. United States, 277 U.S. 438, 470.

3. Discovery and invention have made it possible for the government, by means far more effective than stretching upon the rack, to obtain disclosure in court of what is whispered in the closet. — Brandeis: Olmstead v. United States, 277 U.S. 438, 473.

4. When the Fourth and Fifth Amendments were adopted, "the form that evil had theretofore taken" had been necessarily simple. Force and violence were then the only means known to man by which a government could directly effect self-incrimination. — Brandeis: *ibid*.

5. To declare that in the administration of the criminal law the end justifies the means—to declare that the government may commit crimes in order to secure the conviction of a private criminal—would bring terrible retribution. — Brandeis: *ibid.,* 485.

> Related subjects: Privacy and related subjects; Self incrimination and related subjects.

WISDOM

1. Wisdom, is the union of that virtue, which has ripened under the hardy discipline of principle, with that knowledge, which has constantly sifted and refined its old treasures, and as constantly gathered new. — Story: *Misc. Writings,* 198–99.

2. It is true wisdom, not to blind ourselves to dangers, which are in full view; and true prudence, to guard against those, of which experience has already admonished us.—Story: *ibid.,* 85.

3. It is easy to be wise after we see the results of experience.—Strong: Platt v. Union Pac. R.R., 9 Otto (99 U.S.) 48, 63–64.

4. No doubt the wisdom that is born after the event will engender suspicion and distrust when old acquaintance and good repute may have silenced doubt at the beginning.—Cardozo: Ultramares Corp. v. Touche, 255 N.Y. 170, 179.

5. "Wisdom too often never comes, and so one ought not to reject it merely because it comes late." Similarly, one should not reject a piecemeal wisdom, merely because it hobbles toward the truth with backward glances.—Rutledge: Wolf v. Colorado, 338 U.S. 25, 47.

6. It is the part of wisdom, particularly for judges, not to be victimized by words. — Frankfurter: Shapiro v. United States, 335 U.S. 1, 56.

7. The compassionate wisdom of Lincoln's First and Second Inaugurals bequeathed to the Union, cemented with blood, a moral heritage which, when drawn upon in times of stress and strife, is sure to find specific ways and means to surmount difficulties that may appear to be insurmountable.—Frankfurter: Cooper v. Aaron, 358 U.S. 1, 23.

> Related subjects: Education and related subjects; Intelligence; K n o w l e d g e; Learning.

478

WITNESS

Characteristics 1–4; competency, credibility 5–14; miscellaneous 15–18.

Related subjects: Evidence and related subjects; Self incrimination and related subjects.

———, characteristics

1. It is not every one who can safely venture on the witness stand though entirely innocent of the charge against him. Excessive timidity, nervousness when facing others and attempting to explain transactions of a suspicious character, and offenses c h a r g e d against him, will often confuse and embarrass him to such a degree as to increase rather than remove prejudices against him.—Blatchford: National Meter Co. v. Board of Water Comm'rs, 149 U.S. 48, 66.

2. Witnesses . . . would be unusual to a degree if their conclusions were not, in a measure, colored and partisan.—Clarke: Wise v. United States, 249 U.S. 361, 367.

3. Every lawyer dislikes to take the witness stand and will do so only for grave reasons. This is partly because it is not his role; he is almost invariably a poor witness. But he steps out of professional character to do it. He regrets it; the profession discourages it.—Jackson: Hickman v. Taylor, 329 U.S. 495, 517.

4. Physical objects are not witnesses, even though they have the quality of evidence.—Cardozo: Snyder v. Massachusetts, 291 U.S. 97, 119.

———, competency, credibility

5. The theory of the common law was to admit to the witness stand only those presumably honest, appreciating the sanctity of an oath, unaffected as a party by the result, and free from any of the temptations of interest. The courts were afraid to trust the intelligence of jurors. . . . Steadily, one by one, the merely technical barriers which excluded witnesses from the stand have been removed. — Brewer: Benson v. United States, 146 U.S. 325, 336.

6. Interest creates a motive for false testimony; . . . the greater the interest the stronger is the temptation.—Brewer: Reagan v. United States, 157 U.S. 301, 310.

7. Witnesses whose memories are prodded by the eagerness of interested parties to elicit testimony favorable to themselves are not usually to be depended upon for accurate information.—Brown: Washburn & Moen Mfg. Co. v. Beat 'Em Co., 143 U.S. 275, 284.

8. As a witness, a defendant is no more to be visited with condemnation than he is to be clothed with sanctity, simply because he is under accusation. —Fuller: Allison v. United States, 160 U.S. 203, 210.

9. It must be remembered that men may testify truthfully, although their lives hang in the balance.—Shiras: Hicks v. United States, 150 U.S. 442, 452.

10. A lunatic or insane person may, from the condition of his mind, not be a competent witness. . . . The books are full of cases where persons showing mental derangement on some sub-

jects evince a high degree of intelligence and wisdom on others. The existence of partial insanity does not unfit individuals so affected for the transaction of business on all subjects, nor from giving a perfectly accurate and lucid statement of what they have seen or heard.—Field: District of Columbia v. Armes, 107 U.S. 519, 521.

11. A witness who, at different times, gives different versions of the same transaction, and blows hot or cold as his interest in the particular litigation may require, can scarcely complain if the court fail to give his testimony the weight to which it would otherwise be entitled.—Brown: Richmond Nervine Co. v. Richmond, 159 U.S. 293, 302.

12. Arrest without more does not, in law any more than in reason, impeach the integrity or impair the credibility of a witness.—Jackson: Michelson v. United States, 335 U.S. 469, 481.

13. The touchstone is always credibility; the ultimate measure of testimonial worth is quality and not quantity.—Black: Weiler v. United States, 323 U.S. 606, 608.

14. Our system of justice rests on the general assumption that the truth is not to be determined merely by the number of witnesses on each side of a controversy.—Black: *ibid.*

———, miscellaneous

15. In the classic phrase of Lord Chancellor Hardwicke, "the public has a right to every man's evidence."

— Frankfurter: United States v. Monia, 317 U.S. 424, 432.

16. The influence of lawless force directed toward parties or witnesses to proceedings during their pendency is so sinister and undermining of the process of adjudication itself that no court should regard it with indifference or shelter it from exposure and inquiry.—Jackson: NLRB v. Indiana & Mich. Elec. Co., 318 U.S. 9, 29.

17. The arsenal of every advocate holds two bundles of adjectives for witnesses—such ones as "reluctant," "unbiased," "disinterested," and "honest" are reserved for his own; others, such as "partisan," "eager," "interested," "hostile," and even "perjured," for those of his adversary.—Jackson: Kingsland v. Dorsey, 338 U.S. 318, 324.

18. The basic reason the law has refused to pit wife against husband or husband against wife in a trial where life or liberty is at stake was a belief that such a policy is necessary to foster family peace, not only for the benefit of husband, wife and children, but for the benefit of the public as well.—Black: Hawkins v. United States, 358 U.S. 74, 77.

See also Common law 12; Informer; Juror 46; Litigant 8; Oath 1, 2; Perjury; Trial 1.

WOMAN, WOMEN

1. The civil law, as well as nature herself, has always recognized a wide difference in the respective spheres and destinies of man and woman. Man is, or should be, woman's pro-

tector and defender. The natural and proper timidity and delicacy which belongs to the female sex evidently unfits it for many of the occupations of civil life.—Bradley: Bradwell v. Illinois, 16 Wall. (83 U.S.) 130, 141.

2. History discloses the fact that woman has always been dependent upon man. He established his control at the outset by superior physical strength, and this control in various forms, with diminishing intensity, has continued to the present.—Brewer: Muller v. Oregon, 208 U.S. 412, 421.

3. That woman's physical structure and the performance of maternal functions place her at a disadvantage in the struggle for subsistence is obvious. This is especially true when the burdens of motherhood are upon her. —Brewer: *ibid*.

4. As healthy mothers are essential to vigorous offspring, the physical well-being of woman becomes an object of public interest and care in order to preserve the strength and vigor of the race.—Brewer: *ibid*.

5. The ancient inequality of the sexes, otherwise than physical, . . . has continued "with diminishing intensity." In view of the great—not to say revolutionary — changes which have taken place . . . in the contractual, political, and civil status of women, culminating in the N i n e t e e n t h Amendment, it is not unreasonable to say that these differences have now come almost, if not quite, to the vanishing point.—Sutherland: Adkins v. Children's Hosp., 261 U.S. 525, 553.

6. It will need more than the Nineteenth Amendment to convince me that there are no differences between men and women.—Holmes: *ibid.,* 569–70.

7. Women today stand upon a legal and political equality with men. — Sutherland: West Coast Hotel Co. v. Parrish, 300 U.S. 379, 411.

8. The constitutional right of women to jury duty has lagged behind that of racial groups.—Douglas: *We the Judges,* 392.

Related subjects: Domestic relations and related subjects. *See also* Labor 44; Liquor 7; Person 2; Testimony 5.

WORD

1. A word is not a crystal, transparent and unchanged; it is the skin of a living thought and may vary greatly in color and content according to the circumstances and the time in which it is used.—Holmes: Towne v. Eisner, 245 U.S. 418, 425.

2. Words are the common signs that mankind make use of to declare their intention to one another.—Lamar: Lake County v. Rollins, 130 U.S. 662, 671.

3. This is an attitude that treats words as ends and not as vehicles to convey meaning. — Frankfurter: Pope v. Atlantic Coast Line R.R., 345 U.S. 379, 390.

4. There is no magic in words. — Story: Briscoe v. Bank of Kentucky, 11 Pet. (36 U.S.) 257, 347.

5. The phrase "assumption of risk" is an excellent illustration of the extent to which uncritical use of words bedevils the law. A phrase begins life

as a literary expression; its felicity leads to its lazy repetition; and repetition soon establishes it as a legal formula, undiscriminately used to express different and sometimes contradictory ideas.—Frankfurter: Tiller v. Atlantic Coast Line R.R., 318 U.S. 54, 68.

6. We must translate the idiom of the industry into vernacular English. —Frankfurter: United States v. Felin & Co., 334 U.S. 624, 626.

7. Every group, and even almost every individual when he has acquired a definite mode of thought, gets a more or less special terminology which it takes time for an outsider to live into.—Holmes: *Uncollected Letters,* 163.

Related subjects: Catch phrase; Construction and related subjects; Language; Speech. *See also* Contract 3; Idea 2; Incitement 6; Lawyer 74; Liar; Libel; Logic 1; Logomachy; Mind 13; Obscenity; Platitude 2; Quasi; Style 4; Supreme Court 68; Symbol 13; Technicality 2; Wisdom 6.

WORK

Related subject: Labor. *See also* Effort 5; Good will 2; Leisure; Peonage; Preacher 1.

WORKHOUSE

It was and is what its name implies, —a place of correction and reformation; not of condemnation or infamy, and it might be, to a perpetual criminal career. . . . Its purpose is reformation, instruction in conduct, and diversion from a criminal career.—McKenna: United States v. Moreland, 258 U.S. 433, 440.

WORKINGMAN
See Labor.

WORKMEN'S COMPENSATION ACTS

1. Someone has to take care of an individual who has received . . . an injury which permanently disables him from performance of his work. If employers or the consumers of their goods do not shoulder his responsibility, the general public of a state must.—Black: Magnolia Pet. Co. v. Hunt, 320 U.S. 430, 456.

2. He was to be saved from becoming one of the derelicts of society, a fragment of human wreckage.—Cardozo: Surace v. Danna, 248 N.Y. 18, 20–21.

Related subject: Negligence, industrial accident.

WORSHIP
See Freedom, religion, belief.

WORTH
See Value.

WRONG

1. Wrong is defined in terms of the natural or probable, at least when unintentional. — Cardozo: Palsgraf v. Long Island R.R., 248 N.Y. 339, 345.

2. Something more than the strong probability that an enjoyment will continue must be shown in order to make an otherwise lawful uncompensated interference with it a wrong. —Holmes: Denver v. Denver Union Water Co., 246 U.S. 178, 197.

3. Accountability for wrong is one thing; the wrong is another. — Holmes: United States v. Thompson, 257 U.S. 419, 437.

4. Something more must be shown than ungenerous behavior. — Cardozo: Golde Clothes Shop v. Loew's Buffalo Theatres, 236 N.Y. 465, 470.

5. The act was a wrongful one . . . but in the common speech of men there would be reluctance to describe it as flagitious or dishonest.—Cardozo: World Exch. Bank v. Commercial Cas. Ins. Co., 225 N.Y. 1, 6.

6. A blow in the face seems a fairly palpable fact, but all sorts of mental reservations and concomitants have to be known and estimated before you can determine whether it is to be reckoned as an actionable wrong. The psychical is ever crowding upon the precincts of the physical.—Cardozo: *Law and Literature,* 135.

7. It is not lawful to do evil that good may come. There are plenty of ways in which wrong may be suppressed without resorting to wrongful measures to do it.—Bradley: *Ex parte Curtis,* 106 U.S. 371, 378.

Related subject: Right. *See also* Distinction 2; Equity court 24, 25; Fact 12; Intent 5; Motive 5; Punishment 5; Remedy 7; Rights 44; Sovereignty 17; Suffering 1.

WRONGDOER

1. The loss had to fall on the innocent or the guilty. In such an alternative the law places the loss on the wrongdoer. — Lamar: Westinghouse Elec. & Mfg. Co. v. Wagner Elec. & Mfg. Co., 225 U.S. 604, 619.

2. The wilful transgressor must accept the penalty of his transgression. —Cardozo: Jacob & Youngs v. Kent, 230 N.Y. 230, 244.

3. It is not for him to claim a right springing out of his own wrong.— Johnson: The Arrogante Barcelones, 7 Wheat. (20 U.S.) 496, 519.

4. A person does not become an outlaw and lose all rights by doing an illegal act.—Holmes: National Bank & Loan Co. v. Petrie, 189 U.S., 423, 425.

5. The law may at times refuse to aid a wrongdoer in getting that which good conscience permits him to receive; it will not for that reason aid another in taking away from him that which good conscience entitles him to retain. — Cardozo: Schank v. Schuchman, 212 N.Y. 352, 359.

6. In society, the wrongdoer may be too powerful for the law.—Marshall: Ogden v. Saunders, 12 Wheat. (25 U.S.) 213, 345–46.

7. The transgressor whose default is unintentional and trivial may hope for mercy if he will offer atonement for his wrong.—Cardozo: Jacob & Youngs v. Kent, 230 N.Y. 230, 244.

8. I do not believe that even capital offenses by boys of fifteen should be dealt with according to the conventional criminal procedures. — Frankfurter: Haley v. Ohio, 332 U.S. 596, 602–603.

9. The wickedness of people, shielding wrongdoers, and passing them off (or at least allowing them to pass themselves off) as honest men.—Brandeis: Mason, *Brandeis,* 94.

Related subject: Crime, Criminal.

YOUTH
Related subjects: Child; Infant; Parent-child. *See also* Advice 1; Age (years);

Courage 2; Education 6; War 2; Wrongdoer 8; Zeal 7.

ZEAL

1. Men with more zeal than wisdom.—Field: Beckwith v. Bean, 8 Otto (98 U.S.) 266, 294.

2. Zeal for policies, estimable, it may be, of themselves, may overlook or underestimate private rights. — McKenna: General Oil Co. v. Crain, 209 U.S. 211, 227.

3. Zeal takes care to be explicit in purpose. — McKenna: G r o g a n v. Walker & Co., 259 U.S. 80, 95.

4. Disinterested zeal for the public good does not assure either wisdom or right in the methods it pursues.—Frankfurter: Haley v. Ohio, 332 U.S. 596, 605.

5. Zeal in tracking down crime is not in itself an assurance of soberness of judgment.—Frankfurter: McNabb v. United States, 318 U.S. 332, 343.

6. To use a phrase of Mr. Justice Holmes, one were fired with a zeal to pervert.—Frankfurter: Milk Wagon Drivers Union v. Meadowmoor Dairies, 312 U.S. 287, 298.

7. Obsessed with youth's zeal for the hunt.—Rutledge: Marconi Wireless Tel. Co. v. United States, 320 U.S. 1, 65.

ZEALOT

1. Experience has ... counseled that safeguards must be provided against the dangers of the overzealous as well as the despotic. — Frankfurter: McNabb v. United States, 318 U.S. 332, 343.

2. People with a consuming belief that their religious convictions must be forced on others rarely ever believe that the unorthodox have any rights which should or can be rightfully respected.—Black: Adamson v. California, 332 U.S. 46, 88.

See also Freedom 49; Freedom, thought 153.

ZONING

1. Building zone laws are of modern origin. They began in this country about twenty-five years ago. Until recent years, urban life was comparatively simple; but with the great increase and concentration of population, problems have developed, and constantly are developing, which require, and will continue to require, additional restrictions in respect of the use and occupation of private lands in u r b a n communities. — Sutherland: Euclid v. Ambler Realty Co., 272 U.S. 365, 386–87.

2. Regulations, the wisdom, necessity and validity of which, as applied to existing conditions, are so apparent that they are now uniformly sustained, a century ago, or even half a century ago, probably would have been rejected as arbitrary and oppressive. — Sutherland, *ibid.*, 387.

APPENDICES

I. Parallel References and Court Terms

THE EARLY VOLUMES of the official Supreme Court reports were designated by the names of the respective reporters. The first numbered designation (91) appears in 1 Otto, and thereafter, through 15 Otto and subsequently, the volumes were numbered consecutively, the numbering being exclusive following 15 Otto. For purposes of clarity and brevity, the text employs consecutive numbering from the first volume of Dallas, which, however, contains no record of Supreme Court proceedings. These start in 2 Dallas with the opening of the Court in the February, 1790, term.

Therefore, the dates in the following subdivisions refer to the terms which commenced in the years stated. The terms for the sitting of the Court were originally prescribed by the judiciary act enacted by Congress on September 24, 1789. This fixed two terms to be held in each year, one commencing in February and one in August. By an enactment of February 13, 1801, Congress provided that the Court should hold June and December terms in each year. After the accession of Jefferson to the presidency, the Republicans repealed the act and restored the February, but not the August, term of Court. Since this act was passed on March 31, 1802, the Court was unable to meet until February of 1803 (*see* 1 Cranch *post*). Thereafter, the Court held one term each year beginning in February, until 1827, when, by congressional enactment, the

485

term began on the second Monday in January (*see* 12 Wheat. *post*). This practice prevailed until 1845, when, by the authority granted by a congressional act of June 17, 1844, the Court began to convene on the second Monday of December of each year (*see* 10 How. *post*). Finally, pursuant to the act of January 24, 1873, the commencement of each annual term was set for October (*see* 17 Wall. *post*), as presently set.

TABLE OF REFERENCES
(with dates)

Period (*all inclusive*)			U.S. No.	Reporter	Vol.
			1	DALLAS	1
Feb. term 1790–Aug.	term	1793	2		2
	1794–Feb.	1799	3		3
Aug.	1799–Aug.	1800	4		4
	1801–Feb.	1803	5	CRANCH	1
Feb.	1804–	1805	6		2
	1805–	1806	7		3
	1807–	1808	8		4
	1809		9		5
	1810		10		6
	1812–	1813	11		7
	1814		12		8
	1815		13		9
	1816		14	WHEATON	1
	1817		15		2
	1818		16		3
	1819		17		4
	1820		18		5
	1821		19		6
	1822		20		7
	1823		21		8
	1824		22		9
	1825		23		10
	1826		24		11
Jan.	1827		25		12
	1828		26	PETERS	1
	1829		27		2
	1830		28		3
	1830		29		4
	1831		30		5
	1832		31		6
	1833		32		7
	1834		33		8
	1835		34		9
	1836		35		10
	1837		36		11

Period (all inclusive)			U.S. No.	Reporter	Vol.
	1838		37		12
	1839		38		13
	1840		39		14
	1841		40		15
	1842		41		16
	1843		42	HOWARD	1
	1844		43		2
	1845		44		3
	1846		45		4
	1847		46		5
	1848		47		6
	1849		48		7
	1850		49		8
	1850		50		9
	1850		51		10
	1850		52		11
	1851		53		12
	1851		54		13
	1852		55		14
	1853		56		15
	1853		57		16
	1854		58		17
	1855		59		18
	1856		60		19
	1857		61		20
	1858		62		21
	1859		63		22
	1859		64		23
	1860		65		24
	1861		66	BLACK	1
	1862		67		2
	1863		68	WALLACE	1
	1864		69		2
	1865		70		3
	1866		71		4
	1866		72		5
	1867		73		6
	1868		74		7
	1869		75		8
	1869		76		9
	1869		77		10
	1870		78		11
	1870		79		12
	1871		80		13
	1871		81		14
	1872		82		15
	1872		83		16
Dec.	1872–Oct.	1873	84		17

Period (all inclusive)		U.S. No.	Reporter	Vol.
Oct.	1873	85		18
	1873	86		19
	1873, 1874	87		20
	1874	88		21
	1874	89		22
	1874	90		23
	1875	91	OTTO	1
	1875	92		2
	1876	93		3
	1876	94		4
	1877	95		5
	1877	96		6
	1877	97		7
	1878	98		8
	1878	99		9
	1879	100		10
	1879	101		11
Oct.	1879–Oct. 1880	102		12
	1880	103		13
	1881	104		14
	1881	105		15

OFFICIAL U.S. REPORTS
(dates and volumes)

Term (all Oct.)	Volume	Term (all Oct.)	Volume
1881–82	106	1899	175–78
1882–	107, 108	1900	179–82
1883	109–11	1901	183–86
1884	112–14	1902	187–90
1884–85	115	1903	191–94
1885	116–18	1904	195–98
1886	119–22	1904–1905	199
1887	123–26	1905	200–202
1888	128–31	1905–1906	203
1889	132–36	1906	204–206
1890	137–42	1907	207–10
1891	143–45	1908	211–14
1892	146–49	1909	215–17
1893	150–54	1909–10	218
1893–94	155	1910	219–21
1894	156–58	1911	222–25
1894–95	159	1912	226–30
1895	160–63	1913	231–34
1896	164–69	1914	235–38
1897	170	1915	239–41
1897–98	171	1916	242–44

Term (all Oct.)	Volume	Term (all Oct.)	Volume
1898	172–74	1917	245–47
1918	248–49	1942 (Oct.)	319–20
1918–19	250	1943	321–23
1919	251–54	1944	324–25
1920	255–56	1944–45	326
1921	257–59	1945	327–28
1922	260–62	1946	329–31
1923	263–65	1946–47	332
1924	266–68	1947	333–34
1925	269–71	1947–48	335
1926	272–74	1948	336–37
1927	275–77	1948–49	338
1928	278–79	1949	339
1929	280–81	1950	340–41
1930	282–83	1951	342–43
1931	284–86	1952	344–45
1932	287–88	1952–53	346
1933	289–92	1953	347
1934	293–95	1954	348–49
1935	296–98	1955	350–51
1936	299–301	1956	352–54
1937	302–304	1957	355–57
1938	305–307	1958 (Spec. Aug.–	
1939	308–309	Oct.)	358
1940	310–13	1958 (Oct.)	359–60
1941	314–16	1959	361–64
1942 (July–Oct.)	317–18	1960	364–67

II. Brief Biographies of the Justices

1. The state following the name of the justice represents the state from which he was appointed.

2. The dates of service represent the terms of court during which the justice was eligible to sit.

3. The date of commission is to be distinguished from (1) the date the designee's name was sent to the Senate; (2) the date he was confirmed by the Senate; and (3) the date he took the oath and was installed on the bench.

BALDWIN, HENRY (Pa.). Service: 3 Pet. (28 U.S.), 1830—2 How. (43 U.S.), 1844. Born Jan. 14, 1780; New Haven, Conn.; commissioned Jan. 6, 1830; Yale Univ., 1797; admitted bar, Conn., Pa.; Congress, 1817–22; died Apr. 21, 1844.

BARBOUR, PHILIP PENDLETON (Va.). Service: 11 Pet. (36 U.S.) 1837—14 Pet. (39 U.S.), 1840. Born May 25, 1783, Va.; commissioned Mar. 15, 1836; William & Mary, 1801 (one term); admitted bar, Ky., 1800, Va., 1802; House of Delegates, Va., 1812; Congress, 1814–25; speaker, House of Representatives, 1821–23; judge, General Court, Va., 1825–27; Congress, 1827–29; president, Va. constitutional convention, 1829–30; U.S. district judge, Va., 1830–36; died Feb. 25, 1841.

BLACK, HUGO L. (Ala.). Service: 302 U.S., 1937——. Born Feb. 27, 1886, Harlan, Clay Co., Ala.; commissioned Aug. 18, 1937; Univ. of Ala., 1906; admitted bar, Ala., 1907; police judge, 1911–12; prosecuting attorney, 1914–17; U.S. senator, 1927–37; military service, World War I.

BLAIR, JOHN (Va.). Service: 2 Dall. (2 U.S.), 1790-93—3 Dall. (3 U.S.), 1795. Born 1732, Williamsburg, Va.; commissioned Sept. 30, 1789; William & Mary; Middle Temple, London, 1755; House of Burgesses, Va., 1766–70, clerk, 1770–75; Privy Council, Va., 1776–77; judge, chief justice, General Court, Va., 1778; judge, High Court of Chancery; judge, First Court of Appeals, 1779–1789; member, signer, Constitutional Convention, 1787; resigned Supreme Court, 1795; died Aug. 31, 1800.

BLATCHFORD, SAMUEL (N.Y.). Service: 105 U.S., 1881—149 U.S., 1892. Born Mar. 9, 1820. N.Y.C.; commissioned Mar. 27, 1882; Columbia, Col., 1837; admitted bar, N.Y., 1842; U.S. district judge, N.Y., 1867–72; U.S. Circuit Court, 2d Cir., 1872–82; died July 7, 1893.

BRADLEY, JOSEPH P. (N.J.) Service: 76 U.S., 1869—145 U.S., 1891. Born Mar. 14, 1813, Berne, N.Y.; commissioned Mar. 21, 1870; Rutgers Col., 1836; admitted bar, N.J., 1839; no previous political or judicial service; served on Hayes-Tilden Electoral Commission, 1877; died Jan. 22, 1892.

BRANDEIS, LOUIS DEMBITZ (Mass.). Service: 242 U.S., 1916—305 U.S., 1938. Born Nov. 13, 1856, Louisville, Ky.; commissioned June 1, 1916; Harvard Law Sch., 1877; admitted bar, Mo., 1878, Mass., 1879; in practice, Mass.; active in civic, corporate, labor, and legislative affairs, New England and nationally; no previous political or judicial service; resigned Supreme Court, Feb. 13, 1939; died Oct. 5, 1941.

BRENNAN, WILLIAM JOSEPH, JR. (N.J.). Service: 356 U.S., 1957——. Born Apr, 26, 1906, Newark, N.J.; commissioned Mar. 21, 1957; Univ. of Pa., 1928; Harvard Law Sch., 1931; admitted bar, N.J., 1931; judge Superior Court, N.J., 1949–50, Appellate Division, 1950–52, Supreme Court, 1952–56; military service, World War II.

BREWER, DAVID JOSEPH (Kan.). Service: 133 U.S., 1889—216 U.S., 1909. Born Jan. 29, 1837, Smyrna, Asia Minor; commissioned Dec. 18, 1889; Yale Univ., 1856; Albany Law Sch., 1858; admitted bar, N.Y., 1858, Kan., 1859; commissioner, Federal Circuit Court, Kan., 1861; judge, Leavenworth Co. Court, Kan., 1862; judge, First Judicial District, 1865–69; city attorney, Leavenworth; judge, Supreme Court, Kan., 1870–84; U.S. circuit judge, 8th Cir., 1884–89; commissioner, Venezuela–British Guiana boundary dispute, 1895; died Mar. 28, 1910.

BROWN, HENRY BILLINGS (Mich.). Service: 137 U.S., 1890—203 U.S., 1905–1906. Born. Mar. 21, 1836, Lee, Mass.; commissioned Dec. 29, 1890; Yale Univ., 1856; attended Yale and Harvard Law Schs.; admitted bar, Mich., 1860; deputy U.S. marshal, Mich., 1861; assistant U.S. attorney, Mich., 1863–68; judge, Wayne Co. Circuit Court, 1868; U.S. district judge, Mich., 1875–90; resigned Supreme Court, May 28, 1906; died Sept. 4, 1913.

BURTON, HAROLD HITZ (Ohio). Service: 326 U.S., 1944–45—357 U.S., 1957. Born June 22, 1888, Jamaica Plains, Mass.; commissioned Sept. 22, 1945; Bowdoin Col., 1909; Harvard Law Sch., 1912; admitted bar, Ohio, 1912; in active practice, attorney for utility companies, 1912–35; instructor, Western Reserve Univ., 1923–25; mayor, Cleveland, 1935–40; U.S. senator, 1941–45; resigned Supreme Court, Oct. 13, 1958; military service, World War I.

BUTLER, PIERCE (Minn.). Service: 261 U.S., 1922—307 U.S., 1938. Born Mar. 17, 1866, Northfield, Minn.; commissioned Dec. 21, 1922; Carleton Col., 1887; admitted bar, Minn., 1888; assistant county attorney, 1891, county attorney, 1893–97; in active practice, counsel to railroad companies, 1897–1922; died Nov. 16, 1939.

BYRNES, JAMES FRANCIS (S.C.). Service: 314 U.S., 1941—318 U.S., 1942. Born May 2, 1878, Charleston, S.C.; commissioned June 12, 1941; admitted bar, S.C., 1903; editor, 1903–1907; court reporter, 2d. Cir., S.C., 1900–1908, solicitor, 1908–10; Congress, 1911–25; U.S. senator, 1931–43; resigned

Supreme Court, Oct. 3, 1942; director, Economic Stabilization, 1942; director, War Mobilization Board, 1943; U.S. secretary of state, 1945–47; governor, S.C., 1951–55.

CAMPBELL, JOHN ARCHIBALD (Ala.). Service: 15 How. (56 U.S.), 1853—24 How. (64 U.S.), 1860. Born June 24, 1811, Washington, Ga.; commissioned Mar. 25, 1853; Franklin Col. (Univ. of Ga.), 1825; admitted bar, Ga., 1829, Ala., 1830; legislature, Ala., 1836–42; resigned Supreme Court, Apr., 1861; assistant secretary of war, Confederacy, 1861–65; resumed practice in La.; died Mar. 12, 1889.

CARDOZO, BENJAMIN NATHAN (N.Y.). Service: 286 U.S., 1931—302 U.S., 1937. Born May 24, 1870, N.Y.C.; commissioned Mar. 2, 1932; Columbia Univ., 1889; Columbia Law Sch., 1890; admitted bar, N.Y., 1891; justice, Supreme Court, N.Y., 1914–28, N.Y. Court of Appeals, 1924–32, chief justice, 1926–32; died July 9, 1938.

CATRON, JOHN (Tenn.). Service: 2 Pet. (27 U.S.), 1829—2 Wall. (69 U.S.), 1864. Born 1786, Va. or Pa.; commissioned Mar. 8, 1837; admitted bar, Tenn., 1815; states attorney, 1815; judge, Supreme Court of Errors and Appeals, Tenn., 1824–36, chief justice, 1830–36; military service, War of 1812; died May 30, 1865.

CHASE, SALMON PORTLAND (Ohio). Service: 2 Wall. (69 U.S.), 1864—16 Wall. (83 U.S.), 1872. Born Jan. 13, 1808, Cornish, N.H.; commissioned chief justice, Dec. 6, 1864; Cincinnati Col., 1821; Dartmouth Col., 1826; admitted bar, Washington, D.C., 1829, Ohio, 1830; U.S. senator, Ohio, 1849–54, 1860–61; governor, Ohio, 1855–59; U.S. secretary of treasury, 1861–64; died May 7, 1873.

CHASE, SAMUEL (Md.). Service: 3 Dall. (3 U.S.), 1796—6 Cranch (10 U.S.), 1810. Born Apr. 17, 1741, Somerset Co., Md.; commissioned Jan. 27, 1796; admitted bar, Md., 1761 or 1763; Maryland Assembly, 1764–84; First Continental Congress, 1775; signer, Declaration of Independence; Congress, 1776–79; chief justice, Baltimore Criminal Court, 1788; chief justice, General Court, Md., 1791; impeached, 1804, acquitted, 1805; died June 19, 1811.

CLARK, THOMAS CAMPBELL (TOM C.) (Tex.). Service: 338 U.S., 1948——. Born Sept. 23, 1899, Dallas, Tex.; commissioned Aug. 19, 1949; Univ. of Tex., 1921, LL.B., 1922; admitted bar, Tex., 1922; counsel, federal agencies, 1937–45; U.S. attorney general, 1945–49; military service, World War I.

CLARKE, JOHN HESSIN (Ohio). Service: 242 U.S., 1916—259 U.S., 1921. Born Sept. 15, 1857, Lisbon, Ohio; commissioned July 24, 1916; Western Reserve Univ., 1877; admitted bar, Ohio, 1878; in practice, 1878–1914; U.S. district judge, Ohio, 1914–16; resigned Supreme Court, Sept. 18, 1922, to cultivate world peace; died March 22, 1945.

CLIFFORD, NATHAN (Me.). Service: 20 How. (61 U.S.), 1857—13 Otto (103 U.S.), 1880. Born Aug. 18, 1803, Rumney, N.H.; commissioned Jan. 12, 1858; admitted bar, N.H., 1827, Me., 1828; legislature, Me., 1830–34, speaker, 1832–34; attorney general, Me., 1834–38; Congress, 1838–43; U.S. attorney general, 1846–48; Hayes-Tilden Electoral Commission, 1877; died July 25, 1881.

CURTIS, BENJAMIN ROBBINS (Mass.). Service: 12 How. (53 U.S.), 1851—19 How. (60 U.S.), 1856. Born Nov. 4, 1809, Watertown, Mass.; commissioned Dec. 20, 1851; Harvard Col., 1829; attended Harvard Law Sch.; admitted bar, Mass., 1831; in practice, 1832–51; legislature, Mass., 1851; resigned Supreme Court, Sept. 1, 1857; resumed practice; counsel defending President Johnson in impeachment proceedings, 1868; died Sept. 15, 1874.

CUSHING, WILLIAM (Mass.). Service: 2 Dall. (2 U.S.), 1790—6 Cranch (10 U.S.), 1810. Born Mar. 1, 1732, Scituate, Mass.; commissioned Sept. 27, 1789, confirmed chief justice, Jan. 27, 1796, declined Feb. 2, 1796; Harvard Col., 1751; admitted bar, Mass., 1755, Me., 1760; probate judge, Lincoln Co., Me., 1760; judge, Supreme Court, Mass., 1772; judge, Supreme Judicial Court, 1775, chief justice, 1777–89; died Sept. 13, 1810.

DANIEL, PETER VIVIAN (Va.). Service: 16 Pet. (41 U.S.), 1842—23 How. (64 U.S.), 1859. Born Apr. 24, 1784, Stafford Co., Va.; commissioned Mar. 2, 1841; attended College of N.J. (Princeton), 1805; admitted bar, Va., 1808; legislature, Va., 1809; Privy Council, Va., 1818–35; lieutenant governor, Va., 1833–35; judge, U.S. District Court, Va., 1836–41; died May 31, 1860.

DAVIS, DAVID (Ill.). Service: 2 Black (67 U.S.), 1862—4 Otto (94 U.S.), 1876. Born Mar. 9, 1815, Cecil Co., Md.; commissioned Dec. 8, 1862; Kenyon Col., 1832; Yale Law Sch., 1835; admitted bar, Ill., 1836; legislature, Ill., 1844; judge, 8th Judicial Circuit, Ill., 1848–62; resigned Supreme Court, Mar. 4, 1877; U.S. senator, 1877–83, president, 1881–83, resigned senate, 1883; died June 26, 1886.

DAY, WILLIAM RUFUS (Ohio). Service: 189 U.S., 1902—258 U.S., 1921. Born Apr. 17, 1849, Ravenna, Ohio; commissioned Feb. 23, 1903; Univ. of Mich., 1870; admitted bar, Ohio, 1872; judge, Court of Common Pleas, Ohio, 1886–89; first U.S. assistant secretary of state, 1897; U.S. secretary of state, 1898; judge, U.S. Circuit Court, 6th Cir., 1899; resigned Supreme Court, Nov. 13, 1922; died July 9, 1923.

DOUGLAS, WILLIAM ORVILLE (Conn.). Service: 306 U.S., 1938——. Born Oct. 16, 1898, Maine, Minn.; commissioned Apr. 15, 1939; Whitman Col., Wash.; Columbia Law Sch., 1925; SEC, 1934–39, chairman, 1936–39; military service, World War I.

DUVAL(L), GABRIEL (Md.). Service: 7 Cranch (11 U.S.), 1812—9 Pet. (34 U.S.),

1835. Born Dec. 6, 1752; commissioned Nov. 18, 1811; designee, Constitutional Convention, failed to attend: Congress, 1794–96; judge, Supreme Court, Md., 1796; U. S. comptroller of currency, 1802–11; resigned Supreme Court, Jan., 1835; died Mar. 6, 1844.

ELLSWORTH, OLIVER (Conn.). Service: 3 Dall. (3 U.S.), 1796—4 Dall. (4 U.S.), 1799. Born Apr. 29, 1745, Windsor, Conn.; commissioned chief justice, Mar. 4, 1796; College of N.J. (Princeton) 1766; admitted to bar, Conn., 1771; states attorney, 1777; Continental Congress, 1777–83; judge, Superior Court, Conn., 1784–89; member, Constitutional Convention, did not sign, 1787; U.S. senator, 1789–96; envoy to France, 1799; resigned Supreme Court, Dec. 1799; died Nov. 26, 1807.

FIELD, STEPHEN JOHNSON (Calif.). Service: 1 Wall. (68 U.S.), 1863—165 U.S., 1896. Born Nov. 4, 1816, Haddam Co., Conn.; commissioned Mar. 10, 1863; Williams Col., 1837; admitted bar, N.Y., 1841, Calif., 1850; legislature, Calif., 1850; justice, Supreme Court, Calif., 1857–63, chief justice, 1859–63; professor of law, Univ. of Calif., 1869; Hayes-Tilden Electoral Commission, 1877; resigned Supreme Court, Dec. 1, 1897; died Apr. 9, 1899.

FRANKFURTER, FELIX (Mass.). Service: 306 U.S., 1938——. Born Nov. 15, 1882, Vienna, Austria; commissioned Jan. 20, 1939; College of City of N.Y., 1902; Harvard Law Sch., 1906; assistant U.S. attorney, N.Y., 1906–10; professor, Harvard Law Sch., 1914–36.

FULLER, MELVILLE WESTON (Ill.). Service: 128 U.S., 1888—218 U.S., 1909–10. Born Feb. 11, 1833, Augusta, Me.; commissioned chief justice, July 20, 1888; Bowdoin Col., 1853; admitted bar, Me., 1855, Ill., 1856; legislature, Ill., 1862–64; no previous judicial experience; member, Venezuela-British Guiana Boundary Commission, 1899; member, Permanent Court of Arbitration, The Hague, 1900–10; died July 4, 1910.

GRAY, HORACE (Mass.). Service: 14 Otto (104 U.S.), 1881—186 U.S., 1901. Born Mar. 24, 1828, Boston, Mass.; commissioned Dec. 20, 1881; Harvard Univ., 1845; attended Harvard Law Sch., 1848; admitted bar, Mass., 1851; reporter, Mass., 1854–61; justice, Supreme Court, Mass., 1864–81; chief justice, 1873–81; resigned Supreme Court, July 9, 1902; died Sept. 15, 1902.

GRIER, ROBERT COOPER (Pa.). Service: 5 How. (46 U.S.), 1847—10 Wall. (77 U.S.), 1867. Born Mar. 5, 1794, Cumberland Co., Pa.; commissioned Aug. 4, 1846; Dickinson Col., 1812; admitted bar, Pa., 1817; presiding judge, Allegheny Co. District Court, Pa., 1833–46; resigned Supreme Court, Jan. 31, 1870; died Sept. 25, 1870.

HARLAN, JOHN MARSHALL (Ky.). Service: 5 Otto (95 U.S.), 1877—221 U.S., 1910. Born June 1, 1833, Boyle Co., Ky.; commissioned Nov. 29, 1877; Centre Col., 1850; Transylvania Univ. (Law), 1851; admitted bar, Ky.,

1853; judge, County Court, 1858; attorney general, Ky., 1863–67; Louisiana Commission, 1877; arbitrator, Bering Sea controversy with Great Britain, 1892; military service, Civil War; died Oct. 14, 1911.

HARLAN, JOHN MARSHALL (N.Y.). Service: 348 U.S., 1954——. Born May 20, 1899, Chicago, Ill.; commissioned Mar. 17, 1955; Princeton Univ., 1920; Balliol Col., England (Rhodes Scholar), 1923; admitted bar, N.Y., 1925; assistant U.S. attorney, N.Y., 1925–27; special attorney general, N.Y., 1928–30, 1951–53; judge, U.S. Circuit Court, 2d Cir., 1954–55; military service, World War II.

HOLMES, OLIVER WENDELL (Mass.). Service: 187 U.S., 1902—284 U.S., 1931. Born Mar. 8, 1841, Boston, Mass.; commissioned Dec. 4, 1902; Harvard Univ. 1861; Harvard Law Sch., 1866; admitted bar, Mass., 1867; editor, American Law Review, 1870–73; in practice, 1867–82; professor of law, Harvard, 1882; judge, Supreme Court, Mass., 1883–1902, chief justice, 1899–1902; retired Supreme Court, Jan. 12, 1932; died Mar. 6, 1935.

HUGHES, CHARLES EVANS (N.Y.). Service: 218 U.S., 1909–10—241 U.S., 1915; 281 U.S. 1929—313 U.S., 1940. Born Apr. 11, 1862, Glens Falls, N.Y.; commissioned May 2, 1910, chief justice, Feb. 13, 1930; Colgate Univ., 1876–78; Brown Univ., 1881; Columbia Law Sch., 1884; admitted bar, N.Y., 1884; in practice, 1884–1907; professor of law, Cornell Univ., 1891–93; counsel, N.Y. legislative investigation of insurance companies, 1905–1906; governor, N.Y., 1907–10; resigned Supreme Court, June 10, 1916, to become Republican candidate for president; defeated by Woodrow Wilson, 1916; U.S. secretary of state, 1921–25; member, Hague Court of Arbitration, 1927; judge, Permanent Court of International Justice, 1928; resigned Supreme Court as chief justice, July 1, 1941; died Aug. 27, 1948.

HUNT, WARD (N.Y.). Service: 15 Wall. (82 U.S.), 1872—8 Otto (98 U.S.), 1878. Born June 14, 1810, Utica, N.Y.; commissioned Dec. 11, 1872; Union Col., 1828; admitted bar, N.Y., 1831; legislature, N.Y., 1838; mayor, Utica, 1844; judge, Court of Appeals, 1865–72, chief judge, 1868–72, comm'r of appeals, 1869; last service Supreme Court, because of physical incapacity, 1878; resigned Supreme Court, 1882; died Mar. 24, 1886.

IREDELL, JAMES (N.C.). Service: 2 Dall. (2 U.S.) 1790—3 Dall. (U.S.), 1799. Born Oct. 5, 1751, Lewes, England; commissioned Feb. 10, 1790; admitted bar, N. C., 1771; comptroller of customs, Edenton, N.C., 1768–74; collector of port, 1770–76; judge, Superior Court, N.C., 1777; attorney general, N.C., 1779–81; member, Council of State 1787; died Oct. 2, 1799.

JACKSON, HOWELL EDMUNDS (Tenn.). Service: 150 U.S., 1893—159 U.S., 1895. Born Apr. 8, 1832, Paris, Tenn.; commissioned Feb. 18, 1893; West Tenn. Col., 1849; Univ. of Va., 1851–52; law sch., Lebanon, Tenn., 1856; admitted bar, Tenn., 1856; receiver of sequestered property, Confederacy;

legislature, Tenn., 1880; U.S. senator, 1882–86; judge, U.S. Circuit Court, 6th Cir., 1886–93, presiding judge, 1891–93; died Aug. 8, 1895.

JACKSON, ROBERT HOUGHWOUT (N.Y.). Service: 314 U.S., 1941—348 U.S., 1954. Born Feb. 13, 1892, Spring Creek, Pa.; commissioned July 7, 1941; admitted bar, N.Y., 1913; in practice, 1913–34; counsel for federal agencies, 1934–37; U.S. solicitor general, 1938–39; U.S. attorney general, 1940–41; judge, war trials, Nuremberg, Germany, 1945; died Oct. 8, 1954.

JAY, JOHN (N.Y.). Service: 2 Dall. (2 U.S.), 1790–94. Born Dec. 12, 1745, N.Y.C.; commissioned chief justice, September 26, 1789; Kings Col. (Columbia), 1766; admitted bar, N.Y., 1768; First & Second Continental Congresses, 1774–76; chief justice, N.Y., 1777–79; minister to Spain, 1779; president, Congress, 1778–79; commissioner to negotiate peace with Great Britain, 1782–83; secretary for foreign affairs, 1784–89; wrote Federalist papers on Constitution and foreign affairs; special ambassador to England, 1794; resigned Supreme Court, June 29, 1795; governor N.Y., 1795–1801; confirmed as chief justice, Supreme Court, U.S., Dec. 19, 1800, declined; died May 17, 1829.

JOHNSON, THOMAS (Md.). Service: 2 Dall. (2 U.S.), 1791–92. Born Nov. 4, 1732, Calvert Co., Md.; commissioned Nov. 7, 1791; admitted bar, Md.; Provincial Assembly, Md., 1762; First & Second Continental Congresses, 1774–75; governor, Md., 1777–79; legislature, Md., 1780–81, 1786–87; chief judge, General Court, 1790–91; resigned Supreme Court, 1793; military service, Revolutionary War; died Oct. 26, 1819.

JOHNSON, WILLIAM (S.C.). Service: 2 Cranch (6 U.S.), 1804—8 Pet. (33 U.S.), 1834. Born Dec. 27, 1771, Charleston, S.C.; commissioned Mar. 24 (26), 1804; College of N.J. (Princeton), 1790; admitted bar, S.C., 1793; legislature, 1794–98, speaker, 1798; judge, Court of Common Pleas, 1798–1804; died Aug. 8, 1834.

LAMAR, JOSEPH RUCKER (Ga.). Service: 220 U.S., 1910—238 U.S., 1914. Born Oct. 14, 1857, Elbert Co., Ga.; commissioned Dec. 15, 1910; Univ. of Ga.; Bethane Col., W.Va., 1877; attended Wash. & Lee Univ.; admitted bar, Ga., 1878; legislature, Ga., 1886–89; judge, Supreme Court, Ga., 1903–1905; died Jan. 2, 1916.

LAMAR, LUCIUS QUINTUS CINCINNATUS (Miss.). Service: 125 U.S., 1887—145 U.S., 1891. Born Sept. 17, 1825, Putnam Co., Ga.; commissioned Jan. 16, 1888; Emory Col., Ga., 1845; admitted bar, Ga., 1847; legislature, Ga., 1853; Congress, 1857–60; military service, Confederacy, 1862; special commissioner to Russia, 1862; judge advocate, Confederate Army, 1864; professor of law., Univ. of Miss., 1866; Congress, 1872–74; U.S. senator, 1875–85; U.S. secretary of interior, 1885–88; died Jan. 23, 1893.

LIVINGSTON, (HENRY) BROCKHOLST (N.Y.). Service: 4 Cranch (8 U.S.), 1807—

8 Wheat. (21 U.S.), 1823. Born Nov. 26, 1757, N.Y.C.; commissioned Dec. 17, 1807; College of N.J. (Princeton), 1774; admitted bar, N.Y., 1783; judge, Supreme Court, N.Y., 1802–1807; military service, Revolutionary War; died Mar. 18, 1823.

LURTON, HORACE HARMON (Tenn.). Service: 215 U.S., 1909—234 U.S., 1913. Born Feb. 26, 1844, Newport, Ky.; commissioned Dec. 20, 1909; attended Univ. of Chicago; Cumberland Univ. Law Sch., 1867; admitted bar, Tenn.; judge, Supreme Court, Tenn., 1886–93, chief justice, 1893; judge, U.S. Circuit Court, 6th Cir., 1893–1909, presiding judge, 1907–1909; professor of law, Vanderbilt Univ., 1898–1909, dean, 1905–1909; military service, Civil War; died July 12, 1914.

MC KENNA, JOSEPH (Calif.). Service: 170 U.S., 1897—266 U.S., 1924. Born Aug. 10, 1843, Philadelphia, Pa.; commissioned Jan. 21, 1898; Benicia Collegiate Inst., Calif., 1865; admitted bar, Calif., 1865; county attorney, 1866–70; legislature, Calif., 1875; Congress, 1885–92; judge, Circuit Court, 9th Cir., 1892; U.S. attorney general, 1897; resigned Supreme Court, Jan. 5, 1925; died Nov. 21, 1926.

MC KINLEY, JOHN (Ala.). Service: 12 Pet. (37 U.S.), 1838—13 How. (54 U.S.), 1851. Born May 1, 1780, Culpepper, Va.; commissioned Sept. 25, 1837; admitted bar, Ky., Ala., 1818; legislature, Ala., 1820, 1831, 1836; U.S. senator, 1826–31; Congress, 1833–35; U.S. senator, 1835–37; died July 19, 1852.

MC LEAN, JOHN (Ohio). Service: 3 Pet. (28 U.S.), 1830—24 How. (65 U.S.), 1860. Born March 11, 1785, Morris Co., N.J.; commissioned Mar. 7, 1829; admitted bar, Ohio, 1897; Congress, 1812–16; judge, Supreme Court, Ohio, 1816–22; commissioner, General Land Office, 1822; U.S. postmaster general, 1823–29; died Apr. 4, 1861.

MC REYNOLDS, JAMES CLARK (Tenn.). Service: 236 U.S., 1914—312 U.S., 1940. Born Feb. 3, 1862, Elkton, Ky.; commissioned Aug. 29, 1914; Vanderbilt Univ., 1882; Univ. of Va., 1884; admitted bar, Tenn., 1884; in practice, 1884–1903; assistant U.S. attorney general, 1903–07, U.S. attorney general, 1913–14; retired Supreme Court, Feb. 1, 1941; died Aug. 24, 1946.

MARSHALL, JOHN (Va.). Service: 1 Cranch (5 U.S.), 1801—9 Pet. (34 U.S.), 1835. Born Sept. 24, 1755, Prince William Co., Va.; commissioned chief justice, Jan. 27, 1801; attended William & Mary Col., 1780; admitted bar, Va., 1780; House of Delegates, Va., Council of State, Executive Council, 1782–87, 1789, 1795; Va. constitutional convention, 1788; brig. gen., Va. militia, 1794; minister to France, 1797; Congress, 1799; U.S. secretary of state, 1800; military service, Revolutionary War; died July 6, 1835.

MATTHEWS, STANLEY (THOMAS STANLEY) (Ohio). Service: 14 Otto (104 U.S.), 1881—127 U.S., 1887. Born July 21, 1824, Cincinnati, Ohio; appointed by

President Hayes, not confirmed, 1881, reappointed by President Garfield, commissioned May 12, 1881; Kenyon Col., 1840; admitted bar, Tenn., 1842, Ohio, 1844; editor, 1843–45; clerk, House of Representatives, Ohio, 1848–49; judge, Court of Common Pleas, Hamilton Co., Ohio, 1851; senator, Ohio, 1855; U.S. attorney, Ohio, 1858–61; judge, Superior Court, Cincinnati, 1863–65; U.S. senator, 1877–79; military service, Civil War; died Mar. 22, 1889.

MILLER, SAMUEL FREEMAN (Iowa). Service: 2 Black (67 U.S.), 1862—136 U.S., 1889. Born Apr. 5, 1816; Richmond, Ky.; commissioned July 16, 1862; Transylvania Univ. (Med.), 1838; practiced medicine, 1850; admitted bar, Ky., 1847; Hayes-Tilden Electoral Commission, 1877; died October 14 (13), 1890.

MINTON, SHERMAN (Ind.). Service: 338 U.S., 1948–49—351 U.S., 1955. Born Oct. 29, 1890; Georgetown, Ind.; commissioned Oct. 4, 1949; Ind. Univ., 1915; Yale Law Sch., 1916; public counselor, Ind., 1933–34; U.S. senator, 1935–41; judge, U.S. Circuit Court, 7th Cir., 1941–49; military service, World War I; retired Supreme Court, Oct. 15, 1956.

MOODY, WILLIAM HENRY (Mass.). Service: 203 U.S., 1905–1906—218 U.S., 1909–10. Born Dec. 23, 1853, Newbury, Mass.; commissioned Dec. 12, 1906; Harvard Univ., 1876; attended Harvard Law Sch.; admitted bar, Mass., 1876; city solicitor, 1888–90; Congress, 1895–1902; U.S. secretary of navy, 1902; U.S. attorney general, 1904–1906; resigned Supreme Court, Nov. 29, 1910; died July 2, 1917.

MOORE, ALFRED (N.C.). Service: 4 Dall. (4 U.S.), 1800—2 Cranch (6 U.S.), 1804. Born May 21, 1755, Wilmington, N.C.; commissioned Dec. 10, 1799; admitted bar, N.C., 1775; senator, N.C., 1782–91; trustee, N.C. State Univ., 1789–1807; House of Commons, N.C., 1792; judge, Supreme Court, N.C., 1798; resigned Supreme Court, Feb. term, 1804; military service, Revolutionary War; died Oct. 15, 1810.

MURPHY, FRANK (Mich.). Service: 309 U.S., 1939—338 U.S., 1948–49. Born Apr. 13, 1890, Harbor Beach, Mich.; commissioned Jan. 16, 1940; Univ. of Mich., 1912, LL.B., 1914; admitted bar, Mich., 1914; chief assistant U.S. attorney, Mich., 1919–20; judge, Recorder's Court, Detroit, 1923–30; mayor, Detroit, 1930–33; governor general of Philippines, 1935–36; governor, Mich., 1936; U.S. attorney general, 1939–40; military service, World War I; died July 19, 1949.

NELSON, SAMUEL (N.Y.). Service: 4 How. (45 U.S.), 1846—12 Wall. (79 U.S.), 1870. Born Nov. 10, 1792, Washington Co., N.Y.; commissioned Feb. 14, 1845; Middlebury Col., 1813; admitted bar, N.Y., 1817; judge, 6th Circuit Court, N.Y., 1823–31; judge, Supreme Court, N.Y., 1831–45, chief judge, 1837–45; member, Joint High Commission (Ala. claims), 1871; died Dec. 13, 1873.

PATERSON, WILLIAM (N.J.). Service: 2 Dall. (2 U.S.), 1793—3 Cranch (7 U.S.), 1806. Born Dec. 24, 1745, Co. Antrim, Ireland; commissioned Mar. 4, 1793; College of N.J. (Princeton), 1763, M.A., 1766; admitted bar, N.J., 1769; Second Continental Congress, 1775; signer, Declaration of Independence, 1776; attorney general, N.J., 1776–83; member, Legislative Council, N.J., 1776–77; member, signer, Constitutional Convention, 1787; U.S. senator, 1789–90; governor & chancellor, N.J., 1790–93; remodeled rules of practice and procedure, N.J. (Paterson's Practice Laws), 1799; remodeled laws of N.J., 1800; died Sept. 9, 1806; Paterson, N.J., named for him.

PECKHAM, RUFUS WHEELER (N.Y.). Service: 160 U.S., 1895—214 U.S., 1908. Born Nov. 8, 1838, Albany, N.Y.; commissioned Dec. 9, 1895; admitted bar, N.Y., 1859; district attorney, Albany Co., N.Y., 1869–72; corporation counsel, Albany Co., N.Y., 1881; judge, Supreme Court, N.Y., 1883–86; judge, Court of Appeals, N.Y., 1887–95; died Oct. 24, 1909.

PITNEY, MAHLON (N.J.). Service: 225 U.S., 1911—259 U.S., 1921. Born Feb. 5, 1858, Morris Co., N.J.; commissioned Mar. 13, 1912; College of N.J. (Princeton), 1879; admitted bar, N.J.; Congress, 1894–98; senator, N.J., 1898–1901, president, 1901; judge, Supreme Court, N.J., 1901–1908, chancellor, 1908–12; resigned Dec. 31, 1922; died, Dec. 9, 1924.

REED, STANLEY FORMAN (Ky.). Service: 303 U.S. 1938—352 U.S., 1956. Born Dec. 31, 1884, Mason Co., Ky.; commissioned Jan. 27, 1938; Wesleyan Col., 1902; Yale Univ., 1906; attended Univ. of Va. and Columbia Law Sch.; Sorbonne, 1909–10; admitted bar, Ky., 1910; legislature, Ky., 1912–16; in practice, 1912–29; general counsel for federal agencies, 1929–35; U.S. solicitor general, 1935–38; resigned Feb. 25, 1957.

ROBERTS, OWEN JOSEPHUS (Pa.). Service: 282 U.S., 1930—326 U.S., 1944–45. Born May 2, 1875, Philadelphia, Pa.; commissioned May 20, 1930; Univ. of Pa., 1895, LL.B., 1898; admitted bar, Pa., 1898; first assistant district attorney, Philadelphia Co., 1901–1904; instructor-professor of law, Univ. of Pa., 1898–1918; in practice, 1904–30; special U.S. attorney general, Teapot Dome investigation, 1924; chairman, Pearl Harbor investigating committee, 1941; resigned July 31, 1945; dean, Univ. of Pa. Law Sch.; died May 17, 1955.

RUTLEDGE, JOHN (S.C.). Service: 3 Dall. (3 U.S.), Aug. term, 1795. Born 1739, Charleston, S. C.; commissioned Sept. 26, 1789; studied law in England; admitted bar, England, 1760, S.C., 1761; House of Commons, S. C., 1761–78; First & Second Continental Congresses; president, General Assembly, S.C., 1776–80; governor, S.C., 1779; Congress, 1782–83; minister to Holland, 1783; judge, Court of Chancery, S.C., 1783; House of Representatives, S.C., 1784–90; member, signer, Constitutional Convention, 1787;

retired Supreme Court, March 5, 1791 (never sat); chief justice, Supreme Court, S.C., 1791; recess appointment as chief justice, Supreme Court, July 1, 1795, took seat, Aug. 12, 1795, rejected by Senate, Dec., 1795; died July 18, 1800.

RUTLEDGE, WILEY BLOUNT (Iowa). Service: 318 U.S., 1942—327 U.S., 1948. Born July 20, 1894, Cloverport, Ky.; commissioned Feb. 11, 1943; Univ. of Wis., 1914; Univ. of Colo Law Sch., 1922; teacher, 1915–22; admitted bar, Colo., 1922; professor of law, Univ. of Colo., 1924, Wash. Univ., 1926–35, dean, 1931–35; professor & dean, Univ. of Iowa, 1935–39; judge, U.S. Court of Appeals, D.C., 1939–43; died Sept. 10, 1949.

SANFORD, EDWARD TERRY (Tenn.). Service: 261 U.S., 1922—281 U.S., 1929. Born July 23, 1865, Knoxville, Tenn.; commissioned Jan. 23, 1923; Univ. of Tenn., 1883; Harvard Univ., 1885; Harvard Law Sch., 1889; admitted bar, Tenn., 1888; in practice, 1888–1907; assistant U.S. attorney general, 1907; judge, U.S. District Court, Tenn., 1909–23; died Mar. 8, 1930.

SHIRAS, GEORGE, JR. (Pa.). Service: 146 U.S., 1892—188 U.S., 1902. Born Jan. 26, 1832, Pittsburgh, Pa.; commissioned July 26, 1892; Ohio Univ.; Yale Col., 1853; attended Yale Law Sch.; admitted bar, Pa., 1855; in practice, 1858–92; resigned Feb. 23, 1903; died Aug. 2, 1924.

STEWART, POTTER (Ohio). Service: 358 U.S., 1958——. Born Jan. 23, 1915; Jackson, Mich.; commissioned May 18, 1959; Yale Univ., 1937, LL.B., 1941; admitted bar, Ohio, 1941; judge, U.S. Circuit Court, 6th Cir., 1954–59.

STONE, HARLAN F. (N.Y.). Service: 268 U.S., 1924—328 U.S., 1945. Born Oct. 11, 1872, Chesterfield, N.H.; commissioned Feb. 5, 1925, chief justice, June 27, 1941; Mass. Ag. Col., 1888–90; Amherst Col., 1890–94; Columbia Law Sch., 1895–98; admitted bar, N.Y., 1899; professor of law, Columbia Law Sch., 1903–1905, 1910–1915, 1915–32, dean, 1910–23; U.S. attorney general, 1924–25; died Apr. 22, 1946.

STORY, JOSEPH (Mass.). Service: 7 Cranch (11 U.S.), 1812—3 How. (44 U.S.), 1845. Born Sept. 18, 1779, Marblehead, Mass.; commissioned Nov. 18, 1811; Harvard Univ., 1798; admitted bar, Mass., 1801; legislature, Mass., 1805–1807; Congress, 1808–1809; legislature, Mass., 1809, speaker, 1811; bank president, 1815–35; Board of Overseers, Harvard, 1819, fellow, 1825; professor of law, Harvard, 1829; author of commentaries, *On Equity Jurisprudence, Equity Pleading;* wrote rules of equity practice, U.S. Supreme Court and circuit courts, 1842; died Sept. 10, 1845.

STRONG, WILLIAM (Pa.). Service: 9 Wall. (76 U.S.), 1869—12 Otto (102 U.S.), 1879–80. Born May 6, 1808; Somers, Conn.; commissioned Feb. 18, 1870; Yale Col., 1828, M.A., 1831; attended Yale Law Sch.; admitted bar, Pa., 1832; Congress, 1847–51; judge, Supreme Court, Pa., 1857–68; Hayes-Tilden Electoral Commission, 1877; resigned Supreme Court, Dec. 14,

1880; professor of law, Columbian (Geo. Wash.) Univ.; died Aug. 19, 1895.

SUTHERLAND, GEORGE (Utah). Service: 260 U.S., 1922—304 U.S., 1937. Born Mar. 25, 1862, Buckinghamshire, England; commissioned Sept. 5, 1922; Univ. of Mich., 1883; admitted bar, Utah, 1883; senator, Utah, 1896; Congress, 1901–1903; U.S. senator, 1905–17; resigned Supreme Court, Jan. 18, 1938; died July 18, 1942.

SWAYNE, NOAH HAYES (Ohio). Service: 1 Black (66 U.S.), 1861—12 Otto (102 U.S.), 1879–80. Born Dec. 7, 1804, Culpepper, Va.; commissioned Jan. 24, 1862; admitted bar, Va., 1823, Ohio; legislature, Ohio, 1825, 1829; prosecuting attorney, Coshocton Co., Ohio, 1826; U.S. attorney, Ohio, 1830–39; resigned Supreme Court, Jan. 31, 1881; died June 8, 1884.

TAFT, WILLIAM HOWARD (Conn.). Service: 257 U.S., 1921—281 U.S., 1929. Born Sept. 15, 1857, Cincinnati, Ohio; commissioned chief justice, June 30, 1921; Yale Univ., 1878; Cincinnati Law Sch., 1880; assistant prosecuting attorney, 1881; collector internal revenue, Cincinnati, 1882; judge, Superior Court, Ohio, 1887; U.S. solicitor general, 1890; judge, U.S. Circuit Court, 6th Cir., 1892–1900; president, Philippine Commission, 1900; secretary of war, 1904; president of U.S., 1908–12; professor of law, Yale Law Sch., 1913; joint chairman, National War Labor Board, 1918; resigned Supreme Court, Feb. 3, 1930; died Mar. 8, 1930.

TANEY, ROGER BROOKE (Md.). Service: 10 Pet. (35 U.S.), 1836—1 Wall. (68 U.S.), 1863. Born Mar. 17, 1777, Calvert Co., Md.; commissioned chief justice, Mar. 15, 1836; Dickenson Col., 1795; admitted bar, Md., 1799; legislature, Md., 1799–1800; senator, Md., 1816–21; attorney general, Md., 1827–31; U.S. attorney general, 1831; secretary of treasury (rejected by Senate and resigned), 1833; died Oct. 12, 1864.

THOMPSON, SMITH (N.Y.). Service: 9 Wheat. (22 U.S.), 1824—16 Pet. (41 U.S.), 1842. Born Jan. 17, 1768, Dutchess Co., N.Y.; commissioned Dec. 19, 1823; Col. of N.J. (Princeton), 1788; admitted bar, N.Y., 1792; legislature, N.Y., 1800; judge, Supreme Court, N.Y., 1802, chief judge, 1814; regent, Univ. of State of N.Y., 1813; secretary of navy, U.S., 1818–23; died Dec. 18, 1843.

TODD, THOMAS (Ky.). Service: 7 Cranch (11 U.S.), 1812—10 Wheat. (23 U.S.), 1825. Born Jan. 23, 1765, Co. of King and Queen, Va.; commissioned Mar. 3, 1807; admitted bar, Ky.; clerk, House of Representatives, 1792; clerk, Court of Appeals, Ky., 1792–1801; judge, Court of Appeals, Ky., 1801–1807, chief judge, 1806–1807; military service, Revolutionary War; died Feb. 7, 1826.

TRIMBLE, ROBERT (Ky.). Service: 12 Wheat. (25 U.S.), 1827—1 Pet. (26 U.S.), 1828. Born 1777, August Co., Va.; commissioned May 9, 1826; admitted bar, Ky., 1800; legislature, Ky., 1802; judge, Supreme Court, Ky., 1807–1809; district attorney, 1813–17; U.S. district judge, Ky., 1817–26; died Aug. 25, 1828; Trimble Co., Ky., named for him.

VAN DEVANTER, WILLIS (Wyo.). Service: 219 U.S., 1910—301 U.S., 1936. Born Apr. 17, 1859, Marion, Ind.; commissioned Dec. 16, 1910; Asbury (De Pauw) Univ., 1878; Cincinnati Law Sch., 1881; admitted bar, Ind., 1881, Wyo., 1884; city attorney, Wyo., 1887–88; territorial legislature, 1888; judge and chief judge, Supreme Court, Wyo., 1889–90; assistant attorney general, U.S., 1897–1903; professor of law, Columbian (Geo. Wash.) Univ., 1898–1903; judge, U.S. Circuit Court, 8th Cir., 1903–10; resigned Supreme Court, June 1, 1937; died Feb. 8, 1941.

VINSON, FREDERICK MOORE (Ky.). Service: 329 U.S., 1946—348 U.S., 1954. Born Jan. 22, 1890; commissioned chief justice, June 29, 1946; Ky. Normal Col., 1908; Centre Col., 1909, LL.B., 1911; admitted bar, Ky., 1911; city attorney, 1913; commonwealth attorney, 1921–24; Congress, 1923–29, 1931–39; judge, Circuit Court of Appeals, D.C., 1938–43; chief judge, U.S. Emergency Court of Appeals, 1942; director, Office Economic Stabilization, 1943–45; federal loan administrator, 1945; director, Office of War Mobilization, 1945; secretary of treasury, U.S., 1945; died Sept. 8, 1953.

WAITE, MORRISON REMICK (Ohio). Service: 19 Wall. (86 U.S.), 1873—126 U.S., 1887. Born Nov. 29, 1816, Lyme, Conn.; commissioned chief justice, Jan. 21, 1874; Yale Col., 1837; admitted bar, Ohio, 1839; legislature, Ohio, 1849; in practice, 1839–74; U.S. representative, Ala. Claims Commission, 1871; member, arbitration tribunal, Geneva, 1871; president, Ohio constitutional convention, 1873; member, Yale Corporation, 1882–88; died Mar. 23, 1888.

WARREN, EARL (Calif.). Service: 347 U.S., 1953——. Born Mar. 19, 1891, Los Angeles, Calif.; commissioned chief justice, Mar. 2, 1954; Univ. of Calif., 1912, J.D., 1914; admitted bar, Calif., 1914; clerk, judicial committee, state legislature, 1919; deputy city attorney, 1919–20; deputy district attorney, Calif., 1920–23, chief deputy district attorney, 1923–25, district attorney, 1925–38; attorney general, Calif., 1939–43; governor, Calif., 1943–53.

WASHINGTON, BUSHROD (Va.). Service: 3 Dall. (3 U.S.), 1799—2 Pet. (27 U.S.), 1829. Born June 5, 1762, Westmoreland Co., Va.; commissioned Dec. 29, 1798; William & Mary Col., 1778; admitted bar, Va., 1786; Va. House of Delegates, 1787; county magistrate, Va.; reporter, Supreme Court, Va., 1790; military service, Revolutionary War; died Nov. 26, 1829; nephew of George Washington, executor of his will, and devisee of Mt. Vernon.

WAYNE, JAMES MOORE (Ga.). Service: 9 Pet. (34 U.S.), 1835—5 Wall. (72 U.S.), 1866. Born 1790, Savannah, Ga.; commissioned Jan. 9, 1835; College of N.J. (Princeton), 1808; admitted bar, Ga., 1810; House of Representatives, Ga., 1815–16; mayor, Savannah, 1816–18; judge, Superior Court, Ga., 1824–29; Congress, 1829–35; died July 5, 1867.

WHITE, EDWARD DOUGLAS (La.). Service: 153 U.S., 1893—255 U.S., 1920. Born Nov. 3, 1845, Parish Lafourche, La.; commissioned Feb. 19, 1894, chief justice, Dec. 12, 1910; Georgetown Col.; admitted bar, La., 1868; senator, La., 1874; judge, Supreme Court, La., 1879–80; U.S. senator, 1891–94; military service, Civil War; died May 19, 1921.

WHITTAKER, CHARLES EVANS (Mo.). Service: 353 U.S., 1956——. Born Feb. 22, 1901; Troy, Kan.; commissioned Mar. 25, 1957; Univ. of Kansas City, 1924; admitted bar, Mo., 1923; judge, U.S. District Court, Mo., 1954–56; judge, U.S. Circuit Court, 8th Cir., 1956–57.

WILSON, JAMES (Pa.). Service: 2 Dall. (2 U.S.), 1790—3 Dall. (3 U.S.), 1794–99. Born Sept. 14, 1742, Carskedo, Scotland; commissioned Sept. 29, 1789; educated foreign universities, emigrated U.S., 1761; tutor and lecturer, Col. of Philadelphia, 1766; admitted bar, Pa., 1767; First & Second Continental Congresses, 1774–75; signer, Declaration of Independence, 1776; French *avocat général,* 1779–83; Congress (not continuously), 1778–87; member, signer, Constitutional Convention, 1787; professor of law, Col. of Phila., 1789, Univ. of Pa., 1790; died Aug. 21, 1798 (had financial difficulties and at time of death was seeking to avoid punishment for debt).

WOODBURY, LEVI (N.H.). Service: 4 How. (45 U.S.), 1846—11 How. (52 U.S.), 1850. Born Dec. 22, 1789, Francetown, N.H.; commissioned Jan. 3, 1846; Dartmouth Col., 1809; admitted bar, N.H., 1812; clerk, state senate, 1816; judge, Superior Court, N.H., 1817–23; governor, N.H., 1823; legislature, N.H., speaker, 1825; U.S. senator, 1825–31; U.S. secretary of navy, 1831–34; U.S. secretary of treasury, 1834–41; U.S. senator, 1841–45; died Sept. 4, 1851.

WOODS, WILLIAM BURNHAM (Ga.). Service: 13 Otto (103 U.S.), 1880—119 U.S., 1886. Born Aug. 3, 1824, Newark, Ohio; commissioned Dec. 21, 1880; Western Reserve Col.; Yale Col., 1845; admitted bar, Ohio, 1847; mayor, Newark, Ohio, 1857; general assembly, Ohio, speaker, 1857–61; chancellor, Middle Chancery Division, Ala., 1868; judge, U.S. Circuit Court, 5th Cir., 1869–80; military service, Civil War; died May 14, 1887.

SUMMARY

THE THIRTEEN CHIEF JUSTICES ranged in age at the time of commission from 44 (Jay) to 69 (Stone). Their ages averaged 58. All but one (Marshall) had formal college educations. Six of the thirteen had previous judicial service. Of twelve (excluding Warren, still serving), eight served until death, and four resigned, two because of physical incapacity. When appointed, Jay at 44 and Marshall at 46 were the youngest; Stone at 69 and Hughes at 68 were the oldest. Of the thirteen, two were under 50, six between 50 and 60, and five over 60. Marshall, appointed at 46, had the longest service, thirty-four years; Taney, appointed at 59, had twenty-eight years, and Fuller, appointed at 55, had twenty-two years. The shortest term was that of Ellsworth, who resigned after three years, and Stone served but five years before his death. The average period of service for the twelve whose service has ended was thirteen years and three months.

Of the chief justices, three were appointed from New York, two from Connecticut and Ohio, and one each from California, Illinois, Kentucky, Louisiana, Maryland and Virginia. Two (White, of Louisiana, and Stone, of New York) were elevated while serving on the bench, and one (Hughes, of New York) had previously served on the Supreme Court.

Considering Hughes as having been commissioned twice, the total of all justices commissioned who served (including Thomas Johnson) is 93. Of these, fifteen were over 60 years of age, fifty-three between 50 and 60, twenty-one between 40 and 50, and four between 30 and 40 when appointed. The average age was just over 53.

Of those under 49 when appointed, Story (32), the youngest, served thirty-four years; William Johnson (33), thirty years; Washington (36), thirty-one years; and Iredell (39), nine years. The average length of service of these younger men was twenty-six years, as against the over-all average of fifteen-plus years.

Of those over 60, Holmes served thirty years and lived three years after his resignation, Brandeis served twenty-three years and lived two years after his resignation, and Strong served twenty-five years until his death. The average service of those over 60 was eleven years, as against the over-all average of fifteen-plus.

The greatest length of service was that of the elder Harlan, appointed at 44 years of age. He lacked a month of serving thirty-five years, and was approached only by Story (appointed at 32), Marshall (appointed at 46), and Field (appointed at 47), each of whom served thirty-four years, although Field's senility marred his last years to a point where the justices had to request his resignation.

Of those who resigned, other than Field, Justice Holmes had the longest service (thirty years). The shortest terms were those of James F. Byrnes, who resigned after one year, and Howell E. Jackson, who died after two years.

Of the ninety-two justices, seventy-four appear to have had formal college or law school educations, fifty-four had previous judicial service, forty-nine died in service, thirty-five resigned (including Justice Hughes, who resigned twice), and nine are still alive and serving.

Of the states from which appointments were made, New York ranks highest with thirteen (including Justice Hughes, who was selected twice, and excluding Justice Stone, who was made chief justice while on the bench); Ohio comes next with nine appointees; Massachusetts with eight; Pennsylvania with six; Kentucky, Tennessee and Virginia, with five each; Maryland and New Jersey, with four each; Alabama, California, Connecticut, Georgia and South Carolina, three each; Illinois, Iowa, Michigan and North Carolina, two each; and one from each of the following: Indiana, Kansas, Louisiana (excluding the elevation of Justice White), Maine, Minnesota, Mississippi, Missouri, New Hampshire, Texas, Utah, and Wyoming.

III. The Constitution of the United States

We the People of the United States, in Order to form a more perfect Union, establish Justice, insure domestic Tranquility, provide for the common defence, promote the general Welfare, and secure the Blessings of Liberty to ourselves and our Posterity, do ordain and establish this Constitution for the United States of America.

Article I

SECTION 1. All legislative Powers herein granted shall be vested in a Congress of the United States, which shall consist of a Senate and House of Representatives.

SECTION 2. (1)[1] The House of Representatives shall be composed of Members chosen every second Year by the People of the several States, and the Electors in each State shall have the Qualifications requisite for Electors of the most numerous Branch of the State Legislature.

(2) No Person shall be a Representative who shall not have attained to the Age of twenty five Years, and been seven Years a Citizen of the United States, and who shall not, when elected, be an Inhabitant of that State in which he shall be chosen.

(3) Representatives and direct Taxes shall be apportioned among the several States which may be included within this Union, according to their respective Numbers, which shall be determined by adding to the whole Number of free Persons, including those bound to Service for a Term of Years, and excluding Indians not taxed, three fifths of all other Persons. The actual Enumeration shall be made within three Years after the first Meeting of the Congress of the United States, and within every subsequent Term in ten Years, in such Manner as they shall by Law direct. The Number of Representatives shall not exceed one for every thirty Thousand, but each State shall have at Least one Representative; and until such enumeration shall be made, the State of New Hampshire shall be entitled to chuse three, Massachusetts eight, Rhode-Island and Providence Plantations one, Connecticut five, New-York six, New Jersey four, Pennsylvania eight, Delaware one, Maryland six, Virginia ten, North Carolina five, South Carolina five, and Georgia three.

(4) When vacancies happen in the Representation from any State, the

---

[1] The separate paragraphs of each Section are not numbered in the Constitution. Numbers have been added here for convenient reference.

Executive Authority thereof shall issue Writs of Election to fill such Vacancies.

(5) The House of Representatives shall chuse their Speaker and other Officers; and shall have the sole Power of Impeachment.

SECTION 3. (1) The Senate of the United States shall be composed of two Senators from each State, chosen by the Legislature thereof, for six Years; and each Senator shall have one Vote.

(2) Immediately after they shall be assembled in Consequence of the first Election, they shall be divided as equally as may be into three Classes. The Seats of the Senators of the first Class shall be vacated at the Expiration of the second Year, of the second Class at the Expiration of the fourth Year, and of the third Class at the Expiration of the sixth Year, so that one third may be chosen every second Year; and if Vacancies happen by Resignation, or otherwise, during the Recess of the Legislature of any State, the Executive thereof may make temporary Appointments until the next Meeting of the Legislature, which shall then fill such Vacancies.

(3) No Person shall be a Senator who shall not have attained to the Age of thirty Years, and been nine Years a Citizen of the United States, and who shall not, when elected, be an Inhabitant of that State for which he shall be chosen.

(4) The Vice President of the United States shall be President of the Senate, but shall have no Vote, unless they be equally divided.

(5) The Senate shall chuse their other Officers, and also a President pro tempore, in the Absence of the Vice President, or when he shall exercise the Office of President of the United States.

(6) The Senate shall have the sole Power to try all Impeachments. When sitting for that Purpose, they shall be on Oath or Affirmation. When the President of the United States is tried, the Chief Justice shall preside: And no Person shall be convicted without the Concurrence of two thirds of the Members present.

(7) Judgment in Cases of Impeachment shall not extend further than to removal from Office, and disqualification to hold and enjoy any Office of honor, Trust or Profit under the United States: but the Party convicted shall nevertheless be liable and subject to Indictment, Trial, Judgment and Punishment, according to Law.

SECTION 4. (1) The Times, Places and Manner of holding Elections for Senators and Representatives, shall be prescribed in each State by the Legislature thereof; but the Congress may at any time by Law make or alter such Regulations, except as to the Places of chusing Senators.

(2) The Congress shall assemble at least once in every Year, and such Meeting shall be on the first Monday in December, unless they shall by Law appoint a different Day.

SECTION 5. (1) Each House shall be the Judge of the Election, Returns and Qualifications of its own Members, and a Majority of each shall constitute a Quorum to do Business; but a smaller Number may adjourn from day to day, and may be authorized to compel the attendance of absent Members, in such Manner, and under such Penalties as each House may provide.

(2) Each House may determine the Rules of its Proceedings, punish its Members for Disorderly Behaviour, and, with the Concurrence of two thirds, expel a Member.

(3) Each House shall keep a Journal of its Proceedings, and from time to time publish the same, excepting such Parts as may in their Judgment require Secrecy; and the Yeas and Nays of the Members of either House on any question shall, at the Desire of one fifth of those Present, be entered on the Journal.

(4) Neither House, during the Session of Congress, shall, without the Consent of the other, adjourn for more than three days, nor to any other Place than that in which the two Houses shall be sitting.

SECTION 6. (1) The Senators and Representatives shall receive a Compensation for their Services, to be ascertained by Law, and paid out of the Treasury of the United States. They shall in all Cases, except Treason, Felony and Breach of the Peace, be privileged from Arrest during their Attendance at the Session of their respective Houses, and in going to and returning from the same; and for any Speech or Debate in either House, they shall not be questioned in any other Place.

(2) No Senator or Representative shall, during the Time for which he was elected, be appointed to any civil Office under the Authority of the United States, which shall have been created, or the Emoluments whereof shall have been encreased during such time; and no Person holding any Office under the United States, shall be a member of either House during his Continuance in Office.

SECTION 7. (1) All Bills for raising Revenue shall originate in the House of Representatives; but the Senate may propose or concur with Amendments as on other Bills.

(2) Every Bill which shall have passed the House of Representatives and the Senate, shall, before it becomes a Law, be presented to the President of the United States; If he approve he shall sign it, but if not he shall return it, with his Objections to that House in which it shall have originated, who shall enter the Objections at large on their Journal, and proceed to reconsider it. If after such Reconsideration two thirds of that House shall agree to pass the Bill, it shall be sent, together with the Objections, to the other House, by which it shall likewise be reconsidered, and if approved by two thirds of that House, it shall become a Law. But in all such Cases the Votes of both Houses shall be determined by Yeas and Nays, and the Names of the Persons voting for and against the Bill shall be entered on the Journal of each House respectively. If any Bill shall not be returned by the President within ten Days (Sundays excepted) after it shall have been presented to him, the Same shall be a law, in like Manner as if he had signed it, unless the Congress by their Adjournment prevent its Return, in which Case it shall not be a Law.

(3) Every Order, Resolution, or Vote to which the Concurrence of the Senate and House of Representatives may be necessary (except on a question of Adjournment) shall be presented to the President of the United States; and before the same shall take Effect, shall be approved by him, or being disapproved by him, shall be repassed by two thirds of the Senate and House of Representatives, according to the Rules and Limitations prescribed in the Case of a Bill.

SECTION 8. The Congress shall have Power (1) To lay and collect Taxes, Duties, Imposts and Excises, to pay the Debts and provide for the common Defence and general Welfare of the United States; but all Duties, Imposts and Excises shall be uniform throughout the United States:

(2) To borrow Money on the credit of the United States;

(3) To regulate Commerce with foreign Nations, and among the several States, and with the Indian Tribes;

(4) To establish an uniform Rule of Naturalization, and uniform Laws on the subject of Bankruptcies throughout the United States;

(5) To coin Money, regulate the Value thereof, and of foreign Coin, and fix the Standard of Weights and Measures;

(6) To provide for the Punishment of counterfeiting the Securities and current Coin of the United States;

(7) To establish Post Offices and post Roads;

(8) To promote the Progress of Science and useful Arts, by securing

509

for limited Times to Authors and Inventors the exclusive Right to their respective Writings and Discoveries;

(9) To constitute Tribunals inferior to the supreme Court;

(10) To define and punish Piracies and Felonies committed on the high Seas, and Offenses against the Law of Nations;

(11) To declare War, grant Letters of Marque and Reprisal, and make Rules concerning Captures on Land and Water;

(12) To raise and support Armies, but no Appropriation of Money to that Use shall be for a longer Term than two Years;

(13) To provide and maintain a Navy;

(14) To make Rules for the Government and Regulation of the land and naval Forces;

(15) To provide for calling forth the Militia to execute the Laws of the Union, suppress Insurrections and repel Invasions;

(16) To provide for organizing, arming, and disciplining, the Militia, and for governing such Part of them as may be employed in the Service of the United States, reserving to the States respectively, the Appointment of the Officers, and the Authority of training the Militia according to the discipline prescribed by Congress;

(17) To exercise exclusive Legislation in all Cases whatsoever, over such District (not exceeding ten Miles square) as may, by Cession of particular States, and the Acceptance of Congress, become the Seat of the Government of the United States, and to exercise like Authority over all Places purchased by the Consent of the Legislature of the State in which the Same shall be, for the Erection of Forts, Magazines, Arsenals, dock-Yards, and other needful Buildings;—And

(18) To make all Laws which shall be necessary and proper for carrying into Execution the foregoing Powers, and all other Powers vested by this Constitution in the Government of the United States, or in any Department or Officer thereof.

SECTION 9. (1) The Migration or Importation of such Persons as any of the States now existing shall think proper to admit, shall not be prohibited by the Congress prior to the Year one thousand eight hundred and eight, but a Tax or duty may be imposed on such Importation, not exceeding ten dollars for each Person.

(2) The Privilege of the Writ of Habeas Corpus shall not be suspended, unless when in Cases of Rebellion or Invasion the public Safety may require it.

(3) No Bill of Attainder or ex post facto Law shall be passed.

(4) No Capitation, or other direct, Tax shall be laid, unless in Proportion to the Census or Enumeration herein before directed to be taken.

(5) No Tax or Duty shall be laid on Articles exported from any State.

(6) No Preference shall be given by any Regulation of Commerce or Revenue to the Ports of one State over those of another: nor shall Vessels bound to, or from, one State, be obliged to enter, clear, or pay Duties in another.

(7) No Money shall be drawn from the Treasury, but in Consequence of Appropriations made by Law; and a regular Statement and Account of the Receipts and Expenditures of all public Money shall be published from time to time.

(8) No Title of Nobility shall be granted by the United States: And no Person holding any Office of Profit or Trust under them, shall, without the Consent of the Congress, accept of any present, Emolument, Office or Title, of any kind whatever, from any King, Prince, or foreign State.

SECTION 10. (1) No State shall enter into any Treaty, Alliance, or Confederation; grant Letters of Marque and Reprisal; coin Money; emit Bills of Credit; make any Thing but gold and silver Coin a Tender in Payment of Debts; pass any Bill of Attainder, ex post facto Law, or Law impairing the Obligation of Contracts, or grant any Title of Nobility.

(2) No State shall, without the Consent of the Congress, lay any Imposts or Duties on Imports or Exports, except what may be absolutely necessary for executing it's inspection Laws: and the net Produce of all Duties and Imposts, laid by any State on Imports or Exports, shall be for the Use of the Treasury of the United States; and all such Laws shall be subject to the Revision and Controul of the Congress.

(3) No State shall, without the Consent of Congress, lay any Duty of Tonnage, keep Troops, or Ships of War in time of Peace, enter into any Agreement or Compact with another State, or with a foreign Power, or engage in War, unless actually invaded, or in such imminent Danger as will not admit of delay.

ARTICLE II

SECTION 1. (1) The executive Power shall be vested in a President of the United States of America. He shall hold his Office during the Term of four Years, and, together with the Vice President, chosen for the same Term, be elected, as follows

(2) Each State shall appoint, in such Manner as the Legislature thereof may direct, a Number of Electors, equal to the whole Number of Senators and Representatives to which the State may be entitled in the Congress: but no Senator or Representative, or Person holding an Office of Trust or Profit under the United States, shall be appointed an Elector.

(3) The Electors shall meet in their respective States, and vote by Ballot for two Persons, of whom one at least shall not be an Inhabitant of the same State with themselves. And they shall make a List of all Persons voted for, and of the Number of Votes for each; which List they shall sign and certify, and transmit sealed to the Seat of the Government of the United States directed to the President of the Senate. The President of the Senate shall, in the Presence of the Senate and House of Representatives, open all the Certificates, and the Votes shall then be counted. The Person having the greatest Number of Votes shall be the President, if such Number be a Majority of the whole Number of Electors appointed; and if there be more than one who have such Majority, and have an equal Number of Votes, then the House of Representatives shall immediately chuse by Ballot one of them for President; and if no Person have a Majority, then from the five highest on the List the said House shall in like Manner chuse the President. But in chusing the President, the Votes shall be taken by States, the Representation from each State having one Vote; A quorum for this Purpose shall consist of a Member or Members from two thirds of the States, and a Majority of all the States shall be necessary to a Choice. In every Case, after the Choice of the President, the Person having the greatest Number of Votes of the Electors shall be the Vice President. But if there should remain two or more who have equal Votes, the Senate shall chuse from them by Ballot the Vice President.

(4) The Congress may determine the Time of chusing the Electors, and the Day on which they shall give their Votes; which Day shall be the same throughout the United States.

(5) No Person except a natural born Citizen, or a Citizen of the United States, at the time of the Adoption of this Constitution, shall be eligible to the Office of President; neither shall any Person be eligible to that Office who shall not have attained to the Age of thirty-five Years, and been fourteen Years a Resident within the United States.

(6) In Case of the Removal of the President from Office, or of his Death, Resignation, or Inability to discharge the Powers and Duties of the said Office, the Same shall devolve on the Vice President, and the Congress may by Law provide for the Case of Removal, Death, Resignation, or Inability, both of the

President and Vice President, declaring what Officer shall then act as President, and such Officer shall act accordingly, until the Disability be removed, or a President shall be elected.

(7) The President shall, at stated Times, receive for his Services, a Compensation, which shall neither be encreased nor diminished during the Period for which he shall have been elected, and he shall not receive within that Period any other Emolument from the United States, or any of them.

(8) Before he enter on the Execution of his Office, he shall take the following Oath or Affirmation:—"I do solemnly swear (or affirm) that I will faithfully execute the Office of President of the United States, and will to the best of my Ability, preserve, protect and defend the Constitution of the United States."

SECTION 2. (1) The President shall be Commander in Chief of the Army and Navy of the United States, and of the Militia of the several States, when called into the actual Service of the United States; he may require the Opinion, in writing, of the principal Officer in each of the executive Departments, upon any Subject relating to the Duties of their respective Offices, and he shall have Power to grant Reprieves and Pardons for Offences against the United States, except in Cases of Impeachment.

(2) He shall have Power, by and with the Advice and Consent of the Senate, to make Treaties, provided two thirds of the Senators present concur; and he shall nominate, and by and with the Advice and Consent of the Senate, shall appoint Ambassadors, other public Ministers and Consuls, judges of the supreme Court, and all other Officers of the United States, whose Appointments are not herein otherwise provided for, and which shall be established by Law: but the Congress may by Law vest the Appointment of such inferior Officers, as they think proper, in the President alone, in the Courts of Law, or in the Heads of Departments.

(3) The President shall have Power to fill up all Vacancies that may happen during the Recess of the Senate, by granting Commissions which shall expire at the End of their next Session.

SECTION 3. He shall from time to time give to the Congress Information of the State of the Union, and recommend to their Consideration such Measures as he shall judge necessary and expedient; he may, on extraordinary Occasions, convene both Houses, or either of them, and in Case of Disagreement between them, with Respect to the Time of Adjournment, he may adjourn them to such Time as he shall think proper; he shall receive Ambassadors and other public Ministers; he shall take Care that the Laws be faithfully executed, and shall Commission all the Officers of the United States.

SECTION 4. The President, Vice President and all civil Officers of the United States, shall be removed from Office on Impeachment for, and Conviction of, Treason, Bribery, or other high Crimes and Misdemeanors.

ARTICLE III

SECTION 1. The judicial Power of the United States, shall be vested in one supreme Court, and in such inferior Courts as the Congress may from time to time ordain and establish. The Judges, both of the supreme and inferior Courts, shall hold their Offices during good Behaviour, and shall, at stated Times, receive for their Services, a Compensation, which shall not be diminished during their Continuance in Office.

SECTION 2. (1) The judicial Power shall extend to all Cases, in Law and Equity, arising under this Constitution, the Laws of the United States, and Treaties made, or which shall be made, under their Authority;—to all Cases affecting Ambassadors, other public Ministers and Consuls;—to all Cases of admiralty and maritime Jurisdiction;—to Controversies to which the United States shall be a Party;—to Controversies between two or more States;—between a State and Citizens of another State;—between Citizens of different States,—between Citizens of the same State claiming Lands under Grants of different States, and between a State, or the Citizens thereof, and foreign States, Citizens or Subjects.

(2) In all Cases affecting Ambassadors, other public Ministers and Consuls, and those in which a State shall be Party, the supreme Court shall have original Jurisdiction. In all the other Cases before mentioned, the supreme Court shall have appellate Jurisdiction, both as to Law and Fact, with such Exceptions, and under such Regulations as the Congress shall make.

(3) The Trial of all Crimes, except in Cases of Impeachment, shall be by Jury; and such Trial shall be held in the State where the said Crimes shall have been committed; but when not committed within any State, the Trial shall be at such Place or Places as the Congress may by Law have directed.

SECTION 3. (1) Treason against the United States, shall consist only in levying War against them, or in adhering to their Enemies, giving them Aid and Comfort. No Person shall be convicted of Treason unless on the Testimony of two Witnesses to the same overt Act, or on Confession in open Court.

(2) The Congress shall have Power to declare the Punishment of Treason, but no Attainder of Treason shall work Corruption of Blood, or Forfeiture except during the Life of the Person attainted.

ARTICLE IV

SECTION 1. Full Faith and Credit shall be given in each State to the public Acts, Records, and judicial Proceedings of every other State. And the Congress may by general Laws prescribe the Manner in which such Acts, Records and Proceedings shall be proved, and the Effect thereof.

SECTION 2. (1) The Citizens of each State shall be entitled to all Privileges and Immunities of Citizens in the several States.

(2) A Person charged in any State with Treason, Felony, or other Crime, who shall flee from Justice, and be found in another State, shall on Demand of the executive Authority of the State from which he fled, be delivered up, to be removed to the State having Jurisdiction of the Crime.

(3) No Person held to Service or Labour in one State, under the Laws thereof, escaping into another, shall, in Consequence of any Law or Regulation therein, be discharged from such Service or Labour, but shall be delivered up on Claim of the Party to whom such Service or Labour may be due.

SECTION 3. (1) New States may be admitted by the Congress into this Union; but no new State shall be formed or erected within the Jurisdiction of any other State; nor any State be formed by the Junction of two or more States, or Parts of States, without the Consent of the Legislatures of the States concerned as well as of the Congress.

(2) The Congress shall have Power to dispose of and make all needful Rules and Regulations respecting the Territory or other Property belonging to the United States; and nothing in this Constitution shall be so construed as to Prejudice any Claims of the United States, or of any particular State.

SECTION 4. The United States shall guarantee to every State in this Union a Republican Form of Government, and shall protect each of them against Invasion; and on Application of the Legislature, or of the Executive (when the Legislature cannot be convened) against domestic Violence.

ARTICLE V

The Congress, whenever two thirds of both Houses shall deem it necessary, shall propose Amendments to this Constitution, or, on the Application of the Legislatures of two thirds of the several States, shall call a Convention for proposing Amendments, which, in either Case, shall be valid to all Intents and Purposes, as Part of this Constitution, when ratified by the Legislatures of three fourths of the several States, or by Conventions in three fourths thereof, as the one or the other Mode of Ratification may be proposed by the Congress; Provided that no Amendment which may be made prior to the Year One thousand eight hundred and eight shall in any Manner affect the first and fourth Clauses in the Ninth Section of the first Article; and that no State, without its Consent, shall be deprived of its equal Suffrage in the Senate.

Article VI

(1) All Debts contracted and Engagements entered into, before the Adoption of this Constitution, shall be as valid against the United States under this Constitution, as under the Confederation.

(2) This Constitution, and the Laws of the United States which shall be made in Pursuance thereof; and all Treaties made, or which shall be made, under the Authority of the United States, shall be the supreme Law of the Land; and the Judges in every State shall be bound thereby, any Thing in the Constitution or Laws of any State to the Contrary notwithstanding.

(3) The Senators and Representatives before mentioned, and the Members of the several State Legislatures, and all executive and judicial Officers, both of the United States and of the several States, shall be bound by Oath or Affirmation, to support this Constitution; but no religious Test shall ever be required as a Qualification to any Office or public Trust under the United States.

Article VII

The Ratification of the Conventions of nine States, shall be sufficient for the Establishment of this Constitution between the States so ratifying the Same.

AMENDMENTS

Article I

Congress shall make no law respecting an establishment of religion, or prohibiting the free exercise thereof; or abridging the freedom of speech, or of the press; or the right of the people peaceably to assemble, and to petition the Government for a redress of grievances.

ARTICLE II

A well regulated Militia, being necessary to the security of a free State, the right of the people to keep and bear Arms, shall not be infringed.

ARTICLE III

No Soldier shall, in time of peace be quartered in any house, without the consent of the Owner, nor in time of war, but in a manner to be prescribed by law.

ARTICLE IV

The right of the people to be secure in their persons, houses, papers, and effects, against unreasonable searches and seizures, shall not be violated, and no Warrants shall issue, but upon probable cause, supported by Oath or affirmation, and particularly describing the place to be searched, and the person or things to be seized.

ARTICLE V

No person shall be held to answer for a capital, or otherwise infamous crime, unless on a presentment or indictment of a Grand Jury, except in cases arising in the land or naval forces, or in the Militia, when in actual service in time of War or public danger; nor shall any person be subject for the same offence to be twice put in jeopardy of life or limb; nor shall be compelled in any criminal case to be a witness against himself, nor be deprived of life, liberty, or property, without due process of law; nor shall private property be taken for public use, without just compensation.

ARTICLE VI

In all criminal prosecutions the accused shall enjoy the right to a speedy and public trial, by an impartial jury of the State and district wherein the crime shall have been committed, which district shall have been previously ascertained by law, and to be informed of the nature and cause of the accusation; to be confronted with the witnesses against him; to have compulsory process for obtaining witnesses in his favor, and to have the Assistance of Counsel for his defence.

ARTICLE VII

In suits at common law, where the value in controversy shall exceed twenty dollars, the right of trial by jury shall be preserved, and no fact tried by a jury, shall be otherwise re-examined in any Court of the United States, than according to the rules of the common law.

ARTICLE VIII

Excessive bail shall not be required, nor excessive fines imposed, nor cruel and unusual punishments inflicted.

ARTICLE IX

The enumeration in the Constitution, of certain rights, shall not be construed to deny or disparage others retained by the people.

ARTICLE X

The powers not delegated to the United States by the Constitution, nor prohibited by it to the States, are reserved to the States respectively, or to the people.

[*The first ten Amendments were adopted in 1791.*]

ARTICLE XI

The Judicial power of the United States shall not be construed to extend to any suit in law or equity, commenced or prosecuted against one of the United States by Citizens of another State, or by Citizens or Subjects of any Foreign State. [*Adopted 1798.*]

ARTICLE XII

The Electors shall meet in their respective states, and vote by ballot for President and Vice-President, one of whom, at least, shall not be an inhabitant of the same state with themselves; they shall name in their ballots the person voted for as President, and in distinct ballots the person voted for as Vice-President, and they shall make distinct lists of all persons voted for as President, and of all persons voted for as Vice-President, and of the number of votes for each, which lists they shall sign and certify, and transmit sealed to the seat of the government of the United States, directed to the President of the Senate;—The President of the Senate shall, in the presence of the Senate and House of Representatives, open all the certificates and the votes shall then be counted;—The person having the greatest number of votes for President, shall be the President, if such number be a majority of the whole number of Electors appointed; and if no person have such majority, then from the persons having the highest numbers not exceeding three on the list of those voted for as President, the House of Representatives shall choose immediately, by ballot, the President. But in choosing the President, the votes shall be taken by states, the representation from each state having one vote; a quorum for this purpose shall consist of a member or members from two-thirds of the states, and a majority of all the states shall be necessary to a choice. And if the House of Representatives shall not choose a President whenever the right of choice shall devolve upon them, before the fourth day of March next following, then the Vice-President shall act as President, as in the case of the death or other constitutional disability of the President.—The person having the greatest number of votes as Vice-President, shall be the Vice-President, if such number be a majority of the whole number of Electors appointed, and if no person have a majority, then from the two highest numbers on the list, the Senate shall choose the Vice-President; a quorum for the purpose shall consist of two-thirds of the whole number of Senators, and a majority of the whole number shall be necessary to a choice. But no person constitutionally ineligible to the office of President shall be eligible to that of Vice-President of the United States. [*Adopted 1804.*]

Article XIII

section 1. Neither slavery nor involuntary servitude, except as a punishment for crime whereof the party shall have been duly convicted, shall exist within the United States, or any place subject to their jurisdiction.

section 2. Congress shall have power to enforce this article by appropriate legislation. [*Adopted 1865.*]

Article XIV

section 1. All persons born or naturalized in the United States, and subject to the jurisdiction thereof, are citizens of the United States and of the State wherein they reside. No State shall make or enforce any law which shall abridge the privileges or immunities of citizens of the United States; nor shall

519

any State deprive any person of life, liberty, or property, without due process of law; nor deny to any person within its jurisdiction the equal protection of the laws.

SECTION 2. Representatives shall be apportioned among the several States according to their respective numbers, counting the whole number of persons in each State, excluding Indians not taxed. But when the right to vote at any election for the choice of electors for President and Vice President of the United States, Representatives in Congress, the Executive and Judicial officers of a State, or the members of the Legislature thereof, is denied to any of the male inhabitants of such State, being twenty-one years of age, and citizens of the United States, or in any way abridged, except for participation in rebellion, or other crime, the basis of representation therein shall be reduced in the proportion which the number of such male citizens shall bear to the whole number of male citizens twenty-one years of age in such State.

SECTION 3. No person shall be a Senator or Representative in Congress, or elector of President and Vice President, or hold any office, civil or military, under the United States, or under any State, who having previously taken an oath, as a member of Congress, or as an officer of the United States, or as a member of any State legislature, or as an executive or judicial officer of any State, to support the Constitution of the United States, shall have engaged in insurrection or rebellion against the same, or given aid or comfort to the enemies thereof. But Congress may by a vote of two-thirds of each House, remove such disability.

SECTION 4. The validity of the public debt of the United States, authorized by law, including debts incurred for payment of pensions and bounties for services in suppressing insurrection or rebellion, shall not be questioned. But neither the United States nor any State shall assume or pay any debt or obligation incurred in aid of insurrection or rebellion against the United States, or any claim for the loss or emancipation of any slave; but all such debts, obligations and claims shall be held illegal and void.

SECTION 5. The Congress shall have power to enforce, by appropriate legislation, the provisions of this article. [*Adopted 1868.*]

ARTICLE XV

SECTION 1. The right of citizens of the United States to vote shall not be denied or abridged by the United States or by any State on account of race, color, or previous condition of servitude.

SECTION 2. The Congress shall have power to enforce this article by appropriate legislation. [*Adopted 1870.*]

ARTICLE XVI

The Congress shall have power to lay and collect taxes on incomes, from whatever source derived, without apportionment among the several States, and without regard to any census or enumeration. [*Adopted 1913.*]

ARTICLE XVII

(1) The Senate of the United States shall be composed of two Senators from each State, elected by the people thereof, for six years; and each Senator shall have one vote. The electors in each State shall have the qualifications requisite for electors of the most numerous branch of the State legislatures.

(2) When vacancies happen in the representation of any State in the Senate, the executive authority of such State shall issue writs of election to fill such vacancies: *Provided,* That the legislature of any State may empower the Executive thereof to make temporary appointments until the people fill the vacancies by election as the legislature may direct.

(3) This amendment shall not be so construed as to affect the election or term of any Senator chosen before it becomes valid as part of the Constitution. [*Adopted 1913.*]

ARTICLE XVIII

SECTION 1. After one year from the ratification of this article the manufacture, sale, or transportation of intoxicating liquors within, the importation thereof into, or the exportation thereof from the United States and all territory subject to the jurisdiction thereof for beverage purposes is hereby prohibited.

SECTION 2. The Congress and the several States shall have concurrent power to enforce this article by appropriate legislation.

SECTION 3. This article shall be inoperative unless it shall have been ratified as an amendment to the Constitution by the legislatures of the several States, as provided in the Constitution, within seven years from the date of the submission hereof to the States by the Congress. [*Adopted 1919.*]

Article XIX

The right of citizens of the United States to vote shall not be denied or abridged by the United States or by any State on account of sex.

Congress shall have power to enforce this article by appropriate legislation. [*Adopted 1920.*]

Article XX

SECTION 1. The terms of the President and Vice President shall end at noon on the 20th day of January, and the terms of Senators and Representatives at noon on the 3d day of January, of the years in which such terms would have ended if this article had not been ratified; and the terms of their successors shall then begin.

SECTION 2. The Congress shall assemble at least once in every year, and such meeting shall begin at noon on the 3d day of January, unless they shall by law appoint a different day.

SECTION 3. If, at the time fixed for the beginning of the term of the President, the President elect shall have died, the Vice President elect shall become President. If a President shall not have been chosen before the time fixed for the beginning of his term, or if the President elect shall have failed to qualify, then the Vice President elect shall act as President until a President shall have qualified; and the Congress may by law provide for the case wherein neither a President elect nor a Vice President elect shall have qualified, declaring who shall then act as President, or the manner in which one who is to act shall be selected, and such person shall act accordingly until a President or Vice President shall have qualified.

SECTION 4. The Congress may by law provide for the case of the death of any of the persons from whom the House of Representatives may choose a President whenever the right of choice shall have devolved upon them, and for the case of the death of any of the persons from whom the Senate may choose a Vice President whenever the right of choice shall have devolved upon them.

SECTION 5. Sections 1 and 2 shall take effect on the 15th day of October following the ratification of this article.

SECTION 6. This article shall be inoperative unless it shall have been ratified as an amendment to the Constitution by the legislatures of three-fourths of the several States within seven years from the date of its submission. [*Adopted 1933.*]

Article XXI

SECTION 1. The eighteenth article of amendment to the Constitution of the United States is hereby repealed.

SECTION 2. The transportation or importation into any State, Territory, or possession of the United States for delivery or use therein of intoxicating liquors, in violation of the laws thereof, is hereby prohibited.

SECTION 3. This article shall be inoperative unless it shall have been ratified as an amendment to the Constitution by conventions in the several States, as provided in the Constitution, within seven years from the date of the submission hereof to the States by the Congress. [*Adopted 1933.*]

Article XXII

SECTION 1. No person shall be elected to the office of the President more than twice, and no person who has held the office of President, or acted as President, for more than two years of a term to which some other person was elected President shall be elected to the office of the President more than once. But this Article shall not apply to any person holding the office of President when this Article was proposed by the Congress, and shall not prevent any person who may be holding the office of President, or acting as President, during the term within which this Article becomes operative from holding the office of President or acting as President during the remainder of such term.

SECTION 2. This Article shall be inoperative unless it shall have been ratified as an amendment to the Constitution by the legislatures of three-fourths of the several States within seven years from the date of its submission to the States by the Congress. [*Adopted 1951.*]

Article XXIII

SECTION 1. The District constituting the seat of Government of the United States shall appoint in such manner as the Congress may direct: A number of electors of President and Vice President equal to the whole number of Senators and Representatives in Congress to which the District would be entitled if it were a State, but in no event more than the least populous State; they shall be in addition to those appointed by the States, but they shall be considered, for the purposes of the election of President and Vice President, to be electors appointed by a State; and they shall meet in the District and perform such duties as provided by the twelfth article of amendment.

SECTION 2. The Congress shall have power to enforce this article by appropriate legislation. [*Adopted 1961.*]

The Wisdom of the Supreme Court has been set on Linotype machines in various sizes of the classic Granjon type, one of the most useful faces in the printer's repertory. Granjon was designed in 1924 by George W. Jones, who drew his basic forms from the French Garamond face of the sixteenth century. Four hundred years of continuing use attest to the fitness of this design and to its suitability for a compilation of nearly two centuries of American judicial thought.

UNIVERSITY OF OKLAHOMA PRESS

NORMAN